MISFIRE

THE HISTORY OF HOW AMERICA'S SMALL ARMS
HAVE FAILED OUR MILITARY

•

WILLIAM H. HALLAHAN

CHARLES SCRIBNER'S SONS
NEW YORK LONDON TORONTO SYDNEY TOKYO SINGAPORE

Charles Scribner's Sons
Rockefeller Center
1230 Avenue of the Americas
New York, NY 10020

Book design by PIXEL PRESS

Manufactured in the United States of America

1   3   5   7   9   10   8   6   4   2

Library of Congress Cataloging-in-Publication Data
Hallahan, William H.
Misfire: the history of how America's small arms have
failed our military / William H. Hallahan
p.   cm.
Includes bibliographic references and index.
1. Firearms—United States—History.   I. Title
UD383.H35   1994
623.4'4'0973—dc20   94-1552

ISBN 0-684-19359-0

To every American foot soldier
who ever carried a weapon into battle.

ACKNOWLEDGMENTS

A book of this scope encompasses so many periods of history and so many historical personalities and technical developments that I could not have written it accurately without consulting a number of authorities and experts.

The well-known ordnance specialist and military historian, Charles Smithgall of Lancaster, Pennsylvania (who rolls his eyes when I suggest he write a book), kindly and patiently read the manuscript, made innumerable suggestions and corrections, invited me out on his shooting range to witness the firing of Gatling guns, mortars, and vintage rifles, and then introduced me to other ordnance specialists and historians for additional guidance.

Among others, his pointing finger led me to Valley Forge and to Paulette Mark, Supervising Park Ranger for Visitor Services and Park Ranger Marc Brier, both of whom read the section on the American Revolution, made a number of illuminating suggestions, and added many important facts and insights.

Mr. Joseph Woefling, an ordnance specialist on the 1903 Springfield rifle and another Smithgall colleague, saved me from several errors concerning the World War I Pedersen device on the Springfield rifle

A conversation at the Smithgall farm with Paul Davies of Falls Church, Virginia, an ordnance historian and a specialist on Civil War weaponry, gave me a greater perspective on Ordnance Chief James Ripley and also on the Custer battle at Little Big Horn.

Mr. Fred Pernell at the Still Photograph Section of the National Archives was especially patient and helpful in finding a number of photographs included in this book, while a major part of the Archives was in transit from Washington to its new home in College Park, Maryland.

Historian and teacher and valued friend Frederic Josephson applied his encyclopedic knowledge of American history to a reading of the manuscript which produced many important suggestions.

Charles Flowers's editing is evident on every page and went far beyond the usual vetting of a manuscript. He even suggested the title. This would have been a different and lesser book without his help.

Scribner senior editor Edward (Ned) Chase watched over this book from the time he read the summary proposal, providing me a number of ideas and suggestions and additional sources.

Behind every book of this scope is necessarily an indefatigably dedicated researcher and this book was fortunate to have one who logged endless hours with microfilm screens, computer modems, library stacks, historic sites, and specialist libraries, while outside the sunshine beckoned—my wife, Marion.

Important help and guidance came from the library of the Springfield Armory National Historic Site, where the bulk of the history in this book took place, and from staff members of the Harpers Ferry National Historic Site which still extols the virtues of Hall's rifle with firing demonstrations and lectures and which also located several photos for this book.

There were many others—at the Aberdeen Proving Ground, the Army War College in Carlisle, Pennsylvania, and the museum in Fraunces Tavern in lower Manhattan, to name just three of dozens—whose help furnished key facts and insights.

The errors that remain are my own. I hope they are few in number

CONTENTS

PREFACE

In 1958, one of the country's most gifted military weapons designers, Eugene Stoner, working in the laboratories of the ArmaLite
Corporation in Costa Mesa, California, developed a revolutionary
automatic assault rifle, the AR-15. Delivered to Fort Benning for
tests, the new weapon unleashed one of the most savage bureaucratic wars Washington has ever seen.

Hailed as the deadliest and most reliable automatic weapon ever
designed, before the AR-15 eventually became the army's M16 rifle,
this weapon set off a chain reaction that ultimately involved President
John Kennedy, Secretary of Defense Robert McNamara, his staff of
computer-driven "whiz kids," dozens of generals, the U.S. Army, the
Air Force, the Marine Corps, the Congress, the leading arms
weapons testing laboratories, a number of the Pentagon's interlocking ordnance committees, leading gunpowder manufacturers,
Colt's Patent Firearms Manufacturing Company, an unstoppable
international arms salesman who succeeded in bringing the whole issue to a head, the governments of South Vietnam and South Korea,
a blatantly rigged weapons test, a full-scale investigation by the inspector general, the specially appointed Ichord Congressional Investigating Subcommittee on the M16, the closing of the U.S.
National Armory in Springfield, Massachusetts, and, on the battlefields of Vietnam, the deaths of a number of young American soldiers
killed as they tried desperately to unjam their fouled M16s.

More specifically, this is the history of a deeply entrenched ordnance concept that holds that carefully aimed, long-range rifle fire conserves ammunition and wins battles. This philosophy of the "gravel-belly," as the army sharpshooter is called, has been emphatically denied by critics who present abundant evidence, much of it from the army's own records, that superior firepower, not the best-aimed weapon, wins battles.

Equally as significant as the gravel-belly philosophy has been the armory's often fumbling management methods, whereby, on the eve of almost every U.S. war, the armory has been so ill prepared that no rifles were available for American troops. On several occasions, most notably during World War I, in lieu of rifles, it issued broomsticks for training and had to hastily provide American doughboys in France with borrowed British rifles and borrowed French machine guns and artillery. Three times a sitting president has had to force an ordnance chief to accept an important new rifle the armory was dead set against.

Today, the gravel-belly concept continues to dominate Ordnance thinking. Confronted by other major armies of the world equipped with automatic rifles with a cyclic firing rate of over seven hundred rounds a minute, U.S. Ordnance leaders have armed the American foot soldier with our current assault rifle, the M16A2, that fires three bullets with each pull of the trigger—a weapon Ordnance says conserves ammunition.

A saga, a warning, an often confounding account, the story stretches back to the morning at Lexington when the Minutemen first fired on the British redcoats to record the tumultuous rise and crash of the Springfield National Armory.

PART I

CHAPTER 1

SPRINGFIELD ARSENAL IN THE AMERICAN REVOLUTION

On a wintry day in January 1777, just weeks after the American victories at Trenton and Princeton, Washington's chief of artillery, General Henry Knox, and several of his ordnance officers strode around the high ground overlooking the town of Springfield, Massachusetts, which they were considering as a site for the first American arsenal.

Even though over a year and a half had passed since the Revolution began, Washington and his staff were still fashioning strategies and tactics that would make best use of the colonists' slender— often inadequate, sometimes nonexistent—resources, including ammunition and weapons. What the revolutionists were discovering about warfare under such privation would shape the thinking of the American ordnance department for the next two hundred years.

In a sense, Washington's officers' lack of military experience and training, while a severe drawback, was also an asset, for it opened the door to the very kind of innovation the conservative military mind would resist. In the century ahead, this military stand-pat attitude would leave military men increasingly farther behind technological developments as the Industrial Revolution almost buried them in a Pandora's box of lethal weapons that would change warfare forever.

Nowhere was this resistance to change among military men more abundantly illustrated than in the British navy then patrolling the waters off the colonial shoreline. Twenty-three years before, in 1754, a British navy ship's surgeon, James Lind, published *A Treatise on Scurvy,* which for the first time identified the cause of that dreadful and often fatal disease among British seamen, so widespread and severe it often had debilitated entire warships. It was brought about, he asserted, by a lack of citrus in the abominable navy diet and could be completely eradicated by simply adding a ration of lime juice to the menu. But the required keg of lime juice for each ship was deemed too expensive, and British seamen continued to suffer and die from scurvy for almost fifty years, until 1795, when lime juice was made a compulsory element in the seaman's diet. Historian Barbara Tuchman notes that behind such woodenheadedness lay nothing more profound than a "general reluctance to change old habits."[1]

Lord Howe, in charge of British forces in America, could hardly be accused of such extreme blindness. In his training program, he had even trained his troops in American fighting tactics.[2] But he was a European army man—as were General Clinton and Cornwallis—who would scorn the style of warfare the Americans perforce had to develop.

British infantry tactics were built around the .75-caliber Brown Bess smoothbore muzzle-loading musket, weighing eleven pounds and standing four feet nine inches. But the principal infantry weapon was not the musket but the twenty-one-inch bayonet on the end of it. The musket itself was secondary because it was a fair-weather weapon of uncertain performance. When the trigger was squeezed, the spark from the flint might or might not ignite the powder in the pan, while in rain and snow, once the powder got wet, it would fail to fire. Although the musket in skilled hands was able to hit targets at about one hundred yards, the Brown Bess—which had no rear sight—generally was used as a mass volleying weapon that was not carefully aimed.

The standard British tactic of the day was to close upon the enemy in three—later two—ranks, then, often at less than fifty yards, on command from the officers, to fire a musket volley from military formation into the general area called the "danger range," which might extend two hundred yards ahead on a level terrain, to be followed by a charge with fixed bayonets.[3] There was little time for reloading. Casualties from such encounters were high and only the most brutally imposed discipline would cause men to fight in such fashion.

For increased firepower, an undersize ball was issued, to permit faster loading, allowing four shots a minute under ideal circumstances, but at an additional sacrifice of accuracy.

British army regulars, many of them from the very bottom of society in England, who usually joined only under coercion, had to be trained, their officers believed, by stern—even savage—British discipline, which bred out any impulse to take personal initiative.

At first, the American army relied to a great extent on the Brown Bess, acquired by many colonists during mandatory military service. Increasingly, though, especially after France entered the war, the principal military shoulder arm was the standard French army issue Charleville 1763 smoothbore musket, augmented by muskets from Germany, Holland, and Spain.

While General Washington and General von Steuben, like the British, regarded the bayonet as the first line weapon, they were at first compelled to rely more heavily on the shoulder arm, for untrained American troops were not very skilled with the bayonet; indeed, the weapon, having no place in the colonists' lives, was rarely seen and, in any case, most American weapons did not have the fittings to accommodate it. Such bayonetless firearms were required to be accompanied by a tomahawk. It was said the British going into battle prayed for rain, when their superior bayonet skills could easily rout the colonists. But particularly after the winter encampment in Valley Forge, in the winter of 1777–1778, following von Steuben's training, the Americans proved themselves to be more than a match for the British soldier on the battlefield—as General Clinton was to learn at Monmouth.

British officers believed that, regardless of fighting style, the Minuteman was little better than a country clown whose lack of discipline could not stand up to trained British and Hessian regulars. While it is true that initially Americans were no match for the

British, who used traditional European tactics, they soon developed methods intended to swing the advantage to themselves—methods that would prove unsettling to the British. With their deeply imbued hunting habit of making every shot count, the Americans not only aimed more carefully than the British, they usually aimed at the highest-ranking uniforms, which not only infuriated the officers but also reduced Britain's store of leadership. Worse, from the British viewpoint, the Americans also preferred to stand behind trees to do their firing rather than to draw up in ranks. While this, too, violated European military tradition, it increased the effectiveness of American marksmanship and reduced the effectiveness of British bayonets.

Washington, who admired the British army and really desired to field a British-style army that would be a match for Howe's regulars, initially found this to be impossible. His troops were untrained farmers and clerks, often serving under ninety-day enlistments. What little they knew of military drill had been taught haphazardly from different drill books, often by militia officers who were just one page ahead of them, which produced an army that could not follow uniform commands. Washington had no cadre of trained officers, and for weapons, he had a hodgepodge, most of which were brought from home and included a large number of fowling pieces.

But, especially in that first year of fighting, 1775, ammunition was Washington's greatest concern—torment, in fact. It was so critically short, the American Revolution almost didn't occur. It was not that the American soldiers were inclined to waste gunpowder. As previously noted, the scarcity and expense of gunpowder in the colonies had honed the widely known sharpshooting skills of the colonists. It was the severe scarcity of it. From the beginning, the British understood that ammunition was a key factor in the war. To them, it was a simple three-step equation: No powder meant no arms. No arms meant no army. No army meant no revolution. So the British strictly enforced a long-standing policy, both mercantile and military, that prohibited the manufacture of gunpowder anywhere in the colonies.

The colonists' desperate need for ammunition was the cause of the first encounter between Minutemen and English troops. Before dawn in Lexington, Massachusetts, on April 19, 1775, seventy-seven Minutemen confronted an advance unit of seven hundred British regulars sent to capture a cache of American arms and ammunition believed to be in nearby Concord. Within hours, the muskets of four thousand angry farmers drove the entire British force of fifteen hundred back into the city of Boston with 273 casualties, nearly a fifth of their fighting force.

During the whole first year of fighting, Washington recorded, there were not "more than nine cartridges to a man."[4] A line of American sentries, stretching some thirteen miles around Boston, had not among them a full ounce of powder.[5] Had the American high command played war games at a sand table, as later armies did, this overriding shortage of gunpowder might have persuaded them to call off the revolution. Certainly, no one smiled when Benjamin Franklin suggested that American troops be armed with bows and arrows.[6]

For a graphic example of how dangerously short of ammunition the colonies were, Washington needed to look no further than Bunker Hill. There, twenty-five hundred British regulars in close-order parade confronted fifteen hundred untrained men and boys.[7] For ammunition, the Americans had only the powder appropriated by the New Hampshire militia from Fort William and Mary in Portsmouth.[8] The need to make every shot count led to the famous admonition "Don't fire, boys, until you see the whites of their eyes," generally ascribed either to General Israel Putnam[9] or to Colonel William Prescott.[10]

Twice the British attacked and twice were driven back, both times with heavy losses. It was a critical moment for the British. If they were driven back a third time, they would in all probability not have had enough men left for a fourth assault. And all of Europe would have known soon that British regulars had suffered a significant defeat by a smaller group of untrained colonial farmers.

On the third try, the British did carry the hill,[11] but only after the Americans had run out of ammunition and, using the butt ends of their muskets on the charging British regulars, withdrew from the battle.[12] The Americans sustained losses of 140 killed and 270 wounded; the British lost 226, with another 828 wounded, and would probably have been repulsed with even higher casualties had the Minutemen had enough ammunition. For want of a few thousand rounds more, the Americans had lost a significant victory at Bunker Hill. It is not idle to speculate that such a dramatic American victory—demonstrating so early in the war that Americans were a match for the British in the field—might have brought the French into the war much sooner.

The rifle, used by the British as an auxiliary weapon, primarily for skirmishing and subordinate to the smoothbore musket, became much more important in American hands and served to significantly shape and modify American military tactics. Because of the rifling cut into the inner walls of the barrel, the rifle fired a round patched ball with greater range, a greater muzzle velocity, and a greater accuracy.[13] On the colonial frontiers, the rifle was a tool of survival, needed to help feed growing families and to fend off the attacks of Indians. Consequently, Washington had access to companies of riflemen skilled in the ways of Indian fighting and capable of killing a man at distances up to four hundred yards with one shot. The most admired of all weapons was the Pennsylvania rifle (also called the Lancaster and, later, in a salute to Daniel Boone and his fellow frontiersmen, the Kentucky rifle), the hunting weapon of choice among those who could afford it.

The rifle had three drawbacks that prevented it from becoming the principal infantry weapon. Because of its rifling, it took longer to load. Also, because it was more lightly made than a musket, it was not tough enough to be used as a club in battle. Lastly, it was not fitted with a bayonet. Without it, the rifleman was helpless when the British regular closed with his probing bayonet.

Although representing less than 10 percent of the shoulder arms in the American army, the rifle's long-range deadliness in battle made a major difference.[14] As early as Bunker Hill, a British officer reported that an American rifleman knocked down twenty redcoats with his marksmanship before he himself was felled.[15]

Washington had under his command ten companies of frontier

sharpshooters—six from Pennsylvania, two from Maryland, and two from Virginia[16]—all expert at loading and firing their rifles. Although these frontiersmen proved to be so unruly that the army became disenchanted with them, and although Washington himself, as the historian Russell F. Weigley observed, "wondered whether they were more of a plague than an asset,"[17] in their hands, the rifle was so lethal it became a plague to the British, who in turn relied on hired Hessian mercenaries armed with rifles to try to counter them.

One of the most clear-cut examples of the new role the American rifle carved for itself during the Revolution occurred during the Battle of Saratoga against General Burgoyne's forces in September of 1777. General Washington sent Daniel Morgan and 350 rifle sharpshooters to General Gates, primarily to take care of Burgoyne's Indians, who were terrorizing the entire countryside. Morgan's men, skilled in Indian tactics, turned the tables on the Indians to such an extent, Burgoyne later wrote, that not one of his Indians "could be brought within the sound of a rifle shot."[18] But the rifle soon showed what it could do as a major battle weapon when, firing at ranges far beyond the ordinary musket, Morgan's rifles took such a toll of Burgoyne's artillery officers and gunners as to reduce materially Burgoyne's functioning artillery. In one of Burgoyne's gun detachments alone, Morgan's riflemen killed or wounded the captain and thirty-six out of forty-eight gunners, effectively silencing all the artillery in that unit.[19]

The most emphatic demonstration of the superiority of the rifle over the musket occurred at the Battle of Kings Mountain, North Carolina, in September 1780. Cornwallis's commander in North Carolina was a Scot—Major Patrick Ferguson, of the Second Battalion, Seventy-first Regiment of Highlanders.

Major Ferguson, "perhaps the best marksman living,"[20] was also an outstanding weapons designer who created a rifle that was so unusual it was easily decades ahead of its time. The Ferguson rifle was based on an earlier rifle design by the Frenchman LaChaumette, and among its most noteworthy features was its breech-loading mechanism.

At a time when all weapons—rifles and muskets—were loaded with a ramrod down the muzzle, Ferguson's weapon was loaded— ball and loose powder from a powder horn—through an opening in the breech, just above the trigger. Eliminating the main complaint about the muzzle-loading rifle—the long preparation time—this breech-loading device permitted much faster firing.

The importance of faster firing was well illustrated during the 1777 Battle of Oriskany, in the Mohawk Valley of New York. General Nicholas Herkimer, lying mortally wounded under a tree, observed the attacking Indians watch for the puffs of the American musket volleys before attacking. They had calculated to the second how long it took the Americans to reload and were soon going to overrun the American positions during the intervals. Herkimer instructed his troops to pair off, half the troops to fire a volley in unison, the other half to hold their fire until the Indians attacked and then to open fire. The Indians, caught in an unexpected and murderous short-range volley, paid heavily and withdrew from the battlefield. General von Steuben included such staggered volleying as a principle in his training manual.

On April 27, 1776, at Woolwich Arsenal, England, during a driving rainstorm under high winds, Ferguson put on a stunning shooting exhibition with his rifle that many British ordnance men never forgot. Aiming with a unique elevated rear sight at targets two hundred yards away, Ferguson demonstrated an accuracy no Brown Bess could match, getting off through his breechloader four shots a minute. Then, in a demonstration of walking fire, he strode toward his target, continuing to fire and reload and fire four shots a minute; then, pausing, he raised his speed to an unheard-of six shots a minute. During the entire windblown performance, only three of Ferguson's shots failed to hit the target.[21]

So impressed were his superiors that he was put at the head of a two-hundred-man unit of infantrymen, all armed with his new breech-loading rifle. The unit was to make its first appearance at the Battle of Brandywine, south of Philadelphia, in September 1777.

According to his diary, published after his death, Ferguson had an opportunity to kill George Washington as the general rode by accompanied by a young French officer—identified later as the twenty-year-old Lafayette. But by the time identification was certain, the only target Washington presented was his back, and Ferguson's code of chivalry forbade back-shooting. Major Ferguson lowered his weapon and left historians to wonder ever since what the consequences to the Revolution might have been had he squeezed the trigger.[22]

Unfortunately for the British, Ferguson himself was severely wounded in his right arm at Brandywine prior to the main battle. General Howe, angered at having Ferguson's unit thrust upon him by London without prior consultation, seized the moment to permanently disband the rifle unit and thereby robbed military history of an early lesson in breech-loaded rifle firepower.

Later, in the mountains of North Carolina, Ferguson was in command of a unit of American Loyalists. He sought to scatter a dangerous assembly of rebels by announcing he was going to march over the mountains, destroy their farms and homes, and hang their leaders. He set out to confront them with a unit of more than eleven hundred Loyalists. Fewer than one hundred were armed with his breech-loading rifle, the rest mostly with the British army's .75-caliber Brown Bess. Having heard Ferguson's threat, some nine hundred Tennessee frontier marksmen, all armed with handmade muzzle-loading rifles, rode for thirty-four hours in a downpour to confront the Loyalists. Ferguson chose to face them on the ridge of Kings Mountain, an impregnable position, he felt, even against rifles. The rebels dismounted, surrounded the crest, and, without bayonets, charged up the slope, firing from behind the abundant trees. Major Ferguson led his Loyalists three times in a bayonet charge down the slope and into a slaughter. In half an hour, rifle fire settled the battle, Ferguson's surviving troops were surrounded, and he was slain by a rifle sniper while his panicked white horse galloped away through the trees, riderless. On the ground lay his prized breech-loading rifle.

The rebels suffered 28 killed and 62 wounded. But Ferguson's Loyalists suffered 157 killed and 163 wounded, most of whom later died in the field; 698 Loyalists were taken prisoner.[23]

The rifles at the Battle of Kings Mountain clearly heralded a change in the tactics and strategy of shoulder arms warfare, yet not until the American Civil War did military men finally understand that long-range rifle fire meant the end of the musket, the end of the cavalry, the virtual elimination of the massed infantry charge, and a major change in the use of artillery. New technological developments—like Ferguson's rifle—were changing the face of warfare and giving the advantage to the defense. In short, Ferguson's breechloader, however briefly, had introduced more firepower per man on the battlefield and thus a greater probability of victory.

At war's end, the British army dropped Ferguson's rifle. Historian Barbara Tuchman noted, "As more efficient than anything the British Army possessed, it was, of course, not adopted."[24]

The American Revolution was significant also for the number of clashes between the stand-up volley-and-charge tactics of the British and the behind-the-wall skirmishing tactics of the Americans. This presented General Washington with decided difficulties.

Americans, used to hunting, took to guerrilla tactics naturally. Scattered, crouching, firing from behind trees and rocks, the Americans, driving the British regulars back into Boston, presented less of a target to shoot at, while the British, hurrying along the roadway back to Boston, were open targets. Skirmishing was not new in the colonies. During the French and Indian War of 1754–1763, French and Indian forces, firing from the woods, ambushed and destroyed a British army under General Braddock at Fort Duquesne (later Pittsburgh) and sent the survivors straggling back to Virginia. There was one man in the American Revolution who had witnessed as a young American colonel the slaughter at Fort Duquesne and that was George Washington.

Washington was certainly mindful that his initial advantage—if there was any advantage—lay in irregular tactics. "To lean on the militia," he said, "was to lean on a broken reed. Being familiar with the use of the musket they will fight under cover, but they will not attack or stand in the open field."[25] And that situation was to prevail until after Valley Forge, when the Prussian drill master Baron von Steuben commenced teaching European tactics to the American troops, now not evanescent militia but regular enlisted Continental Army. In the end, Washington won with a medley of tactics, conventional battlefield confrontations combined with the added essential ingredients of skirmishing, daring raids, and guerrilla warfare.

If the Lexington-Concord battle hadn't brought the skirmishing lesson home, Bunker Hill surely did when fifteen hundred untrained men and boys deployed behind entrenchments almost defeated twenty-five hundred British troops. The Battle of White Plains also illustrates the point. Drawn up in conventional style, Washington's army was quickly put to full flight there, and only by a fortuitous rainstorm that rendered British Brown Bess flintlocks inoperative was it saved from certain destruction. Yet, the day before, American skirmishers behind stone walls had absorbed sixteen casualties while inflicting eight hundred on the British.[26] Washington's attack at Trenton and later at Princeton literally saved the Revolution from total collapse. Of that celebrated Christmas-night crossing of the Delaware and the raid that followed, Lord Germain, coordinating British operations from London, observed, "All our hopes were blasted by that unhappy affair at Trenton."[27] Some historians have termed the raid on Trenton the turning point of the Revolution—an accolade usually bestowed on the Battle of Saratoga.

Guerrilla tactics drove the British out of the southern colonies. Skirmishing American rifles at Kings Mountain caused Cornwallis to withdraw from North Carolina, and in South Carolina, he encountered perhaps the greatest master of guerrilla warfare to emerge from the war, Francis Marion, whose devastating exploits against the British earned him the nom de guerre of the Swamp Fox. And at the Battle of Cowpens, in January 1781, a celebrated attack by General Morgan involved a double envelopment—sweeping around both flanks—that brought a great victory over Colonel Tarlton's British forces, which contributed significantly to Cornwallis's removal to Virginia and the final battle at Yorktown.

It is true that Washington was not familiar with these irregular tactics, but neither was he a master of the art of British-style warfare. The bulk of what he knew about soldiering came from a single book, Humphrey Bland's *Treatise on Military Discipline*, a 1727 British tactical manual.[28] In fact, when he took command of the army in Philadelphia, he insisted he felt inadequate to the military role thrust upon him and urged the Continental Congress to appoint General Andrew Lewis rather than himself.[29] During his speech accepting the command, he said, "I beg it be remembered by every gentleman in the room, that I, this day, declare with the utmost sincerity, I do not think myself equal to the command I am honored with."[30]

Probably the most important weapon the Americans had in the field, one the British could not seem to duplicate, was General Washington himself. More than once, when defeat seemed to be in the eyes of every man around him, Washington's will to prevail unquestionably saved the Revolution.

I n one military area—artillery—Washington found an officer who was more than a match for his British counterparts. Henry Knox, a veteran of the Battle of Bunker Hill, became at twenty-seven a brigadier general and Washington's chief of artillery.

When his father, a shipmaster, died, nine-year-old Henry went to work for a Boston bookseller to help support his mother and brother, William. He became an omnivorous reader and acquired a broad liberal education in Greek and Roman classics, even teaching himself passably good French. In his teens, he joined a militia artillery company trained by British officers. Four days after his twenty-first birthday, Knox opened his own "British" bookshop, which soon became a popular Boston meeting place in which he had extended conversations about artillery with British officers. By reading every known work on artillery warfare, he soon became known for his expert knowledge of artillery, as well as for his qualities of leadership,[31] a combination that led to the offer of a commission in the British army, which he declined. When the Revolution began, his studies enabled him to turn American artillery into what Lafayette called "one of the wonders of the Revolution."

Weighing over three hundred pounds and standing well over six feet, with a jubilant personality, Knox was accounted a marvelous conversationalist, a born leader, and a gifted administrator. Often excessively generous, he was always fashionably dressed and had excellent manners. Around his left hand, he habitually wrapped a silk handkerchief to conceal the loss of two of the smaller fingers, blown off during a hunting expedition when a fowling piece had fired accidentally. A fluent, witty writer and an indefatigable correspondent, he left behind at his death more than ten thousand letters.

Over strong objections from her family, at twenty-three, Knox married Lucy Flucker, the strong-willed and vivacious eighteen-year-old daughter of Thomas Flucker, secretary of the province of Massachusetts and a prominent Tory who strongly disapproved of Knox's anti-British sentiments. After his participation at Bunker Hill, Knox and his wife slipped out of Boston, and he soon was in the service of George Washington, thereby commencing a strong lifelong friendship between the two. Washington increasingly put his confidence in Knox's military judgment, and in time, Knox became one of his most trusted advisers.

Knox first achieved fame when he brilliantly succeeded, during the winter of 1775–1776, in dragging through three hundred miles of snowbound wilderness from Fort Ticonderoga fifty-nine pieces of artillery that helped drive the British out of Boston.[32]

Because of Knox's inspired use of artillery and his skill at training others, Washington could rightly claim after the 1777 Battle of Brandywine River, south of Philadelphia, that young Knox's cannons fired more accurately than the English. Eighteen of Knox's guns crossed the Delaware at Christmas 1776 and were a decisive factor against the Hessians on the streets of Trenton. Knox's training and his precepts are credited with giving the U.S. Army's artillery its preeminent place in American military history.[33] Fighting in every major engagement from Bunker Hill to Cornwallis's surrender at Yorktown, Knox was one of Washington's ablest officers. After the Revolution, he became secretary of war of the Continental Congress and then, joining Washington's cabinet, he became the first secretary of war of the new constitutional government.

As the founder of the U.S. Ordnance Corps, Henry Knox is remembered for his successful efforts to set up the first, desperately needed, American arsenal, having impressed on the Continental Congress the necessity for a place "in which shall be prepared large quantities of ordnance stores of every species and denomination."[34] Knox was given urgent orders by General Washington in 1776 to find a site on which to build such an arsenal. Although France was providing the bulk of the revolutionists' ordnance, a place for receiving, storing, and shipping that ordnance was essential.

General Knox and his team had already been to Brookfield, Massachusetts, and to Hartford, Connecticut, twenty-nine miles south on the same Connecticut River, when, in late January 1777, they entered the town of Springfield, Massachusetts, and strode about the hill overlooking the Connecticut River.

In addition to its location, Springfield offered important advantages over Brookfield: it had a vast store of accessible lumber, adequate water power, copper and tin reserves, and a number of resident gunsmiths and artificers. In addition, Springfield offered a vital advantage over otherwise ideal Hartford. The Connecticut River at Hartford was navigable from Long Island Sound, a tempting target to the battle-hungry British navy, prowling out of New York City. So logic drove General Knox upstream, where the Connecticut wasn't navigable, until he reached Springfield.

Viewed from the brow of the hill, Springfield wasn't very prepossessing—just a raw little river town with barely more than one or two streets crowded between the river's edge and the hill. But down there in the town were the forges and foundries of the first Continental Army Cannon Foundry, which was making cannon for Washington's army. From his vantage point on the hill, General Knox could look down on the ford where he had crossed the Connecticut River with the fifty-nine pieces of artillery from Fort Ticonderoga.

Springfield's geography offered a number of unique advantages for an arsenal. Beyond the reach of the British navy, and reasonably safe from the British army, Springfield was centrally situated on the Connecticut River at an intersection of major roadways, to the north and south along the Connecticut River valley, to the east to Boston, and to the west to Albany and the Hudson River. They would thus be capable of sending arms in all directions. Some thirty acres of level ground on the hilltop site would provide more than enough space to contain the various arsenal buildings in which to make ordnance stores, including desperately needed musket cartridges, carriages for cannons of all sorts and sizes, ammunition wagons, tumbrels, harnesses, and the like.

Beyond the physical benefits of Springfield, there were also political considerations. Massachusetts had agreed to pay for erecting the arsenal and therefore favored a site in its own state over one in Connecticut, especially since the new arsenal meant jobs, the purchase of many local services and supplies, and other economic activity.

General Knox wrote to General Washington that, after considering the various sites, and weighing their advantages and disadvantages, "This is the best place in all the four New England states."[35] Washington approved Knox's choice, and even before the Continental Congress had given its endorsement in February, Knox had laborers digging foundations for storehouses, ordnance shops, a powder magazine, and barracks for the troops who would protect the arsenal. March saw the fabrication of the first musket cartridges, and by April 1777, the new arsenal was able to turn out 7,584 cartridges in one week. Meantime, the erection of other buildings proceeded apace.

For the rest of the Revolution, the arsenal proved invaluable—even essential—to the rebels' cause. Its large staff of soldiers and civilians—some of them deserters from His Majesty's Royal Army—made paper cartridges, stored muskets and housed cannon and ammunition, and maintained a large array of wagons and caissons and draft horses that carted military stores to the armies on the battlegrounds all through the colonies. They even built scows and smaller craft to ferry military matériel and horses and wagons across the Connecticut for transport to New York and points south.

Outmaneuvered, trapped beyond the reach of his navy on a peninsula between the James and York rivers, Britain's General Cornwallis angrily struck his colors on October 19, 1781, in

Yorktown, Virginia. He remained in his tent during the surrender ceremony at Yorktown, sending his sword to the detested rebels by way of his second in command, Brigadier General Charles O'Hara.

At war's end, the new nation's military leaders had learned some painful lessons and failed to learn others. While superb fighters like Francis Marion were warmly remembered, largely forgotten were their guerrilla tactics that had done so much to defeat the British. When the U.S. Military Academy was founded at West Point, its primary focus was on military engineering. Skirmishing wasn't even listed on the curriculum.

As for weaponry, General Henry Knox and his fledgling Ordnance Corps could vow never again to be caught short of ammunition—would never forget that the lack of it nearly cost them the Revolution. So well did the Ordnance Corps learn this lesson of conserving ammunition that, in time, it would often put it ahead of more important considerations—as will be shown.

As for the rifle, the most important lesson Ordnance learned was that slow, carefully aimed rifle fire could conserve ammunition and contribute materially to victory on the battlefield. Completely forgotten by both sides was the breech-loading Ferguson rifle. With its brilliant inventor dead at Kings Mountain, the Ferguson was now a curiosity relegated to military museums.

To become a full-fledged eighteenth-century infantry weapon, the rifle needed three things: to be made stronger, to be fitted with a bayonet, and to load faster. Ordnance didn't forget this, and when the new armory at Harpers Ferry was founded, one of its first assignments was the design of a military rifle.

In Springfield, as wartime jobs ended and the soldiers marched away, the town emptied. With its nearest potential enemy far across the ocean, and with little to fear from the Spanish colonies or from the Indians, the new nation felt that the last thing it wanted or needed was an army or an armory. In 1782, the Continental Congress shut down its Springfield Arsenal, and left it, stocked with cannon, ten thousand muskets, a quantity of other small arms left over from the war, and, in the brick powder magazine, a quantity of gunpowder. They placed the arsenal under the meager protection of a few locks and a small staff of military storekeepers under Captain John Bryant from Boston, who was in command later when the Springfield Arsenal became the target of Shays' Rebellion, one of the first grave crises of the new nation, one that would have a significant effect on the writing of the new Constitution.

CHAPTER 2

SHAYS'S REBELLION: HARPERS FERRY ARMORY

By 1787, with the Revolution behind them, the colonies were confronted with dangerous postwar inflation. The farmers were particularly hard hit when they found their paper money so worthless they couldn't pay their debts. In Massachusetts, they looked around for leadership to help them express their views. When they turned to Daniel Shays, matters quickly turned violent. Shays was himself a Massachusetts farmer, a sometime politician, an ex-captain in the American Revolution, a veteran of Bunker Hill, and, while not very sophisticated in the ways of commerce and banking, he felt great sympathy for his fellow farmers in Massachusetts and elsewhere in the country who faced the loss of their farms and even imprisonment for debt.

These farmers felt that their plight was not their fault. The paper currency of the new government was to blame because it was worth so little, they couldn't pay their debts or their taxes with it. As a result, the banks resorted to court action: confiscation and eviction. In angry meetings, these farmers shouted that big business controlled the banks, and merchants controlled the state legislature. Daniel Shays's friends and fellow farmers believed there was a conspiracy against the small farmer and looked to him for guidance.

Shays decided on an extreme solution. Without the courts, he pointed out, the banks couldn't foreclose. So Shays proposed that they save their farms by the simple expedient of closing Massachusetts's courthouses and keeping them closed until the next election, when they could elect more sympathetic representatives. Armed bands of his followers thereupon shut down courts in Northampton and Springfield and a number of other Massachusetts towns.

These roving bands soon coalesced into organized military units, one of which was drilled by Shays himself. More than four thousand angry farmers, believing they were fighting for their very existence, joined him. The news of the rebellion spread quickly throughout the thirteen states, much to the alarm of the nation's leaders, including George Washington. Writing from Virginia, he asked his former general of artillery, now the Confederation's secretary of war, Henry Knox, to assess the situation. Knox's report was bleak. He felt that in Massachusetts and in New Hampshire, Connecticut, and Rhode Island, Shays might soon have as many as fifteen thousand followers. The wartime army had rarely reached this size during all the years of the Revolution. "We are fast verging on anarchy and confusion," Washington concluded.[1]

In November 1786, the Continental Congress met in New York City to discuss the situation. But the Congress had no money and, under the Articles of Confederation, it lacked the power to impose taxes. Delegates considered raising an army anyway, but in the end decided against such a move for fear that the soldiers, unpaid, would join with Shays.[2]

In the town of Lee, in Berkshire County, Massachusetts, a hastily assembled state militia unit threw up a roadway barrier and waited for Shays's marauding army to approach. Shays was ordered to halt, but when his followers wheeled out a cannon, the state militia unit fled, amid the cheers of the Shaysites. To the desperate farmers, the event was grimly funny, but Shays knew he wouldn't be able to use that trick a second time, since the secret was soon out that his followers had trundled up a fake cannon. To succeed, Shays's army needed arms, and to get them, on January 25, 1787, he led several thousand men on a march to the national arsenal in Springfield.

The ten thousand French Charleville muskets and other small arms and gunpowder from the Revolutionary War that were stored in the lightly guarded arsenal could have turned Shays's army into a formidable force. But when they arrived at Springfield, many armed with only pitchforks and field rakes, they found waiting for them two stockade forts and twelve hundred Massachusetts militia, under the command of General Benjamin Lincoln, Washington's second-in-command at Yorktown.

Shays's men marched up Arsenal Hill, reached the junction of Magazine Street and St. James Avenue, and prepared to attack. This time, however, it was the militia who had a cannon, a real one, and this time, Shays had foolishly marched within its range. Grapeshot—a cluster of small cast-iron balls dispersing from a cloth bag when fired from a cannon—killed several rebels, wounded a number of others, and, just a few hundred yards from the Springfield Arsenal, ended Shays's Rebellion, sending Shays in full flight into Vermont with a death penalty on his head.

In the end, statewide elections brought in a more sympathetic Massachusetts legislature, which took specific steps to allay the most vocal complaints by the farmers. It suspended through 1788 the law requiring debts to be paid by specie, and instead allowed payment of debt by personal and real estate, accepting payment of taxes by such goods as beef, pork, flax, leather, iron, and even whale oil. In addition, the legislature suspended the collection of direct taxes during the year of 1787, and passed a general amnesty that pardoned all the rebels, including Shays himself.[3] Improving economic conditions removed most of the remaining grievances,[4] yet Daniel Shays's Rebellion was not forgotten. In fact, his action hastened the writing of the American Constitution because Shays's Rebellion further convinced men like Washington and Adams that the loose embrace of the Articles of Confederation did not bind them into a nation. Singly, the states were too weak to cope with serious internal dissension. Collectively, the confederated states were too weak to cope with serious foreign intervention.

With the Shays crisis over, the questions began. Many felt that the rebellion could have gotten out of hand. If the Shaysites had broken into the arsenal, they might have started a second revolution and, given the anger of the small landholders throughout the country, might have even caused the dissolution of the Confederation.

Despite the profound distrust newly free Americans had of any government, even their own, Washington recognized the "necessity of giving adequate powers to Congress . . ."[5] to enable the nation to cope with its internal problems effectively and also to avoid the appearance of weakness internationally; they feared attracting adventurous nations if "we render ourselves ridiculous and contemptible in the eyes of all Europe."[6]

Agreeing, others like Jefferson felt that while the nation had to become more tightly bound—federated—it must have a written constitution to control the potential excesses of federated government. Hamilton advocated a soundly based national currency and a national power to tax by pointing out that it was the printing of highly inflationary paper currency by the states and by the Congress itself that created the desperate conditions that had raised Shays's Rebellion.

That same year of Shays's Rebellion—1787—a convention met in Philadelphia to discuss the flaws of the Articles of Confederation. People of substance like Alexander Hamilton—property owners and merchants and bankers—wanted a strong national government and military to cope with any other Shays who might be lurking down the road.

Small independent landowners, small farmers, mechanics, agrarians, and rural thinkers like Thomas Jefferson, remembering why they had fought the British throne, feared that a strong national government, especially if it had access to a strong military force, would threaten the freedoms they had just won.

So both the Springfield Armory and Daniel Shays were on the minds of both sides of this argument all through the summer days of the 1787 Constitutional Convention in Philadelphia, and when the delegates had finished, they had managed to address the demands of both the Hamiltonians and the Jeffersonians. The convention wrote a new Constitution, ratified in 1789, that created a strong central government, and by 1791, the distrusters of government had attached the first ten amendments—called the Bill of Rights—which sought to define and protect the rights of the individual citizen.

Today, in retrospect, the Shays episode appears to have been too weak and too poorly directed to have become a serious threat, but at the time, the memory of what a handful of men armed with muskets at Concord and Bunker Hill did to a powerful nation like England was still fresh. It wasn't the specter of marauding mobs roving through the land that galvanized the nation. It was the specter of mobs armed with the abundant weapons in the government's own storehouse. That specter placed the Springfield Arsenal right in the emotional center of the new nation. And once there, the Springfield Arsenal became a profound influence on the writing of the Constitution. James Madison wrote after the Convention that, more than the inadequacies of the Articles of Confederation, it was the threatening moves in Massachusetts and Rhode Island against property that ultimately produced the new Constitution.[7] In the end, the proponents of strong government and the proponents of decentralized government, too far apart on many issues to agree on even when and where to meet, were finally brought together by one phrase more than any other: Springfield Arsenal.

In 1794, the Springfield Arsenal once again occupied the attention of government leaders when the third U.S. Congress met in Philadelphia.

Former friend and mentor, France, had killed its king, Louis XVI, the year before and was now convulsed in a bloody revolution of its own while fighting a war against Austria, Prussia, and Sardinia. Attempting to isolate France and weaken its economy, the British were using their navy to discourage American trade with France. Another American war with England therefore seemed all too likely, although this time, the United States could hardly look to the French government to arm it with necessary ordnance. The country was exposed and inadequately defended and needed to start making its own military arms.

Coincidentally, in the midst of the debate, a new Shays's Rebellion, called the Whiskey Insurrection, broke out in western Pennsylvania. As part of the fiscal program of Secretary of the Treasury Alexander Hamilton, Congress had passed an excise tax on whiskey.

For the backwoods farmers, distilling whiskey was an important method of disposing of excess grain, and they angrily denounced the tax as discriminatory. Matters turned ugly when the farmers formed an army, then burned the home of the regional inspector of excise and tarred and feathered several federal revenue officers who had attempted to collect the tax.

Although the Whiskey Insurrection quickly collapsed when several hundred arrests were made by armed troops dispatched into western Pennsylvania by President Washington, the whole affair, coupled with the unsettled events in Europe, made a strong impression on Congress. So elected officials were quite responsive when, in April 1794, Washington sponsored a bill for the erecting of arsenals and magazines. Congress promptly passed the bill, thereby authorizing the establishment of up to four national armories. Washington was allowed the discretion of deciding how many armories were needed and where they should be placed. He also was given authority to hire and fire superintendents, storekeepers, paymasters, and master armorers, a power that later, in the hands of other administrations, became the source of important political patronage.

Washington's secretary of war, and his former general of artillery, Henry Knox, strongly recommended as one of the choices the Springfield Arsenal, property already owned by the United States, which had many necessary buildings already standing and sited near ample water power, transportation, and other resources. Washington promptly accepted that recommendation.

The selection of the second site, at Harpers Ferry, Virginia, caused almost immediate controversy.

Washington himself chose the location at Harpers Ferry, at the confluence of the Potomac and Shenandoah rivers in northern Virginia near the Maryland border, and gave three reasons for his choice. These were similar to those given for choosing Springfield: abundant water power, convenient location near furnaces and forges, from which the new armory would obtain its iron, and, because of its inland location, security from foreign invaders.[8] But his motives for choosing this site were much more complex, with the manufacture of military weapons among the least of them.

George Washington had been born in 1732 in Wakefield, Virginia, on the Potomac River near the estuary to the Chesapeake Bay. As a youth, he had worked as surveyor for Lord Fairfax, who owned vast tracts of land in the Shenandoah and Potomac River valleys, and, with his surveyor's tools, had charted much of the Potomac River. So Washington knew the Potomac intimately and believed that the area was on the verge of great economic expansion. His views seemed quite sensible to many Virginians; the river had great strategic importance, for it provided a gateway through the mountains into Ohio and points west and another gateway into the Shenandoah Valley, which ran south in western Virginia.

After the Revolution, Washington had turned his attention to the "Western lands"—the territory beyond the mountains into Ohio. From New York south to Virginia and the Carolinas, there were no existing east-west roadways through the Appalachian and Allegheny mountains that could bind the new lands with the original thirteen colonies. So, to gain access to markets, the frontier people of necessity would have to use as their roadway into the world either the Mississippi River, which flowed south via New Orleans—a Spanish (and, later, French) possession—into the Gulf of Mexico, or the Great Lakes and St. Lawrence River to the Atlantic Ocean, dominated by England in Canada. The danger, as Washington saw it, was that either England or France or both could drain away loyalty to the new American nation, especially by populating those territories with new European immigrants who would have no ties at all to the original thirteen colonies. The western territories could thus become a separate nation, even a hostile one.

The answer, Washington felt, was to open new ways through the mountains—via existing mountain passes on navigable rivers. As the nation's new capital city was taking shape on the banks of the Potomac River, Washington dreamed of making it the leading economic hub of the country, carrying manufactured goods and new immigrants upriver and raw materials, farm produce, and even furs from far-distant Detroit downriver. His own community of Alexandria, which he had laid out as a teenage surveyor, would thereby become a thriving tidewater port for the transshipping of goods between oceangoing vessels and river barges. But this would be possible only by making the Potomac navigable for its full two hundred miles and only by making it navigable before other, competitive waterways were opened—through a man-made canal in New York State (which was to become the Erie Canal) or through the mountains south of the Potomac Gap. All these waterways would be needed eventually, but Washington wanted the Potomac waterway to be the first and therefore foremost.

In fact, Washington's vision embraced a growing nation interconnected with a system of canals, constructed by the individual states but orchestrated by the planning of the Continental Congress, "bringing," he said, "navigation to almost every man's door." [9]

After the Revolution, to implement his views, Washington had joined with other businessmen, including his brother, Charles, in a plan to develop the whole area. In 1785, Washington and a group of his associates successfully lobbied the legislatures of Maryland and Virginia for the formation of the Patowmack Company, a joint stock venture, for the purpose of constructing canals around the three rapids of the Potomac in order to make the river a navigable tollway all the way to Westernport, Maryland. The charter specified that the Patowmack Company should do such river improvements as would permit a barge carrying fifty barrels of flour to travel the waterway in the driest season.

Both Virginia and Maryland, wishing to gain the prestige of Washington's participation, voted him fifty shares of stock in the new venture. But Washington was fearful that by accepting the shares, he would be seen as a self-serving opportunist, since he already had landholdings along the Potomac that could be expected to increase in value. As was his habit, he conferred with others he trusted about this seeming conflict of interest, including Thomas Jefferson, who not only urged him to go forth with the project, but also to do it quickly before New York State proceeded with its own canal.

Washington, therefore, placed the fifty shares in a trust, the proceeds of which were to go to the education of poor children, particularly the children of fallen Revolutionary soldiers. Then, to show that he was not a figurehead but a committed member of the venture, he purchased five shares of stock in his own name with his own capital.[10]

Perceiving that the development of the Potomac River Basin and the lands in Ohio meant a major economic, cultural, and political step forward for the country, and great wealth for its promoters, the public quickly subscribed to nearly double the minimum 150 shares necessary to launch the project. And when he became president in 1789, George Washington saw immediately that the nation could gain a vitally needed new armory and the Potomac an urgently needed new economic engine by placing a new arms factory at Harpers Ferry.

Upon the founding of the Patowmack Company in 1785, George Washington became its president[11] and, in August of that same year, conducted a tour of the three rapids that would require canal building, a tour that included an overnight stop at Harper House, the inn at Harpers Ferry.[12] The following year, in 1786, anticipating the effect of the Patowmack Company's activities, Washington's brother, Charles, had laid out Charles Town, five miles from Harpers Ferry, naming the two intersecting main streets George and Washington.

Then, in 1790, General Washington furthered the development of the area by situating the nation's permanent capital—later to be called Washington, District of Columbia—right at the estuary of the Potomac, not far from his birthplace. This, he believed, with a fully navigable river behind it, would make the new Federal City the nation's major economic hub.

Therefore, in 1794, Washington's choice of Harpers Ferry for the armory was another step in the development of the Potomac River basin, strategically placed to attract new communities and industry and to generate canal tolls for the Patowmack Company.

Among the company members were many who warmly endorsed the Harpers Ferry site, particularly two of the board members, businessmen Tobias Lear of Georgetown and George Gilpin of Alexandria. The two directors, close friends of George Washington's, had issued glowing reports about Harpers Ferry as a potential mill site for power generation. Lear in particular regarded a new armory at Harpers Ferry as a powerful economic engine that could help develop the whole Potomac River basin.

But the Harpers Ferry project soon ran into opposition.[13] Secretary Knox and his successor, Timothy Pickering, both objected to the site. Knox felt there were better sites available in Virginia, in Pennsylvania, and in Maryland. Pickering felt that Congress had not appropriated enough money to build two armories. Instead, he urged that the existing facility at Springfield be expanded and that a simple arms depot be set up at Harpers Ferry.

The economic value to the Potomac region of an armory at Harpers Ferry seemed obvious to the Patowmack Company members. But its value there as a military asset was much more questionable. For, in spite of Washington's contentions, physically, Harpers Ferry was not an ideal location for a new national armory. Shaped like an arrowhead, it was located right on the confluence of the Potomac and Shenandoah rivers, seemingly an ideal location. Yet it was quite remote from civilization. The nearest town—Charles Town, seven miles to the south and west—was hardly a town at all, having been laid out by Washington's brother, Charles, only a few years before, in 1786. The nearest, larger, more established town, Frederick, in Maryland, was more than twenty miles away.

As a mill site for generating power for the arms-making facility, Harpers Ferry presented other problems. It was subject to major flooding in the spring and to a serious loss of water volume during dry seasons. The great and devastating flood of 1754 was still recalled by many in the river valley. Harpers Ferry was also malarial, with frequent, often annual, springtime outbreaks of the disease, which was commonly fatal. Little more than a trading outpost in a wilderness providing a ferry crossing of both the Shenandoah and the Potomac rivers, Harpers Ferry had little population there, no supply of labor for building the armory, no housing for outside workers to move into, no available supply of armorers to make the weapons after the buildings were finished, no accessible supply of raw materials. With no social amenities for workers' families, no churches, no schools, almost no stores, and a reputation for malaria, Harpers Ferry would have a difficult time finding and keeping the skilled labor it would need.

Building materials and tooling would have to be transported at considerable expense, often by five-team Conestoga wagons over rough roads from long distances. Pig iron and bar iron, those essential materials for arms making, were not available from nearby sources as Washington thought but would have to be shipped from more than one hundred miles away in central Pennsylvania.[14]

In only one feature was there universal agreement. The wilderness around Harpers Ferry would provide abundant wood for charcoal to operate the forges and for the gunstocks, which represented 40 percent of material that went into a musket.

In 1795, to better evaluate the glowing statements about the site issued by Gilpin and Lear, Secretary of War Pickering sought expert advice from a military engineer, Colonel Stephen Rochfontaine. The French-born Rochfontaine was commissioned to explore various appropriate sites for an armory along the Potomac. His report didn't mention Harpers Ferry. Not an oversight, he admitted. Harpers Ferry was just not a good location. Because of the precipitous slope of the terrain, there was little level land for a factory. There was no ground, he said, on which "convenient buildings could be placed." Also, the annual flooding meant that "no water work would be safe there."[15]

Washington rejected Rochfontaine's findings and became even more determined to site the new armory at Harpers Ferry.

He now appointed Lear and Gilpin his special agents for the acquisition of the necessary land at Harpers Ferry, and they found an entangled situation awaiting them. The 125-acre ferry site they wanted—the tip of the arrowhead—was owned by the Wager family, who were reluctant to sell. An adjacent 230-acre "sawmill" plot, stretching from river to river, was owned by Thomas Rutherford, Jr., son-in-law to General William Darke. A third plot, comprising another 600 acres, was held by George Washington's relative, Burges Ball, under a seventy-five-year lease from the owner, Henry Lee. The Rutherford plot was in litigation between Rutherford and the Wager family, exacerbated by another suit from a man named Bready, whose sawmill was on the Shenandoah side of Harpers Ferry. Negotiations moved slowly, and three years were to pass before the government acquired title to the land in 1797. And when it was purchased, the land came with a stipulation that six adjacent acres would be held by the Wager family, who sold the armory site to the government, for use as a government-guaranteed commercial monopoly for the erection of stores, shops, hotels. For the future of the armory, that agreement turned out to be an unalloyed disaster.

Meanwhile, Washington, refusing a third term, was succeeded by President John Adams, whose secretary of war, James McHenry, evinced little interest in the Harpers Ferry project, and, furthermore, lacked funds to mount a major project at the site. And there matters rested—land but no funds for building.

Only when George Washington came back into government in 1798, now as the commander-in-chief of the new Provisional Army, was the project revived. To Washington, Lear, Gilpin, and other members of the Patowmack Company, the Harpers Ferry project still appeared as "a juicy plum nearly ripe for the picking, and they mustered all their influence to ensure that the tasty morsel would not be snatched out of their hands by equally hungry competitors." [16]

In 1798, only two members of the Adams cabinet were in favor of the Harpers Ferry site for the new armory. One was Attorney General Charles Lee, and the other was Secretary of the Navy Benjamin Stoddert—a native Virginian, a businessman, and a stockholder in the Patowmack Company. After spending two years considering the site, issuing questionnaires to other government members, and gathering advice from many sources, Secretary of War McHenry still hung back from ordering the construction to begin. At last, in August 1798, even though the ground had not been broken for the facility, he appointed John Mackey as paymaster and storekeeper and Joseph Perkin as the superintendent. Perkin and Mackey took an almost immediate and extreme dislike to each other.

• • •

I n 1794, when Congress gave the president authority to establish a system of national armories, the congressional enabling act created three officers to staff the armories—a superintendent, a paymaster/storekeeper, and a master armorer—the familiar structure of most national armories in Europe. In normal nomenclature, the superintendent would be the reigning executive, but the enabling act was vaguely worded, and soon, in both the Springfield and Harpers Ferry armories, the superintendent and paymaster/storekeeper each claimed ultimate authority.

The well-educated John Mackey, a strong adherent to Hamiltonian Federalism, was a friend of Secretary of War McHenry's. Lacking the funds to support the comfortable gentleman's life he desired, Mackey was eager to succeed and rise in the world. Contemptuous and overbearing and arrogantly snobbish to subordinates, yet charming to friends, and unctuous toward superiors, he had little experience to commend him to the post of paymaster and storekeeper of a government armory. The Jeffersonians thought him "unscrupulous and vindictive." Colleagues "considered him vain, overly ambitious and unwilling to share authority." [17]

The English-born Perkin, a practicing Moravian, had a more appropriate background for his appointment. After serving an apprenticeship in gun making in Birmingham, England, he became a skilled arms maker in Virginia's Rappahannock Forge. After the Revolution, he operated a gun maker's shop in Philadelphia, hired out as a part-time gun inspector for the intendant general of military stores in Philadelphia, then became supervisor of the New London Arsenal in Virginia. From there, Secretary McHenry appointed him to superintendent of the Harpers Ferry Armory.

In a situation that paralleled Springfield, Mackey and Perkin were soon at odds over division of authority. In addition, they disagreed about the design of the new buildings, and the choice of an architect. The smithshop, millhouse, and main factory were largely finished by the end of 1799, but construction of the canal to feed water to the mill was delayed. The contract had gone to local businessmen who were members of the Patowmack Company or merchants expecting to do business with the new armory. None had any qualifications for canal building. Work on the canal also lagged because labor to do the hard work of digging was scarce. Manufacturing awaited the availability of water power to operate the machinery.

Meanwhile, Mackey caused strife in other areas. Most notably, he was accused of favoritism in awarding lucrative contracts to friends. In February 1799, his imperious treatment of the workers brought on a strike when the workers refused to eat the "rotten rations" Mackey provided, and accused him of pocketing much of the food money. The workers retired to a nearby tavern, formed a committee, and demanded that Mackey give them the food fund with which they would buy their own food. He got into a quarrel with Perkin and the armorers over wages, and fought with the local Jeffersonian Democrats. At length, Perkin asked the War Department to conduct an investigation of Mackey's conduct.

At the same time, the accountant for the War Department repeatedly objected to Mackey's poor record keeping, complained of a lack of vouchers and incomplete ledgers. Mackey ignored him while still submitting the same inadequate financial reports. At last, the accountant called for an investigation of Mackey's office. In January 1800, citing ill health, Mackey retired, thus avoiding the issue.

As with Springfield Armory, the War Department failed to issue any kind of directive that would help identify the discrete functions of the paymaster/storekeeper and the superintendent, and when Secretary of War McHenry appointed an old comrade-in-arms, Samuel Annin, to replace Mackey, this new paymaster soon drifted into what Perkin considered one of the superintendent's functions, the hiring and firing of workers. Fortunately, the relations between the two men was cordial and matters went on without quarreling. In the meantime, the shortage of available labor continued to be critical. Not until 1801 was the canal project completed.

Like Springfield, the first weapons made were copies of the French Charleville musket. They betray the inexperience of the work staff, and Superintendent Perkin pronounced the work shoddy. Production was no better: in 1804, only 1,472 muskets were turned out. In contrast, during the years 1803–1807, Springfield produced 14,811 muskets.[18] Neither executive seemed disturbed by this. They regarded as the primary function of Harpers Ferry Armory the design and production of the new "short" rifle, which the armorers were making under the directive issued by the War Department. Perkin himself had designed the new rifle, which had so pleased Secretary of War Dearborn that he designated it the U.S. Model 1803 rifle and ordered four thousand copies. It turned out to be Perkin's lasting monument. Today, gun collectors highly prize Perkin's Model 1803 rifle, and consider it one of the finest weapons ever to come from the Harpers Ferry Armory.

In December of 1806, Perkin died from malaria. A new era in the armory began when, in the spring of 1807, Secretary of War Henry Dearborn named to the post of superintendent a Virginian who was to exert a more profound influence on the history of Harpers Ferry than any other single man. His name was James Stubblefield. Although he had been trained in the handcraft tradition as a gun maker in a small country shop, Stubblefield, who was about thirty at the time of his appointment, had no experience in large-scale manufacturing. As was the case with the Springfield Armory, there was still no clear-cut line of authority between Paymaster/Storekeeper Annin and Superintendent Stubblefield. In fact, the next secretary of war, William Eustis, treated Paymaster Annin as the senior administrative officer at Harpers Ferry, even in several letters referring to Annin as superintendent.[19]

From the very beginning, Stubblefield found himself in a conflict of loyalties. As an employee of the War Department, he owed his first loyalty the federal government. Yet he soon found himself at the head of another constituency—the growing town of Harpers Ferry itself. As the superintendent of the town's major manufacturing concern, he controlled jobs and influenced town politics. The townspeople expected him to represent their viewpoint—which was not infrequently at odds with the objectives of the War Department.

CHAPTER 3

SPRINGFIELD:
THE WAR OF 1812

A t the new Springfield Armory, a similar conflict over ultimate
authority between the superintendent and the paymaster/
storekeeper emerged. The quarrel at Springfield was exacerbated
by the pay scale that Congress set up for these officers. Unlike
Harpers Ferry, where both men received $70 a month, in Spring-
field, while the superintendent received a similar $70 a month, the
paymaster/storekeeper there received $125 a month.

The paymaster/storekeeper was Captain John Bryant, formerly
of Boston and a Revolutionary artillery officer. His presence in
Springfield predated the creation of the new armory by thirteen
years, for, since 1781, he had been in charge of the care of the original arsenal's buildings and their contents. A man of some stature in
the town of Springfield, Captain Bryant was by background and experience eminently suited to the position and was retained when
the new armory was created. Because of his extensive experience,
he probably was expected to serve as a guide and counselor to the
new superintendent and the master armorer. His higher pay scale
may have been in recognition of his years of service.

This disparity was to create an area of dispute that festered for
years, particularly in the Springfield Armory, and finally produced a
major crisis some eighteen years later, when the British military
came back on the attack in the War of 1812.

By an act of Congress in 1794, the old Springfield Arsenal now

35

became the new Springfield Armory. Storehouse became manufactory, producing arms for the New England states, while Harpers Ferry Armory a few years later began serving the middle and southern states. Officially, they were called the Springfield National Armory and the Harpers Ferry National Armory.

Significantly, although perhaps unknowingly, Congress had with this stroke created two of the first factories in the United States, and, as such, they were to exercise a profound influence on the development of the mass-production factory system in the United States.

Despite the disparity in pay scales, the first paymaster/storekeeper, Captain John Bryant, and the first superintendent, David Ames, worked reasonably well together. Ames, at thirty-four, was well qualified for his assignment as superintendent of the nation's first armory. A New Englander, he was the son of one of the first men in that region to manufacture iron goods, including guns. Ames grew up in his father's shop, learning iron working and gun making from firsthand experience. He was also a veteran of the Revolutionary War. Such were his talents as businessman and engineer that he went on in later years to successfully pioneer paper manufacturing in the Connecticut River basin.[1]

As for the master armorer, paid $50 a month, well below Ames's $70 and Bryant's $125, his role was obviously and traditionally subordinate to that of the superintendent, so the question of his overall authority was never raised.

Both Paymaster/Storekeeper Bryant and Superintendent Ames were appointed by President Washington, and, under their regimes, the armory was established, new buildings erected, production lines set up, armorers and other personnel hired, and additional property on the hilltop purchased.

The new armory needed two things: a musket to make and a source of water power with which to make it. Funding from Congress was parsimonious, but Superintendent Ames used $400 of those very slender funds to acquire a source of water power by purchasing an acre-and-a-half site on the tumbling Mill River, near the main armory compound. With ample power assured, Ames could create a musket production facility right on the compound.

Ames now faced the next question—what kind of musket to make. For the first and only time in the armory's history, this was a relatively easy question to resolve. Because of the support of the French Royal Arsenal during the American Revolution, the principal shoulder arm used against the British had been the French Charleville musket Model 1763. As a result, the Charleville was now by far the most abundant arm stored in U.S. arsenals, and since it was considered one of the finest weapons of its type, it was the most logical musket to copy. Ames assembled a staff of gunsmiths and artificers and armorers who, first, laboriously measured, weighed, and studied the Charleville, and then, under his direction, invented production-line tooling and mastered fabrication techniques to turn out muskets faster than the customary one-at-a-time handicraft process that had prevailed before the armory's founding.

On June 22, 1795, the new musket emerged from the new production line as America's first military arm, named the Model 1795 Springfield smoothbore musket. A .69-caliber muzzle-loading flintlock, it was almost five feet long and weighed nine pounds. The Springfield '95 was not the finest example of gunsmithy—many years were to pass before the armory developed a staff that could turn out a musket the equal of European arms—but it worked, it was American, and it was quite serviceable.

In 1798, after nearly eighteen years of service in both the arsenal and the armory, Captain Bryant retired. He was replaced by a new paymaster/storekeeper, Joseph Williams, a Springfield resident who had married into a family of some influence. Apparently a man of precise comportment, he found Ames's casual business habits confounding, and soon his relations with Ames soured. The first clash occurred over Ames's accounting methods—specifically, over the manner in which Ames calculated the unit cost of musket manufacture in his annual report to the War Department.

Paymaster Williams complained to War Secretary James McHenry, "I cannot for my part imagine why the Superintendent should Estimate the value of Tools & Work on hand in such *round* numbers, except with the intention to make it appear to Government that he is making the muskets lower than is really the case."[2] He hinted that

Ames was keeping something "behind the curtain." This was a serious charge, suggesting that Ames was falsifying official government documents, and there must have grown a deep bitterness between the two men because in September 1800, a more serious clash occurred. When Paymaster Williams contracted for a load of coal for use in the manufacture of muskets, Superintendent Ames refused to allow the coal on armory grounds, asserting it was short-weighted and filled with foreign matter.

Williams wrote to the secretary of war that Ames "was in the habit of finding fault & even condemning articles procured for the use of the Factory—unless purchased of persons of his own pointing out."[3] Again, Williams's report carried overtones of unethical if not criminal behavior. Affairs in the armory were in stalemate: Ames refused to accept the coal Williams bought, and Williams refused to buy the coal that Ames would accept. The armory was shut down for months while the issue was referred to a new secretary of war, Samuel Dexter. The impasse was resolved only when the commissary general of military stores from the War Department personally stepped in to take charge of the coal contract.

The hostilities dragged on for another year while yet another secretary of war, Henry Dearborn, from Thomas Jefferson's Cabinet, assiduously avoided a direct intrusion. The Springfield Armory historian, Derwent Whittlesey, suggests that President Jefferson and his Democratic administration were secretly pleased with the mess in the armory, since it reflected on both the army, which Jefferson so profoundly distrusted, and on the Federalist party, particularly on former U.S. president and head of the Federalist party John Adams of Massachusetts. Adams, who had appointed the troublesome Joseph Williams as paymaster/storekeeper, was defeated for reelection by Jefferson.

Williams's charges could not have carried much weight with either the Adams or the Jefferson administrations because no action was taken against Superintendent Ames. There were apparently some countercharges made against Williams, for he felt compelled to write an official memo to report "that some false suggestions have been made from a quarter that I never expected—which has had a tendency to create a belief in [Secretary of War Dearborn's] mind that my whole conduct respecting the Coal business was actuated by personal considerations, rather than a regard to the public intent."[4] The issue was resolved finally in October 1802, when Ames angrily resigned, giving Paymaster Williams another excuse to impugn Ames's honesty when he complained to the secretary of war that the departed Ames had turned over all records and papers "except his public Cash Books which he declines giving up as he pretends they are his security."[5] There is no record that Ames ever surrendered the material in question. Eleven months later, in September 1803, Williams himself left office.

Files in the armory's archives suggest that the issue here was a struggle for control. Indeed, in one of Williams's many official memos, he noted that even the secretary of war and the commissary general of military stores could not agree as "to who is the controuling [sic] officer or head of the Department." Williams urged that "for the harmony and well being of the Works, it would be well to have the duties of the Paymaster and Superintendent more particularly defined and pointed out."[6] But still nothing was done. As Whittlesey points out, "The administration, perhaps willing to permit both the Army and New England to discredit themselves, could not be expected to take a hand in a mess so admirably conceived to work harm to both."[7]

David Ames was replaced by a new superintendent, Joseph Morgan, the armory's master armorer. And, the following year, Williams was replaced by James Byers, the owner of two Springfield retail stores. Soon Morgan and Byers were clashing. Byers reported that he had found coal and iron improperly cared for. As paymaster, Byers was required to make payments on all purchases, while, as storekeeper, he had no authority to limit purchases nor to oversee the care of stock of matériel to be used in manufacturing. Fearing that he would be blamed for the consequences, he denounced Morgan for gross mismanagement of the armory, perhaps with some justification, for within two years, for reasons unknown, Morgan was gone. He was replaced in November 1805 by a new superintendent, Benjamin Prescott, another Massachusetts man who seems to have gotten on well with Byers; there were no further eruptions for some six years. In fact, the Byers/Prescott regime was a time of active building construction and expansion of the armory. Prescott is credited with having first established the division of labor in the armory in 1806 as a means of creating more production efficiency. Although still not officially resolved, the issue of authority subsided, and, by 1811, when Byers died in office, it seems to have been all but forgotten.

But then John Chaffee became the new paymaster/storekeeper. This turned out to be a turbulent appointment, for Chaffee was paymaster/storekeeper when, on June 18, 1812, with James Madison in the White House, Congress did exactly what Thomas Jefferson had struggled not to do during his eight years in office as president. Congress declared war on Great Britain.

Despite the overbearing behavior of the British navy, and the impressment of perhaps nine thousand seamen from American merchant ships for service on British warships, the declaration of war was an act of foolish bravado, encouraged in large part by the War Hawks under the leadership of Representative (and later, Senator) Henry Clay, for the United States had few arms, a minuscule army of less than seven thousand men, and a navy of barely more than a few frigates and gunboats.

Prior to the war, management of the military under Madison had been generally indifferent, usually amateurish, and often incompetent. Frugal himself, Madison gathered about him other frugal men. Typical of their attitude was the handling of the army's regiment of light artillery. Created by Congress in 1808 during the Jefferson regime, the new mounted unit caused considerable interest when, with some pomp and circumstance, it paraded before Congress after conducting a route (i.e., informal) march from Baltimore to Washington at an unheard-of six miles an hour.[8] Given the United States' steadily deteriorating relations with England, the new fast-moving mounted artillery would seem to have been an important addition to the military. Yet when William Eustis—a former physician and frugal in the extreme—became Madison's secretary of war the following year, he sold the horses and disbanded the new unit.

In 1810, with the growing intransigence of the British, President Madison and Secretary Eustis asked Congress for twenty thousand regulars and a state-supplied reserve of 100,000 men. At the same time, however, they sought to balance the federal budget by asking Congress to cut the military and naval budget in half. Congress was bemused, and on the day war was declared, Eustis found that he had only some sixty-seven hundred men out of the ten thousand Congress had authorized.[9] Having served as secretary of war for more than three turbulent years, Eustis had waited until the day war was declared to set out to raise an army.

His first step was to order Brigadier General William Hull to hasten to Detroit from Dayton, Ohio, to take command of the forces there in anticipation of a land war along the Canadian border. His next act was to order the Springfield Armory to provide enough muskets to arm a suddenly growing army. The armory had hundreds of thousands of muskets in storage, most of them left over from the Revolutionary War, so Eustis wrote a requisition ordering the armory's staff of gunsmiths to start refurbishing the old muskets. He sent the requisition to the Springfield Armory, addressed to Paymaster/Storekeeper John Chaffee. Now, eighteen years after Congress had passed the enabling bill creating the armory, the flaws in the congressional act produced a wartime crisis, which had become alarmingly apparent when the armory tried to obey Secretary Eustis's order.

The old quarrel over authority reappeared. Secretary Eustis had sent his order for refurbished muskets to Paymaster John Chaffee rather than Superintendent Prescott, presuming that since Chaffee was the most highly paid executive in the armory, he was therefore the man in charge. But Paymaster Chaffee's authority did not extend to the manufacturing facilities in the armory, so he sent the secretary's order to his adversary, armory superintendent Benjamin Prescott. In turn, Prescott was clearly delighted to refuse to obey Chaffee's secondhand order. For in addition to the internecine quarrel, there was a larger public argument going on that had penetrated the walls of the armory.

Like all of New England—which had been nearly ruined by

Jefferson's ill-advised Embargo Act against England—Prescott, a Massachusetts man and an anti-Jeffersonian Federalist, was opposed to the war and felt no urgency to obey an order not addressed to his office.

Thereupon, Paymaster John Chaffee complained to Secretary of War Eustis about Prescott's refusal to obey the order. Secretary Eustis reissued his order to commence work on the old muskets and sent it to Superintendent Prescott. Prescott still did nothing. Even another direct order from the secretary of war failed to move Prescott. Instead, he continued to resist for the remainder of the year of 1812. In fact, even the normal production of *new* muskets— some twelve thousand a year—fell off. Superintendent Prescott could point to a legitimate cause for this: a wartime shortage of both iron and armorers. In fact, practically the entire available pool of skilled labor for gunsmithy in New England was already on the federal payroll, and those who were available in private industry were not in sympathy with Mr. Madison's war. Prescott could blame the reduction in musket production on the war.

Secretary Eustis was evidently not deceived. To deal with the superintendent's intransigence, on August 2, 1812, he send an investigator named Benjamin Moor with direct orders to inspect contract arms at Springfield. It was an interesting choice, for Moor was to have a strong influence over the years on both the Springfield and Harpers Ferry armories.

Born and raised in Springfield, Moor started his career in 1797, when he was fourteen, as an apprentice at the Springfield Armory. Having completed his apprenticeship in 1804, he then worked in both the Virginia State Armory in Richmond and Harpers Ferry and was working in the Philadelphia Arsenal as inspector of contract arms when Eustis ordered him to Springfield. A well-liked and widely traveled man, with an outstanding reputation for integrity as well as for his skills as an armorer, Moor had many friends and supporters in the world of arms making. He was known for his great kindness toward others, and if he had any flaws, it was as a disciplinarian. His confrontation with Prescott came when he ordered the superintendent directly to put all his best available men on the assignment of refurbishing muskets. Still Prescott delayed and the rest of 1812 was lost before he finally complied. When an armory coal house burned to the ground, hampering production even more, Benjamin Moor brought about a full investigation of the armory; as a result, Prescott was summarily sacked and ejected from the premises. Moor dismissed him so quickly, Prescott was unable to clean up his records and files, a situation that was to fester for some time while he lobbied heavily to get his job back.

In December, Congress had had enough of Secretary Eustis, who resigned with a chorus of congressional disapproval ringing in his ears. He was replaced by John Armstrong, who, in his fourteen months in office, seems to have spent most of his time furthering the Pennsylvania–New York faction in the government.[10] He was destined to be the sitting secretary of war when the British, in August of 1814, entered and burned Washington. The next month, he was gone.

Having had enough of antiwar New England Federalists inside the armory, Madison's War Department under Armstrong decided to get production moving by naming a new superintendent of the same political persuasion as the Madison administration—Republican. But rather than resolving all the armory's production problems, the new appointee caused still more dissension.

His name was Henry Lechler, and from the viewpoint of the New Englanders inside the armory, everything was wrong with him. First of all, he was not from Massachusetts, not even from New England. Worse, he was a Pennsylvania German with a funny accent. Worse even than that, he was an old-style gunsmith with a dark suspicion of the new techniques of mass production the armory had so laboriously developed since its founding. He believed in one-at-a-time handcrafted musket making. But perhaps worst of all, like his state, he was a Republican and therefore in favor of the war against England.

He had one supreme virtue in the eyes of the Madison administration, which was desperate for weapons: he was willing to promptly and eagerly obey Washington's order to produce muskets. But Lechler encountered several serious problems. In the armory and in the town, he was unwelcome, and unable to gain support. In addition, iron for manufacturing was hard to come by. Previously, England had been the major U.S. source of iron, but now that nation had not only embargoed its own iron to the United States but British warships were actively preventing other nations from shipping ore into the country.

Lechler blundered into the most serious error of all when he rewarded Benjamin Moor's efforts on his behalf by naming Moor master armorer of the armory. This was always one of the most coveted positions among the armorers and there were many men already on staff who felt qualified for it. To name an outsider to that post was certain to raise a clamor, and Lechler was soon besieged by an intransigent staff. He now encountered nothing but hostility—even open contempt—from the New Englanders who surrounded him, especially Paymaster Chaffee's clerk, who seemed to go out of his way to be deliberately insubordinate. Superintendent Lechler asked Paymaster Chaffee to dismiss his clerk, but this served only to highlight once again the continued split in armory authority—especially when Chaffee refused.

The hostile staff and the iron shortage combined to delay Lechler's attempt to increase musket production. So, on April 13, 1813, with the war with England already ten months old, the new secretary of war, John Armstrong, sent a man named Callender Irvine with full authority to take any action that would get the armory producing again. Close on Irvine's arrival came an order from Generals Dearborn and Lewis for 600,000 flintlocks. But the Springfield Armory could ship only 300,000, holding another 200,000 in reserve.

In the end, primarily because of the shortage of iron, even the combined efforts of Irvine and Lechler were unable to get full production rolling in the armory. When, in October 1813, some ore was obtained to resume manufacturing, Lechler was unable to get anyone to bring it from Boston. A Boston teamster finally carted some three thousand pounds to the armory, but only with a guarantee of a return load.[11] But one wagonload of ore could not have been much help for an armory needing to make enough muskets for an entire army.

The U.S. Army, headed by a combination of inexperienced officers and out-of-practice Revolutionary War veterans, fared badly. An American invasion of Canada was ill timed, incompetently handled, and beaten back by the British, who penetrated into Ohio. British military leadership was not on a much higher plane. When the British built a fleet of ships on the Great Lakes, the United States replied with a fleet of its own. In September 1813, in a ferocious battle, the American fleet under Captain Oliver Hazard Perry hunted out and destroyed the British fleet. As a result, the British were forced to vacate Detroit and were defeated on the Thames River in Canada.

The British sailed with impunity right up the Chesapeake Bay, raiding towns and villages, bombarding Baltimore, and entering Washington to burn the Capitol building and the White House. Despite its effect upon the nation's sense of vulnerability, the Chesapeake foray accomplished little of military value for the British. The Canadian operation fared badly. When a second American fleet destroyed a second British fleet on Lake Champlain, near Plattsburgh, the British general, Sir George Prevost, even with a force of eleven thousand to confront only three thousand Americans, felt his flank was too vulnerable without navy support and withdrew to Montreal.

On December 24, 1814, the Treaty of Ghent formally ended the war between Britain and the United States. Had it not been for the loss of young lives on both sides, as one American historian has pointed out, "it would be easy to dismiss the entire war as a great farce compounded of stupidity, incompetence, and brag."[12]

By January 1815, a few months after the war ended, ex-superintendent Lechler was on his way back to Pennsylvania. To replace him, a new secretary of war, William H. Crawford, made a strange choice. That same month, he reappointed former superintendent Benjamin Prescott, who was now operating a factory in Waterford, New York. From the beginning, Prescott himself treated his recovery of the superintendent's chair as an interim appointment, telling Crawford that he would not remain "any length of time at the head." In fact, he held it for just ninety days. The Springfield Armory historian, Derwent Whittlesey, says flatly that

Prescott recovered the position "because he wanted to supplant Lechler and to get possession of the correspondence of his previous term."[13] Prescott thereupon removed from government files all his old correspondence, in order, he said, to keep the letters from "unclean hands," and although he promised in writing to return the files, he never did. This action has left historians wondering ever since what incriminating material might have been in those files and why someone in the War Department arranged to let him get it.

There may have been one other reason for Prescott's brief return as superintendent. One of his first acts was to fire Master Armorer Benjamin Moor, the man who had contributed to Prescott's downfall and Lechler's appointment. Moor returned to the Allegheny Arsenal in Pittsburgh, where he became master armorer. Later, he returned to Harpers Ferry, to play a significant role in the turbulent events that were to take place there.

CHAPTER 4

SPRINGFIELD: GROWTH
UNDER ROSWELL LEE

E ighteen fifteen was a significant year in the history of the two armories. Congress created the office of chief of ordnance—the person chosen would be responsible for making the armories more efficient and productive. The post was promptly filled by the appointment of Colonel Decius Wadsworth.

By May 1815, in Springfield, Lechler was gone, Moor was gone, Prescott was gone, and the War Department named a new superintendent. His name was Roswell Lee—a recent lieutenant colonel of the Twenty-third Infantry. At the same time, in Harpers Ferry, Paymaster/Storekeeper Samuel Annin retired. James Stubblefield, who had acted in a role subordinate to Annin, was now the senior official in terms of seniority. From this point on, the careers of Lee and Stubblefield were to parallel each other strangely, almost as mirror images, but with vastly different results and vastly different consequences for the two armories.

When Roswell Lee took over as superintendent of Springfield, he encountered chaos—divided responsibilities; confusion of purpose; a capricious, parsimonious, antimilitary Congress; a disaffected staff rife with factionalism, politicking, drinking, goldbricking, and incompetence; an inadequate, inefficient production plant; a low volume of production; and an often hostile community.

A Connecticut Yankee and a disciplined military man, Lee exhibited the ideal characteristics for the job: discipline, patience, and flexibility. With these, he combined honesty, a cheerful disposition, and a military man's imbued sense of duty. He had hoped to continue his commission and serve as military commandant of the armory. Instead, due to pressure from local politicians, the War Department appointed him civilian superintendent, letting his commission lapse.

On his desk, Roswell Lee found a note from his predecessor, Benjamin Prescott: ". . . the men are divided into parties Sum [*sic*] wish A to be Master armorer sum B others are discontented because others occupy situations in the Works that they themselves wish for."[1]

In the end, Prescott, who was a canny judge of men and a very successful owner of his own business in Waterford, New York, seems to have had his judgment vindicated, for Roswell Lee, despite strong internal pressures, kept Prescott's staff appointments in place, at least for a time. And, despite strong political pressure from Washington, Lee refused to reappoint Benjamin Moor to the post of master armorer. While Moor was an outstanding armorer, his recent duty there had left some rancor among others, who felt he had usurped that position. A short while later, when Lee had had time to absorb the magnitude of all the problems before him, he wrote to Captain John Morton of the Ordnance Office in Washington that the problems "are far more arduous and difficult than the command of a regiment even in time of war. . . ." He added, "Much firmness, patience, discretion and judgment is necessary to overcome the prejudices and improper habits that have crept into the Armory."[2] That "much" was much more than Roswell Lee imagined.

One of Lee's most important challenges was the ever-festering problem of the superintendent/paymaster relationship, and he attacked it with his characteristic combination of Yankee shrewdness, patience, and determination. He divided the problem into two parts. First, he set out to eliminate the inequity of pay scales that seemed to elevate the paymaster above the superintendent. He approached this project with his habitual indirection. Instead of trying to raise the superintendent's pay to the level of the paymaster, he set out to get the superintendent's pay level increased on the basis of merit. His plan was really very simple. Joining forces with the superintendent of the Harpers Ferry Armory, James Stubblefield, he petitioned Congress by way of the Ordnance Department for a salary increase. He made no mention of the disparity of pay between his office and that of the paymaster.

In his letter to Congress, Lee said, "I do not ask nor expect a salary that will make me rich, but a compensation that will support me in a manner becoming my station, not in the luxuries but the necessaries of life."[3] He also sought and got the important help of his U.S. senator, James Barbour, and Congressman Samuel W. Dana. His tactic succeeded. His pay was raised to $1,500 a year, and that placed him $300 ahead of the paymaster's annual salary.

With half the problem solved, he next addressed the superintendent/paymaster relationship. Again, he drew Superintendent Stubblefield at Harpers Ferry into his strategy. He broached the possibility of a joint private business venture with Stubblefield and let that be known in Washington. In the meantime, he was campaigning within the War Department to change the relationship with the paymaster. "If you wish to avoid the difficulties that have agitated this Establishment for many years," he wrote to Major George Bomford, assistant to Chief of Ordnance Wadsworth, "permit me to say you will not require the Superintendent to account to the Paymaster who is considered a subordinate officer."[4]

Major Bomford replied, "I am sorry that you entertain any Thoughts about quitting the Armory at Springfield . . . to place the Store Keepers in a State of greater Subordination to the Superintendents. . . . I shall be glad to be favoured with your own Ideas of what is necessary."[5]

Shortly after, Lee's campaigning succeeded, and both he and Stubblefield benefited from it. Under regulations issued on November 29, 1816, the paymaster/storekeeper at both armories was put "under the full charge of the superintendent, and permitted no expenditures not approved of by him."[6] Undoing that piece of mischief from the Congress's 1794 enabling act had taken twenty-three years and the machinations of a consummate executive.

Lee used the same executive skills in reorganizing and modernizing the armory. When he took over in 1815, conditions in the plant were disgraceful. Debt-ridden Congress had failed to pay the workers for three months. The factionalism over the years had created numerous coteries that were stubbornly cohesive. Even elements in the town of Springfield had been drawn into these armory factions.

A longtime friend of the great inventor Eli Whitney, whose shops were a short distance downriver in Hartford, Lee deliberately exposed his staff to fresh new ideas. He regularly sent them to area factories to learn modern production techniques and to study the new machinery that was being invented. Even the secretive Eli Whitney let Lee observe and copy some of his musket-making machinery.

Lee also set out to eliminate the old handcraft methods of making muskets and supplanted them with newly invented tools such as lathes and trip-hammer welders. He expanded the plant, built new buildings, added another water-power plant on the Mill River that now performed a number of arduous operations that formerly had been done by backbreaking human labor.

Roswell Lee also systematically attacked the armory's internal problems. He controlled pricing; established quality control on purchases of raw materials and other supplies; imposed the first discipline among the workers; established regular working hours; brought order to the chaotic wage scales; curbed riotous behavior, drunkenness, and slackness; and introduced proper working conditions, decent hours, and fair wages. Although Prescott is credited with introducing the division of labor, Lee spent eighteen years—from 1815 to 1833—bringing forth a modern facility from the antiquated methods and attitudes he had inherited from Prescott.

And Lee added new techniques of mass production. He is credited with introducing the atmosphere that enabled Thomas Blanchard to create the all-important eccentric lathe—an event of considerable significance. Blanchard, an employee of the armory, as a gifted inventor whose numerous discoveries during his lifetime included a machine to mass-produce tacks, an apple parer, another machine that cut and folded envelopes, and a process for bending large timbers. While working at the Springfield Armory, in 1819, he invented an eccentric lathe for making gunstocks that were previously made by hand, one at a time. Gunstock production leaped, costs fell, output increased—from 7,279 muskets in 1815, the year Lee arrived, to 16,500 in 1833, his last year in office. Annual musket output per man jumped from 35.2 to 63.8. Widely used all over the world today, Blanchard's eccentric lathe is considered one of the great inventions of the Industrial Revolution.[7]

The effort of creating a national armory of international stature had taken its physical toll on Roswell Lee, and, in August 1833, while packing for a vacation, Lee died in his home. He left behind a thriving national armory, reasonable harmony among the staff, and many friends, admirers, and boosters in Springfield who genuinely mourned his passing.

CHAPTER 5

HARPERS FERRY: JUNTO, PORK, AND HALL'S RIFLE

The same month, May 1815, that Roswell Lee had become superintendent of Springfield, at Harpers Ferry, Paymaster/Storekeeper Samuel Annin retired, and James Stubblefield, the superintendent there who had served in a subordinate role for some years, became the senior executive. Unlike Roswell Lee, Stubblefield resolved his conflict of loyalties by putting community demands and wishes ahead of the War Department's needs.

The town of Harpers Ferry, with fourteen hundred inhabitants by 1815, was owned and largely controlled by two families: the Wagers, who originally had owned the site on which the armory stood, and the Beckams, who wielded somewhat greater influence.

The Beckams' control was pervasive. Superintendent Stubblefield's brother-in-law, Armistead Beckam, was the master armorer. Another brother-in-law, Camp Beckam, who was rarely seen working at anything, had a lucrative contractor's job inside the armory for browning (rust proofing) muskets. Fontaine Beckam, who owned a dry goods store, a flour mill, and a cooper's shop, was also the justice of the peace for Jefferson County, and in addition was married to the daughter of Major James Stephenson, one of the most powerful men in northern Virginia. Townshend Beckam operated a large tannery and oil mill, with James Stubblefield as a silent partner. Stubblefield also owned a distillery in partnership with Major Stephenson. Stubblefield's chief clerk, Edward Wager, was a member of the family that had sold the land to the armory, retaining, under monopolistic conditions agreed to by the U.S. government, six commercial acres adjacent to the armory. His mother, Catherine Wager, was now sole owner of that six-acre tract, which had become enormously valuable, since all the town's commercial activities took place there. Completing the interlocking circle of kinship, the Wager family was related by marriage to the Beckam family.

Catherine Wager, by virtue of those six acres of land, was one of two women who dominated the inner circle of privilege and power in Harpers Ferry. The other was Mary Beckam Stubblefield, Superintendent Stubblefield's wife. Catherine Wager claimed that during the sale of the tract to the armory, the Wager family had retained its six key adjacent acres from which the Patowmack Company conceded the Wagers a "monopoly of the mercantile Business of the place." Catherine Wager's control of that tract frequently troubled the War Department, especially since, due to the remoteness of the town from any other commercial centers, armory employees had to pay whatever prices the Wager and Beckam families posted in their shops. As a result, to keep skilled armorers on the payroll, the armory had to pay the highest armorer wages in the country. And, consequently, the cost of weapons at Harpers Ferry was higher than the cost of the same weapons produced in Springfield. The Wager family continued to control prices in Harpers Ferry for nearly thirty years. On average, the armory's monthly payroll of well over $10,000 went directly into the coffers of the local family-owned businesses, including Superintendent Stubblefield's distillery. So powerful was this conjunction of Stubblefield, Beckam, Wager, and Stephenson families that it was known as the Junto.

The Junto's ability to wring profits from every aspect of the town's life became legendary. Often, government- built and -owned houses, intended for the workers, were occupied instead by friends of the superintendent or the master armorer, while the armorers' families for whom these homes had been intended lived in squalid shacks. Other friends of the Junto were allowed to build shops on government property at no charge. The Junto's total control even extended to the polling place, where open balloting during elections made each man's vote visible to the whole town. A wrong vote meant a lost job.

As historian Merritt Roe Smith observed: "Instead of viewing the armory as a national establishment whose purpose was to manufacture arms as rapidly and efficiently as possible, Stubblefield looked upon it as a source of jobs, sinecures, patronage, and profit. . . . [He] and his associates resented and resisted any attempts by outsiders to meddle in what he considered primarily a local affair."[1] And that included the War Department—but not, of course, the two families' pork-barreling friends in Washington, a vitally important source of political power.

Perhaps the unremitting battle between the Harpers Ferry Junto and the Ordnance Department in Washington would have had far less historic significance if Secretary of War John C. Calhoun hadn't introduced, in 1818, the Hall's rifleworks into the Harpers Ferry Armory.

John H. Hall, now generally conceded to be an ordnance and engineering genius, certainly made a major—if highly controversial—contribution to the army's long association with the rifle and to the history of mass production in America.

A New Englander, born in 1781 in Portland, Maine, Hall was one of six children. His father, Stephen, a Harvard graduate, operated his father-in-law's tannery in Portland until he died in 1794. Although his father's untimely death apparently ended the young man's expectations of going to college, he seems to have received an excellent early education, wrote a fluent, legible hand, and spoke with eloquence. Around 1808, he set up shop in Portland as a cabinetmaker, cooper, and boat builder, and in 1813 married Statira Prebel, with whom he had seven children.

Several years before his marriage, Hall had begun experimenting with rifle designs and, without any knowledge of Major Ferguson's British army breech-loading rifle, invented a breech-loading mechanism of his own in 1811. When he sought to patent his weapon, he encountered the superintendent of patents, Dr. William Thornton, who claimed to have already invented a similar mechanism.

When Hall went to see him, Thornton showed him a Ferguson rifle but no model or drawing of his own. Hall contended that Thornton's "thought of a plan" was hardly a patentable item, and, besides, it was so different from Hall's idea that had he produced a model of it, the two rifles could have received separate patents with no conflict. However, Thornton bluntly told Hall to either share the patent with him or receive no patent at all. There's some reason to believe Thornton used the same tactics with other inventors, for when he died, Thornton owned a suspiciously large number of patents.[2]

Hall went to see Secretary of State James Monroe, who told him that half a patent was better than none at all. He also pointed out that the superintendent of patents could protect Hall's rifle from claims from other inventors. Reluctantly, Hall signed with Thornton in May 1811.

By 1818, Hall had invested in his weapon some $20,000 of his own money, much of it from an inheritance from his mother. He was nearly bankrupt. Aware that the major independent arms makers relied on government advances for their production efforts, Hall turned to the government for financing. Even as early as 1811, he had tried to interest Secretary of War Eustis in his weapon, but Eustis put him off. His successor, however, General John Armstrong, ordered Major Bomford to examine it.

The Hall's rifle seemed to solve a number of problems for the Ordnance Department. Rifles were known to be much more accurate, with a greater range, than smoothbore muskets. But because of the spiral grooves in the barrel, it took more care and time to muzzle-load a rifle than a musket. By loading through a breech in the barrel above the trigger instead of through the muzzle, the rifle could be loaded much faster, thereby eliminating one of its major drawbacks.

The army already had manufactured two rifles: the Harpers Ferry Model 1803, the army's first armory-built rifle, a muzzleloader invented by the former superintendent Joseph Perkin, and another muzzle-loading rifle, Harpers Ferry Model 1814. In the military thinking of the time, the rifle was regarded as a specialized weapon to be used by sharpshooters on the flanks of the infantry's main force, which was armed with the traditional musket.

Major Bomford tested five Hall's rifles and five Hall's muskets. His report was so enthusiastic it led to an Ordnance offer to purchase two hundred more, delivery due in December 1814. But Hall didn't have the facilities to make two hundred models and had to refuse the offer.

He returned to Portland to develop a way to make his rifle in quantity. When he wrote again to the Ordnance Department, in 1816, he unwittingly gained immediate attention by announcing he was now ready to make any number of his rifles with completely interchangeable parts so that a thousand guns could be taken apart and reassembled at random.

This was a feature that interested both the army's recently appointed first ordnance chief, Colonel Decius Wadsworth, and his assistant, Major (later Lieutenant Colonel) George Bomford. Because the parts of a handmade shoulder arm were not interchangeable, it could not be repaired on the battlefield. The arm had to be shipped back to the factory and there refitted with customized handmade parts by a skilled armorer. But rifles with interchangeable parts could be repaired immediately on the battlefield by taking parts from other weapons.

Machine manufacture and interchangeability of parts also addressed the second major drawback to the rifle—expense. The Model 1803 rifle, for example, was all handmade, including the time-consuming rifling of the barrel. Consequently, it was more expensive to manufacture. In the 1820s, the Model 1816 musket, a modified version of the Model 1794 musket, even in the inefficient Harpers Ferry plant, cost only about $11 to make, while the Model 1803 muzzle-loading rifle cost about $18. In consequence, the rifle was not distributed to regular troops or to state militia. Machine making interchangeable parts, many in Ordnance felt, could significantly lower the rifle's cost. In fact, parts interchangeability was the elusive goal of many gun designers, including the prolific genius Eli Whitney.

But the Ordnance Department itself was not of one accord on

the matter. Colonel Bomford wanted to replace the muzzle-loading rifle with a breech-loading model, but Ordnance Chief Decius Wadsworth, a determined budget watcher, while very interested, had been skeptical of the rifle concept from the beginning because he felt Hall's rifle, like the Model 1803 rifle, would prove to be too expensive in the end. He also expressed the familiar fear that was to be heard so many times in the ensuing years about wasted ammunition. A faster-firing breechloader, he feared, would lead to "an extravagent [sic] use and waste of ammunition."[3]

Colonel Bomford, who was already enthusiastic about the weapon itself, was now equally enthusiastic about parts interchangeability and more eager than ever to proceed. So Hall had two attractions for Ordnance: a breech-loading rifle, and a way to make it economically in quantity with interchangeable parts.

Hall asked for $40,000 to make one thousand rifles, $40 each. Secretary Armstrong demurred. Hall then offered to make them for $25 each, even though he believed he would lose money on every one. Armstrong countered with an offer to buy one hundred. That was not enough to enable Hall to design the machinery to make the interchangeable parts. But he went back to Portland, and by November 1817, a full month before they were due, shipped the hundred rifles to Captain George Talcott of the Ordnance office, who had already expressed a poor opinion of the weapon. After a test, though, Talcott changed his mind. "I cannot sufficiently praise them," he wrote in his report. He expected they would soon replace the "common" (muzzle-loading Model 1803) rifle in the army.

As a result of those tests, Armstrong's successor, Secretary of War John Calhoun, who, like Colonal Bomford, wanted to adopt the muzzle-loading rifle, invited Hall to supervise the construction of a few of the rifles at Harpers Ferry Armory, making improvements and testing them further. Hall preferred Springfield. Progressive-minded Roswell Lee would have welcomed him eagerly.

But Harpers Ferry was where the U.S. Model 1803 rifle was being made, and Bomford was determined to house the new rifle-making effort there. Superintendent Stubblefield was violently opposed to the idea of setting up a separate rifle-making operation in his domain. For one thing, a fifth of Stubblefield's annual budget—and the power that went with it—would now be paid into Hall's operation. Second, Hall was an independent operator who, in effect, would share power with Stubblefield. Stubblefield quickly suggested the operation be set up in Springfield. The Junto, always distrustful of outsiders, was also strongly opposed to the idea, contending that the Ordnance Department did not have the authority to set up a private gun maker on public property. Nor was Hall destined to endear himself to the armorers. After serving an apprenticeship of thirteen years to master the art of making rifles by hand, they saw Hall's machine methods as a direct threat to their jobs and careers.

Predisposed to dislike Hall on sight, Stubblefield, soon after Hall's arrival in 1819, had ample reason to complain. Hall was brilliant but highly abrasive—an outspoken, scolding eccentric who had something to say about everything in Harpers Ferry, including Stubblefield's management methods, the town school system, and even the appointment of the local postmaster. When Hall complained of the poor workmen and the shoddy material Stubblefield sent him, the two men clashed, and a ten-year quarrel ensued. Stubblefield did find one way to use Hall's presence to advantage: he now blamed his chronic budget deficit on Hall.

Stubblefield and his master armorer and brother-in-law, Armistead Beckam, tested Hall's first weapons and grudgingly admitted the Hall's rifle could be loaded in one-third the time of a muzzleloader and was as accurate and powerful as the Model 1803 rifle. But the four rifles Hall made cost $200 each, which upset ever-frugal Ordnance Chief Wadsworth, who protested, "We can never afford to introduce such Arms into the Service."[4]

In spite of Wadsworth's disaffection, Secretary of War Calhoun remained strongly interested and ordered the weapon to be studied further. Based on three months of testing at Greenleaf's Point in Washington, an army board under Colonel Nathaniel Towson recommended the introduction of the Hall's rifle into the army. They reported that the Hall's rifles had been fired over seven thousand times—more firing than the rifle would undergo in a lifetime—and were still fit to issue to a soldier going into battle. The board cited three features in particular: first, firing speed and ease of loading; second, greater accuracy and less recoil; and, third, less weight.

Hall now expected to receive an order for ten thousand weapons. Instead, Calhoun ordered only one thousand. Under the contract that was issued, Hall would receive a monthly salary of $60, plus $1 royalty on each weapon. He complained that there would be no machine-made economies in such a short run. Furthermore, unable to make the weapons in his own shop because of financial constraints, Hall asked to be allowed to make them in the Springfield Armory, not Harpers Ferry, because of the hostility of Stubblefield's people and also because Springfield was much closer to home.

Calhoun felt, however, he could better observe Hall's activities in Harpers Ferry.

In the meantime, while John Hall was setting up his rifle works on the armory grounds, the battle between the Junto and the Ordnance Department was becoming even more relentless. The office of chief of ordnance had been created by Congress in 1815 to bring greater efficiency and systematization to the national armories.[5] Consequently, the first chief of ordnance, Colonel Decius Wadsworth, spent much of his six-year reign, from 1815 to 1821, attempting to control the high costs at Harpers Ferry and, finally, in 1821, set out to build a store on government property that would sell food and clothing to the armorers at less than the Wagers were charging. By doing that, he felt he could then reduce wages in the plant.

But the ordnance chief's administrative control over the armory was far outweighed by the Junto's political control over the ordnance chief. The Wager family hurried to the War Department, going right to the secretary of war himself, to complain about the projected new store's infringement on their legal monopoly. The new-store plan was promptly quashed. Undaunted, Colonel Wadsworth now shifted the pressure to the armory employees. He imposed a 12.5 percent reduction in armory wages, expecting this would force the armorers to force the Wager-Beckam shops to lower their prices. But that November 1821, before his new policy could have much effect, aging and ailing Colonel Wadsworth left office.

Stubblefield and his coterie had little reason and little time to rejoice in this turn of affairs. Lieutenant Colonel George Bomford became the next ordnance chief. Colonel Wadsworth's principal assistant since the founding of the office of the chief of ordnance in 1815, Colonel Bomford had been a frequent visitor to both Harpers Ferry and Springfield, and had a very poor opinion of the way James Stubblefield ran things. Also, unlike Colonel Wadsworth, he was a dedicated supporter of the hated Hall's rifle. One of the new chief's first acts was to order an additional armory wage cut of 12.5 percent.

A graduate of West Point, George Bomford was married to Clara Baldwin, whose family connections included powerful political and judicial figures. A capable and dedicated engineer, Bomford was intent on introducing more efficient production methods at Harpers Ferry to bring it up to the level of efficiency and volume of Roswell Lee's operation at Springfield. He demanded that Stubblefield's only considerations be the public interest and that he "be influenced in no degree whatever by considerations touching the interest or feelings of those individuals who may be affected by the objects proposed."[6]

Among his many other complaints, Colonel Bomford particularly cited Stubblefield for continuing to run up annual deficits, and for building roads, bridges, and other conveniences for the people of the town with Ordnance Department money.

Stubblefield refused to be governed by Bomford, claiming as his authority the Ordnance Regulations of 1816. These regulations, engineered by Roswell Lee, redefined the relationship of the superintendent and the paymaster/storekeeper, making the latter clearly subordinate. Interpreting those regulations in a way that the orderly and loyal Lee surely never intended, Stubblefield was claiming the armory as his own fiefdom to operate as he pleased. He also never ceased excoriating the Hall's rifle works, and by 1822, he felt he had strong new justification for complaint.

Having set up shop in Harpers Ferry in 1819, Hall had expected soon to have a production line functioning, but his timetable was overly optimistic. Not until the summer of 1822 was he able to design all the tools needed to manufacture his interchangeable parts, and it was not until December 1824 that he finished all one thousand rifles, far later than he and the War Department had expected. Causes for the delay were many—including Stubblefield's intransigence, problems with raw materials and workmen, and the periodic outbreaks of bilious fever. But probably the major cause was the creative bent of Hall himself in designing the tools. Hall had entered an unknown realm when he set out to invent machines to make interchangeable parts, and as often happened with brilliant weapons designers before and after Hall, Hall's allowance for time was overly optimistic and unrealistic.

The army inspector general, who visited Hall in 1822, shook his head and predicted that each rifle would eventually cost more than $50. Hall replied that he was inventing a new system of manufacture that would be used on all the weapons in the armory and eventually at considerably less cost than hand labor. Bomford and Calhoun remained convinced and patient.

During the winter of 1824, with the completion of the thousand rifles, Hall reported to Calhoun and Bomford that he had fully mastered the craft of parts interchangeability. It was a milestone in American manufacturing techniques, but it came at a price: because Hall could make these parts on his machines, operated by quickly trained teenage boys, hostility by the armorers toward Hall increased considerably.

Calhoun and Bomford came to see for themselves, and in July 1824, suitably impressed, they issued an order for a second thousand rifles.

Unfortunately for Hall, soon after, John Calhoun retired and with a new secretary of war, James Barbour, disinterested in the rifle, Stubblefield and the Junto sought to eject Hall from the armory by using their political influence to force a congressional investigation into "the waste and extravagance of the Publick [sic] money on the Patent Rifle."[7]

Under congressional direction, Secretary Barbour ordered Colonel Bomford to test the new rifle thoroughly. Two companies at Fortress Monroe were armed with Hall's rifles. Two other companies were armed with pattern Springfield muskets, and another company was armed with Model 1803 Harpers Ferry muzzle-loading rifles. After five months of testing, the rifle board reported that the Hall's rifle was superior to "every other kind of small arm now in use." The Hall's rifle was praised for its "great and general superiority." The rifle committee was particularly impressed with the parts interchangeability feature.[8]

Congress had also ordered an investigation into costs, so a three-man committee consisting of arms experts who were familiar with the work being done in machine manufacture in plants throughout the country spent days studying Hall's tools and manufacturing methods and then wrote a seventeen-page report. Hall, they said, had achieved what "those engaged in making arms" had "considered almost or totally impossible"—the "perfect uniformity" of parts. The committee was so impressed with what they saw that they described in detail every step of the process, praising the newly invented tools at each step, and particularly praising "the merits of the machinery and the inventor, who we trust will receive that Patronage from Government his talents, science & mechanical ingenuity deserve."[9]

Their report convinced Congress that in spite of the cost, the Hall project was worthwhile. When six state governors called for the Hall's rifle to replace their state militia musket, the demand for Hall's rifles overwhelmed the Ordnance Department. In March 1827, Hall was issued a new contract, giving him an annual salary of $1,450 and a $1 royalty on each weapon he manufactured. He was also given an order for three thousand more rifles to be made on his machines, which he had patented the day before he signed the contract. While Stubblefield's foray had failed, Hall's primary assignment was not to perfect his rifle, but to perfect his system of making the rifle.

This jurisdictional dispute between the Ordnance Department and Stubblefield and the Junto must have been a considerable distraction to Hall. Having festered for years, the quarrel was fully in the open by 1826, when the Junto used its political connections to try to obtain Bomford's dismissal, while the colonel redoubled his efforts to curb Stubblefield.

In addition to his general complaints against the superintendent, Bomford had accumulated many specific charges. Stubblefield was accused of keeping three men on the payroll because they owed him money; of supplying his distillery business partner Stephenson with government firewood; of delivering it with armory teams; of having been inside the armory only twice between August 1824 and April 1825; of leaving day-to-day management to his brother-in-law, Armistead Beckam, master armorer and a man of questionable skills and less administrative ability; of failure to obtain competitive bids as required by federal law; of paying the local Strider brothers 25 cents per bushel of coal, when a nonlocal supplier was offering it at 20 cents a bushel; of requiring suppliers to sell through middleman friends, who then increased the price before selling to the armory. People testified that John A. Smith of Harpers Ferry for years bought rough-sawn gunstocks from Barnard and Sons at 14 cents each, then sold them to the armory for 19 cents each, after having done nothing more than issue a new invoice. Preferential treatment for the iron forge of Peter Shoenberger, whom one witness described as "a Deep Designing Crafty man,"[10] also led the armory to accept in its purchases of pig iron over a period of some years an "emence scrapp heap" of defective iron on armory grounds. Shoenberger was accused of not having the blast furnace needed to make the top-quality pig iron the armory required—a fact the armory should have been aware of and acted on.[11]

When Bomford sent a forging expert named Thomas Copeland to Harpers Ferry to install experimental machinery for making rifle barrels, Stubblefield still insisted on supplying Shoenberger's poor-quality pig iron, while the handcrafting armorers objected to the use of machinery to do what was traditionally done by hand. Reluctantly, Bomford directed Copeland to quit Harpers Ferry and to set up his barrel-making machinery in Springfield, where Roswell Lee and his staff received him with great interest and support.

Never in any year under Stubblefield did the armory reach the War Department's projected goal of fifteen thousand muskets a year.[12] Springfield consistently led in production—and at a lower cost per musket. The reasons for this were many, including the obvious one of poor management. Because of the remoteness of the village, because of the reputation of the Junto, and because of the history of malaria and other diseases, the shortage of skilled labor was chronic. Workers didn't want to move into a town with notoriously bad housing and high living costs brought on by the "baneful influence" of the several families who owned and controlled the town of Harpers Ferry.

The unhealthfulness of the area inhibited production in other ways. With each annual outbreak of malaria, workmen left the factory to escape the dreaded "bilious fever" epidemics, largely brought on by the annual flooding and the sweltering summer heat, which combined to carry off scores of victims, thereby reducing the workforce and closing the plant for weeks on end. Poor drainage, which caused the drinking water to be contaminated with sewage, produced yet other diseases. In the 1820s, improved water treatment and a government housing construction program made armory employment more attractive, at which point jobs became coveted by the people in the town.

The resistance of the armorers to innovations was yet another cause for the low production. After thirteen years of apprenticeship, they wanted no part of any manufacturing process that would diminish the importance of handcrafting. This was in marked contrast to Springfield, especially under Roswell Lee, where new machines and manufacturing techniques were consistently introduced. Harpers Ferry, conversely, was relatively isolated, far removed from the stimulus of new production ideas, so the old handcrafted ways continued to prevail in spite of efforts from the War Department to introduce new ideas—particularly from Springfield.

The division of labor that led to an increase in production at Springfield, credited largely to Benjamin Prescott, was introduced there as early as 1806. Yet years after its introduction at Harpers Ferry, it had failed to materially increase production, since the heads of production divisions continued to be men imbued with the old handcraft tradition.

The quality of Harpers Ferry arms was as poor as the production volume. The rejection rate of rifle barrels was so high—even though many substandard ones were actually put in store—the workers often threw the rejects into the Potomac to conceal them from the visiting government inspectors. Stubblefield was criticized repeatedly for shipping muskets so poorly made that government arsenals were put to great expense to repair them. And this included all armory products—barrels, ramrods, bayonets, and lock mechanisms. Year after year, Stubblefield, due to ill health, outside interests, and waning ardor, failed to keep pace with Roswell Lee's improvements.[13]

In the fall of 1825, Bomford, with the first chief Colonel Wadsworth's efforts to control the Junto as a warning, decided on a new tactic. He ordered Stubblefield to become temporary superintendent of Springfield and Roswell Lee to become temporary superintendent of Harpers Ferry. Both men objected, and while Lee arrived reluctantly in the fall of 1826, Stubblefield, pleading ill health, went to his Berry Hill plantation to recuperate. In truth, in spite of the new drainage system introduced a few years before, there was a bilious fever outbreak in Harpers Ferry that year. Stubblefield's own clerk and relative, Edward Wager, died from it, and some 90 percent of the workforce was incapacitated. But, five months later, Stubblefield still had not reported for duty at Springfield. He never did.

During his stay at Harpers Ferry, from the autumn of 1826 to August of 1827, Lee's brilliant management skills were nearly overwhelmed. While trying to cope with the quarreling factions inside the armory, he also served on a three-man committee set up by Bomford to study the Hall rifle-making machinery in Harpers Ferry, a task that absorbed much of his time. He did manage to introduce Blanchard's eccentric lathe for machine-making gunstocks, thereby eliminating one of the many slow, high-cost handcrafted operations.

Meanwhile, Stubblefield's critics and enemies—like the very angry forging expert Thomas Copeland, who had been forced to transfer to Springfield and who was now back in Harpers Ferry—had become more vocal, and they now took their complaints to Congress. Under pressure, in 1827, Secretary of War Barbour named a three-man investigating committee headed by U.S. inspector general John Wool. All through the investigation, Stubblefield remained unimpressed, still continuing to delegate authority to Armistead Beckam, to ship defective muskets, to spend beyond the authorized budget, and to refuse to obtain competitive bids.

Of Stubblefield's administration, the Wool Report found only a "few instances of neglect of minor importance."[14] Critics said that the board never examined half the witnesses against Stubblefield and that Master Armorer Armistead Beckam and a group of local toughs intimidated other witnesses. One of James Stubblefield's first acts following the Wool investigation was to fire Thomas Copeland.

But then Stubblefield's fortunes changed. Politically, he bet on the wrong horse by stoutly promoting the reelection of John Quincy Adams against Andrew Jackson. When the new Jackson administration took over in Washington in 1828, Stubblefield lost all his Virginia "Old Guard" political strength. His staunchest defender, Secretary of War Barbour, was replaced by Peter Porter. Stubblefield's enemies formed a new coalition against him, while, ever angry and determined, Thomas Copeland filed another complaint against him with the new Congress. Congress passed a resolution requiring the secretary of war to produce a statement of accounts from the armory going back seven years. By January 1829, ten congressmen were calling for a new investigation of the armory.

Reluctantly, in early 1829, Roswell Lee returned as temporary superintendent of Harpers Ferry, and the investigation began in May 1829. Stubblefield appeared to the investigators to be "an honest good hearted man who has been too easy perhaps in dealing with scoundrels,"[15] with the principal scoundrel being his brother-in-law and master armorer, Armistead Beckam.

Beckam was cited for taking bribes, falsifying records, intimidating employees, favoritism, using violence, and fabricating charges against Thomas Copeland. But as superintendent, Stubblefield was the one held culpable. In dismay, the previously unflappable Stubblefield wrote a long, disjointed letter to the congressional board of investigators, admitting the charges but claiming extenuating circumstances. The letter served only to confirm the board in its judgment of him.

At Roswell Lee's urging, Ordnance Chief Bomford, the victor, instead of summarily firing Stubblefield, allowed him to return briefly to his post in order to resign, which he did in June of 1829. Armistead Beckam refused to resign and, strangely, instead of being fired, was ordered to exchange posts with Benjamin Moor, now with the government's Allegheny Arsenal in Pittsburgh.

Following the dismissal of Stubblefield, having lost its political base in Washington, the Junto itself was devastated, never to recover its old power.

As the two superintendents, Lee and Stubblefield, left their positions—Stubblefield by his resignation in June 1829 and Lee by his death in August 1833—nothing could reveal their opposite personalities and talents more than the two armories they left behind. Lee's Springfield was a model gun factory filled with the most recently invented machinery, a high annual production rate, and a low unit cost, "one of the most progressive manufacturing establishments in the United States." [16] Stubblefield's armory was a place of conflict and corruption, of sullenly defended, outmoded handcraft traditions, few machines, low production of poor-quality muskets, and high unit cost.

CHAPTER 6

AFTER LEE, DECLINE

I n November 1833, ninety days after Roswell Lee's death, John Robb was appointed new superintendent of Springfield. An ordinary clerk in the War Department, Robb was a pork-barrel politician, and an enthusiastic supporter of Andrew Jackson. Apparently, his eager loyalty was enough to earn the armory appointment, since Robb had no particular skills of any sort, nor background in administration. In addition, he was totally without experience in gun manufacturing—or any other kind of manufacturing, for that matter.

The astonished armory staff, accustomed to the lofty and unremitting standards set by Roswell Lee, watched as the new superintendent walked through the chambers of the armory without any idea what all those huge and expensive machines did.

With his first act, Robb stamped himself evermore for what he was: he appointed as master armorer a longtime employee and a demonstrated malcontent with local political connections named I. C. Bates. Bates, despite his years in the armory, was in no fashion qualified for the post of master armorer.

Even the leather-skinned Robb could not ride out the furor this appointment raised, and, in time, the secretary of war himself, Joel R. Poinsett, fired Bates and replaced him with Thomas Warner, who was to have a long and successful career as master armorer. Although a decided improvement, this appointment was brought about by the same political practices that led to Bates's appointment and dismissal. Unfortunately, such tampering with the appointment system did significant damage to morale inside the armory, which Robb was never able to repair.

Staff intransigence and administrative incompetence took a heavy toll on output. By 1836, musket production had fallen to 13,500 from 16,500 in the Roswell year of 1831.[1] The army was getting 3,000 fewer muskets for the same dollars. Yet, at the same time, Congress, prodded by the War Department to replace aging equipment, was providing major funding for new tooling all through the thirties and early forties—new machinery that should have raised production, not lowered it.

Discipline in the plant declined. Drinking on the premises and drunkenness on the job not only returned but also increased. With Robb's haphazard financial habits, wages rose abnormally from the levels that he had inherited from the Lee administration. And under Robb's slack reins, the workers were virtually permitted to set their own hours, many of them getting a full month's pay for a few days' work. The quality of manufacture declined, and the number of musket barrels that were condemned by inspectors rose, blamed in part on the inferior iron Robb bought and in part on the slovenly workmanship he permitted.

What is most arresting about Robb's administration is the continued high standards, inventiveness, and pride of performance many of the armory staff continued to maintain. And with the new machines the dedicated few—like Master Armorer Thomas Warner —were able to keep the armory functioning at a far higher level than Robb's incompetent administration deserved, testimony to Roswell Lee's inspiring influence.

Washington pork-barrel practices even reached into the armory's finances. By order of a general circular from the War Department, the armory's bank deposits, an account of considerable worth to any bank, were moved from the Springfield Bank to the Farmers and Mechanics Bank of Hartford, some miles downriver in the state of Connecticut.

Springfield bankers objected vociferously and a political compromise was reached: the two banks shared the profits from the armory account.

During the same period, along with the decline of the Springfield Armory, conditions at Harpers Ferry steadily deteriorated even below the low standards set by Stubblefield. His departure in August 1829 did little to alleviate the problems of the Hall's rifle works in spite of the seeming vindication of the rifle by congressional investigation.

Matters did seem to improve at first. With conditions at Harpers Ferry calling for a new, firm administration, Ordnance Chief Bomford appointed tough, blunt Thomas B. Dunn, superintendent of the Antietam Iron Works in Maryland, as Stubblefield's successor.

Dunn promptly fired a number of "inept and undesirable" workers; rehired others fired by Stubblefield; assigned most of Armistead Beckam's duties to still others; enforced the work regulations inaugurated in 1827 by Roswell Lee in order to eliminate loitering, gambling, and drinking, and absenteeism; established standards of product uniformity and inspection; and began to standardize bookkeeping methods. Hall's rifle works could not but benefit from the efficient, honest administration Dunn was creating.

But four months after Dunn's appointment, on January 29, 1830, an ex-employee named Ebenezer Cox entered Dunn's office, and there shot and killed him. After he was tried and executed, Cox became a folk hero to the armory employees, who liked to suggest this would be the fate of any other superintendent who crossed them.

That same year, 1830, George Rust, Jr., became the next full-time superintendent. Wealthy in his own right, this "Virginia Gentleman of Great Intelligence" was also married to a fortune and wielded great political power in northern Virginia. A gentleman farmer, he knew nothing about factories, manufacturing, or arms. Regarding his appointment as a sinecure, a reward for having supported Andrew Jackson, he frequently delegated his authority to the new master armorer, Benjamin Moor, while absenting himself for long periods of time.

Watching these developments from his rifle works, John Hall had found his stern and abrasive integrity in deep conflict with Rust's pork-barrel methods. Worse still, Hall found himself short-funded again, when, due to Stubblefield's legacy of financial deficits, the Ordnance Department balanced its books by cutting Hall's rifle budget. The results were the loss of some of his key personnel and severe overcrowding. So cramped, in fact, was he in his rifle works that he had to make complete parts runs on various machines, then move the machinery to make room to operate other machines. Given also the small production runs authorized by the War Department, Hall was never able to get his cost per rifle below the $14.50 range. Since it was quite clear to Hall that economy would be a major feature of his "American system" of manufacture, crowded facilities, inadequate manpower, and orders for only short production runs left him in constant frustration.

Hall's mass manufacture concepts were vindicated when, in 1834, Simon North, an arms maker in Middletown, Connecticut, duplicated Hall's tooling and commenced manufacturing the Hall's rifle. The parts made in his plant exactly fit the parts made in Harpers Ferry. Now it was demonstrated that all parts, regardless of place of manufacture, could be interchangeable.

In 1836, a board of examining officers was convened to test the Hall against several new rifles that had appeared—invented by John W. Cochran, Samuel Colt, and Baron Hackett. While Hall's rifle was judged the best of the four weapons, the board opined that the complicated mechanism of breech-loading weapons "deranges and perplexes" the soldier.

In 1837, Rust resigned, leaving the same chaotic conditions he had found. But the new superintendent was no more a friend of the Hall's rifle than the indifferent Rust had been. This superintendent was another Virginian and Democratic political appointee, Edward ("Colonel Ed") Lucas. A lawyer and a businessman with powerful connections within the Democratic party, Lucas was also entirely unqualified to operate a national armory. During his tenure, he fired a number of Whigs on the payroll, many of them "perfectly competent armorers" and replaced them with Democrats of lesser talents, "to the great detriment of the Armoury."[2] He also resisted most of Ordnance Chief Bomford's efforts to direct him in his job, and particularly resisted Bomford's efforts to reduce the size of staff. Several employees later described Colonel Ed as a hot-tempered man prone to fire anyone who expressed even a hint of criticism. Through his political connections, he was able to increase the annual appropriation for the armory and spent far beyond that, having accrued a $46,000 deficit by 1839.

Even more significant damage was done to the Hall's rifle's reputation in 1837 and 1838, when the army reported the five Hall's carbines—made by Simon North—had burst apart when fired. Studies showed that the rifle wasn't bursting; the steamed walnut gunstocks, having grown brittle with age, were. Also there was evidence that poorly trained troops had put too much powder in the breech, causing the gunstocks to shatter. Hall and Bomford both believed this problem was easily remedied. But, by now, opposition to the breech-loading rifle had become overwhelming, especially with the appointment of Joel R. Poinsett as the new secretary of war.

CHAPTER 7

HALL'S RIFLE EXITS:
ARMY CONTROL ENTERS

Secretary Joel R. Poinsett was to have final and decisive influence on the history of the Hall's rifle. A wealthy rice planter, Poinsett was born, in 1779, into a prominent South Carolina French Huguenot family. With great ability and varied governmental experience, he first gained national prominence during the Andrew Jackson administration. Working closely with President Jackson and General Winfield Scott during the South Carolina nullification crisis of 1832, Poinsett emerged as one of the Unionist leaders against J. C. Calhoun's secessionist party in South Carolina, which bitterly fought the Jackson tariff bill, declaring it null and void as they threatened to withdraw from the Union.

Originally intending to be a doctor, Poinsett studied medicine in Edinburgh, but instead of returning home to set up practice, he went to Woolwich, England, to study military science, a subject that fascinated him. He spent the next five years traveling while the Napoleonic Wars raged, visiting Russia, western Asia, and much of Europe. Returning home, he accepted diplomatic missions to Argentina and Chile, where he had more opportunity to study military activities. He spent seven years in the South Carolina legislature, devoting much of his time to the development of South Carolina's communications with the western lands. Then, in 1825, after two terms in Washington as a Democrat in the House of Representatives, he became the first minister to Mexico. When he returned home four years later, he brought with him a native Mexican plant that bloomed at Christmastime. It became known as the poinsettia.

In the mid-1830s, he married a wealthy widow, Mary Pringle, and for a time was content to be a gentleman rice planter. However, he had never lost his great interest in military science, and in 1837, he was called to Washington upon the election of Martin Van Buren to become secretary of war. He quickly became one of Van Buren's most capable cabinet members.

One of the significant achievements of Poinsett's administration as secretary of war occurred in 1840, when he sent a board of American army officers abroad for the purpose of studying European artillery, with the particular assignment of bringing back sample cannon. The effects were felt very quickly when, a little over a year later, the board set up a whole new U.S. Army system of artillery. By the time of the Mexican War, in 1846, when General Winfield Scott was bent on arming American infantrymen with the obsolete flintlock musket, General Taylor asserted that American artillery in Mexico was the pivotal element on which "our success is mainly due."[1]

But Poinsett's inability to cope with the armory problem must have been one of his greatest frustrations. When he took office in 1837, he inherited the embedded political patronage system then prevailing in both armories, with inept John Robb at Springfield and "Colonel" Ed Lucas at Harpers Ferry. As a ranking member of the Democratic party, Poinsett had far less control over the two armories than he would have liked and certainly could not tamper with a spoils system that fellow Democrats in Massachusetts and Virginia had installed in them.

Although he did personally fire the incompetent Bates as master armorer at Springfield, he couldn't touch the equally deserving Robb, the superintendent. To his credit, he replaced Bates with Thomas Warner, one of the most outstanding chief armorers in Springfield's history, yet, after his four-year tenure, Poinsett, upon departing office, could not avoid leaving behind the same shameful conditions in the two armories that he had found.

As the man who removed the Hall's rifle from the U.S. Army arsenal, he exhibited a less than prescient understanding of breech loading and of maximizing battlefield firepower. His crucial decision to remove the rifle was to continue to have repercussions more than twenty years later, when the Civil War started.

In the latter two years of Poinsett's administration, 1840 and 1841, John Hall suffered from increasingly poor health, as well as savage attacks from all sides—from the handcraft traditionalists in the armory; from the civilian superintendents; from the Junto, which believed that the armory should be handmaking muskets, not machining rifles; from the economy-minded in the War Department who failed to see the great economies possible in Hall's methods; from those who felt the rifle was too complex to make and too complex for the ordinary soldier to operate; and from the traditionalists in the army. Secretary Poinsett himself contended that the breechloader's fast firing wasted ammunition.

Wasted ammunition wasn't simply a question of money, but more a matter of ordnance supply lines. If infantrymen fired too many shots in too short a time period, they could soon outrun the Ordnance Corps' ability to resupply them. But what Secretary Poinsett and his Ordnance officers were doing was limiting infantry firepower to the rate Ordnance felt it could supply. And thereby they were throwing away a key to winning battles: superior fire-power. Instead, soldiers should have been trained not to waste ammunition and an ordnance supply system should have been designed that could keep up with breech-loaded rifle fire while continuing to perfect the Hall's breech-loading rifle. In effect, supply was determining demand while reducing the firepower of the foot soldier.

Secretary Poinsett told the chairman of the House Committee on Military Affairs in 1840 that he himself would not have adopted the Hall's rifle and "shall make little use of them" in regular service.[2] In fact, his very jaundiced view of the breech-loading rifle was quite evident in his final report of 1840, when, with a disapproving nod at the Hall's rifle, he commented, "Every attempt to increase the rapidity of firing will fail as they have hitherto done, after involving the government in great expense."[3]

Yet he was wrong. The breechloader did not need to be dismissed, but more carefully researched. Soldiers needed more training in the maintenance and firing of it. Field armorers needed more training and more appropriate tools and gauges. Service-weary Hall's rifles needed to be returned to the armory for refurbishment. All these were standard practices with the musket. More research and development of the breechloader would have led to more improved models, especially in the late 1830s, when more and more American rifle designers were studying the problems and opportunities of the breechloader. The gifted Christian Sharps, after studying under Hall at Harpers Ferry for a few years, was working on the first designs that would produce the legendary Sharps breech-loading rifle that was to see extensive service in the Civil War.

But the truth was, regardless of the merits of the weapon, not enough people really wanted a breech-loading rifle . . . and too many didn't. Like his counterparts throughout American history, Secretary Poinsett was not working with direct information, but rather with information fed to him by the Ordnance system, much of it intentionally negative, despite the best efforts of his ordnance chief, George Bomford, to convince him of the virtues of the breechloader.

In 1841 and 1842, more of the rifle's enemies came into power. Major Henry Knox Craig, who was named first military commandant of Harpers Ferry Armory on April 15, 1841, strongly disliked Hall's rifle. In 1835, he wrote to Ordnance Chief Bomford, one of the few champions of the weapon, "I have always considered it as most clumsily and awkwardly shaped, and as an encumbrance which a fatigued soldier would take the earliest opportunity of getting rid of."

After twenty years of fighting off these various factions, Hall was too worn and sick to fight any longer. A wasting illness—probably tuberculosis—forced him to take an extended leave of absence. He died in the home of his third son in Huntsville, Missouri, on February 26, 1841, aged sixty.

With Hall's death, few remained to speak up for the gun against conservative hostility. The following year, on February 1, 1842, the Hall's rifle lost its last champion when Chief of Ordnance George Bomford left office. The following September, manufacture of Hall's breech-loading arms ceased at Harpers Ferry. All Hall's rifles were removed from service and replaced with the Model 1841 percussion rifle, a muzzleloader that later became famous as the Mississippi rifle. More than twenty years would pass before a breech-loading weapon would again be officially used by the U.S. Army.

Hall's machinery continued to be used, probably up to the Civil War, to make other weapons, demonstrating his major point that his "American System" of machine manufacturing applied to all weapons, including muskets, and to many other types of products as well. But Lieutenant Colonel George Talcott, who replaced Bomford as chief of ordnance in 1842, after serving for years as his assistant, may have had the last word about the Hall's breech-loading rifle and its interchangeable parts system in a letter he wrote in January 1845 to then secretary of war William Willkins:

"The United States long since adopted Hall's rifles, after such trials as appeared to satisfy all objections, and that they were overcome is fully shown by the reports and statements made. . . . The first Regiment of Dragoons when first raised was armed with carbines of this model, and they received the most unqualified approbation. How is it that the opinion of their utility has been changed? It is because no attention has been paid to keep the arms in the hands of troops in good condition, nor have the soldiers been properly instructed in their use. Neglecting to keep the joint closed, a blast has been suffered to exist and ruin the stocks. I am practically acquainted with the use of Hall's arms and assert unqualifiedly that if my honor and life were at stake, and depended on the use of firearms, I would sooner take one of these carbines than any other weapon. But fashions change and what is good today will be cried down to-morrow. Upon due consideration of the subject the department decided on abandoning the manufacture of breech-loading arms, and have followed in the steps of the great powers in Europe, deciding that a diversity of arms was productive of evil, and adopting those of the ordinary construction which are the simplest and easiest managed by the soldier."[4]

With Hall and his rifle now gone, the War Department was still confronted with the problem of shaping up the two armories.

The military was ever painfully aware that the Harpers Ferry Armory had become a "second rate establishment and the source of considerable embarrassment."[5] Common military sense suggested that the two armories were far too important to the nation to be run by destructive, disobedient political hacks. In 1840, the military finally got an opportunity to do something about the situation: the Whig candidate, William Henry Harrison, won the presidential election. Harrison's new secretary of war, John Bell, who replaced Joel Poinsett in March 1841, was confronted with a problem and an opportunity. The problem was the very bad condition of the two armories—just at a time when the new percussion caplock musket was to go into production. The opportunity was the chance to remove a large number of Democrat patronage appointees on the staffs of both armories.

Secretary Bell asked Ordnance Chief Bomford for his recommendations. His choice was obvious: under political appointees, the two armories lay in ruins. John Robb had practically destroyed the Springfield Armory. Roswell Lee's superb production line, after eight years of Robb's neglect, was obsolete and arthritic. As the historian Constance Green observes, "The years of Robb were found to have been wasteful in the extreme, and it is hard to understand why he was allowed to hold office so long, even with the spoils system rampant."[6] Harpers Ferry, after decades of Junto politics, capped off with the regimes of Rust and Lucas, was in even worse condition.

Drawing on his nearly thirty years' experience in Ordnance, twenty of them as chief, Bomford recommended that political appointees, who were loyal to party first and country second, should be replaced by military commandants who were loyal to their country first and foremost. It was, he noted, far easier to remove an incompetent or corrupt army officer than a well-connected politician.[7]

On April 1, 1841, War Secretary Bell accepted the ordnance chief's recommendations. President Harrison, eager to remove Democrats from the armory, quickly issued an executive edict requiring each armory to be headed by a commissioned officer in the U.S. Army. That same day, Bell fired the two civilian superintendents, John Robb at Springfield and "Colonel" Ed Lucas at Harpers Ferry, whose parting gift was a Jacksonian Democrat in every position of importance in the armory except two, plus a deficit of $28,000. Colonel Bomford, with only a meager list of 754 U.S. Army officers to choose from, promptly named two military commandants: Major Henry Knox Craig for Harpers Ferry and Major James Wolfe Ripley for Springfield Armory.

But the fight didn't end there. Among the first to react was Whig congressman William Calhoun of Springfield. Bell's directness had snatched a huge piece of political patronage from Calhoun's hands, and he roundly condemned the move for being "full of mischief in all respects."[8] A military tone in the armory would destroy the "spirit of the establishment." John Strider, a Harpers Ferry businessman who profited over the years from selling coal at inflated prices to the armory, a friend of the Junto, and an active Whig who had waited twelve years to pry the Democrats out of the armory, also saw his town's primary source of political patronage suddenly disappear. He wrote to his Whig president William H. Harrison, claiming the right of the winning party "under a free government" to the spoils of office and urged that Bell's decision be reversed. He warned that the new military administration of the armories would cause great disaffection among the workers.

The battle was carried to the Congress, and it fell to Colonel Bomford's aggressive successor, Colonel George Talcott, to defend it there. Talcott asserted that armory regulations were not being changed—just enforced—and that the armory workers were not being exploited, merely asked to work the same workday as private industry. He pointed out to the Congress that the armorers were in the habit of working only four to six hours a day, with chronic absenteeism of days and even weeks. Under the current arms production system, where each man's work was predicated on the work of

79

others, such absenteeism and slack hours could wreak havoc with production. As for salary, he stated that under the loose and free system the armorers had been following, they got the same monthly pay whether they worked full-time or part-time. In the face of strong opposition, Congress confirmed the president's executive edict and, in August 1842, enacted Statutes at Large 5:512, which passed into law military control over the armories.[9]

Into this political turmoil, with hostile armories and hostile communities awaiting them, on April 16, 1841, Majors Ripley and Craig reported to their new armory posts.

With the establishment of military control over the armories, 1841 proved to be one of the most pivotal years in Ordnance history. Yet still more profound alterations to the armory system occurred that year. In addition to the historically significant change from civilian to military control in both armories, for the first time since its founding, the Ordnance Department was confronted with the choice of a new national shoulder arm. With Hall gone and his rifle discredited, there was no doubt that the new shoulder arm would be a musket, a smoothbore muzzle-loaded musket. But the French Charleville 1763 musket—of which the American Springfield 1794 musket was a direct copy—was now nearly eighty years old. The French had already abandoned it in the face of an international ordnance turmoil. As beneficiaries of the growing European Industrial Revolution, armories there were reaping major developments each year that could be used to improve the speed and killing power of small arms and artillery. In the offing were new small arms with greater accuracy, greater range, and faster firepower.

The development of a new U.S. Army musket was put into the hands of two of the most gifted weapons designers in the country at that time: Benjamin Moor, master armorer at Harpers Ferry, and Thomas Warner, master armorer at Springfield.

This was the same Benjamin Moor who, as inspector of contract arms, was sent during the War of 1812 to Springfield Armory to prod Superintendent Benjamin Prescott into producing muskets for the army and who finally resolved the problem by having Prescott fired. Later, when the ill-fated Lechler was hired as superintendent, he had appointed Moor master armorer. But when Lechler was fired in 1815, Moor, too, had been removed.

Born and raised in Springfield, Moor had started his apprenticeship at fourteen in the Springfield Armory and spent his early years as an armorer working in various arsenals and armories in Pennsylvania and Virginia. After his release from Springfield in 1815, he had returned as master armorer to Allegheny Arsenal in Pittsburgh, where he served for fifteen years, acquiring a reputation as an outstanding armorer. In June 1830, the Ordnance Department requested him to return to Harpers Ferry to replace the infamous Armistead Beckam as master armorer. After being cited by a congressional investigating committee for a number of acts that seemed criminal enough to warrant a prison sentence, Beckam in turn was to become master armorer at Allegheny.

Because of the notorious working conditions at Harpers Ferry, and also because of the lower pay scale, Moor was very reluctant to leave his comfortable position at the Allegheny Arsenal. Only the urging of Ordnance Chief George Bomford led him to accept the post.

An open, friendly man, very popular throughout the entire armsmaking world, and a widely respected armorer, Moor was also a dedicated exponent of machine manufacture of arms. In the face of ramshackle conditions and resistance from the armorers at Harpers Ferry, he made a major contribution as master armorer— and frequently as acting superintendent—in modernizing the plant, despite the several incompetent civilian superintendents he served under. He found conditions there so ingrown and entangled, he confided to a friend, that he felt the only cure was to abandon Harpers Ferry entirely and move the whole operation to Pittsburgh.[10]

In the midst of this major reorganization and retooling of the armory, Moor was also selected by the War Department to design a new musket with completely interchangeable parts, based on John Hall's "American System" and including all requisite production gauges and tools. The project took some six years. The War Department was so pleased with Moor's new musket, it decided to go into production and ordered forty thousand copies. The result was a flintlock musket designated the Model 1840. These Moor muskets were made not at Harpers Ferry, but at Springfield. Production was halted abruptly when the War Department decided to make an even newer musket, featuring a revolutionary new percussion cap system to replace the obsolete flintlock system. Although Moor's Model 1840 flintlock musket was short-lived, the new musket—designed by his close friend and counterpart at Springfield, Master Armorer Thomas Warner—absorbed many of the features of Moor's weapon. This new weapon, the Model 1842 muzzle-loading smoothbore musket, became the first volume-produced weapon with fully interchangeable parts to be made at both armories, a credit to both Moor and Warner. The War Department believed that this new musket gave the American army the finest arm in the world.

Before long, Thomas Warner's Model 1842 musket encountered problems. The all-weather percussion cap that it featured had been invented in Europe in 1816 and represented a revolutionary advance over the old flintlock method, which could not be fired reliably in rain or snow. The new cap freed armies forever from the severe limitation of fair-weather fighting. Its introduction into the arms of the United States was decades overdue, yet even after the Model 1842 was produced, no less a personage than General Winfield Scott, commanding general of the army, pronounced dark suspicions of the cap. Scott thought the mechanical flint action was more reliable, and therefore was firmly opposed to the cap. As a result, the U.S. Army went to war against Mexico in 1845 armed primarily with obsolete flintlocks, while the new percussion cap model remained at home in U.S. arsenals.

Hall's pioneering work was not entirely lost. While his rifle was replaced by more primitive weapons in the military arsenal, his interchangeable parts concept contributed significantly to the "American System" of manufacture that gave American companies a major worldwide lead in the Industrial Revolution and was soon copied avidly by European manufacturers.

Had Hall been allowed to develop his weapon in the more

receptive atmosphere of Springfield, under Roswell Lee, rather than the hostile and repressive atmosphere of Harpers Ferry, under James Stubblefield, he might have been able to bring his weapon and system closer to a level that would have been acceptable to even the most conservative in the War Department. As it was, following Hall's brilliant work, the U.S. Army had taken a major step forward in production efficiency and a major step backward in military rifle efficiency. More than a quarter of a century was to pass before the army once again had a rifle the equal of the Hall's and, even then, it was being left far behind by European rifles, mainly Prussia's, a gap the United States didn't close until the beginning of the twentieth century.

PART II

PART VI

CHAPTER 8

COMMANDANTS CRAIG AND RIPLEY

At Harpers Ferry, unlike Springfield, the handcraft tradition was still deeply embedded, and, with Major Henry Knox Craig's arrival, the final great battle began between the traditionalists and the machine-production proponents.

Major Craig, long associated with Harpers Ferry, was quite familiar with its history and problems, especially the history of the Hall's rifle, a weapon he supervised and strongly opposed, predicting that the foot soldier would at the earliest opportunity throw it away. A graduate of West Point, he had spent much of his career in artillery and ordnance, succeeding to the post of superintendent of contract services at Harpers Ferry in 1832. As commandant, he had the probably pleasurable task of shipping out the last few Hall's rifles and carbines in 1843.

After decades of observing the excesses, abuses, and failures of politically appointed superintendents, now, at the age of forty-nine, Craig had a clear mandate from the War Department to shape up the recalcitrant plant. The armory was to a considerable extent controlled by the workers. Hostile to all outsiders, they came and went largely as they pleased, drinking whiskey, gaming, and taking days off as they wished, and conducting personal business on the premises. They liked to remind themselves and outsiders that the fate of the murdered superintendent Thomas Dunn awaited the person who interfered with their rights and privileges.

Unintimidated, Major Henry Knox Craig announced there would be no more drinking on the premises and then posted the regulations promulgated by Roswell Lee in 1827, which he pledged to strictly enforce. The workday was standardized at ten hours (from eight to six), six days a week. Slackers could be fined and fired. Since private industry exacted twelve hours of labor during each workday, this arrangement was generous, but armorers were spoiled. The workers, believing that skilled craftsmen should not work by the clock, were enraged and, to them, the plant clock became the symbol of the hated machines that pressed in around them.

Their complaints had no effect on Craig, who told them to accept the conditions of employment or find work elsewhere. They did neither, but instead appealed to Ordnance Chief Bomford, who, predictably, backed up his armory commandant. In protest, on March 21, 1842, the entire workforce at Harpers Ferry downed their tools and walked off the job. A delegation chartered a boat to sail down the Chesapeake and Ohio Canal to Washington to complain to President Tyler. They told him they were reduced to slaves, "mere machines of labor."[1] He sent them away with soothing words but no support. The issue was settled, at least for a time, when Congress approved the new military administration of the armories in August of 1842.

But Major Craig's work—and that of his successor, Major John Symington, who succeeded him in November 1844—had only just begun. More than two decades of neglect and resistance by the handcrafters had put Harpers Ferry far behind Springfield. The buildings were all chockablock, having been erected over a period of years without much plan or purpose. The work did not flow in an orderly fashion, and the workers were crowded into too-small work spaces. Under Craig's direction, a number of these buildings were torn down and replaced. Between 1845 and 1854, following Craig's carefully wrought plan, twenty-five new buildings were erected. With stone foundations, brick walls, iron framing, and slate or sheet metal roofs, these new structures housed a boring mill, a forging and smith's shop, a stocking and machine shop, a tilt-hammer and barrel-welding shop, a grinding shop, a sawmill, an annealing and brass foundry, and a rolling mill.[2] The canals were enlarged; fire hydrants installed; larger millwork, to handle more machines, was introduced. Drainage ditches were dug, cesspools sunk, water cisterns built. The grounds were walled and land-scaped, and for the first time, Harpers Ferry looked like a spruced-up spit-and-polish military installation.

This renewal program was orchestrated through the skillful min-istrations of Master Armorer Benjamin Moor, who had begun some of the improvements during the notorious regimes of Rust and Lucas.

At Springfield, the new commandant was going to have to cope with a factory full of political appointees, drunks, malingerers, and incompetents and fend off enduring assaults from a political faction in Springfield while at the same time modernizing the plant, intro-ducing new tooling, and developing a production line on which to make the new musket. For this difficult cleanup job, Bomford probably could not have chosen better. Major Ripley's posture and demeanor announced unequivocally the style of the man within: stiff, autocratic, with erect military bearing. A West Point graduate, he was born the same year as the armory, 1794, and just a few miles downriver, in Hartford, Connecticut. In 1841, Ripley and the ar-mory were both forty-seven.

Some would have described Ripley's high forehead and severe aquiline nose as aristocratic. There was little or no humor in the eyes, and there was no compromise in the small clapped-shut mouth. As he grew older, his face tended toward a choleric red, and when roused to anger, which was frequent, it turned into an apoplectic and intimidating purple. Even his name was intimidat-ing: James Wolfe Ripley.

In 1814, Ripley had been commissioned second lieutenant of artillery and served in the War of 1812. In 1818, First Lieutenant Ripley served with distinction as an ordnance officer in the Semi-nole War in Florida. Even then, his rigid adherence to regulations had become a pronounced characteristic that brought him into direct confrontation with General Andrew Jackson. Ripley had received an ordnance requisition from the general that did not quite follow correct procedure. So the stiff-necked, by-the-numbers young officer refused to honor the requisition. He then received a message from General Jackson that said, in effect, "Honor my requisition immediately or I will send a guard to arrest you and here in my camp I will hang you from the first tree."

Historian Constance Green characterized Ripley succinctly: "His military background supplemented a native inflexibility of attitude, and, where he thought he saw his duty, nor hell nor high water could turn him from any course of action he determined upon."[3]

In the few years preceding his appointment to the Springfield Armory, Ripley had acquired an excellent rating as commanding officer of the Kennebec Arsenal in Maine. He had come to national attention in 1832 when "Old Hickory," Andrew Jackson, was in the White House. South Carolina had declared its extreme dissatisfaction with the new federal tariff and declared it null and void—which was tantamount to secession. Andrew Jackson reacted with characteristic bluntness: "If one drop of blood be shed there in defiance of the laws of the United States I will hang the first man of them I can get my hands on to the first tree I can find."[4]

The threat proved ineffective. A special South Carolina convention passed an ordnance of nullification, prohibiting the collection of tariffs after November 24, 1832. The state then voted funds for the raising of an army. Jackson made some conciliatory moves on revising the tariff but bluntly announced he would raise an army of 200,000, while at the same time strengthening the garrison at Fort Moultrie in Charleston, a sensitive assignment that was given to James Ripley, at that time a captain in the army. President Jackson then directed his anger to South Carolina's leading nullification advocate, Vice President Calhoun. If South Carolina's nullification went through, Jackson warned, aiming his threat directly at Calhoun, "I will hang him as high as Haman."[5] South Carolina had to choose: secession or union, violence or détente. Eventually, the state backed down, but Joel Poinsett of Charleston, later to be Martin Van Buren's secretary of war, wrote to President Jackson about Captain Ripley's "indefatigable exertions to prepare his post to resist the lawless attacks which threatened it, and his gentlemanly deportment have won the esteem and respect of the friends of the government in this city."[6]

This seemingly born diplomat who could handle the prickly residents of a city under threat of revolution was also highly praised by Major General Winfield Scott, commanding officer of the army, to the secretary of war, Lewis Cass: "He has no superior in the middle ranks of the Army, either in general intelligence, zeal or good conduct. . . . His arrangements for [Fort Moultrie's] defense were admirable. . . . No one left a higher reputation, either with our officers or the citizens of Charleston."[7]

But Major Ripley chose not to show this side of his personality to the armory or to the leading figures of Springfield, like Charles Stearns. A self-made man and a Massachusetts politician, Stearns began his working life as a mason, then soon commenced dealing in real estate, coal, lumber, and eventually politics. He styled himself, among other things, a builder and architect. For the interested, he could point to the comfortably appointed superintendent's residence that stood on the northwest corner of the armory, looking down on the central part of Springfield, as his finest architectural accomplishment. "Needless to say," observes historian Derwent Whittlesey, "he aimed, while pushing his town into the paths of progress, to absorb a certain share of the increment attending upon progressive ways."[8] When Ripley became commandant of the armory, Stearns was already a man of stature, having been an important factor in the acquisition of the town's water supply and sewer system. He was also a strong booster of railroad construction that would benefit the local economy.

The condition of the armory that Ripley inherited was similar to the chaotic shambles that his predecessor Roswell Lee had encountered twenty-seven years before in 1815. Both had been confronted with a decaying plant, inefficient production, poor purchasing practices, and everywhere poor morale and incompetence. Both men had first to deal with a defiant workforce.

Roswell Lee never quite eliminated on-the-job drinking, and under Robb's administration, the habit had flourished once more.

When Major Ripley arrived at the armory, he observed that every morning at eleven and every afternoon at four, the men would put down their tools for their traditional booze and sport break. They walked en masse down to a spring behind the shops and there drank liquor—rum, cider, brandy—while cheering on impromptu wrestling matches, hardly the behavior that would appeal to a strict Episcopalian teetotaler or to a military taskmaster. Ripley observed the drinkers, took note of the leaders, and bided his time.

One of Major Ripley's first official acts was to replace the paymaster and military storekeeper, a Jackson appointee named Charles Howard, with a man of his own choosing, Edward Ingersoll, who was to remain for a generation in that post, and who "could and did assume responsibility for the execution of orders from Ripley, which he staunchly adopted as his own."[9]

Major Ripley next took action against the working staff. He announced that budgetary cuts required the laying off of forty men, then personally chose the forty names from his list of drinkers. The dismissals raised a furor—mainly among the employees, their families, and the Democratic politicians in the town, who charged Ripley with partisanship. But the jobs were political patronage appointments and their holders were, to his mind, the worst of the worst. He ignored the criticism.

In August of 1842, Ripley moved again, clearly with the full support of Colonel Bomford's replacement, the new ordnance chief, George Talcott. The major announced that the plant urgently needed extensive repairs and renovation of machinery and shut the entire plant for three months. The staff was furloughed, and an even greater uproar ensued.

When he reopened the plant, Major Ripley issued the list of men to be rehired. Among them was not one of the forty armorers he had laid off initially. Opponents of Ripley's policies quickly coalesced around Charles Sterns, who declared himself Ripley's avowed adversary and indicated that anything Ripley stood for he was against. The protesters held a meeting and drafted a petition to Congress calling for the return of the civilian superintendent's office and lamenting Ripley's treatment of the laid-off armorers and their families. The same group selected a committee—among which were three of the most vociferous of the sacked armorers—to carry the petition to Washington. The major remained indifferent.

While supporting the protesters, Sterns felt that petitioning congressmen wasn't the answer, since they had no jurisdiction over the armory. Ripley, he saw, could ignore them. The solution lay with Ripley's superiors, who could issue orders he would have to obey. So Stearns went to Ripley's superior officer, Chief of Ordnance Talcott, in Washington, to portray the great suffering of the families of those forty furloughed workers. Colonel Talcott, who completely endorsed Ripley's agenda, which put first priority on the elimination of those forty troublemakers, listened politely, bowed Stearns out of his office, and predictably did nothing. Stearns returned to Springfield empty-handed, as had the congressional petitioning committee before him.

Major Ripley's opponents were reduced to ineffectual acts. The major was hung in effigy from his own armory flagpole. A fire broke out on armory property, which was quickly put out but noticeably without aid of the town's fire brigade, whose failure to appear was noted by Ripley. The protesters and their adherents held a meeting once again, and once again Charles Stearns went to the War Department in Washington, in July of 1843, this time to appeal to Colonel Talcott's superior, President Tyler's secretary of war, James Porter.

For Porter, Stearns described a town up in arms, outraged citizens marching, and an armory seriously undermanned, in chaos and half burned down. He felt he was getting somewhere at last when Secretary Porter agreed to personally visit Springfield to investigate Stearns's complaints. Stearns eagerly returned to Springfield, expecting justice to arrive on the next train.

But when Secretary Porter reviewed the armory, he found a well-run military installation undergoing major renovations. The grass had been cut, the buildings painted, new shrubbery planted, walks cleaned, bricks pointed, windows reglazed, footings for new buildings pegged out—a spit-and-polish military operation with a vengeance. Inside, manufacturing and retooling were proceeding on schedule in an orderly fashion. No drunkenness, no lack of discipline, no fires. Everything was exactly paralleling the restoration going on at Harpers Ferry under Commandant Craig.

Furthermore, Secretary Porter did not find the town up in arms as Stearns had claimed. Indeed, influential townspeople came forward to speak on Ripley's behalf. They pointed to the "great improvements, new vigor and economy" in the armory and noted, "Major Ripley has been governed by a strict fidelity to the Government, and has manifested extraordinary ability."[10] They wanted him to stay; they wanted the armory to continue to be run by the army; they did not want another civilian superintendent like Robb.

To Stearns's chagrin, Secretary Porter, based on what he saw and heard, stood by his armory commandant. Another round went to Ripley, who addressed himself to the next item on his improvements list: excessive wages. Under Robb, he had discovered, wages had risen out of all proportion to those paid in private industry. To resolve this matter, he made a general wage cut, which affected the entire workforce of the armory. When the *Springfield Independent Democrat* wrote an editorial attacking him, Ripley threatened to fire any workman who subscribed to it. He also boldly appeared before the Springfield town meetings to face his opponents. At the same time, he sought to cajole people, armory employees in particular, to join his religion—Episcopalianism.

In the meantime, his modernization programs continued. He planned and supervised the erection of a number of new buildings. He directed the refurbishment and restoration of existing old buildings. He ordered the armory's old magazine torn down and used the materials to build a new one. All the buildings in the installation had fresh coats of paint. The grounds were graded and new trees planted. Additional plots of land were acquired.

Inside the buildings, Ripley was creating a modern manufacturing operation. He acquired and installed new machinery and tooling. He helped develop more efficient production-line methods, studied quality control, and introduced new cost-cutting efficiencies into the purchasing operation.

Next, he turned his attention to the armory's power supply. The flow of water had become more and more inadequate for the plant's increasing power needs, especially in times of drought or deep frost. Another source of power was needed and Ripley chose a relatively new one—a steam generator. His methods of acquiring the new steam plant caused a deeper and soon irreparable chasm between him and Charles Stearns.

On a newly acquired plot adjacent to the superintendent's residence, Ripley commenced construction of a new residence. As the structure rose, the handsome lines of its architectural design and the quality of the building materials did not go unnoticed by the town, and particularly by Charles Stearns, who quickly objected to this "magnificent mansion," which he felt was much too good for an army officer.

Major Ripley's next move left Stearns outraged for the rest of his life. When the new home was completed, Ripley moved his family into it and then tore down the original superintendent's residence, which Stearns himself had built and of which he was inordinately proud. Even though Ripley could produce a government survey that indicated that the original residence was in such serious disrepair it needed to be entirely rebuilt, and even though Ripley's authorization to tear it down had come directly from the Ordnance Office in Washington, Stearns would not be mollified. He asserted that he "considered its condemnation and destruction an insult to his business integrity."[11] Ripley did not reply. Instead, he commenced building a new structure on the lot where Stearns's house had stood. The new multistory main arsenal building, capped with a clock tower, housed the steam power plant that would soon free the armory of the vagaries of local water power.

Ripley's work was still not done. With Ordnance Department authority, the major added more property to the fifty acres, added manufacturing room, straightened roads, added roads, and settled old disputed boundary questions. From the chaos left by Robb, Ripley was bringing forth a contemporary military installation in which the production of muskets increased.

Another fire broke out. And, again, the town fire brigade failed to appear. Then a third fire broke out. When it was safely extinguished, to protect the armory from "the temper and disposition manifested by the rabble,"[12] Ripley ordered the entire compound, a circuit of one mile, to be protected with a fence.

Some people in the town objected because the fence would, in effect, separate the armory from the town. Charles Stearns claimed it would block a road leading to one of his properties. Undaunted, Ripley authorized the commencement of the fence's construction. One night, Charles Stearns had his workmen tear a section of the fence down. When armory workmen repaired it, it was torn down again. When Ripley erected it a third time, Stearns sued Ripley for trespass. Ripley referred the matter to the U.S. district attorney, who brought a countersuit against Stearns for forcible trespass. In the end, after the litigation of both Stearns's lawsuit and the government's countersuit, Stearns lost and Ripley erected a high, wrought-iron picket fence that still stands.

The way Ripley built this fence showed how indeflectible his will was once he set himself on a course of action. It also showed the major to be a born Yankee trader. Like all the other structures he had erected in the armory, Major Ripley wanted a top-quality, handsome installation, yet there was little money in the armory fund for an expensive mile-long fence.

First, he addressed the problem of the ornamental wrought-iron fencing. The cost for this alone was well beyond his means. Undismayed, he looked about for a way to get what he wanted at a price he could afford. He had a quantity of surveyed scrap iron—old Ordnance Department cannons and condemned castings of all types—that lay in government installations nearby in Newport, Rhode Island; Portsmouth, New Hampshire; and New London, Connecticut. Ripley struck a bargain with Cyrus Alger & Company, Boston founders, by which he provided the scrap iron for the fencing, which Alger then cast at 3 cents a pound. To pay for the casting, Ripley provided additional scrap iron for which Alger paid him 3.5 cents a pound. In the end, the picket fencing cost the armory a negligible amount of money.

For the foundation, base wall, and posts, he wanted Longmeadow sandstone, a fine-grained native red stone. Confronted again with high costs, he leased a stone quarry four or five miles from the armory and cut all the stone he needed. He saved still more money by having the castings inspected by his own master armorer at the arsenal in Watertown, Massachusetts. The erection of the fencing was interrupted several times during his regime by governmental cutbacks and was not completed until after Major Ripley's departure. The visitor today will find the Springfield Armory compound essentially as it was at the end of Major Ripley's administration, including the still-standing wrought-iron fence.

Ripley's pugnacious temperament was totally indifferent to public opinion. Despite the fact that three times during his superintendency he was hanged in effigy from the armory flagpole, he seems to have been utterly disinterested in the restless scheming against him by his enemies in the town. Only one activity interested him: in the last four years of his administration, "the shop produced annually more arms than in any previous year, and the cost of the arms was reduced."[13]

By 1854, the task of modernization had been nearly completed at both armories. Machine production had gradually forced out most of the handcraft operations, and the transition to modern factory life had been made.

But the politicians had not given up. The House Committee on Military Affairs was composed of a number of politicians who pushed for a return to political control of the armories, the most vocal of whom was the chairman, Charles James Faulkner, from Martinsburg, Virginia, not far from Harpers Ferry. They claimed that there was waste and extravagance under the military commandants and seized on the fact that the military commandants at Harpers Ferry, for all their modernization, had not been able to produce a musket at a significantly lower cost than had the civilian superintendents in 1841. Colonel Benjamin Huger, the Harpers Ferry commandant in 1854, pointed out that the percussion musket cost more to produce and that the quality of muskets was now far superior to muskets made in 1841. The old armory employees were still complaining about the loss of freedom, the enforced regular hours, and the end of handcraftsmanship. And back in Harpers

Ferry, the Beckams and their political cohorts were still pressing for a return to the old days and old ways.

Matters reached a head at the Harpers Ferry Armory when Commandant Symington fired Master Armorer Benjamin Moor. Moor, a brilliant designer of tooling and machines, had been master armorer there since 1830, and since 1841 in particular had been the major instrument in the introduction of new machines and new systems. In fact, in many ways, the modern plant at Harpers Ferry was a monument to his brilliance. Moor and Commandant Symington did not get along well—in fact, they detested each other. In 1845, Symington had tried to oust Moor when he had to take a leave of absence for health reasons. By 1849, relations between the two had grown so difficult that Symington requested—and received—the authority to release Moor on a pretext that Moor had grown old and infirm and had lost his touch.

The firing of Moor proved to be a grave mistake. Furious, Moor entered politics, and within a year—in 1850—had won a seat in the Virginia House of Delegates. From this pulpit, he uttered furious speeches against the military, helping to rouse the enemies of the armory commandant system—Whigs and Democrats alike—who put aside their animosities long enough to form a bipartisan coalition against the military.

Chairman Faulkner welded together the procivilian forces in Harpers Ferry with those in Springfield under the leadership of Major Ripley's old nemesis, Charles Stearns, and now mounted a major campaign in Congress against the military. After years of vituperation on both sides, Faulkner managed to attach a rider to the 1854 army bill of appropriations that restored civilian control to the armories. Although there was considerable opposition, even from the influential secretary of war Jefferson Davis, in August 1854, President Franklin Pierce signed the bill into law. The military was out, the politicians were in, and at Harpers Ferry disaster quickly followed.[14]

Henry W. Clowe, Moor's former assistant, was named superintendent. Paying off old scores, Clowe dismissed more men in four years than the previous superintendents had dismissed in thirteen—

including key armorers with irreplaceable skills. Clowe required all employees to vote for Chairman Faulkner during electiontime. Master Armorer Burton, the man who later became superintendent of the Confederate Richmond Armory, left even before Clowe arrived and, without his strong hand, discipline lost ground. Clowe loaded the payrolls with patronage personnel and raised wages, the armory fell once more into a deficit, contracts went to political favorites, quality deteriorated, and production fell off.

By 1858, Clowe's regime had created such chaos that Secretary of War Floyd, fellow Virginian though he was and fellow Democrat, fired Clowe and replaced him with another Virginia Democrat, Alfred M. Barbour, a lawyer from nearby Charles Town. Congress, embattled with the North-South confrontation, cut the armory budget by 38 percent. Barbour surprised the political cynics. With strict impartiality, he reduced the staff by one hundred and cut wages by 10 percent. With a firm hand, he slowly began to restore order and discipline to the armory and even won praise from the Ordnance Department.

With civil control of the armory reestablished by Congress, Charles Stearns returned to Springfield to prepare in his own way for the departure of Major Ripley and to await Ripley's successor, who had not yet been chosen. But not everyone in Springfield was pleased to see the major go. On September 26, 1854, Ripley and his family were packing, preparing for the journey to his next post, when a group of townspeople brought a petition to him, signed by 175 Springfield citizens, including most of the leading people in town, asking him to set a date for a farewell banquet. Attached to the request was a testimonial containing in flowing prose gratitude for Ripley's service to the armory and to the city of Springfield. Major Ripley declined the invitation. "I cannot," he said, "accept a reward for the simple performance of a soldier's duty."[15] A few days later, he and his family left Springfield.

On October 18, 1854, Charles Stearns sponsored a victory parade. Cannon salutes were fired three times, morning, noon, and evening, and at the evening banquet, Stearns made a speech claiming victory over "military despotism after thirteen years of fight."

Among the banqueters were a number of the forty armorers whom Ripley had discharged. After thirteen years, Ripley's regime left Springfield divided into quarreling factions. But one thing Stearns could not deny: Ripley had taken a shambles and turned it into a well-run, completely modern armory.

On November 14, 1854, the *Springfield Daily Republican* announced the name of the armory's new civilian superintendent: James S. Whitney—a Massachusetts politician. Sizing up Whitney, the *Daily Republican* failed to find in him "any particular fitness for the post" and feared that under his civilian regime, the armory would once again decline.[16]

Whitney fooled the newspaper. Drunkenness did not once again prevail, production did not fall, and the armory did not go into a decline. Instead, Whitney did an excellent job of running the armory, maintaining all of Ripley's policies without change. More than that, Whitney did something Major Ripley never achieved— he got along with everyone in the town and even in Washington.

CHAPTER 9

JEFFERSON DAVIS AND THE
ARMY'S FIRST RIFLE

In 1853, Jefferson Davis became secretary of war in the Pierce administration. That same year, Captain Claude Etienne Minié of the French army invented the revolutionary minié ball, which made the devastating muzzle-loading rifle practicable. As a result, Secretary Davis, who was destined to lead the South into the Civil War against the North, was in the strange position of deciding, in event of secession, what shoulder arm the North would carry into battle against the South.

Few men have exerted such profound and enduring influence on American history as Jefferson Davis. A man whose considerable talents led him to the presidency of the Confederacy, whose great courage helped him endure numbing personal tragedies among his children and vast public tragedies of the Confederacy, he was recalled by many for his great courtly charm and easygoing manner, by some for his utter tactlessness, by others for his iron, unbending will, and by still others for his thin skin and often ungovernable temper that reacted to criticism with violent brawling, even as a senator in Washington. He was a passionate man, fiercely loyal to his convictions and to his friends. As an enemy, his hatred was enduring and formidable—and self-blinding.

Jefferson Davis was basically an introvert and a scholar, yet he loved to party, loved to drink, in youth often to excess. Educated in the classics at Transylvania College in Lexington, Kentucky, before attending West Point, he then self-educated himself far beyond the levels of most of his contemporaries. A man of strong opinions, especially as a convinced slave holder, he taught himself to be a powerful public speaker and formidable debater.

Born in Kentucky in 1808 and raised in Kentucky and Mississippi, he was the son of a horse breeder and clerk of the courts, an elective office. From early life in several schools, Davis resisted all authority and was always particularly difficult to manage. His critics said he could not manage men and could not let others manage him.

Entering West Point in 1824, he was court-martialed for organizing a spiked eggnog party. He escaped dismissal when he was sent to his room for unruliness by the officer of the day before the party degenerated into a thundering riot between students and officials that led to the dismissal of nineteen cadets. He had a winner-take-all fistfight with his friend and fellow classmate, Joseph E. Johnston, later a Confederate general, over a tavern keeper's daughter. Davis lost the fight to the heavier Johnston, and the life-long hatred he carried for Johnston was to have tragic consequences for the Confederacy forty years later, when Sherman was marching through Georgia. Preferring to read his own books over military texts, he was a gifted but indifferent student, graduating near the bottom of his class—twenty-third out of thirty-three.

On duty with the army in the West, he antagonized his commanding officer, Colonel Zachary Taylor—destined to become president of the United States—to the point that Taylor long refused to let Davis have the hand of his daughter, Knox, in marriage.

After seven years in the military, he retired to Mississippi to raise cotton, only to lose Knox, his bride of a few months, to malaria. He remained a widower for some years, while, through deep study, he designed a program of self-governance for his slaves that convinced him of the rightness of slavery under his system.

In 1845, while serving in the House of Representatives, he went off to the Mexican War as a colonel of the Mississippi Rifles. Displaying great bravery, Davis led his unit while severely wounded in the foot and employed brilliant tactics that turned back a superior force of Mexican soldiers.

In 1848, in the Senate as chairman of the Committee on Military Affairs, he brawled with a fellow Mississippi senator—Henry S. Foote—whom he assaulted with his crutch. The two men returned home to run against each other for the office of governor. Foote won in a close election. Still heedless when angry, Davis's temper caused him to challenge W. H. Bissell to a duel for belittling his performance in the Mexican War. The duel was canceled by friends.

Davis saw the rapidly growing industrialization of the north as a grave threat to the future independence of the South and urged southerners to develop more manufacturing capability. The South, with its primarily agricultural turn of mind, ignored him.

Jefferson Davis proved to be one of the ablest secretaries of war ever to occupy that office. The Gadsden Purchase of 1853 brought to the United States for $10 million thirty thousand square miles of land from Mexico and gave the United States a southern transcontinental rail route to California. To care for those new territories adequately, Secretary Davis strengthened the U.S. Army, increased patrols, and convinced Congress to raise the pay of officers and men. He even urged, unsuccessfully, that Congress build another armory on the West Coast. In considering the army's new national role, he was unhappy with the antiquated smoothbore musket. And, at his behest, the Springfield Armory had designed a new military rifle.

What made this prototype rifle so impressive was the lethal bullet it was designed to fire—the revolutionary minié ball that had earned its inventor, Captain Minié of the French army, the enormous sum of £20,000 from the British government. With the Minié design, the Royal Small Arms Factory at Enfield, England, was able to create the first of its famous Enfield rifles, featuring a three-groove rifled barrel of .577 caliber that was soon famous for its great accuracy a half mile from its target. At 250 yards, it was absolutely deadly.

Actually, the minié ball was not a ball at all, but a coned cylinder of lead with an iron cup at its base. When fired, the malleable lead cone expanded against the spiral rifling of the bore and emerged from the barrel with a spin that was much more aerodynamically stable than the tumbling musket ball. The minié flew farther and hit harder and more accurately than anything that had ever been seen before. And when it hit, the bullet caused devastating wounds, tearing huge holes, smashing bone, destroying tissue and organs. What was most important, the minié ball overcame the major objection to the muzzle-loading rifle using the standard lead ball—the difficulty of loading it. The "minnie" made the rifle as easy to muzzle-load as the smoothbore.

The opportunity of choosing the new weapon placed Secretary Davis in a strange, almost anomalous position. As secretary of war, he was required by law to maintain the best military posture for the American army against any prospective enemy. As a political realist, heeding the growing turmoil between proslavery and antislavery factions that was rending the nation, he could see that the most likely adversary to the United States in 1855 was his own South. So Davis found himself in the incongruous position of preparing to make war against himself.

He had to have asked himself what the consequences of the new rifle would be for the South. In the event of civil war, would the South be better off fighting a musket-versus-musket war or a rifle-versus-rifle war?

The longer range of the rifled barrel firing the new minié bullet meant that defenders could start firing sooner at greater distances, knock down more targets, and reload for more volleys before closing with the enemy. Since the South expected its army to be numerically inferior, Davis and the many southern officers who populated the War Department and army would have had to prefer the superior firepower of the rifle.

So the choice of the new muzzle-loading rifle was advantageous to the U.S. Army, particularly in its growing role as a transcontinental power. And it was also advantageous to the South. In 1855, despite the cost of new tooling and the resistance of the armory and private manufacturers, Jefferson Davis ordered the Springfield Armory to commence production of the new Springfield '55 muzzle-loading rifle. Without his firmness, the Union Army would have gone into battle with muzzle-loading smoothbore muskets, little changed from the musket of the Revolutionary War, seventy-five years before. In addition, the secretary ordered that all existing Springfield 1842 muzzle-loading muskets be returned to the armories at Harpers Ferry and Springfield to have their smoothbore barrels rifled.

That same year, Jefferson Davis made another significant military change. Without the experience of combat, no one could foretell what effect the new rifle would have on the battlefield. Yet with its longer range, greater accuracy, and new, devastating minié ball, the new rifle obviously had to have a whole new system of tactics, a whole new way of thinking about war. And there was such a way. William J. Hardee, a career army officer and a gifted tactician who later was to distinguish himself in the Confederate army during the Shiloh and Georgia campaigns, was commandant of cadets at West Point. Known as "Old Reliable," Hardee had carefully studied the effect of the new rifle on infantry tactics and then wrote a manual on the subject titled *Rifle and Light Infantry Tactics*.

Jefferson Davis must have been aware that if he ordered Hardee's tactics to be introduced into the regular army, the bulk of the army's officer corps who would master these new tactics were southerners, who in the event of war would carry those tactics back home, where they would use them to train southern armies. In 1855, the same year the new Springfield '55 rifle was introduced, Jefferson Davis directed the army to abandon its antique Revolutionary War infantry tactics and adopt Hardee's *Rifle and Light Infantry Tactics*.

So, in that one year of 1855, a new rifle and concomitant new infantry tactics were introduced to the U.S. Army and later into the nascent Confederate army.

Given all the divisive events that were now occurring with increasing rapidity in the country, all it would take to push the South into seriously arming itself was one more major unsettling incident. John Brown attempted to provide it. Early in the morning of October 17, 1859, while Harpers Ferry superintendent Alfred Barbour was on a visit to the Springfield Armory, abolitionist John Brown, vowing to raise an army of armed slaves, crossed the Potomac River and attacked the armory's weapons storehouse, which contained over 100,000 rifles.

Brown and his band killed five people, one a free black, and wounded more. Frightened, furious, and, in the end, vengeful, the aroused residents, militia, and vigilantes, many drunk, caused many more casualties. They killed Brown's followers and mutilated the corpses, driving Brown into a small fire-watch building next to the storehouse. Brown was captured the next day. A small force of U.S. Marines under the command of Colonel Robert E. Lee and J. E. B. Stuart restored order. Brown was tried in Charles Town, seven miles away, found guilty, and hanged on December 2, 1859.

Robert E. Lee and J. E. B. Stuart, standing on the armory's premises, could see that Brown had gotten within a few feet of arming 100,000 slaves with rifles. The entire South was stunned. The possibility of an armed slave uprising was its biggest nightmare, and one of the principal reasons southern plantation society maintained a strong military tradition. Brown, they felt, had nearly pulled it off.

In response to John Brown's near success, the South began to arm itself. A few months after the John Brown raid, Virginia started to restore its own armory. Built around the turn of the century, the Virginia State Armory, situated on the James River and the Kanawha Canal in Richmond, had been the first state-owned armory and, with thirty-seven thousand square feet of space, was also one of the largest early factories in the country. In 1860, the facility had fallen into ruins, although the original buildings were still intact. Renaming it the Richmond Armory, the Virginia state government worked urgently all through 1860 to establish a major arms-making capability there.

To fill the essential role of master armorer, the armory, after careful shopping, acquired the services of Salmon Adams, clerk to the master armorer in Springfield. One of Adams's first acts was to draft a list of needed tools and machines for the manufacture of the Model 1855 Springfield rifle. To start production, the revived armory also had to have the drawings, patterns, and schematics of the Springfield rifle. James Burton, the former master armorer at

Harpers Ferry who had adapted the minié ball to the Springfield rifle and who was now superintendent of the Richmond Armory, set out to get them from the Springfield Armory. But the suspicious staff there gave him only a model of the rifle itself, withholding the essential papers and patterns. Burton then turned to the friendlier, prosouthern armory at Harpers Ferry and soon obtained entire portfolios of the Springfield rifle schematics and drawings, which he carried back to Richmond.

In 1860, Jefferson Davis's successor as secretary of war, John B. Floyd from Virginia, who was soon to become a Confederate officer, inaugurated several policies that were to prove greatly beneficial to the South. Ordnance officers at Springfield Armory watched with dismay—and suspicion—as the Harpers Ferry Armory in Virginia received from Washington the lion's share of armory budgets, expanding its rifle-making capabilities with new tooling, while Springfield was almost shut down for lack of work. In fact, one of the major activities of 1860 in Springfield was the conversion of smoothbore muskets to rifles, to be shipped primarily to the Virginia State Armory, where additional rifling of muskets was going on with tooling made from the drawings obtained from Harpers Ferry.

That same year, 1860, Secretary Floyd ordered Springfield to ship 65,000 percussion-lock and 40,000 rifled muskets to "five of our arsenals," in Georgia, Alabama, Louisiana, and North and South Carolina.[1] After John Brown's raid, Floyd ordered 85,000 of the 100,000 rifles in the Harpers Ferry storehouse be shipped to southern arsenals.

Floyd raised a number of eyebrows in Springfield in 1860 when he instructed the Springfield superintendent to open the armory and all its manufacturing data to visits from southern ordnance men. In September 1860, two men from Georgia arrived who, according to Floyd's instructions, were "to procure statistical information as to the cost of erecting an Armory and a foundry for the manufacture of arms and so forth in that State."[2] In December, there arrived "one J. H. Buxton, late of Enfield Eng. [the British armory] now of Virginia State Armory," which had become the largest state armory in the South. He was given full access to armory activities and, unlike James Burton, even obtained detailed drawings of those unique rifle-making machines that Springfield had developed. At the same time, southern armories hired a number of northern armorers to work in their southern plants, where they could be induced to teach their arts.

Accomplishing this quiet arming of the South proved to be relatively easy for Floyd. The War Department was staffed by army officers largely from southern states, most of whom were to join the Confederate army. At the same time, President Buchanan, who owed his election to southern votes, and who had surrounded himself with southern advisers, was fearful of touching off a Civil War by giving offense to the South. Furthermore, his administration was too distracted by the explosive political events of the late 1850s—particularly the quarrel over slavery in Kansas and the Supreme Court's Dred Scott decision, which extended slavery into the new territories, and abolitionist John Brown's raid on the Harpers Ferry Armory—to pay much attention to Floyd's policies. Only the Springfield Armory seems to have taken any note of what he was doing, but it remained incapable of stopping him. The historian Derwent Whittlesey concluded that while southern leaders were making every effort to be ready for the war following secession, northern leaders were "both guileless and helpless to oppose such activity."[3]

CHAPTER 10

CIVIL WAR: RIPLEY
GOES TO WASHINGTON

E ighteen sixty was a presidential election year. Opposed by Democrat Stephen A. Douglas, as well as southern Democrats
and the Constitutional Union party, Abraham Lincoln ran on a Republican platform that called for the barring of slavery in the western lands as they became new states.[1] In protest of Lincoln's
election in November, South Carolina seceded from the Union.
Three months later, on February 8, 1861, the secessionist Congress
of Montgomery, Alabama, comprised of delegates from South Carolina, Georgia, Louisiana, Mississippi, Florida, Alabama, and Texas,
met to form the Confederate States of America. A few days later,
twenty-one northern and border states, including Virginia, attended a Peace Convention in Washington, to try to find a way to avoid
a war, only to break up on February 27 without success.

On the morning of Lincoln's inauguration, March 4, 1861,
Washington was packed as the new administration flooded in while
the old discredited Buchanan administration ebbed. A third group,
southerners in government, were also leaving in large numbers,
most to join their Confederate military units. A great number of the
throng in the city were there to claim appointments from the Lincoln administration in payment for political favors. Everyone waited for Lincoln's inaugural speech to discover if the nation was at
war or not, in one piece or two.

The weather was blustery, with a promise of spring.[2] And so was the president's message to the South. Speaking from a platform on Capitol Hill, Lincoln's tone was conciliatory: he assured the South that southern institutions—meaning slavery—were not being put in jeopardy by his administration. But secession, he said, was not just illegal. It was impossible. He gave the seceded states a choice: return to the fold or face war.

While Lincoln was speaking, the aging chief of ordnance, General Craig, was making a strategic blunder of major significance. He failed to send troops to protect the armory at Harpers Ferry. Southern forces were poised to seize the armory, as well as large quantities of small arms that, as noted, Floyd in previous months had stored in Federal arsenals throughout the South, whereby he helped arm the South and disarm the North. Without having fired his first shot, Floyd's acts could give the Confederacy the equal of a major battlefield victory.

On April 12, 1861, the South replied to Lincoln's speech: Confederate troops declared war on the North by firing on Fort Sumter in Charleston. Five days later, on Wednesday, April 17, 1861, a special convention in Richmond voted that Virginia should secede from the Union. On April 18, in Harpers Ferry, expecting a Confederate attack, Lieutenant Roger Jones, with a meager Union force of some sixty-five men, attempted to raise additional forces from the local militia and failed. At nine that night, he heard that a large Confederate force with artillery was approaching. There were fifteen thousand shoulder arms in the armory's arsenal, the other eighty-five thousand having been shipped south sometime before to put them out of reach of another would-be John Brown. Lieutenant Jones torched the armory and left. When the Confederate force entered the town around midnight, fire had destroyed the fifteen thousand arms along with the main armory building and carpenter shop. The townspeople had put out the other fires.

Working under the direction of James Burton, the former Harpers Ferry master armorer and now superintendent of the Richmond Armory, the Confederates took the armory's entire store of machines, tools, and equipment, packed it in hundreds of crates, and shipped it south to Richmond. In one stroke, the South had acquired a complete national armory, including the new rifle-making machines just installed under Secretary Floyd's regime. Departing on June 14, the Confederates blew up the Baltimore and Ohio railroad bridge, burned the armory buildings, and moved south to Winchester.

On April 14, just before the Harpers Ferry capture, James Wolfe Ripley, now a lieutenant colonel, reported to the War Department in Washington. The city had emptied as suddenly as it had filled on inauguration day. War rumors said that a Virginia army was approaching the capital. Maryland was said to be arming, preparing to link up with Virginia to surround the capital. Everyone who could, fled. Banks of sandbags had been placed around public buildings, barricades were erected on the nearly empty streets. Windows were shuttered; blinds drawn. Unarmed, Washington waited.[3]

After departing from the Springfield Armory, Lieutenant Colonel Ripley had become inspector of arsenals, then chief of ordnance on the Pacific Coast. In 1859, Secretary of War John B. Floyd dispatched Ripley to Japan with a present of military arms for the shogun. Returning to Washington, Ripley met with Secretary of War Simon Cameron and Army Chief of Staff Winfield Scott, among others. The group agreed that the elderly chief of ordnance, Henry Knox Craig, was not the man for the demanding wartime job that lay ahead. Next in seniority to Craig was Lieutenant Colonel Ripley. With few dissenting votes, the group selected Ripley as Craig's replacement.

With Ripley ready in the wings, all that was needed was a pretext to ease out old Chief Craig without disgracing him. The opportunity came quickly. On April 22, General Craig remained home ill with a minor ailment. The War Department chose to view it as a prolonged, chronic illness and, the next day, April 23, little more than a week after the firing on Fort Sumter, Special Order 115 was issued, naming Lieutenant Colonel James Ripley acting chief of ordnance, "during the feeble health of its chief."[4] Although he protested Order 115 vigorously, the general was never allowed to return. The seventy-year-old Craig was replaced by the sixty-six-year-old Ripley.

The Army Ordnance Department was headquartered across from the old War Department in the Winder Building on Seventeenth Street, a seedy, dark building with peeling walls and flaking woodwork varnish. On April 24, Lieutenant Colonel Ripley reported for duty and entered his office on the second floor in a large desk-filled room crowded with Ordnance officers and clerks.

To deal with the Ordnance paper system, he turned to Captain (later Colonel) William Maynadier, an Ordnance officer who had been known for fifteen years as the Ordnance Corps' Master of the Red Tape. Ripley seated Maynadier at the desk beside his and kept him there from the day he arrived until the day he left. As the wartime volume of red tape grew, Ripley kept up with it simply by adding clerks. Yet the paper system was such a burden that even the punctilious Ripley was unable to file his first monthly report for April 1861 until a year later.

The bureaucracy, however, was by comparison only a small problem. Ripley's larger crisis was personnel. Since most of the senior army staff had been southerners who had resigned from the Union army, the United States needed a new cadre of senior officers. Ordnance shared this problem. Authorized to staff only fifty-nine, Colonel Ripley was seriously short of trained Ordnance officers. Even when an act of Congress in 1863 raised the number of Ordnance officers to sixty-four, there were still too few to handle all the affairs of an Ordnance Department.

To outfit an army going into battle, Ripley would be called upon to provide a variety of cannons—rifled Parrotts or smoothbore Napoleons, also Ellsworth, Woodruff, and Wiard cannons, as well as mountain howitzers, mortars, and light mortars known as coehorns. And these might be required in iron or steel or even bronze. For artillery ammunition, there were nine or more calibers, and also a variety of ammunition types that included solid shot, canister, case, plus several types of shells. In all, Ripley was confronted with stocking and shipping ammunition in more than six hundred types and calibers.[5]

Because of this great profusion of weapons and ammunition, any Union army arriving at a battle site was always faced with the grave danger of not having the right combination of weapons and ammunition available, a situation that could force the troops into battle with some of their key weapons silent. Ripley helped solve the problem when he teamed up with General McClellan's chief of artillery, Brigadier General William F. Barry. By standardizing weaponry, by reducing the number of closely similar weapons, by eliminating unnecessary calibers and certain models through the simple expedient of not reordering them, as early as October 1861, Barry had reduced severely the number and type of weapons and ammunition required. Later, after being made inspector general of artillery at Ripley's urgent request, General Barry was able to reduce the number of calibers at Gettysburg in July of 1863 from over 600 to some 140.[6]

While there were not enough Ordnance officers, not enough cannon or ammunition or transport, the most pressing problem of all was the acute shortage of shoulder arms. A quantity of old smoothbore muskets were stored in Federal arsenals—about a quarter of a million. But with the short life of muskets in battle, that wouldn't be enough to supply a burgeoning army of a half million fighting men.[7] To compound the problem, the smoothbores were scattered among state arsenals all over the country, as far west as California. To gather these old weapons, Ripley would have to ship them on rails already struggling to move the freight they had on hand—assuming he could commandeer the necessary freight cars. In any case, smoothbore muskets were of highly questionable military value. Governor Morton of Indiana dismissed them in a single sentence: "It would be little better than murder to send troops into battle with such arms."[8] The Union was facing the prospect of going into battle outgunned by the South.

The raid at Harpers Ferry and the transfer of rifle-making equipment to Richmond made the U.S. situation worse. During the ensuing war, the Confederate armory in Richmond would turn out some forty thousand desperately needed rifles.[9] In a stroke, the South had considerably enhanced its rifle-making capacity, while reducing the North's by almost half. The Harpers Ferry raid left the Union with only the armory at Springfield—where production was running at twelve hundred rifles a month, little more than the normal peacetime production of fourteen thousand a year, far less than was needed by an army of a half million—ultimately more than a million—that the North was raising.

Ripley knew he would have to enter the marketplace and sign orders with every available rifle manufacturing company, while the staff at Springfield Armory would have to provide the expertise, the gun models, tooling schematics, guidance, and control. Many of these firms, lacking the necessary manufacturing facilities, would have to subcontract work out to other firms. Additional problems concerned raw materials and machinery: not enough imported iron for the gun barrels, not enough machine tooling, not enough skilled hands in the country to turn out the needed rifle parts. Ripley could see that even with the greatest effort, American industry would not be able to produce enough rifles to arm the Union army, at least not for several years.

In addition, he was confronted with complaints from all quarters, including state governors intent on getting their state units well armed. He ignored the letters of complaint about him and his abrasive manners that were received in volume by his superior, the secretary of war, Simon Cameron, and by President Lincoln. Besides the anger of the governors, Ripley faced the wrath of the generals, who demanded more and better arms and more ammunition. Ripley answered them all with silence. A number of northern governors—including Governor Morton of Indiana—were actively acquiring weapons for their own state units. Agents from the different states bid against each other and against the Ordnance Department itself—a move that drove prices up—then sent the invoices to Washington for payment.

Among Ripley's first acts when he entered the office of chief of ordnance was to make an assessment report of the army's entire inventory of arms and munitions. As in the War of 1812 and in the 1845 war with Mexico, the U.S. Army was once again going into combat inadequately armed. Ripley, now a brigadier general by act of Congress, took his assessment report to show to his superior, Secretary of War Simon Cameron from Pennsylvania.

Cameron was not a welcome member of Lincoln's cabinet. For despite clear and emphatic instructions to the contrary from Lincoln, Cameron, during the Republican political convention in Chicago, managed to extract a promise of a cabinet seat from two of Lincoln's Illinois floor leaders, delegates David Davis and Leonard Swett, in exchange for delivering Pennsylvania's votes during the balloting for the presidential nomination. Utterly distrusting Cameron, who had a notorious political reputation, Lincoln also believed that he could have had Pennsylvania's votes without Cameron's questionable help.

When Lincoln entered the White House after his inauguration, he looked at the list of available political appointments and then at the army of expectant office seekers plucking at his sleeves and said, "We've got more pigs than teats." [10] Then, with great reluctance, he named Cameron to the War Department post.

For some years, the War Department had been heavily staffed with men from southern families imbued with the military tradition. When these men resigned almost en masse to join their southern military units, Cameron found himself rich with an abundance of political patronage jobs. As fast as the openings came, Cameron filled them—mostly with fellow Pennsylvania politicians.

In his long political career, as a Pennsylvania political leader, as a U.S. senator, and as leader of the Republican party (in 1854), Simon Cameron had served three presidents by 1861: Andrew Jackson, James K. Polk, and James Buchanan, and in the end all three leaders unhesitatingly condemned him. "This is a man," President Jackson said, "not to be trusted by anyone in any way, and as a renegade politician who got elected Senator by selling himself to the Whiggs [sic]." [11] President Polk angrily wrote in his private diary his contempt for a senator capable of such coarseness and vulgarity: "Cameron," he wrote, "is a managing tricky man in whom no reliance is to be placed." [12] President Buchanan, who had been associated with his fellow Pennsylvanian for more than twenty years, called Cameron "a scamp." He's "an unprincipled rascal," Buchanan said, ". . . a disorganizer who put himself first when his personal interest came into conflict with the success of the party." [13]

Cameron immortalized his own persona when he proffered to the world this classic definition of an honest politician. "He's one," he said, "who, when bought, stays bought."[14]

General Ripley was quite aware of Secretary Cameron's reputation. But the Union had few arms, and no quick way to make more, and, as any ordnance man knew, the readiest way to acquire a large quantity of shoulder arms was to buy them on the open market in Europe. General Ripley wanted to dispatch arms buyers abroad immediately, before the Confederate buyers could travel. If the Union moved quickly enough, it could secure an abundance of arms there, and simultaneously prevent the South from acquiring them. Specifically, Ripley wanted to buy 100,000 European muzzle-loading rifles.

This suggestion made Cameron uncomfortable. He was expecting a short war, and thought that if the Union army would indeed soon be composed of more than 300,000 men, that would be more than were needed.[15] Ripley pointed out that these were 300,000 *unarmed* men, for whom he did not have the 300,000 rifles needed. Cameron was reluctant to buy abroad. For years, he had been known as a strict protective tariff man; one did not buy from foreigners, one bought from and supported domestic industry. Ripley cut his request in half—to fifty thousand rifles. Cameron ended the meeting with Ripley and took no action. As events turned out, had Cameron acted then, the South's ability to mount an effective Civil War might have been crushed.[16]

By June, troops arriving in Washington, particularly the New York Seventh, were training all over the city, on fields and farms, raising dust clouds everywhere as they struggled to learn close-order drill. As the army grew, confidence grew, and the town filled again. The tobacco smoke and babble returned to the corridors of the Willard Hotel, the clearinghouse of gossip and political deals. Victory, people told each other, was knocking on the gates of the city. Richmond and victory were just a march down the road.

On Tuesday, July 16, 1861, some three months after the firing on Fort Sumter, amid drums, fifes, and unfurled banners, the Union army of thirty thousand plowboys, factory hands, and office clerks marched out of Washington, urged on by wildly cheering crowds. At the head rode an unsmiling General Irvin McDowell. As he looked at the quickly scraped together army of barely trained men, armed largely with obsolete smoothbore rifles, those who knew him knew of his deep misgivings. Richmond and victory were a long way down the road.

The Union army got no farther than Manassas, Virginia. Only thirty-seven miles from Washington, the troops encountered an equally green Confederate army of about the same size, eager to give battle. The Confederates were commanded by General Joseph E. Johnson and Brigadier General Pierre G. T. Beauregard. And there in Manassas, five days later, on the beautiful Sunday afternoon of July 21, 1861, many Washington residents, wearing their Sunday best and packing picnic lunches, rode out in carriages to watch the beginning of a calamitous Civil War.

Back in Washington, first reports said that things were going very badly for the Confederates. Union forces had swept back Beauregard's left flank. The city waited for news of a Rebel rout. General McDowell wired President Lincoln that the Rebels were in full retreat.

In the evening, rain began to fall while the city anticipated the return of its victorious army. It waited all night until, finally, at dawn Monday, in a heavy downpour, the first Union troops re-entered the city. They carried no captured Confederate banners, they had seized no victory. Instead, they slunk into the city, battered and in full flight. After having turned the Confederate left flank, the Union troops had met for the first time one of the South's great officers, Stonewall Jackson, whose troops, arriving at the last minute by train, ran onto the battlefield and stopped the retreat, then counterattacked, and helped inflict on the Union army its first defeat.

That Monday, Washington had to tell itself the truth. There would be no easy victory after all. In fact, if there was to be a quick decisive defeat, pessimists felt it would come to the North. The South was a formidable adversary—fully aroused, armed, fighting for its life, and led by the finest generals and officers in the land.

That same Monday, the youthful general George McClellan arrived in Washington to assume the formidable task of creating and training a battle-ready army. War Secretary Simon Cameron now galvanized himself into an hysterical lunge for weapons, but the president was long out of patience with him. As General Ripley had urged all along, Lincoln now personally sent Colonel George L. Schuyler on his way to Europe with a $2 million arms fund.

But the order was too late. Cameron had given the South a three-month head start that was to cost the North uncounted lives and fortune. When Schuyler arrived in Europe, the South had already purchased all the top-grade weapons on the European market. To buy what was left—and at soaring prices—Schuyler traveled all the way to Austria and Saxony. He returned home with 120,000 rifles. This episode was not the last time the North let a great military advantage slip through its fingers.

From the very beginning, Abraham Lincoln believed that new weapons and innovations would ultimately win the war for the North. And he tried to create a welcoming environment for inventors of such weapons. All through the Civil War, brilliant ideas flowed into Washington every day, some of which could have had a dramatic effect on the war's outcome. But with the bureaucratic wall erected against change, the inventor had to puzzle his way through a nightmare maze to get his idea considered.

First he could go to the War Department. Here, he usually found shut doors or, worse, found himself shunted to Ripley's Ordnance Office. At Ordnance, he found ears plugged, mouths set in anger, vituperation heaped on his head before he was angrily dismissed. Probably, a number of inventors deserved this treatment. But a few, a significant few, didn't.

If he were really desperate and determined, an inventor could carry his invention out to the generals in their campaign tents right on the fringes of the battlefields. Rejected by the army, he could try his hand at political arm-twisting by visiting representatives and senators from his own state. This often opened doors, but usually not minds. For a really warm reception, he could go to Navy Ordnance, where Rear Admiral Dahlgren, an inventor in his own right, and his ample laboratory eagerly greeted and tested new ideas, often with President Lincoln peering over his shoulder.

But, ultimately, if all else failed, there was one court of last appeal. In all of Washington, the most dedicated seeker of new ideas and new weapons—anything that could win a skirmish, claim a battle, finish the war—was the president himself, Abraham Lincoln. As events were to show, he understood the nature of warfare better than his generals did, and, in the White House, greeted and talked with a number of inventors who had already been refused admission to the offices of the military.

Many of these inventions, to be sure, were not practical. One inventor offered wooden boats for the feet called "Water Walkers" that would enable troops to cross rivers dry-shod. Another proposed the "balloon shell" that would float over enemy lines and fall with a lethal bang. Another wanted to fire canisters of red pepper.

But the list of military innovations that Lincoln pressed on his military is arresting. Most of them had a fundamental and permanent effect on the art of warfare. It was his insistence on the introduction of new weapons into combat that helped shorten and win the war. In every instance, the president faced intractable resistance from the military.

In a real sense, Lincoln was fighting two wars—one with the South and one with his intransigent generals. They failed to understand that new weapons could change the nature of warfare, that the strategies and tactics they had learned as young officers were obsolete. With new weapons, what was needed were new tactics and better field intelligence of enemy positions and movement, better communications, more speed, more firepower—just what Lincoln was trying to give them and just what they were resisting.

At first, one innovation in particular seemed absurd to his generals—the gas-filled balloon. In 1862, during the Peninsula Campaign between the York and the James rivers in Virginia, the president sent twenty-eight-year-old Professor Thaddeus Lowe to join General McClellan's forces. The professor clambered into his balloon and elevated it high above the battlefield. Tethered to the ground, the balloon offered a view nearly fifty miles in diameter, enabling young Lowe, aided with binoculars, to send down priceless military intelligence to the generals below. He could see the entire Confederate encampment, troop placements, supply roads, artillery parks, cavalry positions, and even troop movements. More valuable, Lowe had with him a camera with which he took photographs that when pasted together in a mosaic offered a complete pictorial panorama of the Confederate army. For any general, this kind of information could be of decisive value. In battle, the Union army could now see Lee's moves when they were still in preparatory stages. Lee would thereby be deprived of one of his greatest assets—surprise. The balloon also offered another benefit that was difficult to overestimate. General McClellan authorized Professor Lowe to carry aloft a portable telegraph that could send information back down to ground level. During the Peninsula Campaign, his three balloons—*Intrepid*, *Constitution*, and *Washington*—became a familiar sight over the Union lines, on occasion carrying even Generals Heintzelman and Stoneman to see the Confederate terrain below.[17]

If left to the military, and especially General Winfield Scott, there would have been no balloon corps. General Scott had repeatedly refused to see young Lowe, even at the behest of his president and commander in chief. Only when Lincoln got up from his desk and actually walked Lowe over to the War Department, strode into Scott's office, and commanded him to put the balloons on the battleground for testing, did the army discover the immense value of this weapon.

In response to these northern balloons, the ladies of the South contributed their silk dresses to the making of a beautiful and multicolored Confederate balloon. It was inflated in Richmond, then drawn by locomotive up and down the York River railroad, wherever it was needed, until one day, it was unlucky enough to be attached to a steamer on the James River when the tide ran out. The ship was stuck until high tide, and Union forces, arriving there before the returning tide, captured the balloon. "That," said Lee's General Longstreet, thinking of all those silk dresses, "is the meanest trick of the war."[18] It was the South's first and last balloon.

Professor Lowe's balloon corps of seven telegraphic balloons proved to be an invaluable source of military intelligence and they were singled out for their performance at several major battles in 1862. Unfortunately, the army leaders never succeeded in fitting the balloon into its order of battle. At first, it tried to ignore the balloon, as it often ignored its own civilian telegraph operators—another source of information that was foolishly neglected. Assigned originally to the Corps of Topographical Engineers, Lowe's balloons were transferred to the Quartermasters Department, then to the Corps of Engineers, and finally to the Signal Corps, which, after Gettysburg in 1863, disbanded the unit on the plea that the corps lacked the resources to manage it.[19] After proving itself as a major military weapon, the balloon was indifferently dropped by the army. No one was more delighted than the Confederate army when the balloons disappeared from the battlefield skyline. Lee must have wondered why the North had thrown away such an enormous advantage. For the southerners had on many occasions paid Lowe's balloons the ultimate compliment. They tried repeatedly to shoot them down.

A new communications system fared no better. To learn how to communicate with visual signals, Colonel Albert J. Meyer had studied the signing techniques of deaf-mutes. He then built a system of field signals that was later to form the basis of the Army Signal Corps. What he was seeking was a way to enable command centers on Civil War battlefields to communicate with elements scattered widely over all kinds of terrain. Lacking such a signaling system, infantry officers mounting attacks were compelled to herd their troops onto the battlefield in tightly packed units—ideal targets that left piles of dead behind. Yet during the war, the War Department resisted or ignored Colonel Meyer's semaphore system and thereby threw away another battlefield advantage.

A further innovation ignored by the Union military was the rifled cannon. On April 10, 1862, on Tybee Island in Savannah Harbor, Union colonel Quincy Adams Gilmore looked across the open water to Cockspur Island, where Fort Pulaski stood more than a mile away. Colonel Gilmore then turned his artillery crews to work setting up the Union army's "newfangled" Parrott and James rifled cannons.

Both the army and General Ripley had fought Lincoln about rifled cannon. They preferred the smoothbore Napoleon, which was devastating on the battlefield, firing solid shot, case shot, canister, and anything else that would kill men. And they let it be known they did not like the rifled cannon. Pentagon-shaped Fort Pulaski, the chief defense of Savannah, boasted brick walls an awesome seven and a half feet thick and was considered by army experts to be impregnable. To prove his theory, President Lincoln sent Colonel Gilmore to fire the rifled cannon on those walls.

Ringing in Gilmore's ears was the assertion by Union general Joseph G. Totten, chief of the Army Engineer Corps, that Fort Pulaski "could not be reduced in a month's firing with any number of guns of manageable caliber." Other Union attempts to reduce the fort by cannonballs fired by smoothbore artillery had already confirmed General Totten's opinion.

Colonel Gilmore ordered his artillery unit to commence firing. The first hit carried away a great hunk of Pulaski's brick wall in a cloud of yellow smoke. Another hit produced another great cloud of brick-filled smoke. Steadily, systematically, the cannons pulverized the walls of the fort, reducing them to brick rubble and dust. By late afternoon of the next day, April 1, 1862, what was left of the impregnable Confederate fort struck its colors.

In August 1863, intent on repeating his performance against Fort Pulaski, Colonel—now Major General—Gilmore looked upon an even more symbolic target—Fort Sumter, which guarded Charleston Harbor. Here, on April 12, 1861, the South had struck its first blow of the war by firing on and seizing the fort, thereby igniting the Civil War. To the North, the war would not be won until Fort Sumter was retaken. All Union attempts to take it had failed, including a sustained naval attack by seven ironclad Union vessels that had finally been driven off by Sumter's artillery.

On Morris Island in Charleston Harbor, General Gilmore mounted his rifled cannons—including the terrifying Swamp Angel, a two-hundred-pound, eight-inch Parrott that flung incendiary shells more than five and a half miles into Charleston itself. He aimed them directly at Fort Sumter—a two-and-a-half-mile range that was far beyond the reach of smoothbore cannon. Seven days later, Sumter's engineer in chief described what rifled cannon had done to the fort: "a desolate ruin, a shapeless pile of shattered walls and casemates, showing here and there the guns disabled and half buried in splintered wrecks of carriages, its mounds of rubbish fairly reeking with the smoke and smell of powder."[20]

But equally aware of its symbolic value to the South, General Beauregard ordered the fort held "to the last extremity." When called upon to surrender, he replied the North could have Fort Sumter when it could "take and hold it."[21] Sumter continued to defy surrender even though the Parrotts had rendered it militarily useless.

Lincoln encountered the most resistance of all when he tried to introduce the two most revolutionary new weapons of the war— the breech-loading rifle and the machine gun. Ironically, he found that his most implacable adversary of all was his own chief of ordnance, General Ripley.

General Ripley had one nightmare: failure to keep his troops on the firing line supplied with ample ammunition. In his military lexicon, the first deadly sin was wasting ammunition, yet here he was, confronted with a welter of "newfangled" weapons that seemed designed to do just that. He was also confronted with a commander in chief who most wrongheadedly and stubbornly was determined to introduce those new weapons.

The Civil War covered vast terrains. Armies moved over unpaved roads often deep with mud, crossed rivers, slogged through swamps, stumped through trackless wastes, and to provision them and arm them, horse-drawn wagon trains, often miles long, had to somehow, willy-nilly, follow them.

The general could recite the arithmetic to anyone who would listen. Napoleon had allowed twelve wagons for every thousand soldiers. During McClellan's Peninsular Campaign, the Union army required twenty-six. Six hundred tons of supplies daily—food and matériel—moved over roads and down the gullets of each 100,000 men. One hundred fifty wagons daily just for human food; three hundred wagons a day to feed the horses. To keep these men in battle-ready condition, not one bullet must be wasted.[22]

So Ripley was becoming embroiled in one furious controversy after another, almost all of which had to do with wasting ammunition. Like a king in his demesne, he was defending all borders against all comers in a determined campaign that was far worse than all his quarrels combined in Springfield. Soon his intransigence made him one of the most controversial figures in the whole war effort.

Part of the problem had to do with Ripley's own recent history. He had left Springfield Armory in 1853, and from that time until he became ordnance chief in 1861, he had been in California and Japan, out of touch with all the major technological breakthroughs in small arms design that had appeared, in such weapons as the Spencer and the Henry. General Ripley was, in effect, a technological throwback who was not familiar with the new technology and its profound implications on the battlefield, which, as ordnance chief, he should have been. Also, his rigid, unbending character made him unreceptive to change. In fact, to General Ripley, the biggest troublemaker in the war effort was the inventor who brought a new weapon to Washington. Every day, his office was filled with men who offered him new, faster, harder-hitting weapons. They promised that their weapons could save lives and shorten the war. But what all of them really did, Ripley felt, was waste ammunition. Long before the First Battle of Bull Run, Ripley had made it clear how he felt about inventors. He hated them. He said specifically in 1859 as inspector of arsenals that most of these inventors "owe many of their modifications and much of their successful working to the ingenuity and skill of the mechanics in government employ, for which the inventor obtains all the compensation and lays claim to all the credit."[23]

Time had not mellowed him. If anything, Ripley's abiding hostility toward inventors had grown even more deeply rooted by the time he came to Washington in 1861 as chief of ordnance. On June 11, 1861, he wrote the following memorandum:

"A great evil now specially prevalent in regard to arms for the military service is the vast variety of the new inventions, each having, of course, its advocates, insisting on the superiority of his favorite arm over all others and urging its adoption by the Government. The influence thus exercised has already introduced into the service many kinds and calibers of arms, some, in my opinion, unfit for use as military weapons, and none as good as the U.S. [1855 rifled] musket, producing confusion in the manufacture, the issue, and the use of ammunition, and very injurious to the efficiency of troops. This evil can only be stopped by positively refusing to answer any requisitions for or propositions to sell new and untried arms, and steadily adhering to the rule of uniformity of arms for all troops of the same kind, such as cavalry, artillery, infantry."[24]

To keep the inventors at bay, Ripley developed a foolproof way to dismiss most of them out of hand: army regulations. An inventor was required to present the idea of his invention in writing. If Ordnance thought the idea had merit, the inventor was then asked to submit a test model. And there was the rub. Many inventors could not afford the enormous expense of making a working model of their ideas. As a result, the discussion would end right there, with the army not having actually rejected the idea. If the inventor did return with a model, Ripley had another move: in direct violation of army regulations, he would simply fail to test the new weapon.

As a rule, though, General Ripley avoided the whole issue of dealing with new inventions by simply refusing to see the inventors. The few he did see never forgot the furious red face and bellowing, scolding voice that drove them from his office. In time, his scathing contempt for inventors became so notorious that Ripley found himself under attack by the press, led by the prestigious *Scientific American*.[25]

CHAPTER 11

RIPLEY AND THE REPEATING RIFLE

There was no issue between the president and his chief of ordnance that drew more dogged resistance from Ripley than the breech-loading rifle. To understand the significance of the quarrel, one need just fire the two weapons.

For most of the Civil War, the foot soldier on both sides carried onto the battlefield a nine-pound muzzle-loading rifle, a cartridge pouch, plus a percussion cap pouch. Armed with these elements, he stood on the firing line to load his weapon while facing, amid ground-shaking roars, enemy cannon balls and canisters of metal balls followed by a charge of enemy infantrymen, bellowing and firing, as officers on both sides shouted orders and the wounded men cried out with pain. As a rule, great shrouds of gunpowder smoke from the rifles and cannons obscured the battleground.

In this bedlam, to load his weapon, the infantryman had to stand, erect and fully exposed to enemy fire. From his pouch, the infantryman took out a paper cartridge containing a bullet and a charge of powder. He tore the paper with his teeth and poured the powder down the barrel—carefully, so that none of it blew away. Next, he thumb-pressed the lead minié ball into the bore of the barrel, drew out the ramrod from its tube under the barrel of the rifle, and rammed the ball and powder down the barrel and tamped it several times.

After pushing the ramrod back into its storage tube, he then primed his weapon by raising it, half-cocked, removing the old cap, replacing it with a new cap from his pouch, which he pressed down on the nipple. Now he cocked the rifle fully, raised it to his shoulder, picked a target through the clouds of smoke, and fired.

A skilled shooter might get off two shots a minute.[1] But in the melee of battle, very few did. Some put the bullet in first, then the powder. That would be a misfire. Some would attempt to push the whole paper cartridge in, unopened. Some forgot to remove the ramrod from the rifle barrel, and with a pull of the trigger lost the means of reloading. In many of these cases of misfiring, the rifleman had to step back and patiently clear the barrel, a process that could take some time. The Springfield '55 muzzleloader fouled easily, which increased the difficulty of setting the ball and charge completely inside the barrel. All too often, the excited, distracted soldier would ram home more than one charge.

Nothing can illustrate more eloquently what the excitement of battle did to young riflemen on both sides than the battle statistics that emerged from the Battle of Gettysburg. After that battle, which ran from July 1, 1863, through July 3, gleaners recovered all the dropped rifles from the battlefield and shipped them to Washington for inspection. Of the 37,574 rifles recovered, 24,000 were still loaded; 6,000 had one round in the barrel; 12,000 had two rounds in the barrel; 6,000 had three to ten rounds in the barrel. One rifle, the most remarkable of all, had been stuffed to the top with twenty-three rounds in the barrel. In all, from one-third to one-half of all rifles in the battle at Gettysburg were useless.[2] None of all those many thousand misloaded rifles could have occurred with the breech-loading rifle.

A soldier armed with a breechloader did not have to use a ramrod, so he did not need to stand up fully exposed to enemy fire while loading. He could stand behind a stone wall or a tree, crouch on one knee, or even lie upon the ground. Since a very high percentage of all battlefield wounds were inflicted on the hands and arms of riflemen in the act of loading their weapons, by offering a smaller target to the enemy, casualties could be reduced significantly.

Even prone, loading was a single, quick operation: in the case of the single-shot breech-loading Sharps rifle, with his right hand, the soldier opened the breech above the trigger, put in the entire cartridge of minié ball and powder and shut the breech. Then he primed and fired. There was no biting of the paper cartridge, no dumping of powder into the barrel, no pushing of the bullet in with the thumb, no ramrod to deal with. He could get off six or eight shots at his enemy, who was hard-pressed to get off one or two, rarely three, and chances were that before he reloaded his second shot, a breechloader could have downed him along with several of his comrades. A breechloader was thus the equal of three, four, or more muzzleloaders. In terms of battlefield firepower, a ten-thousand-man unit armed with breechloaders was the equivalent of thirty thousand or forty thousand muzzleloaders or more.

At the Battle of Antietam, Lee threw forty thousand men at McClellan's seventy thousand. The slaughter was so great, both generals were stunned: in a few hours, on both sides, a total of twenty-two thousand men fell—the bloodiest single day of the war.

If the northern forces had arrived with the firepower of breechloaders at that battle, Lee, to achieve the same lethality index, would have needed some 400,000 troops or more armed with muzzleloaders. The South could not have supplied him with such manpower—nor with the 400,000 muzzleloaders needed. A great oversimplification of what happens in battle, these numbers hardly qualify as military science, but they tell a truth about the overwhelming advantage that superior firepower can provide, a situation military experts of the day—including General Ripley—failed to grasp.

Why wasn't the North armed with breech-loading rifles? The weapon had certainly been around long enough. In fact, the armory at Harpers Ferry had made the first armory-built 1803 Harpers Ferry rifle nearly sixty years before the Civil War and had even sent armorers to Springfield the same year to teach that armory how to make them. As previously noted, fifty years before the Civil War, in 1811, the American gunsmith John Hall was issued a patent for a breech-loading rifle and spent many years at Harpers Ferry Armory not only refining the breechloader, but also perfecting the machinery on which to manufacture it. In 1825, two companies of U.S. infantry in Fortress Monroe were equipped with Hall breechloaders made at Harpers Ferry. The cavalry, finding a full-length rifle unwieldy in the saddle, and unable to load a muzzleloader at a gallop, required a shorter version—called a carbine—which could be breech-loaded. Harpers Ferry provided the cavalry with the Hall's carbine Model 1843. Firing a paper cartridge that loaded through the breech, it saw extensive service all through the 1840s and 1850s and during the Civil War, much of it in the hands of Confederate cavalry from Virginia. In U.S. military service, the Hall's carbine demonstrated its superiority over the muzzleloader consistently for twenty-five years.

Successful breech-loading rifles had appeared in Europe in the 1830s. E. Lefaucheux, a famous gunsmith of Paris, developed a reliable French breech-loading cartridge and rifle in 1836. In spite of its record, in the United States, the breechloader continued to be a controversial subject in the U.S. Ordnance Corps, all through the 1840s and 1850s, right up to the Civil War. In 1840, numerous tests were conducted under the direction of Colonel Henry Knox Craig, who had been appointed commandant of the Harpers Ferry Armory on the same day that Ripley was appointed commandant of the Springfield Armory, and who later became chief of ordnance until he was replaced by Ripley. Craig and his superior, Secretary of War Joel Poinsett, looked at a number of breech-loading designs and, feeling that all of them required some redesign and development, became opposed to all breechloaders in general. To Poinsett, a fully developed breechloader, though feasible, could replace the obsolete musket only at great expense. To Craig, the primary flaw of the breechloader was a familiar one. It would waste ammunition.

But, as time was to show, the argument didn't hold up. General Craig, as an ordnance man, had given ordnance supply problems precedence over battlefield firepower. It was easier to deny the infantryman the added firepower of the breechloader than it was to solve the problem of supplying him with ammunition. In fact, Craig actually had no basis for that claim of wastage; there's no record of his having tested it. If he had, he would have found what Ordnance in the Civil War ultimately discovered: troops trained with breechloaders didn't waste ammunition. Just before the Mexican War, however, Joel Poinsett ordered the Ordnance Department to stop making the Hall breechloaders.

But the idea would not go away. Within a few years after Joel Poinsett's decision, Christian Sharps, who had worked for Hall in Harpers Ferry, patented his breech-loading Sharps rifle. It was an awesome performer. Using a cartridge made of linen or nitrate-treated paper that was totally combustible when the rifle was fired, a rifleman could get off eight to ten rounds a minute, outshooting three—even four—muzzleloaders. Introduced while Ripley was still commandant of the Springfield Armory, the Sharps became particularly well known to Army Ordnance, achieving an impressive record with the military during the twelve years that preceded the Civil War. An Army Ordnance board had tested the Sharps as early as 1850 and gave it an enthusiastic endorsement.[3] But it wasn't just fixed-target testing that had built this rifle's reputation. The army liked it so much it bought a quantity of Sharps carbines for its cavalry in the West, where it had established an "exceedingly efficient" record.[4]

During this same period, other gunsmiths introduced important innovations in breechloader design. The fateful decision by Secretary of War Poinsett and General Craig in 1840 to end all research into the breechloader had cost years of vital development time. Yet the idea of a breech-loading rifle had persisted, especially among ordnance men who were watching weapons development in Europe. The Springfield Armory itself was experimenting with breech-loading designs all through the late 1850s. And by 1855, even though the first new Springfield 1855 muzzle-loading rifles had not yet come off the armory production line, there was a strong interest inside the armory in adding a breech-loading mechanism to it. Springfield armorers knew that the breechloader was not only feasible, it was even simple to make, with a quickly done modification to the Springfield '55 muzzleloader that could be performed right on the production line. In fact, in May 1855, Springfield's new superintendent, James Whitney, brought into the armory an adviser on breech-loading mechanisms by the name of George Morse, an inventor who had already devised a workable breechloader himself.[5]

In addition to the armory designs, by the mid-1850s, Secretary of War Jefferson Davis was considering seriously a number of military-grade breechloaders that were available, including the Sharps. In 1860, his successor in the Buchanan administration, Secretary of War John B. Floyd, upon seeing the reworked Sharps with a new vent in the breech mechanism to control gas, was so impressed that he wrote: "The highest efficiency of a body of men with firearms can only be secured by putting in their hands the best breechloading arm."[6]

The Sharps rifle went on to achieve international fame under its nickname of Beecher's Bible during the murderous North/South fight over statehood for Kansas. Beecher was Henry Ward Beecher, a celebrated minister with a rafter-ringing voice and overpowering charm, famous throughout the country as a relentless abolitionist who had fanned the flames of emancipation Sunday after Sunday from his pulpit in the Congressional Plymouth Church in Brooklyn.

One Sunday, he rocked the conscience of the entire country by conducting before packed pews a mock slave auction of a little black child. As he urged the flock to bid for the life of the little boy, standing on a box, women openly wept and men were enraged at the picture of a child being separated from his parents for the profit of the slave owner. Henry Ward Beecher, in a moment of great emotion, professed "to see more moral power in one of those [Sharps rifles] so far as the slave-holders were concerned than in a hundred Bibles."[7] His sister, Harriet Beecher Stowe, was the author of *Uncle Tom's Cabin,* an antislavery novel and later a play that had a profound influence on northern opinion.

Although both Jefferson Davis and John Floyd looked with favor on breechloaders, the same Henry Knox Craig who had killed the breechloader in the 1840s had since been promoted to chief of ordnance, where his influence was even greater. Craig's primary interest was artillery, and while he had not kept up with the twenty years of rifle developments, he remained unalterably opposed to all breechloaders, even in 1859, when Christian Sharps walked into the general's office in Washington with his newly redesigned model to announce he had overcome the general's principal objection to the Sharps rifle—gas that escaped during firing. Craig sent the new model out for tests. And there the Sharps rifle ran into a major Ordnance Department obstacle: no friends. As far as General Craig was concerned, the Sharps still wasted ammunition, and, furthermore, it was .54 caliber, not the standard army .57 caliber, which meant another type of ammunition to be supplied to the battlefield.

Enthusiastic as Secretary of War Floyd was about the Sharps, he was also aware of political events and, with the approach of civil war, must now have seen that the fast-firing, hard-hitting Sharps breechloader was not the rifle the South would want to be confronted with while armed with muzzleloaders—which he was busily storing in arsenals throughout the South. Most of the army high command were southerners who shared Floyd's view. The greater firepower of breech-loading rifles could shorten the war, a war the South would most likely lose.[8] So, in Washington, in the critical years of 1859 to 1861, there was no one of influence to speak up for the new Sharps rifle.

General Craig's closed mind—especially toward new ordnance—was one of the reasons Lincoln sought to oust him. And it was that same hostility toward breechloaders that led his successor, James Ripley, into a protracted confrontation with the president. "Wastes ammunition" was always their answer. Predictably, within weeks of taking office as chief of ordnance, Ripley was on a collision course with his commander in chief, Abraham Lincoln.

With General Craig no longer chief of ordnance, in that spring of 1861, there were many in the ordnance world who waited to see how the question of breech-loading rifles would be handled by his successor, General Ripley. One who waited with particular interest was Commander, soon to be Admiral, John A. Dahlgren, chief of naval ordnance, and therefore Ripley's nautical counterpart. At fifty-one, an open-minded seeker of new ordnance and new tactics, he was a supporter of breech-loading rifles and tested them regularly. He was also very close to Abraham Lincoln, who spent many hours in the Washington Navy Yard studying new weapons with Dahlgren.

General Ripley believed that turning U.S. manufacturers to making breechloaders would reduce their ability to turn out muzzleloaders—which were, in that spring and summer of 1861 before the Battle of Bull Run, in desperately short supply. In addition, General Ripley, like many others in Washington, still believed that there was going to be a short war and a quick victory.

Both Commander Dahlgren and Captain Harwood of the Navy Ordnance Bureau felt Ripley had put forth a lame argument, and Harwood was quick to challenge Ripley. General Ripley, Harwood declared, could have his muzzleloaders and an ever-increasing supply of breechloaders to boot. The captain felt so strongly about it he even wrote an official memo to Navy Secretary Gideon Welles.

The breechloaders, he said, could be made in Belgium, which was one of the major rifle-making centers of Europe. In fact, he believed they could be made faster and cheaper there than in the United States.[9] Harwood's suggestion could have only one effect on Secretary of War Simon Cameron, that zealous protector of home industries. Having already denied Ripley authority to purchase emergency arms from Europe, he could hardly be expected to permit European rifle makers to get such a huge piece of manufacturing business.

As for General Ripley, he employed his usual method of dealing with unwanted problems. He simply ignored Captain Harwood's advice and took no action. His Ordnance Department continued to work night and day to make Springfield muzzleloaders for the new Union army, while the Sharps breech-loading rifle waited in vain for a major arms order from the general.

On analysis, examining the various rifle options open to the Union army, the very worst—the one that would prolong the war the most—was the muzzleloader. This rifle gave the least firepower per man per battle; it gave the South the most usable gleanings from the battlefield and the most chance of winning.

There was another important reason General Ripley championed the Springfield '55. Even though it was not officially issued until after he had left Springfield in 1854, Ripley could claim that the rifle's design and development had begun under his administration, by gifted armory personnel of his choosing who had invented all the machine tools and rifling tools to produce it, and that his successor had completed the rifle by continuing Ripley's policies. The Springfield 1855 muzzle-loading rifle was a notable design and manufacturing achievement that had drawn the praise and admiration of arms manufacturing companies all around Springfield.[10]

But there were forces gathering against the Springfield '55 muzzleloader. While the ordnance chief was resisting the Sharps, other even more advanced rifles were appearing. Three of them were offered to the Federal government before the First Battle of Bull Run—the Henry, the Marsh, and the Spencer—and all three were tested personally by President Lincoln, a noted shooter.

In the early summer of 1861, as the first major battle at Bull Run shaped up, the president decided to see for himself what the Henry and the Marsh could do, and one mild early morning he walked with his secretary, William Stoddard, down the street from the White House to Treasury Park. A recreation field that was later to serve as a military encampment, the park was used by the president for occasional target practice with new weapons. Lincoln carried the newly invented Henry breech-loading repeating rifle. Young Stoddard carried the breech-loading single-shot rifle invented by Samuel Wilmer Marsh.

The Henry repeating rifle was an utterly revolutionary weapon that was to have a pervasive effect on future repeating rifle designs. Just patented by B. Tyler Henry the previous October, this was a true breechloader, but not just a single-shot. It could fire fifteen tube-fed bullets at the astonishing rate of twenty-five shots a minute. One of the most important aspects of the Henry rifle was its cartridge, which was made not of paper but of copper, which was loaded in a tube under the barrel and fed by lever action as fast as the lever could be moved. The metal cartridge completely eliminated the paper cartridge, with its loose black powder and loose minié ball, and completely eliminated the problems associated with the paper cartridge used in the earlier breech-loaders—like the Sharps.

What made it even more impressive was its potential effect on southern ordnance. To survive, the South counted on captured northern rifles for its continued ability to fight—battlefield pick-ups. But it did not have adequate manufacturing facilities to make metal cartridges. Consequently, if it could glean from the battlefield only northern rifles that fired metallic cartridges, it would soon have had few weapons to fight with.

The invention of the metallic cartridge held enormous implications. It silenced many of the military's arguments against breechloaders, eased the problems that the repeating rifle designer faced, and over the next few years spawned a flood of new American breechloaders—including Peabodys, Remingtons, Ballards, later-day Sharpses, Joslyns, Starrs, Chocrans, Whitneys, Millers, Needhams, Robert-Springfield conversions, Allen & Wheelocks, Ball & Williams, as well as scores of others.[11]

The metal cartridge had dealt a resounding blow to the opponents of breechloaders, who had long argued against paper cartridges being used in the breech. If there had been any doubt before, there was none now: with the Henry in the early summer of 1861, before the actual fighting of the Civil War began, the breechloader was developed well enough to go to war as the principal weapon.

Primarily a sporting rifle, the Henry made the president wonder if it was strong enough for the rigors of battle. But he was concerned most of all with its price. As a very frugal Yankee, General Ripley was eager to point out that the armory's newest model—the Springfield '61—cost less than $20, while most breechloaders cost about $35. The Henry was priced at $40, more than twice the price. The army could have two Springfields for less than the cost of one Henry. Lincoln was a convinced breechloader man. He believed that it should be the weapon of the war if he could get the right one at the right price. The Henry, he feared, was too expensive.

The Marsh rifle that young Stoddard held was a converted Springfield '55 muzzleloader. The inventor had simply cut away part of the barrel above the trigger and there added a hinged device that opened for receiving the standard army paper cartridge, then shut for firing. And the price was very tempting. Marsh had created a breechloader that could be made for less than $30. There was no need for the vast expense of tooling up for a new weapon, of casting away huge quantities of old rifles that instead could be easily converted, no need for a two- or three-year manufacturing lead time, and no need for new ammunition. The change could be made in any machine shop, even the smallest. And, to make it even more compelling, if for any reason the breech-loading mechanism failed, the Springfield rifle could be reconverted to a muzzleloader right on the battlefield instantly. At less than $30, this seemed to be the breech-loading rifle the president was looking for.

Both the president and his young secretary took turns firing the two weapons at targets in Treasury Park. At first glance, it seems surprising that Lincoln could shoot the rapid-fire, fifteen-shot Henry, then pass it by. If he could have armed the Union on the spot with the Henry, the impending war might not have lasted six months. But the practical Lincoln realized that it would take a long time to manufacture enough Henrys, while the Marsh was a much easier and faster solution to the whole rifle problem. In fact, he was quite taken with the inexpensive Marsh. When Lincoln returned to the White House, he had it packed off to West Point with an order to have it tested.

At West Point, the Marsh rifle was tested by a young Ordnance lieutenant, Stephen Vincent Benét, who was destined years later to become chief of ordnance and grandfather of two American Pulitzer Prize winners. Lieutenant Benét reported to Lincoln that he had fired the rifle 121 times with no difficulty and got off ten rounds in less than two minutes. Most particularly, unlike some breechloaders, the Marsh breech mechanism effectively sealed against escaping gas. Benét enthusiastically endorsed the weapon as having "great merit."[12]

The inventor, Samuel Wilmer Marsh, of Washington, D.C., and his partner, Gallagher, were overjoyed. Then they met General Ripley. When Marsh approached him, Ripley refused to even consider the weapon. To get rid of Marsh, he used his favorite technique: he simply delayed, and then delayed some more. After months of no response, the completely frustrated Marsh pressed him for an answer. "We do not want such arms as you offer," Ripley replied at last.[13]

On October 14, four months after the president had tested the weapon in Treasury Park, Samuel Marsh visited President Lincoln in the White House to report on the lack of progress. Learning that no manufacturing order had been issued, Lincoln directed Ripley to purchase twenty-five thousand Marshes. But the controversy didn't end there. There are many ways of obeying orders, and Ripley knew them all. Marsh had nothing but a prototype rifle. He had no manufacturing facilities and no capital. But with the president's command ringing in their ears, Marsh and his partner, Gallagher, had formed the Union Firearms Company. Meanwhile, Ripley managed to get the contract entangled in bureaucratic red tape. Marsh and Gallagher did not receive an authorizing requisition. They pressed. Still it didn't come. Delay followed delay. For Marsh, the delays were fatal. By the time the requisition came through, the Union Firearms Company had lost its financial backing. The now-struggling company missed one delivery date after another. Ripley must have been grimly pleased when Marsh and Gallagher were then sued for patent infringement by another firearms company. The company collapsed and Gallagher departed.

Marsh, alone now, and still determined, fought off the patent suit and formed a new company backed by a number of very reputable New Yorkers, including the mayor of that city. He informed Ripley that he had created a new company. Ripley made no reply. Marsh pressed. It was now January 1863, nineteen months after Lincoln had fired the weapon.

Ripley now insisted on confusing Marsh's new company with the defunct Union Firearms Company and refused to recognize it. Marsh announced he was ready to make and deliver up to 100,000 Marsh breech-loading rifles. Ripley used his familiar tactic: he didn't answer Marsh. He did nothing. Marsh pressed him again. Ripley at last replied. "You are in default of 7,000 Marsh rifles," he said. Because of that, he refused to issue any new orders to Marsh. Unable to hold out any longer, Marsh folded a second time and was heard from no more. Not one of Marsh's breech-loading rifles ever saw service. Ripley had waited it to death.[14] There is no record of what Ripley told Lincoln about the extinct Marsh rifle.

In the meantime, Ripley's Springfield Armory and private arms-making companies under contract to it were turning out muzzle-loaders. Every day, the Union army was becoming more completely armed with muzzleloaders, primarily the Model 1861, while the general continued to resist repeaters, treating the generals who inquired about breech-loading weapons with the same disdain he showed the president. When General McClellan asked for a thousand Colt revolving rifles, General Ripley adopted his usual silence and never ordered the Colts.

CHAPTER 12

THE SPENCER
REPEATING RIFLE

New rifle ideas were appearing now faster than General Ripley could cope with them. While he was busy trying to prevent the Sharps—which fired a form of paper cartridge—from penetrating the army ordnance system, he had been confronted with the truly significant development of the metallic cartridge, which President Lincoln had already encountered in the new Henry repeating rifle.

As noted, this was a sweeping technological advance that by itself could have shortened the Civil War. As long as the North continued to arm its troops with paper cartridges and the muzzleloaders that fired them, the South could rely on battlefield pickups to help keep it armed. During the war, the South managed to gather 150,000 northern muzzle-loading rifles from the battlefields, which were immediately put back onto the firing line on the side of the South. Add to that the 40,000 rifles the South was able to make with rifle tooling taken during its raid on the Harpers Ferry Armory, and one can see how dependent from the beginning the South was on northern armaments. Confederate president Jefferson Davis must have awakened many a night and thanked God that he had not, when U.S. secretary of war, armed the North with breech-loading rifles using metallic bullets. Perhaps his successor, John Floyd, uttered the same fervent thanks.

But Ripley's resistance to the metallic cartridge was not his masterpiece of mischief—the Spencer repeating rifle was. This weapon was the invention of a precocious genius in his early twenties by the name of Christopher Spencer, who was born and raised a few miles from the Springfield Armory. "Crit" Spencer was the grandson of a gunsmith, Josiah Hollister, a dead shot with the musket, a skilled gunsmith and cabinetmaker, and, during the Revolution, a soldier and an armorer to George Washington. Christopher Spencer became an apprentice gunsmith at age twelve to his eighty-nine-year-old grandfather. The two formed a close friendship that ended sadly when the old man died a few years later.

By age fifteen, Christopher Spencer had become famous all over New England as a sharpshooter. But what was more interesting about him to the Cheney Brothers Silk Ribbon Manufactory in Hartford was the model steam engine the boy had made from a description he read in a book.[1] He was soon working in the silk ribbon factory as a resident tinkerer and inventor.

With youthful impatience, he began to wander from job to job looking for outlets for his restless, fertile inventiveness. He made machine tools in Rochester and repaired locomotives for the New York Central Railroad, and, ultimately, at age twenty-one, he combined his inventive genius with his love of guns by going to work for Colt's Patent Firearms Manufacturing Company in Hartford, Connecticut. The boy was hired to repair used Colt pistols, the famous six-shooters with the revolving cylinders. The pistols at that stage were still using paper cartridges.

In Hartford, young Spencer made a friendship that was to affect the rest of his working life and lead to one major business success after another. Beside him worked another brilliant machinist, Charles Ethan Billings, who later joined Spencer to form Billings and Spencer, which became known around the globe for its machine tools and forgings, and particularly for one of Spencer's greatest inventions, the automatic screw machine.

Colt was trying to pry its way into the enormous sporting rifle market by using its patented revolver mechanism to create a repeating rifle. Spencer felt that the revolver concept would not work when applied to the long barrel of a rifle. Time proved him right: it was a dead end. While looking for another way to feed the cartridges automatically into the rifled chamber, Spencer conceived two revolutionary inventions that were to have a profound effect on the development of repeating rifles and on the outcome of the Civil War.

One day, in a Hartford gun shop, Spencer found a few brass cartridge cases, probably made in France, and immediately recognized that he'd found the missing element in his concept for a repeating rifle. He approached his old employers and friends, the Cheney brothers—Charles, Ward, and Rush—with his idea. The Cheneys sensed a great opportunity to break into the sporting gun market and brought Spencer back to their shops to work on it.

Two years went by while Spencer struggled with and brilliantly solved a number of design problems. To conquer the biggest problem of all—the repeater mechanism—he had to invent a radically new way to feed ammunition into the breech. After studying the mechanism of Christian Sharps's rifle, he solved the problem by drilling a hole through the wooden rifle stock from the butt end to the breech, then fabricating a spring-fed tube that contained seven of his newly designed metallic cartridges. He inserted the loaded tube into the tunnel through the stock, then, with a lever action by the trigger, pumped a cartridge into the chamber. All the shooter had to do was work the lever, cock the hammer, fire, and work the lever again—to eject the spent shell and insert the new one. In seconds, all seven shots could be fired, the loading tube removed, and a new tube with seven more shots inserted ready for firing. In March 1860, Spencer was granted a patent for one of the first basic repeating rifles. He was twenty-two years old and the outbreak of the Civil War was little more than a year away.

When the South fired on Fort Sumter on April 12, 1861, the Cheney brothers saw an enormous manufacturing opportunity— make the new sporting Spencer rifle bigger and stronger and offer it to the U.S. Army as a military-grade repeating rifle. Spencer agreed. Guided by some of the features in the new 1859 model breech-loading Sharps rifle, with its new gas-venting feature, Spencer took less than two months to make a military-grade model of his rifle.

On June 7, 1861, Spencer and Charles Cheney boarded the Hartford train for Washington. They were on their way to see navy captain John A. Dahlgren, commander of the Washington Navy Yard, who was already famous as the inventor of naval artillery. This door had been opened by Cheney's good friend and neighbor Gideon Welles, secretary of the navy. Spencer personally carried the world's first military-grade repeating rifle in his lap.

The next day, Dahlgren met the young inventor, studied the weapon, then watched Spencer disassemble the weapon and quickly reassemble it, all with a single screwdriver. They took it into the naval testing laboratory and fired it. By now, Spencer was routinely firing twenty-one shots a minute. Captain Dahlgren was so impressed he sat down the same day and wrote to his superior, Captain Andrew Harwood, commander of the Ordnance Office of the Navy Yard. Harwood was General Ripley's naval counterpart, and the man who told the general to buy breech-loading rifles in Belgium. Dahlgren wrote to Harwood that the new rifle "operates so well that I am induced to bring it to your notice." After describing the test, Dahlgren concluded with a recommendation "that a number of these pieces be introduced for trial in service."[2]

The new rifle soon drew a crowd, and Spencer fired it some two hundred times for the navy brass over the next two days, noting their great interest when he got off his usual twenty-one shots a minute. Captain Harwood took Cheney into his office and gave him a contract for seven hundred rifles and seventy thousand rounds of metallic cartridges.

Cheney and Spencer were overjoyed and dismayed simultaneously. They had their first order, but they had no plant, no tooling, no staff—in short, no way to make seven hundred rifles. They walked back to the train station deep in conversation.

The army soon took note of the new Spencer. In August 1861, Captain Alexander B. Dyer, a few weeks before General Ripley appointed him head of the Springfield Armory and some few years before he was to become chief of ordnance himself, tested the Spencer at Fortress Monroe. The rifle was covered with sand, immersed for twenty-four hours in saltwater, and came out firing.

Dyer wrote General Ripley an enthusiastic report. "I regard it as one of the best breechloading arms that I have ever seen."[3]

Dyer's report didn't help. Ripley still would not place an order for the Spencer; worse, he disobeyed Lincoln's expressed orders to be shown all new rifles. Ripley never sent this "new fangled jim-crack" with its "new fangled self-contained cartridges" to him.[4] To break through Ripley's front door, the Cheney brothers hired a professional lobbyist, but he failed to get Ripley's signature on an order, so in November of 1861, the Cheney brothers, attempting to get around Ripley, sent young Christopher himself to demonstrate his rifle for General McClellan.

On November 4, 1861, McClellan watched Spencer's demon-stration and became as interested in the repeater as Dahlgren and Dyer. His three-man testing board had a suggestion—attach the loading tube to a chain so it wouldn't get lost and add some spare springs for the magazine. Otherwise, they found no flaws in the weapon. Compact, durable, and "very accurate," they said, and rec-ommended that it be adopted if it passed a field test.[5]

This was the second army endorsement, but Ripley remained unmoved. Charles Cheney, who was resolute if nothing else, decid-ed on an even more elevated move around Ripley. He used his influence again with Navy Secretary Gideon Welles to get to see one of the most powerful men in the country, Speaker of the House James G. Blaine, also from New England. Blaine was so impressed he called for extensive field tests. Ripley still balked, and so Blaine went over his head and contacted the assistant secretary of war, Thomas A. Scott. Scott pressed Ripley to make a study of the Spencer and the Henry and report on their merits, "as arms such as these are needed by the government."[6]

Ripley uttered a resisting reply. In his mind, he considered the Spencer and the Henry in no way as potential replacements for the Springfield rifle, choosing to categorize them as carbines for the cavalry only. So while others were talking about Henry and Spencer rifles, Ripley would talk only about Henry and Spencer carbines. Besides, he said, both the Spencer and the Henry were too heavy. And he even managed to turn the undoubted improvement of the metal cartridges into a liability: more special ammunition for the overburdened Ordnance Bureau Department to handle. Furthermore, they both had spiral springs that might be bent on horseback (carbines, again) and, the clincher, they were far too expensive. Besides, he said, he had "orders and contracts for nearly seventy-three thousand breechloading rifles and carbines, to the amount of two and a quarter million dollars."[7]

The general was playing games. Since cavalrymen carried carbines and not his full-size Springfield rifle, he didn't care whose carbine they carried. So of the seventy-three thousand weapons he spoke of, only twenty-five thousand were rifles, and these were the Marshes that the president had forced him to order and that he was busy sabotaging. In a sense, then, even though he could wave signed orders, he really was expecting no breech-loading rifles at all. Finally, he even trotted out the old cob—wasted ammunition. The breechloaders he had already ordered (the single-shot Marshes) exhibited "a rapidity of fire that is sufficiently great." This reply could be interpreted as: single-shot breechloaders wasted enough ammunition without adopting the horrendous wastage of repeating firearms like the Henry and Spencer. He still hewed to the old tradition of slow, deliberate fire, and with this priority in mind, the Springfield muzzleloader was the rifle of choice. General Ripley had a one-track mind, and he had become a master of ducking, bobbing, and weaving. Thus, he managed not to order a single Henry or Spencer.

Undaunted, Cheney kept after his prey. Even so, it took the combined efforts of Secretary of the Navy Gideon Welles, Speaker of the House Blaine, and Assistant Secretary of the Navy Scott—and, some said, the direct intercession once again of the president— finally, with an official direct order in writing to compel Ripley to order ten thousand Spencer rifles, priced at $40 each. The contract was dated December 31, 1861, but, in reality, General Ripley had not capitulated. Charles Cheney thought he had walked away with a firm contract, but what Ripley had given him was a ticking New Year's present.

According to the contract, Cheney not only had to deliver ten thousand Spencer rifles, he also had to deliver the first five hundred in sixty days, by March 1, then a thousand rifles a month thereafter. The task was impossible and Ripley, the old rifle production master, knew it. He had done exactly what he had done to Marsh—forcing Cheney into default of delivery, which would forfeit a very large bond and abrogate the contract. Ripley expected he would never see a single Spencer.

B y the beginning of 1862, Ripley had completely undermined his president. With the twenty-five thousand Marshes that Lincoln had compelled Ripley to order, and with the ten thousand Spencers that Assistant War Secretary Scott had compelled Ripley to order, Lincoln thought he would soon have thirty-five thousand breechloaders to test in actual combat, side by side with the old Springfield muzzleloader. With that, and until he had some results to guide him, the president put a temporary halt to any further new weapons testing. Only General Ripley knew that during all of 1862, the president would not see a single breechloader delivered.

But Charles Cheney didn't yet know that. When he returned home with his order, he formed the Spencer Repeating Rifle Company in Boston. The three Cheney brothers—Charles, Ward, and Rush—became directors, and young Spencer became the superintendent of works. Charles set about finding a plant and raising capital. A large part of the Cheney fortune was riding on this new company. He found the building easily enough, sharing his gun-making quarters with an unlikely companion—the Chickering Piano-Forte Company. But then his troubles came thick and fast.

First, he encountered a severe wartime shortage of machine tools and skilled labor. Then he ran into the classic problem of the manufacturer dealing with a creative genius: Christopher Spencer kept finding new—and delaying—improvements for his gun. Although all the changes were considerable improvements that led in the end to the finished rifle that was to become a wartime legend, young Spencer often seemed about to improve the company into bankruptcy. When the scandals surrounding Secretary of War Cameron became public, an Ordnance Investigating Commission was formed, Judge Hunt presiding, and the Spencer contract came under scrutiny.

By February, the company executives knew what Ripley had known all along—they couldn't make the first five hundred rifles by March 1. In fact, even the "pattern" rifle—the production model—wasn't submitted to Ripley for approval until April 23. They petitioned for a delivery delay to the Hunt Commission, saying that first delivery would be in July. The contract was in danger of rupture; the Cheney family fortune was in danger of being lost.

The Hunt Commission revised the contract: delivery of the first Spencers would be June 1, no later. It would be for one thousand rifles, not five hundred, with a thousand a month thereafter. But there was a penalty of 25 percent: the original order was reduced to only seventy-five hundred rifles, with further penalties looming.

The company managed—with extraordinary effort and inspired management, plus $135,000, a great fortune in that period—to finally fabricate such a large production shop that by the end of the year, it had became one of the largest armories in America. But it wasn't until December 1862 that the first rifles came off the line—a full year after the contract was issued. General Ripley was probably surprised they managed to produce even by that late date.

CHAPTER 13

LINCOLN'S
WAR SECRETARIES:
CAMERON AND STANTON

If the Spencer Repeating Rifle Company managed to ride its calamitous organizational and production problems of 1862 to victory, that year was not similarly good for either General James Ripley or his superior, Secretary of War Simon Cameron. Indeed, for Cameron, it was one of the shortest years of his long life. From the day of his appointment to the president's Cabinet, in March of 1861, Simon Cameron had been busy, destructively busy. Under Cameron's direction, the number of Pennsylvania appointees in the War Office shot up from five to twenty-seven, and with their arrival, unbridled, naked corruption became rampant. One of the new Pennsylvanians in the War Office classified a quantity of Hall carbines as worthless and sold them for $2 each. Later, he repurchased them for $22 each. Thomas A. Scott, Cameron's assistant secretary of war, was also vice president of the Pennsylvania Railroad. Unperturbed by the apparent conflict of interest, he specialized in negotiating government contracts for shipping troops and war matériel by rail. Soldiers, for example, were shipped in boxcars for 2 cents a mile, a very profitable arrangement for the railroads. Another Cameron Pennsylvanian, John Tucker, was put in charge of water transportation. His critics claimed he knew nothing about shipping water except how to pay too much. Thurlow Weed, a political partner of Cameron's, formed a group with three friends to increase the size of the Union navy. With personal notes and without a penny of their own that anyone saw, they purchased a lubberly ship dubbed the *Cataline* for a sale price of $18,000. They then promptly chartered it to the government for $10,000 a month. Evidently, it was their fervent hope and expectation that the ship would founder while under government charter: if the *Cataline* sank, the agreement required Washington to pay the four entrepreneurs $50,000.

Other Cameron cronies obtained lucrative contracts without competitive bidding, which they then resold at extravagant markups. One of these contracts—for horses—was so publicly manipulated that most of Washington was scandalized, as was all of Kentucky, even then noted for its horse breeding. The Kentucky state cavalry unit was confounded when it discovered that it would be supplied not with the best that the Kentucky breeders could offer, but with horses shipped by rail all the way from Pennsylvania at great expense. And when they saw the miserable horseflesh that stepped off the train, they raised a furious howl that was heard in Washington. The contract called for the delivery of one thousand horses for military use. One thousand were delivered and paid for. But many were so obviously diseased—"blind, spavined, ringboned, afflicted with heaves and glanders"—that the army was compelled to reject nearly half, 485, of the total. The cost to the War Department was $58,200, plus $10,000 in transit costs.[1]

But the laughter of the town wags over these horse contracts soon turned to anger. Cameron's friends, having pocketed the money, were confronted with the problem of getting rid of the rejected horses. Under another horse contract, this one in Washington, their solution was simple: they tied the animals to posts and trees all through Washington and there left them to starve publicly.

In Congress, Massachusetts's Henry Dawes rose in anger. "A guide can take you around the District of Columbia today," he cried, "to hundreds of carcasses of horses chained to trees where they have pined away, living on bark till they starve and die."[2]

An army at war in the 1860s required vast numbers of horses, and in Washington, Cameron's cronies had executed so many horse contracts they were passed like currency. They were found to be particularly useful for paying back political favors and to salve old political grievances.

A congressional committee was formed. Among many other things, in investigating the affairs of Cameron's political partner, Thurlow Weed, the committee accused him flatly of collecting a stunning 5 percent kickback on every ounce of powder sold to the War Department—5 percent of all the powder that the U.S. Army fired off during the Civil War. The Congress was soon in a towering rage at Cameron. The looting of the government by his pack of Pennsylvanians in the War Department was so naked, so visible, and so astronomical that not even jaded Washington had ever seen anything like it before.

Henry L. Dawes of Massachusetts rose up in the chamber with a shaking finger and a furious, bellowing voice. "Indubitable evidence!" he shouted. ". . . Somebody has plundered the public treasury in a single year of as much as the entire yearly expenses of the previous [Buchanan] government, which the people hurled from power because of its corruption!"[3] Congress, the public, and the press all directed their rage at Simon Cameron. The press actually blamed him for the military defeats at Bull Run in July 1861 and Ball's Bluff the following October.[4] His corruption was blamed for the deaths of Union soldiers, and this finally raised a tide of anger across the entire nation.

Cameron's diabolical astuteness was legendary, and he was quite aware that his days with Lincoln were numbered unless he could come up with a brilliant political move to save himself. So he seized upon the most politically sensitive issue in Washington—the official abolition of slavery.

Lincoln was searching for a way to outmaneuver this ferociously corrupt politician and eject him from his Cabinet. He was forced to bide his time, looking for an opportunity. And, finally, at long last, in January 1862, Cameron gave it to him. For the North, there was one single major issue: preserving the Union. The North believed that secession of the southern states would destroy the whole nation. And on that issue the North united and went to war. The North was not unanimous on the issue of slavery. Many were flatly opposed to putting their lives and fortunes on the line to free slaves. And there was another compelling reason why Lincoln could not endorse the end of slavery: there were several swing slave states that had not seceded. If he announced a policy of abolition, these states would fly into the waiting arms of the Confederacy, and that would probably have given the South the strength and stature in Europe to become recognized as a separate nation.

Yet there was a strong element in Lincoln's own party that believed that once the recalcitrant southern states were conquered and brought back into the Union, slavery would have to be abolished. They pushed hard for announcing the abolition of slavery as a Union cause. And it was to them that Cameron, with his devilish cunning, turned to protect him from the president's wrath.

Simon Cameron became politically reborn as a pious abolitionist. Goodness and love of man oozed from every pore. Cameron was so smitten with his new posture, he announced his newly adopted desires for abolition in his annual report as secretary of war, going so far as to recommend that slaves be armed to fight the South. He even managed to distribute copies before President Lincoln saw it, before he could stop it from getting into the hands of the newspapers. The political damage was enormous.

Cameron had run true to form. By trying to protect his own position in government, he had betrayed his fourth president. But brilliant as Cameron thought his move was, it was topped by an even more brilliant move by the president, one of his political masterstrokes. Lincoln struck on the wintry Sunday night of January 11, 1862.

Alexander McClure was dining at the home of Thomas A. Scott, assistant secretary of war under Cameron, and vice president of the Pennsylvania Railroad. The two men were enjoying after-dinner cigars by a warming fire. McClure was a Philadelphia editor and politician. He had been chairman of the Pennsylvania State Committee at the convention that had nominated Lincoln. He was also Cameron's political enemy. When Lincoln was selecting his Cabinet, right after his election, McClure heard that the new president was reluctantly going to offer Cameron either the post of secretary of the treasury or of war. McClure warned Lincoln that appointing Cameron as treasury secretary would be a major political error. It would, in fact, destroy the Republican party in Pennsylvania. Lincoln asked McClure to put his accusations in writing with evidence. McClure refused, some say wisely.

As a political enemy of considerable power, McClure should have been the last person Cameron turned to. Yet here, in great agitation, came Cameron, right into Scott's dining room. McClure was astonished. Cameron did something even more astonishing. He thrust a letter on the table and said, "Read that!"[5] Cameron told them he had just received it from the White House. The two men read the note. "I have this day," Lincoln had written, "nominated Hon. Edwin M. Stanton to be Secretary of War and you to be Minister Plenipotentiary to Russia."

Cameron asserted that it was a personal affront. It was clear, this action was Cameron's political Waterloo. Simon Cameron wept. He begged McClure, even though they had been political foes, to use his powers to intercede with the president. Intercede? For Cameron? McClure sat back perplexed, then asked Cameron why.

"This is not a political affair," Cameron said to him, "it means personal degradation; and while we do not agree politically, you know I would gladly aid you personally if it were in my power."[6] Lincoln's choice of Stanton as the new secretary of war was brilliant, for Stanton was also from Pennsylvania; indeed, he was the very replacement Cameron himself would have chosen if he had had to choose a successor. With one sentence jotted on White House stationery, Lincoln had trussed and caged Cameron, ready for shipment to Siberia. Cameron was not even to be accorded the honored political custom of being allowed to resign. He was fired, beaten at last by an outraged president that he had tried to betray. Lincoln's move was political execution in its frankest form.

McClure agreed to see the president, and the next day, he went to the White House, where he described for the president the bad political consequences of cutting Cameron's political throat so publicly. Lincoln was persuaded to alter his plan, and a new deal was made. Cameron was to be allowed to submit a predated letter of resignation and Lincoln was to accept it affably in writing.

Some ten months after being appointed secretary of war, Simon Cameron received this face-saving letter from Lincoln:

> My Dear Sir:
> As you have more than once expressed a desire for a change in position, I can now gratify you, consistent with my view of the public interest. I therefore propose nominating you to the Senate next Monday as Minister to Russia.
>
> Very sincerely your friend,
A. Lincoln.[7]

Lincoln had attached a personal note, dripping with an almost hilarious irony. The president expressed "my high personal regard for you and my confidence in your ability, patriotism and fidelity to public trust." The nation applauded Cameron's departure. The *New York Herald* equated Cameron's resignation with a major military victory for the Union. A very reluctant Senate confirmed Cameron's appointment to Russia, while the House in response planned to pass a vote of censure against Cameron as a parting present. Lincoln himself, fearing a rupture with Cameron's Pennsylvanians, had to step in to stop it from passage. As Cameron departed for Russia, his fellow Pennsylvanian, Thaddeus Stevens, Republican leader in the House, seems to have had the last word. In obvious reference to Cameron's quick hands, he said to Richard Dana, "Send word to the Czar to bring in his things of nights."[8]

It was a miracle that Edwin Stanton, the new secretary of war, lived long enough to die of natural causes. Washington was thronged with many who could have eagerly cut his throat, beaten him to death with a horsewhip, or boiled him in oil. The wonder is that no one did.

With his lips pulled back in scalding contempt, he could peel the skin off a man in public, tear his dignity to shreds, then dismiss him with thundering verbal kicks and punches. His legal and political betrayals were notorious. Undoubtedly, this was one of the most hated two-faced men ever to set foot in a city notorious for its legions of hated two-faced men.

Yet one of his greatest detractors, and an ex-friend, Jeremiah S. Black, a power in national and Pennsylvania politics, conceded that Stanton was the greatest lawyer of his time. The political potentate Alexander McClure noted that Stanton's "dominant quality was his heroic mould. He could be heroic to a degree that seemed almost superhuman, and yet at times submissive to the very verge of cowardice. . . . He was a man of extreme moods, often petulant, irritating, and senselessly unjust, and at times one of the most amiable, genial and delightful conversationalists I have ever met."[9]

Here stepping on the stage was one of the most complex personalities ever to appear in Washington. Today, he would be a psychiatrist's prized field specimen, a potpourri of pathological ailments, a lifetime study, and a permanent puzzle. Many people believed he had a deep streak of insanity in him. Two characteristics dominated his personality: an undying ambition to become an associate justice of the Supreme Court and a totally unscrupulous moral code. One historian stops just short of implicating Stanton in Lincoln's assassination.[10]

Born on December 19, 1814, in Steubenville, Ohio, Stanton was the eldest child of a country doctor. Dr. Stanton was a former Quaker who left his meeting when other Quakers objected to his marriage to a woman outside the faith. Dr. Stanton was also a fervent abolitionist who had only to point across the Ohio River to make his point about slavery. For on the other side of the water in Virginia, as the boy often saw, the hands working in the fields were slaves, a few watery yards from freedom, and the slaves must have often looked back with some longing, for Steubenville was a way station on the Underground Railroad for slaves seeking freedom in the North. Having imprinted his son with a lifelong hatred for slavery, Dr. Stanton died when Edwin was only eleven.

Stanton suffered all his life from sudden fits of chronic asthma that struck usually at crucial emotional moments—just before a major courtroom battle or a stressful social appearance. Lasting for a few minutes to a few days, they almost invariably left him exhausted.[11] Even in childhood, Stanton evinced an explosive, uncontrollable temper and a savage personality that were to make him the terror of the courtroom. His treatment of subordinates was the scandal of his law practice, while, socially, his brutal behavior earned him a legion of lifelong enemies. It was widely known that under his waistcoat, in a beautiful sheath, a dagger was always within reach.

An avid reader and an indefatigable worker, he studied law at night at Kenyon College in Gambier, Ohio. On the Kenyon campus in 1831–1832, learning of South Carolina's threats to secede, Stanton became a passionate Unionist. In 1836, at age twenty-one, he was admitted to the bar. Stanton, totally committed to the law and studying night and day, went on to become the most widely known and most formidable lawyer of his era. At the time of his death, he was also one of the wealthiest.

Lawyers, he believed, were the greatest figures of the land, above all other men—even presidents and Cabinet members. Obviously, therefore, the most august body was the Supreme Court. And to that goal—a Supreme Court justiceship—he set his mind and heart for the rest of his life. Fame came from a long series of celebrated Supreme Court civil cases, and with them great wealth. He was also notably gifted as a criminal lawyer. Without hesitation, he cynically defended men he knew to be guilty and won acquittal after acquittal—for stunning fees.

Probably his most lasting influence on American jurisprudence occurred in one of his criminal cases, the celebrated 1859 Sickles murder case in Washington. In the 1850s, members of Congress did not set a very high tone of behavior for the rest of the nation. One of the most notorious acts occurred during the violent 1856 debate over the admission of Kansas as a state. The most vitriolic and most hated man in the Senate, Charles Sumner of Massachusetts, was savagely beaten with a gutta-percha cane right on the Senate floor by Representative Preston Brooks of South Carolina. Another congressman shot a waiter and walked away without serving a day in jail. Gaming, womanizing, fighting duels and grafting, pork barreling and vote swapping, even fistfighting in chambers, were an all too common part of the congressional routine.

One Sunday afternoon in 1859, a New York congressman, Daniel Edgar Sickles, entered Lafayette Square in Washington and there shot and killed his wife's lover, Philip Barton Key, son of Francis Scott Key, composer of "The Star-Spangled Banner." Sickles was clearly guilty and was surely going to prison. He turned to Stanton, who invented and used for the first time in the Sickles case the plea of "temporary insanity." To the dismay of the many people in the country who regarded murder as the gravest possible crime, Sickles was acquitted. The case achieved added significance when Sickles was reelected to Congress, and then, during the Civil War, he distinguished himself repeatedly for valor, rose to the rank of major general, took command of the Third Army Corps, and at Gettysburg led his troops to glory in the desperate Peach Orchard fight, one of the pivotal battles of that encounter.

Stanton's manner toward judges was so overbearing he was often on the verge of being cited for contempt. He terrified witnesses and mauled opposing lawyers with such blistering scorn he was frequently a scant step away from being physically attacked. During an emotional encounter in one of his trials, he roared at another lawyer, "Stop your whining!"

"It's no worse to whine than bark," replied the other lawyer.

"Dogs bark," Stanton quipped. "Puppies whine."

The other lawyer sprang to his feet and rushed up to Stanton and seized him by the throat. The judge adjourned the case until the two recovered their composure.[12] Such courtroom tactics were so crafty many lawyers considered them unethical.

He built a huge practice in Pittsburgh, which in time became so heavily loaded with Supreme Court cases that by 1856, he was impelled to move to Washington. He was soon a familiar figure in capital politics: a short man with a full beard and a quick, spasmodic way of walking and a low growling voice. He was unable to remain in one position long. When roused, he acted like a madman, and many observers privately suggested he was insane. His morbid—some say pathological—terror of death was well known. His first violent reaction to death occurred when he was a law student. His landlady's young daughter died abruptly one day of cholera and by law was buried within hours. Stanton, horrified by the news and by the sudden burial, became convinced she'd been buried alive and in a frenzy dug up the girl's coffin. When his brother committed suicide by cutting his wrists, Stanton again went berserk and ran off. Fearing he might also become a suicide, townspeople formed a search party that located him in deep woods only after a prolonged hunt. He was carried home raving and screaming and for some days thereafter he had to be carefully watched.

In 1844, when he was barely thirty, his growing success in the law brought him the finest house in Steubenville, a noteworthy achievement in that town for one so young. But, shortly after, his young wife died and his grief was uncontrollable. He ordered a copy of her wedding gown for her burial and then refused to leave the grave site. He had so many cases before the U.S. Supreme Court even then that the court was closed for an entire month. Every night for years thereafter, he would lay out her nightgown and cap and weep. He found the death of his baby daughter so unbearable he had her body exhumed and put in a casket that, for several years, he kept on his bedroom mantelpiece.[13] He remained a widower for twelve years, then married the daughter of the richest man in Pittsburgh. His fear of death continued to border on the irrational. When he was secretary of war, the South built one of the first ironclad vessels, the *Merrimac*, and set it prowling the waters off Norfolk, destroying helpless wooden warships at will. Stanton became convinced it was going to sail up the Chesapeake and level Washington. He was terrified, sure he was to be killed in his bed by a bomb. Secretary of the Navy Gideon Welles, disgusted by Stanton's fear, told him flatly that the *Merrimac*'s draft was too deep to sail to Washington. Stanton didn't believe him and remained in a panic.

As a lawyer, while often brilliant, he was not great. He combined a passion for reform with personal opportunism, high principle with double-dealing. Typical of his split thinking were his views on slavery. He was implacably opposed to it, yet he was also firmly convinced, as a lawyer, that there was nothing in the Constitution that made it illegal. Therefore, reprehensible as it was, it merited the protection of the law.

Yet opportunism controlled him, and abruptly in 1856, he abandoned his antislavery political connections in the growing Republican party to join the extreme proslavery wing of the Democratic party. With his usual sedulousness, by 1860, a year before the Civil War, he became Buchanan's attorney general. Critics said he had put political gain ahead of political principle. He was also accused of being two-faced: while now publicly associated with the proslavery party, at the same time, he was still consorting with antislavery leaders, albeit quietly. A double-dealer, his critics pronounced— Stanton wanted to be all things to all men.

By 1860, Stanton saw that the Republicans were going to win the next election. He even foresaw that the next president would be Abraham Lincoln. He quietly made another complete political U-turn and betrayed his proslavery political friends: for his newly adopted Republican party, he spied on his friends inside the Buchanan Cabinet. This unprincipled behavior earned him the undying hatred of Buchanan's state secretary, Jeremiah S. Black, who had been a friend and who now heaped scorn on him.[14] Stanton was indifferent. He was being lauded by the Republicans he formerly hated.

Stanton and Lincoln were both lawyers, and it was well known that Stanton had once levered Lincoln out of the famous and very lucrative McCormick reaper case. When Lincoln came to Washington as president, Stanton repeatedly and publicly went about the city vilifying the new president. He hated him, his political party, and his programs, yet, with an ambition that never gave him any rest, he now set his sights on a position in the Cabinet of the president he hated: secretary of war. He trimmed his sails once more and carefully cultivated two of the most powerful members of Lincoln's Cabinet—Secretary of State William H. Seward and Secretary of the Treasury Salmon P. Chase. These two men held strongly opposed political views, and Stanton played his familiar double-dealing game of convincing each he was of the same mind. At the same time, he was still cultivating the Democrats and thereby achieved the impossible: he had one foot in each camp of Lincoln's party and another foot in the Democratic party. Intellectually, he became a three-legged monster. In his quest for that Cabinet seat, he now added another ally, young General George McClellan, who arrived in Washington the day after the disaster at Bull Run to take over the Army of the Potomac. Within a few weeks, McClellan's massive ego was being stroked by his new and powerful friend, Edwin M. Stanton, who also became his legal adviser. McClellan's would be another voice in Lincoln's ear, urging him to appoint Stanton war secretary.

To get into Lincoln's Cabinet, Stanton needed to make just one more move—get Simon Cameron out. By this time, Cameron's corruption in the War Department was so rampant and the public outcry so great, one last straw would bring him down. Stanton provided an entire bale. Historians are now fairly sure that behind the scenes, Stanton had written the offending passages on emancipation in Cameron's annual secretary of war report that flung him to Siberia.[15]

Stanton now entered yet another phase of his career when he joined Lincoln's Cabinet. Described as a "stubby, whiskered, ill-tempered conniver" who was condemned by many for "all his churlish outbursts and bullyings, his lies, his ready tears," he was now also praised for bringing to the nation a combination of "energy, loyalty and official integrity that was hard to match."[16] Historians now say that Stanton became an enormously effective secretary of war and contributed materially to the North's victory. But his behind the scenes, duplicitous political maneuvering became a constant distress to a wartime president who needed, above all, able, loyal service and not the backstairs political muggings that were Stanton's after-hours specialties.[17]

On January 24, 1862, Stanton, as the new secretary of war, made his dedicated presence felt almost immediately. "As soon as I can get the machinery of the office working, the rats cleared out, and the rat holes stopped, we shall move," he wrote to a New York newspaperman.[18] And with that he shut the door to his office, sat down, and began reading every single war contract his predecessor had issued. With each passing hour, he put to rout more and more of Cameron's rats and ferrets, abrogated manipulated contracts, canceled kickback clauses, ejected corrupt contractors, established an orderly and efficient administration in every office and cubicle of the War Department, then he began shipping to the troops decent food and equipment. By his example and energy, he soon earned the support and respect of his generals, including Grant and Sherman.

When Lincoln appointed Stanton secretary of war, Stanton demanded and Lincoln eagerly granted authority to sweep out all of Cameron's cronies and all the corruption in the War Department. Lincoln also gave him further authority to make appropriate changes in the Ordnance Department for the "success of the military operations and the safety of the country."[19] In short, Stanton was to fire Ripley. All Stanton needed was a qualified replacement, and he believed he had him in the person of Major Alexander Dyer, commandant of the Springfield Armory.

Stanton had hardly been in office forty-eight hours when, on January 27, 1862, in response to a Stanton summons, Major Dyer arrived at the War Department. A pugnacious, redheaded Virginian, and a tough capable officer, Dyer had been appointed commandant of the Springfield Armory just five months previously, in August of 1861, by General Ripley. Under his direction, the armory was undergoing the largest expansion program in its history. In only five months, his success in coordinating the vast enterprise impressed everyone and was one of the few bright spots in the Union war effort. Rifles were pouring out of Springfield. Dyer was so highly regarded, everyone in the War Department, even Ripley, openly acknowledged him as Ripley's logical successor.

When Dyer arrived at the War Department, the place was in a turmoil. True to his promise, Stanton was cleaning out all of Cameron's corrupt and incompetent appointees, restoring order and efficiency, raising morale, and turning the War Department into a model of effective administration that served the Union army throughout the war. Dyer found Secretary Stanton alone in his office. In his brusque manner, the secretary came directly to the point. He asked Dyer to take over as chief of ordnance. Dyer listened quietly, considering the offer. Then he amazed Stanton. "I can be of far greater service," Dyer said, "at the Armory where I am in the midst of large-scale rifle production." He had refused the promotion. And, with that, Major Dyer went to the railroad station and took the train back to Springfield. During his entire administration there, he turned out 1.75 million Springfield '61 and '63 rifles.

Stanton was astonished. He had been so certain that Dyer would accept, he had no other serious candidate on his list. Colonel Craig, the former ordnance chief, at seventy too fixed in his ways and too old for the pressure, was not considered capable even as an interim appointment. Colonel Maynadier of the Ordnance Department, General Ripley's right arm, was "the king of the red tape," and not acceptable. With Dyer gone back to his job in Springfield, Ripley was saved to bring on a new disaster. For in his predictable manner, Ripley soon ran afoul of his new superior. Before he was finished, he almost destroyed Stanton's career and drew down on the Union army the worst possible international calamity, one that could have led to the recognition of the South by foreign governments, which, in turn, could have led to a permanent rupture of the American Union. Once again, the center of the storm was the breech-loading rifle.

One of Simon Cameron's last acts as secretary of war was to order two thousand Sharps rifles for Berdan's Sharpshooters—an elite corps of the finest marksmen in the Union—probably under Lincoln's direct orders. But Ripley held up the order for the Sharps rifles and waited for the new secretary—Edwin Stanton—to arrive. He then persuaded Stanton to delay the order indefinitely. It was a victory for Ripley. He had deliberately thwarted his president. But he also nearly caused a military disaster.

Berdan's Sharpshooters was a special rifle unit of two thousand of the country's finest shots, organized and commanded by Hiram Berdan, himself perhaps the finest marksman in the country. On numerous battlefields, Berdan's Sharpshooters went on to become a Civil War legend. With their rapid-fire breech-loading rifles and their superb marksmanship, these troops were able to lay down such a furious small-arms assault at key moments in the fighting that they were credited with being the deciding factor in many skirmishes and battles. Given the choice of weapons, they were so impressed with the Sharps rifle that they named their unit after it and were growing increasingly impatient for delivery of their weapons.

General Ripley remained obdurate. He flatly refused to order any Sharpses for Berdan's Sharpshooters. They became insistent. Voices were raised and demands were made. Both the president and Secretary Stanton were becoming aware of the outcry. Ripley now tried to hoodwink the Sharpshooters. He offered them one thousand Colt repeating rifles to replace the two thousand Sharps rifles they awaited. But the troops wouldn't accept them. The Colts were inaccurate and unreliable in battle, they said. They were even dangerous to the users. Ripley was quite aware of this. In fact, he knew the Colts would perform badly in battle and thereby give a black eye to all repeating rifles. The Sharpshooters had had enough of Ripley's games. He'd used his usual tactics of silence and delay; when pushed, he indulged in deceit and lies; pushed harder, he resorted to indirection and shifty offers.

In a fury, the Sharpshooters trumped Ripley. They would have their Sharps rifles now or they threatened mutiny. Mutiny—the word had a shocking effect. With morale still frayed by the South's military victories, such a mutiny would have affected the entire northern army and strike another staggering blow to national morale. Berdan himself, caught in the middle and facing certain ruin, in order to put down the mutiny armed one hundred of his most loyal men. Stanton, as secretary of war also facing disgrace, took immediate action. Behind closed doors, he gave his personal word as secretary of war that the Sharps rifles would be delivered as soon as they were available. Meanwhile, the Sharpshooters would be furnished Colts on an interim basis. Ripley realized he'd gone too far. He quickly wired the Sharps Company to send him an order of one thousand breechloaders "as soon as possible."[20]

● ● ●

Eighteen sixty-two belonged to the Sharps rifle: although less than two thousand of them took to the field in the hands of Berdan's Sharpshooters, as the first breechloaders in battle, they altered infantry warfare permanently. In June 1862, at the Battle of Mechanicsville, in one of its first battles armed with the Sharps, a small force of Berdan's Sharpshooters took on an entire Confederate division, under command of General A. P. Hill. The Confederates were astonished to see the Sharpshooters in their dark-green uniforms loading and firing while lying on the ground. Offering minuscule targets, the Sharpshooters proceeded to lay down such a hail of rifle fire that Hill's men were stopped and driven back. Two days later, at Bottom's Bridge, two companies of Sharpshooters mounted such a murderous assault with their rifles on attacking rebels that McClellan's army was able to cross the Chickahominy River relatively undisturbed.[21] At Malvern Hill, Confederate skirmishers encountered a Sharpshooters regiment firing from the protection of a ravine. The Confederates mounted a running charge and suffered heavy losses and retreated. With reinforcements, the Confederates attacked again with another unit flanking the ravine. The Sharpshooters slipped out of the ravine, re-formed in the open, and, with the unprecedented fire of their Sharpses, broke up the second attack.[22]

At Antietam, in mid-September, McClellan faced Lee. A regiment of Berdan's Sharpshooters, assuming again their baffling prone position, knocked down more than half of a confronting Confederate regiment.

Shortly after their very successful stand at the Battle of Antietam, Berdan appeared in Washington. He asked the president to make the Sharpshooters into a separate corps, feeling they would be more effective than they were, scattered as special units throughout the army. He made another request—arm the Sharpshooters with repeating rifles—preferably Spencers. To settle the matter quickly, the president sent for his secretary of war. A very hostile Stanton entered the president's office, still fuming about the Sharpshooters' threatened mutiny the previous January when Ripley had failed to provide them with Sharps rifles. Stanton loudly accused Berdan of being behind the near mutiny. At the end of the furor, Berdan left without his Spencers.[23]

In spite of these contretemps, the president felt that Berdan's successes on the battlefield were justifying his belief in breech-loading rifles. Even some officers who twenty years before had agreed with General Craig's opposition to breechloaders were now reluctantly admitting they were wrong. There were others in Washington who had reason to regret the success of the Sharpshooters. One of them was Colonel Kingsbury. He was so taken with the Sharps rifle he put it in writing—and sent it to General Ripley. "Berdan's Sharpshooters," he wrote, "have demonstrated the value of breechloading arms in the hands of skillful troops. If the organization of new regiments is to be continued, it is suggested that one of the three battalions in each regiment be composed of picked men, that this battalion be exercised almost exclusively as skirmishers [with breech-loading rifles]."[24]

This suggestion was not what Ripley wanted to hear. Furthermore, Kingsbury was the last man he wanted to hear it from, for he had been one of the officers who had opposed Ripley's appointment as chief of ordnance. It turned out to be a monumental mistake to draw the attention of the unforgiving Ripley. Kingsbury was relieved of his command for reasons of health, demoted to major, and packed off to Indian country. Needless to say, the profound significance of Kingsbury's words were wasted on Ripley. In fact, Ripley was falling farther behind every day with revolutionary weapons developments that were taking place on the battlefield, many of them wrought by Ripley's superior, Abraham Lincoln. More and more, Ripley was in the way, impeding the war effort. The uproar over the Sharpshooters caused the final rupture between Ripley and Stanton. Stanton's hatred for Ripley was in the open now, and he did not hesitate to humiliate his ordnance chief in public.

Donn Piat, who knew Stanton well, once wrote: "He was approached by all about him in fear and trembling. And the same ugliness seemed to be contagious. The officer coming from his presence, wounded to the quick, gave to others under him the same treatment."[25] Stanton once summarily summoned Ripley to his office. When he got there, Ripley found Stanton holding a rifle in the midst of a crowd of people. Stanton directed Ripley's attention to the rifle's lock and asked Ripley how many such locks he had ordered. Ripley told him. "Now," said Stanton, "if you dare to adopt another musket of this kind, I will dismiss you from the service."

Ripley tried to protest.

"Not another word," Stanton growled. "You can return to your Bureau." Ripley's face was dark red and he was trembling visibly as he stepped through the shocked crowd and out of the office.[26]

CHAPTER 14

RIPLEY AND
THE MACHINE GUN

W ith Bredan's Sharpshooters now armed with Sharpses, Ripley turned his attention to his next skirmish with the president. And, this time, Ripley tried to block the birth of one of the most revolutionary and murderous war weapons ever invented: the machine gun.

Introduced by Abraham Lincoln over the determined resistance of the military, the machine gun made its uncertain debut early in the Civil War, and, as the dominant weapon on all the battlefields since then, went on to change warfare permanently. The first time he saw it, Lincoln recognized its awesome potential for overwhelming firepower. The first time he saw it, General Ripley recognized its awesome potential for wasting ammunition.

In early June 1862, Lincoln received a visit from a French inventor named Rafael, who arrived in Washington with an introductory note from New York's Governor Edwin Morgan. He called on the president and informed him that he, Rafael, had invented a new machine gun. Captain Dahlgren of Navy Ordnance tested it first and was quite impressed. The machine gun, mounted on a light artillery carriage, fired forty paper cartridges in twenty seconds. At a distance of more than a mile, its lateral deviation was negligible. In one firing pass, sixteen shots were fired at a wooden target six hundred yards away. Nearly all were direct hits. Here was a weapon so powerful, so accurate, so rapid firing, so devastating, that John

Ericsson, the eminent inventor and designer of the *Monitor*, the Union's first ironclad ship, wrote that the Rafael machine gun was "one of many strides which mechanical science is now making to render war too destructive, long to continue the disgrace to civilization."[1] He noted, "One regiment of intelligent men provided with one hundred of these effective weapons can most assuredly defeat and destroy a four-fold number of enemies."

On a swelteringly hot day in August 1862, the president went down to the Washington Navy Yard, led by Secretary of the Navy Gideon Welles. Even Secretary of War Stanton went along. They observed two hours of some of the most astonishing shooting they had ever seen, as the weapon pounded targets set up out on the river. Lincoln was so impressed with the Rafael he later wrote Secretary Stanton to say that he considered it a decided improvement upon what was called the coffee mill gun, "in these particulars, that it dispenses with the great cost, and liability to loss of the steel cartridges, and that it is better arranged to prevent the escape of gas." Lincoln closed by saying he "should be rather pleased, if it should be decided to put it into the service."[2]

Stanton, taking this as a command, sent the Lincoln letter to General Ripley, who felt impelled to have the Rafael gun tested at the Frankford Arsenal in Philadelphia. He was not pleased to read the glowing report that came back. Frankford was very impressed by the fact that the bullets penetrated twice as deep as a rifle bullet. The Rafael fired one burst of sixteen shots in five seconds. Another burst of forty shots took just eighteen seconds. After firing five hundred rounds, it was still performing without a hitch. Members of the testing board even recommended specific uses for the remarkable new weapon: for defending river passages, bridges, and similar key points. In addition, they specifically recommended that a number of new Rafaels be issued to each infantry regiment.

The Rafael underwent three weeks of testing at Sixth Army Corps headquarters in Virginia during April 1863. Two brigadier generals and a colonel praised the machine gun highly, singling out its "simplicity of construction, accuracy, range and frequency of fire." It was, they said, "all that is claimed for it." They saw a much broader use for this remarkable weapon and recommended the army ". . . issue eight to twelve guns per brigade." Brigadier General Pratt asked that at least twenty-four of the Rafael repeaters be attached to his division.

Lincoln received all these glowing reports and sent them to Stanton with an order that Rafael machine guns be issued to the army: "Will the Sec. of War please refer [the weapon] to the Ordnance Bureau, with reference to the propriety of introducing the 'Rafael Gun' into the Service?"[3] The Rafael group offered the government five hundred Rafael machine guns for $850 each. Ripley ignored the Frankford Arsenal report, the Sixth Army Corps report, and the president's command and never purchased one Rafael machine gun.

But the day of the machine gun had dawned. In fact, as early as the summer of 1861, a workable machine gun had arrived in Washington—and in several ways this one proved even more difficult than the Rafael for Ripley to ignore. In June 1861, three men traveled by train from New York and stepped into the notorious heat and glare of Washington's long summer. The city was in turmoil. First Bull Run was a few weeks away. Army units were visible, marching all over the city, carts and supply wagons thundered down the streets, mounted messengers cantered toward the White House, while dust and noise were as oppressive as the heat.[4]

The three men, checking into Willard's Hotel, looked like businessmen or lawyers, perhaps—not the possessors of one of the most lethal weapons ever devised. The first to sign the register was Simeon Draper, a bottom-rung New York politician and an influence peddler with an overly compensating loud voice, a large, long nose, and a well-cultivated potbelly. Time and opportunity had already passed him by.

The second, Orison Blunt, an arms maker and importer and a man of high reputation, carried with him an endorsement by the enormously wealthy and influential John Jacob Astor II. He was currently seeking out vitally needed and often hard-to-find foreign arms for the Ordnance Department and for New York's Union Defense League—at no charge to either body.

The third—who signed his name as J. D. Mill—was an introvert who shunned publicity and attention, a shadowy figure who left little of record for historians to puzzle over. What made the three of them interesting to Washington was the piece of equipment they brought with them from New York. It was called the coffee mill gun, and historians still quarrel over the identity of its inventor— either Edward Nugent or William Palmer, who were in the New York City courts quarreling over ownership when Draper, Blunt, and Mill arrived in the capital.

Blunt was the most persuasive of the trio, and three days later, he clambered up the stairs to the loft of Hall's carriage shop across from the Willard, accompanied by the very curious president of the United States. The three introduced the president to the mechanism of the Union repeating gun, which J. D. Mill then proceeded to demonstrate. No matter who eventually gained credit for inventing it, the Union repeating gun was an ingenious single-barrel machine gun mounted on a light artillery carriage. Standard issue .58-caliber paper cartridges were placed inside steel cartridge cases. These steel cases fed from a hopper into a revolving cylinder where they were placed in the breech and fired, the empty cases then dropping into another hopper to be reloaded by hand with new paper cartridges. It would fire fifty rounds a minute. When the president was shown how the entire mechanism worked, he looked at Mill and said it reminded him of a coffee mill and thereupon called it the coffee mill gun.

Meanwhile, Simeon Draper was busy meeting other people in Washington. Apparently through his friendship with Secretary of State Seward, he actually persuaded General Ripley to watch a demonstration of a firing of the gun on the Washington Arsenal grounds. Also watching were five generals, three Cabinet members, the governor of Connecticut, and President Lincoln himself. General Joseph K. F. Mansfield, who was in charge of Washington's defense, promptly asked the secretary to get a number of these coffee mill weapons for the city's fortifications. "I think it an excellent rampart gun," he wrote, "a good field gun against cavalry & horse artillery, an excellent gun to defend the passage of the bridge and should be thoroughly tested in the field at once."[5]

Captain Dahlgren from Navy Ordnance was equally impressed. Lincoln had grown close to Dahlgren and often spent much time in the Navy Yard, watching Dahlgren test weapons. He now asked Dahlgren for his opinion. Dahlgren suggested to the president that the Union army ought to acquire some coffee mill guns. After hearty handshakes all around, Mill, Blunt, and Draper returned to New York, confident they had made a sale. And indeed they had— to the generals, the Cabinet members, to Dahlgren, even to the president himself. But not to Ripley.

The disaster at First Bull Run came a few weeks later, in July, and by late July, Mill realized that he wasn't going to get an order for his coffee mill gun. Indeed, his letters to Lincoln, which the secretaries routed to Ripley, went unanswered. In late October, J. D. Mill made his ultimate move. He arrived in Washington with ten coffee mill guns and promptly called on the president. Lincoln decided to put on a repeating-gun show for General McClellan at the arsenal. But the general was reviewing troops and refused to attend. Lincoln rode down to the arsenal and bought the ten weapons on the spot at $1,300 apiece. Although J. D. Mill might have shaved the president on the price—Dahlgren at the Navy Ordnance Department felt they cost little more than $600 to make—J. D. Mill had made the first machine-gun sale in history. With the order in his pocket, Mill turned around and offered the president a larger quantity of his coffee mill gun for $1,200 each. General McClellan, with some prodding from Lincoln, turned out to be the cannier buyer. He negotiated the purchase of fifty more at cost plus 20 percent, $735 each. Lincoln himself signed the order on December 19, 1861.[6]

Lincoln now believed that he had on order a large quantity of breech-loading rifles and a large number of machine guns to be tried in the ultimate ordnance testing ground—the battlefield. He didn't think he would have long to wait for test results. But he hadn't put the "Ripley" factor into his equation.

In April of 1862, the assignment of trying out the first two coffee mill guns was given to Colonel Geary, commander of the Twenty-eighth Pennsylvania Volunteer Regiment. Apparently, the guns drove off a cavalry attack at Middleburg in the Shenandoah Valley.

Yet on April 23, 1862, Geary shipped them back as "inefficient and unsafe to the operators."[7] These two were from the first lot of ten bought by Lincoln. That must have grimly pleased General Ripley.

But three days later, General John C. Fremont sent a report outlining the weapon's success and enthusiastically ordered sixteen Union repeating guns. Ripley replied by wire that he had none and that none were on order. Fremont didn't believe him. He reminded Ripley that President Lincoln had ordered fifty on December 19. And, in fact, by April 1862, the order for fifty coffee mill guns was rapidly being filled by the manufacturer—the American Arms Company.

Ripley didn't reply to this wire, nor did he ship the hated weapons Fremont had ordered. Instead, Ripley concealed Fremont's glowing report. In fact, he apparently slipped another unrelated report into his files with the same number as the Fremont report. The Fremont report disappeared and has never turned up. Historian Robert Bruce suspects that Ripley may have deliberately destroyed it.[8] Frustrated, General Fremont turned to Lincoln, who ordered Ripley on May 15 to send the requisitioned coffee mill guns to General Fremont. The weapons might have reversed the outcome of Fremont's battle with Stonewall Jackson that June. But still Ripley refused to ship the coffee mills. He delayed, blatantly disobeying the presidential order. Undaunted, Fremont ordered two coffee mills direct from the manufacturer, but he never got to use them. Fremont, who was a celebrated explorer of the far west, a controversial politician, and a mediocre military officer, angrily resigned his commission after being placed under the command of John Pope, his old enemy from Missouri.

Newspapers reported on the performance of the coffee mill gun, giving the weapon mixed reviews. Apparently, when it worked, it was devastating, but the weapon was cranky. The Forty-ninth Pennsylvania at Golding's Farm reported, "Our Coffee Mill Guns did good work." But the colonel of the Thirty-first New York reported that the weapon "was defective in several particulars." Geary had already returned his two coffee mills. A Washington Navy Yard test reported excessive gas escape from the breech and occasional cartridge-feed failures. The military blamed the problems on "inferior workmanship." The maker blamed "improper usage & neglect." Ripley rejoiced but kept up the battle. When a black regiment from New York ordered eight coffee mills, Ripley refused to ship them. On orders from above, he finally did so. But he sent no ammunition. When the exasperated assistant secretary of war, F. H. Watson, bluntly ordered him to do so, he reluctantly shipped them.[9] Later, the American Arms Company brought out a new and improved coffee mill gun. General Rosecrans saw it test-fired and ordered ten. With conspiratorial eagerness, Ripley tried to discourage the general by recounting the coffee mill's shortcomings. Rosecrans insisted and Ripley shipped him ten—but with the typical Ripley skew. As the guns wended their way to Rosecrans, they encountered one strange delay after another and arrived eventually not at the battlefield of Chickamauga, where Rosecrans waited for them, but in Nashville, Tennessee.

The *Scientific American* seemed to write the gun's epitaph when it reported that the coffee mill guns had "proved to be of no practical value to the army of the Potomac, and are now laid up in a storehouse in Washington."[10]

Yet although the coffee mill gun never received an objective field test, it did have its victories and its proponents and, in the end, Ripley's wrongheaded victory over it proved to be only temporary. For now came forward an authentic engineering genius who brought with him a weapon that even Ripley couldn't exorcise. In the late autumn of 1862, in Indianapolis, Indiana, before a large crowd that included the governor of Indiana, Richard Jordan Gatling stepped behind his new military machine gun, then looked around with great confidence at the expectant throng. They had all come to see what Gatling had promised: something no one on earth had ever seen before—a machine gun. The weapon resembled a small cannon with a crank at the rear. Gatling reached down and turned the crank. The crowd gasped. The weapon fired bullets at an astonishing rate, an awesome show of firepower that indeed no one in the crowd had ever seen before. The governor was so impressed, he wrote to F. H. Watson, assistant secretary of war, to announce the weapon and to urge him to see it for himself. Gatling, an inspired salesman as well as mechanical genius, gave his weapon top billing as "an army in six feet," costing only $1,500. "Two of these at $3,000," he announced, "are equal to a military regiment that costs about $50,000 to assemble and $150,000 a year to operate."[11]

Richard Gatling is still an enigma to military historians and was every bit as complex as Stanton. He seems to have been an amalgam of circus impresario, snake-oil shill, mechanical genius, and scoundrel. He probably originated in North Carolina, for in 1844, he had emigrated from that place to Indiana to put his inventive genius nearer an industrialized center. Gatling began work on his machine gun in April 1861, at the time the South fired on Fort Sumter, and had it ready for patent by November 1862. The six-barrel Gatling fired the standard-issue paper cartridge contained in hopper-fed steel cases. Hand-cranked, the new weapon was presented as an incredible man killer and also an incredible bargain.

Unaware of General Ripley's devout opposition to things new, Gatling confidently approached the Ordnance Office in 1863 and was baffled by Ripley's standard tactic—the closed door. While Gatling was nine-tenths genius, he was also one-tenth fool, and what happened next played right into Ripley's hands. Gatling had taken care not to reveal that he was an active, dedicated member of the Order of American Knights, a group of saboteurs loyal to the southern cause. But in Indiana his reputation caught up with him and he was soon thrown in jail as a Copperhead—a person in the North who was suspected of secretly sympathizing with the South. Only the insistence of President Lincoln himself secured Gatling's freedom. Unable still to sell his weapon to Ripley, Gatling thereupon did what an army of frustrated American gun designers were to do in the decades that followed. Rebuffed by Army Ordnance, they took their weapons overseas to the waiting arms of European governments.

The French were very interested, studied Gatling's drawing with attention, and asked for a model. It was a considerable opportunity, but Gatling overreached himself. He declined to ship a model, offering, instead, to sell a hundred weapons—minimum. The French looked elsewhere. Ultimately, Congress slapped an embargo on the sale of American weapons abroad.[12] Undaunted, Gatling designed a new and improved Gatling machine gun, which he asserted would fire "up to 200 rounds a minute." [13] Thanks to the coffee mill gun, the Gatling machine gun was no longer regarded as a newfangled, unproved weapon but as an improved coffee mill gun.

The new model, firing a one-inch, metal-jacketed cartridge, was tested by Captain Benét in the Frankford Arsenal in Philadelphia. As a result, the Gatling was officially adopted by the army, but, unfortunately for Gatling, the war was in its last stages. Gatling did receive an order, but it was in 1866, after the South's surrender, and it was for only one hundred machine guns. Gatling turned overseas again and there his luck changed.

The British placed a fat order in 1867, the Japanese in 1868, and the Russians, also in 1868, ordered more than one hundred. The Turks then ordered a number to protect their borders with Russia. Fifty more were sold to Spanish Cuba. The world's first effective machine gun, from an American genius and an American factory, was making its way in the world of mayhem and slaughter everywhere but in its native land.[14]

Meanwhile, General Ripley had turned his attention back to his particular bête noire—the breechloader—and here he was rapidly losing running room.

CHAPTER 15

THE SPENCER'S AND
RIPLEY'S LAST DAYS

O riginally, at the beginning of the war, Ripley had argued that
he could not make any new breech-loading rifles in the middle of the war because there was a shortage of the necessary skilled
labor—not enough even for the manufacture of the standard rifle
musket. Besides, he would add, private companies could not make
the new metallic cartridges for those breechloaders. They were busy
making the millions of paper cartridges required by the muzzleloaders—some 470 million by war's end.

He was wrong on both counts. Springfield and private industry
could turn out Spencers—in fact, the Spencer Repeating Rifle
Company did turn them out and in quantity: 200,000 in all, including 60,000 carbines bought by the Ordnance Bureau. Moreover, private industry found the capacity to turn out two thousand
Henrys and could have produced many more if Ripley had ordered
them. Private industry also produced enough Sharpses to outfit
some forty different army units.

At the same time, private industry turned out all the metallic cartridges the army could absorb. Had they not been able to, there
were many manufacturers in Europe with plenty of manufacturing
capability for making metallic cartridges. All this Ripley also knew
and soon everyone knew it. By June of 1862, the army had so many
weapons on hand, Ripley could no longer use a muzzle-loading
shortage as a reason for not introducing breech-loading rifles. By

that month, the Ordnance Department had provided the army with over one million rifles and had well over 300,000 others in reserve inventory.

Even another year later, in 1863, with abundant arms on hand, Ripley was still refusing to provide Spencers. With every battlefield now clamoring for Spencer rifles, General Ripley had developed a new argument. Spencer, he said, was too busy making Spencer carbines to make any more Spencer rifles—yet, at the same time, he was trying to stop Spencer's carbine production.

In February of 1863, he told Assistant Secretary of War Watson that it was not "expedient to continue the manufacture under contract" of the Spencers, meaning he didn't want to renew the Spencer contract when it expired.[1] In March, the general was still contending that the Spencer's "practical value and utility for the military service have yet to be ascertained."[2] He complained about the cost of Spencers and shipped Springfields. In May 1863, Spencer's contract was about to expire. With requests for more production pouring in, company executives came to Washington fully expecting to renew.

Ripley stunned them. "There will be no more orders," he told them, "without special authority from Secretary Stanton." Puzzled, the Spencer executives predictably approached Stanton for a new contract. Predictably, Stanton lost his very short temper with Ripley and demanded to know why Ripley had sent the Spencer executives to him. "I did not send them to you, at all, for any purpose," Ripley demurred.[3] But, by now, the last stand between Ripley and the Spencer was about to be played out. The Spencers were arriving on the battlefields in numbers, and reports of their performances were coming back to Washington.

At Hoover's Gap, on June 24, 1863, a brigade of Union infantry were moving toward the Gap to sweep advance pickets of a large Confederate force. There was one unusual element in this northern brigade: all the foot soldiers were mounted. The North was about to test in battle a new concept for overcoming the slowness of moving infantry by foot. Even though not schooled in cavalry tactics, these foot soldiers were trained to arrive at a battle site at a gallop, then dismount to fight like foot soldiers. The formation of this first mounted brigade was in direct response to the success of a famous Confederate unit of mounted infantry, Morgan's Raiders.

When it was formed, the new northern unit was expecting to be armed with two thousand Spencers. The cavalry had promptly provided the horses, but Ripley, employing his favorite tactic, delayed the shipment of the needed two thousand Spencers. Commanding officer Wilder made each man in the brigade sign a promissory note for $35, and with these, he went to a bank and borrowed the money to order the Spencers direct from the Spencer factory in Boston. They were shipped promptly to Murfreesboro, Tennessee.[4]

While Ripley was still contending that there were no Spencer rifles available from the factory, Wilder's First Mounted Rifles were riding into battle with them. What was about to happen was as much a test of the Spencer as it was of the mounted infantry concept. General Bragg held the Gap with a strong force that outnumbered Wilder's mounted infantry by four to one. Pressing into the Gap with great speed, Wilder's fast-riding mounted brigade had gotten six miles in advance of the main Union army when it came up against Bushrod Johnson's brigade. Johnson promptly attacked. He was thrown back with high losses. He attacked again, and again was driven back by the heavy firepower of the Spencers. Johnson was now convinced he was outnumbered five to one.

Confederate rifled cannons were brought forward to soften up Wilder's unit. Then Bushrod Johnson attacked a third time, and again was thrown back with heavy losses. General Bragg, when informed, was also convinced this was a major attack, and withdrew his entire army through Hoover's Gap and retreated into Georgia along the Chickamauga. Wilder lost 51 killed and wounded, but Johnson lost 156. Thus, "Wilder's Lightning Brigade" was born in fire.[5] The legend of the Spencer had begun. Later, the War Department reimbursed the troops for their Spencers.

On July 1, 1863, one of the pivotal battles of the Civil War took shape when Heth's Confederate infantry brigade, marching toward the town of Gettysburg, Pennsylvania, to forage for desperately needed shoes, encountered Buford's Federal cavalry unit scouting for signs of Lee's army. Armed with Spencer carbines, Buford's cavalry unit of twenty-seven hundred leveled a burst of fire that held up Heth's seventy-five hundred infantrymen for over an hour, while the main armies of both sides converged on the town and hastily drew up battle lines.

The next day, July 2, in Hanover, a few miles east of Gettysburg, George Custer, just made general, raced up to take command of his Michigan cavalry brigade, most of whom had recently been armed with Spencer rifles—not carbines, as was later reported. Colonel James H. Kidd of the Michigan cavalry brigade noted later, "It was here that the brigade first saw Custer." Colonel Kidd heard a fast-moving horse and turned to see the flamboyant boy general ride up in black velvet with gold braid and pale-blue shirt.

Custer immediately took his two thousand mounted Spencers into action in pursuit of Jeb Stuart's Confederate cavalry, which was swinging north and west around the Union army to turn south at Carlisle in order to link up with General Lee at Gettysburg. Custer attacked Stuart again near Hunterstown, six miles northeast of Gettysburg. Custer himself later saluted the Spencers. "I attribute their [Fifth Michigan Cavalry] success," he reported, "to the fact that the regiment is armed with the Spencer repeating rifle, which in the hands of brave, determined men is the most effective firearm that our cavalry can adopt."[6]

As if to illustrate that point, Custer next confronted Stuart in one of the most crucial cavalry battles of the war. On the third and conclusive day of the Battle of Gettysburg, July 3, 1863, General Lee dispatched Stuart's cavalry to sweep General Meade's right flank and attack the Union rear while Pickett was charging Meade's center.

Custer's Fifth Michigan Cavalry intercepted Stuart, dismounted, and poured out such a volume of fire from their 479 Spencer rifles that Stuart's advance was halted, making him believe he was confronted with a much larger force. Custer then led his Seventh Michigan Cavalry in a flailing saber attack that drove back Stuart's cavalry. Following this, Custer's First Michigan, outnumbered three to one but armed with 213 Sharps carbines, charged. Waves of the two opposing mounted units literally crashed into each other, bowling over many horses and riders alike. When both sides reeled back from the violent collision, arms historian Roy M. Marcot notes that the Michigan unit's action "would later be called the greatest cavalry charge and engagement in the western hemisphere."[7] With Stuart's flanking action blunted, the opportunity was lost to neutralize Union artillery firing on Pickett's infantry charge. Custer's extraordinary aggressiveness and the tremendous volume from the Spencers not only saved the day against the Confederate flanking movement, but the repeating rifle had now become unequivocally a major new factor in the Civil War, hastening its end. Lee's effort to conquer the North receded.

Breechloaders were also decisive in the key battle for Little Round Top. Both sides were slow to realize that artillery on top of this ridge would be a dominant factor in the battle. But when Lee sent Longstreet to get up there first with Confederate cannon, Meade, to stop him, and to make way for Union artillery, sent Berdan's Sharpshooters armed with Sharps breechloaders, plus two hundred more Union troops armed with muzzleloaders. For twenty decisive minutes, the Sharpshooters stopped Longstreet, laying down a murderous assault of an unprecedented ninety-five rounds per man. Longstreet's men thought they had encountered two Federal regiments. One Union Sharpshooter, taken prisoner, looked with awe at the condition of the enemy. "It is impossible for me to describe the slaughter we had made in their ranks," he said. "In all my past service, it beat all I had ever seen for the number of engaged and for so short a time. They were piled in heaps and across each other. . . . The doctor would hardly believe that there were so few of us fighting them, thought we had a corps, as he said he never saw lead so thick in his life as it was in those woods."[8] The action of the Sharpshooters was one of the crucial efforts at Gettysburg. All told, the breechloaders delayed Longstreet's sweep by forty minutes. Five minutes less, and Longstreet would have taken the Peach Orchard, swept Little Round Top, and might have delivered a stunning victory to the South. Meade's line held at Gettysburg, when during the monumental final battle, he broke Pickett's charge. But to

Lincoln's great dismay, he failed to follow after the retreating Lee. Some commentators feel that Meade lost an opportunity to end the war then and there. Lee, instead, escaped across the Potomac on the morning of July 4, to fight again and extend the war more than a year.

Colonel Berdan emerged from Gettysburg more than ever an exponent of greater firepower. He was also quite aware of what Wilder's mounted infantry had done at Hoover's Gap with Spencers. And he reasoned that if he had been able to stop Longstreet with the single-shot Sharps breechloader, what could he not accomplish with the seven-shot Spencer? Convinced that he now had a clinching argument, Berdan urged General Ripley yet again to replace his single-shot Sharps rifles with seven-shot Spencer rifles, but found himself once again quickly trussed in Ripley's abundant coils of red tape. Berdan never got a single Spencer from Ripley.

In fact, in spite of the rave reviews the Spencers were getting, it still took the direct intervention of President Lincoln, again, to compel General Ripley to equip Sheridan's cavalry—including Custer's brigade—with repeating weapons. This turned out to be a critical decision, for it was only with the great firepower of those weapons that Sheridan was able to turn the Confederate flank at Petersburg that helped bring about the fall of Richmond.

I n mid-August 1863, more than a month had passed since Gettysburg and the quarrel over the Spencer was still raging furiously. President Lincoln decided to get to the bottom of this quarrel. On the one hand, Ripley was violently, actively opposed to the Spencer; he was not only still refusing whenever possible to supply Spencers, but he was also trying to prevent the company from getting a contract renewal. Yet the field performance of the Spencer was already a legend throughout the entire Union army corps. Every unit was clamoring for Sharpses or Henrys or especially Spencers. President Lincoln decided he would personally test-fire one himself. He contacted Navy Ordnance—Spencer's original customer. Naval Ordnance Chief Wise very proudly showed the president the weapon and explained its working parts.

The president took it out to a target and encountered a serious problem. He couldn't get the ammunition tube out of the chamber that ran through the wooden stock. He tried repeatedly, with no success. Embarrassed, Naval Ordnance issued him a second Spencer, and this time, both Secretary of War Stanton and Chief of Naval Ordnance Wise came along to observe. The president got off two shots in good order but then the mechanism jammed. Since these were two fully finished Spencers that had passed the rigid Naval Ordnance inspection, the navy was quite embarrassed, the president was completely unimpressed, and the Spencer executives had to be quite suspicious. How could failure occur in two copies of a weapon famous for its reliability? Was it more than coincidence that they both failed in the hands of the chief executive of the na-tion—just when the manufacturer was trying to negotiate a new contract?

If someone had wanted to turn the president against the rifle, he had chosen just the right moment. When Major General Hurlbut wrote to Ripley's ally, General Henry Halleck, to ask for Spencers for his mounted infantry, the president himself took the time to reply, outlining in detail his misadventures with the Spencer and closing with: "I am sorry to disappoint you by saying I cannot now order these guns for you. A. Lincoln."[9] Lincoln's note was en-closed with General Halleck's official response, in which the gener-al had the pleasure of refusing to send any Spencers. Halleck told General Hurlbut that mounted infantry would be armed with whatever rifles "the Ordnance Department can furnish." Further-more, "the proposition to permit them to purchase Spencer's Navy rifles cannot be entertained."[10] This all meant that Ripley could supply the mounted infantry not with breechloaders but with muz-zleloaders.

With the chief executive refusing to allow Spencers to be shipped to Union troops, the company faced ruin. Deeply concerned about the cause of those two rifle malfunctions, Cheney quickly contacted his friend and neighbor, Navy Secretary Gideon Welles. Welles then spoke to Lincoln and reminded him of the Spencer's great success-es at Hoover's Gap, at Custer's Battle of Hanover, and at Gettysburg. Welles suggested that Lincoln interview the people who made the Spencer.

Charles Cheney thereupon dispatched Christopher Spencer himself to the White House, carrying a new and improved model of the rifle. It was a momentous meeting. Young Spencer stood for the first time in the presence of the six-foot-four-inch Lincoln, whose mind was tumbling with the phrases he would utter during his Gettysburg Address, to dedicate the vast cemetery of dead young men there. The president found himself looking at the extraordinarily young-looking inventor of the weapon that was causing so much mayhem on the battlefields.

Spencer and the president and the president's son, Robert, and one of the president's secretaries, John Hay, took the Spencer rifle out for some target practice near where the Washington Monument now stands. The president had sent a messenger to Secretary of War Edwin Stanton, but Stanton declined, saying he was too busy to come. On the firing line, at a range of forty yards, the president placed one shot in the bull's-eye and six more around it. Spencer's shooting matched the president's. Hay wrote in his diary that the Spencer was "a wonderful gun, loading with absolute simplicity and ease."[11] The crisis was past. "After that," Christopher Spencer wrote, "we had more orders than we could fill, from the War Department, as well as the Navy, for the rest of the war."[12]

General Ripley now faced his final adventure with the Spencer. Having heard the accounts of "Wilder's Lightning Brigade," and thirsting for the Spencer's enormous firepower and the mounted infantry's great mobility, General Lovell Rousseau, who was credited with keeping Kentucky in the union, approached Lincoln for permission to issue cavalry mounts to his entire infantry division and arm them with Sharps or Spencer rifles. In short, he was proposing the next logical step up from the Lightning Brigade—a Lightning Division. Lincoln agreed readily and Rousseau returned to the war to wait for Ripley to supply him with five thousand Spencers. Ripley predictably looked for a ruse by which to delay. He told Rousseau that the demand for Spencers was so great he didn't have five thousand available. The Spencer company reported it would soon have two thousand rifles, but they belonged to Massachusetts. Massachusetts magnanimously offered the Spencers to Rousseau if General Ripley would provide the latest-model Springfield muzzleloaders to the Massachusetts troops until January, when another twenty-five hundred Spencers would be ready.

General Ripley had the Springfields; the government warehouse was well stocked with them. But he didn't accept the Massachusetts offer. In fact, he urged his superior, Secretary of War Stanton, not to buy any more Spencers. Ever. Then he told Rousseau that he would have to wait until January for his Spencers because the company was busy making Spencer carbines for the cavalry, which made even the January delivery date questionable. This was mid-August—just at the time that young Spencer and President Lincoln were test-firing the newest Spencer model. Ripley had finally gone too far. Lincoln's legendary patience ended. The president decided that Ripley had become a dangerous handicap to the Union effort and had to be replaced immediately. The president reached for the very instrument he needed to cashier Ripley.

Formerly, only the army retirement board had the authority to retire General Ripley. But the Congress felt that too many superannuated Union officers, with their outmoded notions of warfare, were getting underfoot. So it passed a new law that gave the president the authority to retire any army officer with more than forty-five years' military service. Approval by the army retirement board was not required.

Lincoln looked around for Ripley's successor. Two weeks passed while the president conferred with Secretary of War Stanton and the army's General Halleck. Before General Ripley was officially informed of his fate, the story was leaked to the *New York Times* on September 2, 1863, for all of Washington and the country to read. The *Times* capered with glee over the end of "the old fogy Ripley . . . who combatted all new ideas in the fabrication of firearms, artillery and projectiles." The inventor Charles F. Raymond wrote to Secretary Stanton to "congratulate the Country on the removal of that old Fossell Fogy."[13] All of Ripley's many enemies and ill-wishers rejoiced. After serving his country in his own fashion for forty-nine years—since he graduated from West Point in 1814—Brigadier General James Wolfe Ripley was officially retired on September 15, 1863. He was sixty-nine and he had served as chief of ordnance since April 23, 1861, a very damaging period of two years and five months. He was given the sinecure of inspecting the coastal defenses of New England.

To temper the vituperation of General Ripley's critics, the comments of his chief assistant, Captain James G. Benton, testifying before a Senate committee, should be noted. "He may have erred sometimes," Benton said, "and he may have created a great many enemies by refusing to adopt inventions which he thought were unfit or not suited to the service, or were too expensive. But I am very confident, in fact I know, that he was actuated solely by the interests of the service."[14]

Two weeks after he left office, the new chief of ordnance, General Ramsay, received a direct order from Assistant Secretary of War Watson to accept the Massachusetts offer, and ship half of the two thousand Spencers to General Rousseau. With them, General Rousseau achieved a notable victory at Chehaw Station.[15]

Ramsay was no Ripley. He believed in the breechloader. He wrote to the War Department: "Repeating arms are the greatest favorite with the Army and should they be supplied in quantities to meet all requirements, I am sure no other arms would be used. Colt's and Henry rifles and Spencer carbines and rifles are the only arms of this class in the service. Colt's is both expensive and a dangerous weapon to the user. Henry's expensive and too delicate for service in its present form, while Spencer's is at the same time the cheapest, most durable and most efficient of any of these arms."[16] Then he went out and bought every Spencer he could find. They were coming out of Spencer's Boston factory about 150 a day. More manufacturing facilities in nearby Providence, Rhode Island, added to the total, almost all of it in cavalry carbines.

A year later, Ramsay was replaced by a new chief of ordnance, Alexander Dyer, who had once refused Secretary Stanton's offer of Ripley's job. Dyer received a note in early January 1865 that would have empurpled the face of his predecessor, General Ripley. From the head of the newly formed Cavalry Bureau, Major General James H. Wilson, the note read: "There is no doubt that the Spencer carbine is the best fire-arm yet put into the hands of the soldier, both for economy of ammunition and maximum effect physical and moral. Our best officers estimate one man armed with it equivalent to three with any other arm. I have never seen anything else like the confidence inspired by it in the regiments or brigades which have it. A common belief among them is if their flanks are covered they can go anywhere."[17] The phrase "economy of ammunition" would have infuriated General Ripley.

Other officers were praising the breech-loading Sharps rifle, reporting that it proved to be completely reliable through its entire service during the war years. They said it was impressively accurate and had a longer range than the muzzle-loading Springfield. Confederate soldiers had a profound respect for the Sharpses and Spencers. The Spencer soon became known as the rifle that was loaded on Sunday and fired all week.[18]

As an ironic footnote to the Civil War, many of the breech-loading and repeating rifles were supplied not by the Ordnance Department, but by the army units' own state governments. And many soldiers bought them at their own expense. As it arrived in larger numbers on the battlefields, the Spencer rifle was reserved for tried and tested troops, in short, a reward for bravery. Lincoln, the champion of the breechloader, deserves credit for introducing it in the face of widespread army and Ordnance resistance. His belief in it was vindicated before he died. All through 1864, newspapers called for the adoption of breech-loading rifles as the army standard. Finally, in the chief of ordnance's annual report in October 1864, the breech-loading rifle became the army standard.[19] The clearest proof of the enormous effectiveness of the new repeating rifle occurred in April 1865, the last month of the war, when General Phil Sheridan's cavalry mounted such a furious assault with the repeating Spencer it helped turn the Confederate flank and led directly to the fall of Richmond and the end of the war.

General Ripley departed still believing he was right. He was utterly convinced that long-range, deliberately aimed fire won battles and conserved ammunition. But all the long-range, deliberately aimed fire of the South's muzzleloaders and all the carefully conserved ammunition the South could muster couldn't win battles against the murderous firepower of massed Spencer rifles.

How important was the Spencer? One historian has stated flatly that without the Spencers, the war would have gone on six months longer, with an added loss of seventy-five thousand lives on both sides. An officer of the Michigan cavalry brigade said of the Spencer, "If the entire army had been supplied with it the war would not have lasted ninety days."[20] According to a Confederate general, if the North had armed its troops with breechloaders, the South would have been defeated within a year. If northern troops had had a large number of them even by 1862, "Gettysburg would certainly have ended the war. More likely, Chancellorsville or even Fredericksburg would have done it, and history would record no Gettysburg Address, no President Grant, perhaps no carpetbag reconstruction or Solid South."[21]

Once the Spencer armory in Boston got into full production, the Spencer not only won battle after battle, it also won them in astonishingly quick time. From Yellow Tavern to Appomattox, the Confederates were defeated by the U.S. cavalry wielding the Spencer in battles that lasted less than a day. At Cold Harbor, Sheridan sent Confederate forces reeling with a final charge that lasted no more than five minutes. Without his Spencers, there's a good chance that Sheridan would have lost that battle. And his great sweep of the Shenandoah Valley would likely have ended not in victory but in defeat at the key battle at Cedar Creek.[22]

All told, counting those sales made direct to state units and to soldiers in the field, the Spencer Repeating Rifle Company sold some 200,000 seven-shooters to the United States government, state governments, and individual military units.

W hat happened to all the major figures from the Ordnance Wars of the Civil War?

On April 9, 1865, at Appomattox Courthouse, Virginia, almost four years to the day that the South had fired on Fort Sumter, General Robert E. Lee surrendered to Grant. And five days later, on the evening of April 14, while watching a comedy at Ford's Theater in Washington, D.C.—the first five days of peace he had known since taking office—President Abraham Lincoln was assassinated by John Wilkes Booth.

On Wednesday, April 26, twenty-five troopers from the Sixteenth New York Cavalry, under the command of Lieutenant Colonel Everton J. Conger, trapped Booth in a barn on the Garrett Farm in Port Royal, Virginia. Fatally shot, Booth had been armed with a Spencer carbine. The cavalry carbine that killed him was also a Spencer.

Christopher Spencer went on to a very busy life as an inventor. In his eighties, still borne by his tireless enthusiasm, he was enthralled by the invention of the airplane and took up flying. Simon Cameron was politically unkillable. Following the Civil War, after betraying his fourth president, his political machine got him elected to two more terms in the U.S. Senate, and later his son, Don, managed three terms as U.S. senator from Pennsylvania.

Edwin Stanton miraculously avoided being murdered to die a natural death. Stanton was embroiled in the impeachment of President Andrew Johnson, a man he hated, if possible, more than he had hated Lincoln—the impeachment effort failed. But about a year and a half later Stanton's lifelong dream came true when President Ulysses S. Grant appointed him a justice to the Supreme Court of the United States. He barely had time, however, to put his pens on his desk. Four days after his appointment to the Supreme Court bench, on Christmas Eve, 1869, in Washington, he suffered a fatal stroke. He was fifty-five.

Harpers Ferry, effectively closed by the Confederate army in April of 1861 when it removed all the arms-making capability to Richmond, was a battleground all through the Civil War. The town changed hands between North and South eleven times; the railroad bridge was destroyed and rebuilt nine times. At war's end, the firehouse where John Brown had been captured, barely twenty feet from the arsenal with the 100,000 shoulder arms he had intended to distribute to slaves, was the only armory structure that survived. Many of the residents moved away, including most of the idled armorers. Local stores, now bankrupt, were boarded up.

There was some feeble attempt to reopen the armory during the Grant administration, but that hope—along with George Washington's hope of making the Potomac the premier east-west trade route of the United States—was washed away in a series of devastating storms and floods in the 1870s and 1880s.

James Wolfe Ripley retired to his native Connecticut and settled in Hartford to write his memoirs. Born the same year the Springfield Armory was created by Congress and, in retirement, living but a few miles south of it, he died on March 17, 1870. His memoirs, appearing in 1881, declared, "There has been nothing remarkable in my life, nor do I intend to make it appear otherwise."[23]

PART III

PART III

CHAPTER 16

GENERAL ALEXANDER DYER
VERSUS THE INDIANS

By April of 1865, one of the greatest wars the world had ever known was over. Chief of Ordnance General Alexander Brydie Dyer was faced with several questions about shoulder arms, questions so crucial his answers would help determine the kind and nature of weapons the army would have for almost the rest of the century.

A redheaded southerner, Dyer was born in Richmond, Virginia, in 1815, and graduated from West Point in 1837. From the Academy, he went directly to the Second Seminole War in Florida as an artillery officer. By 1846, the thirty-one-year-old lieutenant was serving in the New Mexico campaign as chief of ordnance, Army of the West, where he was wounded in battle in Taos, New Mexico. By 1853, Captain Dyer was in command of the North Carolina Arsenal. And, in August 1861, now a major and firmly opposed to the secessionists, he was appointed commandant of the National Armory at Springfield by Chief of Ordnance General Ripley. As noted, in January 1862, he declined Secretary of War Stanton's offer of the post of chief of ordnance to replace General Ripley. Instead, he remained at Springfield, where he became an essential factor in the production of arms for the Union army, raising the production of rifles to one thousand a day. In the midst of his heavy wartime duties, he found time to invent the Dyer cannon projectile, which was used during the Civil War and for which he refused any compensation. Replacing General Ramsay, he became chief of ordnance in September 1864, with the rank of brigadier general. President Lincoln approved the appointment with some trepidation—he didn't think there was another officer capable of filling the post of commandant at Springfield as impressively as Dyer had. Dyer was breveted major general in March of 1865 and remained as chief of ordnance until his death in 1874.

It is tempting to speculate on what would have happened if Dyer had accepted the post of chief of ordnance when it was first offered to him in January 1862, more than two and a half years earlier than his actual appointment in September 1864. It will be recalled that he had tested the Spencer rifle as early as August 1861, and had written to General Ripley, "I regard it as one of the best breechloading arms that I have ever seen."

As he led the Ordnance Department into its postbellum era, General Dyer could look at an organization that had compiled a distinguished, if turbulent and uneven, seventy-two-year history. Since its creation by Congress in 1794, the Springfield Armory—and to a lesser extent the now defunct Harpers Ferry Armory—had served as the creative center for many important innovations in small arms.

Within its walls, the Springfield Armory had attracted and trained a continuing parade of gifted tool designers and inventors like Blanchard and Allin. Outside its walls, the armory had served as a classroom for all the private arms companies up and down the Connecticut Valley, many of whom were often subcontractors to the armory. For them, the Springfield Armory was a postgraduate university for ballistics studies—gunpowders, gun barrel designs, internal gas pressures, breech-loading devices, rifling tools, production techniques—as well as a vital factor in America's burgeoning world leadership in mass production techniques.

The armory had also been godfather to a number of major arms-making companies—such as Colt and Winchester and Smith & Wesson—which surrounded the armory like satellites around the sun. Unlike Europe, where private ownership of rifles was largely illegal, these companies served a huge domestic market clamoring for guns, and by so doing were spawning the largest aggregation of talented weapons designers anywhere in the world—a group that would turn out an impressive array of new weapons concepts during the rest of the century. Ironically, while the conservative armory would almost invariably reject these new ideas, European armories eagerly studied the work of independent American gun designers and copied them, causing a continuing flow of American designers to settle in Europe.

The problems General Dyer faced offered no easy solution. Along with other military heads, he had to determine what sort of military organization the United States would need in the future, what shoulder arm would best suit that organization, and then try to guess how much money Congress would make available.

Congress had already cut the War Department budget from $31 million in 1865 to $700,000 in 1866, and it had reduced the peacetime army from over one million in 1865 to fifty-seven thousand officers and men in 1866. In 1869, it would cut the number again, to twenty-five thousand. And with these few troops, the army would have to do the work of a military force three or four times larger, patrolling the recently subdued South, handling an explosive Indian problem in the West, and preparing for a military confrontation with a French army in Mexico.

The Indian problem was indeed significant. For some years, the army had been following a policy of containing tribes on western reservations. This policy had worked as long as the Indian lands were not considered valuable—when they were believed to be mostly desert. But after the Civil War, land-hungry immigrants, finding most of the land in the East already claimed and impelled by the Homestead Act of 1862, were pushing westward and there discovering the vast prairie lands of the Midwest, so deep and flat and seemingly limitless that one could literally set a plow at dawn and walk westward to the sunset, leaving behind a day-long furrow without having to turn the plow, without running out of grassland. The problem was that this was Indian land, a fact confirmed by duly executed U.S. treaties. Sodbusters in increasing numbers and Indians were claiming the same land.

Another greatly unsettling factor was the railroad. Ignoring Indian objections, both the Union Pacific and the Omaha and Kansas City railroads were traversing Indian lands, making them completely accessible to both homesteaders and cavalrymen alike, and also aiding the relentless extermination of vast herds of buffalo for hides and sport. The buffalo were vital to the Indian's way of life, forcing him now to fight for his very existence.

As the long wagon trains followed trails westward into Indian territory, and as the railroads relentlessly added more miles of trackage every month, the cavalry was becoming greatly overextended. To protect those trails and those railroads, the cavalry began constructing a series of forts. The trails, the trains, and the forts were too much for the furious Indians, and they turned out in force.

On December 21, 1866, the beginning of the twenty-five-year Indian uprisings was clearly announced with the Fetterman massacre. Captain William Fetterman, leading a cavalry unit of eighty men from Fort Phil Kearny to protect a work party of woodcutters, was set upon by Indians and the entire unit was wiped out.

General Sherman, whose command embraced the Indian territories, indicated he was ready to exterminate every Indian tribe to protect the immigrant trails and the railroads. In effect, he was announcing a new and brutal policy of calculated Indian annihilation. Yet along the entire length of just one of those trails—the Bozeman—which cut diagonally across the territory of the most warlike tribe in the entire West—the Sioux—he had only seven hundred cavalrymen.

General Dyer was also concerned by the threat from the French in Mexico. Observing that the United States was completely absorbed in its Civil War, Napoleon III of France had designated Archduke Maximilian of Austria emperor of Mexico and had sent him with an entire French army to reign over the very reluctant Mexicans. Under the Monroe Doctrine, promulgated by President Monroe in 1823, the United States forbade European powers to colonize the American continents, north or south. Not only was Maximilian clearly defying that Doctrine, but by invading Mexico, he had put a modern army right next door to the United States. Spent from a terrible Civil War, the recently re-United States were faced with fighting another war to dislodge France from Mexico.

General Dyer was also fully aware of a significant ordnance development in Europe that was changing that continent's political geography. In 1864, while military men there watched the great battles of the American Civil War, armories throughout Europe were raising an alarm. They reported to their respective governments that the Prussian army, paying close attention to events on the American battlefields, had armed itself with a new rifle.

Called the Dreyse needlegun, this new rifle, a breechloader that fired a metallic cartridge, gave the Prussians a significant firepower advantage over all the other European armories stocked with old and now obsolete muzzleloaders. Those other armories were impelled to scramble for new rifle designs while their governments groaned at the great costs they were to incur, throwing away old arms and buying new ones, and spending great sums on the ever-increasing costs of rifle-making machinery. The Dreyse needlegun had raised the ordnance ante in Europe to new heights.

In 1864, Prussia put its new needlegun to work. Allied with Austria, its army confronted Denmark—the first step to unify all the loosely confederated Germanic states into a modern centralized Germany. Britain searched for peace and called for a London Peace Conference. Once there, Prussia adopted an inflexible position, and the talks soon collapsed. The rest of Europe watched helplessly as Prussia returned to the battlefield and gobbled up a big piece of Danish holdings.

All the old power-balancing relationships were upset, and a new urgency dominated every national armory seeking a reply to the Dreyse rifle. That same year, 1864, directly after the collapse of the London Peace Conference, the British government set up the Russel Committee to investigate ways and means of obtaining a modern breech-loading rifle. Even though the faster firepower of the American Spencer and Henry warned Europe—even Prussia—that the era of the repeating rifle had arrived, the British were confining themselves to converting their muzzle-loading Enfields to breech-loading single-shots, believing this would bring them roughly up to parity with the firepower of the Prussian Dreyse breechloaders. Yet some thirteen years were to pass—on July 20, 1877, at the Battle of Plevna in Bulgaria, when the Turkish army carried onto the battlefield two kinds of rifles—before Europe witnessed the unmistakable importance of superior battlefield firepower.

The Russel Committee ran an advertisement to gun designers in Europe and America, seeking muzzle-loading conversion designs. The response was impressive—about fifty systems in all were presented.[1] The British armory required many months to work through all the proposals before finally, in 1867, choosing an American design, the Snider conversion mechanism—which American Ordnance had rejected.

With a new Boxer cartridge developed by a British Army Ordnance colonel, the accuracy of the new Snider system exceeded that of the highly prized Enfield muzzleloader. Called the Snider-Enfield, it fired up to eighteen shots a minute. The British regarded their new weapon as just a quick fix, since, with an unwavering eye on the Prussians' new Dreyse needlegun, they were planning a major new rifle design of their own, possibly a repeater. They were impelled to move even faster when another note of urgency sounded: Prussia had just conquered its erstwhile ally, Austria.[2] Britain then adopted the Enfield-Martini, which featured a superb new falling block action invented by Henry Peabody of Boston—also rejected by American Ordnance.

All these European developments were well known to American Ordnance, as it too sought to upgrade its military rifle. On balance, when General Dyer compared American ordnance with European, he could be pleased with the fine war record his Springfield Armory and its civilian subcontractors had compiled—nearly two million .58-caliber Springfield muzzle-loading rifles produced. But he was also well aware that critics—exponents of the breechloading repeating rifle—were saying that Ordnance had done a superb wartime job of producing the wrong rifle. With the invention of the Dreyse needlegun, only the most conservative Ordnance officer would refuse to recognize that the muzzleloader's day had passed. If there were any Ordnance men left who still contended that breechloaders wasted ammunition, Civil War veterans could reply that muzzleloaders wasted lives. If those battle-scarred veterans—North or South—had been asked what shoulder arm to issue to the peacetime army, there could be little doubt about the answer—a breech-loading, repeating rifle.

Clearly, the repeating rifle and the machine gun were the two weapons to focus on in the postwar armory. It was time to develop both of them more fully; it was time to develop new tactics and strategies to exploit their great potential, particularly since even more sweeping technological changes were in the offing.

But inside the entire American military organization—with a few significant exceptions—there was no searching mind at work anywhere. All the top command of the Union army during the war had disliked new ideas. Even Robert E. Lee had dismissed new ideas and new weaponry out of hand. Nor was there a prospect of getting any fresh thinking: the curriculum and faculty at West Point were as dead set against new ideas as the rest of the military. This was in deep contrast to the Prussian armory, which enforced a policy of seeking out and using new ideas, regardless of source.

In short, the armory was confined basically to making hardware. Dominated by production men, it contained inside its walls, along with the tools and technicians, a number of erroneous fixed ideas.

When General Dyer considered the type of weapon he would furnish to the military, there were certain factors he had to accept as givens. First of all, Congress had decided that the future American army was going to be small, under twenty-five thousand men, a size it was to retain for most of the remainder of the century. Circumstances like the Indian wars and the French in Mexico— indeed, the whole westward thrust of the nation—ensured that it was going to be primarily a western army. The vast distances in the West and the nature of the opposition determined that the postwar army was going to be mounted, which meant cavalry and carbines.[3]

Here the general had three choices: a muzzle-loading carbine, a breech-loading carbine, or a breech-loading repeating carbine. In addition, he had to decide what kind of ammunition the carbine would fire. Ordnance had been resisting the metal cartridge for fifteen years, ever since the French Flobert cap—the first practicable metal cartridge—was shown to the ordnance world at the London Exposition in 1851, ten years before the Civil War. When Tyler Henry saw the Flobert cap there, he immediately seized upon it as a principal component of his Henry repeating rifle to replace the paper cartridge. Christopher Spencer was guided by a brass cartridge case that was based on the Flobert cap when he created his Spencer repeating rifle. Yet U.S. Ordnance, which had dropped the breech-loading rifle in 1842 in part because of the troublesome paper cartridge, saw that same Flobert cap at that same 1851 London Exposition and passed it by. In 1865, by cribbing the metal cartridge technology developed by the Henry and the Spencer repeating rifles, General Dyer introduced a new .57 (.5650)-caliber metal cartridge for the new carbine.

Which carbine? General Dyer returned to the cranky issue of wasted ammunition, the primary reason General Ripley had given to block the introduction of the breech-loading and the repeating rifle. For some, the Civil War had settled that issue: troops could be—had been—trained not to waste ammunition. In the three-day Battle of Gettysburg, men armed with breechloaders fired an average of only thirty-two rounds per man, about ten a day.[4] Still, General Dyer worried about wasted cartridges.

The general's choices finally came down to two—develop a device for his one million obsolete muzzleloaders to create a single-shot breechloader as the British were doing, or standardize on and improve the tens of thousands of repeating rifles and carbines he had in store. Technologically, these repeaters, by turning battles into victories, had proved they were decades in advance of single-shot muzzleloaders. They were the most advanced military weapons in the world, with firing speeds that exceeded even Prussia's deadly bolt-action Dreyse rifle. Winchester Repeating Arms Company had already made improvements on the repeater and was ready to introduce its newest model—just in time for the settlers heading West, who needed a fast-firing weapon to fight off the Indians.

General Dyer came to a startling conclusion: the repeating rifle was obsolete. And he auctioned off tens of thousands of them—Henrys and Spencers. In a stroke, he reduced the firepower of the U.S. Army by a significant factor.

Two elements influenced the general's decision. The first was pressure from Congress. Those million-plus muzzleloaders in storage seemed to flummox the Congress. Debt-ridden after the war and pinching pennies everywhere, it could not accept the destruction of more than one million perfectly good rifles, especially if they could be updated and continue to serve. Also, the Ordnance Department itself, despite battle records, still looked upon repeating rifles with grave doubt. The invitation to the ordinary soldier to waste ammunition was just too strong.

But not everyone believed the repeater was obsolete. The Winchester Repeating Arms Company, bringing out a new model of its own Henry repeating rifle, which was soon to dominate the western market, quickly bought Spencers from the government just to get them off the market. Foreign buyers were eager for the Spencers, too. Faced with a much larger Russian army, Turkey was searching urgently for maximum firepower,[5] and when the Spencer company went out of the arms-making business, the Turkish government stepped in and bought its entire inventory of thirty thousand rifles and looked around for more. Most ominously for the U.S. Army, large numbers of Ordnance's cast-off repeating rifles were bought at auction by gun dealers, who in turn sold them illegally to the gun-hungry Indians.

With the question of the repeating rifles resolved, General Dyer set out to convert the muzzleloader carbine into a single-shot breechloader that would fire his new metal-clad .57-caliber cartridge. He called for an open competition of breech-loading ideas from inventors in America and Europe.

The leading contender was the revolutionary Peabody falling block mechanism, which was patented by Henry Peabody of Boston in July 1862. All through the Civil War, General Dyer had resolutely avoided the Peabody device, although some state militia units had adopted it. Now, in the autumn of 1865, General Dyer had his Ordnance staff take its first serious look at the Peabody, and immediately the accuracy of the device attracted everyone's attention. The Peabody could be fired at the impressive speed of up to seventeen shots a minute.[6]

After this 1865 Ordnance Board had reviewed one by one the other sixty-four contenders, the Peabody emerged as the outstanding leader. Another significant entrant, the American Snider system, was turned down, and in disgust, Snider sailed for England and into the waiting arms of the Russel Committee, which, as noted, adopted his system to convert their muzzle-loading rifles to breechloaders, dubbing their new rifle the Snider-Enfield. Even though it was regarded as an interim weapon, the British considered it the match for the Dreyse needlegun.

General Dyer quickly recommended the Peabody to Congress. But that body refused to appropriate the funds needed to retool and modernize the armory, even though the Peabody was later bought by Canada, Austria, Bavaria, Denmark, France, Mexico, Romania, Switzerland, and England, which designed its new Enfield-Martini around the Peabody's mechanism to replace its interim Snider-Enfield rifle.

Turned down by Congress, General Dyer returned to a design created inside the armory in September 1865 by the armory's own master armorer, Erskine Allin. His mechanism was quite simple. He had cut away a section of the barrel of an obsolete 1863 Springfield just above the trigger mechanism, and placed over it a breech-loading device with a hinged lid like a trapdoor that permitted the insertion of a cartridge.[7] General Dyer had Allin put his "cam lock" conversion through some more tests. Twenty modifications later, it passed the Rifle Board standards and, at last, the United States had a sturdy, reliable breech-loading conversion. Erskine Allin's prototype became the Model 1865 .58-caliber "trap-door" Springfield rifle, the first in a series of trap-door models that were the official army rifles until the 1890s.

Allin's design was excellent, but in a field crowded with other gifted designers, it was inescapably similar to at least fifteen other breech-loading devices, including the French Demondion action, which was introduced in 1831, thirty-five years earlier. The Allin mechanism was soon in court for patent infringement, a suit brought by none other than the founder and leader of the legendary Sharpshooters unit of Civil War fame, Hiram Berdan, who claimed that the new Allin breechblock used his single-joint breechblock. The suit dragged through the courts for nearly thirty years, until, in 1895, the court awarded Berdan's widow a judgment of $95,000.

While the armory was making the first batch of five thousand conversions, General Dyer was taking a critical look at his new .58-caliber metal cartridge and decided it was too powerful for the new Allin conversion. Tests indicated that .50 caliber would be better. Erskine Allin now set out to convert the newly created .58-caliber rifle to the new .50-caliber cartridge. The problem was the old .58-caliber barrel was too large for the new cartridge. To solve that problem, Allin reamed the bore of the barrel and brazed inside a liner of steel. On the Springfield firing range, the new .50-caliber cartridge proved to have much less recoil kick than the .58-caliber cartridge. Easier to hold when fired, rifles loaded with the new cartridge were therefore more accurate. Even in this patched-up form, the converted rifle with its new longer-range cartridge was a more powerful and more accurate rifle than the 1861 muzzleloader from which it had been made. With the addition of the simple trap-door breech mechanism, the armory increased the firepower of the Springfield '61 from three shots a minute muzzle-loaded to eight shots a minute breech-loaded.[8] Nearly three times the firepower from the same rifle—and it could have been made in 1861.

Now, all General Dyer needed was some conclusive battle somewhere to demonstrate the worth of the new weapon. He didn't get it against Maximilian in Mexico. That hapless emperor, abandoned by his French troops and left defenseless in a nation of angry Mexicans, was captured and executed in 1867. Instead, General Dyer got the proof he wanted in August 1867, out in Wyoming Territory.

To protect frontier travelers and wagon trains from determined Indian raids, the U.S. cavalry had set up a series of cavalry forts along the Bozeman Trail, which skirts the Bighorn Mountains on its way northwest to Montana. At the end of July 1867, the Powder

River Indian bands met for their annual sun dance on the Little Bighorn River. The Cheyenne Dog Soldiers and Oglala Sioux dominated the great gathering, but there were also Sans Arc Sioux and Miniconjou Sioux and Arapahos.

After the sun dance, they met in war council and planned the destruction of both Fort Phil Kearny and Fort C. F. Smith. While an irregular combination of some eight hundred Indians rode to Fort Smith, the great chief, Red Cloud himself, led one thousand Indians to Fort Phil Kearny.

Several miles from Fort Smith, the Indians came upon a planted field of hay that was being harvested by twelve civilian mowing-machine operators. They were protected by nineteen soldiers armed with the new Springfield breechloaders and new metallic bullets, which the Indians had never confronted before. One of the operators was armed with a Henry repeating rifle. For defense, they had only several log fences.

Armed with bows and arrows, the Indians pounced. The Springfields drove them back. They tried again and were thrown back again. And again they charged and fell back. At last, they dismounted and tried a fourth time. The Springfields shattered their charge. A relief column from the fort finally drove the Indians off. Outnumbered by more than twenty to one, the new Springfields had held off the attackers for six hours. Cavalry casualties: three killed and two wounded.[9]

The next day, August 2, 1867, Chief Red Cloud struck. Five miles west of Fort Phil Kearny, under the protective eye of a detail of cavalrymen, civilian woodcutters were harvesting logs for the walls of the incomplete fort. The cavalry had erected a corral composed of fourteen wagon boxes with their wheels removed. Inside the corral were penned a herd of mules. The Indians announced their presence by driving off the mules.

Captain James F. Powell, caught by surprise, managed to gather thirty-two men—including four civilians—inside the wagon box corral. The new Springfields broke up the attack. Then another and another. A relief column from the fort drove off Chief Red Cloud. In the four-hour battle, outnumbered possibly thirty to one, the new Springfield had proven itself again. The Indians sustained well over 150 casualties. Of the defenders, seven were killed and two wounded.

The lesson for the army: the greater firepower of the new breechloader was the principal factor in turning back the Indian raids. The old muzzleloaders would probably have been overrun. The lesson for the Indians: replace the bow and arrow with rifles. In Washington, no one asked how well the new Springfield breechloader would fare against Indians armed with auctioned Civil War repeaters.

Cavalry officers were not impressed with the performance of the cavalry carbine version of the new rifle. In a mounted skirmish, one officer stated, the single-shot carbine was no match for the bow and arrow, which was just as accurate at close range and which could be fired faster, especially with the notorious carbine marksmanship of the new recruits, who were more likely to hit a horse, a fellow cavalryman, or themselves.[10]

While officially the army was praising the new breech-loading Springfield, on the banks of the Arikara, a stream in Colorado few people had ever heard of, a warning finger was raised to the Ordnance Department. On September 17, 1868, on the Republican River in Colorado, to test the effectiveness of combining frontiersmen, scouts, and Indian fighters into a single military unit, Major George A. Forsyth and a group of fifty were moving up the Arikara fork of the Republican River, near the border of Colorado, Nebraska, and Kansas. They were armed with Spencer repeating carbines.

When they stopped to set up camp on Beecher's Island, they came under a furious surprise attack by a force of six to seven hundred warriors—Oglala Sioux and Cheyenne Dog Soldiers. Three times, the mounted Indians attacked, and three times volleys from the Spencers shattered the attack. For seven days, the scouts and their Spencer carbines held off the Indians until, from Fort Wallace some eighty miles to the southeast, Tenth Cavalry Buffalo Soldiers rescued them. Major Forsyth had been shot twice in the leg, and nearly half his men had been killed.[11]

But as a result of the Battle of Beecher's Island, the army got what it went after: it had clear proof of the great fighting effectiveness of frontiersmen, scouts, and Indian fighters operating as a military unit. As a bonus, the army gathered still more evidence of the murderous effectiveness of repeating Spencers. It seemed also clear to anyone who read the reports that if Forsyth and his men had been armed with new Springfield .50-caliber single-shot carbines, they would not have survived.

The army's reaction was to disband the scout unit. General Dyer took back the few remaining Spencers and commenced arming the entire U.S. cavalry with the new single-shot carbines. The net effect was: just at a time when thousands of Indians were rising up to defend their lands, Congress had undermanned the army and General Dyer had underarmed the men.

Beginning in 1866, the most controversial events seemed to center on one of the most controversial figures of the whole period. On October 7 of that year, in Monroe, Michigan, George Armstrong Custer, the golden-haired, blue-eyed, dashing cavalry hero of the Civil War, was rescued from the worst fate a military man can face—peacetime—when he was given the peacetime rank of lieutenant colonel in the U.S. Army and ordered to proceed to Fort Riley, Kansas, and there take command of the newly raised Seventh Cavalry. His wife, Libbie—Elizabeth Bacon Custer—packed to go with him.

Out on the great plains waiting for him and his newly formed cavalry was a score of tribes—including the Cheyenne Dog Soldiers, the Sioux, the Oglala Sioux, the Pawnee, the Piutes, the Comanche, the Apaches, the Kiowa, the Arapaho, the Ute, and all the other lesser tribes and subtribes fighting to hold their traditional territories against the land-hungry sodbuster, the feverish gold hunter, and the remorseless railroad. Superb guerrilla fighters, they were led by superb leaders—including Crazy Horse, Sitting Bull, Black Kettle, Geronimo, Red Cloud, Chief Joseph, Spotted Tail, Santanta, Satank, Big Tree, and Mescalero.[12]

Bringing with him his designer uniforms, his brilliant talents, and a relentless gnawing ambition, accompanied by four horses, a clutch of dogs, cages of canaries and mockingbirds, a passel of trunks and bags, and his wife, Custer eagerly boarded the train westward to confront the waiting tribes. Astonishingly, this walking Civil War legend was still only twenty-seven. He was soon to become one of the most controversial figures in all of U.S. military history.

George Armstrong Custer's personality was an amalgamation of the most contradictory elements one could find in a single human being. Six feet tall and lean as a cowboy, with blond hair he often wore down to his shoulders, piercing, deeply set blue eyes above high cheekbones, a sharp nose, and a full-grown blond mustache, he was a much-admired horseman. Clad in his unique pale-blue tunic and red scarf, he was considered quite handsome by many women, including Indian women, one of whom, the seventeen-year-old daughter of the famous chief Black Kettle, was said to have borne him a blond-haired son.

As a cadet at West Point, Custer revealed none of the traits that later made him a legend. Scholastically, he ran dead last— thirty-fourth in a class of thirty-four; further, he accumulated so many demerits for poor conduct and slovenliness, he barely escaped expulsion. To cap off his cadet life, he was court-martialed for failure as duty officer to break up a fight between two other cadets and, as a result, almost missed the Civil War.

So undistinguished a student, showing no future promise of any kind, Custer in a normal peacetime year might have been dropped by West Point, but in 1861, the army desperately needed trained officers, and he graduated scant days before the First Battle of Bull Run of 1861. The greenest of the green officers, he literally galloped out of his schoolboy classroom into that battle and into a fabled cavalry career.

The top command first noticed him at the Chickahominy, where his brilliant reconnaissance activities revealed a combination of shrewd war sense, utter fearlessness, and unhesitating eagerness to attack. General George McClellan promptly selected him for his staff, and by 1863, his inspired leadership and courage earned him the rank of brigadier general of volunteers with command of the Michigan cavalry brigade. He was barely twenty-five, the youngest general in the army.

Few other men gained the battlefield glory that gathered around Custer. At the Battle of Gettysburg, his highly praised tactics delayed the efforts of Jeb Stuart and his cavalry to link up with Lee, which is believed to be one of the factors that led to Lee's defeat. Sharing some of the glory and legend with him was the Spencer rifle his troops were armed with there. In the Wilderness and the Shenandoah Valley, as part of Sheridan's cavalry campaign, Custer performed outstanding service. In the Battle of Woodstock, he led a brilliant action, and in the Battle of Cedar Creek was conspicuous for his dazzling tactics. In the last year of the war, he accompanied Sheridan in his last great cavalry raid, won the action of Waynesboro, fought bravely at Five Forks, and as a grand finale, led the last Union cavalry charge of the war at Appomattox Court House, which hastened the South's surrender.

As Richmond was falling, he capped his military career by riding into that city, and with Libbie in his arms slept in the Confederate White House in the bed of Confederate president Jefferson Davis. General Phil Sheridan saluted Custer's brilliant contributions to the winning of the war by presenting Custer's wife with one of the greatest trophies of the entire Civil War—the small table on which General Grant had written the terms of surrender in General Lee's presence.[13]

In 1865, in peacetime, with garlands, praise, and fame showering on him, this ideal dashing cavalry hero and national legend became an unemployed ex-cavalryman, seemingly with his greatest moments behind him, a warrior with no war, and only twenty-seven. He was saved by his orders to report to Fort Riley, Kansas.

In the West, a darker side to the man was revealed. He accumulated bitter enemies. Fellow officers faulted him for a boundless ego and an unslakable thirst for fame. He was hagridden by ambition, they said, and his leading trait was selfishness. He was accused of using other people shamelessly and often badly and of taking advantage of easygoing superiors.

His personality in private life differs sharply with this public persona. He was a tender, loving husband to his doting wife, with whom he exchanged touching love letters and shared poetry readings. He never swore and rarely drank. He could be deeply sensitive to scenes from plays and novels, but, with equal insensitivity, he would describe how he watched the last agonizing death throes of the first man he killed in battle. He often wore the man's sword.

On the plains, other traits were to reveal themselves. In November 1867, he was court-martialed for, among other things, brutal treatment of troops and for being AWOL. Some contended that he was the victim of army politics, that the charges were trumped up, that he was being made the culprit for the badly planned and failed Indian campaign of his superior officer, General Hancock. Nonetheless, the charges held up: Custer was found guilty and suspended for one year without pay.

An impulsive officer, prone to act too quickly and with inadequate information, he was accused of relying too heavily on that incredible "Custer luck" that time and again had rescued him from the disastrous dilemmas his impulsiveness had created. He was afflicted with a childish, furious temper and a juvenile vengefulness.

A few men idolized him. Most eventually hated him. Some said he was mad. A large number openly, publicly condemned him. One officer later described him as cold, dishonest, unscrupulous, universally despised. But from the Indians, his capacity as a warrior initially won him great respect and admiration. They called him Strong Arm and Big Chief Yellowhair and later Son of the Morning Star.

One of Custer's most controversial actions took place on November 27, 1868, before Ordnance had replaced the "obsolete" Spencer carbine with the new trap-door Springfield carbine.

At dawn, to implement General Phil Sheridan's policy of attacking Indians in their encampments during the bitterly cold winter months, burning their tepees, destroying their food stores, and killing their horses, Custer and eight hundred cavalrymen attacked a sleeping Cheyenne encampment along the Washita River valley in Oklahoma during a heavy snowfall in subzero temperatures. Custer's famous impetuousness drove deep into the Indian camp, but he discovered that he had galloped into a large winter encampment of many bands of Cheyenne, Arapaho, Comanche, and Kiowa that stretched for ten miles down the Washita Valley. He had great-ly overmatched himself.

After destroying large stores of winter food and nearly nine hun-dred Indian horses, Custer feinted a charge directly down the valley, causing the attacking Indians to hasten back to their camps to pro-tect their families. Seizing the opportunity to break off the fake at-tack, Custer escaped.

The incident caused controversy. Custer's action was highly praised by General Sheridan because it demonstrated that winter attacks on Indian villages and food supplies could severely hamper the Indians' ability to fight. Other officers, however, accused him of abandoning Major Joel H. Elliot and nineteen men who were cut off, encircled, and slaughtered by the Cheyenne, their bodies muti-lated by Cheyenne squaws. They also said that many of the one hundred dead Indians were women and children. Although others defended Custer, insisting that all the dead were Indian braves, the criticism was to follow him until the day he died. The Indians now nicknamed him "Squaw Killer."

On one fact there was no dispute. A key element in Custer's suc-cess in the Washita was the Spencer repeater carbine his troops car-ried—which Ordnance had deemed "obsolete." He was outnumbered, but the Indians were outgunned. If he had had less firepower, he would have died in that valley along with all his troops.

Perhaps General Dyer believed the stories of the dead Indian squaws and children and blamed that on Custer's troops being caught up in blood lust caused by their repeating arms and too much ammunition. Shortly after the Washita campaign, the general removed the repeating Spencer from the army arsenal and replaced it with some thirty thousand leftover single-shot breech-loading Sharps cavalry carbines that had been converted from the old Civil War paper cartridge to the new .50-caliber metal cartridge.

Then, to make all arms of uniform caliber and quality, the gener-al drafted a plan to acquire a new single-shot rifle and a companion single-shot carbine. In 1872, he ordered Springfield Armory to conduct field trials. With Congress's blessing, General Dyer ordered General Alfred H. Terry, the wealthy bachelor, bon vivant, and famous Indian fighter, to convene an army board with himself as president in order to settle on one uniform system of breech-loading rifles and carbines.[14] What followed was the armory's largest, most comprehensive study of small arms in decades. And it represented a singular opportunity for the army to rearm its troops with the most modern rifle and carbine designs in the world.

Spread before the Rifle Board was an armorer's feast of rifle ideas. One hundred and eight rifle models were submitted, including ten repeaters, and as an index of the importance of American gun designers in world ordnance, only nine of the designs submitted were not American. Perhaps the most important submissions were the dozen bolt-action rifles—a design that was replacing every other type of military rifle in Europe.[15] Prussia had introduced one of the first successful bolt actions in the 1840s, the Dreyse needle-gun, with which Germany was claiming one victory after another. The most important new bolt action was A. A. Chassepot's design, which had been adopted by the French army in 1866 and which was to be modified by Gras two years later, in 1874, to fire a metallic cartridge. The attraction of this weapon design was its increased firing and reloading speed over the trap-door rifle.

After all the testing and talking, economy dominated the decision. The 1872 Rifle Board, probably with one eye on the parsimonious Congress, passed by a number of truly modern weapons and decided to refurbish the Springfield-Allin trap-door single-shot, which was itself a refurbishment of the Springfield '61 muzzle-loader. This decision enabled the armory to continue to use present tooling in which it had a large investment. Acknowledging the limitations of the old, relined Civil War rifle barrels, the armory now fitted out the Springfield single-shot rifle and carbine with a new barrel. In fact, starting with 1873, all Springfield rifles were made from new parts. Finally, the Springfield was rechambered for a new smaller caliber—.45, down from the previous .50 caliber. This meant that the thirty thousand Sharps single-shot carbines that had been refitted for .50-caliber cartridges would have to be refitted again for the .45 cartridge or junked. They were junked.

So, only a few years after the fact, the million old breechloaders from the Civil War that Congress tried to save were finally sold for scrap along with the last of the repeating rifle inventory.

In reality, the new model was an improvement, taking a cut-rate rifle made from used Civil War rifle parts, making it from new parts, and fitting it for a new, more accurate caliber. The reworked model was designated the Springfield 1873.[16] One colonel bestowed an accolade on the new Springfield '73, calling it "a first rate rifle, and probably the best that was ever placed in the hands of troops."[17]

As the 108 submissions demonstrated, rapidly changing technology had made the Springfield 1873 trap-door obsolete even before it was put into production. Worse, the new Springfield '73 carbine, made for the cavalry fighting the Indians, was judged by some experts—ominously, as events were to show—to be too light for the rigors of western duty.

In 1874, in Washington, D.C., after ten years in office, General Alexander Dyer died. As a former commandant of the Springfield Armory, he had been a strong proponent of the single-shot armory rifle, which was designed for slow, long-distance fire and conservation of ammunition. He would be remembered as the chief of ordnance who had armed the "Indian Constabulary," as critics termed the U.S. cavalry, with Springfield single-shot carbines.

CHAPTER 17

GENERAL BENÉT
VERSUS
THE BOLT-ACTION RIFLE

General Dyer's replacement, Stephen Vincent Benét, was to reign as chief of ordnance some seventeen years—from 1874 to 1891.

Born in Florida in 1827, Benét was descended from a Louisiana French family. He originally set out to be a lawyer, and before reaching his teens, under his father's direction, had read his way through *Blackstone's Commentaries*, the basic text for the study of law in both England and the United States. Even after his graduation from West Point in 1849 as a career Ordnance officer, he continued his interest in the law, his *Military Law and the Practice of Court-Martial* being so well received it went through several editions. A fluid writer completely fluent in French, he translated the classic treatise on war by General Antoine Jomini,[1] and, in his personal correspondence as well as in the articles he wrote for newspapers and magazines under various pseudonyms, primarily while an Ordnance officer in St. Louis under future Ordnance Chief Ramsay, he revealed a gift for poetic imagery. This talent foreshadowed the literary careers of his two grandsons, Stephen Vincent Benét, who received the Pulitzer Prize in 1928 for *John Brown's Body*, a narrative ballad about the Civil War, and William Rose Benét, who won the Pulitzer Prize in 1941 for his verse autobiography, *The Dust Which Is God*, and who also co-founded the *Saturday Review*, a literary journal.

As proud of his southern heritage as he was of his French, Benét nonetheless rejected secession and retained his commission in the

Union army. During the Civil War, he drew President Lincoln's attention when, as an Ordnance captain at West Point, he tested the Marsh breech-loading conversion rifle, endorsing it with some enthusiasm. By temperament the opposite of General Ripley, he looked with favor on new inventions and eagerly tested them. Such an attitude quickly found favor with Lincoln, and Benét was asked by the president to test a number of other weapons during the Civil War. At the Frankford Arsenal in Philadelphia, his endorsement of the Gatling machine gun helped earn its acceptance by the Union army. His son, Laurence, was to invent the Benét-Mercié, a French machine gun that became involved in the great machine-gun controversy of World War I.

When General Benét assumed command of the Ordnance Bureau in 1874, there was an unresolved issue in the U.S. military organization that Congress should have addressed but didn't: the relationship between the secretary of war and the commanding officer of the army. The secretary of war's seat in the Cabinet was a political plum, more or less an empty sinecure, the secretary deferring all decisions to the commanding officer, General William Sherman, or to his bureau chiefs. The bureau chiefs, including chief of ordnance, were left more or less to go their own ways, seemingly ensconced in perpetuity in their positions until death or infirmity—or Congress—removed them.

The army was primarily a museum bent on preserving the Civil War in amber. The top officers, all veterans with thrice-told war stories, behaved like curators, reliving and brooding over events of that great conflict. The heroes of the battles had become gods. Everything was carefully dusted and left exactly as it was, no change permitted anywhere. The centerpiece of war was the now glorified 1861 Springfield muzzle-loading rifle that had won the Civil War.[2]

General M. C. Meigs, quartermaster general from 1861 to 1884, stated the widely held attitude of the army command: "The methods that won the Civil War," he asserted, "represent a perfection that cannot be improved upon."[3]

While the nation followed newspaper reports of the cavalry's battles with the Indians, elsewhere, the army was in a thirty-year sleep. The haughty Ordnance Bureau, with its Riplian aloofness and trussing regulations, came in for its usual criticism from other military branches and from civilian bureau heads. Critics said the Ordnance Bureau motto was: "Invincible in peace, invisible in war."[4] Naval Ordnance came in for its share of hostility. Navy men still remembered that naval cannons had performed badly during the Civil War. While enemy fire had killed eleven gunner's mates operating those cannon, friendly fire, mainly exploding cannon, had killed forty-five. In peacetime, sailors were afraid to fire their weapons while Congress was not eager to pay for the ammunition.[5] The navy fell into the hands of the Washington pork-barrelers. Ship repairs became a source of corrupt payoffs, and the new cry of the navy shipyards was: "Don't give up the ship." The decline of the nascent U.S. Navy was so great, a British report said, "there never was such a hopeless, broken down, tattered, forlorn apology for a navy as that possessed by the United States."[6]

With no visible enemies, the country had no visible armed force—except the cavalry, which was pursuing a policy that was leading inexorably to the battles at Little Bighorn and Wounded Knee.

Two years before Bighorn, Custer's Seventh Cavalry was ordered into the Black Hills of South Dakota. Its main purpose was spelled out in a telegram from Custer's superior officer, General Phil Sheridan, which commanded him to prepare an expedition "to investigate rumors of large gold deposits & survey area for possible establishment of Military Posts."[7]

A new Black Hills military post, built near the Sioux villages, would give the Seventh Cavalry a base from which to blunt Sioux raids by retaliating with punishing strikes against their unguarded villages. Custer and his one-thousand-man troop were accompanied by an army mapmaker and mining engineer, plus a paleontologist-zoologist from Yale, a geologist-archaeologist from Minnesota, and a stereoscopic photographer.[8] As armed cavalrymen watched, the "scientific corps" studied the ground and panned the waters of the streams.

Custer wrote to General Sheridan the findings of the science team, which claimed that gold was found during panning operations, and, improbable as it seems, even in the roots of the prairie grass. Someone leaked the story to the newspapers and soon neither the Indians nor the cavalry could handle the situation. Before the winter of 1875–1876 fully set in, fifteen thousand well-armed gold strikers, with axes, shovels, and picks, were trampling all over the Indians' sacred Black Hills.

By sending the Seventh Cavalry into the Black Hills, Washington had violated a solemn treaty with the Cheyenne and the Sioux; by purportedly finding gold, it destroyed them. The Sioux and the Cheyenne were fiercely independent, and they had fought with great ferocity to prevent the Union Pacific Railroad from crossing their land, mounting raid after raid from their Black Hills villages. They were known to attack other tribes that agreed to make peace with the white man. Now the presence of thousands of gold-hungry miners on their sacred land drove them to even more ferocity. Washington decided to settle the Indian question once and for all. It would buy the Black Hills and put the Sioux-Cheyenne on a reservation, along with all the other Indians. But the Sioux and the Cheyenne, passionately attached to their Black Hills and to their freedom, absolutely refused to sell or to be corraled into the white man's reservation.

In the winter of 1875, a directive from the U.S. Bureau of Indian Affairs ordering all Indians onto federally designated reservations by January 31, 1876, set off a series of battles that led to the cavalry's final showdown with Sitting Bull and heavily armed Sioux and Cheyenne.[9]

For nearly a decade, the Plains Indians, having learned the bitter lessons of the Hayfield Fight and the Wagon Box Fight in 1867, and of Custer's devastating raid in the Washita Valley of Oklahoma, had become eager customers of a thriving illicit gun trade, buying or stealing, or gleaning from battlefields, great quantities of rifles, pistols, and ammunition. The preferred weapons were repeating rifles and carbines, ideal weapons for mounted warriors. When the U.S. cavalry set out to drive the Indians onto reservations, the Indians were ready and waiting for the cavalry.

On June 15, 1876, while the United States was preparing for its one hundredth birthday with a coast-to-coast July Fourth Centennial Gala, Custer's Seventh Cavalry entered the Black Hills of Montana, moving toward a battle that military historians and ordnance men have been debating ever since. Hastily, impatiently, Custer led his troop of 650 cavalry up the Rosebud River to the mouth of the Little Bighorn Valley, where he hoped to bottle up an encampment of Hunkpapa Sioux and Cheyenne. Custer was impatient to accomplish his assignment, and in his impatience, he left behind two pieces of equipment: two Gatling guns. As he entered the valley of the Little Bighorn River, Custer split his force of 650 into three units. He personally led a mounted unit of some 210 men. They were armed with the pride of the U.S. Ordnance Corps—the new 1873 single-shot, trap-door Springfield carbine. Among its virtues, said the Ordnance Corps, the new Springfield, by forcing the troops to reload each time they fired, discouraged them from wasting ammunition.

Advance Crow scouts hastened to report to Custer that they had seen in the far distance an Indian encampment along the Little Bighorn River. Custer faced a dilemma. He had no idea of the size of the Indian force ahead of him. His forces were split. His troops and their horses were spent from a thirty-mile day march and a ten-mile night march. He had turned off the course prescribed in General Terry's battle plan—disobeyed orders, many said later—so he was not where Gibbon and Terry, coming from the north, expected to find him. If he delayed taking action, he was afraid that the Indian encampment would escape south before he could block the river valley exit. Yet if he attacked now, it would be a day earlier than the battle plan called for, before Gibbon's and Terry's troops were in position at the other end of the valley. Given the choice of attacking or delaying, Custer's reaction was predictable. Expecting the Indians to follow their custom of avoiding pitched battles by retreating, he decided to drive them north toward Gibbon's troops. Custer attacked.

This time, the Indians were in much larger numbers than Custer expected and this time they didn't retreat. They were waiting for him. From a crest, Custer had one long glimpse of Major Reno's unit under furious attack. By the time he realized that he was facing a huge encampment of Sioux and Cheyenne three miles long, retreat was no longer possible. Needing a great dose of Custer luck, Custer's unit of two hundred troops galloped into battle. Galloping directly at them were fifteen hundred Sioux.[10] And, this time, they were fully armed with illegally gotten rifles and carbines. Custer was trapped just where the Indians wanted him—in open terrain with no cover. Custer's force was quickly surrounded and beleaguered. His troops shot their horses and lay prone behind the carcasses. The battle lasted an hour, perhaps less. Every man in Custer's unit died, including Custer, possibly by his own hand.[11] The 1873 single-shot Springfield carbine had gone up against Spencer, Henry, and Winchester repeaters. Later, critics contended that many of the new Springfield carbines at the Little Bighorn had jammed.[12]

Custer's fellow cavalry officer, Colonel Mackenzie, spoke for most cavalrymen when he made a request in writing that Ordnance replace his regiment's Springfield carbines with repeating Winchesters. The reply from Ordnance Chief Benét in Washington could have been written by General Ripley. The Winchester's range, the general said, was one hundred yards shorter than the Springfield's and its penetrating power less by one-half: request denied.[13]

There was one other element that might have made Custer victorious: superior firepower of a different kind—the two Gatling machine guns he left behind. General Miles, who fought the Indians for much of his career, seemed to speak for most cavalry officers when he said the Gatling was worthless against them. Its range was no better than the rifle, and the bullets were so small "you cannot tell where they strike."[14]

Miles was answered by the famous artillery expert, Colonel Henry J. Hunt, who had been chief of artillery of the Army of the Potomac during the Civil War.[15] The western cavalrymen's care of the weapon was a disgrace, Hunt said. Cavalrymen, considering it an offense to be required to handle the Gatling, hated the weapon. Through slovenly maintenance, they permitted a buildup of black powder residue that would cause the Gatling to foul, overheat, and jam. And this reinforced the cavalry's hostility toward this highly valuable weapon. The fault, Hunt said, lay with the men, not with the weapon. Properly maintained, the Gatling would fire reliably up to seven hundred rounds a minute—a truly devastating weapon. Making matters worse, to draw the despised Gatlings, the cavalry used condemned cavalry horses that were often unable to keep up with a fast-moving column. The Gatling gun, Hunt continued, should not be handled by cavalrymen, who hated the weapon, or even by infantrymen, but by trained artillerymen. And it should be drawn by healthy, well-trained animals. Yet, Hunt added, Custer didn't even have rough terrain and bad horses as an excuse, for the cavalry had been given Gatlings specially designed for cavalry use, easily disassembled and transported by pack mules, then fired either from muleback or by tripod on the ground.[16] Furthermore, Custer could have had not two but four Gatlings—now greatly advanced from the Civil War model, and featuring ten revolving barrels fed by a hopper and fired by a crank. Firing a deadly barrage of seven hundred rounds a minute, the Gatling was the perfect weapon to use on a horde of mounted Indians galloping in a circle like a carousel. Custer made a fatal mistake in leaving his Gatlings behind, Hunt asserted. And if he had taken all four, he would soon have been looking for more Indians to shoot at. Instead, General Hunt said, in his impatience and "arrogant bravado," Custer died as a result.[17]

The Indians' reluctance to face machine guns and artillery was well known and, if nothing else, the Gatling guns might have bought Custer the time needed for help to arrive.

If cavalry officers disagreed with this celebrated artilleryman, it is noteworthy that, following Little Bighorn, the army formed a new cavalry and infantry school at Fort Leavenworth. An important addition to the new cavalry unit: artillerymen—carefully trained and drilled in the use of the portable Gatling gun, drawn by healthy horses.

In retrospect, the worst flaws of the peacetime army had shown up at Little Bighorn. Green troops, single-shot carbines, jammed weapons, bad strategy, bad tactics, disobeyed orders, and left-at-home Gatling guns—all this conspired to wipe them out. In spite of the growing legend of the Winchester repeating rifle, in spite of the object lesson of Little Bighorn, Ordnance Chief Benét rejected the idea that the single-shot Springfield had inadequate firepower and continued to ignore calls by the cavalry to be armed with the fast-firing, lever-action Winchester. Instead, he directed the armory to continue to develop and refine the single-shot rifle, while quietly, a few years later, arming several cavalry units with the same "short-ranged" Winchester model many Indians had carried.

While the wrangling over Custer's ordnance continued, ordnance men all over Europe were talking about a new military rifle that the new nation of Germany had introduced.

On January 17, 1871, in the palace of Versailles in France, with fanfare and panoply, the birth of the new German Empire had been proclaimed. Under the brilliant diplomatic maneuvering of the Prussian Otto von Bismarck and the stunning military victories of the Prussian army, the German Empire was forged in war from a loose confederation of semi-independent German states. The militaristic Prussians swallowed Denmark's Schleswig-Holstein in one bite, overran Austria to eliminate her influence, then humiliated France in 1871 with a victory that claimed two French departments, Alsace and Lorraine, which were duly ceded to Germany in a surrender ceremony in France's palace of Versailles.

In a few short years, Germany became not only the newest nation on the continent; she soon became the most powerful, militarily and economically, dominating the entire continent and completely changing all the old power balances. Many feared that Germany was about to conquer all of Europe. Lights were burning late at night in the foreign chanceries in every capital.

Prussian military men credited their stunning successes to their innovative military tactics and to their Dreyse needlegun, the first successful European bolt-action breechloader. It fired a now-obsolete paper cartridge similar to the earlier breech-loading American Hall's rifle that was discontinued by American Ordnance in the early 1840s. Adopting it in 1864, Prussia had made the muzzleloaders of all the other powers—including the United States—obsolete. The Dreyse had become the terror of Europe.

The Germans themselves had been so impressed with their Dreyse rifle that for a long time they had shut their eyes to any other weapon. But of all the military staffs in Europe, the Germans were the most open to new ideas—and they didn't care where they came from. So by the time of the Franco-Prussian War (1870–1871), realism reasserted itself among German military leaders—every other nation was looking for a rifle that could beat the frightening Dreyse, and the Germans realized that it, too, would soon be obsolete. So they set out to find a successor. In 1871, in a small town in Germany, at a rifle designer's workbench, German ordnance officers found what they were looking for. His name was Peter Paul Mauser and he was a small arms genius.[18]

Mauser was born in Oberndorf in 1838, the thirteenth of thirteen children. The son of a gunsmith and the brother of four others, he started as an apprentice under them in the government firearms factory in Oberndorf. In 1859, at twenty-one, he was drafted into the army, where he had the opportunity to study the Dreyse rifle in action. Back in the armory, he soon had a steady correspondence going with his brother, Franz, who was now working for Remington Arms in New York, and so had continuing access to the torrent of new weapons designs that were flowing from gun shops in America.

As the first step in designing a new rifle, Mauser had turned his attention to designing a metallic cartridge, and Franz sent him abundant information on American metallic cartridge designs. By 1865, Mauser had succeeded in designing his own metallic cartridge. Using it as a keystone, he brilliantly solved a series of engineering problems that had plagued some of the other bolt-action breechloader designs and thereby developed one of the first successful metallic-cartridge bolt-action rifles.

A key feature was his system of automatic cam cocking, which ended the bolt action's dangerous tendency to fire accidentally. Another was a powerful locking mechanism action and breech seal strong enough to withstand the great pressures generated by the powerful military cartridges that were appearing. This was brilliant work for any arms engineer at any age, but particularly for twenty-six-year-old Mauser. Even so, the Prussians, still happy with the Dreyse needlegun at that time, at first rejected his Mauser. But, by 1871, the Germans took a new hard look at the work of Mauser and his brother and business partner, Wilhelm, and issued a contract with which Mauser developed the first successful military bolt action, the M71 Infanteriegewehr. The Germans had their Dreyse successor. They also had found a weapons design genius who could help them dominate all of Europe for many decades.

Mauser's weapons designs were drawn from his close observation of actual battlefield conditions, and no battle was ever to teach him a more profound lesson about battlefield firepower than the war between Russia and Turkey in the summer of 1877, which he saw as a military observer.

In that summer of 1877, Osman Pasha, a Turkish general, went to war and, on the battlefield, taught the rest of the world a stunning lesson about firepower that changed warfare permanently.

On July 20, 1877, 100,000 Russian troops moved through Romania and crowded into the little town of Plevna in Bulgaria to confront 80,000 Turkish troops. All attempts to mediate the Russo-Turkish confrontation had failed. The old Ottoman Empire, having rotted from within, was near collapse. Two years before, it had reneged on payments due on its international debt and was now on the verge of bankruptcy. Big pieces of it had broken away to form separate nations. To preserve what was left, Turkey was slaughtering dissident minority populations within its borders. Czarist Russia, in the grip of a passionate Pan-Slav movement, sought to protect Slav populations inside Bulgaria, an unwilling Turkish province, by sending an army there. So did Turkey. Expecting a quick Russian victory, military observers the world over watched as the two armies formed up for battle. No one could have predicted what was about to happen.

The Russian army considered itself modern, well trained, well equipped, and well motivated. The rifle it carried was invented by Hiram Berdan, the founder and leader of Berdan's Sharpshooters from the U.S. Civil War. These Berdans were loaded with specially designed .42-caliber bottle-necked cartridges. Other Russian units were armed with the .63-caliber Bohemian Sylvester Krinka breech-loading rifle. The Turkish army was felt to be badly led, with an indecisive high command, troops of questionable morale, and arms of doubtful effectiveness. The Turks, however, were led by a man with a plan: General Osman, a highly decorated, battle-hardened ex-cavalryman who had several major military victories to his credit.

On June 22, Russian troops crossed the Danube River and entered Bulgaria. To counter them, Osman Pasha took up a position on the hills north and east of the city of Plevna. On July 20, without preliminary reconnaissance, Russian general Schilder-Schuldner advanced his infantry division in four columns. They attacked General Osman, who then counterattacked. The astonished Russians fell back, turned, and fled. Osman didn't pursue but instead dug in. Around the clock for days, his troops worked on their fortifications: four-foot entrenchments, ten- to sixteen-foot redoubts, fourteen-foot-thick parapets. When he was finished, he had entrenched himself in the Russians' right flank of communication. In a sense, he had seized the Russians by the windpipe; he completely blocked their way south into Turkey while threatening their vital bridge-heads across the Danube. Osman Pasha had to be removed.

This time, the Russians sent General Krudener. He brought forty thousand men with him and 176 guns. Facing them, Krudener knew, the well-entrenched Turks were armed with Peabody-Martini rifles. His intelligence had also informed him that the Turkish cavalry had been armed with some thirty thousand Winchester repeaters. Tyler Henry's latest lever-action tube-loading rifle was the first to bear the name Winchester. The American firm had chambered these rifles specifically for the Turkish .44 rimfire cartridge.

General Krudener aimed an overwhelming blow at Osman, and on July 30, the huge Russian advance began. With it, heavy Turkish defensive rifle fire began, felling Russian troops at well over one thousand yards. At five hundred yards, the Turkish trenches were capped with clouds of smoke from their Peabody-Martinis, firing volley after volley into the advancing Russian line. The massed units of Russians pressed on, revealing large gaps in their lines left by fallen soldiers. At two hundred yards, the slaughter stopped momentarily. The Russians had taken a terrible punishment; the casualties were far greater than General Krudener had expected. But the Russians believed that victory was at hand. They charged—right into a Turkish trap.

The Russian troops were about to learn what Russian intelligence had failed to discover. The Turkish cavalry had been disarmed, and their Winchesters had been turned over to the Turkish infantry, making it the world's first two-rifle army, armed with both the single-shot Peabody-Martini for long range and the repeating Winchester for fast-fire short range. As the Russian troops charged, the Turks laid down their single-shot Peabody-Martinis and picked up their cavalry's lever-action Winchester repeaters. Each infantryman had one hundred cartridges, and beside him a box with five hundred more. The Russian charge slowed, then stopped and turned into a Russian retreat, rout, and terrible slaughter. Some ten thousand Russian troops were in the charge. Less than three thousand came back; more than seventy-three hundred men were lost. Bodies lay all over the battlefield as the Russians went reeling back.

In their retreat, the Russians, expecting Turkish pursuit, had left the vital Danube bridge completely undefended, only forty miles away from Osman and his troops. All Osman had to do was seize the bridge and thereby shut the entire Russian army off from its supply lines into Russia and proceed to destroy it piecemeal. But Osman failed to pursue. He remained in his trenches and missed one of the great military victories of the century.

But the battle was not over. On September 11, the embarrassed Russians, now under the personal command of top-ranking General Skobelev himself, returned a third time. Skobelev brought with him more than enough muscle to do the job, he thought—seventy-five thousand infantry, ten thousand cavalry, and 440 guns, plus an army of Romanians. To be absolutely sure, Skobelev softened up the Turkish troops with days of artillery bombardment. Then he attacked.

The Turks' Peabody-Martinis decimated the charging Russian troops once again, and when the suffering Russian troops then massed for the last charge, the Turks once again picked up their

Winchesters. In another terrible slaughter, far worse than the first, Russia lost eighteen thousand men. The Turks, five thousand men. Again the Russians fell back, and again the Turks, now completely exhausted, failed to attack. In total, thirty thousand Russian casualties on the battlefield had demonstrated conclusively what overwhelming firepower could do on a battlefield.

So the Russians changed their tactics: they turned Osman's strength into his weakness. In their fourth campaign, the Russians gave up the frontal attack and adopted a stranglehold: they encircled Osman to try to starve him out. The Russians kept their troops out of range of Osman's two-rifle system as the weeks went by and Osman's food supply dwindled. By mid-November, the siege had succeeded. Badly wounded, Osman surrendered and was sent off to a Russian prisoner-of-war camp before returning home a hero.

For military commanders everywhere, there were lessons in plenty to be learned from Plevna. Osman had pushed the old ways of military strategy and planning into history books. In addition to demonstrating what superior firepower can do, General Osman's tactics showed clearly that future wars were to favor the defender, a clear portent of the trench warfare of World War I. They also showed that a purely defensive posture will lead to defensive defeat.

Ruefully looking at the war it should have won, Turkey ordered 140,000 more Winchesters and sent arms buyers to Germany to look at a new German rifle. Russia, with thirty thousand casualties from that one campaign, realized its entire armament of Berdan single-shots was obsolete. Obsolete as well were all the other single-shot rifles in all the other armies of the world—including General Benét's favorite single-shot Springfield. For other nations, the lesson was clear: get more firepower, more shots per minute to outgun the enemy.

National armories went looking for the next evolution—a rifle combining the range and hitting power of the Peabody-Martini with the rapid-fire volume of the Winchester. No one discussed conserving ammunition or slow, deliberate, long-range shooting—except the U.S. Ordnance Department. There was one last lesson to be learned: almost all the small arms in that Battle of Plevna had been American-inspired—the Russians had Hiram Berdan's rifle. The Turks had the British Peabody-Martini, built around the American breech mechanism from Peabody, as well as the rapid-fire, lever-action Winchester. Would the next major invention come from the United States?

The Battle of Plevna had had one very important witness: Peter Paul Mauser. What he saw and learned at Plevna sent him hurrying back to his gunsmithy in Germany to work on a new idea.

I n 1878, with the words "Plevna" and "Little Bighorn" still echoing around the military world, Chief of Ordnance Benét and his rifle were coming under increasing criticism. So the general went to Congress and asked for $20,000 so that he could appoint another committee to examine repeating rifles and select one for the U.S. Army.

Because General Benét had indicated many times previously that he had no use for repeating rifles, American gun designers expected the usual Ordnance Department results—a test that would draw lots of new rifle designs, lots of talk, lots of shooting, then finish with the usual decision to stay with the Springfield, which had now become an authentic relic.

Congress gave General Benét the $20,000, and he in turn selected a new Rifle Board to look for a new rifle. The general and his board were aware that all three rifles at the Battle of Plevna were American designs, that two of them—the Peabody and the Berdan—had been turned down by the Ordnance Department, and that the third, the murderous Winchester, was the very weapon Benét had refused to issue to the cavalry following the Little Bighorn massacre. In fact, the ideas of American gun designers were now dominating every rifle in every armory in Europe, most of them having been examined and rejected by General Benét and the Springfield Armory. As a result of armory rejection and foreign acceptance, there seemed to be more American gunsmiths active in Europe than in the United States.

Before the Rifle Board, the new models came in abundance, twenty-nine with a magazine feed; eight of them with bolt actions.

Unexpectedly, the Rifle Board chose a successor for the Spring-field—the Hotchkiss. It was a five-shot, tube-fed rifle invented by Benjamin Berkeley Hotchkiss from Watertown, Connecticut, a short distance from the Springfield Armory. He was one of America's most gifted weapons designers, and he was to go on to create a number of innovations in military ordnance, all of them in Europe.

In fact, Hotchkiss had already abandoned the United States for the more receptive European military market, and the bulk of his inventions would be bought by the French armory. Before leaving for Europe, Hotchkiss had sold the rights to his rifle to Winchester, which was now pressing it on the Rifle Board.[19]

Even though the Hotchkiss had repeating-rifle capability, what the general's Rifle Board liked most about the Hotchkiss was its single-shot feature, the rapid-fire tube of bullets being held in reserve. In short, they picked a repeating rifle that was really a single-shot rifle.

Unfortunately, General Benét was not pleased with the Hotchkiss and killed it with two words: ammunition waster. "The Hotchkiss," he said, "is an improvement on the present Springfield arm only in its ability to empty its magazine of cartridges in one-half the time that the same number of shots could be fired by the latter."[20]

No one should have been surprised, therefore, when the Hotchkiss, under new tests by the Rifle Board, now fared badly, and, once again, the whole quest for a repeating rifle just wound down. The Rifle Committee, content to stay with its old single-shot Springfield, "the rifle that won the Civil War," disbanded.

Yet the pressure on the old Springfield was increasing with each year. The next major innovation in military small arms—perhaps the greatest innovation of the entire nineteenth century—became much more difficult for General Benét to ignore, for it was discovered right inside the Springfield Armory itself.

I n July 1879, James Paris Lee patented his new magazine system as the Lee U.S. Navy rifle, caliber .45-70 Government. This was an innovation of monumental significance—the key breakthrough in magazine design that was being sought by ordnance designers everywhere. James Lee was a weapons designer of major stature. He was also an employee of the Springfield Armory and had invented his new magazine system right on the armory premises.

Here was the very magazine feed that General Benét and his Ordnance people were supposed to be seeking. And it was free—at no cost, no charge, no royalties, for under the armory's employee contract, the armory had unlimited use of any invention developed within its walls while the inventor was free to sell or lease the invention outside.

A naturalized American citizen, the brilliant Lee had been born in Scotland and educated in Canada. His presence on the payroll gave Springfield Armory unlimited access to one of the most fertile gun-design minds of the time.

The Lee U.S. Navy rifle was a milestone in rifle design, for it was a complete departure from the familiar method of loading—through a single-file tube of bullets. Instead, Lee had placed the bullets side by side—so simple, so brilliant—in a clip centrally positioned right below the bolt that fed bullets into the breech.

As an extra benefit, the Lee patent featured another striking idea—a spare magazine so that when the clip in the magazine emptied, the soldier could push in a second loaded magazine without interrupting his firing with manual reloading. Here was a magazine rifle that offered firepower with a vengeance.

Some two years after Plevna, General Benét convened yet another Rifle Board at Springfield to look at this new Lee magazine rifle that could give the United States the most modern repeating weapon in the world. While General Benét hesitated, the Remington Arms Company resolved the issue by hiring Lee away from the armory.

In desperate financial shape and urgently seeking a magazine design for its line of rifles, Remington approached Lee, waving money and opportunity. Sensing a more receptive climate, Lee resigned from Springfield and went to work for Remington at Ilion, New York.

General Benét not only missed an enormous opportunity to take a worldwide lead in a magazine-fed rifle design. He also lost the creative mind of James Lee, whose ideas were soon gracing the finest military weapons of Europe. Lee also performed a singular service for Remington: his magazine system and his other major inventions saved it from bankruptcy.

On July 5, 1881, four years after the Battle of Plevna, two years since Lee presented his new magazine rifle design, General Benét asked Congress to put another $50,000 on the table to develop and test a magazine rifle design.[21] With those funds, General Benét convened the 1881 Rifle Board to look once again at a number of rifle ideas. But this test seemed to be a showdown between a revised version of the Hotchkiss bolt-action rifle that Benét's officers had favored a few years before and the Lee Navy magazine rifle, now also revised and called the Remington-Lee 1882.

After fifteen months of testing, the Rifle Board announced that it had selected not one rifle but three. The group liked the Lee rifle best of all, but it also liked the Hotchkiss and another rifle, the Chaffee-Reece. Significantly, the board took the unprecedented action of recommending that the army regulars make the choice from among the three candidates.

General Benét quickly concurred, and the Rifle Board ordered a supply of all three rifles to be made for field testing. Immediately, the whole program began to drag. Test rifles were not delivered on time. Problems delayed the production of still other rifles. Some rifle shipments were only partial; others were delayed until full shipment could be received. Assembling the test rifles required nearly four years. Not until 1885 did the weapons reach the troops in the field. Then more delays: while some rifle companies had received all three rifles, others received only one; in Texas, the troops selected for testing the rifles were away from camp, chasing Geronimo and his small band of Apaches, who were not captured until 1886. The situation became completely muddied when the armory also shipped a supply of the new Springfield trap-door single-shot model for similar testing. Testing of the three rifles—now four—was not officially completed until 1892, eleven years after the Rifle Board was convened. But the results were obvious long before that. In fact, by December of 1885, General Benét had issued the verdict.

Of the three rifles, Benét told the secretary of war, the troops preferred the Lee, but most of all, they preferred the Springfield single-shot. The reasons the troops gave seemed to have little to do with the firing efficiency of the weapons and were minor objections at best. The magazine of the Lee rifle, they said, was easy to lose, was susceptible to rust, and got in the way of doing the manual of arms, the standard army rifle drill. Cavalrymen said the bolt action was not fit for mounted service.

The test that was intended to determine which of the three was to be the new magazine rifle ended up being a popularity contest among the troops, with the old Springfield receiving the most votes.

It was clear even then that the troops needed more training with the new weapons, that some of their complaints were really a reluctance to give up the familiar old Springfield, and that some revisions to the weapons might be in order.

While on the one hand now presenting himself as a proponent of magazine rifles, a new posture for him, General Benét took the troop's reactions as a mandate to go back to the 1873 Springfield single-shot, trap-door rifle as still the proper weapon for our troops. He reported to Congress that the search had failed, that the three rifles, selected from some forty entries, were flawed and none of them should be accepted. Instead, in light of the contentment the troops felt with the Springfield, the army should wait "a reasonable time" because so many momentous developments were occurring in the world of small arms.[22] Sometime in the future, he felt, the army would look again at magazine rifles. So, with the official test results posted in 1892—after eleven years of looking and eight years of testing—America still had a single-shot army.[23]

The British military magazine, the *Army and Navy Journal*, seemed to catch Benét's real motive in a sentence. "The objection so often and so feebly made, that magazine rifles would entail an enormous waste of ammunition, is not worthy of a moment's consideration." [24]

Meanwhile, Peter Paul Mauser, having observed the Battle of Plevna, was profoundly impressed with the stunning performance of the American Winchester rifle and the piles of bodies it had produced. Back in his Oberndorf plant, his first efforts to design a bolt-action repeating rifle, logically enough, were based on the Winchester's under-the-barrel tube feed. In 1884, the German army accepted the Mauser tube-fed repeater and called it the Infanteriegewehr M71/84. But once Mauser saw the American Lee rifle, he revised the M71/84. Instead of the inevitable Spencer-inspired tube feed in which the bullets were touching nose to toes, Mauser's new rifle had a Lee box magazine right above the trigger, where the bullets lay side by side. Lee had opened many doors for all future weapons designers. In fact, the Lee magazine system had had such a pervasive effect on European rifle design, to protect his patents, Lee had felt compelled to sue several European gunsmiths for patent infringement.[25]

While Germany was adopting the new Mauser bolt-action rifle, General Benét continued to seek improvements in the trap-door '73, adding, in 1884, a long-needed rear sight to allow for the drift of the bullet. The Springfield was becoming not only the finest single-shot, black-powder military rifle in the world, but also the only one.[26]

Benét's position became even more untenable when the British introduced a stunning new rifle designed by former armory employee James Lee. Lee, after working for a time for Remington, had taken his rifle to England to show to the British who were so impressed with the American armory reject, they gave Lee a contract to adapt his design to fit the new Enfield rifle.

Lee thereupon turned out one of the great weapons of the time—the 1888 British Lee-Metford magazine rifle Mark I—which incorporated his Lee magazine system, his Lee bolt action, and the British Metford rifling design, all built around a new British cartridge, the .303.[27]

Benét and his Ordnance team were quite aware that critics were contending that this could have been the new American rifle. Congress was asking questions, wondering why this rifle, invented right inside the walls of the Springfield Armory—this very rifle that General Benét had told them was not fit for U.S. service—was so eagerly copied, to the point of out-and-out patent infringement by other countries. Why was this "unfit" rifle so supremely fit for British service?

If other European nations had already adopted magazine-fed, bolt-action rifles, why was the general telling Congress he could not find such a rifle fit for the U.S. Army? For a nation that was on its way to becoming the most powerful country on earth, the Springfield trap-door rifle was increasingly unacceptable to many influential congressmen.

Unexpectedly in a revolution-prone industry, a truly major revolution—smokeless powder—abruptly made every single military rifle obsolete. In 1884, all the terrible weapons of World War I were made possible when Paul Vieille, a French chemist, announced that he had perfected smokeless gunpowder. This was the ammunition breakthrough that ordnance specialists had been seeking for more than thirty years, ever since the 1860s, when Baron General von Lenk of the Austrian artillery made the first attempts to develop smokeless powder. His experiments with guncotton had been very promising, but guncotton proved to be an untamable giant that, in storage, would explode without warning. After several great gunpowder debacles in plants in England and on the Continent, European armies prudently continued to use black powder.

The Frenchman, Vieille, read von Lenk's studies and a number of others, then hit upon an idea. Experimenting with various solvents, he combined the unruly guncotton—nitrocellulose—with ether and alcohol to form a stabilized gelatin that was safe to handle. He had caged the monster.

Actually, Vieille got more than he had expected. The major problem with black powder was threefold: smoke revealed the firer's position on the battlefield, obscured his visibility, and fouled rifles and cannons. In addition to eliminating those three problems, Vieille discovered that the new smokeless powder was as stable as black powder and much more powerful. It greatly increased projectile velocity, range, and penetration. It offered greater precision and greater accuracy. Artillery and rifles could now fire larger projectiles, and they could fire them much farther and much faster and do much more damage than black powder. Vieille's smokeless powder opened up realms of previously unattainable ballistics performance. By seeking a cleaner-burning powder, he had discovered unprecedented explosive power that quickly brought forth a ghouls' parade of semiautomatic and automatic weapons not possible with black powder. Smokeless powder completely and permanently changed military tactics and made possible a scale of destruction never before dreamed of.

With the composition of Vieille's powder a closely guarded French secret, the other leading European governments, feeling suddenly vulnerable, mounted an urgent quest for smokeless powder, and within a few years after Vieille's discovery in 1884, they would have it.

In 1886, less than two years after the development of the new gunpowder, the French army introduced its Lebel rifle, the first bolt-action rifle to use smokeless powder cartridges. The diameters of both the cartridge case and the projectile were reduced, velocities increased, range extended impressively, and penetration power awesome; with a muzzle velocity of 2,194 feet per second, it was said that "a Lebel bullet can pierce over fifteen inches of oak at 220 yards."[28] The other countries regarded the Lebel as an exceedingly dangerous weapon: "the most vicious small arm in existence."[29] The Lebel was based on the Hotchkiss rifle, one of the many American rifle designs that, turned down by the U.S. armory, had emigrated to Europe. Soon all of Europe was designing similar weapons. The Germans adopted smokeless powder in 1888, giving Peter Paul Mauser the power he needed for his new rifle; the British also adopted it in 1888; and Russia in 1891. Along with the new, much more powerful cartridges of smokeless powder, all of them had also developed new bolt actions capable of withstanding the great new chamber pressures.

With increasing insistence from the army, General Stephen V. Benét and the Springfield Armory had noted the new developments and felt impelled to take some kind of action, if for no other reason than to justify once more the continued existence of the now ancient Springfield rifle. General Benét called up another weapons review committee—the 1888 Rifle Board—at the Springfield Armory. The board would have a difficult time finding excuses for delaying the choice of a new rifle, for all the needed elements were on the table now. There were bolt-action rifles aplenty, metallic cartridge designs in abundance, all kinds of rapid-fire magazine feeds, new barrel rifling and manufacturing technologies, and now there was a smokeless powder that gave the rifle breathtaking power and range.

Benet's response—along with the old guard at the armory—was to turn once more to its venerable Springfield trap-door, making some changes—tinkerings and fine tunings, actually—and pronouncing Allin's basic breech-loading mechanism a weapon that still functioned superbly. This new model, the Springfield '88, was still little more than a converted Civil War muzzleloader. In fact, if one looked closely, one could see some of the original lines of the 1763 Charleville French musket. Completely obsolete even before the pattern model for production was made, the '88 was approved by General Benét, who thereupon ordered more than a half million for the arsenals of the nation.[30]

But other armory officials could no longer remain silent. Colonel Adelbert Buffington, the notoriously temperamental commandant of the armory, publicly criticized the Springfield.

"The Allin breech," he said, "is not strong enough to withstand the pressures of the new smokeless powder."[31] This was another way of saying that the initial velocity of the old Springfield cartridge of only twelve hundred feet per second was no match for the two thousand feet per second of the powerful new European rifles. "A new rifle is needed," he said. If General Benét did not take action, by 1891, the United States would be the only world power without a modern rifle. The question shifted from when to which?

No one was surprised when, in the autumn of 1890, General Benét struck his colors by retiring. Almost as if Benét were taking the old rifle into retirement with him, he and the era of the Springfield trap-door rifle were both gone simultaneously.

CHAPTER 18

GENERAL FLAGLER
AND THE
KRAG-JORGENSEN RIFLE

On January 23, 1891, the War Department in Washington named Daniel Webster Flagler the new chief of ordnance. Born in New York in 1840, he was fifth out of thirty-four in the class of 1861 at West Point, mate to another '61 Pointer, George Armstrong Custer.

General Flagler had served with distinction in the field during the Civil War and had spent his entire career in ordnance. In his time, he commanded several of the major U.S. arsenals and helped design new coastal and field artillery. To appoint Flagler as his successor, General Benét passed over two senior colonels. One possible reason Flagler was chosen was his reputation as a Springfield rifle man.

Flagler, however, was a man of the future and said so in his first annual report: "The United States is years behind other nations in the adoption of a modern type, small caliber, high velocity magazine arm," he declared, "and is suffering in a military reputation therefrom."[1] He exhibited all the characteristics of a new broom.

During his entire seventeen-year regime, General Benét had commissioned one Rifle Board after another to look for a new rifle and then rejected their findings, including the Hotchkiss, the Lee, and the Mauser. To the day he left office, he remained adamantly opposed to replacing the Springfield. But now General Flagler would delay no longer in replacing that outmoded weapon. All the glorified regalia of the "Great Rebellion" must at last be folded in tissue paper and placed firmly in history's file drawers.

In terms of production, manufacturing innovation, precision, pride of product, and team morale, Springfield was one of the finest armories in the world, capable of making a rifle to match any armory in Europe. But as the history of James Lee and other rifle designers clearly demonstrated, Springfield's production-dominated staff couldn't accept a new idea. Aware of this, General Flagler took a momentous step. He created a research and development unit inside the Springfield Armory and named it "The Experimental Department." An excellent move that was long overdue, the new department gave the armory a staff of creative design engineers that might in time transform American military ordnance and make Springfield the creative equal of the finest armories in Europe. But then the general made a significant error. The Experimental Department was put under the direction of the Production Department. Production people would make yes-no decisions on all creative ideas that the designers developed—re-creating the same smothering situation that led to James Lee's departure. This fundamental mistake in authority was to bedevil the armory for the next seventy-five years and ultimately bring on the greatest crisis in its history.

When General Flagler set out to acquire a new rifle that would fire the powerful new smokeless powder, he immediately encountered a problem. The armory needed a large quantity of the new powder for testing, but European armories carefully guarded their powder formulas, and the American armory could not obtain any from them. American powder makers like Du Pont, having had no call from the armory to develop smokeless powder, were just beginning, hastily, to try to catch up, but had not been able to produce a consistent formula of any quantity.

Unexpectedly, in the summer of 1890, from a very unlikely source not known for powder production, the armory got some smokeless powder—from Hiram Maxim, the American inventor of the recoil-actuated machine gun, who had been compelled to create his own powder recipe. In addition, from Belgium, the armory obtained five hundred pounds of Wetteren smokeless powder.

When the Wetteren powder arrived in Philadelphia, the military powder specialists at the army's Frankford Arsenal opened the packages and stood looking at this new monster. Molded into hard black cubes, the powder, capable of killing men like no other gunpowder ever created, smelled like ripe pineapple. There was enough to make 100,000 .30-caliber cartridges at Frankford Arsenal: the U.S. Ordnance Bureau had, at last, taken its first steps into the frightening world of modern military ordnance.

By the end of 1890, Ordnance experts had established the parameters of a new .30-caliber projectile, agreed on the metallurgy of the jacket, determined the composition of the primers, and even worked out the fabrication and rifling of the barrel of a new rifle. They would design the cartridge itself as soon as the magazine system to fire it was selected. Under a directive from its new chief, Daniel Flagler, the armory's Rifle Board was reconvened to decide upon that magazine system—to choose, in effect, America's new rifle.

On December 23, 1890, in the Army Building in New York City, amidst the festive bells and bunting of aVictorian Christmas, the Rifle Board began deliberations. Captain Stanhope E. Blunt of the Ordnance Department was the recorder. The board planned to examine all and any rifles submitted to it—a total of fifty-three, including rifle samples from all the major national arsenals of Europe. Soon spread before the board were the finest rifles in the world— with such awesome power any one of them could kill at a distance of two and a half miles.

The board felt that since all the other major powers had already committed themselves to new bolt-action rifles, the United States, by shopping the entire line, could not fail to end up with the best of all. Thus, U.S. Ordnance decided to adopt the bolt-action rifle nearly fifty years after Johann von Dreyse had invented it, in 1843, just as Ordnance was dropping the Hall rifle. The board adjourned until January 20, 1891, when it was to meet in Springfield to commence testing.

When deliberations began, the Rifle Board was disturbed by one development: there were no American submissions of rifle designs. In fact, the new cartridge presented enormous problems to American inventors. Unlike their European counterparts—and the many American designers working in Europe—American inventors had no experience with the smaller bores, the smaller cartridges, the new powder, or the new, higher chamber pressures. They had a long learning curve ahead of them. As an aid to their researches, General Flagler made available to American inventors, at cost from the armory, new .30-caliber rifle barrels and .30-caliber cartridges.

It soon became clear what the Flagler board was looking for—a rifle that would primarily load cartridges one at a time just like the old Springfield, and, in addition, would include a spare magazine of four or five cartridges that in an emergency could be inserted and fired like a repeater. These were the same characteristics that had attracted General Benét's Rifle Board to the Hotchkiss—a single-shot with emergency repeater capabilities.

The *New York Times* explained the two firing philosophies: "There are two ways of using these magazines, the one as an accelerator of the ordinary rate of fire of the rifle, and the other as a valuable reserve for moments of more than ordinary exigency or peril."[2] By opting for the latter, the Ordnance Bureau was still putting conservation of ammunition ahead of increased firepower.

At every turn, the Flagler board was reminded what a remarkable invention James Lee had developed inside the armory: all the major rifles they looked at were copies or derivatives of the very Lee magazine that the armory had rejected years before. Even France now dropped its lethal Lebel rifle in favor of a new one—the Berthier, which also featured the Lee magazine and fired twenty-eight shots a minute. Many ordnance men around the world pronounced the Berthier the finest rifle of the century.

In the Springfield tests that followed, the first casualty was the German Mauser. A superb weapon, one of the finest, it was the rifle many in the U.S. Army wanted, but the selection process was an exclusive province of the Ordnance Bureau in which other branches were not allowed to intrude. Ordnance was guided by a strict philosophy: technicians know best what the army needs.

The Mauser was clip-loaded five at a time into a Lee-like magazine. There was no way to load only a single cartridge at a time. In fact, the German soldier was not allowed to carry single cartridges; each clip he carried was already preloaded with five cartridges. The Germans didn't want their troops in battle finger-loading single cartridges. They were concerned not about conserving ammunition, but about enabling their troops to get off as many shots per minute as possible—and that meant loading their rifles by the clip, not by the single cartridge. They felt that their stunning past military successes resulted in part from bringing more firepower to the battlefield than their enemy. Flagler's board rejected that philosophy, and so rejected the Mauser.

The Rifle Board was still uneasily awaiting an American submission. Impatient at last, General Flagler set a cutoff date for American rifle submissions of June 30, 1892.

By April, the *New York Times* began to ferret out the truth with a report that Flagler's Rifle Board, like the general himself, did not like magazine rifles.[3] Apparently, even with General Benét retired, many in the armory still wished to spruce up the old single-shot Springfield to take a smokeless powder cartridge and avoid clip-loading entirely. On June 19, the *Times* printed a story that quoted at length a "high source," who did not wish to be identified.[4] The unnamed source noted that "almost to a man the leading ordnance officers at the War Department" believed in retaining the Springfield system in adopting a new small-bore rifle. That clearly included General Flagler and the members of the Rifle Board.

The unnamed spokesman claimed that "I have repeatedly put twenty-three shots in one minute from a Springfield rifle into a target two feet square at 200 feet." Moreover, the source asserted, "the only gain in labor one obtains with a magazine gun over a single-loader is in the handling of cartridges and the time gained in the handling is practically far more than offset by the time lost in shifting magazines and misfires when magazines are emptied."

On September 4, 1892, after months of rumors and story leaks, General Flagler's board officially chose as the new U.S. Army rifle the Danish Krag-Jorgensen. To many ordnance people and to

American gun inventors, the weapon that was chosen was a surprise, but not the reason for the choice: it loaded cartridges singly and thus prevented the wasting of ammunition. The board also noted that, despite the extension of the deadline, not one American rifle had been submitted.[5]

The Flagler board's choice created a major controversy. The Krag-Jorgensen, from the Danish Armory, was a five-shot, bolt-action rifle, firing the new U.S. smokeless powder metal-jacketed .30-caliber cartridge. The rifle was designed by Colonel Ole Hermann Krag of the Norwegian army, who was to become master general of Norwegian Ordnance in 1894. His first version of the Krag was developed in 1868. His 1888 model, which he developed with Erik Jorgensen, became the official rifle of Denmark in 1889, the United States in 1892, and Norway in 1894.

The Rifle Board touted the Krag, saying, "In range, accuracy, and durability it equals or surpasses the best European military rifles." The board noted that the Krag had a smooth-working bolt and horizontal magazine, came with four rifled grooves in the barrel, one right twist per seventeen inches, and weighed a very acceptable 9.2 pounds. The armory asserted that the Krag had a range of four thousand yards—nearly two and a half miles—and would fire forty shots a minute. In all, said the board, it was a well-made, reliable rifle that would do credit to the U.S. Army.

A number of critics soon spoke up. The first reaction to the selection was a furious outburst from American inventors and gun makers. The *New York Times* article had suggested a new reason why American inventors had made no submissions and rebuked American inventors for it. Many American inventors, said the *Times*, felt that submitting anything to the board was "a waste of time; the officers are wedded to the Springfield, and nobody outside the Ordnance ring stands a show."

But American inventors were now saying that, as expected, the Rifle Board all along knew it was going to select the Krag. In fact, the Krag had failed the test rounds five times, and five times it was reworked extensively right in the Springfield Armory, much of it by the inventor himself, Ole Krag, with the supposedly impartial Rifle

Board making suggestions for improvements. The Krag was the only rifle accorded such treatment. The board, they said, was exhibiting extraordinary patience, astounding faith, and grim determination in working with the Krag.

In the same article, the *New York Times* revealed that "the recommendations of the American board came as a great surprise to military experts, and in explanation it is claimed that the board had probably selected the Krag-Jorgensen long before it passed the test."[6]

In the end, the inventors and the gun makers skirted around the Flagler board by having Congress pass a law that prohibited the armory from spending a penny on the Krag for two months, which gave the inventors time to submit their ideas. The waiting period only made matters worse. The inventors were outraged when they found that the same Flagler board members who had chosen the Krag were now sitting in judgment of the new American inventions. Their impartiality was questioned, and several senators went to the office of the secretary of war over the issue, demanding a new board be appointed.

Indeed, the inventors did seem to encounter a good deal of abrasive treatment from Flagler's now truculent Rifle Board, to the point where the inventors demanded that the recorder of the board, Captain Stanhope E. Blunt, be removed for his offensive behavior.

Furthermore, they claimed that the armory refused to provide parts it had agreed to provide; that one invention was broken by the board, and then refused to allow the inventor to repair it before presenting it; and that the board provided the wrong ammunition, which made another invention fail. Most significant, the inventors protested that all the American rifles had been tested to more than fifty thousand pounds' chamber pressure while the Krag was required to pass only a forty-thousand-pound test.

The American inventions were all rejected. This made relations between the armory and American gun designers worse. The Americans now demanded that they, too, be given five chances to rework their weapons.

The quarrel reached its height when the inventors discovered that the armory had gone ahead, against the expressed orders of Congress, and purchased the tooling for manufacturing the Krag before it had finished examining the American weapons. Certainly, such a major military purchase could not have happened without General Flagler's authorization. Such a move indicated, once more, that the office of chief of ordnance had played the usual game with the Americans while it had already made its mind up.

Eventually, the inventors refused to submit their inventions until Captain Blunt—whose behavior they found overbearing—was removed. But General Flagler was equally adamant and Blunt remained.

On Friday, May 26, 1893, the National Board of Ordnance and Fortification announced its acceptance of the report of the Rifle Board. The Krag-Jorgensen was the new U.S. Army rifle. With the $400,000 appropriated by Congress, the Springfield Armory was soon to go into production. In a *New York Times* story, the Rifle Board report also pointed out that American inventors "have not yet made a magazine rifle which can compare with this model of foreign skill."

Hardly had the disgruntled American inventors left the scene than the military critics of the Krag stepped forward. They expressed amazement that the United States had selected the Krag. They pointed out that every major armory in Europe had turned the Krag down. They, too, felt that the armory had in secret chosen the Krag well before the Rifle Board met and had used its new Experimental Department to rework the weapon over and over until it was acceptable.

The critics also noted that the Krag magazine was cumbersome and difficult to load, seemingly intentionally, so that it had to be loaded manually one cartridge at a time and would not permit the use of a loaded clip. This feature was considerably inferior to one of the most important virtues of the Mauser—the clip-loading magazine that would accept five cartridges with one push of the hand.

These critics pointed out that the Krag had a single locking lug instead of the stronger dual front locking lug system of the

Mauser and would therefore tend to break under the high pressures of the new ammunition and that the entire bolting system was inferior to the simpler bolting system of the Mauser. Furthermore, said the critics, before the first Krag came off the Springfield production line, the model was too weak for the newer ammunition charges that were soon to be issued. In short, the weapon was already obsolete.

Privately, Ordnance men in the Navy Department, which had planned to issue the same rifle as the army, felt the Krag was inferior to the Lee Navy rifle, which it already had. The navy had believed that the German Mauser was the finest weapon offered and had planned to issue it.

One rumor held that the Ordnance Bureau had bought the Krag as an interim gun, that its new Experimental Department already had a new design on the drawing boards and was considering others. There must have been some merit to the rumor. Evidently, General Flagler had grown uneasy himself with the choice. On June 8, 1893, while the armory was tooling up for the Krag, the *New York Times* announced that Captain Blunt, the controversial recorder of the two previous Rifle Boards, "will accept for preliminary test such new devices as may be submitted. When enough guns of merit have been secured, he will ask for a board to conduct an examination on the lines and under the conditions of the trials recently held."[7]

As ordnance men often point out, the greatest test of a rifle, as with any other weapon, is the battlefield. And there was one in the offing: the Spanish-American War.

On August 20, 1895, the first public hint that the Krag-Jorgensen rifle was in trouble came from the new six-hundred-yard Willet's Point firing range at the U.S. Military Academy in West Point, New York.

Quoted in the *New York Times*, two training officers admitted that "the Krag-Jorgensen falls far short of the old Springfield rifle for target practice."[8] Nothing serious, they said, but the sight piece was imperfect. They felt that the new Krag model that was due the following September would correct it. On the other hand, they added, the recoil in the Krag is not as great as the Springfield.

In October 1895, a report from Fort Sheridan in Illinois indicated that the Krag was a "failure." Officials were quick to point out that the tests were incomplete; the Krag needed only a wind gauge and lowered sighting, they said.[9] Criticism continued to mount. On December 26, 1895, Brigadier General Wheaton, commanding the Department of the Colorado, stated that the new Krag "had not met expectations."

The report of Wheaton's departmental inspector of small arms practice for the target year 1895 stated that all of the company commanders had complained about the rifle's inaccuracy. The list of problems was alarming. The rifle, said the report, shot too high, while the bullet was easily deflected by the wind. The hits varied after the barrel had heated. The metal of the bolt and chamber was too soft, causing the bolt to jam. Moreover, usage weakened the magazine spring, which then wouldn't keep the cartridge box gate shut. The magazine cutoff was easily pulled off and lost. The front sight would bend. Both the spindle in the safety lock and the hinge bar to the magazine broke constantly. The head of the ramrod was too big and wouldn't clean the barrel. The bolt had to be constantly lubricated, and that damaged clothing. The weapon needed a wind gauge and an automatic drift correction on the rear sight. Furthermore, cartridges had misfired. Gas had perforated the primer, which burned the faces of the shooters and affected their eyes.[10]

General Flagler admitted the weapon had problems,[11] but brushed aside criticism by asserting that such defects were expected when a new weapon is first introduced into service. Rumors that the Ordnance Department would return to the old Springfield '73 were denied. But the problems reported from Colorado were quite substantial, even for a new weapon just introduced into service.

Just as some critics had earlier warned, one new concern worried the Springfield people: the Krag was having problems handling the power of the new smokeless cartridge, and that meant it surely was not going to be strong enough for the more powerful cartridges the armory was developing. General Flagler took the Krag back to the armory for serious reworking.

The next model Krag, the 1896, corrected some of these defects. And, two years later, the 1898 model, very similar to the 1896, was issued with a magazine capacity of five rounds—still hand-fed, to be sure, and still without a cartridge clip, but as a compromising step toward more battlefield firepower, the new model had room for one more round in the magazine.

As it issued the Krag '96, the Ordnance Bureau claimed the Krag was now one of the sturdiest rifles ever made. That thesis was to be tested in Cuba in 1898, two years later.

When General William T. Sherman was retired by act of Congress in 1882, he left behind a superb army. He had created various training schools throughout the military, modernized its shape and structure, gave voice to a philosophy for military organization and war conduct, and brought the army out of its amateur gentleman status. His contribution here may have been more significant than his great contribution as general in the Civil War. In actuality, the superb army he left was all on paper. De facto, there was no army. By 1890, the year of the Battle of Wounded Knee, which ended the Indian Wars, there were fewer than twenty-seven thousand men in the entire army, which was no longer even an Indian constabulary. The U.S. Army had been quietly starved to death by Congress.

Secretary of War Russell A. Alger disagreed with that. A major general of cavalry volunteers during the Civil War, a former governor of Michigan, and a real estate investor grown wealthy—and now recently appointed to the Cabinet post of secretary of war— he felt impelled to make some comments about the state of the U.S. Army to some of his friends. He may have chosen the wrong place to make them.

On August 24, 1897, in Buffalo, New York, at a banquet commemorating the thirty-first anniversary of the founding of the Grand Army of the Republic, a Civil War veterans group, Alger, recently appointed U.S. secretary of war, asserted, "The United States Army, as far as it goes, is the best under God's footstool." Applause interrupted him. ". . . In thirty days," he assured the aged assemblage, "we could put millions of fighting men in the field, and back them up with a wall of fire in the person of the veteran." This produced another ovation.

It was the kind of extravagant verbiage that veterans often heard at such banquets, but this time, unfortunately, the words were uttered by the secretary of war, and reporters were present.

No one in that banquet room knew better than the secretary of war the sorry, threadbare state of the U.S. Army, consisting of hardly more than twenty-five thousand men scattered across a vast continent, almost all of them still armed with Springfield rifles, all breechloader descendants of the original Civil War Springfield carried more than thirty years before by the aging men that now listened to him in the banquet room.

No one knew better than Alger that in the federal arsenal were only a few thousand controversial Krags, still untested in battle.

As for leadership, Alger could look down the organizational chart at the army's tiny peacetime cadre of disgruntled officers, starved for promotions and medals, spending their days bickering and trying to coax a cranky Congress out of more money, which was never forthcoming. The skeletal U.S. Army was sulking its days away, all but forgotten. Actually, with no enemy to confront it and with the protection of two vast oceans, Congress could say that the country had little need for a standing army. All of the listeners in that room knew, as veterans out of service for more than thirty years, that they were now middle-aged men not capable of any action more vigorous than cheering extravagant speeches at banquets.

Alger, of course, was making an oblique threat to Spain. For as he stood there, boasting so vaingloriously, the United States was drifting into a war that was to erupt only a few months hence, a war that Alger should have been furiously preparing for but was not.

Four days later, the *New York Times* took dead aim at Alger and condemned him for his "foolish bragging." The indignant editorial said that Alger knew perfectly well that "we could offer no resistance on either coast to a first-class or second-class naval power, and that two army corps could traverse the country as far as their commanders chose to take them without meeting any effectual opposition."[12]

A few months later, Representative George B. McClellan, Jr., took another shot at Alger. McClellan's father, the famous and controversial Civil War general whose failure to fight Lee nearly drove Lincoln mad, had later become governor of New Jersey four times. McClellan, Jr., asserted that the U.S. Army was just a "clumsily organized national police force."

Perhaps there would have been no Spanish-American War if in February 1896, Spain had not sent a new governor to its colony in Cuba. His name was Valeriano Weyler and he was chosen because he was stern and merciless and determined to stamp out the festering year-old insurgency that was convulsing the island.

Spain had been less than ideal as a colonial master. Only a near revolution had brought about the reluctant abolition of slavery on the island in 1886. The island's population had barely time to get used to its new status when sugar, Cuba's primary export crop, was dealt a paralyzing blow by the worldwide depression of the 1890s. The United States then increased the islanders' suffering when the American sugar trust lobbied through Congress the 1894 revenue bill that raised tariffs on Cuban sugar by a crushing 40 percent.

The islanders' response was revolt. Spain's response was Weyler. And Weyler's response was a series of "reconcentration" camps in which he cooped up as much of the rural population as he could, in order to deny the rebels supplies and recruits. The conditions inside Weyler's camps were scandalous. And soon Weyler was fighting a war against savage guerrillas. The insurgents demanded a Cuba *libre*. A free Cuba. Weyler, now called "The Butcher" by American newspapers, replied with more reconcentration camps.

Many groups in the United States sympathized with the islanders. American business interests, alarmed by the fighting, demanded U.S. protection of their $50 million Cuban investment. Washington pressured Spain, passed a concurrent congressional resolution, and offered to act as mediator—all of which offended the Spanish.

In March of 1897, when the new administration of McKinley came to Washington, bringing Alger in as secretary of war, economic circumstances seemed to be improving. A new Spanish government had promptly recalled Weyler, and made mollifying promises to the islanders. By December, McKinley was able to urge patience with Spain's new programs.

Ultimately, conditions were too far gone. The islanders revolted again; Hearst and Pulitzer newspapers, in a circulation war, dragged bleeding corpses and dead children through their daily columns; and the pacifist McKinley reluctantly acted. He sent the battleship *Maine* to Havana to protect American investments.

Many selfish interests were busy playing on the natural sympathies of the Americans—Cuban insurgents in Washington, hectoring politicians in quest of office, businessmen fearing loss of their investments, newspapers chasing circulation.

In the midst of these explosive conditions, a catastrophe occurred: the battleship *Maine* exploded and sank in Havana Harbor. Spain, the least likely culprit, was blamed by the newspapers, by the revolutionaries on the island, and by American interventionists. Since the likeliest reaction was the sending of American troops, the element most likely to benefit from the explosion was the rebels. The true cause of the explosion was never determined, but the death of 260 American sailors made war almost inevitable.

Dealing with the insurrectionists, Spain couldn't win and wouldn't quit. If it abjectly gave up Cuba, the government in Spain would collapse. Spain needed a face-saving way to get out. The rebels raised the pressure, increased their demands, and intensified their attacks. While McKinley hung back, Congress acted. On April 20, 1898, it passed a joint resolution recognizing the independence of Cuba and authorized the raising of an army. On April 24, 1898, Spanish David declared war on American Goliath, a war it knew it could not win.

Ordnance men the world over shifted in their chairs with new interest. The oncoming war would put America's new Krag-Jorgensen rifle through its paces in a full-scale war against the Mauser rifle carried by Spanish soldiers. This confrontation would settle all arguments.

If it were not so tragic, the war would have been a comedy of errors and incompetence. Congress had never created a planning office in the army, and as a result, during the ensuing rush into war, no one was in charge. The trouble was evident from the beginning. The commanding general of the army, General Nelson Appleton Miles, a man of great presence and appearance with an intimidating war record and a vast ego, refused to acknowledge the secretary of war as his superior—and thereby raised a paralyzing issue at the worst possible time, which was not resolved until after the war.

Among other obstreperous moves, General Miles demanded that the Krag-Jorgensen be replaced by the Winchester—a rifle that had been turned down by the army board in favor of the Krag. Ordnance Chief Flagler resisted; Miles insisted. Reluctantly, Secretary Alger placed a $200,000 trial order for ten thousand Winchesters. General Flagler appointed a board to test them, which, much to Miles's suspicion, declared that the Winchester failed to meet the army's "standards of performance," whatever they were.

The Winchester, the legendary weapon of the Battle of Plevna and the weapon Miles learned to love during his wars with the Indians, would certainly have been a better weapon against the Cubans and the Filipinos than the old black-powder Springfield trap-doors with which most National Guardsmen went to Cuba.

As a standing army, the United States had only twenty-five thousand regulars; its arsenals had only fifty thousand Krag-Jorgensen rifles, and fifteen thousand Krag-Jorgensen carbines. American artillery was equally antique—black powder that was far behind European artillery, far behind the Spanish artillery that waited for it in Cuba.

As usual, up until the day war was declared, the army had made absolutely no preparations for what was obviously coming—a tropical war. All over the country, volunteers waited—to go to camps that did not exist, on railroad cars that were not available, to be drilled by a training cadre that wasn't there, in tropical uniforms that had never been made, shaded from the sun by tropical helmets no one had ordered, in tents that were not available, with mess kits yet to be manufactured, food yet to be grown.

The Springfield Armory's efforts to galvanize itself were equally futile. In March, production of the Krag-Jorgensen rifle stood at about 100 rifles a day. When August came, the factory was turning out little more than 350 a day—this to arm a force that had grown in a few weeks to 200,000 men.

With Alger and Miles as the main event, there were numerous other bureaucratic brawls on the front pages of the newspapers. In the eagerness to go to war, everyone in the army, in Congress, in the military complex, was battling everyone else. No one consulted the supply services or even bothered to tell them what was going on. Instead, the suppliers were just roughly shoved aside, left to guess what to supply and where. The quartermaster had no idea what was happening. Chief Sampson was not told that Congress was issuing a call for 125,000 volunteers; in fact, he may have learned of it first in the pages of the newspapers. The supply services were guided primarily by thirdhand rumors.

Hordes of young men sat in camp in their civilian clothes, while lost on railroad sidings were boxcars stuffed with uniforms and other equipment. Predictably, everyone in the service and all the civilian policymakers were soon raging at the incompetence and stupidity of the service arms.

As a result, 150,000 ill-trained troops went to Cuba in the worst heat of summer wearing heavy wool uniforms and bearing outmoded rifles and inadequate artillery. They had no decent maps and often went stumbling through the brush trying to find the roads that would lead them to the Spanish, drawing heavy enemy fire every time they fired a black powder Springfield rifle or a piece of black powder artillery. The revealing smoke increased American casualties inordinately.

The artist Frederic Remington wrote, "Smoky powder belongs with arbalests and stone axes . . . in museums," not in the U.S. arsenal.

On July 1, 1898, at the Battle of San Juan Hill, ordnance people expected to get their questions about the Krag answered. True, there were too few Krags, only enough for the regular army and for Roosevelt's Rough Riders, but enough to give measure. As they proceeded through the Cuban countryside, American troops soon encountered a terrifying sound—a terrible buzz that turned into a high shriek as it went whizzing by their heads into tree trunks and branches. A man hit in the arm by the force of it would spin on his heels and be slammed down on the ground. This was the first time Americans had heard the sound of the German Mauser. The Spaniards were armed with the latest magazine-fed, bolt-action 7-mm rimless rifle model that featured a new rapid-fire clip loader. The deadly accuracy of the Mauser stopped the Americans' advance more than once with a seemingly incredible volume of fire from such a small force of Spaniards.

The Americans quickly discovered that the Krag didn't have the range or the muzzle velocity of the Mauser bullet. Nor was the obsolete American artillery a match for the modern Spanish artillery. In fact, it proved to be worse than inadequate. In one battle alone, a desperately needed American artillery barrage had to be halted because it was too weak to do the job and, worse, its clouds of smoke drew furious shrapnel fire that created terrible casualties and soon drove off the men of the battery and an adjacent infantry unit.

In the Battle of San Juan Hill, practically without artillery support, Roosevelt led the Rough Riders and the First and Tenth Black Cavalry—all dismounted—from Kettle Hill, which they had previously taken, down into the valley and then up the steep slopes to Spain's main line of defense on San Juan Hill. American army regulars, mounting the slopes of the hill in orderly fashion from another direction, called Roosevelt's action "the school-boy charge."

In all, some five thousand Americans stormed the hill toward the blockhouse on top that held some seven hundred Spaniards. The Americans paid with heavy casualties for every yard, mainly from the punishing rifle fire from the Spanish Mausers. The hill was taken at the cost of thirteen hundred American casualties. For the Spanish, it was a moment of admirable spirit and stubborn resistance. For the Americans, an almost foolhardy act of surpassing courage. The "schoolboy charge" is credited by many with having helped to break the spirit of the Spanish defenders.

Ordnance had its answer and didn't like it: as its critics had insisted, the Krag proved to be no match for the Mauser. In one test conducted between captured Spanish Mausers and U.S. Army

Krags, both rifles were fired at beams of yellow pitch pine. The Mauser's bullets penetrated the wood nine inches deeper than did the Krag's.

W hen the Spanish-American War ended on August 12, 1898, only four months after it had begun, the United States came away with three alarming problems on its hands: Cuba, the Philippines, and its own U.S. Army. The American government had to learn quickly, almost overnight, how to administer the governments of two former Spanish colonies that were both in desperate condition. Also, it had to learn how to restructure the poorest modern army in the entire industrialized world—a product of an "era of insouciant wastefulness, planlessness, and *laissez faire*." [13]

The recent war had demonstrated that there was no overall army command, no overall planning office, no mechanism whatsoever for mounting a full-scale war. Staff departments had bumbled along through the war independent of, and often out of synchronization with, each other.

Many Americans were painfully aware that to the rest of the world, the army's performance in Cuba had seemed badly organized and amateurish. The United States looked like an overgrown helpless military colossus that could not enforce its own Monroe Doctrine against foreign intruders in the Americas. If the United States was to be taken seriously by the international community, the army had to be reorganized from top to bottom. New structures had to be devised, new thinking introduced, and, most pressing, new weaponry developed.

The old had to go—the old black-powder muskets and cannons had to be junked, the old habits of mind had to be replaced, and, most of all, the old moss-backed, backward-looking imperious minds among the top brass had to be turned out.

This wasn't just a temporary flurry that would pass away in due time. Men like Roosevelt returned from Cuba not only heroes, but angry heroes. Roosevelt was angry with the disgracefully inadequate black powder Springfield rifle that the National Guard had carried. He was angry with the underpowered Krag rifle that General

Flagler had put in the hands of the army regulars. He was angry with American artillery that was so inferior to the Spanish. He was angry with the bureaucracy that had created these bad weapons— the insular and arrogant Ordnance Bureau under General Flagler.

But more than that, Roosevelt was angry with the indescribable incompetence of the entire U.S. Army and its antique structure. Of General Shafter, who was the commanding officer of the expedition, he said, "Not since the campaign of Crassus against the Parthians has there been so criminally incompetent a General as Shafter."[14] Of the army's organization and training, he avowed, "No words could describe . . . the confusion and lack of system and the general mismanagement of affairs."[15] The one thing that did not anger Roosevelt was the Spanish version of the German Mauser, whose superb performance, he decided, the American army must have.

President McKinley was uncomfortably aware of all this. He was planning to run for reelection, and to win, he knew, he had to do three things: find a military scapegoat to flog through the streets, appoint a new paladin who could quickly create a modern army, and do it all before the next election.

As for a scapegoat, the newspapers were already in full cry after him. Secretary of War Russell Alger's War Department was redolent with the stench of scandal and corruption. His wartime performance had been so inept that McKinley himself had largely functioned as his own secretary of war. Alger's style of operation had been impulsive, quixotic, and prone to make a hash of things. He was also the self-wounded victim of the inherited system he failed to modernize and tried to operate. Above all, he was an easy, obvious, and highly visible target.[16]

At war's end, the words of his 1897 GAR banquet speech could be quoted by his enemies: "In thirty days, we could put millions of fighting men in the field, and back them up with a wall of fire in the person of the veteran." The press called for Alger's head. McKinley, looking at reelection two years hence, found Alger to be very heavy political baggage. So, after two very damaging years in McKinley's first administration, Alger was ousted.

Russell Alger's GAR speech in 1897 and his departure in 1899 served as bookends, bracketing the major events of the Spanish-American War. With Alger went his romantic concept of the "citizen army," springing whole from the earth in times of crisis to mow down the enemy.

President McKinley now turned to his second objective—a paladin who could raise around him a modern army. Here, McKinley made the most unexpected choice. He had decided that the next secretary of war should have two characteristics: a strong legal background for administering America's burgeoning empire—Cuba and the Philippines—and he must not be connected, in any way, with the discredited military bureaucracy. McKinley chose Elihu Root, one of the nation's leading lawyers, possibly at the behest of Theodore Roosevelt, a personal friend of Root's.

Thin, of medium height, with a full mustache, Root gave the impression at first of being a solemn man with a deliberate lawyerly manner. Under thin receding hair that often fell in a sparse bang high across his forehead was an unwavering pair of quick, sharp eyes—humorless and challenging. But when something amused him, he revealed what Secretary of State John Hay called "a frank and murderous smile."[17]

Root was known for a restless creative mind and a manner that could be impatient, blunt—even ruthless. Fond of challenges, he was an excellent administrator—as his work as secretary of war was soon to demonstrate. From a family of well-known scholars, and himself once a teacher, he was already internationally known as a brilliant corporate lawyer whose name was associated with a number of famous law cases. Among his many renowned clients was Theodore Roosevelt. Root had served as the U.S. attorney for the Southern District of New York, and as a delegate to the New York State Constitutional Convention of 1894. He was the elected head of the prestigious Union League in New York City, that bunker of great wealth, privilege, and power. McKinley had to use some persuasion to lure Root from his comfortable, lucrative practice in New York City into the long hours and poor pay of Washington.

The historian Barbara Tuchman once commented on one of history's great paradoxes, "the pursuit by governments of policies contrary to their own interests."[18] She observed, "Mankind, it seems, makes a poorer performance of government [which surely includes war making] than of almost any other human activity. In this sphere, wisdom, which may be defined as the exercise of judgment acting on experience, common sense and available information, is less operative and more frustrated than it should be. Why do holders of high office so often act contrary to the way reason points and enlightened self-interest suggests? Why does intelligent mental process seem so often not to function?"

Months away from the beginning of the twentieth century with the vast technological developments it heralded for military affairs, Secretary Root must have asked the same questions when he confronted the entrenched bureaucracy and conservatism in the U.S. Army. Why, he must have wondered, does the military mind become stubbornly resistant to change, to new and better ways of operating, to new and better weapons systems, clinging tenaciously, instead, to the obsolete? In particular, he must have wondered at the mind of Nelson Appleton Miles, commanding general of the American army, who had caused great mischief by categorically refusing to accept the secretary of war as his superior.

As is almost invariably the case, General Miles had been assigned the post of commanding general in 1895 because, to the military seniority system, he seemed eminently suited to it.[19] First of all, he looked the part, a tall, commanding presence, powerfully built— "strapping" was the popular word of the day—dedicated to personal physical fitness, handsome, and a leading media figure, encapsulated in the legends of both the Civil War and the Indian Wars, where his name was linked with names like Sitting Bull, Geronimo, and Chief Crazy Horse.

General Miles did not attend West Point. Born in 1839 into a stern antislavery Baptist farm family in Massachusetts, he enlisted in 1861 in the Union army with the rank of captain in the Massachusetts Volunteer Infantry. As part of the Army of the Potomac, he fought in most of its major battles including Fredericksburg and Chancellorsville. His courage and battle sense led to a series of promotions, and the rank of brigadier general by the time he was twenty-five in 1864, commanding an army corps in the Wilderness and Petersburg campaigns.

Generals Grant and Sherman backed him in his quest for a colonelcy in the peacetime army. His political influence grew significantly when he married Mary Hoyt Sherman, whose uncles were General William Sherman and his brother, Senator John Sherman, Ohio Republican, author of the landmark Sherman Antitrust Act and also a bitter rival of Russell Alger, secretary of war in President McKinley's Cabinet.

In the West, in command of the Fifth U.S. Infantry, he added to his legend when he and his unit fought in many of the major campaigns against the Comanche, Apache, Sioux, and Cheyenne. Miles made headlines when he captured the elusive Geronimo in 1886, then in 1890–1891 put down the last Indian uprising, the Sioux Ghost Dance Revolt, displaying throughout the years in the West the same qualities of leadership, military skill, and pugnaciousness he exhibited in the Civil War. He rose in rank to brigadier general by 1880, major general by 1890, senior major general by 1895. As a result of his years of campaigning, he developed a high respect for the Indian and his tribal ways of life, treated captive Indians humanely, and learned to use negotiation in lieu of combat. Later, his strong sense of honor led him to defy Washington—even the president—with his demands for proper treatment of the Indian.

Revered in the West, he was the recipient of many honors there, including testimonials, parades, and even jeweled swords. In 1895, amidst talk of running him for president, he replaced Schofield as commanding general of the army. Unlike many of his fellow officers, he maintained an interest in new combat tactics and weapons and urged the army to study the bicycle and the automobile for military use.

Yet, as commanding general, his great failure brought about the termination, by Congress, of that office. Critics accused him of self-dramatics and having an enormous ego, as well as being overly sensitive to criticism. "Pompous," says the historian Cosmas, "conceited, politically ambitious but gullible and naive."[20] Because of his love of publicity, particularly his eagerness to ride a horse at the head of every parade that would have him, he drew the accusation from Secretary of War Lamont of being "a newspaper soldier."[21] It was whispered that, because of overambition, he stole the credit for the capture of Geronimo from the famous scout officer Charles Gatewood, who died a lieutenant.[22]

In Washington, his quarrelsomeness raised an array of opponents, extending even to the House Appropriations Committee. He refused to acknowledge Secretary of War Alger as his superior, insisting instead that he had sole control over all military operations, which added enormously to the confusion and contretemps during the Spanish-American War. He was the sitting commanding general of the army when Elihu Root came to Washington to reform the U.S. military.

Soon after he arrived in Washington in the oppressive heat of July 1899, Root was spending his days reorganizing the War Department and his nights reading deeply in the world's literature on military organization. He became familiar with everything written—from the two-thousand-year-old work *The Art of War*, by Sun-tzu, to Prussian general Karl von Clausewitz's seminal book, *On War*.

He studied the structure of the German army, the British army, the French, and any others that might teach him something. In a remarkably short time, he grew from a man who knew nothing about military matters to one of the country's—perhaps the world's—leading experts on the subject. Of Root's knowledge of military matters, Lord Richard Haldane said, "Really, you know, I do not need to know anything about armies and their organization, for the five reports of Elihu Root, made as Secretary of War in the United States, are the very last word concerning the organization and place of an army in a democracy."[23]

That was high commendation from an authoritative source. Lord Haldane was Root's counterpart in England, secretary of war in the 1905 Campbell-Bannerman Cabinet. A considerable authority on military structure himself, he was to bring about the complete re-organization of the British army.

One of the most significant works Root found on the subject of war was in the U.S. Army archives—a nearly forgotten and largely unread manuscript by a nineteenth-century American military officer. His name was Emory Upton, a brevet major general and Civil War hero, who served in the post–Civil War army, studied military organization, and left a searching monograph on the flaws of the American army structure in a democracy when he committed suicide. When Root found and read Upton's manuscript, he was so impressed with it that he had it published and pressed copies on anyone he could buttonhole.

In effect, Upton had predicted that America's "civilian army" would ultimately produce the War Department mess now confronting Root. Upton blamed it on the minds of amateurs like Alger, boasting of raising an army from the earth overnight. Upton, a proponent of the professional army, had the deepest contempt for the "citizen army" concept. Looking around at the shambles of the War Department in the aftermath of the Spanish-American War, Root felt impelled to agree with much of Upton's thesis. The Alger/Miles way was not the way to run an army.

"The real object of having an army is to provide for war," Root said.[24] He not only designed a new American army, but also saw its primary function as a stabilizing influence, an extension of foreign policy, a peacemaker in a violent world. He had become a dove in olive-drab feathers.

"Walk softly," Theodore Roosevelt said, explaining the philosophy behind his foreign policy, "and carry a big stick." Agreeing, Root was fashioning the stick. Following the lead of his nightly studies, he made fundamental changes in the army structure, all the while trying to anticipate and silence potential opposition from the entrenched old guard, especially in the person of the ever-obstreperous General Miles, and at the same time avoiding the anti-imperialist faction in the Congress.

He eliminated the military seniority system that, with such notorious consequences, promoted the incompetent, of which the

Ordnance Bureau had had its share. He created a General Staff to be the brain of the army, then created the War College to provide the "intellectual exercise" that would guide the General Staff in its planning. He convinced Congress to permanently establish and fund the core of a modern army that could be expanded through National Guard units. To break up the entrenched nests of autonomy set up by some senior officers, including the chief of ordnance, he limited the service time in staff assignments to four years.

Deft as he was, he soon roused opposition inside the army old guard, who hurried to their contacts on Capitol Hill and sought by such indirection to block Root. General Miles, as expected, led the guerrillas.

Root showed his political skill, and an impatient man's capacity for patience: rather than fight General Miles, he outwaited him. In fact, he waited until August 8, 1903, General Miles's sixty-fourth birthday—when by military regulations he was required to retire. One week later, before Miles's chair had grown cold, and before Miles had fairly gotten off his campaign to run for president, Root had guided through Congress a bill that founded the General Staff Corps.

Among other vital elements of that bill, it abolished the anomalous maverick office of commanding general that Miles had used to cause so much turmoil and replaced it with a chief of the General Staff, who was chosen by and reported to the secretary of war.[25] From then on, the military was firmly under the command of the civilian government, free of the circus element of divided command that Miles had introduced. This broke the back of the outmoded army structure and formed the essential underpinning of a new and modern army structure in the United States, which later war secretaries were to need for the further development of the army command. Elihu Root even performed the feat of getting the army and the navy talking and cooperating by forming the Joint Army-Navy Board.

There were two specific developments in American armaments. Under his administration, the Ordnance Department developed the Model 1902 three-inch smokeless powder field gun. It fired both high-explosive and shrapnel shells and featured optical sights and a recoilless carriage. It was heralded as the equal of the famous French 75-mm gun, which was considered by many to be the hallmark of that type of artillery. And of the most profound significance, under Root's administration, the Ordnance Bureau went in search of a new rifle to replace the Krag-Jorgensen—an adventure whose consequences were to last for more than thirty years.

W hile Elihu Root was fighting one of Washington's oldest and most deeply entrenched bureaucracies, Lord Haldane, secretary for war in the Bannerman Cabinet, was conducting a similar battle of twentieth-century technology striving against the entrenched nineteenth-century British military bureaucracy—which unfortunately had served as a model to American ordnance leaders.

Lord Haldane came to ask precisely the same questions that historian Barbara Tuchman and Secretary Root had, concerning "the pursuit by governments of policies contrary to their own interests."

Lord Haldane was even confronted with his own General Miles—in the person of the duke of Cambridge, commander in chief of the British army, who can be safely credited with one of the most reactionary minds in all of Europe's armies of the nineteenth century.

Born in Hanover, Germany, in 1819, His Royal Highness the duke of Cambridge, first cousin to Queen Victoria and a career officer since his eighteenth year, was appointed lieutenant general in 1854, at age thirty-five, when the Crimean War against Russia broke out. He was present at the battles of Alma, Balaklava, Inkerman, and the siege of Sevastopol. Here he had abundant opportunity to observe firsthand the ways that the British army had rusted from peacetime disuse and been pushed unprepared into war. This situation revealed all its major flaws, including command incompetence and breakdowns in supply lines, all of which led to the near starvation and freezing of British troops, while in store were abundant winter supplies. At war's end, in 1856, at age thirty-seven, he became commander in chief of the army, a post he was to hold with autocratic powers and the unquestioning support of the queen for almost the next forty years.

With the British public clamoring for postwar reform, Cambridge, still "young and keen,"[26] at first used his sweeping powers to respond to the great changes that were taking place in military affairs. He introduced new educational standards for officers, doubled the enrollment in the Royal Military College at Sandhurst, and set it apart as a separate Army Staff College. He expanded the curricula, which previously had stressed mainly mathematics and surveyor skills, to include the study of military history and strategy and even dispatched observers to Europe to study the structure of other armies. At every juncture, he evinced a lifelong concern for the welfare of the British soldier.

The four decades of his administration were to witness revolutionary technical changes wrought by the Industrial Revolution: the replacement of smoothbore artillery and small arms with new, more powerful and more accurate rifled artillery and small arms; the replacement of black powder with the much more potent smokeless powder; the introduction of the machine gun, which completely changed infantry warfare; the stunning rise of a newly unified Germany that, using new tactics based on the new weapons, scored lightning victories over Denmark, Austria, and France and placed in boldface type England's urgent need to modernize its army.

It was the crushing German victory over France in 1870 in particular that so alarmed the British government and led Secretary for War Edward Cardwell to introduce proposals for major changes in British military structure. But the call by reformers for the establishment of a general staff would have reduced the duke's powers and made him subordinate to the secretary for war. Cambridge, fifty-one in 1870, had grown conservative and opposed to change. Supported by a majority of the British officers, who were strongly attached to the old and outmoded regimental system, the duke aggressively challenged many of Cardwell's proposals. Even with the passage of some reforms, the British military system was still, as described by British military historian Barnett, "ramshackle."[27]

Critics accused the duke of Cambridge of having become opposed to any originality of thought. Inflexibly dedicated to the system of seniority, he often blocked the way of younger officers of
special ability. As a result, in each decade, the British army fell pro-
gressively farther behind the armies of Europe. So rickety was the
British military, between 1860 and 1880 alone, eighty-nine official
studies of the armed forces were conducted. Yet Cambridge remained implacable. "His conception of the army was pre-industrial,"
says Barnett.[28]

Opposition to him became so pervasive, even Queen Victoria's
private secretary wrote of Cambridge, "At a time when Army reform was under discussion he was not just conservative but hopelessly reactionary, and not only opposed change, but quarrelled
with those who proposed it."[29] The 1890 Hartington Commission
concluded that the concentration of power in the office of commander in chief was stultifying and urged the formation of a joint
navy-army council headed by the prime minister. The duke's post
of commander in chief would have been abolished. Now in his sev-
enties, still backed by the unflagging support of the also-aging
queen, Cambridge predictably fought the Hartington Commission.
His resistance prevailed for so long that by the time age finally forced
him to step down in 1895, even his longtime critic and
replacement, reformist General Sir Garnet Wolseley, had himself become aged and slow and his views on warfare also largely outdated.[30]
Not until the grueling war with the Boers made the flaws in the
British military system glaringly public in 1904 did the Hartington
Commission's recommendations begin to make headway, fourteen
years after their introduction. British army training was so antiquated that military historian Barnett Correlli portrays the British
regular during the Boer War as "no more than a mindless brick
in a moving wall of flesh, instantly responsive to the orders of his
superiors."[31]

Ultimately, it remained for Lord Haldane to almost single-
handedly rescue the British army from its antiquated bureaucratic
morass. The similarities between Haldane and Root are striking. A
brilliant lowland Scot, Haldane appeared in the Bannerman Cabi-

net a few years after Root's appearance in the McKinley Cabinet. Like Root, he was a noted lawyer and a brilliant administrator with absolutely no military background—trained in philosophy at the University of Edinburgh, with a "first class intellect." Haldane had the same incisive mind as Root, the same capacity for extraordinary concentration and hard work. Coming like Root from an educational background, Haldane was credited, more than any other, with the creation of the new teaching universities outside Oxford and Cambridge.[32]

To clean out the military and introduce new administrative apparatus, Haldane turned for help to the cadres of younger officers with new post–Boer War thinking. Under Haldane, the British army received the first administrative manuals in its history—manuals that proved crucial in the mobilization of the British army at the outbreak of World War I. When he introduced plans for the reorganization of the army and reserve system, which included a mobilization program that reduced the time needed to field an army from two months to fifteen days, the outraged resistance of the tradition-bound military bureaucrats brought Haldane his greatest fight. Conflicts between France and Germany, precursors of the onrushing world war, served as an imperative to Haldane's efforts. In the face of military and political opposition, Haldane had to turn to Parliament for authorization to compel his changes. The needed bill was passed only after savage attacks.

Even with Haldane's great efforts, the duke's "Colonel Blimp" legacy remained a strong impediment to the army right into World War I, as will be seen.

PART IV

CHAPTER 19

GENERAL CROZIER AND THE SPRINGFIELD '03 RIFLE

C hief of Ordnance Daniel Flagler, the godfather of the Krag, died in office on April 1, 1899. In a real sense, like Benét, who took his obsolete Springfield '73 with him when he left office, Flagler took his discredited Krag-Jorgensen with him.

Military men checked their seniority lists to see who would succeed Flagler. It was a touchy question. After the war, the ballistics men at the Springfield Armory had taken a hard look at their battle-tested offspring, the Krag-Jorgensen. It was more like the post-mortem of a corpse. They compared it extensively with Spanish Mausers captured in Cuba and also the newest Mauser, the Gewehr '98, the weapon of the German army. The comparisons were painful: ballistically, Flagler's Krag was hardly the rifle that the 7-mm Mauser was. In fact, if the Mauser wasn't the greatest rifle in the world, Ordnance men would have been hard put to say what other rifle was.

Troops who had been in Cuba were saying bluntly that Flagler and U.S. Ordnance had let them down, that the American army had been outgunned there, that standing on the firing line amid the din and excitement of battle, firing single shots or, worse, trying to shove cartridges one at a time into that difficult side magazine—all the while your enemy is emptying clip after clip at your head —is not the way to be armed, and certainly not the way to win battles. A poor second in a two-gun race, the underpowered Krag rifle may have conserved ammunition, but it didn't conserve lives. Furthermore, since the Rifle Board had tested both rifles in the early nineties, it must have known the Krag's inferiority.

In these postmortem meetings, armory personnel felt that there was a way to work out the problem of the Krag magazine so that it could be clip-loaded—with a Mauser-type clip. But that wasn't the major problem. The Krag simply couldn't handle the more powerful charge that the Mauser used to fire its 220-grain round-nosed projectile. To do so, the Krag would have to increase its muzzle velocity from 2,000 feet per second to 2,300 feet per second. This improvement would raise the pressure inside the Krag from 30,000 to above 40,000 pounds per square inch. For the Mauser's double-locking lug, that was no problem. But for the Krag's single-locking lug, it was: at those pressures, the Krag would blow open.

This was proof, critics said, that Flagler and his Ordnance team had rigged the original tests in 1892 to make the Krag win. The Krag had been tested only for some 30,000 psi, while others had been tested up to 40,000 psi. Too weak the day it was accepted, the Krag was far from being the best of the rifles that had competed in those 1892 tests. It was time to make a change, and the man to make the change was the new chief of ordnance, Adelbert Buffington.

General Buffington was an odd choice for ordnance chief. True, he was an inventor of some stature in the ordnance world, even a "genius," some said. But he was temperamental in the extreme and capable of such offensive interdepartmental bickering that he was once charged with and found guilty of conduct unbecoming an officer, a minor offense that would not affect his movement up through the seniority system. In fact, that seniority system, not merit, gained Buffington's appointment for him—he was the next man on the list. But with less than eighteen months left before mandatory retirement would sweep him out of the army, he was a lame-duck interim appointee whose slow and imperious ways were bluntly criticized by the *Army and Navy Journal*. The Ordnance Department, it said, "spends too much time splitting hairs and in experiments that lead to no final result. With all of his excellent qualities General Flagler was slow to learn, and let us hope his successor will be less disposed to forget that the Ordnance Department exists for the Army, and not the Army for the Ordnance."[1]

In early 1900, soon after he was appointed the new chief, Buffington directed the Experimental Department to redesign the Krag rifle around the new, heavy 220-grain bullet the Mauser fired. On October 2, 1900, at Springfield Armory, General Buffington's Rifle Board was convened to test the new Krag-derivative rifle submitted by the Springfield Experimental Department. Still a recognizable offspring of the 1896 Krag-Jorgensen, the weapon was reported to be able to fire the 220-grain bullet with a muzzle velocity of the mandatory 2,300 feet per second.

While the Rifle Board was testing the new weapon, the American people had reelected William McKinley to a second term as president. His running mate, the new vice president of the United States, was America's favorite war hero—Teddy Roosevelt—a man who was very interested in a new army rifle.

For two months, the board tested the new model and then, in December of 1900, it recommended two changes. Noting that the new model was still not easy to load, the board recommended that it be redesigned. Also, the new design should fire rimless cartridges.

In effect, the board had rejected the reworked Krag. The two changes were so significant they really required a whole new rifle design. Making the rifle easier to load meant making it easier to fire rapidly. The only way to make it easier to load was to introduce a preloaded clip, the very element that Flagler and his staff had rejected. Evidently, the proponents of increased firepower were wringing concessions from the proponents of ammunition conservation. More significant, introducing rimless cartridges meant redesigning the rifle chamber. Both changes represented a major step away from the old Krag design. The board ordered two new experimental models that would incorporate these changes.

The order for changes in the new rifle came directly from Teddy Roosevelt himself, even though he was not to be inaugurated as vice president until March, three months away.[2] Remembering the terrifying sound of those 220-grain Mauser projectiles as he charged up San Juan Hill, Vice President Roosevelt was said to be determined that the U.S. Army should have an equivalent weapon and should never allow itself to be outgunned again.

When the work was finished, the new rifle didn't look at all like the Krag, with its single-locking lug, but more like the German Mauser Gewehr 1898—with its double-locking lug, Peter Paul Mauser's improved version of the Spanish Mauser Roosevelt had faced on San Juan Hill.[3] The transitional Springfield M1901—or, more formally, the U.S. magazine rifle, caliber .30, Model 1901, bolt-action and clip-loaded—handled the new, more powerful 220-grain projectile, and weighed 9.47 pounds. With this model came an interesting feature: instead of the familiar blade bayonet, the M1901 sported a rod bayonet—similar to the 1888 Springfield trap-door—that would also serve as emergency ramrod to clean or unjam the rifle.

The inventor, Captain William Crozier of Ordnance, suddenly, on June 1, 1901, stepped into national prominence. The *New York Times* on that day reported that Buffington was soon to retire—on his sixty-fourth birthday in November—and, when he did, his replacement would be Captain William Henry Crozier.[4] Under Elihu Root's army reforms, his term would be limited to four years. There would be no more life-tenure chiefs of ordnance.

The news caused a thundering bureaucratic war inside the War Department. Crozier was only a captain; critics complained that army regulations required that the new COO hold at least the rank of lieutenant colonel. Worse than that, Crozier would be jumping over the heads of thirty senior officers.

In October 1901, the *New York Times* was back with more bad news for the old guard. Not only was it even more definite that Crozier would be the new panjandrum, he also was being chosen for "high scientific attainments." That meant he was more qualified than all the thirty officers ahead of him in spite of their superior experience and time served. His appointment, added the *Times*, "will mark another step by Secretary Root toward the vitalizing of the important army bureaus by placing young men at the head."[5]

On November 21, Buffington, on his sixty-fourth birthday, was required to retire. On November 23, 1901, it became official:

Secretary of War Elihu Root appointed Captain William Henry Crozier COO—Chief of Ordnance—with the rank of brigadier general.[6]

The old guard didn't take it without a fight. They ran to their friends on Capitol Hill and soon had the Senate Committee on Military Affairs balking at confirmation. Captain Crozier, said the Senate Committee, was appointed to a staff position while holding a rank lower than lieutenant colonel—a clear violation of army regulations.[7]

The obstreperous General Miles, ever at odds with Secretary of War Root, whom he still refused to accept as his superior, eagerly, loudly, testified in Senate chambers against young Crozier. Jumping thirty places was just too much and, besides, Crozier, as an inventor of some stature, would use the office to adopt his own inventions and reap some lucrative royalties as a result.

In response, Root pointed at the new law, Section 26 of which gave him power to abrogate the seniority system. Further, the requirement that new appointees hold the rank of at least lieutenant colonel applied only to line appointments.[8] Finally, Captain Crozier announced that, while in office, he would accept no royalties from his country for any of his inventions.

It was Teddy Roosevelt—now president of the United States following McKinley's assassination in September 1901—who then played the trump card. Name one officer, he demanded of the army, who gave "more conspicuous proof of fitness" for the office. Name one who was more qualified than—or even as qualified as—General Crozier.[9] With Crozier's intimidating résumé widely known, no one replied. In fact, a number of those officers over whose heads Crozier jumped heartily endorsed the appointment.[10] After seven months of political skirmishing, the old guard was beaten back. On June 21, 1902, the U.S. Senate in executive session confirmed General Crozier's four-year appointment by a vote of 44 to 12.

Together, Root and Roosevelt had cleaned up a mess: no more kings entrenched for a lifetime in an invincible fortress at Springfield, beyond the reach of reason and reform, no more superannuated prehistoric thinking and autocratic ways. There could be no question: William Henry Crozier was Teddy Roosevelt's personal choice. And from the viewpoint of Roosevelt and Root, Crozier seemed an ideal man for the job.

He was forty-seven, born in Carrollton, Ohio, February 19, 1855. He graduated from West Point at the top of his class in 1876, the year of Custer's defeat at Little Bighorn. He was a military teacher, having taught at West Point and having recently declined another opportunity to teach there—as professor of natural and experimental philosophy. He was a battle veteran, with three years fighting the Sioux and the Bannock Indians. He was an ordnance administrator, having commanded, before he was thirty, the Watertown Arsenal from 1884 to 1887. He was an inventor, having created, among other things, a gun, several ordnance appliances, and, most important, with General Buffington, the Buffington-Crozier coast artillery disappearing gun carriage, and so was obviously open to new ideas—an astonishing trait in a chief of ordnance. As an ordnance officer, he was fully experienced: because of his considerable skill with artillery, in 1888, the Ordnance Bureau had sent him abroad to study European ordnance, and on his return placed him in full charge of the construction of gun carriages for the army—which, in 1896, led to the Buffington-Crozier carriage.

During the Spanish-American War, he was inspector general for the Atlantic and Gulf coast defenses. In December 1898, his stature was such he was selected to be the U.S. military representative to the Hague Peace Conference to work out the details of a peace treaty with Spain. Later service in the Philippines rounded out his experience.

More than all that, his record seemed to suggest he was willing to drop the Ordnance Bureau's usual bunker mentality and let other branches of the army participate in the selection of weapons. In fact, he recommended the formation of an Infantry Board that would do just that. This type of advisory panel, Crozier said, would allow for "the expression of opinion from constituted authorities in the Cavalry and Infantry as a basis on which to proceed with the improvements suggested or needed."[11] On the surface, this seemed to be not just a fresh wind in the Ordnance Department, but a full-blown gale.

Yet, when the new Infantry Board convened in March of 1903, it was still an advisory board only. Final decisions remained firmly in the hands of General Crozier. And he could quote that law verbatim. Like the ordnance chiefs who had preceded him, he was also firmly convinced that "the technician knows best what combat troops require." By "technician," he meant the ordnance chief. Under Crozier, the Ordnance Bureau was going to continue to select the army's small arms.

Crozier even looked like the ideal American army commanding officer. Straight of posture, tall and strong, handsome in his uniform and boots, with a dashing military mustache, he gazed loftily at the world with those hawklike unwavering eyes expected of a commanding presence. Here, his every move and gesture said, was the decisive leader needed to mount a charge against the enemy or face down a recalcitrant bureaucracy.

In short, here was a young, creative, popular Ordnance man looking ahead at America's new international role—not back at the faded glories of the Civil War. Just the man to wean Ordnance away from its antique rifle ideas and to godfather a rifle worthy of the most powerful nation on earth. His friends cheered his appointment, expecting him to become one of the best ordnance chiefs of all time.

On April 7, 1902, William Crozier, a mint-new general, took charge of his new rifle and authorized $1,700 for the production of a small number of the new Springfield '01s. The samples were to be given to a board of officers for full-scale field testing of the rifle, clips, bandoleers, cartridge belts, and the rod bayonet. And less than a year later, on February 16, 1903, at the Springfield Armory, the limited run from the model shop was completed; the weapons were ready for testing; and an examining board gathered at Springfield to put the new rifle through its paces.

With modifications and after firing ten thousand rounds of a new round-nosed cartridge from the Frankford Arsenal, the rifle had passed one grueling test after another and had won the endorsement of 223 officers and 4,669 men on ten posts. Two models were presented to the infantry at Fort Leavenworth and to the cavalry at Fort Riley.[12]

Both boards, without reservation, recommended the new rifle. With that kind of unanimity, in June 1903, the secretary of war approved Crozier's recommendation that the army replace the Krag with the new rifle: the clip-fed, bolt-action Springfield 1903 rifle, firing the new powerful Mauser-like round-nose cartridge.

The only cloud, a tiny one, in the Ordnance Bureau's blue sky was the rifle's design. It had an uncomfortably close similarity to the patented features of the Mauser. The cloud soon grew larger.

The following year, after continued testing, the M1901 cartridge clip was found not completely satisfactory. The 1903 model Springfield needed a new clip design. A new design proved to be an outstanding performer but also similar to a patented feature on the Mauser clip.

President Roosevelt didn't like the rod-type bayonet. And said so in writing. In January 1905, he wrote to Secretary of War William Howard Taft, "I must say that I think that ramrod bayonet about as poor an invention as I ever saw."[13] One wonders if the president knew it was selected by his own choice for ordnance chief, General Crozier himself, from a previous rifle.[14] In any event, in March 1905, the M1903 got a regular sixteen-inch knife bayonet.

There was yet one final—and major—change to be made to the new '03, a new and more deadly cartridge. Produced as a direct result of the Rifle Board's request for a rimless cartridge, it was long and slender, with a sharply pointed nose and a tapering boattail at the back. It was best known as the spitzer, from the German *spitzgeschoss*—pointed bullet. Germany had been studying the spitzer for some years and finally adopted it for its Mauser 1904. France produced its own spitzer at about the same time. Because of its aerodynamic configuration, the spitzer bullet traveled at a much higher velocity and had a flatter trajectory than the round-nosed bullet. It also was less affected by wind drift, one of the major complaints with the old Krag. The new spitzer turned the Springfield '03 into a super rifle, firing a faster, harder-hitting—and lighter—bullet at a greater rate. In short, more firepower.

When Du Pont developed a new cooler-burning Pyro single-base powder to fire it, the resulting new 1906 .30-caliber cartridge became known as the .30-'06, the famous "thirty-aught-six." When the Springfield '03 rifle was rechambered to accommodate the new cartridge, the result was considered a masterpiece.

Yet, with universal praise ringing in its ears, the Ordnance Department was about to be publicly embarrassed. On March 15, 1904, while the first armory production run of thirty thousand '03s was under way, there were urgent conversations going on behind closed doors in Washington. The words "patent infringement" were being whispered. Ordnance experts and government patent attorneys, comparing the Springfield '03 rifle and cartridge clip with the Mauser rifle and clip, shifted uncomfortably in their chairs. Patent infringement was evident to every eye. In spite of the armory's design changes, the Springfield rifle was such an obvious copy of the Mauser rifle that Mauser could sue for patent infringement. Worse, he had an excellent chance of winning. The army chief of staff, the secretary of war, and even the president himself had to be informed. The implications were enormous. The Mauser people in Germany would soon enough have some samples of the new Springfield '03, and their patent lawyer would be knocking on the door of the War Department.

This was an uncomfortable moment for Crozier. The Springfield '03 was his gun. He had been associated with it from the beginning, when he was still a captain. As indicated, President Roosevelt made no secret that he wanted the German weapon for the U.S. Army. Author James Fallows states flatly that Roosevelt "ordered the War Department to buy Mausers for American troops." But, Fallows adds, "there was little enthusiasm in the army for a rifle that came not only from outside its own system but also from outside the country."[15] Therefore, instead of licensing the Mauser from Germany as the Flagler regime had done with the Krag-Jorgensen, General Crozier had come close to duplicating it.

One ordnance expert states unequivocally that the new American rifle was not as good as the German rifle it purportedly copied: "Various departures were made from the Mauser design, and in every instance the designers laid an egg. If these departures were made as an improvement, they failed. If they were made with the worthy notion of avoiding royalty payments to Paul von Mauser, the inventor of the Mauser action, they also failed."[16]

On March 15, 1904, an official letter, over the name of Brigadier General William H. Crozier, Chief of Ordnance, was addressed to Waffenfabrik Mauser, Württemberg, Germany. The letter said, "As an examination would seem to indicate that some of the features of the cartridge clip recently adopted for the United States Army may be covered by your United States letters patent Nos. 402,605; 482,376; and 547,932, it is requested that your attorney in this country call at this office for determining what, if any, of its features are covered by your patents and if so, to arrive at an agreement as to the royalties which should be paid therefore."[17] The Germans must have had a solid case. Crozier was waving royalties at them even before the first conversation.

On May 4, 1904, Arthur Frazier, the American attorney representing Mauser interests in the United States, came to the office of the chief of ordnance in Washington, D.C., to talk with General Crozier about the Mauser cartridge clip patents. Although General Crozier's letter had mentioned just the clip, Frazier soon understood that there was more to discuss. In the end, it was agreed that the attorney would send to Springfield Armory for not just an M1903 clip but the entire '03 rifle as well. The general waited for Frazier's return.

On June 16, 1904, Arthur Frazier met with General Crozier again. The Mauser people, he reported, had now carefully examined the Springfield '03 rifle and clip. As for the clip, the general's expectation that there was a patent infringement was incorrect. There was not a single patent infringement on the clip. There were two. General Crozier asked, assuming the U.S. government agreed with Mauser, what kind of an arrangement could be made.

Mauser, Frazier answered, was asking for a dollar royalty for every one thousand clips made for the Springfield '03. General Crozier took that under advisement.

But the meeting was not over. Frazier stated that the Mauser people had also examined the new Springfield '03 rifle and found not one but five infringements. Mauser required a dollar royalty on each Springfield made.

Arthur Frazier then delivered more disturbing news to General Crozier. The American-made Krag-Jorgensen rifle also infringed on Mauser patents. In other words, the United States had been in-fringing on German-held Mauser patents since 1892, when it first issued the Krag-Jorgensen to its troops. Frazier made a conciliatory offer. If, he suggested, the United States were to be cooperative in a settlement of the seven M1903 patent infringements, such an ami-cable arrangement might induce Waffenfabrik Mauser to waive the Krag-Jorgensen infringements. The general took the offer and went off to see his lawyers and his superiors.

On December 22, 1904, the lawyers gave the U.S. Ordnance Bureau another unhappy Christmas. Mauser, they said, clearly had U.S. Ordnance over a barrel. Since the armory had already gone to the enormous expense of obtaining and setting up the production tooling to make the Springfield '03 rifle, the Ordnance Bureau was hardly in a position to dicker unless it wanted to abandon the enor-mous sum expended on the Springfield '03 and go in search of an-other rifle.

The general now had no choice but to walk up to the negotiating table with his hands up and his wallet open. At the next meeting, General Crozier and Frazier reached an agreement. After a review by the comptroller of the Treasury and a few revisions, the agree-ment was submitted through Frazier to his client, Waffenfabrik Mauser, in Württemberg, Germany.

On March 27, 1905, Waffenfabrik Mauser accepted the offer. And the final agreement was ratified by the comptroller on April 5, 1905. The United States agreed to pay Waffenfabrik Mauser 75 cents for each Springfield rifle made. And 50 cents per thousand clips made. All royalty payments would cease after total payments reached U.S.$200,000.

Between November 6, 1905, when the Germans received a Trea-sury check for $11,367.53, and the July 1909 Treasury check for $8,117.25, the U.S. Armory made nine payments to Waffenfabrik Mauser for the specified total of $200,000.

In most aspects, the transaction seems a bargain.[18] The United States was embarrassed, but now had clear title to one of the finest rifles in the world. Everyone seemed satisfied with Crozier's handling of the matter, and on November 19, 1905, President Roosevelt reappointed him to a second four-year term as chief of ordnance.[19]

But a few days before he was officially reappointed, there occurred another event that seemed to reflect directly on his capability. As chief of ordnance, and as an expert on coastal artillery, General Crozier had been personally involved in the placement of the American coast-artillery system.

Between November 12 and 15, 1905, in New York City, during a three-day gala, Britain's Admiral Prince Louis Battenberg (who Anglicized his German name to Mountbatten during World War I) arrived in New York with a British fleet on a courtesy call. During a newspaper interview, he said he was not impressed with the naval defenses of the city. In fact, he stated that two British fleets "could reduce the city to atoms in less time than it would take his cook to make an omelet."[20]

With American pride and his own reputation at stake, General Crozier flatly denied Prince Battenberg's assertion, saying that coast artillery could sink all his warships long before they got through the Narrows or through Long Island Sound. The *New York Times* ran an editorial praising the general, but now there were questions in the minds of many. The fiasco of the Spanish-American War was still fresh in America's memory. Just how ready was the United States for war?

In 1907, an additional damaging blow was dealt to the new rifle when General Crozier had another German visitor, also bearing patent infringement papers and representing Deutsch Waffen-und-Munitionsfabriken, Berlin, Germany, the manufacturer of the spitzer rifle cartridge for the German Mauser rifle. This cartridge, the Berlin firm announced, was covered by U.S. patent 841861, issued on January 22, 1907, and the U.S. Army was infringing on it with the manufacture of the U.S. .30-'06 cartridge for its Springfield M1903 rifle.[21]

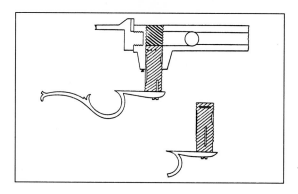

Invented in 1776, the British Ferguson was the first operational breech-loading military rifle. Although 100 were in use during the American Revolution, after the death of its inventor, Patrick Ferguson, during the 1780 Battle of Kings Mountain, the British army abandoned it.
(BRITISH PATENT OFFICE, 1776)

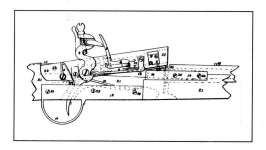

The 1819 Hall's—the first breech-loading rifle in U.S. service and the first military weapon to be mass-produced with interchangeable machine-made parts. In the face of traditionalist opposition, Ordnance dropped the Hall in the 1840s in favor of a hand-made muzzle-loading smoothbore musket. (HARPERS FERRY NHS ARCHIVES)

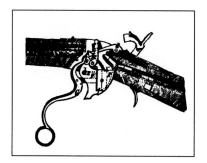

The most controversial weapon of the Civil War was the seven-shot Spencer repeating rifle, condemned by Gen. James Ripley as an ammunition waster.
(SCIENTIFIC AMERICAN, 1862)

Richard Jordan Gatling, inventor of the first successful hand-cranked machine gun (Civil War era). Multibarrel Gatlings might have saved Custer and his men had they not been left behind in camp.
(SMITHSONIAN INSTITUTION, #42496)

Chief of Ordnance James Wolfe Ripley (1861–64). Critics contend his adamant opposition to the repeating rifle extended the Civil War by many months and caused many thousand more casualties.
(MASSACHUSETTS COMMANDERY, MILITARY ORDER OF THE LOYAL LEGION, AND THE U.S. ARMY MILITARY HISTORY INSTITUTE)

Chief of Ordnance Alexander Dyer (1864–74). Hailed for his rifle production while commandant of the Springfield Armory during the Civil War, he is the father of the single-shot, breech-loading Trap Door Springfield rifle and carbine, which supplanted the repeating rifle and carbine.
(MASSACHUSETTS COMMANDERY, MILITARY ORDER OF THE LOYAL LEGION, AND THE U.S. ARMY MILITARY HISTORY INSTITUTE)

Chief of Ordnance Stephen Vincent Benét (1874–91). He kept the Trap Door Springfield rifle in service long after it was obsolete, despite the shortcomings revealed at Custer's Little Bighorn debacle.
(MASSACHUSETTS COMMANDERY, MILITARY ORDER OF THE LOYAL LEGION, AND THE U.S. ARMY MILITARY HISTORY INSTITUTE)

*Chief of Ordnance Daniel Webster Flagler (1891–99).
He chose the Krag-Jorgensen bolt-action rifle in
1892 because it conserved ammunition. During
the Spanish-American War it was outgunned by the
Mauser, the rifle Flagler had rejected.*
(U.S. ARMY ARMAMENT, MUNITIONS AND CHEMICAL
COMMAND [AMCCOM] HISTORICAL OFFICE,
ROCK ISLAND, ILLINOIS)

*Chief of Ordnance William Henry Crozier
(1901–18). His war preparations
plus his personal quarrels with Isaac
Newton Lewis over the Lewis Machine
Gun led to a Senate investigation
and Crozier's dismissal in 1918.*
(U.S. ARMY MILITARY HISTORY INSTITUTE)

*The Springfield '03 bolt-action .30-caliber rifle. Considered one of the
U.S. army's greatest shoulder arms, its similarities to the German Mauser
rifle cost the United States $200,000 in patent infringement payments.*
(SMITHSONIAN INSTITUTION, #72-5105)

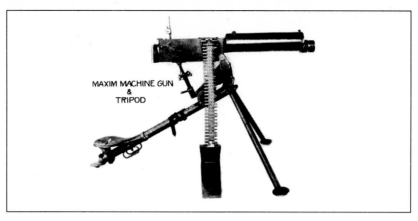

The Maxim machine gun. Possibly the most efficient small arms mankiller of all time, the Maxim, in its Russian, German, and British versions, slaughtered tens of thousands of soldiers during the trench warfare of World War I. Its rejection by Ordnance Chief Crozier in favor of the less reliable French Benét-Mercié brought on a major machine-gun controversy. (NATIONAL ARCHIVES, #165-WW 385-G-2)

Col. Isaac Newton Lewis, inventor of the Lewis machine gun. After Ordnance Chief Crozier rejected it, the British adopted the Lewis as their primary automatic weapon in the trenches of World War I. (U.S. MILITARY ACADEMY ARCHIVES)

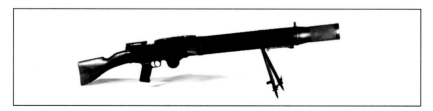

The Lewis machine gun became an issue in Woodrow Wilson's presidential campaign of 1916 and contributed to Ordnance Chief Crozier's dismissal in 1918. (SMITHSONIAN INSTITUTION, #78-16422)

Second Lt. Valentine A. Browning, son of inventor John Moses Browning, demonstrates his father's heavy machine gun to men of the 1st Platoon, Company A, 315th Machine Gun Battalion, 80th Division, Meuse, France. (NATIONAL ARCHIVES, #111-SC-31973)

John Cantius Garand, Canadian-born inventor of the World War II M1 semiautomatic .30-caliber rifle. (SPRINGFIELD ARMORY NATIONAL HISTORIC SITE)

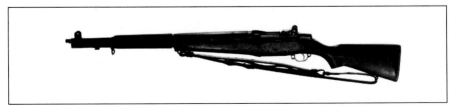

The Garand M1 semiautomatic rifle allowed such rapid fire operation that many German soldiers believed they were confronted by automatic weapons. The Japanese army attempted, too late, to copy it. (SMITHSONIAN INSTITUTION, #84-10079)

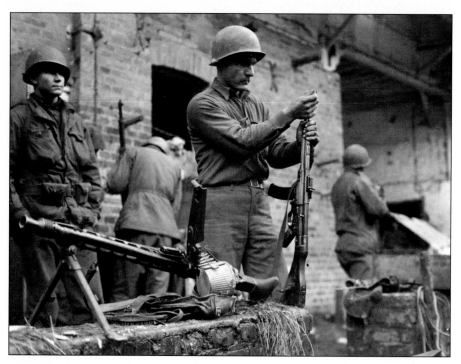

A captured Sturmgewehr 44 automatic rifle being cleaned by Pfc. Henry P. Riggan, Ninth Army, in Germany in the fall of 1944. The first true assault rifle, its cyclic rate of six hundred rounds a minute could have made a major difference had the German army introduced it earlier in the war. In the foreground, the devastating German MG42 machine gun. (NATIONAL ARCHIVES, #111-SC-197095)

Reconnaissance scout trainees receive instruction on the Soviet-made AK47 assault rifle. Designed by Russian army sergeant Mikail Kalashnikov at the end of World War II, the AK47 is probably the most widely used automatic rifle in the world. (NATIONAL ARCHIVES, #111-SC-653832)

Col. Rene R. Studler, Chief of Small Arms Development Branch of the Springfield National Armory. His brilliant early career was overshadowed by his failed efforts to design an automatic rifle that would fire the overpowered .30-caliber cartridge. His refusal to consider a smaller cartridge severely affected U.S. post–World War II relations with England and Belgium. (U.S. ARMY MILITARY HISTORY INSTITUTE)

Springfield Armory, Springfield, Massachusetts, on a site chosen by Washington's Ordnance Chief, General Henry Knox. It was the scene of the Ordnance Department's greatest triumphs and failures. Closed in the midst of the M14 production scandal in 1966 by Secretary of Defense Robert S. McNamara, it now houses the Armory's Small Arms Museum (lower foreground). Colonel Ripley's "palatial" commandant's residence is lower left. (S.A.N.H.S.)

A landmark in political porkbarreling, Harpers Ferry Armory stands at the confluence of the Shenandoah and Potomac rivers, shown here in July 1865. Founded by President George Washington, it was the scene of John Brown's raid in 1859. Today it is a National Historic Park.
(NATIONAL ARCHIVES, #165-SB-26; HFNHP/E HARPERS FERRY)

The uncontrollable M14 automatic rifle, being fired by M/Sgt. Otto Hanel at the Aberdeen Proving Ground, March 1961. Manufacturing problems led Defense Secretary McNamara to stop M14 production and close the Springfield Armory.
(NATIONAL ARCHIVES, #111-SC-580103)

President John F. Kennedy examines the ArmaLite AR-15 automatic rifle, militarized as the U.S. M16. The Ichord congressional investigating subcommittee characterized U.S. Ordnance handling of M16 production as "bordering on criminal negligence."
(JOHN F. KENNEDY LIBRARY, #ST-C85-1-63)

This assertion made the armory top brass exceedingly uncomfortable. If they paid this bill, they could look very bad in the eyes of the international arms world. People could say that not only did U.S. Ordnance copy the Mauser rifle (with credit for good taste in copying a very fine rifle), and not only did it copy the brilliant Mauser clip design that loaded the Mauser rifle, but it even copied the revolutionary spitzer cartridge that went into the Mauser clip that went into the Mauser rifle. Critics could say the United States copied the whole system, lock, stock, and barrel; infringed on seven or eight German patents; and were forced to pay royalties.

This time, General Crozier assigned the problem of replying to Lieutenant Colonel John T. Thompson, acting chief of ordnance whenever Crozier was absent. Colonel (and later General) Thompson, who was to invent the Thompson submachine gun, went to a gathering of government patent attorneys and listened to their analysis of the situation. Deutsch, they assured him, had a very weak case and told him not to pay. Deutsch, they felt, could be beaten in court.

Colonel Thompson contacted Deutsch and informed them that the United States felt there was no case. When Deutsch pressed for a settlement, Thompson refused. On July 18, 1914, Deutsch brought suit against the United States in the U.S. Court of Claims, asking for royalty payments on a quarter-billion M1906 rifle bullets at a dollar a thousand for a total of a quarter of a million dollars. The timing was ironic, just ten days before the start of the worst war the world had ever seen, in which many millions of rounds of spitzers would be fired.

On July 28, 1914, Austria-Hungary declared war on Serbia, precipitating World War I. The Deutsch suit was deferred. When the United States declared war on Germany in April 1917, the U.S. alien property custodian seized the Deutsch spitzer patent and the U.S. attorney general dismissed Deutsch's suit.

But in 1920, Deutsch reopened its claim in the American court. A U.S. tribunal did not try to determine whether Deutsch had a patent infringement suit. Rather, it focused on the wartime seizure of the German patent, which was covered by a U.S. treaty with

Germany. On July 2, 1921, the tribunal stated that the United States was in open violation of that treaty and awarded Deutsch $300,000 in damages. The U.S. government appealed and the case was in the courts for more than seven years before it was finally settled, on December 31, 1928. After twenty-two years of on-again, off-again litigation, Deutsch won. With interest, the $300,000 award for damages had grown to $412,520.55—another Christmas present for the Ordnance Bureau.[22]

CHAPTER 20

THE MAXIM MACHINE GUN

T he war that had interrupted Deutsch's patent suit in 1914 was known then as the Great War. In spite of the new and lethal rifles that were used, the most controversial weapons were three machine guns that came to dominate—indeed, create—trench warfare from 1914 to 1918.

All three were invented by Americans—three men of genius. All three machine guns were fundamentally different from one another, all destined to write an unforgettable history during the Great War. All three had an impact on the U.S. Army Ordnance Bureau during the regime of General Crozier.

The military organizations of Europe and the United States required years to digest the awesome implications of the machine gun, which so basically and permanently changed the nature of warfare that the military mind was at first loath to even study it.

The first of the three guns appeared in 1887, twenty-seven years before the Great War. In fact, it can be said that the war of 1914 to 1918 actually began in London in 1883, when research on the weapon began in the London laboratory of a Yankee by the name of Hiram Maxim.

Military science, in the age of the Industrial Revolution, was already in turmoil. War, which had always been a closed world of general against general, was now a stage crowded with intruders—politicians, military historians, military theorists, a new freewheeling player called the arms merchant, and, worst of all, inventors with disturbing ideas that were coming so quickly one could not adapt new tactics fast enough to keep up. In that conservative, and in many ways cloistered, world, military men were soon to be confronted with a completely revolutionary weapon—the Maxim machine gun.

As might be expected, the inventor, Hiram Maxim, was an expatriate American, in fact, a Down East Yankee from Sangersville, Maine, where he was born in 1840. Before he died seventy-six years later, he had incontestably become one of the world's great mechanical geniuses and the brilliant progenitor of automatic small arms. He began life with several key advantages. He had no science education, but he claimed he thereby escaped the university blinkers that were blinding other minds to what was so clear to Maxim. Also, Maxim had a clear, frank, unflattering view of the frailties of the world, of people, and of his own family. Of his French Huguenot ancestors, he said, "They came to America because here they could worship God according to the dictates of their own conscience and prevent others from doing the same."[1] From them, he inherited his huge physique and extraordinary physical strength. Although he had no formal education, he absorbed a quite extensive rough-and-ready technical education by studying the existing technical volumes of the day and by working at a series of different occupations—from operating water-powered machinery to wood turning. In each of these occupations, he sought to design items that would improve them. As an inexpensive substitute for slate blackboards, he designed a new kind of paint for use on plastered classroom walls. He even designed the proverbial better mousetrap that was later to be sold in large quantities, although Maxim himself never earned any money from it.

After traveling extensively in the United States and Canada, wandering, and engaging in a number of occupations, Maxim went to work in his uncle's metal casting company in Fitchburg, Massachusetts. There he had invented an automatic illuminating gas machine that worked so well a New York firm agreed to take every one the company could make. But before the shop could get production fairly under way, Maxim saw a way to simplify it and reduce the manufacturing cost. When he showed it to his uncle, the man became indignant. He felt Maxim should have thought of the new design first, and in consequence fired him.

Undaunted, Maxim, then twenty-five, went to Boston to work for a firm making automatic illuminating gas machines and, before he was thirty, had a number of inventions to his credit, including the first gas-density regulator and the first automatic fire extinguishing system, which still forms the basis of all fire sprinkler and alarm systems. He moved to New York, where, becoming affiliated with one of the wealthiest men in the country, he designed and developed the first electric lightbulbs used in New York City.

None of these inventions heralded the remarkable work that was to come. In 1882, he went to Europe to attend an electrical industry show. In Vienna, he talked with another American inventor. "Hang your chemistry and electricity!" the man told him. "If you want to make a pile of money, invent something that will enable these Europeans to cut each other's throats with greater facility."[2]

Maxim pondered that idea. Although almost all of the new weapons inventions had come from Americans, there was no significant military weapons market in America. Springfield Armory, under Ordnance Chief Benét, after flirting with new ideas, always returned to its revered trap-door Springfield. Weapons inventions ended up in European arsenals. Maxim decided that if he were to design guns, he should remain in Europe. London seemed to be the best place, so he set up shop there. He already had a gun idea he wanted to work on—to make the first automatic machine gun, one not dependent on the cranking of the handle by an operator, like the Gatling, something more efficient, more lethal.

From the beginning, he had great difficulty getting the idea from his head into reality. English gunsmiths warned him to forget the whole thing, one in particular asserting, "You don't stand a ghost of a chance in competition with regular gunmakers. You are not a gun man. Stick to electricity."[3]

Years before, Maxim had spent some time firing an old Springfield .45-70 rifle, and the ferocious kick of the weapon left his shoulder bruised. He had wondered ever since if there was some way to use the power of the recoil to do some other work for the rifle. Now he returned to that question, and within a year, he had his first success. He developed a recoil action for the rifle that ejected the spent cartridge, chambered the next cartridge, and recocked the rifle. It was a major discovery, the first automatic firearm, and, although Winchester Repeating Arms, which readily bought the device, never found an important market for it, Maxim himself had gained the serious attention of all the major gun makers in Europe.[4]

But a new rifle was not what Maxim was after. He had now decided that there was an enormous potential market for a reliable machine gun. He soon discovered why no one had been able to invent one. There was a vast gap between the relatively simple design of a bolt-action rifle and the design of a complex automatic weapon that would fire, eject, reload, and fire an endless supply of cartridges. He wasn't seeking just a single invention; he was seeking a series of them, each growing from the previous one. This was the kind of creation that would normally evolve from the work of many gifted designers over a period of time—just as the rifle had. Perhaps he had been mistaken; maybe there were easier conquests to be made elsewhere, for this was a realm with no maps, no roads, and a number of major obstacles. But this realm had never been entered by a mind like Maxim's. He got out a piece of drawing paper and began to attack the problems one by one.

Hiram Maxim had invented not only the first mechanically operated machine gun, bristling with so many brilliant inventions that it would take years for other gun designers to absorb them, but also the first cartridge-feed belt, which he had devised because no other system existed that could feed the bullets as fast as his gun would fire them. With these ammunition belts linked in a series, the Maxim machine gun could fire as long as a finger was on the trigger. More than that, he had designed his gun so that any piece in the weapon could be replaced by hand in six seconds without the aid of a single tool. And having created all the parts by hand, Maxim then made the jigs and tools that would mass-produce his new gun.

It is difficult to overvalue the brilliance of Maxim's work. The problems he solved and the insights he developed—especially in the face of the discouraging doubts that other gun designers pressed on him—are regarded today as the mark of true genius. His weapon was so completely developed and thought out, none of the brilliant designers who came after him ever produced a significant refinement. Between 1883 and 1885, while Europe watched, Maxim obtained an impressive series of patents on every aspect of automatic recoil, a number of which later appeared in most weapons of the world.

Selling his weapon proved to be as difficult as designing it. His attempts to get publicity drew only scornful stories in the newspapers, to whom the weapon sounded too good to be true. But the stories did serve to get the attention of ordnance men, and in 1883, one of the most important, His Royal Highness the duke of Cambridge, the commander in chief of England's military forces, arrived with an entourage to see for himself. During the demonstration, the Maxim gun produced a tremendous noise and clouds of black powder smoke, while, as the duke attentively watched, firing off six hundred rounds a minute tirelessly without jamming to leave its target in shambles. The duke congratulated Maxim, but left without issuing a order.

Maxim continued to improve his machine gun and continued to present it to ordnance men—including Mauser and Mannlicher—who praised it without buying. Maxim soon discovered why. His way was being blocked by the greatest and most unscrupulous arms dealer of all time—the legendary Basil Zaharoff, the original Merchant of Death.

Zaharoff, representing the Nordenfelt Company, was selling a hand-cranked, multiple-barrel so-called machine gun that was little better than the Gatling gun. But if he didn't have the best gun, he was the better—albeit unscrupulous—salesman, and wherever he went all over Europe, Zaharoff maintained a relentless whispering campaign against the new Maxim gun.

When Maxim brought his weapon to Vienna in 1885 for a demonstration before the archduke himself, Zaharoff attempted to deter the archduke by asserting that the weather was much too hot to journey thirty miles to see a weapon that always malfunctioned.[5] But the Maxim didn't, and Zaharoff was faced with the loss of his Austrian market. Tale-tellers in the arms trade claimed that Zaharoff bribed workers in Maxim's plant to sabotage some of the parts of the machine gun destined for the next Austrian test. He also spread rumors all over the Austrian government about the unreliability of the Maxim. During the late 1880s, Maxim put on three demonstrations in Austria, the last before the emperor Franz Joseph himself, who saw his initials spelled out with Maxim machine gun bullets. Zaharoff efforts succeeded when Maxim received a cautious order for only 160 guns. Small as it was, it was larger than Maxim's first order, which came from the British in 1887 for three weapons. Even though the three passed the British ordnance tests handily, the Maxim was still not officially adopted by the British. In an effort to solve his sales problems, Maxim formed a coalition with Albert Vickers, the British arms maker, and later even with Zaharoff himself.

Yet 1888 still brought no major sales. The Springfield Armory tested the weapon that year, but with the Indian Wars winding down, there seemed to be no enemy at which to aim the Maxim. Besides, the machine gun violated a primary armory dictum against wasting ammunition.

A break came a short time later, in the Spandau Arsenal, in the presence of the kaiser himself, when the Germans tested the two-man Maxim against their four-man, hand-cranked Gatling. The kaiser was so impressed that he designated the Maxim gun as the official machine gun of the German army.[6] Quickly, all the arsenals of Europe had to put the Maxim gun into their strategic military thinking. Still, military thinking couldn't encompass the significance of the machine gun and orders remained small.

Even though the kaiser himself had approved the Maxim, German ordnance men were still leisurely testing the weapon. The Austrians, while very impressed, developed the Schwarzlose, which was inferior to the Maxim. In the United States, the Ordnance Bureau barely acknowledged Maxim's existence.

Even Vieille's development of smokeless powder in 1885, which, because of its greater explosive power, made the machine gun more lethal than ever, didn't immediately help. The military mind seemed unwilling to confront the great significance of the new weapon and the equally significant effect it would have on military tactics. All through the 1890s, sales were modest. Maxim needed something dramatic to demonstrate the terrible powers of his weapon.

He got it. The Maxim gun was the main reason the European powers were able to slaughter their way through the continent of Africa. The British adventurer, soldier of fortune, and officer Frederick Lugard used one to win a key battle in Uganda. In another battle, against Chief Mwanga, with one Maxim gun in one action, German troops killed over a thousand Hehe tribesmen. In three separate battles, the British South African police, using five Maxim guns, destroyed the Matabele warriors of Chief Lobengula. In 1895, in Afghanistan in the Chitral campaign, fanatical tribesmen who attacked the Maxim were wiped out to a man.

As the list of battle names grew with each year, none was more impressive than the Battle of Omdurman, Sudan, Africa, which took place on September 2, 1898. Sir Horatio Herbert Kitchener, British field marshal, led an Anglo-Egyptian force into the Sudan against a fanatical Dervish sect of Baggara Arabs who were followers of the theocratic Mahdi—Muhammad Ahmad. Near Khartoum, and just outside Omdurman, the capital city of the Khalifa Abdullah, the ultimate battle of the campaign took place. Anglo-Egyptian forces were heavily outnumbered by the Dervishes. With the river at his back, Kitchener drew his army up in formation and awaited the Dervishes' attack. The Arabs, armed with spears, mounted a suicidal charge as human waves of their warriors drove toward their enemy. Under Kitchener's heavy defensive fire, the Arab charge faltered, broke, and fell back. Spread out in front of the British troops, the vast battleground was covered with the bodies of the Arabs. Military records show that the British lost twenty-eight; the Egyptians, twenty; and the spear-carrying Dervishes, eleven thousand.[7]

The power of the Khalifa in the Sudan was over, and the British Union Jack flew over another vast piece of Africa. Today's military historians recall the battle as one of the last great cavalry charges of modern times. Among the riders was young Winston Churchill. British newspapers of the day drew a different lesson. They heaped praise on the British soldier for his dash and élan—for his superior fighting ability and courage in bringing Christianity and civilization to the heathen. Kitchener was admitted to the peerage as Baron Kitchener of Khartoum.

Only one British writer, Sir Edward Arnold, credited the true victor of the battle—the six Maxim machine guns: "The battle was won by a quiet scientific gentleman living in Kent."[8] The Maxim was officially credited with killing more than three-quarters of the Dervishes.[9]

If military men still needed proof that the machine gun was properly the central piece in infantry firepower, the Boer War produced it. Both the British and the Boers had Maxims and used them with frightening effectiveness against each other.

In the 1890s, despite the early and deep depression, Europe enjoyed a period of growing prosperity; a modicum of comfort began to reach down into the working classes. Expectations for better living conditions rose. Yet the will to war grew. The colonial aspirations of the British and the French and the Germans and the Belgians and the Italians, particularly in Africa, came into repeated conflict. With each friction-filled year, a growing nationalism increased hostilities and diminished the willingness to negotiate or to reason through conflicts. All through the nineties, the arms race accelerated as the European nations raised armies with which to intimidate each other. By 1899, armies were training diligently, arsenals were bulging to overflowing, and investments in war-making machines were causing national budgets to groan. Every nation had a plan for defeating its enemies. Unable to get at England any other way, Germany was planning to confront her on her domain, the seven seas, openly building a modern navy that would challenge the British fleet.

There were many causes for the war that finally came, but underlying all of them were two essential causes: people wanted to fight, and science had given them the most horrible weapons ever invented with which to fight. With each clash, there was less willingness to negotiate. Finally, Europe shut its mind and endured the war it said it didn't want.

The Germans were the first to finally recognize the significance of the machine gun, and that was fifteen years after Maxim had invented it. In 1899, watching the Boer War—watching the Boer Maxims wipe out one British artillery unit after another—the Germans realized that the machine gun had become a key piece in future wars. They acquired the Maxim and issued it as the Spandau MG08, which they began manufacturing in volume at the Spandau Armory. The German high command did more than just acquire a weapon. They made wide-scale tactical studies of the Maxim and completely rethought infantry tactics as a result. Their Spandau MG08 was to become their terror weapon of World War I.

The military world—including U.S. Ordnance—got a major lesson on the revolutionary role of the machine gun during the Russo-Japanese War of 1904–1905. For the first time, massed Maxims, in batteries of six to eight pieces, were pitted against massed French Hotchkisses. An air-cooled, gas-piston-operated, clip-fed machine gun, the Hotchkiss, which exhibited a nasty tendency to jam, was outgunned.

U.S. Ordnance had tested the Maxim as far back as 1888 and declined it. The Springfield Armory observed with little interest as the British began buying the remarkable new machine gun from its American designer. U.S. Ordnance men had a chance to look again at the Maxim when American troops in the Philippines captured some British-made .303-caliber Maxims from the Spanish. And they still failed to see the significance of what they were looking at.

CHAPTER 21

THE BROWNING MACHINE GUN

The second machine gun appeared within a few years of the Maxim and it came about through a completely different concept, from a completely different kind of mind. It involved General Crozier directly in 1901—in a way that would haunt him for seventeen years.

In January 1901, General Crozier received as a guest John Moses Browning, an ordnance genius in mid-career, at the height of his powers, with an extraordinary record of inventions already, yet with some of his best work still ahead of him, for he was ultimately to become the greatest and most prolific gun designer of all time. Browning had something the United States would soon desperately need—a remarkable new machine gun.

General Crozier knew that many people in the United States and abroad regarded Browning as one of America's greatest mechanical geniuses. He was also familiar with the Colt 1895 machine gun that Browning had invented and that the U.S. Navy had issued to its Marine Corps. In fact, Crozier's predecessor, General Buffington, had issued a number of Browning Colt machine guns as "non-standard" ordnance. Crozier himself was destined to acquire, in 1911, Browning's now legendary M1911 Colt .45 military pistol as the official U.S. sidearm.

To know John Browning you had to peel him like an onion. On the surface, he was a lanky cowboy from Utah with the cowboy's rangy saddle slouch when he walked. He loved the West, the open range, and hunting. He was born in Ogden, Utah, in 1855, in a Mormon family of twenty-two children. His father, three times married and sire of his last child at seventy-one, was a skilled gun designer who owned a gun manufacturing shop in Ogden, where he had his young son, John, building rifles before the boy was twenty.

John was still a small boy when he became a dead shot with a rifle, shooting rabbit and small game to help feed his large family of brothers and sisters. Before he was twenty, to get the job of bagging game done better, he invented and built his own rifle.

Peel another layer, and you met the raconteur with the mirthful one-eyed squint—a cross between Will Rogers and Mark Twain. This was the showman that would have been happy performing in a rodeo, like Annie Oakley shooting the lights out, the showman who loved to perform before the world's leading ordnance men with his remarkable weapons.

Peel another layer and you met the family man who never smoked or drank, in a family business with his brothers and half brothers—Matthew and Samuel and George and Ed—and, later, sons and nephews, handmaking rifles in Ogden, Utah, the land of the large frame farmhouse and large families, bound together by the strong traditions of the Mormon religion.

There were other layers: the international John Browning who dealt with princes and cabinet ministers, generals and scoundrels, the genius with his latest gun in his hands. And there was that most vital layer: the great mechanical genius and inventor, enormously wealthy, bedecked with medals from foreign countries, applauded and honored, who remained totally unaffected by the world's fussing at him. He returned always to Ogden and his family, where he was just another member of the Browning clan, and where the medals and awards all lay stuffed in the bottom drawers of his old desk, while he sat with a stub of a pencil drawing his ideas always on a piece of brown wrapping paper.

This modesty was no pose. Browning declined several honorary doctoral degrees on the grounds that he never accepted anything he hadn't earned. And during World War I, when the government urged him to accept the commission of colonel to help in his work with the military, he declined in a speech of record length for him, some thirty or forty words, allowing that while he might enjoy being called colonel around the factories and proving grounds, "I'd never dare take the title West."[1]

In the deepest layer was the religious Mormon and the patriot who surrendered to his government and country millions of dollars in royalties on weapon purchases.[2]

When the father, Jonathan, died, John and his brother Matthew took over the gun-making business, and they quickly introduced a new policy. Over the years, the boys had watched their father fabricate one custom-made gun after another, on order to some of the worst gun cranks in the West. There was endless reworking, and as a result, the father seemed to make little profit from his efforts.

Matthew decided that was not the way to prosper in the gun trade. Brother John, he saw, was a gifted gun designer, so he set him to work designing weapons while he himself ran the business. It turned out to be a fortuitous arrangement.

When John invented his dropping block, single-action rifle, Matthew was ready and waiting. First, he and John patented the device and then actually built six hundred copies on a rudimentary production line in their shop. The price was right—lower than the major gun makers' rifles. Also, the dropping block—which slid the breechblock vertically for fast cartridge ejection and loading—provided great breech strength and exceptionally high accuracy.

The story of their new rifle with the dropping block quickly spread, and one day, a representative of the famous Winchester Repeating Arms Company visited their operation. Executives at Winchester knew a dangerous competitor when they saw one and promptly acted. They bought the rights to make the Browning rifle and the six hundred rifles as well, and they then bought the inventor himself, hiring John to design a new lever-action Winchester for them in his shop.

The two brothers, feeling they had gotten the best of that deal, took the proceeds and opened a sporting goods store. The sign, complete with misspelling and stretching the full width of the old frame building in Ogden, soon became famous:

THE BROWNING BROTHERS
GUNS, PISTOLS, AMUNITION AND
FISHING TACKLE.

They knew their market. Utah in the 1880s was wide-open, still-untamed country, full of game and hunters: gun country. Browning Brothers was soon known for its gun inventory, including a wide choice of known brands of guns, as well as fishing tackle and other sporting supplies. Upstairs, John had his design shop, where he could have happily remained for the rest of his life except for his re-markable inventiveness. The world was waiting for those ideas that were churning around in his head.

Meanwhile, Hiram Maxim, half a world away in London, was struggling to create his machine gun. The year was 1884, and John Browning, now twenty-nine, designed and patented the celebrated lever-action rifle that Winchester marketed as their famous Model 1886, a lever-action gun with a tube-fed magazine, made in various calibers. That was the first in a series of guns he produced for Win-chester to their mutual advantage. He created the Winchester .22-caliber pump-action Model 90 rifle; the Winchester Models 92 and 94—the latter one of the most widely used deer-hunting rifles in history; the Winchester Model 95 magazine rifle, which was used extensively in World War I by the Russians—who never forgot what beat them in Plevna. With the invention of his Winchester pump-action shotgun, Browning quarreled with Winchester over financial arrangements. The firm was not to see him again in its plant until World War I. Colt eagerly signed Browning up, and for them he designed a long list of revolutionary weapons, sporting and military.

In an age when revolutionary gun ideas were appearing with pre-dictable regularity, Browning had one of the most revolutionary of all: when a gun is fired, there's a blast of gas and air that explodes out of the muzzle with the bullet. Browning wondered if he could harness that energy. If he could, then he could use it to perform automatically some of the functions of the gun that were still often done by hand: opening the breech, extracting the spent shell, inserting a new shell, shutting the breech.

How he solved the question shows how the mind of a genius works. Browning prepared a five-pound cube of iron, four inches by four inches by four inches, and drilled a hole in it big enough to fire a rifle bullet through. He mounted a rifle on a workbench, aimed it through the hole, and with a lanyard, pulled the trigger. The bullet went through the hole and hit a target. But the gas and air that came out with it was so powerful it blew the five-pound iron block across the room. Browning's method, although crude, taught him that there was plenty of energy available.

Next, he made a steel cone with a hole in it. This he fitted just in front of the muzzle. Now, when he pulled the trigger, the cone leaped forward, jerking some strings and levers that reloaded the bench-mounted rifle automatically—all Browning had to do was yank the lanyard. He had found the way to use the spent gas to operate the rifle automatically. The significance was enormous, for while Maxim was using the energy from recoil, Browning was blazing a completely different path by using the energy from gas.

He wasn't home yet. The strings and levers had to be translated into gun parts. He next designed an escape hole to tap the gas to operate a piston. This unlocked the breech, extracted the spent shell, and reloaded the rifle with a live cartridge. He had created the first gas-operated rifle.

Now he turned his attention to making the first gas-operated machine gun. It was 1890, and he sat down and wrote a letter from his Ogden workshop to Colt's Patent Firearms Manufacturing Company. He announced that he had invented a new type of machine gun with extraordinary firing capacity. Colt wasn't enthusiastic, since any new weapon based on something as untried and unfamiliar as gas power would have to confront the now well-established Maxim gun, using recoil power. But Browning's great stature was reason enough to set up a demonstration.

In the spring of 1891, Browning set his weapon up on the Colt firing range and aimed it into their firing tunnel. Before everyone was fairly settled, Browning pulled the trigger. In seconds, with astonishing speed, the gun fired two hundred rounds, ". . . so fast," Browning said later, "nobody could think. . . . When the last empty shell spanged on the floor, with not a hitch in two hundred, Hall and his men were too bug eyed to see the hammer marks on the gun. . . . [Their] changed expression put a pound of fat on my ribs."[3]

Colt quickly signed up to develop it. By November 1891, they had prototype models. And by 1893, they had the U.S. Navy testing the new Colt machine gun. The gun performed well enough to cause the navy to order more test samples. Then came an opportunity to show it to the Army Ordnance Bureau in a test against the hand-cranked Gatling gun. It should have been no contest. On June 14, 1895, Browning arrived and demonstrated his new weapon to Flagler and his Ordnance Board at the Springfield Armory .

The board dutifully wrote a full report. "The mechanical [Gatling] machine gun," it wrote, "is preferred over the automatic [Browning] machine gun." Clearly fixed on mechanical operation and distrusting the first gas-operated weapon it had ever seen, the board's report went further and was more emphatic. The Browning machine gun, it said, "is not suitable for ordinary service and has no place in the land armament."[4] It was June 1895, and the Colt sales team transferred their sales quest to Europe.

Even though the Browning gun had some design problems, the ordnance chiefs in Germany and Austria didn't agree with Flagler's assessment. They watched the extraordinary speed of Browning's weapon, studied the unique gas operation mechanisms, and ordered samples. For the European market, Colt was soon making test models of the Browning machine gun in various national calibers.

Even the U.S. Navy didn't concur with Flagler's people. In 1896, the Navy Ordnance Board ordered fifty Colt machine guns in the 6-mm cartridge that the navy used for its Lee rifle. Two years later, the navy ordered 150 more for marine training. In 1899, a special Machine-Gun Board at the Springfield Arsenal tested three machine guns—the French Hotchkiss, the Maxim, and the Browning Colt and found all three "suitable" for use by the army. Unfortunately, it didn't rank the weapons in order of performance, so General Buffington selected the Browning Colt as a nonstandard issue while continuing to issue as standard the Gatling gun.[5]

The following year, Buffington reported that U.S. military men had not agreed on what part should be "assigned to machine guns in the operations of war, nor what troops shall use them, nor what shall be their organization."[6]

That same year, 1900, John Browning turned to heavy machine gun design and agreed with the Maxim design concept—using mechanical recoil operation rather than gas operation. In 1901, he obtained a patent for a water-cooled, short-recoil machine gun. This was one of his greatest inventions and was to have a profound influence on future gun designs the world over. When Browning contacted the Ordnance Bureau, General Buffington was retiring, and the new chief of ordnance was to be General Crozier. Browning, a born salesman, brought his new idea to Springfield, explained the concept, and asked for funds to develop the weapon.

As General Buffington had reported, American ordnance men, like many of their military counterparts in Europe, could not seem to visualize how the machine gun was changing the battlefield. One of the main problems with selling a machine gun to American Ordnance at that time was the background of the ordnance chief. Crozier was an artilleryman. So was his predecessor, Buffington, and so was Buffington's predecessor, Flagler. All were schooled in the deliberate, carefully aimed fire of large artillery pieces. One did not waste ammunition by firing before the target was identified and locked in by range and bearing.

Rifles to them were small cannon. A well-trained infantryman did not fire until he sighted on the appropriate target, and he did not fire two bullets when one would do. He did not waste ammunition. If an infantry weapon increased the rate of firepower—as the Gatling gun and the Maxim machine gun so clearly did—it was also increasing the rate of wasted ammunition.

In fact, in 1902, Ordnance itself had conducted a very successful experiment by coupling a Gatling gun to an electric motor, which improved the Gatling's rapid-fire rate. Yet, despite all the reports on the devastation wrought by machine guns on many battlefields around the globe, the ordnance chief and his staff still "could not envision a situation which would require such a voluminous amount of firepower, and because of the high expenditure of ammunition, the project was abandoned."[7]

The Croziers and Buffingtons and Flaglers were just not disposed to like such a heedless, prodigal bullet waster as the machine gun. General Crozier, like Buffington and Flagler before him, did the predictable—he declined. In turn, Browning did the predictable, what all the machine-gun inventors did—Gatling, Maxim, and, later, Colonel Isaac Lewis: he went to Europe, and once there, he decided that he was more interested in designing for the sporting gun market than for the American military ordnance market. Filing his revolutionary machine-gun concept, he walked into the welcoming arms of Fabrique National Works in Belgium. It proved to be a perfect marriage of American gun genius and Belgian craftsmanship. For there, John Browning amassed a huge fortune designing for F. N. Works an unending cornucopia of hunting rifles and shotguns. At the same time, to reach the American market, he designed for Colt's Patent Firearms Manufacturing Company in Connecticut a long line of automatic military pistols, including the most famous U.S. Army pistol of all time—the 1911 Army Colt .45 model.

While the Maxim was being manufactured in huge numbers for World War I armies, and while Browning's new machine gun was lying in General Crozier's Ordnance files where it would remain all but forgotten for the next sixteen years,[8] another American machine gun was about to be born to write its own turbulent history with General Crozier's armory. It was called the Lewis, and it was originally conceived as a weapon for the burgeoning military aircraft field that was developing with astonishing speed.

CHAPTER 22

THE LEWIS MACHINE GUN

O ne development that accelerated thinking about warplanes occurred on July 25, 1909, when Louis Blériot, a thirty-seven-
year-old French inventor and owner of an airplane factory in
Issy-les-Moulineaux, arrived in Calais, France, to try to become the
first man to fly across the English Channel. He had already won the
Prix de Voyage for flying from Étaples to Orleans in 1907, and held
another record for cross-country flying from Tours to Arthenay.

This day he was after one thousand English pounds—the prize
from the *London Daily Mail* for the first Channel flyer. He took off,
turned west, and soon landed in Dover, England, to claim the reward. A milestone in aviation history, to some observers it was also
a milestone in military aviation history, for although it was some
time before that fact came home to the English, Blériot ended England's military impregnability.

To be a military threat, however, the airplane needed bombs and
a machine gun, and five years before the start of the Great War, military aviation pioneers went looking for both those weapons. In
1911, an American daredevil pilot, Riley Scott, created a device that
would calibrate the exact moment a bomb should be dropped in
order to hit a selected target. Scott arranged to show this first aerial bombsight to his country's leaders. The U.S. War Department
sent observers to a demonstration, then, predictably, announced
that the War Department was not interested.

Riley Scott followed the pattern adopted by so many other American inventors. He took aviation's first accurate bombsight to Europe and, finding that Michelin in France was holding a contest for accurate aerial bombing, immediately entered.

The target was 375 feet by 124 feet. The bomb was to be dropped from an altitude of a half mile, a challenge that was far beyond the known skills of the day. Riley Scott dropped fifteen bombs in a row and stunned all the observers when eight of his fifteen bombs hit inside the target area. His device was promptly bought by burgeoning European air forces.

Now European military airmen set out to find a good aeronautical machine gun. With it, they would be able to create the first fighter bomber. There was a growing sense of haste in their researches: in 1912, any shrewd observer could see that a war was coming in which the military airplane would make its fearsome debut.

In 1910, one year after the Blériot flight, the third major machine gun of the Great War was introduced as the aerial machine gun everyone was seeking. Invented by an American Army Ordnance officer, the weapon was to cause the greatest scandal inside the Ordnance Bureau since its founding in 1794.

For an inventor, he was aptly named: Isaac Newton Lewis, and in 1910 he was fifty-two, with thirty-five years of service in the U.S. Army. He was already a well-known inventor. Born on October 12, 1858, Lewis graduated from West Point in 1879. By 1894, he'd had a distinguished career as an ordnance man specializing in artillery. For four years—until 1898—he was a member of the Coast Artillery Fire Control Board in New York Harbor, then became regulator of the Board of Ordnance and Fortification in Washington, D.C. That duty led to the invention of a number of fire-control devices.

That same year, 1899, the Ordnance Bureau selected him to travel to Europe to make a study of ordnance there. His report, coming after the disastrous performance of American artillery in Cuba, caused a sensation in the Ordnance Bureau and led to the rearmament of American field artillery. By 1900, Lewis was known in America and Europe as an inventor of, among other things, a series of very important range finders and other coast artillery fire-control devices. From 1904 to 1911, he was instructor and director at Fort Monroe of the Coast Artillery School. In 1911, he was made lieutenant colonel, and a full colonel in 1913, the year he retired at fifty-five.

Three years prior, in 1910, the Automatic Arms Company, sensing that there was market for a new lightweight machine gun, gave him a contract to develop such a weapon for them. Automatic Arms already had a machine gun that had been invented by Samuel Neal McClean, who had assigned the rights to it to Automatic Arms as the McClean-Lissak rifle. The weapon had never found a market.

After Lewis invented such revolutionary elements as his draft cooling system, his rate-of-fire regulator, and clock-type mainspring, and added them to the McClean-Lissak, the renamed Lewis gun became one of the most lethal machine guns ever invented, air-cooled, gas-operated, designed to fire the Springfield '06 rifle cartridge from a top-mounted pie-plate magazine that came in two sizes, one containing forty-seven cartridges, the other ninety-six. Because there was no cartridge belt on the Lewis, one operator could comfortably carry the twenty-six-pound weapon. From a manufacturing standpoint, the design was so simple six Lewises could be made as quickly as one Vickers (the British version of the Maxim). The Lewis gun was the first truly portable system of its type.

When it was ready for its debut, Lewis, still thinking of his weapon as an aircraft machine gun, took it to his fellow officers in the Ordnance Bureau to test, stipulating, as he had many times before, that he would forgo all inventor's royalties from his government. And there he encountered the presence of General Crozier. These two men had known each other for decades. Indeed, their backgrounds, their interests, and their accomplishments were very similar—West Point, artillery commands, coast artillery boards, significant inventions, sensitive foreign assignments skillfully accomplished, merit promotions, and increasing rank and stature. Fame. By most standards, they should have been the closest of comrades. But, with their proponents and boosters inside the Ordnance Corps, they had a history of rival inventions, and as a result, the two men actively disliked each other. The autocratic demeanor of General Crozier was confronted by the "determined manner" of Lewis, who was, historian George M. Chinn notes, "no respecter of person, rank or position in life and he had already acquired the title of 'stormy petrel of the service.'"[1] Predictably, they clashed in the first demonstration of the Lewis gun in 1910. Crozier dismissed the weapon out of hand, and by rejecting the design, he was rejecting the man. Lewis took his weapon back to his laboratory and reworked it. The situation quickly became explosive when, a year later, in 1911, Lewis returned with his weapon now fully finished. Again, he submitted it for tests and again clashed with Crozier over the terms and conduct of the test, causing the collapse of the second audition.

Lewis was so upset he now set out to get the gun tested by ordnance people not controlled by Crozier. On June 28, 1911, he went to General Leonard Wood, who was then army chief of staff and also president of the Board of Ordnance and Fortification. Lewis offered the gun to Wood and, with it, all his royalties on the gun. There was one stipulation: Lewis wanted a test conducted by the army but independent of General Crozier or his Ordnance Bureau. The Automatic Arms Company, maker of the weapon, because of its own troubles with Crozier, backed Lewis in his irregular request. General Wood agreed to arrange for a test by a Cavalry Board and an Infantry Board at the School of Musketry in Monterey, California, and another before the Artillery Board at Fort Monroe, just south of Washington, D.C.

By April 1912, Automatic Arms had the four Lewis guns ready and asked for a test. But General Wood now asked for a letter from Automatic Arms outlining its reasons for not wanting to submit its weapons to General Crozier or to any boards controlled by General Crozier.

Automatic Arms complied, and in the letter of July 1, 1912, the company accused the Springfield Armory of giving to Colt's Patent Firearms Manufacturing Company a "practical monopoly insofar as concerns the commercial manufacture and supply, in this country of such small arms as rifles, pistols and revolvers."[2] This practice became so scandalously pervasive in later years inside the Pentagon that it was given the pejorative label: single sourcing. Automatic Arms charged that, at a time when the Ordnance Bureau was holding competitive tests between a Colt pistol and another from the Savage Arms Company in Utica, New York, Crozier's Ordnance officers had appeared in a patent infringement trial between Colt and Savage on the same two weapons, and had given testimony so clearly slanted toward Colt that Savage lost the case. Shortly after, Automatic Arms charged, Crozier placed a large order with Colt for its pistol.

Automatic Arms said that the Colt–Savage Arms situation was pertinent because Automatic Arms was confronted with an almost identical situation. It, too, was preparing to bring a patent infringement suit against Colt, since Colt was the licensed American manufacturer of the Benét-Mercié machine gun from France, a weapon that was infringing on an Automatic Arms patent. The Benét-Mercié was in competition with Automatic Arms's Lewis gun in Springfield machine-gun tests.

The Benét-Mercié weapon had been invented in France by Laurence Benét, former U.S. ordnance officer and son of the former U.S. chief of ordnance, Stephen Vincent Benét. With the highly favored Colt company sponsoring Benét's gun, Automatic Arms felt that under the circumstances, it could not get a favorable reception for the Lewis gun at the Springfield tests. The company contended that Ordnance had a clear conflict of interest in the matter and should withdraw itself.

This was a very serious accusation. In its dealings with the arms world, the Ordnance Bureau felt it was essential to preserve a reputation for impartiality. The bureau had not forgotten that charges of partiality toward the ill-fated Krag-Jorgensen rifle had greatly damaged the credibility of General Flagler's Rifle Board. Obviously, General Crozier wasn't going to accept these charges or seem to acquiesce to them by letting another branch of the army test the Lewis. The precedent could destroy Crozier's autocratic autonomy.

No one who knew War Department politics was surprised, therefore, when the Board of Ordnance and Fortification refused to go along with its rambunctious chairman, General Wood, and instead insisted that the Lewis gun could not be tested anywhere but at Springfield.

To both Colonel Lewis and Automatic Arms, such a test was a waste of time and they withdrew from negotiations. But even Crozier couldn't stop the talk among army men about Lewis's new weapon. Colonel Lewis had many friends who could campaign for the Lewis gun, who had fired it, and could claim that it was a great weapon—perhaps the greatest machine gun of all time—and deserved its chance to be considered. In addition, by not making some accommodation to test the now controversial weapon, the War Department was letting serious accusations stand and a bad situation fester. Pressure mounted inside the army for the issue to be resolved.

On February 13, 1913, General Wood approached Automatic Arms again, asking them to visit him in the capital, where, four days later, he indicated to the corporate secretary of Automatic Arms that the government was very interested in the Lewis gun. He then arranged a meeting between the secretary and Colonel Birnie, acting chief of ordnance, in Birnie's office. To break the impasse with Crozier, Wood had proposed two tests—one at Springfield under Crozier and a duplicate test elsewhere, away from the influence of Crozier and his Ordnance Board. Colonel Birnie accepted. Automatic Arms accepted. But Crozier wouldn't. Instead, when he heard of the plan, the general moved to block it. On February 18, 1913, Colonel Birnie sent Automatic Arms a terse telegram. The proposed double test was postponed—indefinitely. Lewis had had enough. "Discouraged and disgruntled," he resigned his commission in the U.S. Army, and followed the many other American arms designers to Europe.[3]

Unfortunately, the politicking inside the War Department hadn't ended. Colonel Lewis still had high standing there as an officer and as an inventor of considerable stature. Many of his proponents could point out that while the United States was determinedly looking for a new machine gun—even preparing to test soon the Maxim and the Benét-Mercié—it was letting perhaps the finest of all leave the country. They urged, not unreasonably, that some way be found to give the Lewis gun an audition.

In 1913, Automatic Arms was summoned again to Washington. A new test for the Lewis gun was proposed, this one to be administered by a board drawn from the infantry and the cavalry. The armory was willing to test the Lewis first as an aerial machine gun and afterward as an antiaircraft gun. But the test site would still be the Springfield Armory. However, as a gesture of impartiality, following the test at Springfield, the armory also was willing to give the Lewis a full field test among various army units.

Lewis, in Europe, was emphatically set against the plan. The investors in Automatic Arms were also dead set against it. Yet somehow, a "tactical mistake was made," according to the company, and someone in Automatic Arms agreed to the test.[4]

The test was to take place in September 1913, against a new Vickers-Maxim machine gun and the "service" gun, as the Benét-Mercié machine gun was called. Unfortunately, Lewis and Crozier clashed again when the board came to the aerial tests, scheduled for College Park, Connecticut. Colonel Lewis offered an airplane, a pilot, and, for an aerial gunner, his own son. He asked the board to present a supply of official .30-'06 service ammunition that the armory customarily issued for such tests.

Colonel Lewis later stated that General Crozier refused "to furnish American ammunition to fire the gun."[5] He went on to say the "rebuff was one of the things that decided him to abandon further efforts to interest the [U.S.] government and to take his gun to Europe."[6]

The Lewis test guns ran into performance trouble in the next test inside the armory firing range. Certain metal parts of the test guns had been incorrectly tempered and soon began to break. This was not an uncommon occurrence with handmade test models of new weapons—the Krag-Jorgensen had failed repeatedly during its initial tests. Automatic Arms requested permission to withdraw the Lewis guns from the test in order to prepare properly tempered parts for a future test. Permission was granted.

The board's records show that during that test, the defective Lewis guns scored 206 jams, 35 broken parts, and 15 parts not broken but requiring replacement. The Benét-Mercié scored 59 jams, 7 broken parts, and no other parts that needed replacement. The Vickers-Maxim scored 23 jams, no broken parts, and no other parts that needed replacement.

Lewis expected to have the new parts in time for the upcoming field tests in 1914, and since these were the tests he had been trying to get for his weapon all along—among dispersed army units in various army camps, away from the control of General Crozier—Lewis immediately began his test preparations. The colonel felt that here, against the two-man Maxim and Benét-Mercié, all firing .30-caliber rifle cartridges, the lightweight and highly portable Lewis, capable of being fired like a rifle by one man, would soon display its superior characteristics.

General Crozier, however, announced that since the Lewis gun had failed the armory tests, it had not qualified for the field tests. General Crozier dismissed Colonel Lewis and his machine gun.In the field tests, the Vickers-Maxim outperformed the Springfield Benét-Mercié, and the board recommended that it be adopted.

General Crozier must have been satisfied with the results of this encounter with Lewis. He had fought off the incursions by Chief of Staff Leonard Wood into Ordnance's domain. He had fought off the challenge to his authority from Automatic Arms. He had prevented the Lewis gun from being tested outside Ordnance precincts and, instead, had compelled the Lewis gun to submit to his authority by allowing itself to be tested on his turf—the armory where, he could say, the Lewis gun had publicly and spectacularly failed; and, finally, he had prevented the Lewis gun from participating in either the aircraft test or the infantry field tests.

If, as some were charging, he had wanted the Benét-Mercié to be the United States' official army machine gun all along, luck seemed to favor him there.[7] For the war was starting in Europe, and he was able to report that there were no surplus supplies of the British

Maxim gun available—he reported that he tried to buy 135. By default, the Benét-Mercié became the official weapon and was manufactured by Colt—Crozier's favorite arms company, according to Automatic Arms.[8]

General Crozier had emerged from the fray with his domain intact, his authority firm, and himself the clear winner, and with what he felt was official proof that the Lewis gun was unfit for U.S. Army service. Reviewing the entire affair in the autumn of 1913, he surely could not have seen that his handling of the Lewis gun matter would two years later make nationwide headlines, rock his reign as chief of ordnance, draw criticism of his professional ability from the British, shake the War Department to the very top, and affect a very closely contested presidential election.

He had his first inkling of trouble a short time later—from England, while the Springfield Armory machine-gun tests were still going on. In that tumultuous year of 1914, when all of Europe was arming for war, Colonel Lewis was submitting his machine gun to a field test at Bisley, England, in the presence of Major General Sir Stanley Brenton von Donlop, master general of ordnance of the British army, Crozier's counterpart, and a number of the highest-ranking officers of the British Ordnance Department.

The weapon's performance caused a sensation. "The British promptly accepted the gun and pronounced it the greatest machine gun yet invented."[9] The British army quickly placed the Lewis gun in service and furnished their troops with thousands of them.

These same British Ordnance officers had tested the Benét-Mercié machine gun, Crozier's choice, and had declined it. France, home of the Benét-Mercié, had also tested and rejected it.

With substantial orders for his weapon, Lewis went on to Liège, Belgium, and formed a new company, the Armes Automatiques Lewis. But there, he discovered, the Germans were as enthusiastic about the Lewis gun as the British and were making a determined effort to get it: Lewis discovered that his Belgian company had quietly been taken over by German officials. Before they got their hands on his drawings and models, Lewis switched to the Birmingham Small Arms Company in Birmingham, England. When the

British demand kept rising, Lewis turned to the Savage Arms Company in Utica, New York. Savage was soon making four hundred Lewis guns a week.[10]

To see how the Lewis lived up to its British billing, one has to look to the battlefields in France and the nature of the fighting that took place there. General Crozier soon had reason to watch its wartime role very closely.

CHAPTER 23

MACHINE GUNS
IN THE TRENCHES

On June 28, 1914, in Sarajevo, Bosnia, a teacher, a carpenter, a printer, and four students, all under thirty, four under twenty, all suffering from tuberculosis, all armed, and all Bosnian Serbs, set out to free Bosnia from the rule of the Austro-Hungarian empire.

They succeeded in killing Austria's Archduke Franz Ferdinand in an entourage and thereby set off World War I. Like firecrackers on a string, each setting off the next, the various pacts and interlocking treaties of Europe fired off in a series: Austria-Hungary declared war on Serbia; Germany declared war on both Russia and France; Britain declared war on Germany; Austria declared war on Russia; Serbia and Montenegro, already threatened with extinction by the Austria-Hungary armies, declared war on Germany; France declared war on Austria; Britain declared war on Austria; Austria declared war on Belgium; and in a grand finale for the summer of 1914, Russia, France, and Britain all declared war on Turkey.

Europe quickly gathered up its staggering collection of super-weapons, its scrolls of strategies and tactics, its map cases and food rations, its fifes and drums and merry banners, its uncontrollable hatreds, bigotries, and blood lust—and loaded all this on the backs of an entire generation of millions of young men and sent them off to war. Everyone expected a quick battle, a short war and victory. Few saw that there was going to be nothing quick or short about it, and there was to be no real victory for anyone. Certainly not for the appalling number of young men who never came home again.

In September 1914, in the midst of harvest all over Europe, Germany abrogated its promise to honor the neutrality of Belgium and bludgeoned its way through that nation with such ruthless brutality to the civilian population it contributed greatly to the turning of world opinion against Germany and became a major emotional reason for the entry of the United States into the war on the Allies' side.

In the First Battle of the Marne, the German army was stopped by the French. There, both sides burrowed into trenches that were to stretch ultimately from the North Sea four hundred miles southeastward to the Swiss border. For the next four years, until the Armistice, that battle line didn't move as much as ten miles one way or the other. Almost before it began, Clausewitz's concept of the war of movement ended in a permanent stalemate.

Most of Britain's original army of professional soldiers were killed in the first battles, and newspapers reported that for France alone, the first month of the war brought a death toll of 200,000 men. America was stunned—appalled—by the incredible carnage.

When the Great War began, few military men realized that the machine gun was to be the dominant weapon that would dictate the very nature of the combat. More than any other weapon—and right from the start—its killing power was so great neither side could attack with success. Thus, the machine gun created immobilized trench warfare and turned the Great War into a defensive war.

All through the years of fighting, both sides relied on the same machine gun—for the British Vickers *and* the German Spandau were Maxims—and both sides continued to evolve machine-gun strategy and tactics. Right up to their last offensive in the autumn of 1918, the Germans were adjusting their infantry structure to make the machine gun more dominant.

When the British were shown Colonel Lewis's gun in 1914, they quickly added it to their machine-gun arsenal, with such effect that the Germans made a concerted effort to copy it. As noted earlier, at the height of the war all up and down the front, the British Lewis gun was relied on so extensively that the British reported it was firing fifteen million cartridges a day at the Germans.

Historian John Ellis's figures show the consequences of the British combat learning curve. Prior to 1914, he notes, Vickers was selling eleven machine-guns a year to the British War Office. The figure jumped in 1915 to about twenty-four hundred a year, and by 1918 to more than thirty-nine thousand. The War Office bought during the war years "a grand total of just under a quarter million machine-guns." Of these, 133,000 were Lewis guns.[1]

In the beginning, the Germans not only had more machine guns, but they also used them more effectively, with more advanced machine-gun tactics than the Allies. German machine gunners were trained to work in concert and, removed from the infantry, were placed in separate machine-gun companies that could be moved up and down the battle line. Whenever Allied troops gathered for an advance, the Germans were able to quickly mass their machine-gun units to beat back the attack, inflicting enormous loss of life.

In 1918, the Germans introduced new machine-gun attack tactics in which light machine guns and automatic rifles were used to spearhead an assault, leaving the rifle-armed infantry behind to mop up. Like the Allies, the Germans were trying to break out of the defensive stalemate.

Taking note of the new German strategy, on September 6, 1918, a page-one headline in the *New York Times* reported, "Light Maxim Weapon Replacing Rifle in General Reorganization of Kaiser's Army."

The report went on: "The infantryman as such has ceased to exist in the German Army. All the German forces are being organized not on the old basis of the number of rifles to a force, but on the basis of the number of machine guns." The article added that two machine gunners were able "to do the work of fifty or more riflemen." On the limited scale that they were able to mount at that late stage in the war, the German strategy appeared successful and might have helped break through, but it came too late. Germany had run out of men and was unable to continue the fight much longer.

The British came to appreciate their own Vickers-Maxim very slowly. It was late in 1915 before they set up a separate Machine Gun Corps, long after the Germans had shown them the effectiveness of such an arrangement. One of the hindrances to evolving new machine-gun strategies was an element inside the British army command who, in spite of the evidence before their eyes, failed to recognize the great change in military tactics wrought by the machine gun.[2]

The civilians in the British government, newly come to the realities of war, saw at once that machine guns meant superior firepower. Superior firepower meant greater casualties for the other side. Greater enemy casualties meant a more timely surrender. The side that ran out of young men first would lose, and, hence, World War I became the war of the machine gun and the gravedigger.

In November 1915, Lloyd George, England's minister of munitions and future prime minister, did some simple arithmetic that seemed to be beyond the ken of his generals—arithmetic that predicted the events of the rest of the war. Fifty thousand machine gunners, his pencil told him, were more than equal to a quarter of a million riflemen. He then took General Kitchener's estimate of machine-gun requirements and said to his assistants, "Square it, multiply that result by two—and when you are in sight of that, double it again for good measure."[3]

The military continued to be so uninclined to devote that many thousands of men to machine-gun training—preferring to send them to France as simple riflemen—that the British War Committee, to assure the army of an abundant supply of machine gunners, had to order the Army Council to set up a permanent machine-gun training program that would process ten thousand trainees at a time.[4]

When one British officer, in charge of a machine-gun training school, early in the war recommended the formation of a separate machine-gun corps, he later discovered his memorandum in a GHQ file labeled "Of No Further Interest." When he recommended to GHQ that the number of machine guns per unit be increased from two to four, he was told to mind his own business.[5]

The historian John Ellis observes that "all power had passed to the defensive" mainly because of the machine gun, yet it took British commanders three years to accept this change. Even on the eve of the Battle of the Somme, the British high command was still obsessed "with obsolete attacking formations" and "a fierce emphasis upon the bayonet. . . . The German machine guns made sure that all but a handful of men never got near enough to stick their bayonets into anybody."[6] Even after abundant battlefield experience, the British army was still confining basic training to close-order drill and bayonet practice. There was practically no training in such vital battlefield matters as digging trenches and setting out barbed wire.

Nor were French practices any better. Slower than even the British to recognize the significance of the machine gun, they had only a few thousand on hand when they went to war. At one point, French dragoons without horses were ordered to attack a German position armed only with their lances "at the ready."[7]

The generals, lifelong students of war, failed to understand the lesson of greater firepower. Even as late as 1918, after years of unprecedented slaughter by the machine gun, some still dismissed it. Courage, élan, glory, invincible confidence, pride, battle ribbons, regimental colors, all the manly virtues—these counted for more than any weapon. The European officer was a romantic, socially isolated from the great Industrial Revolution that was pouring new weapons onto the battlefield and, along with his fellow officers, "still believed in the glorious cavalry charge and above all the supremacy of man as opposed to mere machines."[8] The "epauletted marshals . . . and their staffs rarely visited the front."[9]

Britain's General Haig refused to admit that it was mainly the machine gun that had already wiped out whole armies of British soldiers he himself had sent into battle. The machine gun was, he believed, no match for real soldiering, and he persisted to the end, as did his German and French counterparts, in sending hundreds of thousands of young men to their deaths charging entrenched machine-gun nests. "The machine gun," he said, "is a much over-rated weapon."[10]

Like General Haig, all the other generals refused to see that new technology had changed all the concepts of warfare. They had new war tools and old tactics. France's General Joffre refused to use the telephone. When the tank clanked suddenly onto the battlefield and into the nightmares of every infantryman, Kitchener dismissed it as "a toy." When the generals in the British War Office twice refused to develop and introduce the devastating trench mortar, an Indian maharaja gave a British Cabinet member the money to develop and make it.[11]

Haig, a cavalryman to the death, maintained a number of spit-and-polish mounted units near the front lines throughout the entire war, waiting for what he described as "the charge," that moment when the infantry would break through and open the way for the cavalry to make a mad dash all the way to Berlin. The few times that Haig stubbornly used cavalry to charge machine guns waiting behind impregnable barbed wire, the results were heartbreaking. Even King George V, speaking to him in Buckingham Palace, was unable to make Haig see the futility—and great expense—of maintaining cavalry.

The American General Pershing, no student of his own country's Civil War, it seems, wherein devastating firepower by 1862 had made cavalry obsolete, also brought cavalry to no-man's-land. Like Haig, he also expected to win the war with a cavalry charge. Getting in the way everywhere, his idle horses performed only one function well—they ate their way through tons of expensive fodder and never set a hoof on the battlefield. While the munching cavalries waited, the slaughter of young men went on. Yet the battle line never moved.

Just how effective was the machine gun? There was probably nothing more lethal on the battlefield than the machine gunner's "two inch tap." "By constant practice," John Keegan records, "the machine gunner learned to hit the side of the breech with the palm of his hand just hard enough to move the muzzle exactly two inches against the resistance of the traversing screw. A succession of 'two inch taps' first on one side on the breech until the stop was reached, then on the other, would keep in the air a stream of bullets so dense that no one could walk upright across the front of the machine-gunner's position without being hit."[12]

Ellis notes as a typical example that in March 1915, at Neuve-Chapelle, two German machine guns and about a dozen German soldiers stopped two battalions of British infantrymen—about fifteen hundred men. The exact same thing happened in September in the Battle of Loos. A single machine gun almost completely wiped out two British battalions—the Seventh Green Howards and the Tenth West Yorkshires—and required only three minutes of firing to do it. On one other day, 173 British battalions during a massive attack suffered 50 percent casualties—75 percent among their officers—much of this caused by German Maxim machine-gun fire.[13]

The historian Sir Llewellyn Woodward recorded similar machine-gun devastation during the Battle of the Somme. "On July 1, 1916, the first day of the Battle of the Somme, more than 1000 officers and 20,000 other ranks of the British Expeditionary Force were killed, fatally wounded, or reported missing; over 1300 officers and 34,000 other ranks were wounded. Most of the casualties were caused by machine-gun fire."[14]

England's prime minister Lloyd George estimated that 80 percent of all casualties were caused by machine guns. The *New York Times* confirmed this, reporting that out of every ten Americans killed, eight died by machine-gun fire.[15] This is in marked contrast to the effectiveness of the rifle prior to the introduction of the machine gun. Dupuy notes that during the Civil War, "infantry rifles inflicted 85 to 90 percent of the casualties, while artillery accounted for only 9 to 10 percent."[16]

When Berlin declared all the waters around the British Isles a war zone in February 1915, German submarines strained America's determined efforts at neutrality. Many Americans were uneasy. This war was not turning out to be a short one, and the longer it went on, the more likely it was the United States would to be drawn in. President Wilson sent a peace mission to Europe that failed. Certainly, by that February of 1915, the United States should have been preparing for war. But President Wilson hesitated, with unforeseen tragic consequences.

On May 7, 1915, in the North Atlantic off the coast of Ireland, a German U20 submarine sank the British liner *Lusitania*. Twelve hundred passengers died, including 128 Americans. Extremely reluctant to face the possibility of America at war, and torn by his divided Cabinet, President Wilson delayed until the following November to ask Congress for the first funds for military preparedness.

During most of 1916, the Battle of Verdun raged. Forty-three divisions of German troops and sixty-six divisions of French troops attacked each other in a campaign that lasted ten months, from February 21 to December 18. The fighting was so ferocious, with French artillery alone firing more than ten million shells, the two opposing armies were decimated, yet the battle line barely moved.[17] During the same year of 1916, from April 4 to May 27, the Second Battle of Ypres blazed. Germany introduced poison gas against French troops. The French panicked and the Germans gained three miles. But the gas proved uncontrollable even in the slightest breeze, and French machine guns soon pinned down the Germans once again. Stalemate resumed.

The Battle of the Somme began a few weeks later and ran from July 1 through November 11, 1916. British and French troops mounted repeated assaults on German lines, charging into massed machine guns and wheel-to-wheel German artillery. The Germans repeatedly counterattacked Allied machine guns and artillery. After six months of fighting, the British broke through the German lines expecting now to fight a war of movement. But after a five-mile gain, they were stopped by German infantry, backed by machine guns. Trench stalemate returned. In the five-month campaign, British casualties alone were 410,000.[18]

Yet another massive campaign marked that tragic year of 1916— September 25 through November 14, 1916, during the Third Battle of Artois. Attacks by the French at Artois and Champagne and by the British at Loos brought some gain of territory, but losses of life were now beyond belief. In this battle, the Germans suffered 141,000 casualties and the Allies 242,000.[19]

CHAPTER 24

GENERAL CROZIER
SELECTS A MACHINE GUN

On November 24, 1916, as the United States moved closer to the Great War three years after it had begun, while thousands of Maxim machine guns were firing relentlessly on the battlefields of both the Western Front and the Eastern Front, Sir Hiram Maxim, the gun's inventor, a British citizen since 1900 and knighted in 1901, died in London at the age of seventy-six. For an inventor whose weapon dominated one of history's greatest wars, he left the surprisingly small estate of $159,000.[1]

The U.S. Army had a number of military observers on the battlefields of Europe who, daily, found the power and importance of the machine gun more inescapable. As a result of information coming from the battlefields, infantry commanders of the U.S. Army should have had three thoughts uppermost on their minds: the increasing likelihood that they would soon be drawn into the war in Europe; the immediate need for a troop training program built around the use and tactics of the machine gun; and the need to be fully armed with tens of thousands of the most modern machine guns. Yet General Crozier still had not selected one. On hand in U.S. arsenals were a handful of Benét-Merciés of questionable value.

Nineteen sixteen was a presidential election year, and all through that autumn, the campaigning paralleled the Third Battle of Artois. With each passing week, the candidates' voices became increasingly emotional and turbulent. President Wilson campaigned on the platform "He kept us out of war," a theme that struck home with most Americans, who were reading of the hideous slaughter in the trenches. But Wilson faced a tough fight for reelection, as he was running against Charles Evans Hughes, in what would turn out to be almost a dead heat.

Theodore Roosevelt campaigned for Hughes as though he himself were running for office. He wanted the United States in the war against Germany. He wanted a nation armed, a nation morally indignant menacing its enemies. As he pounded fist to palm to emphasize every word, he bellowed the same message from podium to podium across the country: we must prepare for war.

The campaigning became Machiavellian. Theodore Roosevelt was a very close friend and war comrade of General Leonard Wood, former army chief of staff and now commanding the Department of the East of the U.S. Army. Roosevelt and Wood were proponents of full military preparedness. And both of them, despite their original support, were now highly critical of General Crozier. In fact, after the Lewis gun affair, Wood and Crozier had openly become adversaries. Like Roosevelt, whose support was critical to the elevation of Crozier to ordnance chief in 1901, Wood thought Crozier was a major reason why the United States was not prepared. If Wood could make that charge stand up, then Crozier was a way to attack Wilson, whose reluctance to prepare for war became a major issue during the campaign.

All these ingredients in the political stew of 1916 did not auger well for General Crozier. In fact, for him, the whole year started off inauspiciously. On January 25, 1916, while the insistent headlines talked of the trenches and the upcoming political campaigns, the Senate Committee on Military Affairs summoned General Crozier to outline the state of the nation's arsenal. They wanted the general to tell them how prepared he had made America.[2]

General Crozier and his Ordnance Department felt they could look over the army's weaponry with some confidence. The army's artillery piece—a 3.2-inch howitzer—was by all accounts the equal of the French 75-mm gun, a battle-seasoned weapon considered the best in the world. In addition, the army had the Springfield '03 rifle, which also by all accounts was the equal of the German Mauser, a battle-seasoned rifle considered by many to be the best rifle in the world.

General Crozier's Achilles' heel was an army machine gun. In 1913, just before the Great War started, he halfheartedly settled on the Benét-Mercié from France, apparently as an interim weapon. Since then, for three years, he had done nothing. With the likelihood of war increasing, the army needed forty or fifty thousand machine guns in reserve plus forty or fifty thousand more if war came. On hand, the army had only eleven hundred Benét-Merciés. Of the new American howitzer, which American ordnance men felt was the equal of the famous French 75, the first deliveries were two years away. Of the millions of Springfield rifles the army would need, General Crozier had on hand less than a few hundred thousand.

When the senators totted up the columns of figures, they asserted that the nation was completely unprepared for war. Worse, General Crozier, the chief ordnance officer of the country, had no contingency plans to acquire the necessary weapons and, most baffling of all, didn't seem to feel the need to make plans.

The senators asked the general if the Springfield Armory could not at least put in reserve duplicate sets of the rifle dies, tools, and machine attachments, as well as the '03 patterns and blueprints, so that in time of war, these duplicate sets could then be distributed to America's commercial gun makers, who could then quickly convert to making the '03.

General Crozier agreed, not seeming to understand that, as a professional Ordnance head, this was a proposal he should have been presenting to these civilian senators, not receiving. With $275,000, he estimated, he could set aside those dies and parts and plans, with which in a matter of months he could make America's production of the Springfield leap from fifteen hundred a day at the government armories to fifteen thousand a day at private rifle factories. During further questioning, the general admitted that, without such a contingency plan, to increase rifle production to wartime needs would require a year or more. It was the same story, he added, as the artillery.

Obviously then, the senators agreed, the indicated action was for General Crozier to immediately start making duplicate sets of '03 rifle drawings and dies. By the end of the meeting, they authorized the necessary funds and expected the general to promptly proceed with the program.

With all the headlines from the trenches in Europe, the senators' real concern was the machine gun. They asked General Crozier if he believed that the Benét-Mercié was the best machine gun for the U.S. Army. If the general felt this was a calculated question, he might have been right, for stories still persisted that, through pettiness and jealousy, he had let a great weapon, the Lewis gun, get away from the American army and that he continued to block its introduction in spite of the praise it was receiving from the British all along the European battle line. There were now some thirty thousand Lewis guns n British service, nested in the trenches of Belgium and France, and firing some fifteen million rounds every twenty-four hours at the German army. Since the war began, British Lewis guns had fired between five and seven billion rounds with notable reliability and telling effect. Later, the Germans were reported to believe that the Lewis gun was the best of the various machine guns.[3]

The senators were uncomfortable with the relentless barrage of criticism that was coming from former President Roosevelt's good friend, General Wood, and his faction in the War Department. One of General Wood's favorite complaints was that the Lewis gun was invented right under General Crozier's nose and he let it get away, even chased it away.

Also, the senators seemed to be suggesting that the general lacked a sense of urgency, having just spent three years studying the machine-gun market without a conclusion.

In mid-August 1916, to make the blueprints and patterns for the '03 rifle, General Crozier turned to an ideal source for help: Frederick Colvin, the editor of *American Machinist*, a widely influential technical publication. Colvin was recognized as an unmatched expert and voluminous writer on tooling, machine tooling, and machine manufacturing. Colvin was assigned an office in the Springfield Armory to begin measuring, documenting, and blue-printing every inch of the Springfield '03 rifle.

Colvin later wrote about the shock he felt when he examined the rifle production line in the Springfield Armory, a collection of machine antiques from the previous century. "The speeds and feeds," he noted, "were almost leisurely and the methods employed were of about the 1890 vintage."[4]

With an assistant, Colvin started with the barrel and studied the rifle piece by piece, as he followed the rifle through the production line, detailing on paper the entire process for duplicating it in any rifle plant in the country. "We reported on the kinds of material used, the tools and cutters, feeds, and operating speeds, cutting lubricant, heat-treatment and time required for each operation." The preparation of the hundreds of illustrations and detail drawings consumed, all told, four months.

While compiling the master patterns, Colvin decided that the rifle was overmanufactured. The band that held the barrel on the stock, the butt plate, the sling-strap swivel, and a number of other parts were drop-forged—expensive, time consuming, and completely unnecessary. Worse, all the parts of the rifle, without exception, were made to exact specifications. There were no plus or minus tolerances. Either the part matched specs exactly or it was thrown in the waste bin. More than just wasteful, this exactitude went far beyond the needs of the rifle. Colvin felt that making rifles in such a manner took too long and cost too much. In the late fall of 1916, with war coming, this excessive process on those antiquated armory machines was not the way to produce the rifles the army needed.

Confiding his concern to Secretary of War Newton Baker, Colvin pointed out another serious defect in the Ordnance Department: "There is a great need for officers around here who know modern production methods more than they know military regulations."

Secretary Baker asked Colvin for a detailed report and added, "Make sure you mark your report Confidential."[5] Colvin sent his report to Baker with the requisite word "Confidential" stamped on the envelope. Colvin then received a letter from General Crozier, informing him he was no longer welcome at the armory and that the magazine, *American Machinist*, was to send a replacement. When Colvin went to Springfield to see the general about the matter, he was refused admission to the armory. In Washington, Secretary Baker's office informed him that during the secretary's absence, Colvin's report had been sent in error to General Crozier.

Under Baker's orders, Colvin was readmitted to the armory. When news of the contretemps leaked out, the local Springfield newspaper went after Crozier, and for some days, the story made front-page news.[6] In addition to his inability to complete his responsibilities in timely fashion, General Crozier was revealing an ominous inability to accept the slightest criticism.

The scandal did not end there. Colvin's path was to cross Crozier's a few months later, and then Colvin's behavior was guided by his knowledge that General Crozier was wearing a dangerously thin skin.

More scandals stalked the general during most of 1916. During March of that year, the U.S. Thirteenth Cavalry, under General "Black Jack" Pershing, was sent down to the New Mexican border to deal with threatening gestures made by the Mexican insurrectionist Pancho Villa. On the night of March 24, Villa led a daring raid across the Mexican border into the town of Columbus, New Mexico, and attacked the Thirteenth Cavalry bivouacked there. The nation was outraged; the United States had been invaded.

Reports came from the border states that during the firefight, the general's machine gun of choice, the Benét-Mercié, repeatedly jammed.[7] The cavalry was almost defenseless against Villa, who was armed with Maxims that didn't jam. For Crozier critics, the inference was clear: this would never have happened if Crozier had armed the cavalry with the Lewis gun.

Actually, the Benét-Mercié was getting bad press. A year later, it was demonstrated that the Benét-Mercié machine guns down in New Mexico had performed fairly efficiently and with few jams. The true problem was the difficulty of loading them, especially in the dark. But the damage had been done—enough to condemn an army weapon that had never been popular with American troops

319

anyway. For three years, since 1913, the troops had been complaining about a number of the gun's characteristics, particularly the difficulty of loading it. Crozier had always explained the problem as the result of poor training.

To silence the critics, Crozier acted quickly. In April 1916, he announced he would test three machine guns: the Benét-Mercié from France, the Vickers-Maxim from England, and the Lewis gun. Politically, this move was fraught with difficulty for him because a good performance from the Lewis gun could reflect negatively on his previous evaluations.

When the Springfield Armory test results were posted, once again, as in the 1913 test, both the Benét-Mercié and the British Vickers finished in a dead heat with both weapons judged acceptable. As for the Lewis gun, Savage Arms, the domestic manufacturer, had submitted two Lewises—one chambered for the American .30-'06 cartridge and one for the British .303-caliber cartridge. The American Lewis, General Crozier reported, "did not do well." He asserted that the Lewis gun couldn't handle the stronger American charge, a curious accusation since Colonel Lewis originally designed his weapon around the American cartridges and had adapted it to the British caliber only after he had carried it to England. The British Lewis gun "did well but not as well as the Benét-Mercié or the Vickers."

Crozier announced that the Vickers-Maxim machine gun would be chambered for the American .30-'06 cartridge under license to the Ordnance Bureau's most favored gun maker, the Colt factory in Hartford, Connecticut, to replace all eleven hundred Benét-Merciés in the U.S. Army. His choice begged the question: since the Benét-Mercié and the Vickers finished in a dead heat, why replace the Benét-Mercié?

Apparently, Crozier expected his choice of the Vickers-Maxim would be universally accepted. Germany was using the Maxim, which it called the Spandau MG08, with deadly effect. England was also armed with the Maxim, which it called the Vickers, also with unparalleled results. So a Maxim by any other name in the American army should have pleased everyone.

Instead, General Crozier's announcement caused an uproar. Even the British were baffled by his test results. With extensive battlefield experience using the Lewis as their first-line weapon and the Vickers-Maxim as their second-line weapon, the British felt they were experts on these two weapons. As for the Benét-Mercié, they had tested it and rejected it.[8] A British correspondent reported that Lewis guns were in use not only by the British army, but also the French, Russian, and Italian armies. He criticized the American government of "action mainly of a personal or political character."[9] The *Cleveland Press* asserted that the British army had not found any other weapon "of so much real use . . . as the Lewis machine gun. It has done wonders." British army officers were reported to be astounded when they heard that American troops were not armed with the Lewis gun.[10] The *New York Times* reported that Lord Hugh Cecil told the House of Commons that the Lewis gun was "a weapon that is the envy of all Europe." The *Times* added, "For many months, the Germans have been making frantic efforts to duplicate the gun for use in their own armies."[11]

General Wood flatly disbelieved Crozier's test results. He reported that the highest-ranking officers in the U.S. Army, during a demonstration of the Lewis gun in New Mexico, had all enthusiastically endorsed it. These rankers included Major General Leonard Wood himself; Major General Frederick Funston, commanding officer at the Mexican border; Brigadier General John "Black Jack" Pershing, soon to be commander of the AEF in France; and the commander of the Aviation Section of the Signal Corps, Colonel George O. Squier, who asserted that the Lewis gun was also the greatest aerial machine gun in the world, performing spectacular service on thousands of British airplanes.

General Wood's adherents claimed that Crozier had carried a personal grudge against Colonel Lewis for some years, and had never given his gun a fair field test. "The real test," Wood told the *New York Times*, "is being made daily on the battlefields of France and Belgium. What do our backyard tests amount to in the face of that evidence over there?"

To document his assertions, Wood announced a public show-down between the Benét-Mercié and the Lewis, away from the control of General Crozier. Timed for August, just a few months before election day, he appointed a board to go to the military camp in Plattsburgh, New York, to "fair test" the Lewis against the Benét-Mercié. General Crozier was pointedly not invited. Had he been, he most certainly would not have attended.

The Dorey Board, so called after Captain Dorey, who headed it, unanimously, with great enthusiasm, chose the Lewis over the Benét-Mercié. The Benét-Mercié was the equal of the Lewis in one area only—portability.

When informed of the test, General Crozier dismissed it as not "official"—that is, not under the control of the Ordnance Department.

The quarrel became public on September 18, 1916, on the front page of the *New York Times*—the worst possible time for the Woodrow Wilson campaign, just weeks before election day. The headline is several inches deep:

AMERICAN GUN,
REJECTED BY US,
WINS FOR BRITISH

LEWIS RAPID-FIRER, ENVY OF
ALL EUROPE, ONCE OFFERED AS
GIFT TO OUR ARMY.

ORDINANCE BUREAU BARS IT

GOOD FAITH OF THE
BUREAU AND ITS CHIEF,
GEN. CROZIER, ASSAILED.

The article presented rave reviews from British troops in the trenches. It was also harshly critical—even condemnatory—of General Crozier for refusing to accept the world's finest gun because of a personal grudge against Lewis. The article reported the results of the Dorey Board tests and published Crozier's reply, in which he presented the results not of the tests of the past April Machine Gun Board, but of the 1913 tests, three years before. He detailed fully the 1913 poor performance of the Lewis gun, including the 206 jams, without revealing that the metal parts had been defective and that the gun had been withdrawn.

The *Times* article suggested that there was a belief in some quarters that General Crozier had plotted against the Lewis gun, driving it across the ocean to the British. The portrait of Crozier implied by the facts presented was devastating: a petty, vindictive, brassbound officer, jealous of a fellow officer's great success, violating his sworn duty by blocking the adoption of a great machine gun that the nation desperately needed. The story, crushing to Crozier, was certainly a disaster for Woodrow Wilson, campaigning in the last two months of a very close presidential election. Crozier responded in the *New York Times*: "In the opinion of the board, the question as to whether or not it [the Lewis gun] can be developed to a satisfactory degree of reliability and dependability is an open one." Since the *Times* had already noted that the Lewis gun was being fired at the rate of fifteen million rounds a day in France by highly enthusiastic troops, the general's doubts about the weapon's reliability were hardly creditable. In fact, with patriotism approaching flood tide as 1917 approached, Wood's tests were making Crozier seem unpatriotic.

Wood's timing had been perfect. He had dragged Crozier right into the middle of the presidential campaign. He stuck a black hat on Crozier's head and set him up in a six-gun shootout against the white-hatted, sainted, superpatriot Isaac Newton Lewis, who was selflessly waiting to pour into the American Treasury the royalties from the remarkable gun that was saving England.

The next day, September 19, 1916, in a story in the *New York Times*, Robert N. Calfee, an attorney from Cleveland and the legal counsel for the Automatic Arms Company, the manufacturers of the Lewis gun, added to the clamor. He accused General Crozier of "a determined effort . . . to prevent any test of the Lewis gun at Springfield and to prevent absolutely any tests of the gun in connection with aeroplane work."[12]

CHAPTER 25

SECRETARY OF WAR BAKER SELECTS A MACHINE GUN

Secretary of War Newton Baker rushed back from the campaign trail to Washington to conduct some fast damage control. His office announced that 353 Lewis machine guns would be furnished to militia serving on the Mexican border, apparently to replace the Springfield-made Benét-Merciés that were alleged to have failed. The announcement added that the Lewis was chosen only because it was the only machine gun available on the American market. Yet this move served only to draw attention even more to the most fundamental question: Why hadn't General Crozier in three years produced a U.S. Army machine gun in the first place? And that, for Crozier, was the question that would not go away.

The next day, the *New York Times* reported that Secretary Baker was appointing a blue ribbon committee to perform new tests on the "American Gun," as the Lewis gun was termed. General Crozier was not to be part of the test group. Right next to this front-page report was quoted a letter to the *Times* from General Crozier, denying everything. The headline ran: "Gen. Crozier Denies Lewis Offered His Gun Free; Tested and Rejected by Best Agencies, He Says."[1]

The timing seemed to indicate that Crozier's rejection of Lewis's patriotic royalty-free offer was bothering Baker and the Democrats. But the Crozier denial was offset by an adjacent story stating that those in the War Department "Confirm Word of Inventor." The net effect of the stories made Crozier seem to be a liar.

What Secretary Baker didn't announce that day was that he had appointed another investigator, Brigadier General E. A. Garlington, inspector general of the army, to investigate claims that Lewis had offered his gun free. General Garlington's investigation would be done behind closed doors, undisclosed to the public, for if he did find documentary evidence that Lewis had made such an offer, Baker wanted to be in command of all the facts before he spoke publicly. If not, there would be time enough later to effectively deny the allegation.

Buried in that same *Times* story was a statement that few people seem to have noticed: "The War Department has knowledge that an American inventor intends to submit to the Government for tests an entirely new type of machine gun." The report did not disclose the inventor's identity or any facts about his new type of weapon.

The attack continued. On September 20, 1916, the *Times* reported that a high Washington official "insists Lewis waived right to royalties on gun used in army; Automatic Arms Co said to have objected to tests of Lewis guns offered by Crozier." On September 22, Colonel Lewis himself wrote a letter to the *Times*, answering Crozier and reiterating the claim that his gun was offered royalty-free to his American government in repayment for the education and nurture he received at West Point. He had set but one condition: his machine gun was not to be tested by General William Crozier, by the Springfield Armory, or by any group controlled by General Crozier. He also reported how General Crozier managed to prevent the aerial test of the Lewis that had been authorized by the War Department: he said that General Crozier had simply refused to issue bullets for the test.

With each passing day, public statements printed in the newspapers were creating the portrait of a villain sitting in the chief of ordnance's chair. The issue now became completely politicized. Secretary of War Newton Baker sent Crozier out of town to inspect arsenals beyond the reach of the press. He gagged General Wood, and then, seemingly acting on the principle "If you can't convince, confuse," Baker adroitly set his blue ribbon panel to brilliantly answering the wrong questions.

The board he named was hardly qualified to answer in a few days the questions that General Crozier had been dealing with for three years. Consisting of five officers and two civilians, the board was headed by Colonel Francis H. French of the Army General Staff, picked by the adjutant general (who reported to Baker), and included a retired colonel of Ordnance, a colonel for the Coast Artillery, a colonel from the Cavalry, and a captain from the Signal Corps. One of the civilians was Bascom Little, former president of the Cleveland Chamber of Commerce, with "a deep interest in military matters," and B. M. W. Hanson of Hartford, Connecticut. The last appointment was strange, since Hanson was the president of Colt's Patent Firearms Manufacturing Company, the firm that was accused of holding a virtual monopoly over armory arms production and licensee of the disputed Benét-Mercié machine gun.

The assignment Baker gave them seemed to ignore the questions raised by the reports in the newspapers: Did General Crozier conspire for personal reasons to wash out the Lewis gun? Was the Lewis gun washed out in a rigged test? And, lastly, did Lewis offer his gun to his government free of royalties? Instead, Baker asked his blue ribbon board to decide which machine gun was best for the army—a lightweight gun or a medium-duty gun. Or both. The Lewis-Crozier issue seemed to be safely sanitized until after the election.

On October 8, with at least one great machine gun available— the Maxim—and no doubt two that could have been put into immediate production—the Maxim and the Lewis—and given the urgent need to arm American troops, the Machine Gun Board was calling for inventors to submit ideas for new machine guns. No mention was made of the "entirely new kind of machine gun" that had been reported in a previous *Times* story.

And then after the election was safely passed, on November 11, with the president reelected for a second term, the Baker board announced its decision. The *Times* reported:

VICKERS GUN WINS
BOARD'S AWARD

LEWIS GUN
PREFERRED FOR THE
LIGHTER BRITISH
AMMUNITION—

FURTHER TESTS OF
LIGHT GUNS[2]

There hadn't been enough time—a few weeks—to mount major tests of the weapons, so the board was reissuing the results of General Crozier's April tests, which General Wood had rejected. Again the Lewis gun was dismissed as a British-caliber gun that needed further developing, suitable only for "certain special purposes, such as aeroplanes and use of skirmishers, etc." Meanwhile, the board was opening a whole new round of tests open to any machine gun from anywhere in the world.

The test was not to occur until the following May 1917. This seven-month period was given to the inventor of the "entirely new machine gun," whose name still had not been revealed. With the nation just months away from going to war in Europe, Secretary Baker didn't have seven months to find a new machine gun, plus the additional year or more to develop tooling and get into production. With the usual production problems, it could take up to two years before the first new machine gun would come off the production line.

Since the Maxim and the Lewis were available and in production, Baker was laying himself open to charges of politicking with the security of the nation. He apparently, however, felt he had a winning trump card. In the interim, he would order the Maxim—forty-six hundred of them, an absurdly low number for a major war—plus any additional machine guns to be purchased on an emergency basis on the open market: Lewises, Colts, anything.

On November 22, Secretary Baker reassembled the Machine Gun Board. Congress had appropriated $12 million for machine guns, and Baker was reluctant to spend it all on Vickers-Maxims, since the army needed a light machine rifle like the Lewis. Hence, he asked the board to authorize the expenditure of some of that money for the purchase of Lewis guns. Secretary Baker then tried to restore the public standing of his Ordnance Department. He announced that General E. A. Garlington, the inspector general of the army, had investigated the alleged offer from Colonel Lewis of his gun free of royalties. There was no official record of such an offer, said General Garlington.

General Garlington had also looked into allegations that General Crozier had displayed gross partiality in the selection of a machine gun. Not so, said the inspector general: General Crozier's comportment throughout had been correct and professional. Colonel Lewis had been given every opportunity to display his weapon. Rejection of it came not from General Crozier but from the entire War Department.

Secretary Baker waited for public reaction to the inspector general's report. An answer came on December 19, 1916, when the House Committee on Military Affairs summoned Chief of Ordnance General William Crozier for questioning about the Lewis gun affair. Reporting on the committee's move, the *Times* noted that "the alleged discrimination against the Lewis gun had become of such a nature that there would be a number of questions asked concerning it."[3] The investigation was not to be a whitewash. The committee wanted to go out on the firing range and witness the Lewis's performance. But before anything else, the committee wanted to talk with Secretary of War Newton Baker.

On January 22, 1917, as newly re-elected President Wilson was preparing another peace mission to Europe, Germany announced that after February 1, all ships—Allied and neutral—headed for Allied ports would be sunk without warning. The Germans were convinced that, denied American war matériel, the Allied war effort would collapse. On February 3, 1917, the USS *Housatonic* was torpedoed. The German ambassador was handed his passport, and the United States severed diplomatic relations with Germany. On February 24, 1917, the British turned over to the White House the contents of the intercepted Zimmerman note, in which Germany offered Mexico its "lost territories" of Texas, Arizona, and New Mexico if it would declare war on the United States. During March, German submarines torpedoed five more U.S. merchant ships. Inevitably, the United States declared war on the Central Powers on April 7, 1917. From March through June 1917, military casualties continued in the three Battles of Arras, and

Messines Ridge, when British, Canadian, and French troops attacked Germany with little gain. The French offensive at Chemin des Dames, which produced 120,000 casualties, almost proved to be that nation's undoing. Fifty-four French divisions, fully half of the French army, mutinied. By June, there wasn't a single French division between Soissons and Paris prepared to engage the enemy.

General Pétain, touring the exhausted battle line, managed to gain control of his troops only by promising there would be no more campaigns like the failed and costly offensive by General Robert Nivelle, whom Pétain replaced. France, he vowed, would wait for the Americans, as Marshal Joffre sailed for the United States. He told President Wilson that the only thing between Germany and victory was a very battered British army and begged the president for troops. At least one division. The United States did not have one battle-ready division.

By March, the country's sons were in camp, without uniforms, without army shoes, without tents or blankets, marching in their ranks with broomsticks on their shoulders. A campaign was created to mail the broomsticks to Congress as a reminder of its poor scores on military preparedness. That same month, there was progress of sorts. The broomsticks were replaced with wooden rifles. By April 20, on the authority of the Machine Gun Board, the U.S. government purchased six thousand Lewis guns, half for the army and half for the navy and marines. For an army of a half million men, with another million to be drafted in 1918, the machine-gun count was up to ten thousand. In the meantime, there were still only a few hundred thousand rifles for the infantry.

On April 28, Secretary of War Baker had a heartening announcement to make. He had found an unlimited supply of rifles that would serve until production of the American Springfield rifle could catch up. True, Frederick Colvin had done the engineering book on the Springfield—the illustrations, drawings, and dimensions—as a guide to the rifle manufacturers to start making the gun. But even so, production was a long way off. No mention was made of the tools and dies that General Crozier was to have made.

In the interim, as Baker knew, not many rifles were going to come out of that antiquated armory factory in Springfield.

Baker announced that American troops would be armed with the British army P-14 Enfield as an interim weapon. He pointed out that for some years, three production lines right in the United States had been turning out thirty thousand Enfields a day for the British army. These plants were fully tooled, had complete sets of dies, and large staffs of trained men working in shifts.

The Enfield might not have been the Springfield—it was heavy and rather clumsy—but it was a fine rifle, British quality throughout, with one of the sturdiest constructions in the rifle world. The primary manufacturing plant couldn't have been more ideally situated—from Washington, it was a short railroad ride away in Eddystone, Pennsylvania, outside Philadelphia, an easy hundred miles distant.

To make matters even better, the man in charge of British rifle production at Eddystone was a retired officer of the U.S. Ordnance Bureau, an expert in both U.S. Ordnance and British Ordnance: General John T. Thompson.

Rechambering the Enfield from the British .303 caliber to the American .30 caliber was all that needed to be done—a small change, quickly accomplished—in order to start the production lines rolling once more.

Baker was well aware that many Americans were going to say that the people responsible for preparedness—the Congress, the president, and the War Department—had let America down. With the newspapers digging into the story, it was not the best time to be the chief of ordnance.

In spite of that, the Enfield was a salvation. The nation could expect American-style British Enfields to be soon flowing off the production lines at Eddystone, at Winchester, and at Remington—if all went well. Thinking he had that problem solved, Secretary Baker handed the production problem off to General Crozier. Baker turned his attention to his Machine Gun Board and the upcoming tests in May, at which time it was expected the mystery inventor would introduce his radical new machine gun.

• • •

330

In May 1917, the name of the mysterious gun designer was revealed. The Machine Gun Board's call for submissions drew two entries from one of the towering figures in gun design, John Moses Browning. When he appeared to present both his candidates, a heavy machine gun and a lightweight portable machine gun, the board members, walking to the firing line, were not at all prepared for what they would see.

Water-cooled, belt-fed, and weighing thirty-six pounds, the Browning heavy machine gun fired the standard Springfield .30-'06–caliber rifle cartridge. During the test, Ordnance men fired twenty thousand rounds of ammunition through the Browning at six hundred rounds a minute. There was not a single jam, not a single hitch. This feat seemed so improbable that the Machine Gun Board appeared to doubt what it had just seen.

To show that this wasn't a fluke, the commanding figure of John Browning himself stepped up to the firing line with another Browning machine gun. He set it to firing automatically while he casually linked together belts of ammunition that fed endlessly through the gun, which fired continuously as the minutes ticked by. Box after box of ammunition belts were opened and attached to the previous belt, and box after box of belts with empty cartridges came chattering out the other side. The gun ran like a sewing machine, without overheating, without jamming, without laboring. Finally, the only thing that stopped the weapon was the board. When it signaled for an end, the Browning heavy machine gun had fired for forty-eight minutes and twelve seconds. The Browning had entered the munitions world by destroying all records for performance and reliability.

Then, as a grand finale, Browning the salesman—the showman—stepped before his machine gun and tied a blindfold around his eyes. With no tools, he disassembled the gun, reduced it entirely to its seventy component parts. Then, still completely blindfolded, he reassembled the gun with an elapsed time of fifty-five seconds. So important was this feature in battle, blindfolding became part of the standard military training program when the gun was issued to American troops.

Next, Browning followed up this striking success by introducing his Browning automatic rifle—the BAR. It, too, fired the standard Springfield .30-'06 cartridge. A rifleman stepped up to the line, poked a clip of twenty into the weapon, and fired the entire clip of twenty bullets in two and a half seconds. Two and a half seconds reloaded the weapon and two and a half seconds emptied the second clip. The BAR weighed only thirteen pounds, was fully portable, and was in every sense a machine gun. A rifleman could fire this weapon as he walked or even charged. It, too, could be disassembled and reassembled by hand in minutes.

The Machine Gun Board was looking at a great new heavy machine gun and a great new light machine gun ready for production—and also at a great problem. Introduced years late, these weapons were test models. They needed to be developed, quirks worked out, and the parts redesigned to be handled by an automated production line. With luck, without production hitches, working at top speed, a whole year might pass before any could come off the production line, while hundreds of thousands of American doughboys were about to embark for France with no machine guns at all.

Sitting there accusingly was the Lewis gun, serviceable, battle-tested, with production lines ready to run night and day in America and Canada and even England. In a few months, American military units could ship out for the trenches fully armed with Lewis machine guns. Significantly, the Lewis gun had also passed the board's test "very successfully." General Crozier's previous tests of the Lewis gun looked suspect. But if, after all the quarreling, the board picked the Lewis, the political implications were enormous. General Crozier and the Ordnance Department would lose all credibility and thereby the whole War Department. The board went with the Browning.

There was one final problem. Because of production capacity, the ideal maker—possibly the only maker—of the new guns was Winchester. The firm's executives wondered if the sixty-two-year-old Browning could put aside his old animosities. To serve his country, Browning said, he could and would. He gathered up the working drawings of his guns and, for the first time in twenty-two years, entered the Winchester plant to expedite the design, the tooling, and production.

On July 2, 1917, the army ordered four thousand more Lewis guns and ordered the new Browning guns into preproduction development. By July 22, the army called for forty-five thousand machine guns: ten thousand Browning heavy machine guns, ten thousand Browning BARs, and twenty-five thousand Lewises.

The same day the nation learned that the U.S. Army had a supply of only six hundred pieces of various artillery, General Crozier quickly announced that there was plenty of artillery: the Allies—France, in particular—could supply all we needed. "We have neglected our ordnance for fifteen years," the general said, "and now are faced with the logical result of our failure to keep up."[4] "We" meant Congress and the American people.

The Allies had fifty thousand artillery pieces in action. The United States was preparing to send an army over there with six hundred pieces, hoping that France would supply the rest.

On July 4, 1917, on the Champs-Elysées, in Paris, a battalion of the American Sixteenth Infantry, behatted with the "chapeau de cow-boy," and under the command of General "Black Jack" Pershing, marched through wildly cheering crowds of war-exhausted Frenchmen. Arriving in France barely armed with rifles, and bringing no machine guns and no artillery, the Americans found waiting for them on the battlefield all those American inventions that had been rejected by the American Ordnance Bureau over the years before being eagerly accepted by the European armies.

There was the German Maxim machine gun, the Spandau MG08, the English Maxim machine gun, the Vickers, the English Lewis gun in use as a trench gun, a tank gun, and an aerial gun, the airplane, the bombsight invented by the American Riley Scott, and a multitude of other items and impedimenta of war, including range finders, hand grenades, telephones, and trucks.

The American army was to go into battle armed with British rifles, French and British airplanes, French and British machine guns, French artillery, French and British ammunition, French and

British tanks. Oddly enough, the Americans excelled in one area: trucks.

American troops also arrived with a single airplane—the De Havilland. A cranky, poorly designed, and at times completely uncontrollable craft, it was nicknamed the Flying Coffin and soon crashed.

From July 31 through November 10, 1917, in the Third Battle of Ypres (also called the Battle at Passchendaele), Britons, Australians, and Canadians fought for yards as they advanced toward Passchendaele. A complete failure, the battle produced 200,000 casualties. The Allies applied increasing pressure on General Pershing to commit immediately all his American forces. Feeling they were only half trained and refusing to portion them out to the various Allied armies, Pershing steadfastly refused.

CHAPTER 26

CROZIER'S LAST DAYS

B y September, General Crozier was on the griddle again. Defective ammunition had arrived in France for General Pershing's army, and it was blamed on bad chemicals at the Frankford Arsenal in Philadelphia. Warned by arsenal experts to change the chemicals, the Ordnance Department had failed to take timely action and consequently the troops were preparing to go into battle with defective small arms ammunition. Congress formed a committee to investigate and the *New York Times* wrote an editorial to admonish: "The remembrance of General Crozier, Chief of Ordnance, and his aides is singularly defective in this matter. Perhaps they have so many other important matters to trouble them that they cannot spare the time for cartridge primers which might doom thousands of American soldiers to sure death. Public interest in this matter will be increased by the recent reports of General Crozier's amazing attitude toward the Lewis machine gun, an American invention rejected by our Ordnance Bureau, but used by the British Army in the present war. The United States Government might have owned this gun. Now it is compelled to buy it at the market rates, which the foreign demand has made high."[1]

Crozier was now attacked from another side. A new major flap occurred over the Enfield rifles that were supposed to be rolling off production lines at a rate of 100,000 a month—and weren't. In August 1917, in the Winchester Repeating Arms Company plant,

Fred Colvin, the production engineer and editor of the *American Machinist* magazine who had prepared the blueprints for the Springfield '03, was on an inspection tour, and when he entered the plant, what he saw angered him. He found no Enfields coming off the production line. The workers were playing cards and checkers, chatting, reading newspapers, and drawing full pay. Ever since Secretary of War Baker announced the adoption of the modified British Enfield, the workers had been waiting for the okay to start up the production line again. Days had passed, then weeks, and now months—in all, lost production of a quarter of a million rifles—while draftees were marching and drilling with broomsticks. Colvin took pictures of the scene, then stormed out.

The delay was inexcusable. All that had been required was a change in the rifle's chambering to handle the American cartridge. He found the culprit very quickly: General Crozier. He and his staff were holding up everything while they resolved some design questions about parts interchangeability. Colvin felt no design problem could possibly require months to solve.

At Colvin's behest, his magazine, the influential *American Machinist*, wrote an infuriated editorial. Before it was published, General Crozier learned about it and "went," said Colvin, "to considerable pains to have that issue of the *American Machinist* suppressed or impounded." Ultimately, he failed, and the editorial appeared.

It was a stinging rebuke to Crozier. It accused him of "inexcusable and dangerous loss of time." The magazine pointed out that "England was forced by bitter experience and delays of this kind to eliminate Bureaucratic control of all munition manufacture, and place this work in the hands of those qualified by experience to decide quickly between the essential and the nonessential." The editorial indicted General Crozier as a man who was "incapable of coming to a decision."[2]

The editorial caused a furor, and, shortly after, Colvin was "requested" to attend a meeting of Ordnance officers. General Crozier refused to have any contact with Colvin and didn't attend. But his right-hand man was there—General John T. Thompson— and with him were three other generals.

The presence of General Thompson was significant. He had

been in charge of Springfield Armory production under General Crozier. He was the officer who had dealt with the German maker of the spitzer bullet that sued the United States for patent infringement. After the war, he was to become famous as the designer of the Thompson submachine gun—the Tommy gun of the Bootleg Prohibition Wars. In 1914, he had retired from the army to become civilian head of production at the arsenal in Eddystone, Pennsylvania, making the 1914 Pattern Enfield Repeating Arm (ERA) for Britain.

When Springfield Armory couldn't make enough Springfield '03s, Thompson returned to service in April 1917 (the month the United States declared war on Germany) as chief of the Small Arms Division, Ordnance Department. Then he was brought back to Eddystone to head up the production of the American M1917 version of the Enfield rifle. In short, he was to go on doing for the United States what he had been doing for the British—producing Enfield rifles—only now he would do it in an American army uniform. Thompson was in charge of all three plants—at Midvale Steel's Eddystone Arsenal, at its Remington Arms Company, and at the Winchester Repeating Arms Company.

The feeling of the three officers was that since Colvin had never fired a gun in anger in his life, he couldn't know anything about rifles or any other kind of weapon. They explained to him that there was an overriding reason for the delays: the need to assure the interchangeability of parts made in the different factories. Under the British program, rifle parts from one factory didn't interchange with parts from another factory.

Colvin pointed out that their own words had shown the error of their ways. The British had no parts interchangeability because they didn't think it was important, and they had managed to fight the biggest war in history for three years without it, and during that time, they had made hundreds of thousands of rifles every month on the same machines. Colvin accused them of shutting down the production lines in order to agonize over trivia. He told them their obsession with exact dimensions was an absurdity. They had to make rifles the way the British did—with plus or minus tolerances. And they had to make them now.[3]

The bruising meeting cleared the air. Colvin had made his point, and soon the three plants began to turn out rifles in quantity. But with the desperate need for rifles unabated, Colvin was still angry with Crozier's inexcusable insouciance and sloppy, inefficient manufacturing methods. He decided to attack the general personally. In the fall of 1917, the *American Machinist* ran another editorial, titled "Wanted—A Master Hand." It said:

> Work is being duplicated by different committees; gauge inspection is being scattered instead of centralized; the army and navy bid against each other for delivery and occasionally in price; red tape, seniority and precedent stand in the way of the hearty cooperation that makes for the most efficient conduct of any business.
>
> The time has come to put the right man in charge of all munitions and end the inevitable delays and inefficiency of the present system. . . . Delays mean needless loss of life, unnecessary sorrow and suffering and war taxes that may be avoided.[4]

The magazine's accusations were hardly an exaggeration. In December 1917, after Crozier had wasted months dawdling, the British had 100,000 fewer troops than they had begun the year with—and their manpower well was about run dry; Germany, after the collapse and surrender of Russia, had shifted an entire army of battle veterans to the Western Front to confront a British army stretched almost to the breaking point and a French army near mutiny. The magazine was calling for a professional production expert—a civilian—to replace General Crozier. By then, so were many other people.

Now it was autumn 1917, and from November 20 through December 7, 1917, during the Battle of Cambrai, the British introduced tank warfare, broke through German lines, but soon lost captured territory. Battle lines were still more or less where they had been in 1914.

Back in the United States came the unforgettable December of

1917, when everything came tumbling down—for the War Department, for Secretary Baker, and particularly for General William Crozier. In December, the nation had had enough of the incredible mess that had occurred as the military tried to raise, train, and ship an army to France. The first contingent of American troops arrived at the battlefield half trained, with no weapons. Men were training in army camps still wearing their civilian clothing. In the winter weather, the army worried that disease would break out. The Senate was swarming with angry committees set up to study everything in the War Department. A committee created to study the scandals surrounding the shortage of uniforms focused on a "Rag Ring" accused of conspiring to control the manufacture of uniforms and pocket enormous profits while the men in camp had no winter clothing. Another committee studied the scandals in the sugar industry; another, the coal industry; another, the railroads; while another took a bead on General Crozier once more: it wanted to find out why he could not seem to produce guns. An angry set of senators summoned Crozier and found themselves facing an angry general.

Crozier had been attacked from every side. His shortcomings had been held up for the whole world to see. His notoriously thin skin had worn through. His testimony revealed that he was absolutely, utterly convinced that in the whole affair, he was blameless. For five days, in the Senate Military Affairs Committee room, the senators pummeled him with questions. When they asked him why there were so many delays, Crozier told them it was their fault. Congress hadn't appropriated the war funds soon enough. He also blamed armory workmen who had quit the ordnance plants to go to higher-paying war jobs. The method of handling contracts was to blame—contracts let without competitive bids that the War Munitions Board had to approve, which caused a major bottleneck. He denied that the Ordnance Bureau had let the army down, contending that there was no shortage of munitions or guns with the U.S. Army in France. It was being equipped with artillery by England and France. He told them that his staff alone had increased from eighty-five to twenty-one hundred to handle the demand. On

December 14, during Crozier's second day of grilling, President Wilson sent him a Christmas present. He reappointed Crozier as chief of ordnance for another four-year term. But what seemed like a vote of confidence wasn't.

When the senators turned to machine guns, Crozier dropped a political brick. He blamed his boss, Secretary of War Newton Baker, and the Baker Machine Gun Board for taking so long in choosing a weapon. Crozier did not remind the senators that Baker formed the Machine Gun Board because he, Crozier, had failed to settle on a machine gun after many years of searching. He reported that factory production of Enfield rifles in the country had fallen from ten thousand a day prewar to five thousand a day currently, without noting that he and his staff had shut the Enfield rifle production lines down for months while they debated minor points of parts interchangeability. The senators felt that they weren't getting enough information from the general and they took him, on the third day, into secret session so that he couldn't hide behind national security. Even there, with the doors shut, the exchanges were heated. They wanted to talk about Crozier's failure to produce a machine gun. He denied it was his fault. Still not liking his answers, the Senate committee asked more blunt questions. They asked Crozier what he did with the $5 million they gave him in August 1916, when he said he would develop patterns and dies for the Springfield '03 to give to rifle factories. Crozier told them he spent it on pistols. The senators decided to hold the general over for another day of questions in closed-door executive session.

That same day, Secretary Baker stated publicly that he assumed full blame for the slowness of his Machine Gun Board. He added, "It was perfectly proper for General Crozier to tell the Senate that."[5] He also reported that every available plant in the country was making machine guns for the army.

On December 18, the fifth day of his testimony, General Crozier blamed red tape in the War Department for the lack of artillery. When the senators pressed him, he blamed the nation's steel makers for failing to cooperate with the government after the price of steel had been fixed. So far, Crozier had blamed Congress, factory workers, Secretary Baker, bankers, contracts, circumstance, time, red tape, and the steel industry, among others, for the country's lack of ordnance—everyone but himself. In five days of testimony, he had succeeded only in increasing the anger of the senators facing him.

Senator Chamberlain, the committee chairman, seemed to sum up the committee's frustration when he said, "You had money for machine guns, and you haven't got the machine guns yet. You had money for small arms, and you have spent it for pistols instead of rifles." Crozier answered, "We were shorter of pistols."[6]

The committee dismissed him.

General Crozier could take cold comfort in knowing that in another Senate hearing room, General Sharpe, quartermaster general of the army, was being shredded and destroyed. Army Surgeon General Gorgas reported that the shortage of clothing plus overcrowding in camps had brought on a significant number of pneumonia cases. The camps were in danger of being overswept by infectious diseases. He asked that the army delay the arrival of more recruits until the problem was solved. As if to underscore this terrible failure of the quartermaster general to provide warm clothing for the troops, a vast and bitterly cold weather front settled over much of the nation—one of the coldest winters in memory. Temperatures of thirty below zero were reported from the Midwest, eighteen below in Utica, New York, and when the thermometer dropped to twenty-three below zero in Fort Devens, Massachusetts, military drills were suspended. At Camp McArthur, in Texas, confronted with a camp filled with troops with no clothing, a thermometer well below zero, and fearing an outbreak of pneumonia, military authorities went into all the retail stores in the Waco area and commandeered all uniforms and overcoats they could find.

In the meantime, on December 22, Secretary Baker announced the formation of a Military War Council to be staffed by the heads of the five different branches of the army. This infuriated, among others, Representative C. B. Miller of Minnesota. He demanded that General Crozier, chief of ordnance, and General Henry G. Sharpe, quartermaster general, be superseded and also dropped from the newly formed Military War Council. But Secretary Baker was ahead of Miller. He had put the two generals on the new council, while at the same time relieving them of their other staff duties. Both men were effectively removed from administering their bureaus of ordnance and supply.

Before the Senate Military Affairs Committee, General Crozier's enemies came to testify against him. The next day, Representative Medill McCormick of Illinois, just back from France, appeared before the committee and promptly challenged everything General Crozier had said about French and British ordnance supplies to American troops, claiming that those two countries were near collapse and could not possibly supply the unarmed American army there. In fact, he said, "unless the United States speeded up the manufacture of guns and ammunition, its forces in France will suffer a serious handicap, even to the possibility of losing the war."[7]

Then came the most damaging testimony of all—from the heads of the nation's leading arms-making companies. Louis E. Stoddard, president of the Marlin-Rockwell Company, testified that before the war started, he offered to make machine guns for the Ordnance Board, but the board held meetings over gun types and design changes that wasted six months of potential gun production. In contrast, Admiral Earle, chief ordnance officer of the U.S. Navy, and Crozier's counterpart, had told Stoddard to go ahead and make every machine gun he could. But Crozier, Stoddard said, wouldn't even listen to him. If he had, Stoddard said, the U.S. Army would already have had American machine guns in the trenches with them.

Henry Kimball, vice president of the Remington Arms Company, testified that he personally had offered his entire factory at Eddystone, Pennsylvania, for the making of Enfields to Crozier in February, before the war started. Crozier didn't take over the plant until July, after having made changes in the Enfield seventeen times. Kimball added, "There was nothing we could do to make [him] comprehend the necessities of the situation."

J. E. Otterson, vice president of the Winchester Repeating Arms Company, told the same story of Crozier and his Ordnance people indignantly rejecting suggestions, of delaying production of the Enfield for months to make seventeen changes—and this for a changeover that should have taken only thirty days.[8]

The *New York Times* wrote another editorial faulting Crozier for two flaws—his inaction for months on end when confronted with a crisis and his unwillingness to take any blame for the mess. "Perhaps," said the editorial, "the most exasperating aspect of the General's testimony was his evasion of responsibility, his twisting and turning to escape the painful effects of his testimony."

The only comfort Crozier received was from a suspect source. M. W. Hanson, vice president of the Colt's Patent Firearms Manufacturing Company, the firm accused by Automatic Arms Company of holding a monopoly on gun making from the Ordnance Department, stated that the U.S. Enfield as modified by the Ordnance Department was twice the gun of the original British Enfield. The Lewis gun was not much of a gun for army use since it had always failed with American ammunition.

Frederick Colvin appeared to recount his dealings with the Ordnance Bureau, and recommended that ordnance affairs be put under the control of a minister of munitions, adding that the government was "too antiquated."[9]

On December 22, the day General Crozier was relieved of his Ordnance command and named to the Military War Council, Colonel Isaac Newton Lewis appeared. He stated that he had already turned over to the Treasury two checks for royalties on his weapons amounting to $17,500, for which he had received no acknowledgment except the cashed checks. He had since offered another $2.5 million to Secretary Baker, who had not answered his letter. He stated that there was an Ordnance Ring, and only those in it did business with the bureau. He also said the Lewis gun fired American ammunition and, in fact, was originally designed around American ammunition. He maintained that Crozier knew of the Lewis gun's capability and had fired the gun himself many times as early as 1912. He accused Crozier of being absolutely autocratic and "hopelessly inefficient. There hasn't been a new idea or a new development in ordnance for fifteen years." Lewis blamed the

Ordnance Bureau's problems on "Crozierism," a one-man machine. Before that, it had been "Buffingtonism," under the regime of General Adelbert Buffington, General Crozier's predecessor. Of the range finder he invented, Lewis said General Crozier "had opposed its introduction to the bitter end."[10]

A. Borie of Automatic Arms later seemed almost prescient when he said that the Ordnance Bureau should be run by businessmen who would not "pussyfoot around" but take responsibility and make decisions.[11]

After all this testimony, much of it flatly contradicting Crozier's testimony, on December 31, the Senate Committee on Military Affairs called Crozier back "to clear up a few details," and grilled him once more. This time he blamed the entire United States for the lack of ordnance, "because it had failed to adopt a preparedness policy in peace time." Once again, he denied any bias against Colonel Lewis and refused to concede that the Lewis gun had any merit.

Senator Wadsworth challenged him by saying that the machine-gun division of the Seventh Regiment of New York broke all records with the Lewis gun on the Mexican border in 1916. Admitting that it was true, General Crozier insisted that in nearly every other border test, the Lewis gun simply did not come up to requirements.[12]

Apparently, the *New York Times* had not heard of any of the "many adverse reports" against the Lewis gun either. An editorial suspiciously dismissed them in one line: "Requirements can be too exacting." The *Times* added, with a last dig at Crozier's choice of the Benét-Mercié, "It was not the Lewis Gun that went wrong when Villa raided Columbus."[13]

General Crozier was now attacked from yet another side. In an accusation that was devastating for a career soldier, another Senate investigating committee was impugning his loyalty to his country in the Tauscher affair.

The whole issue centered around one Captain Hans Tauscher, a German national who was the American representative of German arms makers, including Krupp, and, as such, had many contacts with Crozier and his Ordnance staff. Tauscher had been accused of plotting to blow up the Welland Canal in Canada and had offered to plead guilty in exchange for a fine with no jail sentence. When the plea bargain failed, he was brought before a jury in New York in June 1916 and unexpectedly was acquitted—according to the federal prosecutor—largely on the strength of a testimonial letter provided by General Crozier. Others were contending that the general, at Tauscher's behest, refused to sell the British some 200,000 desperately needed old Krag-Jorgensen rifles in 1914. Crozier replied that he had been legally restrained from selling arms to any belligerent in 1914 by the congressional neutrality act. Another critic alleged that Crozier's personal efforts helped Tauscher obtain a safe conduct pass through belligerent lines back to Germany.

The Tauscher affair did still more damage to General Crozier's badly impaired public image. With Crozier's appointment on December 22, as noted, to the purely advisory post on the Military War Council, the authority of the office of ordnance chief was further undermined when Secretary of War Baker announced a complete organizational overhaul at the Ordnance Bureau. It was basically a copy of the structure of the British Ministry of Munitions, which the British had adopted after a similar scandal of unpreparedness racked that nation in 1914. As a key provision of the new overhaul, the ordnance chief was now required to have an administrative and advisory staff of competent businessmen. These would be the first civilians in authority inside the Ordnance Bureau since the Civil War. The military citadel had been breached. Still technically chief of ordnance, General Crozier had to surrender his responsibilities and authority to General Charles B. Wheeler, acting chief of ordnance. Meanwhile, Crozier's renomination as chief of ordnance was still awaiting Senate confirmation.

The final blow to the general's career came when Representative McCormick returned from France and stated publicly that Pershing's officers were calling for the removal of both General Sharpe, quartermaster general, and General Crozier. "Superseded" was the word he used. McCormick quoted Pershing's officers as saying, "If

Sharpe and Crozier do not go, we do not know what may happen."[14] The seventeen-year Crozier regime was nearly over.

The last shreds of power were taken from him the following year, on July 14, 1918, when President Wilson assigned him to command of the Northeastern Department, a line position and a sinecure. As he left, he could claim that under his regime the United States had developed the three finest small arms weapons in the world: the Springfield '03 rifle, the Browning automatic rifle (BAR), and the Browning heavy machine gun, all coordinated to fire the American spitzer bullet M'06. But, his detractors could point out, with the army already in Europe— already in the trenches—none of the weapons was yet in volume production.

Yet there was one claim the general didn't dare make public. Among all the papers, files, and impedimenta that he took with him, General Crozier also took a dark secret that would have brought howls of dismay from the Senate Military Affairs Committee. The two new Browning machine guns were not all that new. The heavy machine gun was basically the same weapon that John Browning had first offered to General Crozier in 1901 and that General Crozier had summarily rejected. The plan for this gun had languished in Crozier's files for seventeen years while Browning, the greatest military gun maker of them all, was off making guns for the sporting market. The Browning water-cooled heavy machine gun had been patented in the U.S. in 1910.

The plans for the 1901 Browning machine gun were still tucked into General Crozier's files when he set up his 1913 Machine Gun Board that selected the far inferior Benét-Mercié. They were in his files in 1916 when he appointed another one of his Machine Gun Boards that again resulted in the choice of the Benét-Mercié. And they were still in his files in May 1917 when Browning himself appeared before the Baker Machine Gun Board to present the 1901 and 1910 weapons in model form.

The lighter "walking fire" Browning automatic rifle, an outgrowth of the same mechanism, was developed in 1914, at the outbreak of the war, when Browning, sensing the United States would soon need a lightweight machine gun, prepared it to be ready for the Ordnance call for new weapons—a call that came belatedly in 1917, only after Secretary Baker took the program over from the dilatory Crozier.

The two machine guns could have been in the U.S. and Allied arsenals before the beginning of the Great War.

On September 13, 1918, German troops in their trenches heard a frightening new sound as the American Seventy-ninth Division cut loose with its new BARs, the first time they were used in battle. Strangely, General Pershing almost immediately pulled them out of the troops' hands, offering as an implausible reason his fear that the Germans would get them and copy them. So the machine gun that the army could have had in 1901 arrived in France in 1918, seventeen years later, just a few months before the war ended and were immediately secreted away from the troops.

The Lewis gun suffered its final indignity from American Ordnance in France. The French had created a machine gun called the Chauchat—which Americans called the Sho-Sho. According to one commentator, the Chauchat "was probably one of the crudest, most unreliable and cheaply made guns ever to come into service."[15] Unfortunately, desperate for any kind of machine gun, the U.S. Army signed an order with the French manufacturer of the Chauchat to produce over thirty-seven thousand of them. The problem was the guns were inspected indifferently at the French factory, and the U.S. Army by contract had to accept them "as is." They turned out to be so poorly made American troops threw them away as quickly as they were issued.

American marine divisions arrived on the Western Front carrying Lewis guns that the U.S. Navy had purchased. When these marine units were placed under the control of the American army, Army Ordnance rounded up all their Lewis guns and sent the marines into combat with the infamous Chauchat machine gun.

In November 1918, the Germans made their fourth—and last—gamble of the war and lost. Their reserves of men and matériel had run out; confronting them were vast infusions of American matériel and five million fresh American troops under arms, two million in France alone, and more coming to relieve the British and French in the trenches. The Germans were finished. In early November, as the German army began to retreat, the German high command sued for peace. At the eleventh hour of the eleventh day of the eleventh month, 1918, the last shot was fired and the horror ended.

While Springfield Armory made 265,000 Springfield '03 rifles, and Rock Island Armory (established in Illinois in 1863 to replace the Harpers Ferry Armory) made forty-seven thousand, over two million M1917s (American Enfields) were made in Eddystone. The American infantry had gone to war preponderantly armed with a British rifle.

General Crozier remained hostile toward Colonel Lewis to the end. When the colonel sent the U.S. Treasury a total of $1 million —his entire share in the royalties of Lewis guns sold to the U.S. Army—Crozier suggested that the money be rejected because it looked like a bribe. Yet when John Browning gave to the Treasury all but $750,000 of his $12 million in federal royalties, the general failed to make the same judgment.

World War I can justly be called the war of the machine gun, because, of the 65 million combatants, the machine gun was the dominant weapon on the battlefields where were killed over 8.5 million men, including 1.7 million Germans, 1.3 million Frenchmen, 1.7 million Russians, well over 1 million Austrians and Hungarians, 650,000 Italians, 335,000 Romanians, over 900,000 from the British Empire, and 126,000 Americans. More than 20 million men were wounded, many of them maimed or crippled for life. Three-quarters of all Russian and French troops were casualties. Nine out of every ten Austrians and Hungarians were killed or wounded. Total casualties: over 37 million.[16]

Yet, even with these facts before him, General Crozier, ever more baffled by the nation's concern with machine guns, failed to see the devastation that weapon had wrought. He could write in 1921 with apparently unintended irony, "The most important weapon with which nations go to war is the infantryman's rifle."[17]

Britain's General Haig, after four years of directly observing the carnage in the trenches, seemed equally blind to what had happened. "Aeroplanes and tanks are only accessories to the man and the horse, and I feel sure that as time goes on you will find just as much use for the horse as you ever have done in the past."[18]

Nothing could delineate more the great change in operating philosophy that had taken place in the Ordnance Bureau than these two trademark sentences: General Crozier had said repeatedly, "The technician knows best what combat troops require." Major General Clarence Williams, the new ordnance chief, said simply, "If the fighting men want elephants, we get them elephants."

PART V

CHAPTER 27

THE ARMY CONFRONTS
THE TANK
AND THE AIRPLANE

O n June 28, 1919, on the fifth anniversary of the assassination of Archduke Franz Ferdinand in Sarajevo, in the Hall of Mirrors, at Versailles, France, the German delegation came to sign the peace treaty ending the Great War with terms dictated by an angrily victorious England and France. France's leader, Georges Clemenceau, was unhesitating in his bitter condemnation of Germany. He blamed that nation of having committed "the greatest crime against humanity and the freedom of the peoples that any nation calling itself civilized has ever consciously committed."[1]

He charged Germany with starting the war, raping Belgium, introducing poison gas, deliberately bombing and shelling civilians, indulging in submarine warfare, enslaving thousands and removing them to Germany for forced labor, and subjecting prisoners of war to barbarities. He insisted that the German war be treated as a crime against humanity, calling for the strongest punishments. In the end, the Allies, with armies massed to overrun a resisting Germany, imposed on the infuriated Germans a war-reparations program so punishing it could soon bring on another war.[2]

Few Europeans had any illusions about the permanence of the peace treaty. René Gimpel, one of Paris's leading art dealers, wrote in his diary on January 18, 1919: "Today the peace conference, out of which the next war will come, opened at the Ministry of Foreign Affairs."[3]

In the 1920s, inflation in Germany went raging through the land and the economy nearly collapsed. The German people listened to the voice of Adolf Hitler while the German military, vowing revenge, as predicted, quietly girded for another war. Unaware how intertwined were all the national economies of Europe, the Allies were paying the price for the German collapse with their own severe economic woes. Although, as John A. Garraty points out, "Wilson had achieved a remarkably moderate peace, one full of hope for the future,"[4] World War I had settled nothing and had proved nothing. While the victors had learned nothing, the loser had learned a great deal—an ominous lesson.

It is often observed that the victors in any war continue to rely on the weapons that won the war for them. The vanquished abandon the weapons that lost the war for them and develop new ones. Hence, all through the twenties and thirties, while France foolishly slept behind its ultimate trench, the steel-and-concrete Maginot Line, and while England, deluding itself with what it believed was the ultimate moat, the English Channel, refused to spend an extra penny on military arms, German military men studied World War I. They extracted the lessons therefrom and quietly developed or improved the weapons they would need to win the next war— including the ferocious Tiger battle tank, the screaming Stuka dive-bomber, the brilliantly designed Messerschmitt fighter plane, and pulverizing 88-mm artillery. Most important, vowing never to be trapped in trenches again, Germany developed military tactics of such explosive speed that it was called blitzkrieg—lightning war. Germany also developed a new and devastating assault rifle—which would ultimately become the fully automatic Sturmgewehr MKb42, and which was capable of firing up to four hundred rounds a minute.

While Germany rearmed, the U.S. Army returned home to a peacetime war of its own—between those who wanted change and those who were determined to block it. Sitting invisibly on the table of every War Department committee meeting were three pieces of war equipment—the tank, the airplane, and the Springfield '03 rifle.

Resisting change were those who would lose most by it: the infantry, who didn't want the great tactical changes tanks would bring and who saw no need to drop the great battle-proved '03 rifle; and the cavalry, whose very existence was at stake. For them, change meant extinction. Since this camp involved most of the top-ranking officers in the army, it was able to control most of the events inside the War Department during the twenties and thirties.

Proponents of change saw that war was forever altered. To prepare for it, they wanted to design a new semiautomatic rifle, to develop tank and mechanized warfare unencumbered by outmoded infantry and cavalry strictures and traditions, and to create a separate airarm out from under the control of the ground-bound army. But these advocates of new technology, with a few exceptions, were mostly younger men—low-ranking and powerless.

Actually, the issue was far more complex and revolutionary than a single rifle, airplane, or tank. Army men have often been poor students of their own military history. In the 1920s, they should have been holding a complete and long-running postmortem, to review the war and its lessons. They didn't, and by resisting such studies, they were resisting not just new weapons but new thinking—new technologies, new strategies, new tactics.

The issue of developing an American tank is a perfect example of what was happening in the postwar U.S. Army. All through the twenties and thirties, the cavalry didn't want anything to do with a mechanized cavalry idea—for mobility, they wanted horses and only horses. In the 1930s, seventy years after General Henry J. Hunt galloped his mobile artillery units onto Civil War battlefields and forever blew the cavalry away, less than ten years after unused and unusable British and American cavalry units during the Great War had demonstrated to everyone but cavalrymen that the horse soldier was an anachronism, the U.S. Army still had ranking officers who persisted in believing that horses belonged in combat.

Into this muddled military mentality came a man with a brilliant idea. J. Walter Christie.[5]

On December 12, 1922, on the New Jersey side of the Hudson River, Christie, one of the great automotive designers and engineers of the time, invited General S. D. Rochenbach, an American tank leader from World War I, and his party to a cinder track that looked across to the wintry New York City skyline for a special presentation. There on the track stood a strange-looking vehicle, some kind of army tank, to be sure. At Christie's signal, the driver started the engine and climbed into the tank. The vehicle turned, left the track, and promptly astonished the military observers as it climbed one hundred feet up a steep bank. If Christie had stopped there, that feat alone would have made a lasting impression on General Rochenbach. But as Rochenbach watched, the tank now climbed down the other side of the embankment, clambered over a six-foot stone wall, and plunged into the Hudson River.

Rochenbach fully expected the Christie tank to sink, but as he watched, the world's first fully amphibious tank drew away from the shore and crossed the choppy tidal river to Manhattan. There it turned north against a tremendous tide, cruised for about a mile, then climbed a twenty-foot railroad revetment and rode on the railroad tracks to 205th Street in Manhattan.

General Rochenbach later remarked, "It was the most remarkable performance that I have ever seen or heard of."[6]

That was 1922. During the next few years, Christie further developed and tried to sell his tank design to a resisting Ordnance Department. Yet only one man in the military seemed to completely understand the vast implications of the tank—General Adna Romanza Chaffee. Chaffee saw, as German innovators like Guderian were also seeing, that the tank had changed everything in warfare, that in the future, war strategies, battle tactics, and overall military thinking had to be built around it. The tank was not an infantry weapon, Chaffee asserted, not a mechanized cavalry weapon—it was a totally new and separate instrument of war, and brought with it totally new concepts for warfare.[7] Chaffee's published studies were so seminal, German tank men were reading them with close attention.

In 1927, General Chaffee went to Rochester, New York, to see a new model tank sponsored by the Ordnance Department. Designed by James Cunningham and Sons on plans supplied by the

Ordnance Department at the behest of Chief of Infantry Allen, this tank weighed seven tons and could reach a maximum speed of eighteen miles an hour.

With the Cunningham tank fresh in his mind, General Chaffee left Rochester to attend another tank demonstration at Meade, New York, that featured the latest experimental tank built by J. Walter Christie, who, at age sixty-eight, was still one of America's most prolific inventors. As General Chaffee watched, Christie's latest development, a ten-ton battle tank mounted on tracks, raced past him at forty-two and a half miles an hour. Another model, mounted on wheels, roared by him at seventy miles an hour. Its performance up steep embankments, through mire and mud, through thickets and other obstacles, was so spectacular it completely outperformed the Cunningham tank. Chief of Ordnance Major General Samuel Hof dismissed the Christie, contending that it was structurally unsound and good only for flash demonstrations. But it was obvious to all observers that if the two tanks had to go to war against each other, the Christie would quickly blow the Ordnance tank off the battlefield. Although Ordnance continued to favor its own tank design, the Christie became the tank that wouldn't go away.

The Ordnance Department issued a new regulation that no tank could weigh more than seven and a half tons, the maximum carrying capacity of the army's even then obsolete bridging equipment.

People like General Chaffee tried to point out that tanks were going to play a major role in any future war and that these tanks were going to be behemoths, heavily armored and bristling with powerful weapons. Obviously, due to the armor they would have carry to resist modern artillery, they were going to have to weigh much more than seven tons. Chaffee called on Ordnance to junk the obsolete bridging equipment and fabricate designs that would be able to carry the weight of the new tanks. But General Hof and his Ordnance team ignored Chaffee's protests. The weight-limiting rule stood and was soon involved in the first bureaucratic tank war.

The new chief of infantry, General Stephen O. Fuqua, was so impressed with the Christie, he enraged the Ordnance Department in 1928, when he took Congress's infantry appropriation for tank development, which Ordnance Chief Hof thought would be spent on the Ordnance-sponsored Cunningham tank, and instead ordered six Christie tanks. General Hof went to Army Chief of Staff Summerall and protested that the Christie tank, when finished, would weigh more than the mandated seven-and-a-half-ton limit of a light tank. In fact, at fifteen tons, it would weigh double the limit. The Christie would be classified as a heavy tank. Since Army Chief Summerall was himself interested only in a light tank that could be supported by existing military bridging equipment, Hof won his support against the Christie.

Hof didn't kill the Christie or countermand Fuqua's order. He simply cut the order from six to one, for $62,000, and then returned the balance of Congress's quarter-million-dollar tank appropriation to the U.S. Treasury.

The *Chicago Tribune* exploded. "Another Ordnance Fiasco," bellowed its headline. One Christie tank was not enough to prove or disprove anything. The *Tribune* called for the shutdown of the entire Ordnance Department, to permit each arm to buy its own weapons.

A congressional committee summoned military leaders to a hearing, some for and some against the Christie tank. The committee rejected the Ordnance Department's Cunningham tank, and ignoring the Ordnance-mandated weight limitation, decided the Christie should be given a full airing. It reappropriated its quarter of a million and specified that the funds be spent on just Christie tanks, no Cunninghams.

But the decision failed to address an even more deeply rooted tank dispute among military men. At issue was the question of who would design and build the tanks—Ordnance or some other branch—who, in effect, would control the tank—the infantry or the cavalry? It was a crucial question affecting the future shape of the U.S. Army: Would the tank be an infantry weapon under the control of the foot soldier or a tin horse under the control of the cavalry?

The quarreling among military leadership, still clinging to traditional pretank thinking and doubtful of these new battlefield concepts in which the tank would play a decisive role, eventually caused an impasse. Disgusted with the quarreling, J. Walter Christie followed the well-established tradition of previous American inventors and went to Europe.

He found an England that was highly receptive to new tanks. Under the influence of two brilliant military thinkers and writers—Fuller and Liddell Hart—the British had become harshly critical of the tunnel vision tactics of its Great War generals under whose leadership hundreds of thousands of young Englishmen were slaughtered trying to break through impregnable defensive positions. Like Chaffee in America, Fuller and Liddell Hart were teaching mobile warfare—battle tanks plus motorized reconnaissance, plus motorized infantry, plus motorized supply, all controlled by radio. Wars would once more be mobile and offensive, with a technology that increased the speed and terror of destruction.

Even though their burgeoning program had died when Parliament, ignoring the diligent German rearmament program and focusing on the looming British recession, cut the British military budget, the British marveled at the Christie and snapped up the rights to make it—which formed the basis of their World War II tanks.

The Germans were even farther along than the British. With their policy of accepting good ideas no matter their source, they amalgamated the ideas of Britain's Fuller and Liddell Hart and America's General Chaffee and quickly added the American Christie tank. With these components combined with their own studies, the Germans eclectically designed a terrifying Tiger tank.

The Russians also recognized the virtues of the Christie and with just two models developed their outstanding heavy tank T-34, which helped save Russia from the German onslaught during World War II.

Meanwhile, the American army, having turned its attention away from the Christie, continued to struggle with the seven-and-a-half-ton weight restriction and consequently could produce only light tanks like the "General Stuart" tank, better known as "Honey," which was so light in weight, so lightly armed, and so thinly armored, it could not be used seriously in battle when World War II came.

The United States didn't develop a medium tank until 1939, and never did have a heavy tank in World War II fit to face the American-inspired German and Russian tanks, which became more indispensable as the war wore on. Even General MacArthur, as chief of staff in the early thirties, seems to have failed to understand what was so clear to the Germans, the Russians, and the English. He resolved the bitter interarm quarreling by issuing an order that rejected Chaffee's separate armored force recommendation and instead directed each arm to separately explore its own views of mechanization. As a result, the cavalry and the infantry, by going in different directions, dissipated their efforts.

The battle tank wasn't the only new weapon confounding the American army. Its efforts to digest the airplane recalled its struggles with the Civil War observation balloon. In fact, the resistance to the battle tank was mild compared with the furious resistance the military mounted against the "airship." That quarrel finally focused on one highly outspoken man, a visionary who took on the entire military establishment—including the U.S. Navy—in a fight to the finish: Billy Mitchell.

William Mitchell was compounded of all the elements of the all-American hero, and he entered the life of an adventurer while still a teenager. The son of Senator John Lendrum Mitchell of Wisconsin, in 1898, he watched from the Senate gallery as his father voted with great reluctance to go to war against Spain. Young Mitchell, barely eighteen, enlisted. He saw service with the Army Signal Corps in Cuba and later in the Philippines, where he distinguished himself laying telegraph communication lines under fire. His further adventures while laying telegraph lines in Alaska and his spectacular role in the relief of earthquake-torn San Francisco could have filled pages of the *Boys Adventure Magazine*. Possessed by the dream of flying, he taught himself aeronautical science and engineering, and after passing the qualifying test, he was brought back to Washington as the youngest captain in the army.

In 1908, he was on hand at Fort Meyer, Virginia, when Orville

Wright delivered to the Signal Corps its first aircraft, and from that moment, Mitchell was an unstoppable exponent of airpower. During World War I, as a lieutenant colonel, he went to Europe to be General Pershing's air adviser, and was confounded to discover that the American air force consisted of one French Newport airplane and one pilot—himself. By now, his grasp of airpower bordered on the visionary. To break up the trench stalemate, he proposed that twelve hundred American bombers air-drop the entire U.S. First Division, armed with twenty-four hundred machine guns, at the German rear. Although the idea was far ahead of its time, General Pershing approved, but before the air fleet could be assembled, the major rollback of German defenses by Allied ground forces effectively canceled the air maneuver before the twelve hundred planes could be acquired. Other Allied aviation commanders came to regard him as a gifted air strategist. He was put in command of Allied air services and personally conceived the largest concentration of Allied airpower of the war during the Battle of the Argonne—when some fifteen hundred British and French bombers flew concerted bombing runs. He also conceived the first air blitzing strategy, attacking from three sides the entrenched German salient at Saint-Mihiel that jutted into American positions. He returned home a heavily decorated brigadier general and a dedicated exponent of military airpower and walked into his first major controversy. Billy Mitchell was convinced that there had been a deliberate sabotaging of U.S. airpower in Europe by an army coterie in the War Department in Washington. His charges were so convincing, Congress ordered an investigation that largely confirmed his accusations. Of a billion and a half dollars in appropriations, intended to buy large fleets of fighter planes and bombers, only 109 American aircraft—all De Havillands, the infamous "Flying Coffin"—reached Europe.

Thereafter, his view of his own military comrades darkened. In peacetime, he developed a new campaign. Having now a deep distrust for the army, he asserted that the military air service had to be freed from the army, and set up as a separate arm. This idea quickly encountered determined army opposition.

He also asserted that, because of the airplane, naval power had to be completely restructured and refitted and even boldly announced that airpower could sink a battleship—which drew an angry reaction from navy men around the world, who rose to condemn his assertion, often in the most intemperate language. One of his avowed naval opponents, Assistant Secretary of the Navy Franklin Roosevelt, went before the Senate Subcommittee on Military Affairs to emphatically denounce the idea. Navy Secretary Josephus Daniels himself offered to stand bareheaded at the helm of any U.S. battleship Mitchell cared to attack. Naval experts hastened to assure the world that airplanes could not sink battleships. The idea was so preposterous that navy men refused to even consider a test of plane versus ship.

A joint resolution of Congress was required to prod the navy into a showdown. Believing its future as a fighting arm was at stake, the navy chose what it considered two targets—both prizes of war: the German battleship *Ostfriesland*—which was deemed capable of withstanding the largest aerial bomb—and the German cruiser *Frankfurt*. The navy sought to cinch its case by demanding a limit on both the size of the aerial bombs and the number that Mitchell would be allowed to drop.

Mitchell, with intensive preparations, designed new bombs that revolutionized ordnance—one weighing a ton and filled with a thousand pounds of TNT—and another weighing two tons. For practice, he sent a flight of bombers to attack the old battleships *Texas* and *Indiana*, which the navy had already tried—unsuccessfully— to sink with aerial bombs.

On July 18, 1921, off the Virginia capes, the entire U.S. Atlantic fleet was assembled within sight of the German prize of war—the cruiser *Frankfurt*—waiting for the Mitchell attack. The navy was convinced it had an invincible position—an unsinkable ship facing aerial bombs that, it had insisted over Mitchell's protests, be limited to six hundred pounds each. Under Billy Mitchell's direction, six army bombers took off from Langley Army Airfield and flew southeast to the target.

The waiting navy spectators soon sighted the planes coming over the horizon and watched as one at a time the bombers attacked the

Frankfurt. The bombs shook the ship, tore gaping holes in it, and, within thirty-five minutes, had put the *Frankfurt* at the bottom of the sea. All the navies of the world had suffered a staggering setback.

Navy men responded by insisting that there had been a hidden flaw in the *Frankfurt* and demanded—and won—a rematch. This time, the U.S. Navy towed into position the German *Ostfriesland*, a full-size battleship weighing twenty-seven thousand tons and deemed by navy men to be unsinkable. The navy anchored the *Ostfriesland* sixty miles off Cape Charles Lightship.

On July 21, 1921, two days after the sinking of the *Frankfurt*, with the full U.S. Atlantic fleet again in attendance, plus hundreds of top-ranking guests, numerous foreign military observers and naval engineers, the navy expected its views to be fully vindicated. The *Ostfriesland* had been built by German naval engineers specifically to shrug off the worst that the British navy could throw at it—and that was far worse than any aerial bombardment six bombers could inflict.

Once again, the six Mitchell bombers appeared, flying at little more than two thousand feet. Each bomber turned, made a direct run for the *Ostfriesland*, and released a single bomb—six of the heaviest permitted by the navy. This attack took less time—within twenty-two minutes, the unsinkable was sunk and sent to the bottom. Having dramatically announced the advent of airborne warfare, Billy Mitchell returned to Washington, expecting apologies and applause.

Instead, his resounding conquest of the navy led to silence, sullen anger, or outright defiance. Neither the navy nor the army wanted to acknowledge his victory. His attempts to publicize military airpower and the changing nature of warfare fell on deaf ears. Mitchell became an embarrassment. His strident voice, his trenchant pen, his unbending manner infuriated people who disagreed with him—and many of these were his own military comrades. He became one of the most hated men in uniform. He refused to be silenced. To put him out of sight, the army broke him in the ranks, reducing his brigadier generalship to the permanent rank of colonel, and shipped him out to an inferior post in San Antonio, Texas.

When the dirigible *Shenandoah* was struck by lightning in a storm over the Ohio River and broke up, Mitchell, in a great rage, spoke out. He accused both the War and Navy departments of "incompetency, criminal negligence and almost treasonable administration of the national defense."[8] Under direct orders from President Coolidge, he was court-martialed for defiance of his superiors. The prosecution described him as a "self advertiser and wildly imaginative, hobby-riding egomaniac." Mitchell counterclaimed that the indictment ignored the main issue. He accused both the army and the navy of heedlessly keeping airpower in an auxiliary posture, under the control of men who neither understood nor favored it. This, he asserted, "absolutely compromises our whole system of national defense."[9]

Mitchell was found guilty of making statements to the prejudice of good order and military discipline. One of the officers on the panel who voted not guilty was Major General Douglas MacArthur. Rather than accept five years' suspension from military service, Billy Mitchell resigned his commission. Freed from military rule, he became more of a thorn in the side of the military than ever. He wrote voluminously on the subject of airpower and a separate air arm. Books, articles, and pamphlets came steadily from his typewriter. He became a tireless platform speaker, criticizing the army without cease. His predictions gained worldwide attention. "Some fine Sunday morning," he warned on a number of occasions, "the Japanese will attack the United States."[10]

While no one in the U.S. military seems to have wanted to listen to him, his thinking and his actions had drawn the closest attention from the Germans and the Japanese.

In 1936, Billy Mitchell died. Having gone on a visionary campaign that inspired some, convinced some, and infuriated many, having angrily talked himself into a court-martial, and having spent his last years driven by his mission, he departed in his fifty-seventh year, not sure he had accomplished anything. His prophetic words would be remembered five years later with the Sunday-morning bombing of Pearl Harbor.

CHAPTER 28

GARAND VERSUS PEDERSEN: SEEKING A SEMIAUTOMATIC

A mid the confused and often hostile military thinking that greeted the tank and the airplane, the Ordnance Department set out on its own tortuous path in search of a new military rifle.

As the new major power of the world, the United States should appropriately develop the world's finest rifle—one that reflected the nation's great industrial leadership. To that end, the Springfield Armory assigned two of the leading rifle designers of this century to the task. For many in the army, this two-man arms race promised to be the most memorable ordnance event of the times.

On July 15, 1919, General C. C. Williams, the postwar chief of ordnance, who had promised elephants for any military men who wanted them, set out to undo some of the great damage done by General Crozier and his coterie on the Ordnance Board, who over the years had alienated the infantry, the cavalry, and the artillery by steadfastly refusing to give them enough influence in the selection and development of new weapons.

General Williams had superseded the old Crozier board with a new one named the Ordnance Committee, open to representatives of the combat commands and technical services, as well as liaison personnel from other interested branches, and scheduled to meet every Thursday. All were encouraged to make recommendations to the Ordnance Technical Staff for developing new weapons.

Since the representatives were limited to making recommendations only, and since research and development were still firmly under the control of the armory Production Department, Williams's new body was little advanced over Crozier's except in one important particular—C. C. Williams himself was much more open than the imperious Crozier had been. One of the first pieces of business before the committee was the development of a new rifle.

The problem with the Springfield M1903—and there were many who did not agree that there was a problem—was the familiar and highly esteemed Mauser bolt action. To eject the empty shell and insert a new one into the firing chamber, the bolt had to be manually operated with each firing. During rapid fire, operating the bolt was tiring, distracting, and time wasting. The army wanted to replace it with a self-loading mechanism that would fire, eject, reload, and cock with just the pull of the trigger, semiautomatically.

On that summer's day of July 15, 1919, in the first meeting of the new Ordnance Committee, Lieutenant Colonel Harry J. Maloney of the Ordnance Technical Staff offered a set of specifications for the proposed new rifle. As they listened to the proposals, no one on the committee had any illusions about the difficulties that lay ahead. The Ordnance Department had already spent sixteen years—from 1901 to 1917, when the Great War intruded—searching for an effective semiautomatic, and had tested and rejected more than twenty designs.

The U.S. Army, Colonel Maloney told the meeting, wanted a simple, rugged weapon that would be easy to manufacture —preferably on the existing '03 machinery. It should fire the standard Springfield .30-'06 cartridge. Maximum weight, he said, was 4.3 kilograms—9.5 pounds. As he read the rest of the list, it became obvious to all that Colonel Maloney was describing a semiautomatic version of the now-hallowed Springfield M1903.[1]

Four months later, on November 4, 1919, John Cantius Garand, a thirty-one-year-old small arms weapons designer, joined the research and development staff at the National Armory, Springfield, Massachusetts. Garand found a tradition-bound, production-dominated bureaucracy that for more than thirty years, through its various committees, would often frustrate his best design efforts. To the production men who ran the armory, a resident arms designer was merely a backroom employee with no power, no status, and no hope of advancement. Most capable designers would have preferred positions in private arms-making companies, where a designer's stature was much loftier and where chances for financial rewards were much greater. But before his career ended, Garand held fifty-four patents, all designed within the precincts of the armory.[2]

Considered now one of the great mechanical geniuses of American arms design, Garand was born on a small farm in St. Rémi, Quebec, Canada, on January 1, 1888.[3] When he was ten, his parents moved to Connecticut, and there the die may have been cast when, for some years, he helped his brother operate a shooting gallery. From there, he went to work as a floor sweeper and bobbin boy in a New England textile mill, became a tool and gauge maker for Browne and Sharpe, then foreman and machine designer for Federal Screw Corporation in Rhode Island.

While working in New York City during the Great War as a design engineer for a precision instruments factory, he became aware of the public debate in the newspapers over America's lack of a reliable machine gun. He couldn't understand what all the fuss was about. He was guided by a simple platitude: good guns came from good design; bad guns came from bad design. Anyone with a sound grounding in machine design could solve the machine-gun problem, he felt, and decided to try his hand at it.

In March 1917, just as Newton Baker's Machine Gun Board was calling for new machine-gun ideas, Garand found a backer named John W. Kewish, a financial broker and something of a gun designer himself. Impressed with Garand and his idea, and with the tremendous opportunity the government was offering, Kewish put up the money for development, plus an added salary for Garand of $50 a week.

By June 1918, Garand had a firing model of his gun. He showed it to Hudson Maxim, a somewhat eccentric inventor and brother of Hiram Maxim, who had invented the Maxim machine gun. Hudson Maxim recommended that the gun be presented to the Naval Consulting Board, which was receptive to new weapon ideas. The board sent Garand and Kewish to the army.

Armory personnel felt Garand's machine gun, while an excellent weapon, did not offer a significant improvement over existing weapons. They were, however, impressed with the most unusual primer-actuated mechanism that operated the gun and with the designer himself. Garand had a very rare combination of talents. He could produce remarkably fresh weapon concepts and then, because of his unrivaled knowledge of machine tooling, he could design the machines to make them.

At first glance, with his thick head of hair and his friendly eyes, John Garand didn't look like the familiar American gun genius. He didn't have the flamboyance of a Hiram Maxim, or the mirthful, dramatic style of a John Browning. One was struck, rather, with his thoughtful, quiet manner. Fortunately, he was also endowed with the great patience needed to endure the very trying political world of the armory. Behind his solemnity and strength of purpose, few saw the uncomplex man who enjoyed playing checkers.

As one of his first assignments, the armory handed him a design order for a new self-loading rifle, based on the primer-actuation concept of his machine gun.

Many Ordnance men had a wonderful war story or two to tell about the Springfield '03. Although more American troops had carried the American Enfield, the Springfield's great wartime performance record was surrounded by anecdote and legend. Defenders could point out that its bolt action was still state-of-the-art, and since no other major nation seemed to be seeking a semiautomatic rifle, why change? Besides, a semiautomatic would waste ammunition.

These defenders were equally articulate about the .30-caliber cartridge, especially with its new and improved cartridge construction and new gunpowder. The army's traditional gravel-belly marksman had won numerous championship rifle matches with the combination of the '03 rifle and the .30-'06 cartridge. Many Ordnance men declared it to be one of the greatest long-range shooting combinations in ballistics history. They were certain a caliber change was not needed.

Opponents disagreed. On April 27, 1923, during the Thursday meeting of the Ordnance Committee, representatives of the "using services"—the infantry and cavalry, primarily—announced that they felt the caliber of the official army cartridge was one of the key problems blocking the development of a new semiautomatic. The .30 caliber, they said, developed excessive heat and weighed too much. Also, Ordnance had difficulty supplying it on the battlefield. The new rifle, they suggested, needed something less than .30 caliber.

They proposed that the committee invite the noted designer J. D. Pedersen, to hear his startling new recommendations for a less-than-.30-caliber cartridge, including his new studies on wound ballistics—more specifically, the lethality index.

No Ordnance man would casually refuse this request. No less an authority than John Browning considered Pedersen to be the greatest living arms designer, perhaps the greatest in history, with his best work still ahead of him. Like John Garand, Pedersen had the very rare ability not only to design new weapons brilliantly but also to create the tooling necessary to produce them.

This dual capability helps explain his impressive design record. On his list of credits were the Remington Model 1910 repeating shotgun, the Remington slide-action .22 repeating rifle Model 12, the Remington slide-action, high-power repeating rifle Model 14, and the Remington automatic pistol Model 51. But most of all, among Ordnance men, the Pedersen device had made him a legend.

This device was an automatic bolt designed specifically to allow a modified Springfield '03 rifle to fire a .38-caliber pistol cartridge semiautomatically from a forty-cartridge clip. The U.S. Army had set out secretly to manufacture a half million of these devices. The plan was to have the entire American army in France instantly, without warning on a day in March 1919, convert their Springfields to semiautomatic rifles, go over the top, and charge the German lines with more lethal firepower than the war had ever seen. The consequences could have been staggering—the combination of tremendous firepower and surprise could have torn at least one gaping hole in the German lines and thereby helped to collapse the whole German defense.[4]

The plan was abandoned when the war ended in November 1918. Sixty-five thousand Pedersen devices had come off the production line, along with sixty-nine million rounds of ammunition—all of which had to be scrapped—plus 101,000 modified Springfield '03 rifles, but the War Department never forgot this brilliant design and the plan it made possible.

Furthermore, J. D. Pedersen had another considerable advantage over every other rifle designer. In addition to his intimidating reputation for rifle design and machine crafting, he was also an expert on infantry tactics. Over the years, he had studied all the literature on the subject and knew far more than the typical army officer. There were few military men who would challenge him on infantry tactics, and far fewer who could win the argument.

When J. D. Pedersen approached the War Department with an idea for a .27-caliber automatic rifle, he reached a number of attentive ears. In a meeting attended by a number of ranking Ordnance officers, he uttered a whole new semiautomatic philosophy that had a profound influence on their thinking. He maintained that .30 caliber was too strong for a new self-loading rifle. The ideal cartridge for the job should be shorter, lighter, with less recoil, and generating less heat. He presented abundant data to back up his contention that .27 caliber was the optimum size.

The smaller cartridge, Pedersen told them, would generate less heat—a noteworthy 60 percent less, which meant less chance of jamming; less recoil—an eye-opening 42 percent less, which meant less punishment for the shooter and more accuracy. The cartridge also had a flatter trajectory, which enabled it to travel faster, with less drop-off and more shooting accuracy. In addition, a lighter bullet and a lighter cartridge case meant enormous potential savings of expensive metal during a major war. Finally, the lighter bullet meant the soldier could carry more ammunition and stay on the firing line longer without being resupplied.

Pedersen capped all this with a truly arresting offer. He would build, right in the armory, a .27-caliber, self-loading rifle that met all the Ordnance Department guide sheet specifications, and he would make it without either the gas-operating system or the recoil system, and so avoid the drawbacks of both.[5]

Pedersen was one of a very small number of world-class weapons designers who could get serious attention with such an astonishing offer. What made his offer especially irresistible was the history of wound ballistics.

Nearly a half century before, in Europe, specialists in wound ballistics had made a surprising discovery that small arms experts had been discussing ever since. A smaller bullet often did a great deal more damage—had a greater "lethality index"—than a larger round. Smaller-caliber projectiles tend to be more unstable. When they hit flesh, they are more likely to tumble and behave like a whirligig, creating huge wounds. Under similar conditions, higher-caliber bullets tend to remain more stable and inflict smaller wounds as they pass through the flesh. In short, the .27 caliber can be more lethal than the .30 caliber.

In all, Pedersen's offer contained an irresistible combination of ballistic virtues to an Ordnance man. So the Ordnance Department authorized a quest for a semiautomatic rifle of a caliber near .30 but not less than 7 mm (.276 caliber). Pedersen was given a contract and the entire Springfield Armory to work with—and at the munificent salary of $10,000 a year, with a promised royalty on every weapon if successfully developed and adopted.[6]

Pedersen's concept wasn't without critics. They quickly pointed out that the small caliber didn't make as good a tracer bullet. Furthermore, .27 caliber provided less power than .30 caliber for armor-piercing bullets. Nor could a lighter-weight cartridge be as accurate or match the long-distance range of a .30-caliber bullet. It certainly wouldn't be suitable for long-range machine-gun fire.

So, they went on, that meant there would be two calibers in use, one for the rifle and another for the machine gun, a very undesirable situation in combat that would overburden supply lines. Critics were also concerned with costs: changing over to a smaller caliber would be expensive. But, they urged, most of all, why change? Why abandon the '03 rifle, why change the .30-'06 cartridge? Why drop the ideal arrangement? Finally, they argued, the smaller caliber could affect morale. The bigger the bang, the greater the troops' confidence. This all sounded like so much carping to Pedersen's spokesmen, but it was a warning of conflicts to come.

Like John Garand, John Pedersen represented a thumping bargain to the Ordnance Department. With his great tooling knowledge, experience, and skill, instead of making model after model and change after change to test his concepts, "he knew what would work and what would not, without having to make up a gun [model] to find out."[7] Typically, it could take 100,000 man-hours for a production department to tool up a rifle. But Pedersen needed only a fraction of that enormously expensive time, since as he designed the piece, he also made the actual tools and jigs and fixtures and gauges for each production step. When he presented a weapon, the production equipment was presented with it. John Garand was perhaps the only other man who could do this.

J. D. Pedersen was installed in the new Experimental Department Building in Springfield with appropriate staff. During the same period, 1923–1924, not far away in the same armory complex, John Garand was developing his 1924 .30-caliber semi-automatic rifle.

Anyone who worked in the armory during that time had a front-row seat to one of the most exciting gun design competitions ever. And with the two top rifle men working on the semiautomatic rifle assignment within feet of each other, the armory felt it could not lose: it would end up with the world's finest semiautomatic rifle, be it called Garand or Pedersen. What made the competition eternally interesting was the contrasting personalities of the two men.

John Garand was a quiet, dedicated, intuitive genius who had little interest in material gain or fame—forever a salaried employee who wanted only to follow his creative impulses. In the end, he showed a profound and shrewd understanding of weapons, tooling, and Ordnance Department politics.

John Pedersen was a genius of a different stripe—in fact, a pinstripe. Well dressed, well groomed, dignified, with a trim mustache, accustomed to leading and directing, accustomed to boardrooms and profit-and-loss sheets, he suggested in every gesture the man of breeding and education. Having an extensive background as a production engineer with Winchester—one of the largest arms makers in the country—he could immediately dominate any meeting he attended. Articulate, with charts and documents, he could make his case forcefully and totally. Here was a truly great weapons designer and a great salesman.

The first order of business for John Pedersen was to design a .276 cartridge around which he would build his rifle. He actually designed two types for testing. The results were so impressive, the Ordnance Committee was convinced they were on the right track. The new cartridge was called the Pedersen .27 caliber. The committee now waited for the rifle to fire it.

In the autumn of 1925, within two years of commencement, and right on schedule, J. D. Pedersen produced the first model of his new rifle. The sleek-looking weapon exhibited a finish that was complete right down to the sights. As promised, the new rifle featured a new breech-operating concept that avoided both gas operation and recoil operation. Equally impressive, it weighed only eight pounds, two ounces.

Never has a rifle worked through the armory gauntlet with so few hitches. From the commencement of the on-line firing tests, the rifle performed so well, the Ordnance Committee became convinced it had found the solution to the semiautomatic problem—a truly brilliant and flawless solution. For the first time to anyone's knowledge, the armory was testing a rifle that had been born unblemished.

There were two concerns about the new rifle. To minimize friction, the Pedersen action required cartridges that had been lightly coated with hard wax. Anyone disinclined to like this weapon could use that feature as a club to attack the entire rifle. Also, the rifle had to be loaded by way of a ten-shot clip. Critics pointed out that if a rifleman lost his clips, he lost his rifle. Without clips, the weapon was useless.

Proponents felt these were two minor complaints. It was time to show off the Pedersen to all the top brass right on the firing line—a crucial moment in any rifle's life. On May 10, 1926, at the National Armory in Springfield, the Pedersen .276 semiautomatic rifle debut became such a major event that officers as high as the chief of infantry and chief of cavalry attended, coming up from Washington just for the presentation.

As the visiting brass hefted the notably light weapon, then fired off clip after clip of .27-caliber cartridges, heads began to nod with approval. Feeling the reduced kick and seeing the resulting increase in firing accuracy, they were also impressed by the greater firing speed that came from the elimination of the bolt action. The weapon performed superbly. The armory men felt they had made a sale when infantry and cavalry officers pressed around them to ask the key question: When can we get samples for field tests?

On June 15, 1926, barely a month after the Pedersen rifle presentation at Springfield, the U.S. Army Infantry Board met at Fort Benning, Georgia, to test John Garand's Model 1924 primer-actuated semiautomatic rifle against several other candidates. Unlike the Pedersen, the Garand was a .30-caliber rifle and used the standard .30-'06 army cartridge.

After all the prescribed, grueling tests, the board selected the Garand, pending some design modifications concerning accuracy and trigger pull. The significance of this test was the next stage that evolved from it: the Garand was to be tested against the Pedersen.

Garand must have shaken his head at the strange world of the armory he now lived in. Working alone before joining the armory, he had required only a year and a half to develop his machine gun. Pedersen, working with a staff but behind closed doors, away from any intrusions and interruptions from Army Ordnance men, had taken two years. But Garand, working in the armory as a staff designer and constantly burdened with endless interruptions, intrusions, changes, and layers of conflicting committees, consumed nearly six years in developing his self-loading rifle.

Following the Fort Benning meeting, Garand went back to Springfield to make the required design changes. But disaster had already struck his new rifle. Another series of interlocking Ordnance committees had developed a new military rifle cartridge containing a new type of gunpowder that didn't work in Garand's primer-actuated mechanism.

Furthermore, the new cartridge presented a significant design change: a newly developed crimped primer pocket at the base of the cartridge, where it was struck by the firing pin. While this was a major cartridge improvement, the Garand semiautomatic action was built around the characteristics of old primer pockets, and the firing pin couldn't be modified to fit the new primer pocket. This was another blow to Garand's rifle. Since a rifle was ineluctably wedded to a specific cartridge, when the old cartridge was phased out, so was the Garand 1924 rifle.

The Ordnance people were working at cross-purposes again—while one set of committees was developing a cartridge configuration with a new primer pocket, another set of committees was wasting six years of great talent designing a new rifle that would not be able to use that cartridge. With the permission of the Ordnance Department, Garand decided to abandon his primer-actuated rifle. After all those years of unremitting effort at Springfield, he had ended up with a rifle that was destined for a display case in the Armory Museum. The firing mechanism of the Pedersen was unaffected by the new design.

There was one interesting result from the creation of the Garand M1924. While John Pedersen was convincing many in the Ordnance Department that a semiautomatic rifle had to be made in .27 caliber, Garand had built a successful semiautomatic rifle that fired .30 caliber.

In place of his obsolete primer-actuated M1924, Garand now set out to develop a gas-operated turning-bolt semiautomatic rifle. When it came time to choose a caliber, Garand made a decision that was to affect the future course of the entire Ordnance Department. Garand parted company with Pedersen.

Unlike Pedersen, he believed that a semiautomatic rifle could be made in .30 caliber. In fact, he felt he had already proved it with his M1924. But now he had to build a rifle around the new .30-caliber cartridge. Since the new .30 cartridge was much stronger than the old one that the 1924 had fired, he had a far more difficult challenge. There was a very good chance Garand would fail.

More than just rifle caliber was involved in this Pedersen/Garand contest. After six years in the Ordnance Department, Garand had acquired a canny understanding of armory politics; he sensed that no matter how right Pedersen's .27-caliber arguments were, the top men in the Ordnance Department would never be able to convince Congress to accept the enormous cost of making a new weapon in a new caliber. The army would either get a new semiautomatic rifle in the .30-caliber range, or it would be told by Congress to live with the old Springfield M1903.

For confirmation, he had only to look around the armory. The Congress of the 1920s was savaging the military budget once more. In 1923, the Experimental Department had been chopped from sixteen people to four, not counting John Garand—and the last job on the assignment list of the overburdened four was making a new rifle. So the only experimental rifle money being spent was John Garand's salary. This was not the setting for selling a new rifle, a new caliber, and millions of dollars in new tooling to Congress.

But while John Garand was quietly betting that the .27-caliber concept would not survive, he was far behind the Pedersen design, which had already been completely designed and built and sold to an enthusiastic top brass. Garand seemed to be entering a race that had already been run. And won.

Yet by July 1926, Garand was showing a new gas-operated semi-automatic in .30 caliber. By then, the Ordnance Committee, completely smitten with the .276-caliber Pedersen, ordered but a single model of the new Garand .30 semiautomatic to be made for testing. So while .30 caliber was not dead yet, it was hanging by a thread.

Distant as it was, the Garand dogged the tracks of the Pedersen. On December 5, 1927, the Ordnance Committee examined Garand's new gas-operated rifle. The committee decided that it exhibited a number of interesting characteristics, but it was in the wrong caliber. The group ordered Garand to make his new gas-operated rifle in the Pedersen .276 caliber for full-scale field tests. Then it ordered all .30-caliber rifle studies to be terminated. Although he was still the darkest of dark horses, far back in the field, Garand had moved a few steps closer to Pedersen.

On December 15, with the excellent new .276-caliber Pedersen rifle in hand, the Ordnance Committee reversed itself again and called for ideas from inventors for semiautomatic rifle designs ranging in caliber from .25 up to .30, with .30-'06 preferred. The specifications contained an interesting sentence: "Information concerning the desired caliber is not definite at this time." The Ordnance Committee was exhibiting indecision about caliber, drawing away from its new .30-caliber cartridge toward the old .30-'06 cartridge, hesitating over the Pedersen .276, and even considering .25 caliber, with none of them favored. The indecision suggests strong disagreement behind the scenes.

On April 16, 1928, the Pedersen passed another major hurdle with great success. The Cavalry Board, after a continuing series of comparison tests extending over a period of months, issued a glowing report on the Pedersen rifle. It indicated that in a four-minute nonstop firing session, the manual bolt-action Springfield rifle M1903 had exhausted four riflemen. Conversely, in a four-minute firing session with the Pedersen, they experienced no "appreciable fatigue or other ill effects." Furthermore, while the Springfield rifle barrels became so hot they scorched their wooden stocks, none of the Pedersens overheated.

This report seems to confirm John Pedersen's evaluation of the .30-caliber cartridge as generating too much heat and too much recoil for semiautomatic use. The case for .27 caliber seemed stronger than ever, and by April 30, 1928, the Pedersen seemed to have scored a complete victory because, two weeks after the Cavalry Board report, the Infantry Board, concluding an exhaustive series of tests of its own, declared the clear winner to be the Pedersen .276. The report urged, "This rifle is suitable and should now be adopted for Infantry use as a complete replacement for the service rifle [the Springfield M1903] and the Browning automatic rifle."[8]

The infantry report, like the cavalry report, noted that the Pedersen was much less fatiguing than the Springfield. In effect, both reports came to the same conclusion: that a lighter-caliber semiautomatic is less fatiguing than a heavier-caliber manual bolt-action.

This was an exciting time in the armory. It seemed possible that soon the United States would become the world's first major army to have a semiautomatic rifle. Further, the Pedersen was such a handsomely designed weapon, other ordnance men around the world were bound to regard the United States with new admiration and respect.

In spite of the flawless performance and the enthusiasm of Ordnance men and field troops alike, some on the committee were still hesitant. For them, the question of caliber had not been resolved. More exhaustive tests were required. They wanted to be absolutely sure that John Pedersen's very convincing evidence concerning the superiority of the .276 cartridge over the .30 would hold up in practice. Let's test them on living flesh, they said. Then let's ask the frontline soldier. Let's convene a board drawn from the U.S. Army, Navy, and Marine Corps to study those wound ballistics tests, and to air out the whole question of caliber for semiautomatic weapons.

CHAPTER 29

PIGS, GOATS, AND
MACARTHUR'S DECISION

During most of the summer of 1928, a series of wound ballistics studies, now called the Pig Board tests, were conducted at
the Proving Ground in Aberdeen, Maryland. The army had never
done anything quite like this before. The only wound ballistics tests
it had ever conducted on flesh had involved hanging sides of beef;
none on living flesh of any type.

Grimly determined to get some answers, members of the Pig
Board shipped eighteen living pigs to the Aberdeen Proving
Ground, where three medical officers and a member of the Ordnance Department would witness the effect of gunshot wounds on
the pigs' anesthetized bodies. Intended to be exhaustive and definitive, the tests extended all through June and July. The range of firing
was in increments from three hundred yards up to twelve hundred
yards. The results gave everyone pause.

At three hundred yards, the worst wounds were inflicted by the
lowest-caliber bullet in the test—the .256, followed by the next
lowest, the .276. At six hundred yards, all calibers were about equal
with the .256, still the most damaging by a slight degree. At one
thousand yards, the new .30 caliber created the most severe
wounds. At twelve hundred yards, all calibers can kill or maim.

The tests indicated smaller caliber for shorter distances, higher
caliber for longer distances. The results begged the question: What
does the infantry want in a weapon—short-range killing power or

long? And that raised the larger question: What would be the role of the infantry rifle on the battlefield of the future?

With the results of the Pig Board study in hand, on July 2, 1928, the War Department appointed a board to recommend a specific semiautomatic rifle caliber. Composed of a dozen officers from the U.S. Army, Navy, and Marine Corps, it became known as the Semiautomatic Rifle Board. Going over and over the Pig Board report, it debated—sometimes heatedly—for two months. In September 1928, it issued a report that recommended that "a caliber of .276 inch be adopted as standard for the semiautomatic shoulder rifle to replace the present shoulder rifle caliber .30 M1903."[1]

The board also had some thoughts for those who still defended the .30-caliber system. It asserted that armor-piercing ammunition in a rifle was of "questionable value," thereby setting aside one of the strengths of the .30 caliber. In addition, it noted that the average citizen soldier could be trained to use a semiautomatic rifle in half the time of the hand-operated, bolt-action type, a significant advantage during the hasty assemblage of a conscription army during an impending war. It also dismissed the old complaint against having separate calibers for rifles and machine guns. Even when they are the same caliber, the board noted, the cartridges are supplied separately in battle, anyway. So, in practice, they're treated like two different calibers. The board presented an additional reason for the smaller caliber: lighter weight. A full clip of .27 caliber made the rifle weigh less. In combat, the rifleman can carry much more .27-caliber ammunition—can, in effect, go longer without being resupplied.

As a follow-up to its decision, the board called for immediate tests of the various .276 cartridges with a 125-grain bullet.

The army felt it had two reasonably hard pieces of information. Based on the Pig Board's wound ballistics, the .27-caliber cartridge was the best choice for semiautomatic rifles. This put the board on the side of short-range rifle power. Based on the Semiautomatic Rifle Board's report, the lighter .27 caliber was the best choice, since it enabled the rifleman to carry more ammunition. As it stepped closer to an official .27-caliber cartridge, the committee still had one question left—Pedersen or Garand? On October 1, 1928, the War Department shut the door on .30-caliber concepts once more when it called for inventors to submit ideas for the new semiautomatic rifle—in one caliber only: .276.

Nine months later, in July 1929, the Semiautomatic Rifle Board met again to look at rifles that had been offered as a result of its October invitation. Six rifles had been submitted, including the Pedersen and an unknown, relatively untested new weapon— a .276-caliber, gas-operated Garand.

As the tests proceeded, the Rifle Board began weeding out the weakest weapons until, finally, amid the gunfire and the close scrutiny of the target tally sheets, the board eliminated four of the six entries. Only two rifles passed all tests—the Pedersen, as expected, and the Garand. As the Pedersen proponents exchanged uncomfortable glances, the Garand had suddenly become a serious contender in a two-gun race.

The board ordered that certain minor defects in both models be corrected and that twenty Garand models be made in the .276 caliber. These would then be submitted to the Infantry and Cavalry Boards for full-scale field tests, which would be compared with the completed field tests of the Pedersen.

There was another significant surprise for the Pedersen proponents. Almost as a footnote, the board ordered John Garand to provide twenty test models of his .27-caliber gas-operated rifles chambered to fire .30-caliber cartridges. Behind the scenes, in his spare time and on weekends, John Garand, still convinced that Ordnance would ultimately refuse to adopt .27 caliber as standard, had built his gas-operated rifle around the new, more powerful .30-caliber cartridge, the one that was supposed to be too strong for semiautomatic fire. For some members of the Ordnance Board, this was a disturbing development because it brought back into the confusing equation the question of caliber, which had supposedly been eliminated .

Abruptly, on February 21, 1929, the Ordnance Department was ordered to discontinue making the twenty models of the .30-caliber Garand. Reason: The .276-caliber cartridge had been approved. The caliber issue seemed to have been now settled permanently: .276 was it. The .30 caliber was history.

But, back in Washington, proponents of the .30 caliber were not done fighting. The chief of infantry, a gravel-belly sharpshooter and a determined .30-caliber '03 man, presented a new objection to the .27-caliber cartridge tests. Pigs were not men, he said. Their fatty flesh was not like human flesh. How would humans react to being shot by a .27-caliber bullet? Was there an animal flesh more closely related to human flesh?

Yes, he was told. Goats. Goats have a flesh closer to humans. So the Pig Board now became the Goat Board. At Aberdeen Proving Ground, the 1930 Goat Board gathered to perform tests on anesthetized goats. Riflemen were assembled. Military surgeons and a proof officer arrived. The parameters were established and posted. The results were very similar to those of the Pig Board. Lower calibers made nastier wounds at short ranges; .30 caliber was more effective at longer ranges. These tests seemed to convince only the convinced, while the skeptics remained skeptical.

While the chief of infantry was still deeply concerned about the new caliber, Vickers Limited of England, sensing that the Pedersen .276 semiautomatic rifle was about to become the winner of the U.S. tests, began to tool up in expectation of finding an international market for it under Pedersen's patents.

In that year of 1930, the sharpshooting tradition seemed to be losing ground. As he had been for the past hundred years in the peacetime American army, the gravel-belly sharpshooter was still the darling of the Ordnance Corps, for this constant stressing of long-distance marksmanship reinforced in the minds of the Ordnance Corps the premise that aimed fire, the fire of the marksman, was of the utmost importance in combat. Slow, deliberate fire that could hit the bull's-eye of a target five, even six, football fields away, this was the standard by which to measure soldiers. Slow and deliberate fire wasted less ammunition, and put less strain on supply lines. Guided by this philosophy, there were many in Ordnance who simply did not like automatic weapons.

While the Infantry Board and the Cavalry Board both favored

the new .276 caliber, the chief of infantry and the chief of cavalry both hung back. Like many others in the Ordnance Department, they cast a longing glance at the .30-'06 cartridge. Moreover, there was that .30-caliber Garand that had been shelved. Despite its abandonment by the board, Garand had continued to work on it in his spare time with even more impressive test results.

After having ordered all work on the .30-caliber semiautomatic rifle be stopped in its meeting of February 21, 1929, the Rifle Board changed its mind again, now suspecting that it was feasible to make a semiautomatic weapon in .30 caliber. Perhaps, board members said, Pedersen was wrong. Doubt decided them to take another look at both calibers.

On November 14, 1929, a scant few weeks after the stock market crash, the Semiautomatic Rifle Board convened at the National Armory in Springfield. Day after day, bad economic news flooded the front pages. Amid the mood of fear and helplessness, the board ordered the Springfield Armory to make a pilot model of the Garand gas-operated semiautomatic rifle, caliber .30.

At the Infantry Board Semiautomatic Rifle Tests in Fort Benning, Georgia, the showdown came at last. In an extended field test by the army's top sharpshooters, the Garand .276 was tested directly against the Pedersen .276, the Springfield '03, and the Browning automatic rifle.

The Garand outperformed them all. In fact, the report can only be described as glowing. "The Garand," concluded the Infantry Board, "is the best semiautomatic rifle that we have tested to date." It added, "A rifle of caliber .276 is preferable to one of caliber .30 for use as the basic Infantry weapon."[2]

On August 29, 1931, the Cavalry Board Semiautomatic Rifle Field Tests tested the Garand .276 against .30-caliber rifles. And it concurred with the Infantry Board, preferring the .276 caliber to the .30-caliber cartridge.

However, the chief of infantry was still not convinced, accepting the .276 over the .30-caliber cartridge only because he was told the .30 caliber was too strong for semiautomatic fire. In addition, the chief of cavalry still preferred the .30-caliber cartridge for armor piercing because it is "very destructive to the tracks and tires of vehicles."[3]

On October 9, 1931, at the Combined Services Semiautomatic Rifle Board Meeting, at the Aberdeen Proving Ground, came the final showdown test, Garand against Pedersen. This was the Rifle Board's third and final round of tests and evaluations. Members looked at four semiautomatic rifles: the new Garand .30 caliber, the Garand .276 caliber, the Pedersen .276 caliber, and a new contender, a .276-caliber rifle submitted by J. C. White of Boston, which had impressively passed the armory's tests.

In a race tightly packed from the beginning, trouble struck the Garand .30 caliber. It had been performing well until it developed a cracked bolt. Withdrawn from the tests, it was returned to Springfield. The board faced a dilemma: all tests had to be concluded and the rifle budget spent before the year expired. The board ordered the tests to continue without the Garand .30 caliber. This meant, in effect, that, after taking thirteen years to develop serious contenders for the official new rifle, the board had to rush its decision at the last and most critical stage—and thereby eliminate one of the serious contenders from consideration.

In the three-way race that continued, the White rifle was eliminated first, then, as the scores came in, the board ruled that the winner was the Garand .276. The army had a new rifle. In awarding the Garand the crown, the 1932 Rifle Board presented these conclusions:

- A .30-caliber semiautomatic weapon was impractical because it overheated too readily, was not free of malfunctions, was too heavy, had too much recoil for the soldier, and caused fatigue.
- The caliber, therefore, should be fixed at .276.
- The rifle that best met military requirements was the Garand T3E2 .276 semiautomatic rifle.
- The T3E2 was recommended for limited procurement.

Even though it ruled the .30 caliber out of consideration, the board, with lingering doubts, and pressure from the unconvinced in

Washington, contrariwise, recommended that research on the .30-caliber semiautomatic rifle be continued.

The Rifle Board's report was forwarded to the Ordnance Committee, which debated the findings before finally concurring: the Garand .27-caliber rifle should be the standard army weapon. All that was necessary now was a confirming approval by the War Department.

It seemed that, for those who were inclined to celebrate, the time had come to break out the champagne. Then, General Douglas MacArthur himself stepped into the dispute. As the army's chief of staff, General MacArthur read the report with close attention and misgivings. He saw the situation from a different angle. He was hefting the War Department's purse and found it very light. The country was in a deep and growing Depression. There were breadlines everywhere, bonus marches on Washington, and a Congress taking a mace to every budget in sight. He looked at the probable cost of introducing the new caliber as standard army issue and the numbers made him frown. Congress wasn't going to give him that much money, he felt. Therefore, no new money, no new caliber. It was that simple. But his reasoning didn't stop there.

He was also looking at a large inventory of .30-caliber ammunition and weapons, just as the War Department in 1865 had looked at an enormous supply of leftover Civil War muskets and ammunition. Confronting him, he felt, was an isolationist Congress, disillusioned by the cynical 1919 peace treaty and by the floundering efforts of the League of Nations. If France was hiding behind an inadequate Maginot Line of bunkers, and England relying on its no-longer-adequate military moat of the English Channel, Washington was slumbering behind its two shrinking oceans, unaware it was almost totally defenseless against attack. Let the rest of the world and its military quarrels go hang. The United States was not going to end up in a European war ever again.

Furthermore, MacArthur reasoned, if the new caliber was not suited to long-range machine-gun fire, it meant a two-caliber army. Despite the army board's countervailing arguments, the general rejected this situation. He had obviously heard about the Garand .30

rifle, for he also noted that more studies could produce a semiautomatic rifle in the .30 range. With the strong recommendation of Chief of Ordnance Samuel Hof, General MacArthur said no to the Garand .27-caliber rifle.

At first, army personnel could not believe MacArthur's decision. After more than thirteen years of mutual negotiating and testing and retesting and disputing and quarreling, the army had produced a rifle, a fine rifle, that was rejected.

John Garand had been right all along. The War Department would not buy a new caliber. All the committees—the Ordnance Committee, the Cavalry Board, the Infantry Board, the Combined Services Semiautomatic Rifle Board, the Cavalry Board Semiautomatic Rifle Committee, the Infantry Board Semiautomatic Rifle Committee, the Pig Board, the Goat Board—all were thrown into confusion. For a time struck dumb, they reread MacArthur's memo, which ordered them to take their rifle research money and build seventy-seven models of the Garand .30 caliber and test it thoroughly.

The Ordnance Committee hurried back to John Garand's .30-caliber, gas-actuated semiautomatic rifle. It was in the armory having its bolt repaired—the single model of the .30-caliber Garand. Cinderella's foot slipped into the glass slipper: suddenly, the armory couldn't do enough fast enough to finish developing the Garand .30.

In March 1932, at the Aberdeen Proving Ground, John Garand's new .30-caliber rifle performed all its tests with great aplomb to enthusiastic praise. When Douglas MacArthur saw the new .30 caliber weighing in at only slightly more than the .27-caliber Garand, he was elated. The new weapon solved in one stroke a great number of his problems—military and political. His decision was vindicated. The U.S. Army had the world's finest semiautomatic weapon, and it was still a one-caliber operation. Eighty copies were now ordered and full-scale field tests were scheduled.

One could look back at the great efforts, the generous budgets, the large staffs, and the serious coddling that had backed up the various rifles. It was a great irony that the weapon that finally saved the day had been developed part-time, with no budget, no staff or support, by a genius who alone had solved enormous design problems that would have taken ordinary staffs years and would have defeated many other rifle designers entirely. Miraculously, by himself, John Garand had created one of the great rifles of all time. He had won not just once; he had won twice. His .276 semiautomatic beat out all contenders, then, when it was rejected, as Garand had expected, his .30-caliber rifle saved the day.

When it came time to make the eighty models, Garand himself had to step in to design the basic tools—the jigs, the fixtures, and gauges—then supervise the production of them. The eighty models were finished in May 1934 and shipped to the Infantry and Cavalry Boards for field testing. The Garand was hammered and battered and tested and fired by dozens of enlisted troops, dragged through mud, immersed in water. When the tests were completed, the rifle was unanimously recommended for adoption as the official army rifle, replacing the M1903. Procurement was authorized in November 1935. The Garand was baptized with a new name: The M1.

The armory was confronted with the enormous job of tooling up for mass production of the M1. For this job, it was completely out of practice, since it hadn't tooled up for a new rifle since 1900, thirty-five years earlier. Worse, the Congress, since World War I, had just about starved the Springfield Armory to death. Many of the key tooling and production men had been laid off, left for other jobs, or retired. The few remaining were nearly of retirement age. Barely a handful of men were left who knew how to tool up for this remarkable new rifle. Fortunately, one of them was John Garand.

Making a rifle was an enormous undertaking. The process required two thousand separate operations to make each weapon, and, for each, someone had to make a jig or a fixture to hold the work, then fashion a tool to do the cutting, then provide a gauge to measure the finished job. After studying the M1, the armory production managers announced they were rejecting the new rifle, contending that it couldn't be mass-produced. They summoned one of the nation's top tooling companies, whose experts came and looked at the armory's equipment, some of it dating back to the tool-up of the Springfield rifle in 1900, and some of it even dating back to General Ripley's day, before the Civil War. Tooling antiques, they asserted. Then they studied John Garand's rifle and announced their conclusions: they needed 20,000 man-hours of study time just to plan production and another 200,000 hours of engineering and design time just to get the tooling equipment ready to begin production.

John Garand stepped forward once again and performed a feat of genius. Undaunted by the clamoring voices around him, with great patience, in the armory's machine shop, Garand designed all the tools needed to produce his rifle. In each instance, his machine designs turned out to be the most efficient way to produce the four million rifles the army needed in World War II. In each case thereafter, any production problem that cropped up was the direct result of production men not consulting with Garand or of their failing to follow his orders. In every aspect, the M1 was John Garand's rifle.

Garands began coming off the production line in September 1937, and by September 1, 1939, when Hitler invaded Poland to begin World War II, the United States was producing one hundred M1s a day. For the first time in its history, the U.S. Army was going to war with the lead in small arms development.

After this astonishing performance of design, perseverance, and tooling legerdemain, Garand got his reward from the armory's Production Department. With his role in the creation of the new rifle completed, the Production Department, engrossed in its Garand-designed machining operations, dismissed him from their thoughts. One high-ranking officer, confronted with the chronic shortage of appropriations from the parsimonious Congress, recommended that Garand be repaid for his sixteen years of brilliant and unremitting service by being dropped from the armory payroll to save his annual salary of $3,600.[4] Colonel Hatcher notes that this "monstrous" proposal, greeted in the Ordnance Office "with indignation,"[5] was rejected.

The 1930s—when the Garand was born—were not good times in America. The country lay stunned under the greatest Depression it had ever known. Armies of men stood on breadlines, mile after mile of farms across the country lay abandoned or fore-closed, everywhere were packing-crate cities of derelicts, many of them fathers who, unable to face their hungry children, had run off. Countless thousands of plants were closed. People lost everything, and yet each day awoke to find the Depression still there, behaving more and more like a permanent visitor.

The country was disillusioned and cynical toward the Great War, feeling it had been hoodwinked by France and Germany and Eng-land. Distrust of the peacetime military, always just below the sur-face, fueled the mood in the Congress for military cost cutting. The army's banners fell into tatters in their arsenals. With little training material available, some reserve officers kept up on military matters by taking correspondence courses privately.[6] All through the twen-ties and well into the thirties, the size of the army trended down-ward from over 230,000 in 1921 to less than 135,000 in 1932. The army's stature with the public descended even more when it was called out in Washington, D.C., to rout the Bonus Army, composed of World War I veterans looking for a desperately needed war bonus.

In October 1936, replacing General Douglas MacArthur as chief of staff, General Malin Craig called a meeting of the Army General Staff in the midst of a number of very gloomy international events. Rearming in violation of the 1919 peace treaty, Germany reoccu-pied the Rhine, the Spanish Civil War began, France devalued the franc, Italy the lira, Germany and Italy proclaimed the Rome-Berlin Axis, and Chiang Kai-shek declared war on Japan.

Sensing the onset of another war, the General Staff made a list of things it would need to field an army. More than a list, it presented the General Staff with a frightening warning. We have, the Staff noted, no airplanes, no tanks, no combat cars, no scout cars, no antiaircraft guns, no searchlights or antiaircraft fire-control equipment, no .50-caliber machine guns, practically no gas masks or radio or telephone equip-ment, no medical equipment, no military engineering equipment, and practically no ROTC units or reserve units. The Staff looked in vain for military equipment of any kind anywhere suitable for a major com-bat. In the face of ominous international developments, the Staff's assessment was alarming. The United States had fewer arms than the punishing peace treaty of 1919 allowed to the defeated Germans. The country was nearly defenseless.[7]

Even more frightening, the members of the General Staff admitted they had no plans—or the money to prepare plans—for new equipment: no designs for a modern tank, no concepts for fighter planes or bombers, no research and development of any modern artillery. In 1936, the U.S. Army was on the breadline with the rest of America.

Part of the problem—a large part of the problem, as always—was Congress. Less than 1 percent of the minuscule military budget was set aside for new weapons research. Russell Weigley, the military historian, has noted, "The army may have been less ready to function as a fighting force than at any time in its history."[8]

England behind its moat, France behind its trench, the United States wrapped in a cocoon of isolationism—all watched while the Germans trained for war and the Japanese seized one colonial prize after another. This time, America's weakness invited outside attack. As Billy Mitchell predicted, the attack came on "some Sunday morning" at Pearl Harbor on December 7, 1941, to push the United States into the greatest war the world had ever known, wrest it out of its determined isolationism, and put it onto the path of a world power.

When, in 1942, the United States went off to war, despite its steep decline in the peacetime Depression years, and its severe shortage of weaponry, it carried into battle one weapon that outgunned its counterparts in every other army in the field—the M1 Garand rifle.

If there were any lingering doubts about the Garand, its performance in combat dispelled them. In surf and sand, dragged through the mud and rain of tropical rain forests, sun-baked, caked with volcanic ash, covered with European snows that melted, then refroze inside the breech, beset by rust and mildew, mold and dirt, the Garand still came out shooting. German troops often believed that every American GI was carrying a machine gun.

The Garand was praised by the GI for its few faults and its many virtues, and especially for its trustworthiness in the midst of terrible battle abuse. With the Garand, an American squad could match the firepower of an entire Japanese company. "Accurate," "Powerful," "Quite reliable": these were the terms that commonly appeared in the M1's battle reports.[9] Of considerable significance, officers noted that in spite of the worst fears of the Ordnance Department, GIs and marines did not waste ammunition. It was very rare for any unit to run out of bullets.

It doubled the strength of American troops in both defense and offense. A soldier got off more shots at a fleeting or moving target and gathered more knockdowns. Unlike the bolt-action, the Garand did not distract the rifleman from the battle by the need to manually operate his weapon. By getting off those extra shots, the M1 saved the lives of many a GI.

Lieutenant John B. George labeled the M1 "the best military hand weapon ever placed on the battlefield in appreciable numbers."[10] "By all past standards," said another report, "the infantryman's perfect weapon."

General Douglas MacArthur, who commanded the Allied forces in the southwestern Pacific during World War II, praised the rifle in his guarded prose: "The Garand has proved itself excellent in combat in the Philippines. Under combat conditions it operated with no mechanical defects and when used in foxholes did not develop stoppages from dust and dirt. It has been in almost constant action for as much as a week without cleaning or lubrication."[11]

The Garand's highest praise was contained in one sentence from General George Patton, Jr. "In my opinion," he said, "the M1 rifle is the greatest battle implement ever devised."[12]

The M1 was one of the very few bright spots in the U.S. military's dismal ordnance record in World War II.[13] As previously noted, American ordnance leaders declined the considerable design gifts of the Christie tank in the 1920s—gifts that helped create the battle tanks of both Germany and Russia, including the fifty-six-ton German terror called the Tiger. The United States belatedly produced a tank in 1941 that was vastly and obviously inferior to them. The thirty-two-ton Sherman tank was so lightly armored that its propensity to burst into flames when hit earned it the nickname of the Ronson, after a popular cigarette lighter of the day. Unlike the 88 tank gun the Germans were using, the Sherman featured a 75-mm cannon that was so underpowered it couldn't penetrate the armor on the front of German tanks. Only by sheer numbers was the Sherman tank able to cope with German tanks on the battlefield. In one notable Normandy battle, two hundred U.S. Shermans and British Cromwells of the British Seventh Army were beaten back by six German Tiger tanks. America's top-heavy tank destroyers couldn't destroy tanks. And while the U.S. semi-automatic M1 was no doubt a better rifle than the German bolt action, the German infantry unit wasn't built around the rifle. Intent on superior firepower, it relied on its awesome MG42 machine gun, capable of firing twelve hundred rounds a minute. Opposing it, the United States had to rely on obsolete U.S. Brownings, which had a cyclic rate of less than half that.[14] Moreover, German infantry carried sixteen MG42s per company compared with the American's eleven Brownings. In every instance, the Germans came onto the battlefield with considerably more firepower—which they measured by the most shots fired. The Americans, still hamstrung by Ordnance's ammunition-conservation philosophy, measured firepower by the most shots that hit a target.

When the Germans realized that their Mauser bolt-action rifle was inadequate, they were ready with the MP44, the world's first automatic assault rifle, quickly producing over four hundred thousand of them, each firing more than five hundred rounds a minute. Had the war lasted another year, the entire German army would have been armed with automatic rifles fifteen years before the U.S. Army got its first automatic rifle, the M14.

And even though America's Dr. Robert Hutchings Goddard almost single-handedly invented rocket science—developing all the mathematics and physics, the propellant pumps, the gyro controls, and instrumentation in his laboratories all through the 1920s and 1930s—the Germans, not the American military, put the first jet fighter in the sky. Given another year, German jets would have been able to take a fearsome toll of American and British bombers while their six-engine jet bombers could have gone back on the attack in England.

Given another year, the Germans would also have been able to introduce a cornucopia of missiles—ground-to-ground, air-to-ground, and air-to-air, and even ICBMs—to go with their V1 buzz bombs that did such fearful and terrifying damage to London.

To list the failures and shortcomings of U.S. ordnance equipment in World War II requires mention of the American submarine torpedo. Because of the Naval Bureau of Ordnance—which was so notoriously hidebound it was called the Gun Club and was described by Professor O'Neill as "an enemy second only to Japan,"[15] U.S. Navy submarines were armed with Mark XIV torpedos so slow a Japanese warship could outrun them and so unreliable they bounced off Japanese hulls without exploding or missed them entirely. While the U.S. Navy was desperately fighting a superior Japanese navy in the Pacific, American submarines waited nearly two years before the total defeat of the Gun Club finally produced effective torpedos.

American ordnance had years to study the superb Japanese Zero fighter plane in action in Asia, yet didn't discover its considerable superiority over the American Grumman Wildcat until after Pearl Harbor, when it was also forced to recognize the utter worthlessness of the American Devastator torpedo plane.

Most troubling of all, one of the reasons for American urgency and secrecy in making the A-bomb was the knowledge that the Germans were making one. Historians still ponder the consequences of a Nazi Germany with the first atomic bomb.

For the Allies, World War II ended just in time.

PART VI

CHAPTER 30

MIKHAIL KALASHNIKOV
AND THE AK47

W hen America came home from the war, the military had
ample indication that the M1 rifle had been a key factor in
the winning of the peace. And although many Ordnance men would
have hotly denied it, the semiautomatic M1 was also obsolete. The
first fully automatic lightweight assault rifle had already appeared in
dramatic fashion on the Russian front in 1942.

The German army had gone to war using infantry tactics struc-
tured around its new machine gun, the MG34 and later the MG42,
backed up by World War I bolt-action Mausers and submachine
guns firing pistol cartridges.[1]

But even as the army marched off, German Ordnance officials
were reevaluating the World War I Mauser bolt-action rifle and
found it wanting. Because of its 7.92-by-57-mm cartridge, the punishing recoil was too fatiguing for sustained firing; the range was far
more than the average foot soldier could use; the weapon was too
heavy and fatiguing to carry; the extra weight reduced the amount
of ammunition the troops could carry; but, most of all, the Mauser,
with its laborious bolt action, was too slow. It lacked firepower.

Ordnance decided that the German army needed a fully automatic lightweight rifle that could replace the light machine gun,
the bolt-action rifle, and the submachine gun, all in one. However, for such a rapid-fire weapon, the standard 7.92-by-57-mm
rifle cartridge was too powerful. German Ordnance men were

confronted with two choices: either reduce the power of its 7.92-mm cartridge or increase the power of its pistol cartridge. They chose the former—reducing the length and power of its rifle cartridge—which was cheaper and conserved the expensive material that went into the longer cartridges. Developed in 1941, the new intermediate cartridge, now only 33 mm long with 24.6 grains of propellant (as opposed to the 45 to 50 grains in the previous cartridge), was titled the 7.9-mm Infanterie Kurz Patrone, a name that was to become famous.

As a parallel assignment, German Ordnance set out to design an automatic rifle around the new cartridge. Both Haenel and Walther worked on the project, and the result was the 1942 MKb42 machine carbine, which was introduced in July. By then, the German army in Russia had discovered the limitations of the old bolt-action rifle and the submachine gun and were looking for more firepower. Within months, the MKb42 made its stunning debut in battle. In November 1942, on the Russian front, a German army unit—the Kampfgruppe Scherer—was surrounded by Red Army units and under heavy attack, with the Russian noose slowly tightening.[2] Unexpectedly, salvation fell from the skies when the German air force air-dropped the new MKb42 rifle to the beleaguered unit. The Kampfgruppe's sudden and tremendous increase in firepower enabled it to break out of the Russian noose to fight another day. A deadly new dimension had been added to infantry warfare—more rifle firepower than any army unit had ever had before, a lethal four hundred rounds a minute.[3]

In the following spring of 1943, Hugo Schmeisser of the Haenel arms firm refined the MKb42 to produce the Sturmgewehr assault rifle series known as the MP43 and MP44. By February 1944, Germany was producing some five thousand a month, 400,000 by war's end, with a cyclic rate of five hundred per minute.

During World War II—called the Patriotic War by Russia—through desperate fighting against the invading German armies, the Russians also had discovered the shortcomings of the combination of bolt-action rifles and massed submachine guns firing pistol cartridges. In the midst of a raging war, with the continued existence of Russia in the balance, a young sergeant, Mikhail Timofeyevich Kalashnikov, in his early twenties, set out to design Russia's first automatic assault rifle. He was almost killed before he got his idea down on graph paper.

On the surface, Kalashnikov was an unlikely candidate to invent a rifle. He was born on November 10, 1919, to a peasant family in Alma-Ata in southeastern Kazakhstan, far from any technical schools, military weapons, or even vocational training. In 1936, after high school, he went to work for the Turkestan-Siberian Railroad. He didn't have much chance to learn anything there, because by 1938, he was in the Red Army. There, in an armorer's training program, he discovered a fascination with small arms, and, later, as a tank driver, he earned his first chance to use his creative instincts, designing a fuel consumption gauge, then an improved tank track assembly. He was promoted to sergeant and sent to a factory in Leningrad as an adviser on the production of his fuel gauge and tank track. As a senior sergeant, he went off to war against the German invaders as a tank commander and distinguished himself for bravery. In September 1941, in the Battle of Bryansk, his T34 tank was hit by a German shell and he received a severe shoulder wound. He was shipped back to a military hospital where his recuperation was slow: his wound was not healing well and he was in considerable pain. To fight off the pain, he turned his mind to ideas about automatic weapons. A helpful hospital librarian searched for books on ordnance design and brought back a book that changed his life: *Evolution of Small Arms* by the great Russian weapons designer V. G. Federov.

"That was my lucky day," Kalashnikov recalled. From Federov's book, he ingested the major principles of small arms design.[4] One day, he was notified by hospital authorities that he was to be decorated for his bravery in battle with the Order of the Red Star. He was also informed that he could not yet return to duty. At a time when Russia was desperately scratching for men to fight the Germans, his wound remained so severe he was sent home for a six-month convalescent leave. Returning to Alma-Ata, he spent his time visiting a local hospital and working on a concept for a new small arm—a submachine gun. He systematically studied all the existing models and when, in 1942, the Red Army established a competition for a new submachine gun, Sergeant Kalashnikov found himself up against several of the leading weapons designers of the Soviet Union—G. S. Shpagin and V. A. Degtyarev. In his remote part of Russia, Kalashnikov had little access to design facilities or to machine tools, had no formal training and no experience. The submachine gun he designed was eclectic, derivative, crudely made from hand tools, not very pretty, and while it didn't win the competition, it worked effectively enough to urge him on.

He was twenty-four. His arm was still not healed properly and he was restless. He needed a place to work—a machine shop where, lacking an engineering education, he could make with his own hands the ideas he had in his head. He appealed to his friends and associates on the railroad and was allowed to use the railroad's machine shop facilities after hours. With the help of his machinist friends, he soon had a working model of his newest weapon. But he quickly discovered that designing was only half the job. Isolated as he was in a little town, he saw that to get official attention, he needed a sponsor. He tried various paths, but the Communist bureaucracy thwarted him at every turn. There had to be another way, through a sponsor higher up on the bureaucratic ladder. When he took his new weapon to the secretary of the Central Committee of the Communist Party at Kazakhstan, that official was as impressed with Kalashnikov's Red Star medal as he was with his gun and he opened doors for the inventor.

Kalashnikov was admitted to the model shops of the Moscow Aviation Institute, which had been evacuated from Moscow to Alma-Ata. His Red Star decoration opened still more doors, and soon Kalashnikov was finishing his weapon with the expert guidance of the dean of the Faculty of Rifle and Cannon Armament and his staff. When Kalashnikov submitted his weapon to the Ordnance authorities, he was totally unprepared for what was to happen. In an experience that paralleled John Garand's, Kalashnikov's weapon was turned down as being similar to existing weapons, but its design and its designer both caught the attention of General Anatoliy

Arkadaevich Blagonravov, chairman of Infantry Weapons at the Dzershinskiy Artillery Academy, a distinguished weapons designer. The chairman beckoned and Kalashnikov was brought to the Red Army Small Arms Proving Ground in Ensk, where, as a member of the staff, he met the leading weapons designers of the Soviet Union and had the opportunity to broaden his technical background significantly. His designs earned him two "author's certificates," the Russian equivalent of patents.

Yet another door opened for him when he obtained a supply of Russian Model 1943 7.62-by-39-mm cartridges. The Russians had encountered the same problem as the Germans: the standard Russian rifle cartridge was too strong for automatic fire. When either the Tokarev AVT40 rifle or the Simonev AVS36 was fired as an automatic weapon, they became completely uncontrollable. As a result—and perhaps aware of the German Kurz Patrone—the Soviets developed a similar intermediate-power .30-caliber cartridge. Like the German Kurz Patrone cartridge, the Russian cartridge was shorter than standard rifle length; it was also rimless. Kalashnikov immediately recognized that this was the very cartridge he needed to make his design ideas work. Getting ever closer to an automatic rifle, he developed, for another open competition, his first semiautomatic carbine. Although he was again a runner-up—this time to the SKS45—he was undaunted; his learning was taking quantum leaps and he had gotten several important new ideas. He was still only twenty-five—one of the youngest men in the Soviet arms design world. With many of the leading arms designers in the country—the men he was competing against—approaching retirement age, he felt time was on his side.

The moment had come to design an automatic rifle. Like John Garand, he based his design on gas operation, and with sheets of drafting paper, he explored its possibilities in sketch after sketch. Each time he modified one part or dimension, he had to change all the other parts. Each change required another complete new set of drawings, but each change brought him closer to the design he had in mind. Finally, he felt, he had it—a simple, rugged automatic rifle. He was quite excited: if it performed as well as he expected, such a weapon could vastly improve the effectiveness of the entire Red Army. Although by now it was 1946 and too late for his weapon to help win the Patriotic War, a dream he had cherished, Kalashnikov shipped the drawings to the Main Artillery Commission in Moscow. A short time later, his design was selected for development.

Kalashnikov was suddenly busy. He was given an entire staff of engineers and specialists to help him, and soon the group had a model of his weapon ready for testing. Made with a stamped sheet-steel receiver and weighing nine pounds—ultimately less than seven pounds—it was a stunning weapon in every respect. From a thirty-round clip, working as a semiautomatic or automatic, it fired up to six hundred rounds a minute. Army Ordnance tested it thoroughly and kept testing even as it was being reworked. The rifle successfully passed through the battery of proving ground tests and then the brutal gauntlet of field testing with Russian army troops. When the testing was over, the Kalashnikov had passed every test the Russian Ordnance people had thrown at it.

In 1949, three years after he had submitted his drawings, Kalashnikov's rifle was accepted. As the Avtomat Kalashnikova 1947—the AK47—it became the official rifle of the Red Army. Kalashnikov was now an arms designer of international stature, with his own considerable design group. He went on to design a whole family of small arms to go along with his AK47, and in time collected a number of awards and citations.

But nothing matched the importance of the AK47 in the decades that followed World War II. In time, according to estimates, between thirty million and fifty million AK47s and AKMs—a modified version—were made. The AK47 proved to be the ideal weapon for Communist insurgency groups who soon confronted the United States in a Cold War that stretched around the world.

Unfortunately, the United States was much slower to recognize the need for an automatic rifle. Bemused by the stellar wartime record of their own M1, which, they were convinced, was the finest semiautomatic rifle in the world, U.S. Ordnance men failed to appreciate the significance of the German automatic rifle even when it was used against them. At war's end, they gained more impressive evidence of the power of an automatic weapon when, in 1945, a roving team of American Ordnance experts drove up to the remains of the Mauser Werke in Oberndorf, Germany. This was just one of many teams fielded by the Allied Combined Intelligence Objectives Subcommittee to comb through the wreckage of the Third Reich's military ordnance system.

The Mauser Werke were historically significant ruins because this was the manufacturing and design complex where Peter Paul Mauser had created in the previous century his celebrated and much-copied Mauser bolt-action rifle. But history was not what had brought these American Ordnance men here. They were looking for the files and sample drawers of the Mauser Werke's Ordnance Experimental Shop. When they located them in the rubble, they found two new weapons—the Gerat 03 and Gerat 06. Both designs had been chambered for the 7.9-mm Infanterie Kurz Patrone round and both exhibited a number of unusual breech designs the team had never seen before. The two weapons were sent to Springfield Armory and examined with great interest by weapons designer Cyril Moore, who could only speculate on what these two automatic weapons might have done had Germany had time to put them in production.

What was probably of more interest to Ordnance was the German MP44 automatic rifle—first used, in an early version, by the surrounded German Kampfgruppe in Russia. In 1944 and 1945, the MP44 proved so successful that the Germans were urgently replacing all their bolt-action and semiautomatic rifles with it. But they were too late: the Allies were pounding the nation from all sides and there was neither time nor manufacturing facilities to complete the switchover. The MP44 joined other might-have-been relics that provide idle speculation for military historians. But it did have a profound influence on postwar weapons thinking. Having never seen automatic rifles before, American Ordnance men had much to learn from this brilliantly conceived and made weapon. However, when a supply of MP44s reached the Springfield Armory, the traditionalists there failed to perceive the significance of the weapon. They saw what they dismissed as cheap stampings, flimsy construction, unreliability, and a cut-rate appearance. Only later did the attentive eyes of other designers like Eugene Stoner, inventor of the M16, learn the lessons of the MP44.

Two lessons Springfield failed to learn: the .30-caliber, full-power rifle cartridge was an overpowered ballistics antique, and the overengineered, overmanufactured rifle like the M1 was finished. For despite the views of many American Ordnance men, the German MP44 was not a product of desperate war shortages but of new technology. The Germans had raised machine stamping and welding to a high technology. As a result, the parts made from sheet steel, stamped and welded, turned out to be just as durable and just as reliable and accurate as machined and forged parts. What was more significant for the rifleman who had to carry the weapon, because of its stamped sheet steel, the MP44 was lighter. Furthermore, the MP44 could be made much faster, much of it in ordinary machine shops, and more cheaply than traditional rifles. Most important, because the MP44 was lighter, the infantryman could carry more ammunition. He didn't need to be resupplied as often and faced less risk of running out of ammunition. Instead of wasting ammunition, this system could take pressure off the supply lines. In fact, here were the same virtues that were to make the Soviet AK47 the most popular small arm in the world. The United States would have to include these virtues in its own fully automatic rifle in order to meet the AK47 on future battlefields.

CHAPTER 31

COLONEL STUDLER
STARTS THE SEARCH

D uring World War II, few in the United States saw that the whole structure of the Ordnance Department desperately needed rethinking. The thirteen-year search in the 1920s and 1930s for a semiautomatic rifle that only by the greatest good luck—and in spite of the Ordnance committee system—produced the Garand was ample testimony of the department's inefficiency. The nation simply could not afford to acquire new weapons through the Ordnance Department's bureaucratic power games anymore. But the United States received not a new Ordnance acquisition system but the old Ordnance system's idea of an automatic rifle—the M14.

During the war, the army brought pressure on the Ordnance Department to create an all-purpose selective-fire rifle—lighter in weight than the M1 with full automatic capabilities. The Garand M1 was a fine weapon, but even its proponents realized it was not perfect. Weighing in at nine and a half pounds, it was considered heavy, the magazine system needed reworking, and some felt its rate of fire was too slow, although, in contradiction, traditionalists said its rate of fire was too fast, encouraging ammunition wastage. The Browning automatic rifle—one of John Browning's two machine guns from World War I—had plenty of firepower and, in fact, had established an outstanding record during World War II. But it also was too heavy. The army's carbine—a shorter version of the M1 rifle—was light enough, but it was underpowered. The Thompson submachine gun had the volume, but its range was far too short; besides, it was heavier than the Garand M1.

This was the same path that the Germans, and later the Russians, had trod—seeking to replace many weapons with a single lightweight selective-fire fully automatic rifle. The assignment to develop such a weapon for the U.S. Army was given to Colonel Rene Studler, in the U.S. Ordnance Department, who started his quest in May 1944, at the height of the fighting of World War II—just when the Germans were air-dropping the new Sturmgewehr MP44 to their beleaguered Kampfgruppe in Russia, and just when the Russians were urgently developing their own selective-fire automatic rifle.

Colonel Studler seemed to be the perfect man for the quest. A fully experienced Ordnance officer, just under fifty, with twenty-seven years in the military, he had an unusual and quite outstanding background. In 1917, with a bachelor's degree from Ohio State, he started his career as an Army Signal Corps pilot. Five years later, he decided the Ordnance Corps was more to his liking and struck a deal with the army in 1922: he switched to Ordnance and was promptly shipped to the Massachusetts Institute of Technology. A year later, he returned to the Ordnance Department with an MIT degree in mechanical engineering and began working his way upward through the Ordnance system.

In 1923, the peacetime army was living on a very slender budget, and opportunities for distinction were not common. But he continued his diligent engineering studies on the job inside the armory and quickly acquired a substantial technical background in ordnance. By 1928, he served as proof officer during the Pig Board tests in Aberdeen. In the early 1930s, the army sent him to Europe to study European ordnance. Among his qualifications were an extensive technical background, facility with several European languages, and an independent income that he used to supplement his meager army pay.

He was on the European scene during the crucial years of 1934 through 1939, watching the Germans rearm and launch a new war.

Wide-ranging, meeting key people in all the European armies, he filed hundreds of reports. No one in Washington read them. But by the time he returned in 1939, he was one of the army's top experts on small arms. His influence on weapons development from that point on was enormous. "Studler, in a real way," observes Dr. Edward Ezell, curator of the National Firearms Collection at the Smithsonian Institution, "single-handedly shaped the course of American infantry and aircraft arms development until his retirement in 1953."[1]

His star rose rapidly during the war years as he turned out one successful product after another. He introduced the "Carbine" Williams M1 carbine, the M3 machine gun, the M1 steel helmet, and the shoulder-fired recoilless artillery rifle, a major new infantry weapon. In the process, he successfully reorganized the structure of the research and development programs inside the armory, but his efforts to improve the management of the Ordnance Department itself were less successful. He found himself face-to-face with the officer group that ran the armory's production line. They emphatically declared that research was not the armory's primary job— producing rifles was. As a research man, he was not part of their team.

By 1943, he had became chief of the Small Arms Development Branch, with an office in the Pentagon, and by May 1944, when he began the quest for the army's new, all-purpose, fully automatic rifle, he had developed an emphatic—critics said autocratic— method of dealing with the Ordnance system. He liked to give orders and he liked to have them obeyed with a minimum of fuss or delay. Because of his string of product successes, he had great stature with his superiors as the man who could accomplish the most difficult assignments. With stature came power, and with power, a growing imperiousness, a trait that recalled General Ripley. He had one other Riplian trait: once he'd made up his mind, it was almost impossible to make him change it.

If Colonel Studler could add an automatic rifle to his other successes, his way to the very top of the Ordnance Department would be wide open. He would be much closer to becoming General

Rene Studler, army chief of ordnance. This new rifle was a political creature from its inception, and to create it, Studler would have to satisfy some unavoidable and conflicting objectives. The infantry wanted the faster firepower and lighter weight that only an automatic rifle could provide. Others inside the Ordnance Department concerned with supply logistics wanted a rifle that would remain basically a semiautomatic rifle—the M1, in effect—in order to prevent infantrymen from wasting ammunition. Other Ordnance men—upholding the gravel-belly marksman tradition—were determined to keep the .30 full-power cartridge, for carefully aimed, long-range fire. Last, armory production men wanted a rifle they could make on their existing M1 machinery. Strangely, with all these conflicting objectives, no one regarded this weapon as a new rifle, simply an improved M1.

Drawing on his deep technical knowledge of rifles, Colonel Studler set forth the parameters of the new rifle in great and precise detail. This was one rifle that would satisfy everyone in the Ordnance Department—including his adversaries—while giving American troops the finest automatic rifle in the world.

This "modified" M1, he determined, would still be primarily a semiautomatic rifle, to be sure—which wouldn't waste ammunition. But when the occasion required, a switch would convert it to a fully automatic rifle with a twenty-shot magazine—to satisfy the infantry. Mounted on a bipod, and featuring a folding stock, a flash hider, bayonet, and detachable telescopic sight, the weapon would also launch rifle grenades—for those who wanted many weapons in one. Yet, with all this equipment, plus the added weight of a twenty-shot clip, its weight would be no more than nine pounds—a full half pound lighter than the M1—again, to satisfy the infantry. Furthermore—to accommodate his most trying opponents, the armory production men—the new rifle would be manufactured in the armory on the M1 tooling with little or no tooling changes. Most challenging of all, the modified M1 was expected to fire full-power .30 cartridges—thereby satisfying the gravel-belly traditionalists. The new weapon was designated T20.[2]

A month before D day, in Normandy, June 1944—when Allied forces invaded France—Colonel Studler issued his job order. With haste, the new rifle could be in service in time to win battle kudos —a fitting crown to his Ordnance career. The assignment was turned over to Ordnance's top talent and chief miracle worker: John Garand.

The inventor of the M1—and, some said, the savior of the Ordnance Department—Garand pondered the problem. Trying to make an automatic rifle out of a semiautomatic rifle raised an overwhelming number of new problems: hundreds of shots a minute created heat great enough to burn the wooden stock. Added to that were tremendous muzzle blast, bone-bruising recoil, and uncontrollable climb. Garand also felt that the new weapon needed a new gas chamber, a complex design stricture that meant no bayonet, no grenade launcher, no flash hider. With such design changes, the new weapon might not be made on the old M1 tooling.

Just as the Germans and Russians had, Garand focused on the one problem that aggravated all the rest—the excessive power of the .30-'06 cartridge. When fired at the rate of four hundred to six hundred a minute, the cartridge produced a recoil no one could hold. Colonel Studler was vehement. No change in the .30-caliber cartridge. Ever! Having lived through the 1920s and the terrible consequences of trying to introduce the Pedersen .276 cartridge, the colonel was unshakably determined to find a way to make an automatic rifle that would fire the full-power .30-caliber cartridge.

To gain the benefit of others' thinking, in September, Colonel Studler turned the same project over to the Remington Arms Company. When the full-charge .30-caliber requirement was explained to them, Remington officials were doubtful. They carried the project back to their research department, where their weapons designers were equally skeptical.

On October 12, 1944, the Ordnance Technical Committee met in Washington, D.C. Composed of representatives of the army ground forces, other agencies, and of the Ordnance Department itself, the committee had come together to approve a formal request from the infantry for an automatic rifle. The men around the table read the description of contradictory characteristics. Each saw that his own were included, and all were told that Colonel Studler already had both John Garand and Remington Arms working on the project. Everyone was accommodated, and the committee had consensus.

Unfortunately, these specifications were describing an impossibility and should never have been allowed to leave the committee room. Yet Studler—the man who could do the impossible—announced he would return in a few months' time with the rifle they wanted. Consequently, the committee members left feeling they would have a new weapon in time to help win the war in the Pacific. With old lessons unlearned, Ordnance was once again attempting gun design by committee. Unless someone interceded, the department was heading for a fiasco.

That same month—October 1944—the Armory Model Shop announced that the Garand Model T20 was ready and met all specifications except one. With all the new equipment and attachments, the rifle weighed not eight and a half pounds, but over thirteen pounds. The committee increased the weight limit to over twelve pounds, turning the lightweight automatic rifle into a heavyweight automatic rifle. Within weeks, Remington returned with its first model—the T22.

With the two weapons before the committee, disagreements appeared. Production people at both the armory and at Remington warned that if the board wanted a selective-fire rifle in time to see action in the Pacific theater, there could be no major production line changes in the basic mechanisms of the M1—particularly the receiver and bolt. Yet Garand's new model had a slightly longer spring, and that meant some new tooling. In November, while design engineers pondered this problem, the Garand T20 and the Remington T22 were shipped off to the Aberdeen Proving Ground for testing.

Progress was made. By the spring of 1945, with modifications and design changes, John Garand's new T20E2 met all the given parameters: fitted with a flash hider, bipod, bayonet, and detachable telescopic sight, it fired an astonishing seven hundred .30-

caliber shots a minute. Fully equipped, it weighed 12.5 pounds. Stripped of the extra equipment, the T20E2 weighed 9.61 pounds. A muzzle brake even took some of the furious kick out of the recoil. Most important, it could be made on M1 tooling. Far from ideal, as an interim wartime model, it met the urgent need of American troops in the South Pacific. While Remington continued to modify its T22E1, the committee focused its attention on Garand's T20E2.

In August 1945, as it was preparing to authorize production of 100,000 T20E2 rifles—now designated the M2—America dropped the A-bomb on Japan. Overnight, the project died. In fact, by September 1945, with peace celebrations in the streets and the lights going on again all over Europe and Asia, the pressure lessened on the automatic rifle project. Colonel Studler decided to shelve both the Garand T20E2 and the Remington T22E1 and, rather than modify an existing weapon, plan a wholly new automatic rifle.

He soon learned, in 1945, that he was now confronted with an ominous new challenge. At war's end, statesmen on both sides of the Atlantic began serious discussions on forming a new multinational European military force called the North Atlantic Treaty Organization—which was to be formed four years later, in 1949—and to be armed with an all-NATO lightweight automatic rifle, a single common weapon for all the armies of the European allies and the United States. Several other foreign armories were already scrambling to design that weapon. For the first time in its history, the U.S. Ordnance Corps found itself in a situation no entrenched bureaucracy can endure: outside competition. The Springfield Armory would not be able to form a committee to declare its rifle the winner. To be chosen as the new NATO rifle, the American entrant had to be demonstrably the best out on the firing line.

America found itself in a sort of World Cup of ordnance. It was about to learn how good it really was, with the whole ordnance world watching. National prestige was at stake. If Colonel Studler failed in this quest, the American army could find itself armed with an automatic rifle of foreign design. Unlike any Ordnance officer who had preceded him, the colonel was in an international political situation that went far beyond the parochial machinations of the prewar Ordnance Department.

As he assessed the situation, Studler saw that competition was coming primarily from two formidable sources—the British and the FN Armory in Belgium, the latter one of the oldest and greatest armories in the world. The British were proceeding in a very brisk businesslike manner. Like the Germans and the Russians, the British Ministry of Supply started by taking a hard look at their .303-caliber cartridge through a group called the Small Arms Ideal Calibre Panel. Observers were betting they would reach a conclusion similar to the Russians and the Germans: reduced power.

There was a third source of competition. From Germany, Studler now had samples of Schmeisser's brilliantly designed Sturmgewehr 44 automatic rifle with its .30-caliber Kurz cartridge. From battle veterans who had seen that high-volume rifle in action came pressure to design a weapon just like it. Colonel Studler was not impressed with the German Kurz. He said its combat range was too limited, the bullet too light, the muzzle velocity too low. It failed to meet the fixed tradition of the gravel-belly long-range sharpshooter that haunted the halls of the Pentagon.

Behind all other entrants, dimly perceived, was a fourth competitor: in Russia, twenty-six-year-old Senior Sergeant Mikhail Timofeyevich Kalashnikov was finishing the design of his AK47, which would go into production in 1949. The AK47 proved to be the weapon to beat.

Colonel Studler set out to redesign the American .30-caliber cartridge, around which he could build an automatic rifle—in fact, a whole family of small arms. For his new cartridge, he turned to the Olin Chemical Corporation's new "ball"-type gunpowder. This more powerful powder gave him a .30-caliber cartridge in a shorter case—yet with the same power as the longer cartridge. So Colonel Studler nailed his banner to the flagstaff: he declared he would build the rifle no one else could—a fully automatic weapon firing a full-power .30 cartridge, the weapon other countries had declared impossible.

In the new cartridge with less metal, shorter meant lighter, enabling the soldier to carry more. Shorter also meant a shorter breech mechanism in the rifle, another important weight saver. The shell used less expensive metal, still another cost saving. On paper, the design was formidable: smaller, lighter case, lighter rifle, faster firepower, long range: just what the infantry wanted, but only if the recoil could be reduced.

CHAPTER 32

EARLE HARVEY
AND THE T25

To design the new weapon, Colonel Studler chose Earle M. Harvey. Harvey was a Connecticut Yankee, born not far from the Springfield Armory in 1908, in a small town where, in his youth, he had been an avid hunter of small game.[1] Guns remained a lifelong interest.

Actually, Earle Harvey hesitated at a career crossroads for several years before he chose the life of a weapons designer. He started out as an engineering student at the University of Connecticut, then switched to English at Brown University, graduating in 1933 with honors. With a depressed job market, Harvey decided on graduate studies and matriculated at Yale. Indecisive still, he switched from English to history, then to psychology, to philosophy, then, in February 1937, he changed back to his original interest, engineering.

The reason for the final switch occurred in June of 1934. While walking downtown in New Haven, he got an idea for the locking mechanism of a self-loading rifle. With a few pennies' worth of brown wrapping paper, bought in a local drugstore, he sketched his idea, then took it to the Winchester Repeating Arms Company. While impressed with the design concept, Winchester executives indicated they were more interested in the designer. They suggested that Harvey consider a career as a weapons designer with them. In fact, they offered to put him through Winchester's factory training course. Harvey thought about it for over a year before accepting.

When he went back, Winchester was still ready to hire him, but they suggested that an even better career opportunity awaited him at Remington Arms. In 1937, at Remington, he began his career as an apprentice in the Design Work Program, in which he remained until September 1939. With the war, Remington had cut back on commercial design; Harvey didn't like the alternative assignment. He went to work for Savage Arms as a commercial designer, had the same problem, and decided to find a job designing military arms.

Then he made a fortuitous mistake—he sent a letter of application to the wrong place. The Aberdeen Proving Ground tested weapons, but it didn't design them and didn't, therefore, hire designers. Aberdeen sent Harvey's letter to Washington, where it was routed to Colonel Studler's office. Studler's office hired Harvey, sending him, in October 1941, to the Springfield Armory, where he remained until March 1945. Then, with the war's end near, Studler brought him to Washington to work on the lightweight rifle design project.

The colonel's original parameters were still basically unchanged—except that the new lightweight automatic rifle was going to be really lightweight, not nine pounds but seven, and to be many weapons in one, replacing the M1 rifle, the carbine, the Browning automatic rifle, the infantry sniper rifle, various submachine guns, and the antitank grenade launcher.

The new objectives were more difficult than those John Garand's T20E2 rifle had faced. They were, in fact, incompatible. From the beginning, Earle Harvey knew that a seven-pound rifle could not contain the recoil of the new .30-caliber powerhouse capable of penetrating a piece of ten-gauge steel plate. Against the shoulder of the shooter, the recoil was punishing; in automatic fire, the rifle would climb out of control. This was simple physics understood by any ordnance man.

The idea of a multipurpose weapon was even more unattainable. The T25 simply could not be a BAR and a sniper rifle and a submachine gun, to select just a few from the long list. These were all different weapons, with different design parameters and different performance requirements. When Earle Harvey asked that the parameters be changed, his request was refused.

Originally, Studler gave the assignment to three men: John Garand, Earle Harvey, and Cyril Moore. Moore's project was abandoned early: his assignment had been to adapt design elements from the Sturmgewehr models recovered at war's end in the Mauser Werke in Oberndorf, and since these designs called for machine stamping and welding, the production people dismissed them out of hand as being flimsy and unworthy of an American military rifle.[2] With no developmental money appropriated, Moore's project was not heard from again.

John Garand had lost none of his innovative brilliance, and he produced a remarkable rifle that sought to eliminate the three bugbears of that .30-caliber cartridge—muzzle blast, muzzle flash, and, most of all, recoil. His ingenious design may have come closest to accommodating the unattainable parameters. But by answering the design requirements with an extremely short rifle stock and an ammunition clip behind the trigger, the weapon didn't look like an army rifle, and the Ordnance Committee refused to consider it. There was no written committee record of this. Like the Moore weapon, its funding was simply ended. Had John Garand, acknowledged as one of the outstanding weapons designers of his era, spent his career in a more receptive environment, he may have created many more weapons designs than he did. The armory was a poor environment for his kind of talent and this, his last assignment before retirement, served to illustrate it.

By default, almost from the beginning, the Harvey weapon—designated the T25—became the only real candidate. Colonel Studler, by placing his whole career and the prestige of the American armory on one rifle and one caliber, had left himself no other options after 1946. Actually, he had chosen an excellent gun design to bet on. Among the various features of Harvey's T25 rifle, one major virtue stood out: an unusually strong breech, stronger than the M1. That was exactly what Colonel Studler felt his new .30-caliber cartridge needed. But while Harvey had solved several stubborn technical problems with his weapon, in the eyes of the armory production men, the T25 had one insuperable flaw: it could not be made on M1 tooling.

Development of the Harvey rifle proceeded very slowly. From the outset, it was an orphan with no one seeming to support it, no one to fend off the undisguised hostility from the armory Production Department. The project was starved for money, with only one design engineer assigned to it, Harvey himself, who was able to work on it only intermittently. Harvey was burdened with numerous other—often vapid, frequently demeaning—assignments that weren't even part of his job description, yet often took precedence over his T25 project.[3] He found little time to work on the new weapon himself. Indeed, there wouldn't have been a T25 at all if, like Garand before him, Harvey hadn't done much of the original design work on his own time. In the face of the determined team efforts in England and Belgium, his weapon was the armory's sole project for a new automatic rifle. Critics could make a strong case that the Ordnance Department—especially Colonel Studler—wasn't seriously trying to develop the world's finest automatic rifle. Then a new study appeared that challenged all the ordnance concepts about the nature of the military rifle and the men who fired it.

In 1947, General S. L. A. Marshall published *Men Against Fire*.[4] One of the most important studies on warfare ever written, the book described in copious detail—fully documented with many case histories—exactly how American infantrymen behaved in battle during World War II. General Marshall, a noted military historian, had set out to determine just exactly what happens when the shooting starts. His study was so seminal, it led him to make an even more important and extensive study of the war in Korea a few years later.

General Marshall had taken teams of military historians onto the battlefields of Europe and the South Pacific, who observed infantry behavior in battle and then interviewed soldiers on the spot. The study covered hundreds of battles and skirmishes and many thousand troops. His conclusions, which stunned everyone who read them, should have been mandatory reading for every person in the Pentagon, especially Colonel Studler.

Only one-quarter of the men on the battle line actually fight, General Marshall reported. The rest—all 75 percent—stand and watch, unless compelled by junior officers, and even then fight only briefly. They will face the danger but will not fight—even when their position is being overrun by the enemy. They are not shirkers or malingerers or cowards. They simply do not act. This was a ratio of fire far below the usually assumed 60 to 80 percent. In fact, the 25 percent figure was high: in the preponderance of cases, General Marshall said, "we have found that on an average not more than 15 per cent of the men had actually fired at the enemy positions, or personnel with rifles, carbines, grenades, bazookas, BARs, or machine guns during the course of an entire engagement."[5]

He went on: ". . . The man didn't have to maintain fire to be counted among the active firers. If he had so much as fired a rifle once or twice, though not aiming it at anything in particular, or lobbed a grenade roughly in the direction of the enemy, he was scored on the positive side. Usually, the men with heavier weapons such as the BAR, flamethrower or bazooka, gave a pretty good account of themselves, which of course is just another way of saying that the majority of men who were present and armed but would not fight were riflemen."[6]

The figure was consistent in both the Pacific and the European battlefields. Type of terrain didn't affect the finding, nor did degree of battle experience. All battle plans that postulate a firepower efficiency rate higher than this would have to be false. General Marshall also found that from battle to battle, the same men did the fighting. And the same men did the watching. As a consequence, contrary to the beliefs of the American leaders in the Pentagon, conserving ammunition in battle was not the problem. Getting three-quarters of the troops to fire it was.

Another significant observation emerged from the general's research: most officers had little or no knowledge of how their men fought individually. When interviewed, not one of them realized that as few as fifteen men in a hundred under them were doing all the fighting. And the higher the officer's rank, the more distant he was from the battlefield, the less he knew about how men in battle fight. Ergo, the least knowledgeable would be the highest-ranking men in the army and in the place most distant from the battlefield: in the Pentagon.

All the cherished beliefs about heroism and battle behavior were false, the general noted. No one could predict in advance during training who would do the fighting. Many were model soldiers, but "there were men who had been consistently bad actors in the training period, marked by the faults of laziness, unruliness, and disorderliness, who just as consistently became lions on the battle-field. . . . They could fight like hell, but they couldn't soldier."[7] The general noted also that no amount of training would make men in battle aim carefully and fire long-distance. It just didn't happen. In fact, firing distances in combat are much shorter than official doc-trine teaches.

General Marshall was not concerned specifically in his study with the efficacy of various calibers and different weapons, but anyone reading his work had to conclude that men are much more likely to fire automatic weapons than semiautomatic or single-shot weapons. Three-quarters of them will not fire rifles. Also, long-range shooting, careful aiming, and conserving ammunition are all myths that don't stand up to the facts of battle. "If anything," observes historian Thomas L. McNaugher, "the Army's training emphasis on carefully aimed fire seems to have been counterpro-ductive. Trained to fire at targets, soldiers who could not see targets fired no shots."[8]

In light of General Marshall's study, Colonel Studler and his full-charge, .30-caliber associates were trying to make a rifle that was based on 150-year-old parameters that were completely wrong.

In 1947, the long-range rifle concept suffered another challenge. That summer, as part of their program informing the United States on their studies for a new NATO rifle, a group of Britain's leading ordnance experts traveled to the United States to present their newly completed Beeching study on infantry rifle caliber.

The high-water mark of the British visit was the warm reception they received from private American weapons designers who shared their conclusions about the lower-caliber cartridge needed for an automatic weapon and who also admired the German Sturmgewehr "intermediate power" Kurz caliber.

The reception by the American team of U.S. Ordnance officers led by Colonel Studler was far cooler. The British Beeching report contradicted much that American Ordnance men believed about caliber. In fact, the British reported, their Small Arms Ideal Calibre Panel, after full and extensive testing, had concluded that the maximum effective cartridge range for a rifle was six hundred yards. The two thousand yards postulated by the American Ordnance Department were more than three times that and therefore excessive. The British acknowledged that in consequence of these studies, their old .303-caliber cartridge "overkilled at rifle ranges,"[9] and they had therefore abandoned their long-cherished gravel-belly marksmanship tradition, and with it, the full-power, long-distance, carefully aimed cartridge. They were convinced that neither they nor the Americans could design a new lightweight rifle around such a powerful charge. The ideal caliber, their study indicated, was .28. This was not a complete surprise to American Ordnance men. It will be recalled that, in 1924, John Pedersen's brilliant .276-caliber rifle had nearly become the official army rifle, based in large part on Pedersen's persuasive evidence concerning the lethality index of smaller calibers.

Colonel Studler rejected the British recommendation for a .28-caliber cartridge as not being "full power." Based on American battlefield experience, he said, the U.S. Army's new NATO rifle was to be .30 caliber.

This announcement stunned the British. Since 1945, they had been regularly informing American Ordnance on developments in their new rifle program and had assumed the Americans were replying in kind. Instead, they were learning for the first time from Colonel Studler that the Americans had developed a new .30-caliber cartridge called the T65 and had been designing a new rifle around it for some two years—a very long lead time over the British.

420

When they returned home, the British team tried to determine why they'd been given such brusque treatment. British-American relations had certainly grown cooler. Brigadier Dixon summarized the American meeting succinctly: "We took a mauling at the hands of American Ordnance." Among themselves, the British said, "We've been Studlered again."[10] Whatever the cause, the British realized they were going to have to design a rifle of their own in competition with the soon-to-be American weapon. Unexpectedly, Britain found itself in an arms race with the United States.

That historic meeting heralded a major battle over the choice of a uniform NATO rifle cartridge and rifle. Before the choice was made, a British government was nearly toppled and the Americans were painted into a caliber corner that threatened to bring on a military and a Pentagon disaster.

Meanwhile, with the continued hostility of armory production people, development of Harvey's T25 rifle was proceeding with incredible slowness. Yet the first serious test-firing, delayed for more than two years after the test models were made, posted some impressive scores: in January 1948, the Bennel Machine Company of Brooklyn fabricated four T25s and tested them in a Manhattan National Guard armory. The T25s posted above-average scores in performance, effectiveness, and accuracy. In April, Bennel engineers found that the T25 could endure pressures up to an impressive 130,000 pounds per square inch with no parts breakage.[11]

In June 1948, Colonel Studler ordered a T25 delivered to his office. Wondering if some weight could be removed without harming its overall great strength, he ordered the T25 to be lightened from 7.5 pounds to 6.8 pounds—nearly three full pounds lighter than the M1 semiautomatic. So lightened and modified, the T25 confronted the crucial test on automatic fire with the .30-caliber cartridge. Still strong, but much too light for such powerful automatic fire, the T25 climbed and bucked and was absolutely unmanageable. The weight was increased to 7.5 pounds and even more. But the T25 was still uncontrollable. Harvey added a muzzle brake to absorb some of the powerful recoil, but the weapon continued to climb. In test after test, the climb persisted. Colonel Studler was receiving firsthand irrefutable evidence that full charge and light-weight were incompatible. Yet despite the T25's adverse performance as an automatic rifle, despite the caliber experiences of the Germans, Russians, British, and Belgians, and despite the battle-field studies by General Marshall, the colonel continued to believe that a way would be found to solve the excessive power problem to give him a fully automatic, full-power, .30-caliber rifle. Toward that goal, he continued to order additional tests.

In September 1948, the Aberdeen Proving Ground in Maryland posted still more good news for the T25. In a test against two M1s as controls, two T25s proved to be more accurate. They also performed well under adverse conditions. When added to the results of the armory tests in Manhattan, these Aberdeen tests provided some creditable credentials for the T25. Subsequent Aberdeen tests encouraged Harvey even more. Two thousand rounds were fired from each T25 with no parts failures. Slight defects that turned up were deemed to be easily corrected. The T25 was strong enough to handle the new cartridge; the soldiers' shoulders weren't.

After years of international preparation, the North Atlantic Treaty Organization was formally established in Brussels in 1949. U.S. Army Ordnance Corps people attended a meeting of the newly formed NATO Alliance to discuss standardization of all weapons and calibers for all NATO participants. As far as the Americans were concerned, attendance was an empty formality. U.S. Ordnance was still firmly committed to its American .30-caliber cartridge with its powerful long-distance charge. If there was going to be a single caliber for all armed forces in NATO, it was going to be .30 caliber. Caliber was not negotiable. While not surprised, the British, still convinced that the American .30-caliber cartridge was too strong for an automatic rifle, were disturbed to learn that the American position had not changed since their visit to the United States in 1947, two years before.

In March 1949, as Mikhail Kalashnikov's brilliant AK47 was going into production as the official Russian army rifle, Earle Harvey's T25 was heading for infantry tests at Fort Benning, Georgia. It is difficult to fathom what was going on in Colonel Studler's mind. After nearly four years of seeking, all he had to show his superiors was a rifle that couldn't be controlled during the automatic-fire test and that the armory Production Department hated. His attitude seemed to be: If feasible, the United States will have a .30-caliber automatic rifle or else it will stand pat with a .30-caliber semiautomatic rifle. Despite such growing evidence like General S. L. A. Marshall's study and the British Beeching report on small caliber, the hallowed fixed idea hadn't budged a millimeter: long-range, aimed fire conserves ammunition and wins wars.

Colonel Studler had one other option—the original T20. This was the upgraded M1 that John Garand had modified during the war to fire automatically. The armory had come close to producing 100,000 of it for the South Pacific campaign. The armory Production Department strongly favored the T20, which, although chambered for the old, longer, cartridge, could be made on existing M1 tooling.

The Harvey T25 rifle reached Fort Benning for a debut before the Army Field Forces Board Number 3. Even though the T25 still couldn't pass the automatic fire test, the infantry liked the weapon and praised its accuracy. The infantry's affirmation, the closest the T25 ever got to acceptance, may have aroused the Springfield production people, and perhaps they warned Studler again about their feelings. For Studler now seemed to become indecisive. First he ordered 110 T25s, hardly a resounding expression of confidence, and then cut the order to 50. At the same time, he renewed his interest in John Garand's T20 automatic-fire version of the M1 by ordering that it be chambered for the new T65 light-rifle cartridge. Both moves suggest that he had lost his commitment to the T25 and was looking elsewhere for a new rifle.

Suddenly, strangely, Harvey's T25 was beset with problems: design changes, delayed delivery of new models, fault-finding with metallurgy—every day seemed to bring forth new rifle problems.[12] Then the infantry ordered that the T25's straight in-line wooden stock be replaced by a drop stock to make it look more like a rifle. It was a capricious change that made the weapon even more uncontrollable. The rifle that had no friends seemed to have found many calculating enemies.

Nearly another year passed—April 1950—before twenty T25 test rifles were delivered. Now nearly five years since Harvey was first assigned the design project, the U.S. Army still had no automatic rifle. Two months later, UN forces would be at war with North Korea. Another year and a half was to pass before the second batch of twenty T25 rifles was delivered, nearly six years after the Lightweight Rifle Program had begun. There seemed to be no one in the Ordnance Department who could step in and stop the behind-the-scenes quarreling. The Production Engineering Branch of the armory continued to resist the T25, calling for changes in the metals and in the engineering drawings and claiming that the T25 was not designed for mass production. No progress was being made on the program to develop an automatic rifle, and respect for the Ordnance Department had fallen greatly. "All the delays," Dr. Ezell of the Smithsonian notes, "pointed to institutional rejection of Harvey's new rifle."[13]

In February 1950, just four months before the Korean War began, the British military came back to Washington. Believing that Studler was about to push the T25 as the standard American weapon, they were ready to make a strong case for their weapons system. Yet Colonel Studler met them head-on and absolutely refused to consider the British .28-caliber system. He appeared to be unconcerned that he had failed to produce an automatic rifle. Then Studler found that the British had left their usual good manners home. They were getting tough, calling for a showdown on the caliber and ammunition issue. When Studler refused, the foreign offices of both countries became involved, because the caliber quarrel deeply affected both armies. When British politicians pressed for action, Studler found he had run out of maneuvering room. The Pentagon ordered him to conduct joint caliber studies with the British. In compliance, Colonel Studler scheduled caliber tests in two phases—first at Aberdeen, then at Fort Benning.

Since the dispute was over caliber, the Americans did not

seriously expect the British to arrive with a firing rifle. In fact, for the meeting with the British at the Aberdeen Proving Ground on February 14, 1950, Harvey was told he would probably not have to fire a shot from his T25; just parade it up and down, then catch the evening train back to the armory. In truth, the T25 was far too underdeveloped to be ready for major competitive testing.

When the American team arrived, they were given a Saint Valentine's Day surprise. The now polite-but-firm British did arrive at Aberdeen with a firing rifle—with, in fact, two firing rifles, for along with their own EM2, they also brought the Belgian Fusil Automatique Leger (FAL) rifle, both chambered for the .280. Furthermore, they arrived with A. W. Duneclift, one of the team that developed the .280 ammunition, and with S. Kenneth Janson, the man who designed the EM2 rifle for the .280 cartridge, plus a squad of British infantrymen trained to fire and maintain the rifles. The Harvey T25 was soon in a fight for its life.

Both the EM2 and the FAL were based on the Sturmgewehr MP44. The FAL was an eight-and-a-half-pound, twenty-shot, semi-automatic/automatic selective-fire rifle. Like the German MP44, it was designed to be a low-cost weapon, made from high-grade stampings on standard production tools.

The extremely different American and British views on the ideal military rifle became quickly apparent. The Americans didn't like the .280 cartridge. The range was too short and the cartridge too weak to handle special-purpose ammunition like tracer, incendiary, and armor-piercing projectiles. The British countered by saying that their ammunition wasn't intended for such unnecessary seven-hundred-yard distances. They insisted that the new American T65 cartridge was too strong for an automatic rifle and excessively strong for modern battlefield conditions. In sum, the British were willing to make reasonable caliber concessions to get an effective automatic rifle, while the Americans didn't want an automatic rifle at the price of the T65. Someone was wrong, but neither side yielded. The caliber controversy had reached a philosophic standoff.

Grueling tests of the three rifles were scheduled for seven months later, in September 1950. In June, the United States abruptly found itself at war with North Korea and equipped U.S. troops with its World War II M1. Even though Colonel Studler was to claim that the semiautomatic M1 was performing admirably in Korea, Dr. Ezell notes that the M1s were not adequate "against a numerically superior enemy equipped with large numbers of automatic weapons."[14]

With the shooting in Asia as a backdrop, the great rifle showdown under the sponsorship of the Army Field Forces Board Number 3 was held at Fort Benning, Georgia, on August 31, 1950. Harvey's weapon, with its already demonstrated great strength and superior target accuracy, could be expected to perform well on some tests, but bad luck—and perhaps some malice—continued to dog the T25. The T65 ammunition proved defective and adversely affected the Harvey's performance. The armory failed to properly "Parkerize" some of the T25 operating components with an external rust-resistant finish, which caused excessive friction in the breech mechanism. With bad ammunition and bad metallurgy, the T25 did not perform well. Even though Harvey managed to get some "Parkerized" parts during the final tests—which enabled the T25 to outperform the European weapons in some tests—the damage had been done.

The physical appearance of the British EM2 bothered the conventional members of the Rifle Board. Like John Garand's T31 automatic rifle, the ammunition clip was placed behind the trigger, the stock was a metal shaft with a metal shoulder butt, and the whole effect bore little resemblance to traditional rifle contours. But its poor performance during the Arctic tests—especially significant in a war against Russia—seems to have finished it.

The Belgian FAL failed to perform as expected by its proponents. In fact, the results at Aberdeen and later at Benning were disappointing for all three weapons. Actually, the test was premature, for none of the three rifles was developed enough to be considered seriously for NATO standardization.

The board recommended that the British EM2 be dropped from

future trials, that the T25 be given a rematch, but only after several modifications were made, and that the FAL—which the board liked the most, but without the .280 cartridge—be refitted to fire the American T65 .30-caliber cartridge.

The British may not have convinced the Americans to change caliber, but they did have the cold comfort of seeing Studler's T25 also perform poorly. And they were vindicated on another point: just like everyone else—German, Russian, Belgian, British—Studler had not been able to develop an automatic rifle to fire a full-charge, .30-caliber cartridge.

The Ordnance Department's stubborn adherence to the .30-caliber charge caused some very serious international mischief. When the British returned home, they announced that the British army was standardizing on the EM2 and the .280 cartridge. This caused a great flap in Parliament between those who felt Britain could not go it alone on such a matter, outside NATO, and those who wanted to return to the glory days of British independence. The debate grew so passionate, the British government was nearly toppled, and the NATO proponents won the day. As a result, a political conference was arranged by Canada in Washington, where the Americans clearly snubbed the British. During the conference, the American technical spokesman was Colonel Rene Studler, who recited the old arguments—the cost of dropping .30-caliber tooling, the inadequate stopping power of the .280 caliber, the need for armor-piercing power, the danger of change during the Korean War. The British argued for the .280 to no avail and felt they had been Studlered again.[15] No one's mind had budged a millimeter, and, in the end, it was money that won the argument. On the diplomatic level, NATO was forced to accept the American .30-caliber cartridge as standard—not because it was superior, but because the Europeans were dependent upon the billions of dollars the United States was sending to Europe as part of the Marshall Plan to help restore war-ravaged economies—and the Europeans were reluctant to seem ungrateful.

When the British and Belgian weapons were rechambered for the American—now NATO—.30-caliber cartridge, they, too, proved to be too light to control it on automatic fire. As a result, NATO had a single caliber but no automatic rifle to confront the revolutionary Russian AK47. U.S. Ordnance had painted the Europeans into the same .30-caliber corner.

In September of 1951, for the army in Korea, the armory ordered more M1s—nearly a million and a half. This was no time to consider changing to another rifle, Ordnance said.

Meanwhile, the Europeans returned home believing that the United States, in exchange for European adoption of the .30-caliber cartridge, had made a commitment to adopt the FAL as the standard American infantry rifle. Instead, the Americans resumed testing their own rifle.

I n spite of everything, the Harvey T25 was finished. Colonel Studler had tried for six years to make Production accept it, to make the infantry endorse it, to make it flawless, and on all three fronts he failed. Yet there were some who believed that given adequate development time and money—neither of which he ever had—Harvey could have made a lightweight automatic .30-caliber weapon out of his troubled rifle. But recriminations came too late. The army quietly buried the Harvey T25 by the traditional committee method. The rifle was exposed to tests it wasn't ready for and joined other rifles in the Ordnance museum.

"Observers of the rifle development scene have concluded," comments Dr. Ezell, ". . . that extensive competition can be one of the worst enemies of a developmental rifle."[16]

I n March 1952, while the Korean War moved back and forth over the 38th parallel, and efforts by North Korea and the UN in Panmunjom to negotiate a cease-fire repeatedly failed, there appeared a new study challenging the appropriateness of the .30-caliber military cartridge. From the point of view of the .30-caliber proponents, the study stated absolutely the wrong thing at absolutely the wrong time.

Entitled *An Effectiveness Study of the Infantry Rifle,* the study was conducted by Donald L. Hall, a civilian engineer attached to the

Ballistics Research Laboratories at the Aberdeen Proving Ground. Hall had based his research on ballistics studies he had previously conducted at Aberdeen, plus current information from various sources—from the British and Belgian caliber studies, from the Korean War commentary of General S. L. A. Marshall, and from other studies derived from that conflict.[17]

The Hall report asserted:

- On the typical battlefield, to achieve the most hits, the maximum range for most rifle fire is only 500 yards. In fact, the optimum is only 120 yards. Ranges beyond that, obviously, are superfluous.
- While the .30-caliber charge is more effective at killing at longer range, the .22-caliber charge is more effective at killing in the shorter range. To prove it, Hall presented the precise kind of evidence that the Pig Board had sought in 1928. Among other studies, he had tables of wound ballistics from Korea.
- A .22-caliber projectile has a higher striking force than a .30-caliber projectile. Therefore, it will inflict a more severe wound.
- The caliber that is most effective under 500 yards should be issued in preference to the caliber that is most effective over 500 yards.

The British could point to this American report as further proof that the .280 EM2 or the FN FAL should supersede the .30-caliber T25. The case against .30 caliber could not have been more bluntly stated: according to Hall's report, all of the .30-caliber's virtues were actually flaws. The .30 caliber was too strong, its range too great, its killing power not great enough. Conversely, a .22 caliber offers the right strength, the right range, the greatest number of hits, and the best killing power.

These conclusions could not have been more damaging to the official American .30-caliber position, nor could they have come at a worse time. At that moment, the small/large caliber quarrel was the centermost explosive issue in the NATO alliance, and this impressive new evidence substantiated much of what the British and the Belgians were saying about rifle caliber against American contentions. Most embarrassingly, the Hall study came from one of the army's most respected research centers.

Colonel Studler didn't accept any part of these findings. He still went on trying to push the American .30-caliber round through NATO—the most difficult battle Studler had ever fought and one of his last acts before retirement. Strangely, the Hall study had been sponsored by Colonel Studler himself, who had provided the two hundred .22-caliber cartridges Hall had used in the ballistics test.[18]

But matters didn't rest there. In the same month, March 1952, that the Hall study appeared, the gravel-belly philosophy was firmly reasserted in front of the whole military world—including, presumably, NATO proponents of the .28-caliber FAL rifle—when General Lawton Collins, army chief of staff, declared in the *American Rifleman*:

"My personal view is that we need a lightweight rifle that can be used for semiautomatic fire, or, when required, full automatic fire. I am personally quite skeptical about making all weapons fully automatic. Automatic shoulder weapons waste too much ammunition . . . you can get more hits with a semiautomatic rifle than with a full automatic. I am confident that the automatic wastes ammunition. And it's difficult enough to get ammunition to the front without wasting it."[19]

Only three months later, in June 1952, this enduring gravel-belly concept received another blow—following the Marshall studies, the British studies, and the Hall report—when the Operations Research Office at Johns Hopkins University in Chevy Chase, Maryland, issued the Hitchman report. This proved to be the most devastating proof ever assembled of the wrongness of the gravel-belly rifle philosophy. Written by Norman Hitchman, a civilian researcher with the ORO, this stunning document was entitled: *ORO-T-160: Operations Requirements for an Infantry Hand Weapon.*[20]

When Congress created the air force as a separate military service, the air force was beset with so many technical problems that it set up a think tank in California that it named the RAND Corporation (an acronym for R and D, research and development). The Pentagon realized it needed help as well in establishing scientific methodologies for producing new weapons, particularly for nuclear warfare and, toward that end, set up the Operations Research Office (ORO) in Baltimore.

While the ORO was sponsored by the U.S. Army, civilians were actually in control and managed to evade many of the smothering effects of the military pecking order. When the ORO set out to study the ideal attributes of the rifle, it was beyond the reach of the Ordnance Department's committee system. The ORO had come at the subject of wound ballistics from the opposite end of the rifle. It originally set out to help design infantry body armor. That led to questions about wounds, which led to questions about the weapons that caused wounds, which led to questions about the nature and function of the assault rifle.

For the eleven years of its existence, the ORO's outspoken research was a stone in the army's shoe, and never more so than with the Hitchman report, which concluded that the army was looking for the wrong rifle. ORO asserted that the rifle procurement procedure was all wrong. Under the existing army system, the Infantry Board decided on the characteristics it wanted in an assault rifle and the armory R&D produced the weapon. The infantry, however, was using battlefield experience from World War II, which was obsolete, and in consequence was asking R&D to make an obsolete rifle. To correct the situation, the ORO set out to develop a science of weapons design for the infantry.

The Hitchman report reached many of the same conclusions as Donald Hall's report had, confirming that the most cherished ideals of the gravel-belly infantryman were patently, flatly, demonstrably false. Moreover, the report contained overwhelming proof from an irrefutable source: the army's own files on some three million casualties from World War II. ORO also had General Marshall's verbatim interviews with GIs on the battlefields of World War II and the Korean War, plus masses of other material.

The Hitchman report concluded:

- The rifle was most frequently effective at less than three hundred yards.
- Most infantry kills were done by rifle at ranges under one hundred yards.
- Marksmanship with a rifle is satisfactory only up to one hundred yards. Beyond that, it tails off to a low of three hundred yards.
- Hits could be significantly increased by replacing slow, aimed fire with a hand weapon using the pattern dispersion principle at ranges up to three hundred yards, i.e., an automatic weapon spraying shots. More firepower; less aiming.
- The very expensive, finished weapon the American armory was turning out was overengineered and could be made cheaper without significant loss in hit effectiveness.
- Smaller calibers can do as much wounding as the .30 can—and do it with significant logistical and overall military gains over the .30 caliber.
- The smaller caliber with low recoil could improve dispersion control and hit probability over the higher recoil of the .30 caliber.
- Rifles like the T20 and T25 were valueless on separated man-sized targets.
- The army in Korea, armed with the M1 semiautomatic rifle, was being outgunned by North Koreans armed with automatic weapons.
- All future wars would be characterized by close combat; long-range firing would be useless.
- Therefore, the American infantryman needed to be armed with maximum firepower for close-range fighting, i.e., a low-caliber, high-volume automatic rifle.

The long-standing fixed idea of the Ordnance Department had never been more emphatically refuted. Hitchman said flatly that what the army believed was wrong, not borne out by battlefield experience. He called on the army to drop the .30-caliber cartridge and the whole gravel-belly philosophy behind it. He even called on the army to prove his assertions for itself by setting up tests comparing the two weapons.

The opposition to the gravel-belly was mounting. Starting with General S. L. A. Marshall's study of men in battle from World War II, an increasing volume of studies like Norman Hitchman's and Donald Hall's and the British Beeching report, drawing on irrefutable statistical studies from battlefield and laboratory, were hammering home the same point: smaller-caliber bullets were more effective than the .30-caliber bullets.

Meanwhile, London was still waiting for Washington to specify the FN FAL as the official NATO rifle for the United States, and U.S. Ordnance was still getting ready to test it—against the old Garand T20, the modified M1 designed for automatic fire by John Garand himself in 1945, during the last months of World War II. The T20 had one supreme virtue: production liked it because it could be made on the M1 tooling. This, in fact, was the weapon armory production people had wanted all along.

Garand's T20 was renamed the T44.

CHAPTER 33

THE M14 AND CONTROVERSY

I n spite of a growing pile of impressive low-caliber ballistics
research, thinking inside the armory had not changed. Thirty
caliber was still king. Production still ran the armory. R&D was still
kept half-starved in a back room. The infantry testing boards continued to set what Ordnance R&D felt were unrealistic test sched-
ules and demanding impossible weapons designs. After seven years
of dissension, with the T25 buried and the T20 exhumed as the
T44, Armory Production felt it had won and Colonel Rene Studler
had lost.

In March 1953, Lieutenant Colonel Miles B. Chatfield, chief of
the armory's Research and Development Division, went to a meeting at the Pentagon, where he was told that the T44 was up for
retest by the Army Field Forces Board Number 3 against the FN
FAL on July 1, 1953. Both would then go to Arctic trials in October. The time schedule was unrealistic. The T44 was just not
ready—and could not be made ready—to face the FN FAL. The armory R&D looked at the list of changes that had been recommended by the previous tests, made as many as they could, and sent the
inadequately developed weapon off to Fort Benning.

Strangely, after refusing to allocate the necessary preparation
time for the T20/T44, the Infantry Board was offended by the unprepared state of the weapon it received. At moments like this,
commentators look for shadowy figures behind and in between the

committee meetings. Had some U.S. ranker with connections in NATO ordered that the FN FAL be selected? Demanding that T20/T44 be submitted before it was prepared was a sure way to kill it, leaving the field to the FAL.

The selection of a national rifle is an act of great significance. To the Belgians, the NATO choice of the FAL rifle meant a great technological victory, international prestige, and wealth. To the British, American acceptance of the FAL was the payback for the NATO acceptance of the American caliber. But to many in the Pentagon and in the armory, accepting the FAL rifle would have been a defeat and a loss of face, a blow against national prestige. Yet, realistically, even the most dedicated .30-caliber man had to admit that the T44 would probably be no match for the FAL at the Fort Benning trials. In fact, by July 20, 1953, *Newsweek* was predicting that the FN FAL would be the new American assault rifle, thereby fulfilling what Belgium and England believed to be their understanding with Washington.[1] When the results of the test came out in August, no one was surprised—least of all the armory R&D. The Infantry Board recommended that the FN FAL be adopted as a limited procurement item and the T20/T44 be dropped. For the second time, John Garand's automatic rifle seemed dead.

A few weeks later, on August 31, 1953, Colonel Rene Studler retired as chief of the Small Arms Research and Development Division. Like General Ripley and his Springfield muzzleloader, General Benét and his Springfield breechloader, and General Flagler and his Krag-Jorgensen, Colonel Rene Studler took the Harvey T25 into retirement with him. After a brilliant early career, his latter years were marred by the quarrels within the walls. As a legacy, he left a caliber few people wanted and a rifle no one wanted. He was replaced by his subordinate and protégé, Dr. Fred H. Carten, a former major in the Ordnance Corps, a resolute champion of the .30-caliber cartridge, and a man from the production side who would back the Garand T20/T44 to the bitter end.[2]

With little warning, with the concurrence of the army chief of staff himself, the Pentagon decided that the T44 should be sent to the Arctic as a control during the cold weather tests of the FN FAL. It would be T44's last official appearance before being put into a glass case in the armory's museum. Lieutenant Colonel Rayle of the armory knew that the FAL had not been fully tested under Arctic conditions, and he wondered if there was an outside chance something might happen to it in the Alaska cold testing. If the FAL failed, and if the Garand T44 survived, perhaps he could make a case for further development of the T44.[3] Everyone believed it was a lost cause—that the T44 was a "dead duck" and the FAL was the next U.S. rifle.

Armory R&D personnel knew that they were held in low esteem by the Congress and the Pentagon, that regard for their "research and development capabilities had already sunk to an all-time low."[4] Perhaps some of their tattered prestige could be rescued by a good showing of the T44. It was certainly one R&D project that even the intractable Production Department could get behind, for as a makeover of the old M1, produced on existing tooling, this was their favored weapon.

Colonel Rayle talked with the Springfield engineers, then went to see the armory commandant, Colonel W. J. Crowe, to propose a serious effort to ready the T44 for the Arctic tests. Crowe approved of the idea and sent Rayle to see the chief of ordnance, General E. L. Ford. Ford, approving, sent Rayle upstairs, and ultimately the army chief of staff himself, General Matthew B. Ridgway, approved the T44 Arctic testing.

The armory galvanized itself. The engineering staff went over the magazine design time and again, polished and lubricated each magazine, worked on the springs that might react to the cold, developed a winter trigger just for Arctic mittens, reinforced the gunstock with steel, put a pressure relief valve on the gas system, and did a number of other things that would winterize their last best hope. A new enthusiasm seemed to infuse the armory's shops and corridors.[5] Still flawed in many ways and still not fully developed, the spruced-up T20/T44 was packed off to Alaska. The only way it could survive would be if it passed the cold tests and if the FAL failed them—an outcome that seemed the longest of long shots.

The improbable happened. Despite the best efforts of FN engineer Ernest Vervier, the FN FAL did turn in a poor Arctic performance. The Alaska test team didn't fall in love with the T44, but in Arctic temperatures, it had proved more dependable than the FAL. Perhaps that was enough to give it a new lease on life.

Rayle kept trying. Earle Harvey, the developer of the defunct T25 and head of the Rifle and Hand Arms Section, said that due to the shortage of engineers and the heavy workload, R&D needed two years to debug and fully develop the T44. The same was true in the Model Shop. But Rayle didn't have two years. So he went outside the armory to the retired John Garand. Matthewson Tool Company, a specialist in prototype small arms, hired Garand and put him to work once more on his own weapon.

Another unexpected decision complicated the process: Washington had decided to Americanize the FN FAL—that is, to convert it from the metric system to the American system—and to give this very challenging assignment to the already understaffed armory.

The armory's future seemed more precarious than ever. Its engineers were now charged with developing both the T20/T44 and the Americanized FN FAL. If armory personnel did their best for the FAL, it might oust their own favorite, the T44. Yet if they failed to do their best for both weapons, their reputation, already low, would be ruined.

The Arctic tests seemed to have caused a change of heart in the Pentagon. For now, suddenly, in June 1954, General Ridgway gave General Medaris, chief of Ordnance's Industrial Division, permission to make five hundred T44s and five hundred FAL rifles.[6]

In Asia, during the previous month of May, an ominous event occurred that cast a long shadow over the armory's quest for an automatic rifle. On May 7, 1954, in Dien Bien Phu, Vietnam, after eight years of relentless, harassing, unforgiving attack, Viet Minh forces surrounded the French and defeated them. France was through. Perceiving Vietnam as part of the international Communist conspiracy to take over the world, the United States began providing military support to the South Vietnamese. Army Ordnance men were disturbed. If the United States was drawn into a shooting war against the Viet Minh, the army still had no automatic weapon to use against Ho Chi Minh's AK47 and SKS. This situation added a sense of real urgency to the tests between the FAL and the T44.

The armory decided to make the necessary five hundred Garand T44s on armory tooling, while, at the same time, it issued a contract to Harrington & Richardson, Inc., to make the five hundred FALs. Harrington & Richardson immediately contacted the retired Ivan Swidlo, former chief of the Industrial Division of the Springfield Armory, a longtime opponent of the Harvey T25 rifle and a proponent of the T20/T44. He agreed to come out of retirement to direct the FAL production program.

The activity was furious. To translate the FN drawings into English and into English dimensions, the armory turned to French-speaking engineers in Canadian military ordnance.[7] Earle Harvey must have wondered what would have become of his T25 rifle if it had ever received this kind of attention.

The next Arctic test was scheduled for December 1953 in Fort Greeley, Alaska. For that test, the armory now shipped six reworked Garand T44s, six Americanized FALs, and six of the original Belgian FALs. Five of each were also shipped to Fort Benning for continued tests there.

Although the testing board noted significant improvements in both weapons, none of the models scored high in Alaska. Greeley called for more reworking of the two models. Then came the most heartening news of all to the armory—the Fort Benning testing board was beginning to favor the T44 over the FAL. Colonel Rayle, it seemed, had managed to turn things around.

The focus was now on the trials at Fort Benning. There, during 1954, dust, sand, and mud tests almost did in the FAL—its parts were deemed to be machined too close, too sensitive to fouling. The T44 was judged much superior. Tests were suspended while the armory reworked the FAL.

Armory personnel visited the British National Armory at Enfield Lock to confer with British engineers who had had the same sand test problems in the Sudan. They went on to confer with FN at Liège, Belgium, on ways to make the FAL perform better.

In September 1955, with six new rifles of each type, the Infantry Board members at Fort Benning resumed their tests. In this race, the T44 came in first, FN FAL second, and the Americanized FAL third, followed by the old semiautomatic M1, entered as a control. In successive tests over the combat course, the T44 performed significantly better. Then, due to poor performance of the Belgian FAL, tests were suspended once more with the Infantry Board now definitely leaning toward the T44. Everything awaited the arrival of the rest of the five hundred production models.

There was considerable political agitation at this point. Britain, Canada, and other Commonwealth nations, along with Belgium, West Germany, and several other countries, had all designated the FAL as their national rifle to fire the American .30-caliber round. These NATO nations were putting pressure on the United States to live up to its tacit agreement to adopt the FAL. They were quite disturbed with the events at Fort Benning.

The mounting international political pressure affected the trials. The field tests set for September at Aberdeen and the marine base at Quantico were put off until December. The official reason given: the FAL production models were breaking their firing pins. The board announced it would not conduct full-blown field tests after all. The tests it did perform produced a near dead heat between the two weapons. The board, declaring either weapon suitable, refused to choose between them. After all the effort, the reworkings, the trips between the United States and Europe, the great number of hours, the vast number of dollars, there was no winner. The Infantry Board had passed the problem to the Pentagon, which was feeling great pressure from European allies, who pointed out that the Belgian FAL had been adopted by England, Canada, Belgium, and several other nations. The Pentagon delayed making a decision. A year went by.[8] Finally, the issue came to rest on the desk of the chief of staff, General Matthew B. Ridgway. He noted that the deciding factor was not political or technical but rather economic: the T44 could be made on M1 tooling, while the FAL could not. The difference represented millions of dollars. He therefore designated the T44 the new official rifle of the U.S. Army. The production team at the Springfield Armory had won the argument with a weapon that had literally come back from the dead twice. After twelve years of fighting off all threats, production finally received approval for the rifle it could have had in 1945, when John Garand had first modified it.

On February 12, 1957, after twenty years of development and the expenditure of well over $100 million, the Ordnance Corps presented its new automatic rifle—the M14—to the military, the press, and the public at the Aberdeen Proving Ground with fanfare and charts and slides and logic. Platform presentations included a rigorous selling of the "full charge" American .30-caliber bullet. Frowns began to appear.

First of all, critics quickly pointed out, the new M14 sacrificed too much to meet new field demands for a truly lightweight weapon.

Retired Marine General Vernon E. Megee, "a rifleman's rifleman," dismissed the new weapon with one sentence. "They labored mightily and brought forth a mouse." John Garand worried about the new rifle in combat. He condemned the White gas system in the M14 as "bunk. I tested it and it doesn't work the way they claim." The White system had been invented in 1921 and rejected by the army in 1930.[9]

Other observers noted the ferocious kick of the weapon when on automatic fire. It was virtually uncontrollable and the aim was wildly inaccurate. Several marksmen on the line got nosebleeds from the kicking weapon, and stories circulated that the new M14 had already broken noses. The only way to control the M14 was to set it on semiautomatic. "This is nothing more than the M1 Garand," said the editor of *Army Times,* "with a semi-automatic position and an uncontrollable fully automatic position."

Since only two men in each squad would receive a selective-fire, fully automatic M14, for all practical purposes, the M14 was basically a semiautomatic weapon.[10] Unless another Garand miracle happened, this would be the weapon U.S. troops would take to Vietnam—against the Soviet Kalashnikov AK47. Because so many highly placed Washington officials had "their names on the M14 fiasco,"[11] which was ultimately to cost $500 million,[12] Ordnance felt that, despite the criticism, there was little choice other than to go ahead with the introduction of the new weapon.

On May 1, 1957, Secretary of the Army Wilbur M. Bruckner made it official: the reworked Garand—the original M1, metamorphosed into the T20, then the T44—was now the M14, the official U.S. Army automatic .30-caliber rifle. Facing the armory now was the task of manufacturing the rifle many army men didn't want. But just as manufacturing was about to get under way, unexpectedly a revolutionary new automatic rifle appeared. For the proponents of the M14, the timing could not have been worse, nor could the source. For the new rifle came from outside the armory.

PART VII

CHAPTER 34

THE M14
VERSUS THE AR-15

In 1953, Richard S. Boutelle, president of Fairchild Engine and Airplane Corporation, Hagerstown, Maryland, invited to his office George Sullivan, an aeronautical engineer, patent attorney, and highly successful salesman with connections in Lockheed Aircraft Corporation. Sullivan had an idea for a new type of rifle and Boutelle wanted to discuss it.

Sullivan, with characteristic enthusiasm, talked of the wealth of new space-age materials on the market that were much lighter and tougher than some of the older materials—including lightweight metal alloys, nonferrous metals, expandable plastics, and fiberglass. With such materials, Sullivan believed he could create a major new type of space-age firearm, fully automatic, with a streamlined in-line profile made primarily of fiberglass and aluminum, extremely lightweight—perhaps seven pounds—and tough, impervious to the weather, with a carrying handle that would also be the gunsight and scope mount. Such a shoulder arm, he felt, could revolutionize the military firearms market.

Boutelle was very interested for two reasons. He was looking for ways to diversify his corporation's aircraft activities and, second, he was a self-styled gun nut—indeed, he often staged target-practice events for friends and fellow gun enthusiasts on his farm in Hagerstown, near his offices. Boutelle decided to pursue the idea.

On October 1, 1954, Boutelle established a Fairchild Engine and Airplane Corporation subsidiary, ArmaLite Division, in Costa Mesa, California. George Sullivan was chosen president.[1] Under the company's provisions, ArmaLite would design, build, and test new weapons, with manufacturing to be done by outside firms under license from ArmaLite. With such a structure, Fairchild planned to avoid the prohibitive cost of establishing its own arms production facility.

Sullivan brought into the company his brother-in-law, Charles Dorchester, an experienced plastics engineer, as plant manager and research assistant. For chief engineer of the firm, Sullivan chose Eugene Stoner, an ex-marine and a technician with U.S. Army Ordnance. Many today consider him the most important weapons designer since John Browning.[2] Stoner's design concepts were to change military small arms ordnance permanently.

The firm soon produced a series of rifle designs, including a sporting arm that could also be militarized as a sniper rifle, a commercial-type .308-caliber rifle, a commercial-type shotgun, and an AR-5 air force survival rifle. While the sale of AR-5 never materialized, the weapon made a great impression on the air force, and ArmaLite's reputation in the military market grew significantly.

ArmaLite's next weapon, the AR-10, embodied the original rifle concept that Sullivan had described to Richard Boutelle and was utterly without precedent in the military world. Its sleek appearance had immediate appeal to weapons fanciers, and its seven pounds of aluminum alloy and fiberglass imparted a sense of incredible lightness. One feature in particular drew the attention of many military men: it was designed to fire automatically the army's .30-caliber NATO cartridge from a twenty-round clip. Sullivan took his new product on the road, but his timing could not have been worse. It was 1954, and the armory at Springfield was in the midst of weapons trials at Fort Benning, Georgia, which pitted the T44 against the Belgian FAL. The armory's weapon, reputation, and future were all at risk.

Sullivan therefore should not have been too surprised by the reception he received at Springfield Armory. He reported later in a magazine interview that he was told, "We'll send you home in one day with your parts in a basket."[3]

On the firing range, he observed a test staff member write on his report form: "This is the best lightweight automatic rifle ever tested in the Springfield Armory." Sullivan reported that a few minutes later, the man's supervisor erased every word.

The following year, in December of 1955, Sullivan presented his AR-10 to the Infantry Board in Fort Benning, Georgia. With the T44 now leading the FAL in the field trials there, American Ordnance men were more affable, and George Sullivan was accorded a much warmer reception. After his presentation, the board urged Ordnance R&D to immediately investigate the AR-10 as a military rifle. By late spring of 1956, he had made a number of sales calls on the military with it. Commanding General Willard G. Wyman and his staff at the Continental Army Command (CONARC) shared the enthusiasm of the Infantry Board and endorsed its recommendation. Sullivan now faced the possibility of having the AR-10 tested against the American T44 and the Belgian FAL (the T48), which were still in the throes of the Fort Benning trials.

But, to be considered, the AR-10 needed much more development. ArmaLite now faced the choice of either gracefully withdrawing its AR-10 or trying to perfect it at high speed and high investment. Even then, it might be too late to qualify. The temptation to take the risk was enormous and the ArmaLite board voted yes.

Within months—in the fall of 1956—ArmaLite delivered the AR-10A to the Springfield Armory. Armory research people put it through some of the tests used on the T44 and the T48. As a prototype, the rifle made a good impression, but it developed a number of problems, including failure of the muzzle brake/flash suppressor, extractor breakage, sear failure, and failure to eject. The AR-10, said the armory, needed more development.

Unable to get the army to slow its rifle selection plans, ArmaLite rushed back to its test labs and, by January 1957, less than three months later, was back in Springfield with a modified AR-10 that eliminated many of the original problems. There were more tests, more impressive performances, but also more failures. It was clear that with some more reworking, the AR-10 could become a contender against the T44 and the T48, but there was not enough time. General Ridgway had made his decision, and the next month, February 1957, the Pentagon introduced the new official army rifle— the T44 (now the M14).

ArmaLite had gambled and lost. The company had spent a fortune to come in third in a three-gun race. Because of the time constraints, Sullivan could say the AR-10 was never seriously in contention. Yet Ordnance was so impressed, it offered ArmaLite direct financial support to help fully develop the AR-10. One hitch: the army wanted "ultimate proprietary rights to the finished weapon." ArmaLite would not be allowed to retain even foreign marketing rights. Since ArmaLite was sure there was a vast international market for their weapon, the company turned down Ordnance's offer.

Richard Boutelle, president of Fairchild, the parent company of ArmaLite, looked for another market for his weapon. To showcase it, he threw one of his target-practice events on his farm in Hagerstown and invited members of the international arms community. Sam Cummings, president of Interarms, a leading arms sales firm, picked up the AR-10, fired it, and fell in love with it. "This," said Cummings, "is the most advanced weapon of its kind I have ever seen."[4] He obtained sales rights to it for South America, all of Africa south of the Sahara, plus Norway, Sweden, and Finland. Sidem, another international arms firm, was given exclusive sales rights to Western Europe and North Africa. And Cooper-Macdonald, Inc., an arms agency from Baltimore, took Southeast Asia. Fairchild kept the U.S. market for itself. Worldwide manufacturing rights of the AR-10 went to Artillerie-Inrichtingen of Zaandam, near Amsterdam.

The AR-10 had made a lingering impression on many military men, and in December 1957, General Willard G. Wyman visited ArmaLite's chief of design, Eugene Stoner, in his laboratory in Costa Mesa, California.

Ten months had passed since the Ordnance Department had

presented its new M14 rifle, and the general was not at all pleased with it. If there was one lesson that General Wyman had learned from the Korean War, it was that more than ever, the United States urgently needed a new automatic assault rifle. And the M14 was not the weapon. Field commanders described what was needed: a weapon of short range and split-second rapid fire that could pin down obscure, fleeting targets. In short, an American AK47. Confronted by Ordnance's intransigence, he made the fateful decision to go outside the Ordnance Corps to obtain what he wanted. This was a clear index of the armory's low standing. By going outside the armory channels, General Wyman was going to raise a storm in Springfield.

The general, having been very impressed with the AR-10 and with Eugene Stoner, considered him an ideal choice to design a rifle that would take advantage of the lethal payoff of the small bullet.

Stoner was just as displeased as the general with the .30-caliber NATO cartridge he had designed the AR-10 around.[5] He said it was too strong for automatic fire. It bucked like a goat and was uncontrollable. This was exactly the same conclusion reached by the Germans, the Russians, the British, the Belgians, Earle Harvey, the Field Forces Board Number 3 in Fort Benning, the Hall study, the Hitchman report, General S. L. A. Marshall, and a growing list of other anti-M14 critics.

Stoner said that the Russian Kalashnikov AK47 .30-caliber cartridge, which carried a lesser charge, was a better choice than the American cartridge, but that .22 caliber was better than either.

The CONARC specifications that General Wyman gave Stoner were specific: full and automatic fire, twenty-shot magazine, loaded weight six pounds. The bullet had to penetrate both sides of a standard army helmet and .135-inch steel plate at 547 yards—which was beyond the distance set by Hitchman and other studies and hence a compromise with traditionalists.[6] Stoner went back to his design board.

Significantly, a .22-caliber cartridge with the military characteristics Stoner needed didn't exist, so Stoner designed his own .223

caliber, basing it in large part on a commercial .222-caliber cartridge marketed by Remington Arms Company and ordered a customized lot of ammunition. Around it, he designed his new rifle: the AR-15.

Since most military men were delighted with the space-age appearance of the AR-10, ArmaLite wisely retained the same appearance in the AR-15 and the same aluminum alloys and plastics. When Eugene Stoner delivered ten test models of the AR-15 to General Wyman, the rifle featured a twenty-five-cartridge clip and weighed a remarkably light 6.13 pounds.

Stoner himself demonstrated the rifle for General Wyman, who was so impressed he placed an order on the spot for ten more to be used at an Infantry Board trial on May 6, 1958. Stoner personally delivered the ten new rifles to Fort Benning on March 31, with one hundred rounds of ammunition. Benning kept four, three were sent to other stations for tests, and three were sent to Fort Greeley in Alaska for Arctic tests.

Since there were no instruction manuals for the AR-15 yet, Stoner remained during the Fort Benning tests to conduct instruction classes on the new weapon. Everyone agreed that it was essential for Stoner to attend the Arctic tests in Fort Greeley when they became scheduled.

When the Ordnance representatives arrived at the Infantry Rifle Board tests at Fort Benning, Georgia, they were collectively in an angry state of mind. Criticism of their new M14 rifle was swarming from every quarter. The last thing they wanted was to be confronted with a remarkable new fully automatic assault rifle from outside the armory—especially one with advance billing as the deadliest and most reliable small arms weapon ever devised, greater than the great Russian AK47. To gore the bull even more, it was only .22 caliber, smaller than the British .28 caliber, which they had already rejected.

When they arrived at Fort Benning, they had their first look at the new AR-15 and beside it stood the designer. The AR-15s were tested against newly minted and carefully prepared M14s from Springfield Armory. "It was as rugged a test condition as I have ever seen," Stoner recalled, with simulated battle conditions, tightly strung barbed wire, and rough obstacles.[7] During the rifle trials, Stoner said, the uniforms on the troops were entirely shredded between sunup and sundown, and boots were destroyed in just a few days.

The results were stunning and were soon known throughout the Pentagon and especially at the Springfield Armory. In a one-on-one showdown under simulated battle conditions, the upstart still-unfinished AR-15 outperformed the M14. On the firing line, the AR-15 in three clean starts fired 3,578 semiautomatic shots. Over-all malfunction rate was 6.1 per 1,000 rounds. The handpicked M14 fired 2,337 rounds. Overall malfunction rate was 16 per 1,000 rounds—close to three times more malfunctions for a military rifle presumably ready for combat than for a still-developmental rifle.[8] The Infantry Board suggested that the AR-15, when fully developed, might be a suitable replacement for the M14.[9]

The Infantry Board was used to dealing with outside suppliers who were completely familiar with the inner working of the military and were staffed for complete research and development. But without a large engineering staff to back him up, and without a full-scale research and testing facility, Stoner turned the rifle over to the Ordnance people to let them research it, a move that turned out to be a mistake.

Everyone—civilian and military alike—in the Ordnance Corps who attended the debut of the Stoner rifle felt immediately threatened by this new weapon. The AR-15 was not a gravel-belly's or a technician's weapon. Coming from outside the Ordnance Corps, the weapon had a ridiculously small caliber—.22. Ordnance men called it a popgun—a Mattel toy. But the AR-15 fired six hundred rounds a minute and could be mass-produced from stamped parts and plastic at a fraction of the cost of an M14.

Back at Springfield, Dr. Fred Carten was confronted with a major dilemma. Since the Springfield Armory was in the advanced stages of planning for mass production of the M14, the army as yet was without an inventory of its new rifle, with first production at least two years away—1960. If a sudden crisis occurred in the world, there would be no M14s for U.S. military forces. The armory would have to go back to producing the old M1, like the Crozier scenario from World War I. However, if, while Springfield Armory went ahead with the enormous cost of tooling up for the production of the M14, the Congress learned that the Infantry Board had recommended a new rifle to replace it, there were those in Congress who could and would stop everything. Worst of all, the AR-15 was a .22-caliber rifle. If it became the standard army rifle, it would be the only rifle in NATO not .30 caliber—the caliber that the United States had literally rammed down the throats of other NATO members in 1953. The choice of either going ahead with production of the M14 or delaying for possibly another year while the AR-15 was developed was probably one of the most difficult decisions any U.S. Ordnance head had ever faced.

To turn around at this late date, declare the M14 not the rifle the infantry needed, and to plunge wholeheartedly into the development of the .22 rifle must have seemed inconceivable to Dr. Carten. The Ordnance Corps would loose all credibility. Such a reversal of policy would sound the death knell of the army's ordnance system.[10] Dr. Carten, in his darker moments, must have believed that the Ordnance Corps was at bay with its life at stake.

The Ordnance Corps' standing in its tightly wound little world of the army was already badly damaged. Many military men were not pleased with the M14, which was held up as an example of the inability of the Ordnance Corps to develop and produce a satisfactory rifle. With each passing week, the M14 was attracting a growing chorus of articulate critics. The last thing Springfield needed was a major new rifle of the wrong caliber and from the wrong place—private industry.

Eugene Stoner returned to his laboratory in Southern California to work on the short list of very minor corrections to be made in the AR-15 design. The Fort Benning tests gave him good reason to feel that the AR-15 was very close to being the next army rifle.

A few months later, Fort Benning tested Stoner's modified AR-15s and approved them for field trials by other army stations. Soon troops were firing away at targets all around the country. But it was clear that a full-blown test between the two weapons was needed where performance really counted—in a side-by-side contest under extended simulated battle conditions. The face-off was not long in coming. In a winner-take-all atmosphere, the two weapons were tested the following autumn—from November 1958 through February 1959 at the U.S. Army Combat Development Experiment Center (CDEC) in Fort Ord, California. Elite troops, many of them combat veterans from the Korean War, were brought to Fort Ord.

As one week led to the next and the weeks led to months, endurance became a major consideration and the results became worse for the M14. The AR-15 was simply overwhelming it. Repeatedly, in the hit distribution and capability test, the AR-15, with only a seven-man squad, outscored the M14, which had an eleven-man squad. In overall combat potential, the AR-15 far outdistanced the M14. CDEC personnel urged the "early replacement of current rifles."[11] ArmaLite had good reason to believe that AR-15 was showing itself to be—as billed—the most reliable, most lethal automatic rifle ever devised.

Even before the AR-15 had posted its overwhelming performance at Fort Ord during the autumn of 1958, Fairchild's president, Richard Boutelle, feeling there was now an enormous worldwide sales potential for both the AR-10 and the AR-15, wanted to go into production. With the unofficial test results from Fort Benning in his hand, he went before his board and presented a plan to manufacture the AR-10 and AR-15 right there in ArmaLite's own California plant. The board thought and fought and concluded that manufacturing would require too much capital. License the new rifles to other manufacturing firms, they told him, and take a percentage. Undeterred, ArmaLite salesmen went calling on the U.S. Navy, the Air Force, the Coast Guard, and the FBI, and waited for a favorable reaction.

In the meantime, Army Ordnance came under even greater pressure when in January 1959, in Hanoi, North Vietnam's Central Executive Committee, headed by Ho Chi Minh, issued Resolution 15, which renounced the fragile truce with South Vietnam and dropped its own policy of "political struggle." Instead, the committee announced, North Vietnam would pursue a policy of "armed struggle." Ho Chi Minh already controlled a huge network of underground forces inside South Vietnam, with major concentrations in the jungles of the southern Mekong Delta, as well as along the Cambodian and Laotian borders. U.S. military analysts feared that in a shooting war, Ho Chi Minh would have a quick and easy time conquering the south. Yet twelve years after the invention of the AK47, the U.S. Ordnance Corps still had not produced or accepted an automatic rifle that could matched it.

CHAPTER 35

DR. CARTEN'S DILEMMA

The army's continuing one caliber (.30) policy must have given Dr. Carten some encouragement to proceed with production of the five million M14s the army needed. What would make him feel completely sure would be a test that revealed a flaw in the AR-15 great enough to wash out the entire weapon, including the .22-caliber system. As Dr. Carten well knew, many a prototype weapon like the AR-15 had developed insuperable design problems that removed them from further armory consideration. He could point to a number in the Springfield Armory's museum cases.

Testing, however, created other problems for him. The next tests for the AR-15 were scheduled at Aberdeen Proving Ground. From Dr. Carten's view, Aberdeen was enemy territory. The ballistics engineers there were civilians. The Hall report, so critical of the .30-caliber philosophy, had come from there; moreover, as a group, Aberdeen engineers had already expressed interest in—had made studies of, had expressed enthusiasm for—small-caliber cartridges. Indeed, to stop them from additional studies on smaller calibers, Dr. Carten himself had cut off their funding. He had given as the official reason at the time that the Frankford Arsenal in Philadelphia, not Aberdeen, was the established facility for studying ammunition.

Ideally, Carten would have liked to obtain some AR-15s for his armory, where he could conduct some tests of his own. But

ArmaLite quickly scotched that and refused to provide test rifles. Springfield was an armory, not a testing facility. To make sure Dr. Carten did no testing in the future, ArmaLite turned to a friend now working for ArmaLite's parent company, Fairchild Engine and Airplane Corporation, retired General Devers. The general had friends in the Pentagon, and to them he raised the question of Dr. Carten's impartiality. The general's friends agreed: it was ordered that future AR-15 testing be done at Aberdeen.

Of all the outspoken civilian engineers at Aberdeen, the most blunt and direct on the whole staff, Lawrence F. Moore, was chosen to test the AR-15. For years, he had been the principal civilian test engineer for the Development and Proof Services of the Infantry and Aircraft Weapons Division. More than a laboratory theoretician, Lawrence Moore was a dedicated and nationally rated shooter and marksman who was well known for his careful and critical testing of small arms. Dr. Carten had often been unhappy with his thoroughgoing critiques of armory rifles. Moore took the AR-15s and also some Winchester .224-caliber rifles and went to work.

By February 1959, he had completed his AR-15 tests, and, as required, sent his report, including his closely reasoned recommendations, to Dr. Carten. The report was highly favorable to the AR-15. In effect, the recommendations said that the AR-15 was an exceptionally promising design, with no significant faults, and that the development of the weapon should proceed.[1] As was the practice at the time, after Dr.Carten had read it, Lawrence Moore's report was published by Dr. Carten's office, but without Moore's list of recommendations.

In the pages of test data and charts and conclusions, Dr. Carten found results he could construe as a major flaw in the AR-15. In the rain test, Moore reported that he had exposed both the AR-15 and the Winchester .224-caliber rifle to simulated rainfall. With water in the bore, both rifles were fired and both barrels split. To Moore, it meant that the barrels needed redesigning—a correctable problem. To Carten, it meant a major flaw that could jeopardize the AR-15. Eugene Stoner had no problem with the split barrel. He simply made another barrel that was two ounces heavier. When

Aberdeen put it through the rain test and fired the rifle, response was normal.

Dr. Carten, however, felt that the rain-in-the-barrel issue would probably wash out the AR-15, and on the strength of it decided to begin the lengthy preparations required to produce the M14. The wheels and gears of the Ordnance production system began to work, with the expectation that a few years later, private contractors would have produced five million M14 rifles for the nation's arsenals.

On September 19, 1958, CONARC issued its *Report on Project NR 2787, Evaluation of Small Caliber High Velocity (SCHV) Rifles*. This was the Infantry Board's final report on the AR-15 test and, in contrast with the original enthusiasm, it was extremely solemn in tone. The AR-15 and a Winchester .22-caliber rifle, said the board, had both failed the rain test again. While the board felt that both rifles were still potential candidates for continued development, it insisted that the rain in the bore was a major deficiency. Both models were therefore rejected until the problem was corrected. The report told both makers to rework and resubmit their weapons for retesting.

ArmaLite felt the board was highly exaggerating the problem of rain in the bore, hardly serious enough to justify the sudden flagging of the board's original enthusiasm. While the board gave new life to the issue of rain in the bore, it gave Dr. Carten little else to celebrate. The group didn't find much to like in the M14. The board felt that because of their lightness and ease of handling, both the AR-15 and the Winchester were superior to the M14. A soldier, the board noted, can carry 650 rounds of AR-15/Winchester ammunition, but only 220 rounds of the M14. Three times as much—a decided battlefield advantage. Furthermore, said the board, the AR-15 beat both the M14 and the Winchester for ease of assembly and disassembly. But, most damaging of all, the AR-15 showed greater "reliability under simulated combat conditions"—which is a rifle's most essential attribute.[2] The judgment must have made Dr. Carten wince. The AR-15 weapons system provided three times more ammunition in combat and was more reliable than his combat-ready M14. Had the AR-15 been the control weapon and the M14 the contender, this report would have been enough to kill the M14. Instead, it was the AR-15 that was in trouble. For the problem of rain in the rifle's bore would not go away. The AR-15 took in water during the 1958 Infantry Board tests, then again at the Springfield Armory in 1959, and yet again at Aberdeen in 1962.

The problem was the rifle's small bore. Dr. Carten was quick to point out that M14's larger bore didn't have this problem. He had the AR-15 on the defensive. Eugene Stoner redesigned the barrel yet again to overcome the rain danger, but Aberdeen reported that the problem was still present. When Stoner contended that Dr. Carten was exaggerating the danger, Carten countered by claiming that the rain hazard was so great that the whole .22-cartridge program should be booted out of contention—AR-15 and all.

Believing the AR-15 was now in serious trouble, Dr. Carten could feel a little easier about having authorized production of five million M14s. Yet in spite of the rain-in-the-bore issue, the AR-15 had done real damage to the acceptability of the M14. In the AR-15, Army Ordnance was confronted with the very characteristics its own M14 was supposed to have and didn't: true light weight—6.35 pounds versus 9.32; true automatic fire, fully controllable; extremely high reliability in simulated combat; and a gun buff's Christmas list of other features including a sexy space-age design.[3]

Most damning of all, while Ordnance had taken twelve years to produce the roundly criticized M14, Eugene Stoner, working alone and free of the many and varied intrusions that befell a John Garand or an Earle Harvey, was able to produce his remarkable rifle in less than nine months.

Everyone was aware of the tension between Dr. Carten and Eugene Stoner. What the army did next escalated the battle into a full-blown war. In December 1958, contrary to agreement with Stoner, the army sent three AR-15s to the Army Arctic Test Board in Fort Greeley, Alaska, without telling Stoner.

As was the case with the Fort Benning Infantry Board tests, no one in Fort Greeley was familiar with the AR-15, so it had been considered very important for Stoner to attend the Arctic tests in order to familiarize Fort Greeley personnel with the weapon before they attempted to test it.

Stoner first learned about the Arctic testing of his rifle when, in that same month, he received a request from Alaska for spare parts. Stoner flew to Alaska with the required spare parts, to find out why they were needed. When he arrived, he could not believe what he saw.[4]

"My examination showed that the front sights had been removed from a couple of weapons and were loose." Stoner had designed the front sight to be held in place with taper pins. The sights were not supposed to have been removed or even touched during the tests. In fact, during accuracy tests, the loose sights would certainly have caused poor performance.

"One of the rifles had the pins driven in from the wrong side," said Stoner in his report to R. W. "Bobby" Macdonald, president of the Cooper-Macdonald arms company, who was interested in Asian market sales of the AR-15, ". . . the other rifle had ground down pieces of welding rod substituted for missing taper pins." There were other homemade parts in the rifles that he felt could definitely have caused the reported malfunctions.

Since accuracy of firing under extremely cold temperatures was a key test at Greeley, the AR-15s had been literally crippled. The test weapons could not be accurately aimed. Worst of all, test results from such damaged weapons could wash the AR-15 out of Ordnance contention permanently. Stoner said later to the Ichord Congressional Investigating Committee: "I was given the opportunity to fire one weapon while dressed in full arctic clothing. This weapon had been outside and subjected to low temperature for several days. I fired 400 rounds and had no malfunctions of any kind."[5]

Stoner made a written complaint about the condition of his weapons and demanded that the Greeley Test Board retest his AR-15 with undamaged rifles. He thought he had an agreement on this issue and left Alaska to attend a meeting at CONARC headquarters.

At CONARC, Stoner attended a meeting held by a special rifle review board under the direction of General Herbert B. Powell. Stoner was asked to present his rifle. During his presentation, General Powell interrupted him. "What," he asked, "is your opinion of the Arctic tests?"[6] Stoner stated that the difficulties had been corrected.

Unfortunately, they hadn't been. Stoner later learned that the general had the results of the Arctic test in his hand during that entire meeting. The results had arrived at the same time Stoner had. Stoner's trip to Fort Greeley had been a waste of time. His repair of the damaged weapons had also been pointless, because no Arctic retest with the correctly fitted AR-15s was ever made. The results of the original tests with loose sights was what Fort Greeley sent to General Powell. The Arctic test report made the AR-15 unacceptable for military service. Who had loosened the sights and why has never been determined.

Prior to the meeting of the Powell board, General Wyman, who had originally asked Stoner to prepare the AR-15, had retired, still convinced that the AR-15 should replace the M14. General Powell, appointed personally by General Wyman to the board, had watched, "alarmed," as the chief of ordnance made such an issue of the rain test failures that the Infantry Board rejected both the AR-15 and the Winchester .22 rifle as "not acceptable at this time."[7]

General Powell was deputy commanding general of CONARC under General Wyman, and four months after the Powell Rifle Board meeting, he showed where he stood on the AR-15 issue. In spite of the Arctic tests, the Powell board recommended the purchase of 750 AR-15s for further testing. But the Army Small Arms Research and Development staff moved quickly to stop the purchase. On the staff were Dr. Carten and A. C. Bonkemeyer—the two men who had headed up the program to develop the M14 and, as such, the last two men who should have been allowed to sit in judgment of the AR-15. The staff said that the results of the tests of the AR-15 didn't warrant further testing of the weapon since it would be a direct violation of the NATO .30-caliber agreement.

Then Dr. Carten made a surprising proposal: since the size of the bore of the AR-15 was the cause of the rain test problem, why not make the bore larger? Develop a .258-caliber rifle, he said, which would be an intermediate caliber between the .22-caliber (5.56 mm) and .30-caliber cartridges. Dr. Carten's suggestion meant that the AR-15 would have to be completely reengineered from .22 to .258 caliber.

The Powell board accepted Dr. Carten's proposal, recommending that the AR-15 now be chambered for .258 caliber and then retested, while the M14 would continue to be the army's official "automatic" rifle. Stoner returned to his Costa Mesa laboratories and waited for Ordnance's new .258-caliber cartridge, around which he was to redesign the AR-15. Although he received a number of different concept drawings at various times, stretching over a number of months, no final samples of the approved new .258-caliber cartridge arrived. At last, he personally went to Ordnance in Washington to inquire about the long-delayed new cartridge and learned that the project had been dropped because the new .258-caliber cartridge was "too marginal an improvement over .30 caliber." By then, Dr. Carten had issued the first manufacturing contracts for the M14.[8]

The whole Small Caliber High Velocity Program had been led down a blind path—the design and testing of .258-caliber cartridges—that diverted money and manpower away from the .22-caliber program for some two years before it petered out.[9] During the same period, the question of .30 caliber versus .22 caliber reached the desk of General Maxwell Taylor, the army chief of staff. He wasn't pleased with the AR-15. Like General MacArthur before him, he worried about changing the infantry to a new rifle and a new cartridge. He worried about NATO's reaction if the United States were to abandon the American caliber that the NATO countries had already adopted. Such a change would introduce nonstandard calibers into NATO once more.

The general's dilemma must have caused wry smiles on the faces of many Europeans: it was General Taylor who had decided to adopt the M14 rather than the FAL, which many Europeans, especially the British, felt America had been morally bound to. Years later, he felt he had to stay with the .30-caliber cartridge, which the United States had forced NATO to accept over their recommendations for a smaller caliber. They must have been bemused by the general's logic.

The general was caught up in a political issue and made what seemed a prudent political decision. In the face of all the studies documenting the need for an automatic rifle, the only problem was the M14 barely qualified as such. In fact, 90 percent of M14s were ultimately issued without the automatic firing position, making them purely and permanently semiautomatic rifles, and, many felt, not as good as the semiautomatic M1 they replaced. The NATO FAL, a superb .280-caliber weapon, suffered the same fate. Rechambered to handle the overpowered .30-caliber cartridge, it, too, was issued strictly as a semiautomatic.

In February 1959, the fight was over. General Taylor made the full-scale production of the M14 official. He ordered that no more AR-15s be purchased. As a consolation for its efforts with its .224 rifle, Winchester was awarded a contract to make thirty-five thousand M14s, the first such civilian contract ever awarded. For its pains, ArmaLite received nothing.

One wonders what Dr. Fred Carten was thinking. By throwing back the AR-15, he had beaten astronomical odds and had shown himself to be a great master of bureaucratic gamesmanship. His success must have been hugely satisfying. Like a head on a pike, ArmaLite's small-caliber AR-15 rifle was headed for the armory's small arms museum, right next to that other trophy, ArmaLite's .30-caliber AR-10 rifle, and adjacent to three others: the .280-caliber FN FAL, the .30-caliber FN FAL, and the EM2 British rifle. Dr. Carten had won this battle. The official U.S. Army rifle cartridge remained the .30-caliber NATO, and the official U.S. Army rifle, the M14.

But one wonders if he ever had doubts about his victory. He had witnessed the AR-15 roundly—decisively—defeat his M14. He knew that many testing boards and military men regarded his M14 as an inferior weapon not worthy of the army. He knew about all the studies that said his M14 was the wrong caliber. Furthermore, as historians Stevens and Ezell note, by dismissing the AR-15 as "devoid of merit . . . [Dr. Carten] undermined the credibility of the Army's technical services, polarizing and demoralizing the Ordnance technical community," which was to have serious repercussions for him and the armory.[10]

Three years before, in 1956, the armory had officially obtained its first Russian AK47s[11] and tested them extensively, so Dr. Carten knew what a superb and formidable weapon his M14 was up against. Did he believe that the M14, having been mauled by the AR-15, could outfight the AK47, another excellent automatic rifle? On the day General Taylor declared the M14 a winner, the United States was just a few years away from one of the most savage wars in its history. In the streets of the inner cities, in suburban fields, on ranches and farms, all across the United States, at play were hundreds of thousands of young boys, most of them barely in their teens, who would soon be drafted and sent into battle in Vietnam to fight for their lives against the AK47 with the rifle Dr. Carten had selected for them—and without the rifles he had fought to keep out of their hands. How sure was he that the M14 was the right rifle?

Many of his critics believed they knew the answer, and in a few years, history would produce the definitive answer from Southeast Asian rice paddies and jungles. In the meantime, the fight with the AR-15 had left a lot of blood on the floor of the Pentagon and of the Ordnance world as a whole. Dr. Carten had a lot of cleanup to do, as well as the production of five million M14s.

Back in California, ArmaLite was beaten. For its pains, the company had been mauled by the OCO bureaucracy and now was out of pocket almost $1.5 million in AR-15 development costs. Worse, Fairchild, the parent firm, was in serious financial trouble, and its president, Richard Boutelle, knew he didn't have the money to carry on the fight against the M14 and the Ordnance bureaucracy. Having had enough of the mandarin games of the Ordnance Corps, Boutelle decided to do what Maxim and Browning and all the other American gun designers had done. He cast his eyes abroad. As a result of licensing the foreign sales of the AR-10, he believed there was a huge foreign market waiting for the AR-15 if he could only find someone to tool up and manufacture both weapons for him.

CHAPTER 36

THE MACDONALD
WHIRLWIND SALES CAMPAIGN

B outelle telephoned an old comrade in arms, the military weapons salesman Bobby Macdonald, which, with a plot twist right out of a spy novel, unexpectedly turned out to be very unlucky for Dr. Carten. Robert W. "Bobby" Macdonald was a principal in Cooper-Macdonald, Inc., arms merchants based in Baltimore, not far from the Hagerstown offices of Boutelle's Fairchild Company. Bobby Macdonald was a highly successful international arms salesman in one of the toughest markets in the world. In his line of weapons were Colt handguns, Remington rifles, ammunition, shotguns, the .30-caliber AR-10, and more. His favorite territory of many years' standing was one of the world's toughest, Southeast Asia. He was used to turndowns, betrayals, and corrupt competition, but also to many victories. Macdonald was known as a salesman who lived by the sales cliché of "not taking no for an answer."

Boutelle had Macdonald come to the rifle range on his farm to test-fire the AR-15. Macdonald was so impressed that he wanted to immediately take it on a sales tour. Boutelle offered Bobby Macdonald a fee to find a company to tool up and make the ArmaLite AR-15 for the international market.

Macdonald traveled to Hartford, Connecticut, the home of Colt's Patent Firearms Manufacturing Company and of Macdonald's friend Fred Roff, Colt sales manager and later president. Colt had the manufacturing capability Fairchild needed, but it also had two problems.

First of all, the manufacturing equipment was quite old; it hadn't been updated for nearly a century, since the Civil War, in fact. Also, in 1958, arms makers had their ribs showing; since the end of the Korean War, neither the civilian nor the military markets were very active. Colt was in an even more precarious financial condition than Fairchild—and actually fighting off bankruptcy.

Yet the AR-15 presented such enormous potential to Colt that negotiations between Fairchild and Colt went forward. In February 1959, a new board of directors at Colt signed a production licensing agreement with Fairchild for the AR-10 and the AR-15. Bobby Macdonald's Cooper-Macdonald, Inc., was given a percent of all future production. The only money that changed hands was an advance check of $5,000 from Colt to Bobby Macdonald as expense money to enable him to seek out weapons orders so that Colt could start production.[1] Ironically, Macdonald's mission began practically on the day General Taylor banned the purchase of any more AR-15s.

Bobby Macdonald contacted Eugene Stoner and together they carried demo models of the AR-10 and the AR-15 to Southeast Asia, following a sales trail that was to lead back to Dr. Carten's doorstep. Macdonald and Stoner were soon blazing away at demo targets in the Philippines, Malaya, Indonesia, Thailand, Burma, India, and, finally, Italy. They quickly discovered that the small-statured Asians preferred firing the .22-caliber AR-15 to the .30-caliber AR-10—so much so that Macdonald gave away six thousand rounds of NATO 7.62-mm (.30-caliber) ammunition in the Philippines "because nobody wanted to shoot the AR-10. Everybody wanted to shoot the AR-15. So I didn't see any point in carrying [the 7.62-mm ammunition] any further."[2]

Macdonald later told the Ichord Congressional Investigating Committee: "We fired eight thousand rounds through that one rifle in the course of getting to India, and that means all the Malayans, everybody had a shot with it under all sorts of conditions. And as I recall, we had exactly one malfunction, and that was easily traceable to a lip on the magazine which somebody had bent. . . . It was the finest, most foolproof weapon I have ever seen in my life." Macdonald's experience convinced Colt to tool up for the AR-15, but not the AR-10.

Although the AR-15 was greeted with enthusiasm in the Asian market, no one placed an order. Four of Macdonald's largest potential purchasers—including the Philippines—told him they could not buy his rifle because they had signed a military assistance pact with the United States. To get U.S. mutual aid funding, those countries could purchase only standard U.S. military hardware— the M1, the BAR, and soon the M14, but not the AR-15. There, in Asia, Bobby Macdonald discovered that all roads led to Dr. Fred Carten. Macdonald told the Ichord committee how he reacted to that.

"I made a deal with both Fairchild and Colt that if they would get out of the way and turn over the whole business to me, I would make a great effort to try to get the rifle tested here and adopted by the U.S. government, not so much to replace the M14, although it was capable of doing so, but to supply our small-statured allies with this type of rifle which has very little recoil, as you know."[3]

Macdonald saw that the only way to keep alive the weapon billed as the greatest, most reliable rifle ever invented was to sell it to the man who hated it, Dr. Carten. That idea seemed so improbable that Fairchild believed the AR-15 was dead, as also must have Eugene Stoner, who left ArmaLite the following year.

Finally, a break came from a totally unexpected source, and for a brief time, Dr. Carten was totally unaware of the threat. On July 4, 1960, as was his custom, Richard Boutelle celebrated his and the nation's birthday with a party on his farm in Hagerstown, Maryland. Bobby Macdonald later described the Boutelle farm for the Ichord committee: "His farm was all set up outside Hagerstown, with a skeet field, trap field, archery, pistol ranges, you name it. It was beautifully equipped from a shooting angle."[4]

Boutelle invited his old air force buddy General Curtis LeMay, who was then air force vice chief of staff and who was later to run for vice president on the George Wallace states' rights ticket.

Boutelle and LeMay often went hunting with another friend, the star of his own radio and television show, Arthur Godfrey. LeMay was a very serious competitive shooter and a noted marksman.[5] He was also one of the top men in the world's largest air force, and, as such, he was looking for a huge number of military-grade rifles to be used in air base security. General LeMay had tested the new M14 extensively, but after careful consideration, he had turned it down as too heavy, too bulky, and uncontrollable. What air base security patrols needed, he knew, was a lightning-fast, lightweight, heavy-traffic, totally reliable automatic rifle.

It was no accident that also present at the picnic was Bobby Macdonald, nor was it an accident that he had with him three watermelons and a number of AR-15s, including abundant ammunition.

Macdonald placed one watermelon 50 yards away, and a second 150 yards away. When the general fired the AR-15, both watermelons exploded, and LeMay, like every other gun fancier who'd fired the AR-15, was smitten.

Bobby Macdonald recounted what happened: "He shot both of them and as you probably know, the explosive feature of the bullet takes all the water out of the watermelon. So he walked up to both of them and put his hand down in there and picked this stuff up, and I won't say what he said, but it was quite impressive—he was impressed. So I asked him, 'Do you want to shoot the other one?' He said, 'Hell no, let's eat it.' So that's [what] we did."[6]

While General LeMay left the Boutelle farm determined to have the AR-15 for his huge ground force, Richard Boutelle soon found himself out of the AR-15 situation entirely. As Macdonald explained: "In the meantime, Colt was taken over by another group of financiers, and in the course of it they fired all the people that I had been doing business with. . . . Fairchild also went through a change in management several times. Based on this rifle and on the F-27 airplane, Mr. Boutelle got fired."[7]

While General LeMay was studying the AR-15, the new group at Colt looked at the history of the AR-15, its performance against the M14, and decided they had the best rifle, not Dr. Carten. They also decided that they couldn't play the usual bureaucratic game against the labyrinth of committees and tests. That was Ordnance's game, Ordnance's turf, from which the AR-15 had already been ejected. Instead, Colt executives decided to take on the entire Ordnance Department in a public relations contest. They would conduct a publicity campaign against the M14 and the Ordnance Department in national magazines. If their campaign failed, Colt would lose everything, but if it succeeded, Colt would own one of the most valuable rifles in the world, a goal worth fighting for. No handicapper on earth would have given Colt very good odds, but Dr. Carten now faced adversaries more pugnacious than the last.

Colt started at the very peak of the pyramid when it attempted to resell the AR-15 to the top brass in Washington. As its opening move, in June 1960, Colt asked for a retest of the AR-15. The first response was predictable. Dr. Carten refused Colt's request for the retest because of "the lack of any military requirements for such an arm."[8]

Colt went public. "We're up against the NIH factor," Colt president George Strichman said. "Not Invented Here. The rifle's basic problem was that it hadn't been invented by Army arsenal personnel." Pointing a finger at the armory, he said, "They got the M14 adopted, then tried to cover their tracks. They resented the AR-15 being thrust upon them."[9]

Meanwhile, General LeMay arrived back in Colorado with a model of the AR-15 to show to his air force associates there. They watched the AR-15 through the toughest tests they could improvise and were clearly satisfied that this was the kind of weapon they needed for protecting air bases around the world. With their favorable reaction, on August 23, 1960, General LeMay invited Colt's representatives to the U.S. Air Force Academy to discuss acquisition of the AR-15. As a result of that meeting, Lackland Air Force Base submitted a request to the Pentagon to qualify the AR-15 as a potential candidate for replacement of the air force's World War II M2 carbines.

Since this request was to replace not the M14 but the obsolete air force carbine, this air force action overrode Dr. Carten's refusal to reconsider the AR-15. Meanwhile, Colt was continuing its campaign, and now congressmen were asking questions about the armory's treatment of ArmaLite.

Dr. Carten himself was required to arrange the air force test at Aberdeen Proving Ground. This assignment came as a double blow to him: the air force was absolutely rejecting the new M15 (the carbine version of the M14) as a replacement for the obsolete M2 carbine, and the AR-15 was back in his life.

The test date was set for September 26, 1960. Colonel Dubia at Aberdeen was advised by wire from Dr. Carten to expect some interested observers: "General LeMay, DCS, USAF, and Lt. General Trudeau, CRD, are expected to attend, along with other representatives of Air Force and Army."[10] The air force was not concealing the strong interest it had in this weapon and didn't want anything to go wrong with the testing. The testing engineer, Lawrence Moore, had tested the AR-15 originally two years before. As a control, Aberdeen used two other rifles—the old M1 semiautomatic from World War II and the M14.

Aberdeen's test report—*Development and Proof Services Report 96*—was issued in November 1960. The AR-15 had turned in an exceptional performance in each test and had outgunned both the M1 and the M14. In addition, in the unlubricated, dust, extreme-cold, and rain tests, Moore reported that the "AR-15 gave near-normal performance." This result was a very curious turn of affairs, since the AR-15 had previously failed the same rain test and the extreme-cold test. More than anything else, failure of these two tests had caused the AR-15 to be removed from consideration. Two years later, the same rifle passed both tests easily, which must have raised the same question in the Pentagon and at Colt: How could the AR-15 easily pass tests it had failed repeatedly two years before?

Dr. Carten was undoubtedly displeased to see that, once again, the AR-15 had been compared directly with his M14—and, once again, far outperformed it. He released the Aberdeen report with just two words of faint praise: the AR-15, he wrote, was "reasonably satisfactory."[11] As requested, the AR-15 was approved for air force tests.

Later, at the Lackland Air Force Base, Texas, the AR-15 was subjected to various firing tests against the obsolete M2 carbine and the

M14. These tests convinced the air force that they had found their weapon: the AR-15. When General LeMay requested permission to purchase eighty thousand rifles, he ran into some severe difficulties. In the summer of 1961, in Congress, the House Watchdog Sub-committee on Defense Department Appropriations decided against having another rifle in the military system. LeMay's request was de-nied. The following fall, President John F. Kennedy test-fired the AR-15 at a Sea Power demonstration and that December, General LeMay asked the president for his AR-15s. Predictably, with the two-caliber issue raised again, he was turned down.

Bobby Macdonald, the salesman who never took no for an an-swer, kept searching for a yes with phone calls and letters to many leaders on Capitol Hill and in the Pentagon, reiterating the facts about Ordnance's handling of the AR-15. His order pad, however, remained blank, and without orders, Colt continued to slowly sink.

By December 1960, South Vietnam had 243,000 men under arms to fight Ho Chi Minh's invasion forces, which were construct-ing the Ho Chi Minh Trail, a seventeen-hundred-mile transporta-tion road, much of it built in Laos and Cambodia, starting from North Vietnam, just above the 17th parallel demilitarized zone (DMZ) and ending at Tay Ninh, in southern South Vietnam. The trail's terminus was a short distance from the strategic city of Saigon. U.S. military intelligence expected most of the North Viet-namese insurgents to be armed with the Kalashnikov AK47. The South Vietnamese infantrymen were armed with the M14. At this point, nine hundred U.S. military personnel were on duty in Vietnam.[12]

In April 1961, a few weeks after John F. Kennedy's presidential inauguration, an insurgent force from Florida attempted to invade Cuba by way of the Bay of Pigs. At the last minute, U.S. air cover was canceled and Cuba easily defeated and captured the insurgents, severely damaging the stature of the administration of President Kennedy.

Despite this setback, everyone in Washington was aware that there was a whole new Kennedy team who presented themselves as bright young men with new ideas and new management methods.

One of these was Robert Strange McNamara, the new secretary of defense, and his broom was aimed right at the bureaucratically paralyzed Pentagon. High on his list was the U.S. Armory.

A retired World War II army air force lieutenant colonel, McNamara had joined the Ford Motor Company and ascended the ladder of power to the office of president, then finally director. A proponent of the new computer technology, McNamara brought with him a team of Ph.D. systems analysts. He wanted to open all the windows of the Pentagon and let the computer winds blow out all the dust. His program was intended to replace what he considered an entangled, inefficient, and old-fashioned Pentagon structure with a new streamlined one. The Pentagon did not like these new brooms, their new methods, or their imperious attitudes. The relationship between McNamara and the Pentagon quickly became confrontational.

In the meantime, in the following January 1962, at the U.S. Air Force Academy in Colorado Springs, Colorado, with General LeMay's personal backing, and with no objection from the secretary of defense's office, the air force made the AR-15 its standard weapon. And the following May 1962, General Curtis LeMay, as the new chief of staff of the air force, ordered from Colt eighty-five hundred AR-15s, and, from Remington, 8.5 million rounds of ammunition. An additional nineteen thousand AR-15s were ordered the following year—1963. Neither order went through the Ordnance Department.

Secretary McNamara now had the whole Pentagon system under his scrutiny, and he was particularly interested in the armory's very vulnerable production methods. By the summer of 1962, the armory, feeling at bay, was governed more and more by a siege mentality.

Into the midst of this angry situation, the tireless, relentless arms salesman, Bobby Macdonald, impelled by a Colt manufacturing plant desperate for a substantial arms order, was about to open the final tumultuous act of the drama. Smelling a potential sale in Vietnam, he flew there with demonstration models of the AR-15. A special American army unit, called the Combat Development Test Center, had been sent to Saigon in 1961 to study the needs of the

Army of the Republic of Vietnam (ARVN). Remembering how much difficulty the small Asian soldiers had with the hard-kicking .30-caliber ArmaLite AR-10, and how much they preferred the .22-caliber AR-15, Macdonald approached the unit's head, Colonel Richard Hallock.[13]

Macdonald told Hallock he had a weapon that could make all the difference in the fighting capacity of ARVN. Hallock was interested. Macdonald pointed out that the average Vietnamese soldier, standing five feet tall and weighing ninety pounds, was too short and slight to handle the walloping and exhausting recoil of a full-power, .30-caliber M14. Hallock agreed. Macdonald then said he had a ferocious killer with practically no recoil—the ArmaLite AR-15, which, he asserted, was the perfect weapon for the smaller soldier. Colonel Hallock test-fired the AR-15 and did what everyone else outside the armory had done. He was completely won over by it and ordered four thousand AR-15s for the ARVN for tests. Ordnance interceded and the request was denied. The Pentagon told Colonel Hallock to use the M2 carbines, which were in stock.

Hallock asked for ten AR-15s, a quantity so small it slipped past the vigilance of the armory. The diminutive Vietnamese soldiers and their American advisers took the ten AR-15s into combat and came back praising the weapon. Macdonald had gained more converts to the AR-15, but still no order. Colonel Hallock resubmitted his original order of four thousand, stressing that these AR-15s were not for general issue to American troops but for tests by American adviser units and their Vietnamese allies only.

"Finally," Bobby Macdonald told the Ichord committee, "we got the . . . order, December 27, 1961."[14] Secretary McNamara's office had signed the order, but it was for only one thousand weapons. Yet McNamara's signature indicated a change from his original position as a proponent of the M14, a change brought about by the persistent comments about that rifle's defects and the superiority of the AR-15. He believed those thousand weapons might tell him just how well the AR-15 would perform in combat in comparison with the M2 carbine and alongside the M14.[15] The order for one thousand AR-15s saved Colt from financial collapse but only for a month or two. If Secretary McNamara wanted more AR-15s in the future, he was going to have to promptly place a new order for a substantial quantity. At Colt, they were down to counting days.

Air-freighted to Vietnam by Cooper-Macdonald, the first AR-15s arrived in January 1962. The U.S. Army supplied them to various ARVN units, along with M2 carbines, then went off into the bush as observers to see what would happen.

What happened caused a sensation in Washington. The AR-15 won the highest praise from the ARVN in the rice paddies—praise that had a familiar ring to it, echoing many previous tests. In all categories—ease of disassembly, marksmanship, ruggedness, durability, safety features, effects of tropical environment, and brush penetration—there was no comparison between the M2 and the AR-15, particularly with reference to the exceptional reliability of the latter under the most adverse jungle conditions. The Advanced Research Projects Agency of the Defense Department, which conducted the test, was emphatic: remove the M2 carbine from service and arm the entire Army of the Republic of Vietnam with the AR-15.

Verbatim reports on the performance of the AR-15 in actual combat followed. From the Vietnamese jungle came the first evidence of the lethality of small-caliber bullets on human flesh that had been sought since the Pig Board tests in the 1920s. There was nothing borderline about these results, which were lurid enough to satisfy the most bloodthirsty.

According to one report, an ARVN ranger platoon took on a Viet Cong unit estimated to be company strength. Five Viet Cong were killed, all by AR-15s. The first was killed by a back wound, which caused the thoracic cavity to explode. The second died of a stomach wound, which caused the abdominal cavity to explode. The third died from a buttock wound, which destroyed all tissue of both buttocks. The fourth died from a chest wound, which destroyed the thoracic cavity. The fifth died from a heel wound that split the leg all the way to the hip. All died instantaneously except for the Viet Cong with the buttock wound: "He lived approximately five minutes."[16] Five men hit, five men dead—one from a heel wound normally not mortal; the number of men involved was small, but the level of lethality suggested that a major new killer weapon had entered the battlefield.

The commander of the U.S. advisory group in Vietnam ordered twenty thousand AR-15s, giving Bobby Macdonald reason to be hopeful. Those twenty thousand rifles would save Colt for another several months. If it could be arranged, arming all of the ARVN with AR-15s would save Colt. But Ordnance immediately moved to block the order for AR-15s on the grounds that it would cause complicated logistics problems. Admiral Harry Felt, commander in chief, Pacific Forces, heeding the complaint, had the order canceled—fearing that the cost would be taken from his budget—and later the Joint Chiefs of Staff supported his decision. As a result, the M14—which had already been condemned as being too heavy, too long, too punishing and uncontrollable for six-foot American soldiers—was issued to the five-foot, ninety-pound ARVN troops, who were then sent off to fight the Viet Cong, who were armed with the AK47.

Bobby Macdonald, whose patience must have been extraordinary, decided to take his case to the highest court. He flew back to Washington and went directly to Secretary McNamara's office. Rounding up a large assortment of McNamara's top people, Macdonald took them all to a shooting range and put on a shooting show with AR-15s, M14s, and even AK47s. The staff members came back to their offices enthusiastic about the AR-15 and determined to discover the reason for the armory's opposition to it.

In the process, McNamara's staff went back to the 1920s, to the Pig Board, the Goat Board, and all the studies and tests for the Pedersen .276 rifle, then went through all the other studies and battlefield reports, back up to current times. Attaching their own studies of the AR-15, M14, and AK47, they wrote a report to Secretary McNamara that included a cost effectiveness study.

Issued over the signature of the comptroller of the Defense Department, Charles Hitch, on September 27, 1962, the report was known afterward simply as the Hitch report. Its attack on the M14 was comprehensive.

"In over-all squad-kill potential the AR-15 is up to five times as effective as the M-14 rifle," the report said. With a nod at the terrible production problems the M14 had encountered, it went on, "The AR-15 can be produced:

- with less difficulty
- to a higher quality
- at a lower cost than the M-14 rifle."

The report continued: "In reliability, durability, ruggedness, performance under adverse circumstances, and ease of maintenance, the AR-15 is a significant improvement over any of the standard weapons including the M-14 rifle. . . . The M-14 is weak in the sum of those characteristics. . . . It is significantly easier to train the soldier with the AR-15 than with the M-14.

"Three times as much ammunition can be carried on the individual soldier within the standard weapon and ammunition load." In the most significant statement of all, the report observed that while "the M-14 also appears somewhat inferior to the M1 rifle of World War 2 and decidedly inferior to the Soviet combat rifle, the AK-47 . . . U.S. armed forces armed with the AR-15 would have marked firepower advantage over Soviet forces armed with the AK assault rifle."[17]

CHAPTER 37

A RIGGED TEST
AND THE DEATH OF A RIFLE

M atters had reached the boiling point at the office of the secretary of defense. Not only was the controversy with AR-15 out in the open, armory problems with production of the M14 also had become critical. Even as early as 1956, the armory's industrial engineers had warned solemnly that a production disaster was in the making. They stated that an M14 industrial engineering package was needed to establish inspection standards and methods for production of the rifle. In any manufacturing plant, this industrial engineering package is considered essential.

What the armory engineers were saying was: since the M14 is a new rifle, as it goes through manufacturing and testing and research, a number of production-line bugs will be uncovered and engineering will learn many important things about elements like metallurgy and assembly and tooling. With such feedback, engineering will learn how to make the M14 better. It can then recycle data back into the process over and over until the engineers get all the bugs out and get a new high-quality rifle endlessly duplicated.

Without an industrial engineering package, the engineers won't capture the new technical data and therefore they won't make corrections. They'll make mistakes. They'll be less efficient and make the same expensive mistakes over and over. In short: a good plan is needed to make a good weapon. Without such a plan, there will be an endless parade of headaches, lost time, lost money, inferior product.

The Ordnance Office in Washington rejected the request. The engineers pressed again for the package in 1957. Ordnance rejected it again. And twice more, in 1958 and 1959.

The armory also seemed to lose all sense of time. To begin the funding of the production process, armory production people needed a simple but essential document—the item report. Instead of taking the normal few days to write it, the Ordnance Technical Committee took six months. As a result, money to make the new M14 rifle wasn't requested from Congress until 1958. A whole year was lost. In 1958, the Ordnance Weapons Command ordered the armory in effect to rush into production of the M14 without enough time for even the simplest technical data package to be prepared. Further, Command failed to give the armory the funds needed for the rush job. And so some refinements to the rifle were dropped, which, engineers felt, could affect the rifle's performance.[1]

They warned the Ordnance Department that it was building problems into the production process that would last as long as the rifle was manufactured. This situation, they warned in writing, would produce a poor-quality rifle and add significantly to the cost. Ordnance refused to listen. Instead, needing five million new M14s in a hurry, Ordnance continued its hasty, unorganized, unplanned rush into production. As a result, the Springfield Armory blundered into one production problem after another.

The bid invitation was sent to an outdated list of thirty-eight manufacturers from World War II and the Korean War. A number of those firms lacked the capability to make the weapons. Others, unwilling to make a great investment in new tooling for such a small order, only seventy thousand, declined. All the problems that should have been uncovered in the preproduction industrial engineering package now began to surface. For example, Raritan Arsenal, on reinspection of one of the first batches of M14s, turned up 1,784 rifles with defective cartridge receivers.[2] Metallurgical analysis found that a critical heat treatment process required much closer controls than expected. New controls had to be introduced into the manufacturing process. This requirement halted production and drew complaints from the two manufacturers.

To make a number of critical parts, the manufacturers discovered that they had to order new machines no one had planned on. This unexpected retooling led to more delays and inevitably more costs. Two parts-making machines the government purchased for Winchester cost $6 million.[3]

The mandatory stockpiling of raw material was overlooked as well, and when American steelworkers went on strike in 1959, no stockpiling of steel had been ordered. M14 production lines sat in darkness for two full months while the strike went on. Because of errors in inventory control and material handling, Harrington & Richardson production people used the wrong steel in making some M14 receivers. These parts disintegrated when fired and had to be destroyed. The manufacturers began missing their delivery dates, and when deliveries were made, they were only partial orders.

Armory inspectors rejected quantities of weapons; the manufacturers blamed the defects on the army's excessively close tolerances. The problem here lay with the very sensitive "sliding valve" White piston and cylinder that had replaced the loose-fitting, reliable, and battle-tested piston and cylinder built into four million M1s. The White system had been invented in 1921 and rejected by the army in 1930. John Garand himself called the White sliding valve "bunk," adding, "I tested it and it doesn't work the way they claim."[4] Why, then, was it accepted? Garand stated that more than thirty years after it had been rejected, the White sliding valve people were still trying to sell it, and that "somebody" in the Pentagon liked it. He said that an outside firm that had tested it reported not what happened, but "what the Ordnance people wanted to hear." A manufacturing tolerance is the allowable degree, plus or minus, that a given part exceeds a precise dimension. The manufacturing tolerance of the White system was seven times closer than the tolerances the M1 required, and the manufacturers simply were not able to meet them. Even if they were, the resulting rifle was prone to clogging and "possibly dangerous to use."[5]

Tempers frayed. Angry quarrels erupted. Increasingly hard feelings came to dominate the relations between the armory and its suppliers, and by the time the armory managed to inject a spirit of teamwork into the process, it was nearly too late. By 1961, the whole rifle production program had to be reformed. More time lost. More money lost. With international crises popping up everywhere, the army waited for its new rifle while M14 production ran—or walked—years behind schedule.

On July 28, 1961, in front of Congress and the whole nation, Secretary of War McNamara publicly and angrily attacked the armory's M14 program. "I think that it is a disgrace the way the project was handled. . . . It is a relatively simple job to build a rifle compared to building a satellite . . . or a missile system."[6] The armory had made a hash of things and was losing friends everywhere. Its reputation was at the lowest level ever.

Nineteen sixty-one was a year that thundered with events. John Kennedy was inaugurated president and was almost immediately submerged in the catastrophic Bay of Pigs invasion of Cuba. The Russians built the Berlin Wall, and newspapers reported that the five thousand American troops in Berlin were armed with old World War II M1s. When fifteen hundred U.S. Army reinforcements arrived in Berlin in August, they, too, were armed with the M1. The scandal of the failed M14 production program reached a new level.

Nineteen sixty-two was the year of reckoning for the Ordnance Corps. Secretary McNamara, with his computerized automotive production background, decided to take charge. Having confined previous studies to the relative performance merits of the M14 and the AR-15, he sent in his own team to conduct a similar investigation of the M14's production process. He then appointed Brigadier General Elmer J. Gibson with orders to cut all the red tape. The general instituted many long-overdue basic reforms, and a number of them had a permanent effect on the armory's weapons procurement system. By the fall of 1962, production was running at 300,000 rifles a year. But, at that point, McNamara's office was asking why we needed the M14 at all. His staff was becoming increasingly interested in the AR-15.

The final grim irony focused on the M1 rifle production machinery. All through the controversies surrounding the quest for an automatic rifle, armory production people had fought bitterly to get a rifle that could be made on the old M1 machinery, citing the millions of dollars that could be saved. After years of skirmishes, after causing the downfall of the Harvey T25 rifle and probably of Colonel Studler himself, the M1 machinery turned out to be the pivotal argument that led General Ridgway to adopt the M14, thereby causing great consternation among the NATO allies and considerable muttering about welshing on a promise to adopt the FAL rifle.

But, in the end, the M1 machinery proved to be worse than useless. Because the design of the M14 was just different enough, the M1 machinery could not be used. Efforts to use it cost great amounts of time and money. "Using M1 tooling led Harrington & Richardson into great difficulties. . . . Indeed it proved cheaper not to use that equipment."[7]

It was the well-managed and efficient third civilian contractor, Thompson Ramo Wooldridge (TRW), that paid for the armory's sins of omission. From the beginning, it had gone about making the M14 by the numbers, investing substantial sums and setting up, step by step, an efficient production line, and turning out a quality product. The company was barely beginning to recoup its huge upfront expenses when abruptly Secretary McNamara shut down the entire M14 program. With a factory full of unneeded tooling, TRW lost a fortune.

On January 23, 1963, when Secretary McNamara ordered a halt to purchases of the M14, he told the Senate Appropriations Committee it was canceled because there was a rifle better than the M14 in the offing. He was not referring to the AR-15. In the interim, the army would make do with existing M14s and whatever else was in the Ordnance cupboard. The Springfield Armory's small arms procurement system had failed, and its disgrace stirred up murmurings among McNamara's staff that it should be shut down.

In the meantime, the AR-15 hung like a baleful star in the skies of Ordnance Corps—the weapon that would not go away. With the damning report from his Assistant Secretary of Defense Hatch in his hands, Secretary McNamara decided he had to get this M14/AR-15 issue settled one way or the other. First, he revamped the Ordnance organization from top to bottom. The Ordnance Corps was no longer. In its place appeared the Army Materiel Command (AMC). Ordnance field command became the WECOM (Weapons Command). Among the many wide-reaching effects of the shakeup, Dr. Fred Carten, as chief of the Technical Branch of the Research Division of the Army Materiel Command, was transferred from the Springfield Armory to the U.S. Army Arsenal in Rock Island, Illinois.

The previous October—1962—Secretary McNamara confronted the issue of the M14 versus the AR-15. He ordered the army to reexamine the three weapons—the AR-15, the AK47, and the M14. Even President Kennedy became involved. Having read a summary of Comptroller Hitch's report, the president directed Secretary McNamara to report to him on the state of the rifle controversy. McNamara in turn told General Earl Wheeler, army chief of staff, to have a report on his desk by the end of January 1963, little more than three months away. He ordered two sets of tests, one tactical and one technical, to be conducted on army bases in four locations—the United States (Georgia and Alaska), Europe, and the Caribbean. The tactical test was written by Dr. Fred Carten and his staff—who later evaluated the results.

The marks of haste were everywhere evident in the tests. Rather than just testing three rifles, the whole program quickly degenerated into a raging philosophic war: the long-range, deliberately aimed, ammunition-conserving, high-caliber gravel-belly sharpshooters' group on one side, and the short-range, high-velocity, high-volume, small-caliber pattern shooters' group on the other. Within two months, the whole research effort collapsed into a shouting match with Colt loudly claiming that the tests were out-and-out "rigged" in favor of the M14.[8] Guided by Dr. Carten's testing procedures, both at Fort Benning and at Fort Greeley in Alaska, army testers used the 1954 standards for military rifle characteristics. This was absurd—or calculated: since these 1954 standards described the .30-caliber M1 performance characteristics as the ideal, the M14 met the standards handily, but the AR-15 didn't. In one instance, the AR-15, having been deliberately designed for a maximum range of five hundred yards, predictably did not pass the eight-hundred-yard firing tests. Designed for greater range, the M14 did. The test skirted the very issue that raged around the two weapons—should a modern military rifle have a range of eight hundred yards or less? Proponents of the AR-15 felt the test itself had the results built in—in favor of the M14.

In another of Dr. Carten's tests, ammunition was issued on a per-round basis, rather than per-pound basis, thus negating before the test even began another great advantage of the AR-15. During the accuracy test, the M14 was allowed to fire on the semiautomatic position, while the AR-15 was required to fire from the automatic position. AR-15 proponents rejected the resulting aimed-fire scores as being rigged, biased, and completely misleading. In addition, all the troops used in the tests were all carefully trained with the M14, but none had ever handled the AR-15 before and had little time to become familiar with it before they were thrust into tests. On top of all this turmoil, Bobby Macdonald and the Colt field maintenance crew discovered that the Remington ammunition supplied for the AR-15 rifles was defective, made with little or no quality control before being shipped to the test sites. Primers fell out of cartridges. Bullets fell out of their cases. Defective cartridges thus failed to eject on firing, while loose primers got stuck in the breech mechanisms. The jamming rate of the AR-15 soared. It had eight times the malfunction rate of the M14. In addition, some of the AR-15 rifles themselves had been poorly made and barely inspected.

At the most crucial moment in the life of the AR-15, in front of the whole Ordnance world, the AR-15 had been crippled by bad ammunition and several poorly made rifles. With uncontrolled fury, Bobby Macdonald accused Colt and Remington—both suppliers to the armory—of deliberately sabotaging the AR-15.[9]

With the results in hand, General Wheeler wrote the army's summary of the tests. He scored the AR-15 as not fitting the

assignment—which was to be usable by U.S. armed forces anywhere in the world. The AR-15 did not fit into the NATO uniform
caliber agreements. The AR-15 was no match for the M14 at distances beyond four hundred meters. General Wheeler conceded
the obvious: the AR-15 was judged superior to the M14 in terms of
weight, total hit capability, and automatic fire accuracy. But he
scored the AR-15 unacceptable for reliability and night-sighting
characteristics. Wheeler finished by asserting that the AR-15 was
not yet a fully developed weapon and not ready for full-scale production and distribution to the troops: "The AR-15 is not now acceptable for the Army for universal use."

The Aberdeen Proving Ground test gave low scores to both the
AR-15 and the M14. The AR-15 was cited for a lesser performance
in mud, rain, and cold. Surprisingly, the M14 was shown to be less
accurate than the AR-15 during semiautomatic fire. Neither
weapon showed exceptional accuracy during fully automatic fire.
Finally, Aberdeen said, these tests could not reproduce the extraordinary performance of the AR-15 as reported by the Advanced
Research Projects Agency (ARPA) of the Defense Department and
the comptroller's report.

"The AR-15," the report said, "although lighter than the M14, is
not considered suitable as a replacement because: it is less reliable,
it has poor pointing and night-firing characteristics, its penetration
is marginally satisfactory and its adoption would violate the NATO
standardization agreements." In sum: "Only the M14 is acceptable
for the general use in the U.S. Army."[10]

The report on the AK47 test was presented in secret, but with fifteen years of battle performance, its reliability was well established.

With the test results in hand and the AR-15 proponents yelling
foul, and "disturbing rumors . . . circulating the corridors of the
Pentagon," less than a month before the president's deadline, Secretary of the Army Cyrus Vance sent the inspector general of the
army to investigate. Look at the tests, he told him, and determine if
they were in any way biased or rigged.[11]

The inspector general replied with a well-documented yes. He
reported that there had indeed been bias in the testing, that the

M14s used in the test were customized "match-grade" weapons (prepared for marksmanship match competitions) while the AR-15s were taken straight from the box. The M14s had also been carefully "coddled" with excessive care and preparation.

In short, not only had the tests been skewed in favor of the M14, the skewing had been pervasive. The inspector general asserted that a planning conference had been held at the Army Materiel Command Headquarters on October 22, 1962. Representatives from the Ballistics Research Laboratories, the Development and Proof Services, the Army Test and Evaluation Command, and the Army Infantry Board attended. The representative of the Army Infantry Board wrote an official memorandum of the meeting, which stated, "The U.S. Army Infantry Board will conduct only those tests that will reflect adversely on the AR-15."[12]

Equally damaging, the inspector general learned that General Frank J. Besson, the commanding officer of the Army Materiel Command, had favored the AR-15, but, caught between his superiors who wanted the M14 and the old Ordnance Corps personnel now within his command, he was overridden.

The army inspector general's report did great damage to the public standing of the Pentagon.[13] The following month, April 1963, the AR-15 gained more valuable public image from the carefully orchestrated publicity campaign that was being mounted against the M14 by Colt. In that month, there appeared two magazine articles that were highly critical of the M14.

True, a high-circulation general men's magazine, published an article by John Tompkins titled "The Blunderbuss Bungle That Fattened Your Taxes." Simultaneously, *Gun World* magazine ran an article by Jack Lewis titled "The M14: Boon or Blunder." Both were detailed attacks on the M14. Both wanted the M14 replaced with a new rifle. ArmaLite and Colt did not miss the opportunity to generously distribute reprints of these two articles. So far, only the Ordnance Corps was opposed to the AR-15, while in favor were the air force, the airborne units of the army, the ARVN, the Green Berets, the U.S. Marines, and the CIA. Joining the growing clamor were the civilian heads of the Defense Department, Cyrus Vance and Robert McNamara, and even the president, John Kennedy himself.

With General Wheeler's report, and with the inspector general's counterreport on the army's bias in the testing, Secretary McNamara had to decide what to do next. While he was deliberating, the Army Small Arms Development Staff confided to him that it would soon have a radically new weapon that would make both the M14 and the AR-15—and, yes, even the AK47—obsolete. A product of a secret program the army had in place called the SPIW—the Special Purpose Individual Weapon—this new rifle would fire a cartridge loaded with flechettes—small lethal darts that hit their target with a large pattern of lethality. This revolutionary rifle concept, if realized, could make each infantryman a one-man killing machine.

The SPIW concept caused the secretary to hesitate over his decision. Although the idea had been around for years, the Army Materiel Command had only recently begun to design the weapon in its ordnance labs. Critics quickly pointed out that this was 1962, many years after the AR-15 had been created. Why, they asked, had the Army Materiel Command—the Ordnance Corps under its new name—taken so long to get started with research into their new, radically different weapon?

Dr. J. A. Stockfish, a former senior research associate with the Institute of Defense Analysis, and a staff member of the RAND Corporation, provides a blunt answer. In his book on the Defense Department, he calls the SPIW "a political tactic." Army thinkers, he says, "conceived the program as a way of heading off a possible major purchase of M16's [the army designation of the AR-15]."[14] If the idea behind the SPIW was to impel McNamara to kill the AR-15, while producing the M14 as an interim weapon, the effort failed.

For instead of canceling the AR-15, Secretary McNamara killed the M14 and along with it the old concept—after nearly 170 years—of long-range, deliberate fire. Production of the M14 would be discontinued at the end of 1963. Ultimately, the M14 machinery would be sold by the armory to the Chinese government in Taiwan. The secretary ordered the AR-15 to become the interim gun and authorized the purchase of eighty-five thousand AR-15s for the army and another nineteen thousand for the air force. Expecting to stand pat with that hand until the SPIW was developed three years later, McNamara wasn't able to foresee the huge demands the Vietnam War was to make for rifles—nor the scandalous disaster it would cause.

In October 1962, the nation faced the Cuban missile crisis. President Kennedy demanded that the Russians remove missiles set up in Cuba. At the last minute, with World War III as a distinct possibility, Russian ships carrying more missiles turned back from a course set for Cuba. Missiles in Cuba were removed. A few months later, in December 1962, the army in its year-end report noted that there were 11,300 American military personnel in Vietnam, up from 3,205 the year before.[15] Almost imperceptibly, the United States was being drawn into the war against Ho Chi Minh, while the U.S. Army still had no automatic rifle, except for the severely criticized and now nearly defunct M14.

In January 1963, in Ap Bac, South Vietnam, the ARVN (Army of the Republic of Vietnam), armed with the M14, suffered its first major defeat by the Viet Cong, armed with the AK47. Early in 1963, with the strong backing of President Kennedy and Secretary of Defense McNamara, the Special Forces (Green Berets) received approval to issue the AR-15 as their standard weapon. Then the army's own airborne units in Vietnam were also granted approval. Even the CIA acquired it. The legend of the AR-15 among units operating in Vietnam was growing, accompanied by the same litany: light weight, lethality, reliability, and low cost.

CHAPTER 38

ORDNANCE "MILITARIZES" THE AR-15 AS THE M16

It was now 1963, and with orders in hand from the air force for nineteen thousand AR-15s (now officially designated as the M16) and from special army units for another eighty-five thousand, Secretary McNamara had to decide what procurement unit would purchase these weapons and all the subsequent AR-15s. There were several options. Each service could buy its own, or some services could buy their own separately, while others could buy theirs through a joint purchasing operation. Secretary McNamara concluded that in the interests of efficiency and uniformity, there would be a single AR-15 procurement agency for all the services. In the light of the still very fresh bad blood and factionalism between the adherents of the AR-15 and the M14 in the Pentagon, the secretary made a decision that had tragic consequences. He turned the job of producing the AR-15 over to the Army Materiel Command, the new name of the Ordnance Corps. Many of the people who would be charged with making the AR-15 were M14 adherents who had every reason to hate this weapon. However, to impel the AMC to do a good job, Secretary McNamara issued a blunt four-part order to the Ordnance Corps:

1. Produce the M16 (AR-15) in volume.
2. Produce it immediately.
3. Make only the most nominal and essential modifications.

4. Make those changes or modifications, if any, only in close consultation with Eugene Stoner, the inventor of the AR-15.[1]

On March 6, 1963, Ordnance (the AMC) created the special Office of Project Manager for AR-15 Rifle Activities. Lieutenant Colonel Harold T. Yount was named project manager. As Stevens and Ezell note, his orders were to "achieve the earliest possible acquisition and deployment of the AR-15 system."[2] From that point on, all the services were to make their purchases of AR-15s through Yount's office. One of his army colleagues described him as "bright, industrious, highly motivated, eager to learn and professionally competent."[3] Until the day he assumed his duties, Colonel Yount had never seen an AR-15.

To make sure the committee got the McNamara message, his deputy secretary of defense, Roswell Gilpatrick, reinforced his boss's orders with specifics: "To avoid the cost, delay, and management difficulties of quality assurance, parts interchangeability, and acceptance test standards programs of previous rifle procurement . . . limit interchangeability requirements to those parts which can be realistically changed in the field."[4]

Frustrated with the antique military bureaucracy that had botched the production of the M14 and intent on introducing modern management methods, McNamara was usurping functions that had traditionally belonged to the military, with very unsettling effects in the Pentagon, which regarded the M16 with "teacher's pet" hostility. Nor did Ordnance like the newfound voices of the U.S. Navy, Marines, and Air Force in the committee rooms telling it how to make a rifle. All three branches were acquiring M16s and had definite ideas on how they wanted their new weapons made.

The defiance began almost immediately. Instead of obeying McNamara's written order to make only the most nominal changes in the AR-15, and only in conference with Eugene Stoner, Ordnance promptly declared the AR-15 to be inadequately "developed" and announced that it would "militarize" it.

And instead of immediate volume production of the M16, the Ordnance Corps, in a leisurely pace that recalled General Crozier's lackadaisical production of the Enfield, spent month after month studying the weapon so it could "finish developing it." A Technical Coordinating Committee (TCC) was formed in April of 1963, and, under the chairmanship of Colonel Yount, was staffed with representatives of the U.S. Army, Navy, Marines, and Air Force, plus a representative from McNamara's office. Various members soon proposed some 130 changes in the ammo-gun system. Quarreling began. No one would budge, and so the production contract authorizing Colt to proceed with production was postponed repeatedly. All through the spring, summer, fall, and even winter of 1963, the production authorization remained unsigned. What McNamara ordered not to happen had happened.

First off, the army declared that the reliability of the M16 was poor. Ordnance therefore would add a manual bolt closure to ram home a cartridge manually if it refused to seat itself properly. But on April 3, 1963, in a hastily called meeting at the Pentagon, the air force and the marines objected vehemently to the new bolt action. With three years of AR-15 experience, the air force deemed the addition totally unnecessary and useless. In those three years, the air force had never encountered a single instance of the kind of AR-15 malfunctioning that the manual bolt closing device could have corrected. Furthermore, the new bolt would increase the cost, weight, and complexity of the M16 and, rather than improve its performance, would actually reduce its remarkable reliability. Eugene Stoner later told the Ichord committee he thought the new device was useless. "I never saw an instance where it would have done any good." Further, by adding such a device, he went on, "you are buying yourself more trouble."[5]

By forcing the bolt on the AR-15/M16, the army was damaging its last bits of credibility with McNamara's office and destroying any vestige of harmony inside the Technical Coordinating Committee among members of the other services. In effect, the army was causing open war within the TCC. Any decision made by the committee was subject to immediate and irrevocable overruling by the distrustful representative from Secretary McNamara's office, who was determined not to let the Ordnance people turn the M16 into another M14. The AR-15/M16 was regarded at the office of the secretary of defense as the work of a genius, perfect in every way.

The TCC conflict was now out in the open: the committee room had become the battleground where McNamara's people were determined to flog the recalcitrant army into producing a weapon it didn't like or want. And Ordnance was fighting back in every way it could.

On May 15, 1963, the Army Materiel Procurement Agency designated Colt as the single-source manufacturer of the M16. Without a production contract, Colt was further prohibited from selling the AR-15—its own version of the M16—abroad. Colt warned that it was going to go broke while the TCC bickered over the absurd new manual bolt. The bickering continued.

In May 1963, in Springfield Armory, Ordnance decided to make another major design change in the M16—in the rifling inside the barrel. Eugene Stoner had made one twist for every fourteen inches, a major factor in the lethality of the weapon and one of its most celebrated features. The air force reported that its tests on the M16 showed that the accuracy of the rifle was impaired in the denser air of Arctic temperatures of 65 below zero. To correct some of the wobble, the air force suggested that the twist be once every twelve inches. Ordnance concurred and ordered Colt to make up several models with the new, shorter twist. The tests that followed showed conclusively that the extra twist in effect made the bullet more stable but less lethal on impact—40 percent less lethal, according to some commentators.[6] The army argued that without the added twist, the weapon could not meet its all-environments test, which required it to perform from minus 65 below zero to 125 above. So the extra cold-weather twist was added just in time to send the rifle to the steamy jungles of Southeast Asia with a significant loss in its lethality.

Caught up in the complexities of ballistics science, Secretary McNamara personally approved the twist change on July 26, 1963, with reluctance. In the autumn of 1963, another problem arose: Colt announced that due to the unresolved four-service quarrel over the addition of the manual bolt, its idle M16 manufacturing plant was facing imminent bankruptcy. Accordingly, Colt was soon going to shut down its M16 production line, retool, and start making a more profitable item on those machines. There would be no AR-15s available. Since Colt owned the patents on the AR-15, the army could hardly turn to another manufacturer to make the rifle. The implications were clear: either give Colt a significant production order or go back to the discredited M14.

McNamara had to take action. Instead of getting the interim rifle he wanted quickly, the TCC was bogged down in endless bickering. The four services hadn't even worked out a solution to its original dispute—the added manual bolt—and there were still the rest of the 130 proposed changes on the agenda. McNamara had originally stipulated that all four services had to agree with all changes in order to end up with one "all-service" rifle. That rule was now coming back to haunt him.

The problem was the technical nature of ballistics. In spite of all their computer techniques and management sciences, McNamara's "whiz kids" had no experience with proving and preparing a military weapon. Unable often to distinguish between the serious efforts of highly qualified gunsmiths and what they suspected was petulant foot-dragging, McNamara's people regarded every problem encountered in the Technical Coordinating Committee as another act of army intransigence.

On October 25, 1963, with Colt's announcement of the imminent breakup of its M16 production line, McNamara rescinded his rule of "one rifle." He ordered that the air force be given its rifles without the bolt. The army could have the same rifle with the new bolt or, if ongoing tests indicated, without—whatever it wished. Production therefore could proceed immediately. Questions like the firing pin changes—a new issue raised in the maddening TCC—could be answered later, during production.

On November 4, 1963, Secretary McNamara's office issued Contract "508" to Colt for some $13.5 million worth of Stoner's rifles, which placed the M16 officially into production. The contract also saved Colt. The air force was to receive nineteen thousand rifles in addition to those it had already purchased. This air force model was called the M16. The army was to receive 104,000 rifles with the highly controversial manual bolt, renamed the XM16E1. At $121 per rifle, that unnecessary bolt added $9 to the $112 cost of the M16.[7]

Why did the army insist on the bolt closure? Stevens and Ezell quote the U.S. Army's superintendent of the NATO North American Regional Test Center for ammunition, Bill Davis, who was involved in this phase of the M16 story: "It is my personal opinion that the stubborn stand taken on this issue by the Army . . . was provoked by the frustration that they felt at the impotence to which the TCC had been reduced by the much-used veto power of OSD [Office of Secretary of Defense] on every issue, great and small. It was unfortunately a weak issue on which to take such a symbolic stand."[8]

The question of ammunition next became an issue. Some ammunition explodes quickly; some burns more slowly. This characteristic determines where the gas port in the rifle will be placed. When the CONARC people asked Stoner to design the M16, it did not give him a finished .22 round to design his weapon around. Consequently, he designed his own, based in large part on a commercial .22 cartridge manufactured by Remington. Stoner designed his AR-15 for a powder called the IMR (Improved Military Rifle) which was made by Du Pont. Its principal component was nitrocellulose, a fast-burning powder that leaves little residue. Nitrocellulose was the ammunition which the air force tested in the AR-15 and which had established the weapon's highly praised reliability in Vietnam. Eugene Stoner specified IMR powder because it required fewer moving rifle parts and because it reduced the weight of the finished weapon.

Army Procurement wanted to order a supply of the new cartridge, so it asked Frankford Arsenal to detail the military characteristics of the cartridge to go on the purchase order. Frankford Arsenal obtained Remington's technical data package on its commercial .223 cartridge and discovered that Remington had been unable to mass-produce bullets to Stoner's original specifications and had quietly over the years changed the design of the bullet. While this bullet did not meet Stoner's original specifications, it was the ammunition that helped establish the reliability and lethality that had sold the enthusiastic air force and that had also earned those glowing reports from Vietnam.

Frankford Arsenal made another discovery. The Remington cartridge delivered slightly less muzzle velocity than the 3,300 fps everyone thought it did. Frankford Arsenal recommended that the M16 return to Stoner's original cartridge design as being more aerodynamic with better-resulting lethality.

But in the Technical Coordinating Committee, Frankford's recommendation incensed McNamara's representative. He summarily dismissed the whole idea. He was not interested in 3,300 fps muzzle velocity. In effect, he wanted the same ammunition that the air force had been using, the same ammunition that led to the rifle's great success in Vietnam. In truth, this was hardly the time to change the ammunition on a so-called interim rifle, yet the discrepancies between the original specifications for the AR-15 and the performance characteristics of the actual cartridge and powder as delivered raised technical questions that should have been resolved.

The TCC then issued a call for bids. But all three of the qualified ammunition manufacturers declined to bid on making the existing M16 round because they couldn't make it within the limits imposed by the TCC staff. In fact, the TCC's specifications for the M16 cartridge were so tight that even the ammunition that had been used in the M16 for the previous five years didn't qualify.

The ammunition makers said that the state of the art of the industry could not reach the army's tight parameters. To get the ammunition it needed, the TCC had to relax its IMR specifications because the army would soon need 130 million rounds of M16 ammunition. In December 1963, in Vietnam, a month after John Kennedy's assassination, the army reported that there were now 16,300 U.S. troops in Vietnam, most still armed with the M14.[9]

On January 17, 1964, rather than broaden its specifications for the IMR powder, and thereby introduce wide variations in performance, the Technical Coordinating Committee temporarily solved the ammunition problem by waiving the requirements for the first million rounds. But the TCC was still confronted with the problem for the next 129 million rounds. Before this issue could be resolved, ammunition requirements rose to 164 million rounds, with the first M16s due to come off the production line within two months—in the spring of 1964. The TCC found itself under terrific pressure to produce an ammunition almost overnight.

There must have been many in Ordnance who secretly exulted over the angry frustration in McNamara's office, especially when Du Pont withdrew itself from consideration as a bidder on the enormous potential M16 cartridge order. It announced that it would no longer make the IMR4475 powder around which Eugene Stoner had designed the AR-15. This cost the committee a crucial fallback position, forcing it now to find a totally new powder for the M16.

This withdrawal by Du Pont proved to be a disaster for the rifle, because now, whatever gunpowder the TCC chose, it would be an ammunition for which the M16 had not been designed and with which it had never been tested. Yet the army didn't seem to object to Du Pont's stunning decision. There must have been many in the military who felt that the army, by its silence, was letting the secretary of defense unwittingly bring on a disaster.

To find a new propellant, Ordnance called on its ammunition suppliers to present alternate gunpowders for the M16. This request was a move of profound significance. A rifle is designed around a specific cartridge, which is comprised of a multitude of characteristics—type of powder, quantity, grains of weight, diameter of the cartridge, configuration, and much more. Changing any of the specifications of the cartridge requires a redesign of the rifle, followed by extensive tests. With the exception of the representative from Secretary McNamara's office, there was not one man on the Technical Coordinating Committee who did not know this. Since the ammunition makers could not provide the ammunition stipulated, standard operating procedure indicated that the production of the M16 rifle be stopped and the designer, Eugene Stoner, given the problem to resolve.

This action was doubly indicated, since under McNamara's direct orders, the TCC was to make no changes in the weapon without Stoner's permission. The moment when this action should have been taken came and went. If the committee, for some political reason, could not return to Stoner—even though McNamara's directive required them to—then a prudent alternative would have been to turn to another weapons designer for help. Instead, the committee sent the problem to three ammunition makers.

Further complicating matters, the committee changed the recipe for the gunpowder. Instead of calling for a clean-burning gunpowder like Du Pont's, the committee called for a slow-burning ball powder that was known to leave a residue.

On that same day, the Technical Coordinating Committee changed another specification, and again without consulting Stoner, allowing the maximum chamber pressure inside the rifle to be increased from 52,000 psi to 53,000 psi. Ordnance said this was a very temporary solution.[10]

Three gunpowder makers submitted a powder for consideration. These were tested at the Frankford Arsenal and eventually two powders qualified: Du Pont's CR8136 and Olin's WC846. Contrary to McNamara's express orders to clear every change with Stoner, no one in the TCC or in McNamara's own office informed the designer of the new ammunition. He didn't learn of this profoundly significant change for some weeks afterward, after contracts for millions of rounds had been let.

Long after Secretary McNamara's instructions required it, after many major changes in the M16 had been made, the Technical Coordinating Committee sent Frank Vee of the comptroller's office to visit Stoner to obtain his endorsement for the new gunpowder. Vee brought the armory's technical data package for the AR-15/M16 with him.

Stoner told the Ichord committee later that Vee asked him for his opinion of the set of changes in the rifle and its ammunition. Basing his reply not only on his own design and development work with his rifle but with the field experience in Asia of the AR-15, particularly in Vietnam, Stoner answered, "I would advise against it."

Stoner pointed out that because of the new ball powder, residue inside the gas tube and chamber would cause the rifle to jam chronically, thereby destroying the rifle's reliability.

In addition, Stoner asserted that the new powder also increased the rifle's cyclic rate from 750 to 800 rounds per minute to 1,000, which could cause the rifle to break down and jam and would be exacerbated by the new higher twist of the barrel. "This is not the rifle I gave you," Stoner told Vee.[11]

This was a serious turn of events: the designer of the weapon had rejected the changes wrought by the Technical Coordination Committee and the committee, in turn, ignored the objections. Contrary to Stoner's warning, no long-term testing of the new powders in the M16 was scheduled, an omission that opened the committee to future attack.

The choice of powder was removed from the TCC's authority when the chief of ordnance made the ammunition change mandatory. He ordered that all small arms ammunition—not just for the M14 and the M16—be loaded with ball-type powder. The chief had his reasons: ball powder was used in the NATO 7.62-mm round, among others, and to assure uniform quality, Ordnance wanted to buy it in large quantities. Ball-type powder was also described as safer and cheaper to manufacture. This move was part of the armory's often criticized single-sourcing practice.

In the event of any future dispute, the record would show the chief of ordnance—not the TCC—was requiring the M16, the army's newest rifle, to use a powder designed for the M14, the dead rifle waiting to be phased out of the army. And they were to use that powder as standard even before anyone had determined what effects the M14 powder might have on the performance of the M16.

"From a technical standpoint," Stoner told the Ichord Congressional Investigating Subcommittee, "it was absolutely wrong."

The first sign of a problem with ball-type powder occurred in the inspection department at the Colt manufacturing plant on March 24, 1964. In the standard testing procedure, the Colt test staff presented the new rifles in horizontal gun racks ready for inspection and test-firing by in-house government inspectors. Acceptance was based on successful test-firing with a maximum allowable firing of 850 rounds per minute. Almost all M16 rifles that were tested with the last of the old Du Pont IMR4475 passed the test and were accepted. But six out of ten of the M16s tested with the new WC846 ball powder exceeded the 850 rounds per minute maximum called for by the army's specifications. Colt realized that such a rate could soon fill a warehouse with rejected rifles and put the company on the road to bankruptcy.

Colt's experts held a meeting to make certain that the problem lay not with the rifles but with the WC846 ammunition the army was supplying. Colt asked the army to accept rifles that fired up to nine hundred rounds per minute, a higher rate caused solely by the new powder. Under pressure, with M16s coming off the production line in volume now, the army reluctantly raised the acceptable rate to nine hundred rounds per minute, effective with April's run. This specification was extended each month that summer of 1964—when Eugene Stoner declined to endorse the powder change requested by Frank Vee. So the TCC was caught in a trap: it had rejected the IMR4475 ammunition for not meeting standards, then replaced it with WC846, which also did not meet standards.

The army inspectors referred the excessive firing problem to army ballistics experts at the Frankford Arsenal in Philadelphia. Frankford conducted a study that showed that the WC846 was producing gas port pressures 500 psi higher than the IMR powder. WC846, concomitantly, put more heat in the gas tube, an undesirable side effect. With the report, Frankford Arsenal pointed out that no one knew the M16's allowable upper firing limits of rounds per minute, nor of the maximum allowable port pressure with the new powder. At what point does the weapon begin to foul and jam, when will it explode? The Frankford study finished with this ominous statement:

"In the final analysis, the tests required to establish tolerable port-pressure limits for the AR-15 are weapon tests." But the only weapon tests in the offing were in combat in Vietnam. In other words, the only way the army would discover performance limits of the WC846 powder was in the hands of American soldiers facing off with Viet Cong armed with AK47s.

On March 30, 1964, the air force received the first of its rifles bearing the new designation M16, when Colt presented it to Major General E. J. Gibson at the Hartford plant. On May 26, the army's first XM16E1 was presented to Army Chief of Staff General Wheeler in his office by Paul Benke, Colt's president. No one commented on one glaring oddity about the new rifle. In the Springfield '03, in the M1, in the M14, in every other weapon of recent vintage, the army issued a cleaning kit—including bore brushes, cleaning patches, and lubricants—that was stored inside the gunstock. But the M16 had none—no cleaning tools of any type and no maintenance manual. And yet the rifle was being issued with an ammunition that left a residue behind. Everyone who has ever carried a rifle in the army has been imbued with the sacred ritual of rifle cleaning. It takes precedence over everything else. A clean rifle is a religious precept, a holy act.

On April 24, 1964, the TCC was confronted with a need to change another M16 performance standard. The Frankford Arsenal in Philadelphia produced more technical bad news. The air force had a test requirement: the rifle bullet should pass completely through ten-gauge mild steel plate at a range of five hundred yards. This test was originally established for the official 7.62-mm M80 round. The M1 passed this test; so did the M14. But the 5.56-caliber bullet fired from the M16 was not designed to pass such a plate penetration test. It, however, could penetrate ten-gauge steel consistently at 450 yards, fifty yards less. The Technical Coordinating Committee referred the problem to the Frankford Arsenal, where, in June 1964, during penetration tests conducted jointly by the air force and army, the new M16 ball ammunition passed penetration tests at 450 yards. So this became the new plate standard—ten gauge at 450 yards, fifty yards less than the original specification. This specification was the third new test parameter that had been created after the new ball powder failed the previous more-stringent tests. Everybody on the TCC seemed to like the new powder, except the rifle itself.

Frankford Arsenal called once more for some bona fide testing of the new M16 rifle/cartridge as a system to determine whether they were compatible. There were plenty of indications that they were not. In calling for more serious testing, Frankford Arsenal once again raised a cautionary finger and called for a return to the original .223-caliber cartridge that Stoner designed. The warning went unheeded.

Meanwhile, all through the summer of 1964, the hostility between the TCC and representatives from McNamara's office continued to exacerbate the struggles to cope with swarming technical problems. If the McNamara representatives were conducting themselves in an overbearing, scornful manner, vetoing committee decisions, upbraiding committee members, and showing a lack of experience in rifle science, most of the committee members were reacting with truculence. Their combined activities seemed to cancel out the dedicated efforts needed to produce the best possible rifle for infantrymen in battle.

On August 1964, a new ammunition from Du Pont—CR8136—became available, and Colt began using it in the qualifying firing tests for the M16. CR8136 produced lower port pressures than WC846. Therefore, the cyclic rate under the CR8136 fell below the 850 allowable maximum. The 900 rpm waiver for the WC846 was allowed to expire.

On September 4, the TCC received the first reports from troops at Fort Bragg on the army's version of the M16—the XM16E1, with the added bolt. For the test, the troops had been issued a new cleaning rod, M11. The troops reacted favorably to the rifle, but not to the new cleaning rod, which was generally faulted for being flimsy and easily broken. More significant: the troops said that the rifle lacked a brush that could be used to "clean the space between the bolt locking lugs and chamber, in barrel extension."[12] The army failed to take action on that recommendation.

In June 1964, General William C. Westmoreland replaced General Paul Harkins as U.S. MACV commander (Military Assistance Command Vietnam). Only a few weeks after General Westmoreland assumed command, the U.S. destroyer *Turner Joy* reported that it had been attacked by North Vietnamese patrol boats in the Tonkin Gulf off North Vietnam, and on August 7, 1964, the U.S. Congress passed the Tonkin Gulf Resolution, which in effect gave President Lyndon Johnson—and later Richard Nixon—authority to conduct full-scale war against North Vietnam.

Two months later, on October 30, a North Vietnamese attack on Bien Hoa Air Base destroyed six U.S. B-57 bombers and killed five American service personnel. That same month, Communist China exploded its first atomic bomb, while in a continuing series of proving tests on M16 rifles as they came off the production line, the Development and Proof Services at the Aberdeen Proving Ground published a report that should have alerted every member of the Technical Coordinating Committee. DPS had test-fired the M16 with samples of ball powder and recorded nineteen malfunctions— sixteen of them after firing a thousand rounds without cleaning or lubricating. The DPS warned that this meant the rifle should not be fired beyond a thousand rounds without cleaning and lubricating. Echoing the recommendation issued at Fort Bragg a few weeks before, on September 4, 1964, the DPS report also stated that the M16 should be equipped with special brushes for cleaning sensitive areas, including the chamber, the locking lugs in the barrel extension, and the inner chamber of the bolt carrier, where carbon residue accumulated.

Another ominous development occurred during the same tests, when, after eighteen hours at temperatures of 125-plus degrees Fahrenheit and relative humidity of 90 percent, the M16 cam pin rusted. This made opening the bolt very difficult and indicated that the M16 needed special care in tropical environments. To that end, the Development and Proof Services recommended that a proper cleaning kit be included with all M16s, along with a rust-preventive lubricant. This marked the second time in as many months that the TCC had been warned that the M16 rifle needed, as standard issue, cleaning and lubricating equipment, cleaning instruction literature, and, by implication, cleaning training.[13]

In its year-end report in December 1964—a year after the assassination of John Kennedy and in the first year of Lyndon Johnson's administration—the U.S. Army reported that U.S. troops in Vietnam had now reached 23,300, up from 16,300 in December 1963. The South Vietnam Armed Forces (SVNAF) troop count was 514,000, up from 243,000 a year before.[14] And that same December, without the required authorization of Eugene Stoner, in direct violation of the command of Secretary McNamara, the Technical Coordinating Committee's continued production of the M16 encountered a major problem at the Colt plant. Du Pont's CR8136 powder, which Du Pont had created as a replacement for its IMR formula, was also withdrawn from the market. This development came at a very sensitive time. The new Du Pont powder was being used to proof-test the M16 rifles as they came off the Colt production line. The other new powder accepted by the Technical Coordinating Committee—Olin's WC846 powder—was not used because it caused cyclic rates above the allowable limit of 850 per minute. The reason Du Pont gave for withdrawal was the inability of its manufacturing process to maintain the very narrow specifications that the Technical Coordinating Committee required. When Colt consumed its existing supply of Du Pont powder for proof-testing, the TCC would be left with one powder, Olin's, which did not fit army specifications. Colt warned that the M16 most likely would not pass the proof-test with Olin powder. Having rejected the original IMR4475 ammunition as failing to meet specifications, the Technical Coordinating Committee accepted a new ammunition that also failed to meet specifications and that, furthermore, could cause serious jamming problems, which Du Pont's IMR4475 never did.

In the meantime, the U.S. role in the Vietnam War was escalating. Three months after the ammunition problem occurred at the Colt plant, on March 2, 1965, the U.S. Air Force commenced Operation Rolling Thunder, which sought to stop the flow of North Vietnamese military supplies south by bombing targets in North

Vietnam. On March 8–9, 1965, the first U.S. combat troops—the Third Marine Regiment, Third Marine Division—arrived in Vietnam from Okinawa to defend Da Nang airfield. On April 6, 1965, President Lyndon Johnson authorized the use of U.S. combat troops for the first time in offensive operations in South Vietnam.

That August in 1965, Colt's manufacturing proving rooms witnessed another heated exchange when Colt executives expressed their anger and frustration with the army inspectors. Colt had used the last of Du Pont's CR8136 cartridges, which enabled the M16 to pass the army's acceptance test. The only powder available was Olin's WC846, but test after test showed that WC846 made the M16 fire too fast and then jam. The factory was crowded with M16s that had been rejected because they could not pass the army test. The rejection rate had risen to 50 percent. Colt executives claimed that the Olin ammunition the army supplied was going to put the company out of business.

At this meeting, Colt announced that it could no longer be responsible for getting the M16 past the army's acceptance test and asked that the cyclic rate be allowed to increase to 900 rpm. As a result, an urgent meeting was held in the Office of Army Materiel Procurement in the Pentagon, during which the ranking officers in Procurement drafted an official letter permitting Colt to use any ammunition it wished for the proving tests. In this same meeting, however, it was agreed that the army would continue to ship those rifles to Vietnam with ball powder. The army said it did not recognize the "theories" that ball powder caused the rifle's problems, so the powder that Colt used for its acceptance testing was immaterial.[15] As a result of this letter from the TCC, Colt was permitted to return to using its dwindling supply of discontinued Du Pont ammunition to test the M16. In short, the army tested the M16 rifle with one ammunition, then shipped it with another ammunition that caused the rifle to overheat and malfunction.

Colonel Yount and the members of the Technical Coordinating Committee put themselves in a vulnerable and dangerous position: they had been put on notice that they were shipping weapons that could jam in combat and leave U.S. troops defenseless in the face of enemy fire. In the months ahead, the TCC was to ship 330,000 M16 rifles, most of them to Vietnam, 90 percent of them with ball powder.[16]

The next major crisis occurred only weeks later, in the autumn of 1965, when Colt used the last of Du Pont's CR8136 test cartridges that enabled the M16 to pass the acceptance test. Thereafter, the only powder available was Olin's WC846, which was producing a rejection rate by army inspectors of an astonishing 50 percent. Colt executives argued that since the rifle couldn't pass the test, the test should be altered to fit the rifle. They wanted the TCC to increase the acceptable firing rate with ball powder to 900 a minute. When the TCC refused, Colt suspended manufacture of the XM16E1 for the army, but continued to make the M16 for the air force, which would accept the 900 rpm cyclic rate.[17]

In response to Colt's action, while the army was gearing up for battle with the North Vietnamese army and the Viet Cong, the TCC called for more tests at the Frankford Arsenal in Philadelphia and asked the powder makers to submit new powders. Olin refused, asserting that major and expensive research would be required to improve its WC846.

In September 1965, in Philadelphia, the Frankford Arsenal completed the tests requested by the TCC and presented some disturbing results. The tests concluded first off that "none of the test propellants appears capable of consistently meeting the current XM16E1 rifle cyclic rate requirement of 750+/- rpm."[18] Furthermore, of the powders tested, the WC846 "gave the greatest amount of visible accumulation of residue in the bolt assembly area." After 1,000 to 1,500 rounds without cleaning, "WC846-loaded cartridges will cause stoppages attributable to excessive fouling in the bolt mechanism."[19] The TCC was being told by yet another test that the M16 rifle, capable of firing WC846 ammunition up to 750 rounds a minute, could jam soon after being introduced in battle.

Frankford recommended that a new powder—EX8208 from Du Pont—be approved, and that Olin be encouraged to reduce the cause of fouling deposits from its WC846 powder. Since Du Pont's EX8208 powder was not available until June of 1966, nine months later, the army's build-up in Vietnam had to be accomplished with M16s provided with WC846. The army had wasted nearly three critical months to learn officially, in writing, from its own testing laboratory in Philadelphia what Colt had been telling it vociferously for many months: without careful rifle cleaning, WC846 powder could cause the XM16E1 to jam after firing a few clips of ammunition. Yet the army was not to ship a single new chamber brush to Vietnam until late 1966, and by June 1967, brushes were still in short supply.[20]

Reluctantly, the TCC accepted a new cyclic rate of 900 rpm from the Colt test labs and M16 production resumed.

The first major engagement between American and North Vietnamese forces took place November 14–16, 1965, in the Ia Drang Valley of South Vietnam. The U.S. Third Brigade, First Cavalry Division, green troops in their first combat, took on the battle-hardened Thirty-second, Thirty-third, and Sixty-sixth North Vietnamese regiments. The Americans were armed with the unmodified M16 (the original AR-15), which performed outstandingly and received high praise from the troops and their officers. Most significant, these green American troops roundly defeated the NVA. Thereafter, the North Vietnamese dubbed the AR-15 "the Black Rifle" because of its black case, and in future engagements would avoid American units armed with it.

In marked contrast, the M14 was causing the U.S. Army in Vietnam grave concern. On the same day that the Third Brigade was defeating the North Vietnamese with the M16, November 16, 1965, General Westmoreland and his senior military advisers, in an urgent meeting in the general's headquarters in Saigon, discussed how badly the M14 was fairing against the enemy's AK47. Nineteen sixty-five was the year the U.S. troops were committed to full combat in Vietnam and most of them carried the M14. But, Westmoreland's advisers told him, American troops found that the M14 was inaccurate and uncontrollable and no match for the enemy's Soviet AK47, firing six hundred rounds a minute. Conversely, the battle at Ia Drang showed that the M16 could defeat troops with the AK47. American soldiers who could afford it were buying the AR-15 on the black market for $600, six times the original list price of $100.

The consensus of the meeting held that American troops with the M14 were being mauled, with casualties mounting significantly. Westmoreland's officers decided that the M14 had to be replaced by the EM16E1. Knowing how adamant Ordnance was about the M14 and anticipating a tough fight, Westmoreland personally made an urgent request for 100,000 EM16E1s.

One needs to wonder, since battle reports demonstrated that the M14 was no match for the AK47, what the U.S. Army in Vietnam would have done for the rest of the war had there been no M16 in the army's arsenal.

To induce Ho Chi Minh to come to the negotiating table, President Johnson suspended Operation Rolling Thunder, which was heavily bombing North Vietnam. Ho Chi Minh sent his reply publicly—he counterattacked American forces.

In December 1965, Frankford Arsenal engineers tested the M16 with ball powder and with IMR. The results were conclusive: the M16 had a failure rate six times higher with ball powder than with IMR. That same month, the air force strongly objected once again to Ordnance's changes in the AR-15—this time to ball powder, which it did not want. The air force called for the clean-burning IMR powder. Once again, Ordnance ignored the complaint.

In its annual report on December 31, 1965, the U.S. Army reported that military personnel now on duty in Vietnam had been increased to 184,300. Six hundred and thirty-six Americans had been killed in action to date. SVNAF troop strength remained at 514,000.[21] Large antiwar rallies had been held throughout 1965 in Washington and forty other cities.

During the winter of 1965–1966, at Fort Ord, the army conducted an extended series of new tests with the M16, the M14, and the Soviet AK47. A number of the personnel who participated in these tests had participated in a series of M16 tests three years before. They were surprised to discover that "three years of 'development' had done more harm than good."[22] The tests themselves provided the specifics; the M16 had suffered breakdowns, jamming and fouling, all of which was directly attributed to ball propellant ammunition. Even though the testing troops maintained a more-stringent cleaning standard than troops in combat could meet,[23] ball propellant had measurably diminished the M16's reliability. Ironically, the most reliable weapons in the tests were Soviet AK47s, despite the fact that while all the M14s and M16s were mint condition, the AK47s were battlefield pickups from Vietnam. However, in terms of performance characteristics—pointing, accuracy, ease of handling—the M16 was deemed the most effective weapon of the three. These Fort Ord tests provided the TCC with still more evidence from an outside source of the direct correlation between ball powder and M16 malfunctions. Yet Ordnance was shipping more ball powder to Vietnam than ever.

Dr. William Payne, chief of the Office of Operations Research, Office of the Secretary of the Army, in Washington, D.C., received a copy of the Fort Ord report the next month, January 1966, and was very disturbed by the findings. If malfunctions were happening to carefully cleaned M16s, during carefully controlled tests, then what must be happening in the down-and-dirty war in Vietnam? He wrote a memo, asking the Frankford Arsenal to conduct a comparison test of the two ammunitions in the M16. In February 1966, the test Dr. Payne requested—similar to the test the previous December—produced the same unequivocal results: the M16 suffered a greater number of malfunctions with ball propellants.[24]

In that same January 1966, the TCC made its own moves to correct the ball propellant problems. Rather than fit the ammunition to the rifle, the TCC would alter the M16 to fit the ammunition.[25] To slow the cyclic rate of the weapon, the committee decided to increase the weight of the recoiling parts of the rifle by adding a heavier recoil buffer. The new buffer did slow the cyclic rate, but by solving one problem, it degraded overall performance. Compounding the problem, despite the urgent requests from American troops in Vietnam for M16s, the new buffer was not to be incorporated into the M16 until December 1966—eleven months later.

Those 100,000 M16s General Westmoreland had ordered were distributed quickly, and by midsummer of 1966, he had informally asked for 100,000 more—to be issued to American troops, to the ARVNs, and also to the Korean troops who were eager to be rid of the old M1s they were carrying. General Chu Chinn of the ROK (Republic of Korea) army pressed hard for M16s.[26] Ordnance ignored General Westmoreland's informal order. To get the new weapons, he would have to go through formal channels.

CHAPTER 39

OUTCRY FROM VIETNAM

B y October 1966, M16s had begun to jam in battle. Up and down the firing line in Vietnam, in the jungles and rice paddies, in desperate firefights with the Viet Cong and the North Vietnamese army, the M16s became fouled with the residue of the ball powder and stopped firing. American troops were dying as a direct result.

By that month, only 45,000 of the 385,000 U.S. troops in Vietnam had been armed with the M16 rifle, but the jamming of the brand-new weapon became so widespread that even the TCC heard about it.[1] Ordnance officials said the complaints only proved what they'd been claiming all along, that "it was a lousy rifle."[2]

Despite the growing clamor, the army still shipped the M16s with poor or misleading maintenance instructions. And no cleaning equipment. Contrary to army practice with every other weapon in the U.S. arsenal, and in spite of repeated warnings for two years, the army was still shipping the M16 with no cleaning kit—no bore brushes, chamber brushes, cleaning patches, or lubricants. Even if such a kit were provided, the M16 still lacked the customary place in the butt stock to store the kit. Many of the troops were sent into combat without any training whatsoever on the care and cleaning of their M16s—a shocking omission of the most important ritual in an infantryman's life.[3]

Desperate for cleaning equipment, American soldiers had already begun to buy by mail order a rifle lubricant called Dri-Slide. One soldier wrote the Dri-Slide company that some of his best buddies died in a firefight. "I personally checked their weapons. Close to 70 percent had a round stuck in the chamber and take my word for it, it was not their fault. Sir if you will send three hundred and sixty cans along with the bill, I'll 'gladly' pay it out of my own pocket. This will be enough for every man in our company to have a can."[4]

Parents received letters. "These rifles are getting a lot of guys killed because they jam so easy," wrote one soldier. "Please send me a bore and a 1¼ inch or so paint brush I need for my rifle."[5] The parents sent the cleaning material, then, along with many other parents, contacted their representatives and senators. Even the Viet Cong, who had at first avoided American troops armed with the AR-15, now stripped dead Americans of everything but the M16, which they considered "worthless."[6]

Senator Gaylord Nelson of Wisconsin received this letter:

"The weapon has failed us at crucial moments when we needed fire power most. In each case, it left Marines naked against their enemy. Often, and this is no exaggeration, we take counts after each fight, as many as 50% of the rifles fail to work. I know of at least two marines who died within 10 feet of the enemy with jammed rifles. One Marine [was found] beating an NVA [North Vietnamese Army] with his helmet and a hunting knife because his rifle failed— this can't continue—32 of about 80 rifles failed yesterday."[7]

The Ichord Congressional subcommittee, formed to investigate the M16, reported after its visit to Vietnam: "The reported death of one corporal, killed while running up and down the line of his squad pushing out cartridges which failed to extract with the only cleaning rod in the squad, was confirmed by our investigation."[8]

Kanemitsu Ito, a member of the Colt team that was sent to Vietnam, later told the Ichord subcommittee that because of the acute shortage of cleaning equipment, he found troops attempting to clean their rifles with "wire, shoe strings, nylon cord, string and bamboo strips." They also tried to clean the rifle bore with "solvents, gasoline, JP-4 aircraft fuel, diesel oil, motor oil, LPS, WD-40, Dri-Slide, Mil-L-46000, insect repellent, and water."[9]

The outcry caused Colonel Yount to send his assistant, Lieutenant Colonel Underwood, to Vietnam. He found many M16s in appalling condition, some never having been cleaned and, in almost all of these cases, troops who had never been trained in cleaning their weapons. The fewest jamming problems occurred in military units that had received maintenance training.

Lieutenant Colonel Underwood called Colonel Yount to persuade him to come to Vietnam, which Yount did. After studying the problem, Colonel Yount identified the cause: a lack of proper maintenance. In other words, the troops were at fault for not cleaning their weapons.[10] By December 1966, the army, officially echoing Colonel Yount, was saying that the jamming was a problem of improper maintenance. In response, officials were sent on inspection tours in Vietnam to instruct the soldiers on cleaning their M16s. But this directly contradicted statements contained in the literature that accompanied the rifle, which told the infantrymen: "This rifle will fire longer without cleaning or oiling than any other known rifle. . . . An occasional cleaning will keep the weapon functioning indefinitely."[11]

The army in Vietnam now instituted maintenance training for the M16, and at the same time issued a flow of new instructional literature. For the first time, many troops learned that the M16 bolt, which officially didn't need to be oiled, needed to be oiled. They also were told to tape a cleaning rod to the rifle and to never leave a cartridge in the chamber overnight, where it could swell and jam.

Even after the troops were conducting proper maintenance on their M16s, the problem of the ball propellant remained. Some eighty-nine million rounds of ball propellant were to be fired before the army acknowledged that the ball-type propellant was causing the M16 to malfunction.[12] Not until the new buffer, authorized by the Technical Coordinating Committee in January of 1966, finally reached Vietnam in December of 1966, nearly a year later, did the jamming largely clear up.

On December 6, 1966, in his headquarters in Saigon, General Westmoreland and his staff were once again reviewing the rifle situation. Although the jamming problem was abating, a severe shortage of M16s still remained. And, at the same time, the shortcomings of the M14, "semiautomatic and too heavy for the jungle,"[13] had proved over and over that it was no match for the enemy's Soviet AK47. Those troops not armed with M16s were taking more of a mauling than ever from the enemy as the mounting American casualties indicated.

Unable to get a favorable response from Ordnance to his informal request, General Westmoreland sent a formal requisition for 100,000 M16s through official channels, and the next day, December 7, Ordnance issued a production order to Colt for 100,000 M16s.[14] Even with Colt's new production order, Ordnance still didn't give General Westmoreland everything he wanted. Some 68,000 M16s were reserved for the U.S. Army, 32,000 for the Marines, but none for the ARVN and the ROK. All of the 100,000 M16s would be provided with ball powder only.

This condition was dismaying to the ARVN. Years after they could have first used the M16—and had asked for it—against the ferocious attacks of the Viet Cong, the ARVN still waited for their first M16, with little expectation of ever getting any. In the face of the rapidly rising involvement of U.S. forces in Vietnam, and while Colt's production was barely able to operate a single shift per day and was scratching for more orders, the U.S. Army had no plans to order more M16 rifles beyond General Westmoreland's requisition for 100,000—not in 1967, 1968, or 1969.[15] Simultaneously, the army ordered that the M16 not be used in Europe or the United States; it would not replace the M14 as the army's standard assault weapon.

In its year-end report in December 1966, the U.S. Army reported that the number of U.S. troops now in Vietnam had reached 385,300. That level was due to rise to 485,600 within the next twelve months. The number of American troops killed to date was 6,664. Another ten thousand young men were to die in the twelve months ahead. The South Vietnamese armed forces, carrying either the M14 or the M1, now had 735,000 men under arms, a huge jump of some 200,000 men. To date, 47,712 South Vietnamese soldiers had been killed.[16]

When complaints against the M16 reached Congress, that body was baffled by the outcry. The M16 had been introduced as the most lethal and the most reliable assault rifle ever invented. Congressmen recalled that only two years before, when the M16 had first been introduced into Vietnam in large numbers, an untested U.S. cavalry regiment, in fighting as fierce as any ever experienced by American troops, beat back and drove off several brutal North Vietnamese attacks, killing thirteen hundred of them in the process. It was an awesome first performance for troops never before in battle and a major victory, and the regiment's commander, Moore, had proclaimed in headlines around the world, "Brave soldiers and the M16 brought this victory."[17] Moore and his men told General William C. Westmoreland that "the M16 was the best individual infantry weapon ever made, clearly the answer to the enemy's AK47." Congress felt it had found the weapon that could defeat Ho Chi Minh's troops.

But praise turned to political heat. Letters were arriving from all over the country—from parents quoting letters from their sons in Vietnam, from wives, from friends, relatives, people who read accounts in newspapers. What had gone wrong with the M16? On May 7, 1967, Representative Mendel Rivers, chairman of the House Armed Services Committee, formed a subcommittee under the chairmanship of Representative Richard Ichord, Democrat from Missouri, and assigned two other members to the committee: Speedy O. Long, Democrat from Louisiana and William G. Bray, Republican from Indiana. Rivers ordered the troika, designated the Special Subcommittee on the M16 Rifle Program, to conduct a full investigation into the M16 situation.[18]

The Ichord committee acted quickly, and by mid-May 1967 was down in Fort Benning, where the U.S. Infantry, feeling it had made great strides in eliminating the problems with jamming, was the eager host. It proved to be an embarrassment.

In full view of the Ichord committee, the M16 malfunctioned on the firing range. The Ichord team then traveled to another demonstration at Camp Pendleton. More M16s malfunctioned.[19] These two failures did considerable harm to the army's defense that it was adequately handling the problems with the M16. The committee could draw only one conclusion from what it had seen. If the weapon could fail during a carefully prepared and controlled presentation at two military firing ranges, then it certainly could fail in battle.

As if to underscore the firing range failures, a still-greater outcry against the M16 occurred just as the Ichord committee was visiting the two military bases. During April and May 1967, a North Vietnamese army had moved artillery up on three hills—Hill 861, Hill 881 North, Hill 881 South—overlooking the U.S. combat base and airstrip at Khe Sanh, with the objective of attacking and overrunning the base. In response, two battalions from the Third U.S. Marine Regiment, which had been flown into that airstrip, moved toward the three hills, supported by Marine Corps fighter bombers and 175-mm artillery, and soon engaged North Vietnamese Regiment 325, C Division, in a ferocious firefight. Both sides mounted a heavy small arms assault, and both sides suffered heavy casualties.

The marines began to experience jammed M16s and became highly vulnerable to enemy fire as they broke open their weapons, urgently passing back and forth an inadequate number of cleaning rods. Many were shot dead as they struggled with their weapons. Casualties mounted as the jamming increased. A young marine from New Jersey wrote an account of the battle in a letter to his family, which they permitted to be published on May 20, 1967, as part of an article in the *Asbury Park Evening Press* headlined: "Causing Deaths—Marine Hits Faulty Rifle."

It was reprinted in the U.S. *Congressional Record* on Monday, May 22, 1967, when Representative James J. Howard, a Democrat from New Jersey, a member of the House Public Works and Transportation Committee, and himself a World War II navy veteran who served in the South Pacific, stood up to address the House.

"Mr. Speaker: the Members of the House, as well as millions of Americans, have been greatly disturbed over recent reports that the M16 rifle presently being used in Vietnam is unreliable. A special subcommittee of the Armed Services Committee of the House under Representative Ichord is presently holding hearings concerning the M16. I have, this morning, brought to the attention of Secretary of Defense McNamara and the Ichord committee disturbing information that has come into my hands concerning our fighting in Vietnam in general, and the M16 rifle in particular."

Omitting the marine's name, the congressman read the short letter into the *Congressional Record*:

Dear ———:

I just got your letter today aboard ship. We've been on an operation ever since the 21st of last month. I can just see the papers back home now—Enemy casualties heavy Marine casualties light. Let me give you some statistics and you decide if they were light. We left with close to 1400 men in our battalion and came back with half. We left with 250 men in our company and came back with 107. We left with 72 men in our platoon and came back with 19. I knew I was pressing my luck. They finally got me. It wasn't too bad though. I just caught a little shrapnel. I wish I could say the same for all my buddies.

The ratio was something like 8 to 1 confirmed. We don't know how many they dragged away. It was a lot from all the blood we saw, believe it or not, you know what killed most of us? Our own rifles. Before we left Okinawa, we were all issued this new rifle, the M16. Practically every one of our dead was found with his rifle torn down next to him where he had been trying to fix it. There was a newspaper woman with us photographing all this and the Pentagon found out about it and won't let her publish the pictures. They say they don't want to get the American people upset. Isn't that a laugh?

All this just because we had to take some hills with numbers on them. The ones we caught hell on were 861 and 881.[20]

Representative Howard demanded that Secretary of Defense McNamara and the Pentagon provide an immediate explanation. Congress was in no mood for an M16 problem. There were over

385,000 U.S. troops in Vietnam fighting one of the most vicious and stubborn and wily enemies the United States had ever faced. By the end of 1967, some sixteen thousand Americans were to die there. Congress was feeling the heat from a nation that had had enough. This M16 controversy was more fuel on a growing fire of American anger.

As a result, Chairman Mendel Rivers directed the Ichord committee to go personally to Vietnam for a firsthand look. The committee left on June 1 to question hundreds of army infantrymen and marines on the firing line in combat. The group returned on June 11, 1967, convinced that Ordnance had seriously botched the conversion of the AR-15 into the M16.

Back in its committee hearing room, the Ichord committee began to peel away the layers of accrued history and conflicting viewpoints to discover who was responsible. The group summoned a long list of witnesses, including three major generals from the U.S. Army, a major general from the U.S. Air Force, a major general from the Marine Corps, a brigadier general from the Marine Corps, a deputy assistant secretary of the State Department, an assistant secretary of the army, an assistant secretary of the air force, a number of top officials from America's leading arms manufacturing companies and gunpowder makers, and, significantly, the inventor of the AR-15 himself, Eugene Stoner.[21]

The investigation lasted all through the summer of 1967, and its testimony filled six hundred pages of closely packed type. The Ichord committee published its report on October 10, 1967, and submitted it to Representative Mendel Rivers, chairman of the parent House Armed Services Committee. Congress and the American public were finally getting as close to an answer on what had gone wrong with the M16 as they would ever get.

The Ichord committee was not satisfied that all the witnesses had been fully forthcoming. Most of the witnesses were unable to say where the various standards that changed the M16 had come from: the tighter twist in the barrel, the FPS rule, the reasoning behind the added bolt, the switch to the ball powder ammunition. "I don't remember" was a frequent reply.

Under questioning, Colonel Harold Yount finally told the congressional committee who had decided to add the highly disputed bolt closure: the army's chief of staff himself, General Earl Wheeler.[22] Why the top-ranking military officer in the country intruded himself into the arcane and complex design problems of a military rifle was never explained. Members of the Ordnance Corps testified that they had a hard time remembering who issued key orders that so significantly affected the performance of the M16. They defended the rules for Arctic performance, sought to justify the choice of ball powder, which kept the chamber pressure below 52,000 fps, and a few even blamed the rifle's problems on the soldier "the draft was dredging up these days" who would not keep his weapon clean.[23]

The Ichord committee's conclusions severely damaged the few shreds of stature the Ordnance Corps still retained with the rest of the military. Under "Findings and Recommendations," the committee impaled the entire Ordnance bureaucracy with such stunning disapproval, the text reads more like a grand jury indictment against a criminal conspiracy than a congressional report. What made the summary even more interesting to military historians, many of the committee's thirty-one points of condemnation sound like a historical bill of particulars against all the other eras of Ordnance Department history—including the regimes of Ripley and Benét, and Flagler and Buffington and Crozier—right through the regimes of Studler and Carten. Here are a few of the points it made:

- The major contributor to malfunctions experienced in Vietnam was ammunition loaded with ball propellant.
- The change from IMR extruded powder to ball propellant in 1964 for 5.56-mm ammunition was not justified or supported by test data.
- The sole-source position enjoyed by Olin Mathieson on ball propellants for many years and their close relationship with the army may have influenced the decision makers at Army Munitions Command, Army Weapons Command, and the Army Materiel Command.

- The number of modifications to the M16 rifle were made necessary only after ball propellant was adopted for 5.56-mm ammunition.
- That the AR-15/M16 rifle as initially developed was an excellent and reliable weapon.
- Certain modifications made to the rifle at the insistence of the army were unnecessary and were not supported by test data.
- Two of these modifications increased the unit cost of the rifle substantially and another decreased its performance characteristics. These modifications were the bolt closure device, chrome plating of the barrel chamber, and the change in barrel twist.
- Officials in the Department of the Army were aware of the adverse effect of ball propellant on the cyclic rate of the M16 rifle as early as March 1964, when it was brought to the attention of the Technical Coordinating Committee, yet continued to accept delivery of additional thousands of rifles that were not subjected to acceptance or endurance tests using the ammunition of greatest density in the field and in the supply system (ball-propellant-loaded ammunition). Up to September 1966, about ninety-nine million rounds of 5.56-mm ammunition were consumed in Vietnam, of which eighty-nine million rounds were loaded with ball propellant.
- The rifle project manager, the administrative contracting officer, the members of the Technical Coordinating Committee, and others as high in authority as the assistant secretary of defense for installations and logistics knowingly accepted M16 rifles that would not pass the approved acceptance test. . . . Colt was allowed to test using only IMR propellant at a time when the vast majority of ammunition in the field, including Vietnam, was loaded with ball propellant.
- The failure on the part of officials with authority in the army to cause action to be taken to correct the defi-

ciencies of the 5.56-mm ammunition bordered on criminal negligence.

• The manner in which the army rifle program had been managed was unbelievable. The existing command structure was either inadequate or inoperative. The division of responsibility made it almost impossible to pinpoint responsibility when mistakes were made. There was substantial evidence of lack of activity on the part of responsible officials of highest authority, even when the problems of the M16 and its ammunition came to their attention. It appeared that under the present system, problems were too slowly recognized, and reactions to problems were even slower. . . . It was possible that internal politics and jealousies between the Army Weapons Command and the Army Munitions Command were roadblocks to the successful management of new weapons systems.

James Fallows, author of *National Defense,* may have had the final word when he says, "It is the purest portrayal of the banality of evil in the records of modern American defense."[24]

In response to the Ichord committee report and complying with Congress's call for a complete review, the chief of staff ordered a sweeping study of the whole small arms weapons procurement program including a history of the AR-15/XM16E1/M16A1 weapon system.

As an almost amusing—certainly absurd—bureaucratic gesture toward thoroughness, following the Ichord hearings, and long after the M16 was given its Arctic tests, the Institute for Defense Analyses was ordered to conduct at Fort Sherman in the Panama Canal Zone the M16's first "tropical tests"—after hundreds of thousands of M16s had taken a far more severe tropical test in Vietnam.

In June 1967, Colonel Yount was removed as production manager of rifles and reassigned to Korea. Many felt that he had handled an impossible job with considerable talent and dedication and for his reward became the official scapegoat.[25]

Over the many years of its life, as this study has shown, the

Springfield Armory seems to have received its worst turns of fortune during Christmastide. In a climactic coda in December 1967, the armory suffered its worst turn of fortune. One hundred seventy-three years after it was established by Congress, the National Armory at Springfield, Massachusetts, found the ultimate lump of coal in its Christmas stocking: official closure.

The action occurred by direct order of Secretary of Defense Robert McNamara, after the Defense Department "had examined its Arsenal System and identified additional excess capacity that is no longer needed."[26]

Springfield closed its doors 191 years almost to the month after General Henry Knox and his survey team first strode about the barren acreage in January weather, stepping off the dimensions of needed ordnance buildings, while the birth of the new nation was still in grave question.

The main arsenal building that General Ripley had constructed on the site of the original superintendent's house is today the Springfield Armory Museum, administered by the National Park Service. A stroll along the many glass cases there reveals the entire history of the durable gravel-belly philosophy that, as the next chapter will show, still thrives unchanged—deliberate, long-range fire conserves ammunition and wins wars. The idea has never yielded an inch to the proponents of the opposing idea that wars are won by superior firepower.

Inside the glass cases, the history of that idea, as it wound its way through war and peace, economic cycles, politics and technological revolutions, is marked off in rifles, starting with the first Springfield musket, copied from the Charleville French musket and perfected under the administration of Roswell Lee. Nearby is the Hall's rifle, that lost opportunity of military arms leadership, still reminding the historian of the tumultuous, improbable days at Harpers Ferry Armory that ended when all the rifle-making machinery was carried off to the Confederate armory in Richmond. The Springfield 1855 rifled musket stands in its case not far from the now-darkened factory buildings where it was born under the aegis of General Ripley. Beside it rests the Springfield 1865 conversion with its Allin breech-loading device as developed by General Dyer and perversely preserved beyond its prime by General Stephen Vincent Benét. The Spencer is there, having had to fight its way past General Ripley on to the battlefields of the Civil War. Obsolete even before it was put into production, the ill-fated, underpowered Krag-Jorgensen has its place in one of the cases, recalling the bitter quarrel between various American weapon's designers and General Flagler and later its severe defeat by Spanish Mausers on San Juan Hill. One of the armory's greatest weapons, the Springfield '03, recalls the embarrassing royalty payments made to Mauser by General Crozier, while near it is the British 1917 Enfield, manufactured in Pennsylvania and carried by American doughboys to France following General Crozier's failure to prepare the Springfield '03 for war. Easily found are the Pedersen and Garand .27-caliber rifles, around which swirled the quarrels of the Goat Board and the Pig Board. The museum proudly displays the M1, the brilliant part-time product of the armory's own gifted John Garand, and perhaps the armory's greatest weapon. The M14 is there as a sad reminder of gravel-belly bureaucrats gone astray, of Colonel Rene Studler's quarrel with the Europeans about the overpowered .30-caliber American cartridge and of Dr. Carten's quarrel with Eugene Stoner's AR-15, which is also there with a placard noting that the rifle was never produced in the armory. The M16 stands beside it, the result of the Technical Coordinating Committee's often inept efforts to "militarize" the AR-15 and the subject of the angry denunciations from the Ichord Congressional Subcommittee.

Outside the museum building stand unused the long and very old two-story brick factory buildings where most of these rifles were made. Adjacent to the museum, General Ripley's "magnificent mansion," the commanding officer's house, remains unoccupied, while around the perimeter of the grounds marches his wrought-iron fence. The armory's main administrative building now houses the Springfield Technical Community College.

At its closing, the armory was the first and oldest U.S. government bureaucracy. Few other federal institutions had such a long and interpenetrating relationship with American national government nor affected so many thousands of young men, officers, politicians, statesmen, diplomats, and inventive geniuses. The empty buildings stand as a monument to the central role the armory played in the development of the American mass-production factory system.

As we shall now see, the gravel-belly philosophy has no place in the museum among the extinct weapons, because it continues to prevail in the modern-day Ordnance Corps, its history still being written.

In 1969, the U.S. Army's Aberdeen Proving Ground Museum in Aberdeen, Maryland, which houses an outstanding collection of military small arms and offers the interested visitor a stroll through its park of military tanks—American, German, and otherwise—established a Wall of Fame to salute those who have made major contributions to American Ordnance. Among the first inductees onto the Ordnance Wall of Fame, complete with photo and thumbnail biography, were Chief of Ordnance James Wolfe Ripley and Chief of Ordnance William Henry Crozier.

PART VIII

CHAPTER 40

THE RETURN OF
THE GRAVEL-BELLY

I n 1970, there seemed to be strong evidence that the gravel-belly philosophy had expired. Once the fouling and jamming problems had been dealt with, that antithesis of gravel-bellyism —the M16—had emphatically established itself with its performance in Vietnam; the last great effort of the old Ordnance system, the M14, had ended in failure; and the doors of the old citadel, the Springfield Armory, had been closed permanently. The notion, however, that gravel-bellyism was dead proved to be false.

Some of the significance of the Ichord committee's hearings was lost because by the time the report was published, a number of the most critical reliability problems of the M16 had been resolved. With a mounting outcry against the war in demonstrations all across the nation, the Ichord committee's final report was little noted by the press and accepted with silence by the Congress, which seemed glad to have that explosive issue behind it. Authors Stevens and Ezell felt the Ichord hearings produced "little other than some biased, not to say, rabid, anti-Army publicity."[1]

The closing of Springfield Armory may not have been in the best interests of arms procurement research and testing. Nearly five hundred R&D personnel, highly specialized and virtually irreplaceable, were expected to move to the Rock Island facility in Illinois.

Only twenty did. The others either resigned and found other jobs or took early retirement. Years passed before the armory system recovered from this loss.[2]

In the fall of 1969, some twenty years after Colonel Studler impelled NATO to accept the American .30-caliber cartridge, the U.S. Army made a decision with widespread and unpleasant repercussions: the .22-caliber (5.56-mm) M16A1 was issued to all American armed forces in Europe. "Outrage" is the term one writer used to describe the British reaction.[3] After their .27-caliber automatic weapons system had been brushed aside by the Americans as being underpowered, the British found the Americans returning to the small arms table with a weapon of even lower caliber.

However, many Ordnance men on both sides of the Atlantic felt that the .30-caliber NATO round was obsolete. Indeed, it had been accepted in Europe only with the greatest reluctance, and during the ensuing years, it had decidedly lost ground with European armories, which were looking for a new (and smaller) caliber replacement. England had set off on its own course with its testing of a new 4.85-by-49-mm-caliber cartridge, while Germany was studying a 4.7-by-21-mm-caliber caseless cartridge.

With all these divergent studies under way, commonality was in danger. New NATO trials were needed to establish a common smaller caliber, which would be second to the still-official American .30-caliber cartridge for which most European machine guns were chambered. There were "strong economic, industrial and political considerations" among the eleven participating nations to have their own national candidates chosen as the new NATO common rifle.[4] Consequently, a very strong competitive atmosphere hung over the trials.

Seven years were required to bring everyone back to the table. In June 1976, members of NATO signed an agreement to test and evaluate various calibers and cartridges. There was a very faint secondary hope that the participants could agree on a single rifle for all armies.[5]

A major factor in the discussions that followed was the M16's rifling of one in twelve-inch twist, which had been reduced from Eugene Stoner's original one in fourteen-inch twist. The Belgian FNC 5.56-caliber rifle had a twist every seven inches, which increased the ballistic stability of its SS109 cartridge, but with a controversial trade-off—its killing power was decreased.[6]

As a result of these NATO studies, in 1980, the 7.62-mm caliber remained the NATO standard caliber, while the American 5.56 caliber was chosen as the standard second caliber, but Belgium's SS109 was chosen as the standard 5.56 cartridge. Even though the SS109 had a lower lethality index than the American XM777, it had won this endorsement after it had penetrated a 3.5-mm soft steel plate at 640 meters, a German helmet at 1,150 meters, and a U.S. helmet at 1,300 meters—"in every case better performance than with the 7.672 (.30) caliber NATO round."[7] On paper, NATO had become a two-caliber military force with 5.56 (.22) caliber for rifles and light machine guns and 7.62 (.30) caliber for medium machine guns.

These NATO studies also established as standard a one in seven-inch twist in all future NATO rifles. In the six years that followed, ninety thousand American rifles were rebarreled to the new tighter twist. There was no agreement on a new NATO rifle.

Germany and England headed off in directions of their own. All through the late 1970s, other countries introduced new 5.56-caliber weapons. West Germany developed its Heckler & Koch's HK33 rifle and HK13 machine gun. Belgium FN armory introduced its FNC rifles, Italy adopted its Beretta Model 70 rifle, France its FA-MAS, Israel its Galil, and Austria its Steyr AUG.[8]

That the long-range, aimed-fire gravel-belly philosophy was still very much alive in the United States became apparent when, in 1979, the U.S. Marine Corps took a long look at the M16. The Corps felt that the weapon's range was too short and the strength of both the barrel and the buttstock was inadequate for the rigors of battle. The marines investigated a modified M16 from Colt, designated the M16A1E1, which made some major and highly controversial changes in the M16A1. Of greatest significance, the new model sought to replace the original fully automatic capability with an automatic three-round burst with each pull of the trigger. The reasons for the change were given in the official marine report on the performance tests: "Increased ammunition conservation and more effective use of ammunition" and "Increased effectiveness at long ranges (more hits, better accuracy, and greater penetration)."

Since the U.S. Marines still train their troops to fire at targets beyond three hundred meters—the only fighting unit in the world to continue to do so—the original armory philosophy of long-range, deliberately aimed, ammunition-conserving fire had reasserted itself.[9] The marines designated their modified M16 as the M16A1E1 (and, later, the M16A2) and officially adopted it in September of 1982, ordering some seventy-six thousand weapons from Colt.[10]

The army adopted the same basic model in November 1983 and began to issue it in appreciable numbers in 1986. The M16A2 remains today as the official U.S. military weapon. While still a 5.56-caliber weapon, the M16A2 fires new, heavier, more powerful M855 ammunition for greater range. The rifle weighs more, nearly 8 pounds, up from the 6.8 pounds of the original M16A1, with a heavier barrel and one twist per seven inches, up from the previous one twist in twelve inches, and from Stoner's original one twist in fourteen inches. The range has been increased from the A-15's 460 meters "into a full scale all terrain main battle rifle with considerably improved range capabilities." But the most significant and most controversial change is the elimination of the M16A1's automatic firing capability. The new "automatic" version is now, in effect, semiautomatic, firing a burst of three bullets with every trigger pull. These changes in the original M16 were so pervasive that many commentators regarded the new model as "a different weapon."[11]

This return to the old gravel-belly philosophy encountered some decided opposition. Shortly after the army adopted the new M16A2, the army's Mellonics Systems Development Group in Fort Benning issued a memorandum for record in which it singled out and rejected every single "improvement" in the new M16A2. Noting that the M16 had been adopted because American troops armed with the M14 felt "outgunned" by the enemy armed with the AK47, it repeated the conclusions of General S. L. A Marshall's study by observing that 85 percent of the troops in World War II and Korea failed to fire their semi-automatic weapons. Yet almost all soldiers in Vietnam armed with the fully automatic M16s returned fire. As for the fear that soldiers would waste ammunition and thus outrun their supply lines, the report acknowledged that while "much" of the fire in Vietnam was "wasted" (i.e., hit no target), troops in Vietnam who ran out of ammunition were the "rare exception." The fully automatic fire might not have made any difference, the report acknowledged, but "the soldiers thought it did"—and that was a decided psychological asset. The Mellonics report warned that U.S. troops armed with the three-shot gun would be facing all future enemies armed with "individual weapons with full automatic capabilities."

Striking at the heart of the traditional gravel-belly philosophy, which contended that the three-round burst was more accurate and conserved ammunition, the report rejected both claims. The three-round burst was not more accurate nor did it conserve ammunition, the report asserted. A thirty-round burst took two and a half seconds, yet ten three-round bursts fired the same number of rounds in five seconds. The report also contended that the new one-in-seven barrel twist was adopted to stabilize the Belgian SS109 tracer cartridge, while the fast twist caused an increase in fouling and erosion,[12] and that the tighter twist reduced the killing power of the M16A2.

The whole idea of aimed fire was also challenged. In Vietnam, the M16 was often called upon to provide an unaimed "suppressing fire" that would keep the enemy pinned down while American infantry units could move forward.

Despite these criticisms, the return to the gravel-belly philosophy prevailed, and in 1984, the M16A2 was adopted as the official army rifle. Another group of gravel-belly proponents in the military wanted to abandon the M16 rifle entirely and reintroduce the 7.62-mm (.30) caliber rifle.[13]

In the midst of this American controversy, Canada set up a study group of its own to choose its new NATO rifle—to be either the Belgian FNC or the U.S. M16A1. Canadian troops who tested the two weapons found that they both offered an equivalent hit proba-bility, but that the M16A1 was "significantly" more reliable and won the overall preference of the Canadian troops.[14] The new Canadian C7 rifle is basically the fully automatic M16A1.

In choosing the M16A1, the Canadian armory rejected the three-round burst device of the M16A2 as more expensive and less reliable than the fully automatic M16A1. The Canadians consider control over fully automatic fire—avoiding ammunition wastage—a training function and not to be accomplished by "some add-on device or gadget."[15]

Today, most nations of the world arm their troops either with some form of the .30-caliber AK47 or with some form of a full automatic 5.56-caliber rifle. The German rifle—the Heckler & Koch G41—is a 5.56-caliber rifle offering the infantryman sin-gle-shot, three-shot, and full automatic fire options. The Belgian 5.56-caliber FNC rifle provides a three-shot and an automatic fire option and is widely used among nations as diverse as Sweden and Indonesia. The British Enfield XL64 5.56 caliber offers single-shot and full automatic modes. The Italian Beretta AR70 5.56-caliber rifle is full automatic. The U.S. M16A2 three-shot is still the official weapon of the U.S. military today and the only modern rifle that does not offer full automatic capability.

The conclusion seems inescapable that U.S. Ordnance continues to reject its own overwhelming battlefield experience of the last fifty years, especially from Korea, where automatic weapons out-gunned the semiautomatic M1, and from Vietnam, where the AK47 outgunned the M14 and was matched only by the M16. Instead, Ordnance persists in believing that long-range, carefully aimed rifle fire wins battles and conserves ammunition in the face of oppo-nents armed with fully automatic rifles.

That philosophy is no more clearly exemplified than in the modified semiautomatic M16A2. The original AR-15 was the exact opposite of the gravel-belly's ideal weapon. A medium-range, low-powered, high-velocity rifle, the AR-15 provided automatic firepower with a tumbling bullet that created devastating wounds and maximum payoff in the lethality index. The M16A2 was reworked into a gravel-belly's weapon by increasing the power of the .556-caliber cartridge, increasing the range, increasing the rifling to one turn per seven inches, increasing the velocity with an attendant loss of lethality, and decreasing the firepower to a semiautomatic three-shot. In short, the gravel-bellies have converted the fully automatic AR-15 into a semiautomatic M14, albeit more effective and efficient than the original but with the same limiting characteristics.

One has to ask why, in light of its own experience, the Ordnance Corps insists on maintaining its discredited gravel-belly posture and persists in rejecting the maximum-fire concept accepted by all other major national armies. The answer seems to be in the corps' own troubled historic relationship with the enlisted man. When one takes a thoughtful look back on the Ordnance Corps' historic attitude toward the common soldier, the move back from the fully automatic M16A1 to the not fully automatic M16A2 does not seem so surprising.[16]

The Ordnance Corps began its career in 1794 by copying France's musket and Britain's army tactics, along with the British army's attitude toward its common soldier, which was largely contemptuous. When the Hall's rifle was invented, despite its greater breech-loading firepower and unmatchable accuracy, Ordnance continued to prefer the muzzle-loading musket, contending that the Hall's (i.e., the foot soldier armed with the Hall's) wasted ammunition. The conscripts' wasting of ammunition was the reason for General Ripley's condemnation of the Spencers and the Sharpses and other breech-loading rifles. Even though ample battlefield evidence clearly recorded that foot soldiers armed with repeating rifles during the Civil War did not waste ammunition, postwar Ordnance leaders continued to distrust the ordinary soldier's ability to conserve his ammunition and, during the Indian wars, removed all the "obsolete" repeating weapons like the Spencers from the hands of the troops. And this despite the evidence at the Republican River, where Spencer-armed scouts survived repeated Indian attacks they would surely not have survived armed with the Springfield single-shot breechloader. This event was paralleled by Custer's raid on the Washita Valley Indian camp, where only the greater firepower of his repeating Spencers saved his corps from certain disaster.

The army felt justified with this posture because of the quality of the cavalry recruit. Living often in rotting log cabins full of centipedes, suffering all too frequently from scurvy caused by poor army rations and from venereal disease, typically given to drunkenness, usually illiterate, with no skills, the cavalryman came from the lowest levels of society. To maintain discipline, the cavalry meted out savage punishment, including hanging by the thumbs, marching to exhaustion with a knapsack full of bricks, dunking in a stream, confinement in a sweatbox, bucking (being tied hands and feet in a sitting position, which was so painful most men would weep after several hours), and even flogging, although this was officially ended in 1861. Cavalry life was so severe that in one year alone, 1871, eighty-eight hundred men deserted. With little rifle-range training, the cavalryman was often a notoriously bad shot and so not to be trusted with a repeating rifle.

Distrust of the common soldier's ability to conserve ammunition was an almost overriding factor in the choice of the Krag-Jorgensen in the 1890s, which could be used primarily as a single-loader with a five-cartridge magazine in reserve. The much superior Mauser was rejected by Flagler for only one reason. It had no single-shot capability, but fired from a loaded clip that he felt could permit the wasting of ammunition.

If General Flagler's distrust of the common soldier in the 1890s seems reactionary, one should keep in mind that the U.S. Ordnance Corps modeled itself largely on the British army, which still regarded the ordinary British soldier during the Boer War at the turn of the century as "a mindless brick in a moving wall of flesh."[17]

General Crozier's failure to select a machine gun for World War I went beyond any pettiness and jealousy he may have felt for Colonel Lewis's machine gun. Despite the reports of the great machine-gun slaughters in the trenches in Europe, he persisted in rejecting machine guns as ammunition wasters by, obviously, recruits who, regardless of training, could not be relied upon to conserve bullets.

It will be recalled that the highly advanced Browning machine gun, when it reached France, was taken from American troops by General Pershing on the plea that the German's might copy it. Such a mystifyingly illogical reason for disarming troops going into battle suggests to the skeptic that General Pershing was really thinking about green conscripts wasting ammunition.

During the twenties and thirties of this century, Ordnance continued to have a jaundiced view of the recruit. Stories abounded of young men in court given a choice by judges of either prison or military enlistment, hardly the sort of recruit who would inspire trust and confidence in a spit-and-polish career Ordnance officer.

After World War II, Ordnance seemed more determined than ever to keep rapid-fire weapons out of the hands of the common soldier. One of the key arguments for the M14 was that it would be largely a semiautomatic weapon with automatic firing allowed only during the most demanding situations and to be controlled by infantry officers. Contrariwise, one of the major objections to the M16 by the proponents of the M14 was the wasting of ammunition. Ordnance clung to this hostility to the M16 even when the M14 was clearly outgunned by the AK47 in Vietnam, making the urgent need for the M16's higher firepower glaringly evident.

In Vietnam, the draft, with its loopholes for college students, was clearly biased against youths from the poorest sectors of society. During the Ichord hearings, the low respect the Ordnance Corps had for these Vietnam conscripts was barely concealed. Ordnance regarded Vietnam as a haven for an ammunition-wasting rifle in the hands of an ammunition-wasting conscript.

After the Vietnam War, Ordnance could feel justified in its scornful view of the conscript who in its eyes did waste ammunition with great abandon in the jungles and rice paddies. The evening television news abounded with footage of Americans holding M16s over their heads to fire blindly over walls during the Tet offensive. With eighty-nine million rounds of U.S. rifle ammunition fired, any gravel-belly could claim ample evidence that wartime conscripts had heedlessly and needlessly fired off enormous quantities of ammunition.

As was pointed out earlier, ammunition is often expended on to-day's battlefield, not to hit anything, but to keep the enemy from firing, from regrouping, from attacking, or to cover infiltrating American soldiers. According to gravel-belly doctrine, this is wasted ammunition, but from the battlefield tactician's standpoint, such rifle fire can be an essential element in the winning of skirmishes and battles.

While the United States finds itself surrounded by a world bristling with hostile anti-Americanism and millions of fully auto-matic select-fire battle rifles, the question raised here is not over the relative tactical merits of three-burst versus fully automatic rifle fire. German and other select-fire national rifles offer three-burst capability for those occasions that require it.

The question concerns the absence of the fully automatic option for the American weapon. Obviously those other nations do not agree with U.S. Ordnance that three-burst fire alone can cover every battlefield situation as they have given their soldiers a choice between three-burst and fully automatic fire. As noted, even neigh-boring Canada dismisses the three-burst M16A2 as the wrong approach to conserving ammunition, preferring a select-fire auto-matic weapon preceded by proper training.

Why isn't the American soldier entrusted with the same option as these other nations? How can U.S. Ordnance be so sure the American soldier will never need it?

Today's U.S. Army enlistee can hardly be compared with the brutalized British redcoat during the American Revolution, but it is predictable that the Ordnance Corps is as distrustful as ever of the enlistee of the 1990s. Attracted by the offer to "Be All You Can Be in the Army," most new recruits sign up not to become gravel-belly career sharpshooters, but to learn a skill useful in civilian life, or to accumulate credits for higher education, or both—one-hitch birds of passage, garnered largely from the socioeconomic groups most in need of career opportunities.

The army is well aware that today's recruit with a high school diploma doesn't measure up to the recruit of twenty years ago *without* a high school diploma. Before basic military training can begin today, recruits need to be put through a BS&K (Basic Skills and Knowledge) program which will teach them such fundamentals as how to measure with a ruler and how to read an index to a training manual. Consequently, even after basic military training, the army feels that today's recruits don't have the skills to manage a fully automatic weapon—that is to say, the fully automatic position has been removed from the M16A2 not because it isn't necessary but because today's troops can't be relied upon not to waste ammunition.

The army's solution (and the marines') to this problem is not more training but less rifle. That suggests that the new "Be all that you can be" army will field an undertrained foot soldier with deliberately reduced fire power to face enemy troops trained to handle the highest fire power. Who can be expected to win that battle?

Has conserving ammunition been placed ahead of battlefield fire power once again? Does the army still believe that deliberately aimed long-range rifle fire—not superior firepower—wins battles while conserving ammunition? Are we going to be caught in a major war with the wrong rifle again? As this history shows, U.S. Ordnance has been more often wrong than right

NOTES

CHAPTER 1

1. Barbara Tuchman, *The First Salute*, 130.
2. Some of the material in this chapter was gained through notes and conversation with Paulette Mark, supervising park ranger for visitors' services, Valley Forge National Historical Park. Portions of the material on revolutionary small arms were drawn from comments and notes provided by Marc Brier, park ranger at Valley Forge.
3. The Dupuys, father and son, offer more interesting material on this subject. See appendix I in their *Compact History of the Revolutionary War*.
4. Tuchman, *First Salute,* 7.
5. William Addleman Ganoe, *The History of the United States Army*, 6.
6. Russell F. Weigley, *History of the United States Army*, 61.
7. *World Book Encyclopedia*, vol. 2, p. 587.
8. Weigley, *History of the United States Army,* 32.
9. Marcus Cunliffe, *George Washington, Man and Monument*, 82.
10. James C. Neagles and Lila L. Neagles, *Locating Your Revolutionary War Ancestor*, 12. But the command may be apocryphal.
11. *Encyclopaedia Britannica*, vol. 12, p. 329.
12. Tuchman, *First Salute,* 7.
13. One of the longest kills on record traveled four hundred yards to strike one of British Colonel Tarleton's horses. Valley Forge Briefs, No. 35.
14. Valley Forge Briefs, No. 35.
15. Ganoe, *History of the United States Army,* 9.
16. Weigley, *History of the United States Army,* 29.

17. Ibid., 66.
18. Don Higginbotham, *Daniel Morgan*, 65.
19. John R. Cuneo, *The Battles of Saratoga*, 51.
20. Merritt Roe Smith, *Harpers Ferry Armory*, 27.
21. David F. Butler, *United States Firearms*, 31.
22. Smith, *Harpers Ferry Armory*, 27.
23. David Barr Chidsey, *The War in the South*, 110.
24. Tuchman, *First Salute*, 204.
25. Corelli Barnett, *Britain and Her Army*, 223.
26. Ganoe, *History of the United States Army*, 33.
27. Page Smith, *A New Age Begins*, vol. I, p. 827
28. Weigley, *History of the United States Army*, 11.
29. *Encyclopaedia Britannica*, vol. 23, p. 383d.
30. James T. Flexner, *George Washington and the New Nation (1783–1793)*, 16. Some of his detractors, however, noted that Washington had come to Philadelphia in full uniform.
31. Louis Birnbaum, *Red Dawn at Lexington*, 62.
32. Allan R. Millett and Peter Maslowski, *For the Common Defense: A Military History of the United States*, 62.
33. Weigley, *History of the United States Army*, 70.
34. Constance Green, "History of the Springfield Armory," vol. I, bk. I, p. 2.
35. Derwent Stainthorpe Whittlesey, "The Springfield Armory," 14.

CHAPTER 2

1. John A. Garraty, *The American Nation*, 145.
2. James T. Flexner, *George Washington and the New Nation*, 18.
3. Merrill Jensen, *The New Nation*, 310.
4. Garraty, *The American Nation*, 145.
5. Ibid., 146.
6. Samuel Eliot Morison et al., *The Growth of the American Republic* 1:242.
7. Ibid., 240.
8. Merritt Roe Smith, *Harpers Ferry Armory*, 32–33.
9. Flexner, *George Washington and the New Nation*, 75–76.
10. Ibid.
11. Dave Gilbert, *Where Industry Failed*, 35.
12. Ibid., 25.
13. Smith, *Harpers Ferry Armory*, 29.
14. Ibid., 34.

15. Ibid.
16. Ibid., 32.
17. Ibid., 38.
18. Ibid., 53.
19. Ibid., 73.

CHAPTER 3

1. Derwent Stainthorpe Whittlesey, "The Springfield Armory," 73.
2. Ibid., 74.
3. Ibid., 75.
4. Ibid., 76.
5. Ibid., 78.
6. Ibid.
7. Ibid.
8. Russell F. Weigley, *History of the United States Army,* 111.
9. Ibid., 112.
10. Ibid., 122.
11. Whittlesey, "Springfield Armory," 96.
12. John A. Garraty, *The American Nation*, 199.
13. Whittlesey, "Springfield Armory," 97.

CHAPTER 4

1. Derwent Stainthorpe Whittlesey, "The Springfield Armory," 99.
2. Ibid., 101.
3. Ibid., 114.
4. Ibid., 115.
5. Ibid.
6. Ibid., 116.
7. Blanchard's lathe is exhibited at the Springfield Armory Museum in Springfield, Massachusetts.

CHAPTER 5

1. Merritt Roe Smith, *Harpers Ferry Armory,* 151.
2. Ibid., 189.
3. Ibid., 156.
4. Ibid., 194.
5. Ibid., 106.
6. Ibid., 152.
7. Ibid., 153.

8. Ibid., 206.
9. Ibid., 207.
10. Ibid., 166.
11. Ibid.
12. Ibid., 74.
13. Ibid., 102.
14. Ibid., 174.
15. Ibid., 179.
16. Ibid., 247.

CHAPTER 6
1. Constance Green, "History of the Springfield Armory," bk. I, p. 60.
2. Merritt Roe Smith, *Harpers Ferry Armory*, 261–62.

CHAPTER 7
1. Russell F. Weigley, *History of the United States Army*, 184.
2. Merritt Roe Smith, *Harpers Ferry Armory*, 218.
3. Irving B. Holley, *Ideas and Weapons*, 6–10.
4. Talcott to secretary of war, January 14, 1845, as quoted in R. T. Huntington, *Hall's Breechloaders*, 89–90.
5. Ibid., 262.
6. Constance Green, "History of the Springfield Armory," bk. II, p. 72.
7. Smith, *Harpers Ferry Armory*, 267.
8. Ibid., 268.
9. Ibid., 275.
10. Ibid., 279.

CHAPTER 8
1. Derwent Stainthorpe Whittlesey, "The Springfield Armory," 272.
2. Ibid., 276.
3. Constance Green, "History of the Springfield Armory," bk. I, p. 74.
4. John A. Garraty, *The American Nation*, 266.
5. Ibid., 267.
6. Robert V. Bruce, *Lincoln and the Tools of War*, 24–25.
7. Ibid., 25.
8. Whittlesey, "The Springfield Armory," 177.
9. Ibid.
10. Ibid., 184.
11. Ibid., 187.

12. Ibid., 183.
13. Ibid., 196.
14. Merritt Roe Smith, *Harpers Ferry Armory,* 303.
15. Ibid., 206.
16. Ibid., 205.

CHAPTER 9
1. Merritt Roe Smith, *Harpers Ferry Armory,* 217.
2. Derwent Stainthorpe Whittlesey, "The Springfield Armory," 218.
3. Ibid.

CHAPTER 10
1. John A. Garraty, *The American Nation*, 396.
2. Robert V. Bruce, *Lincoln and the Tools of War*, 29.
3. Ibid., 27.
4. Ibid., 29.
5. Ibid., 124.
6. Ibid., 125.
7. Joseph E. Smith, *Small Arms of the World*. As an indication of the tremendous loss of shoulder arms in battle, Smith reports that some thirty-seven thousand rifles were picked up following the Battle of Gettysburg, pp. 44–45.
8. Bruce, *Lincoln and the Tools of War,* 39.
9. It is difficult to overvalue the importance of the Richmond Armory to the Confederate cause. During the Civil War, it turned out 323,231 infantry arms, of which one half had been repaired or captured. Some of these arms are on exhibit in the Atlanta, Georgia, Historic Museum.
10. Shelby Foote, Civil War historian, television interview.
11. Burton J. Hendrick, *Lincoln's War Cabinet*, 65.
12. Ibid., 51.
13. Ibid., 66.
14. Ibid.
15. Bruce, *Lincoln and the Tools of War,* 43.
16. Ibid., 87.
17. John S. Blay, *The Civil War*, 246.
18. Ibid.
19. Ian Drury and Tony Gibbons, *The Civil War Military Machine,* 84.
20. Bruce, *Lincoln and the Tools of War,* 247.

21. U.S. Department of the Interior, *Fort Sumter, Anvil of War*, 39.
22. Russell F. Weigley, *History of the United States Army,* 224.
23. Constance Green, "History of the Springfield Armory," 97.
24. Bruce, *Lincoln and the Tools of War,* 69, quoting Official Records, series 3, I, p. 264.
25. Ibid., 71.

CHAPTER 11
1. John S. Blay, *The Civil War,* 161.
2. Joseph E. Smith, *Small Arms of the World,* 44–45.
3. Robert V. Bruce, *Lincoln and the Tools of War,* 112.
4. Ibid.
5. Constance Green, "History of the Springfield Armory," 101.
6. Ibid.
7. Bruce, *Lincoln and the Tools of War,* 112. This was also a play on the Breeches Bible, published in 1560 in Geneva, so-called because it substituted the word "breeches" for the fig-leaf coverings made by Adam and Eve.
8. Ibid., 102.
9. Ibid., 107.
10. Ibid., 42.
11. Smith, *Small Arms of the World,* 45.
12. Bruce, *Lincoln and the Tools of War,* 108.
13. Ibid.
14. Ibid., 252.

CHAPTER 12
1. Justin O. Buckeridge, *Lincoln's Choice,* 5.
2. Roy M. Marcot, *Spencer Repeating Firearms,* 28.
3. Buckeridge, *Lincoln's Choice,* 11.
4. Marcot, *Spencer Repeating Firearms,* 31.
5. Ibid., 29.
6. Ibid., 34.
7. Ibid., 35.

CHAPTER 13
1. Burton J. Hendrick, *Lincoln's War Cabinet,* 222.
2. Ibid., 221.
3. Ibid., 221–22.
4. Ibid., 223.

5. Ibid., 277.
6. Ibid., 278.
7. Ibid., 277.
8. Bruce Catton, *Terrible Swift Sword*, vol. II, p. 141.
9. Hendrick, *Lincoln's War Cabinet,* 237.
10. See ibid., 282, for more.
11. Ibid., 239.
12. Ibid., 289.
13. Ibid., 241.
14. Ibid., 237.
15. Ibid.
16. Robert V. Bruce, *Lincoln and the Tools of War*, 154.
17. Hendrick, *Lincoln's War Cabinet,* 267.
18. Bruce, *Lincoln and the Tools of War*, 154.
19. Ibid., 167.
20. Ibid., 155.
21. Ibid., 204.
22. Ibid., 105.
23. Ibid., 206.
24. Ibid., 205.
25. Ibid., 169.
26. Ibid.

CHAPTER 14

1. Robert V. Bruce, *Lincoln and the Tools of War,* 209.
2. Ibid., 210.
3. Ibid., 251.
4. For a compelling picture of the capital during wartime, see Margaret Leech, *Reveille in Washington*.
5. Bruce, *Lincoln and the Tools of War*, 119.
6. Ibid., 123.
7. Ibid., 195.
8. Ibid., 197.
9. Ibid., 250.
10. Ibid.
11. John Ellis, *The Social History of the Machine Gun,* 26.
12. Ibid., 28.
13. Ibid., 29.
14. Ibid.

CHAPTER 15

1. Robert V. Bruce, *Lincoln and the Tools of War,* 253.
2. Ibid.
3. Ibid.
4. Justin O. Buckeridge, *Lincoln's Choice,* 41.
5. Ibid., 42–43.
6. Ibid., 58.
7. Roy Marcot, *Spencer Repeating Firearms,* 54.
8. Bruce, *Lincoln and the Tools of War,* 256–57.
9. Marcot, *Spencer Repeating Firearms,* 56.
10. Ibid., 56; see also Bruce, *Lincoln and the Tools of War,* 261.
11. Marcot, *Spencer Repeating Firearms,* 58.
12. Buckeridge, *Lincoln's Choice,* 68.
13. Bruce, *Lincoln and the Tools of War,* 264.
14. Ibid., 264–65.
15. Ibid., 286.
16. Buckeridge, *Lincoln's Choice,* 68.
17. Bruce, *Lincoln and the Tools of War,* 290.
18. Ibid., 285.
19. Ibid., 288.
20. Buckeridge, *Lincoln's Choice,* 19.
21. Ibid., 16.
22. Ibid.
23. Bruce, *Lincoln and the Tools of War,* 298.

CHAPTER 16

1. Joseph E. Smith, *Small Arms of the World,* 46.
2. Ibid., 47.
3. The length of the standard military rifle was too unwieldy for a man firing from a saddle. Consequently, cavalrymen were traditionally armed with a shorter version, called a carbine.
4. Robert V. Bruce, *Lincoln and the Tools of War,* 105.
5. Justin O. Buckeridge, *Lincoln's Choice,* 238–39.
6. Smith, *Small Arms of the World,* 50.
7. An exhibit of Allin's design is on display in the Springfield Armory Museum.
8. Springfield Armory National Historic Site, Fact Sheet No. 3, "Evolution of Springfield Weapons."
9. Robert M. Utley, *Frontier Regulars,* 124.

10. John Robert Elting, *American Army Life,* 166.
11. Utley, *Frontier Regulars,* 148.
12. For a full and readable history of the Indian wars, see Robert Utley's *Frontier Regulars: The United States Army and the Indian.*
13. This is now on exhibit at the Smithsonian in Washington. It was given by Mrs. Custer. There is a similar table in the Confederate Army Museum in Richmond, Virginia, next door to the Confederate White House. On the underside of the table is scratched the name "Custer." However, the provenance of this table has not been established.
14. Utley, *Frontier Regulars,* 70.
15. Smith, *Small Arms of the World,* 61.
16. Ibid.
17. Utley, *Frontier Regulars,* 70.

CHAPTER 17

1. It is interesting to note that Jomini, a veteran of the Napoleonic Wars and considered one of the great military theorists, wrote a widely read treatise on the Austro-Italian War of 1866, which dealt with the influence of the breech-loading rifle.
2. Robert M. Utley, *Frontier Regulars*, 72.
3. Russell F. Weigley, *History of the United States Army,* 288.
4. Frank Comparato, *Age of Great Guns,* 196.
5. Ibid., 194.
6. J. A. Stockfish, *Plowshares into Swords*, 55.
7. D. A. Kinsley, *Favor the Bold,* 156.
8. Utley, *Frontier Regulars,* 244; see also Kinsley, *Favor the Bold,* 157.
9. Utley, *Frontier Regulars,* 248.
10. Wayne R. Austerman, *Guns at the Little Bighorn*, 25.
11. Kinsley, *Favor the Bold,* 230.
12. Utley, *Frontier Regulars,* 70.
13. Ibid., 72.
14. Ibid., 72–73.
15. Ibid.
16. John Ellis, *The Social History of the Machine Gun,* 74.
17. Ibid.
18. Joseph E. Smith, *Small Arms of the World,* 73–74.
19. Sidney B. Brinckerhoff and Pierce Chamberlin, "The Army's Search for a Repeating Rifle, 1873–1903," 21.
20. Ibid., 22.

21. Ibid., 23.
22. Ibid., 26.
23. Smith, *Small Arms of the World,* 63.
24. Brinckerhoff, "The Army's Search for a Repeating Rifle," 26.
25. Smith, *Small Arms of the World,* 62.
26. Weigley, *History of the United States Army,* 290.
27. Smith, *Small Arms of the World,* 62.
28. *New York Times*, December 23, 1890, p. 3:1
29. Ibid.
30. Springfield Armory Fact Sheet No. 2.
31. Brinckerhoff and Chamberlin, "The Army's Search for a Repeating Rifle," 23.

CHAPTER 18

1. Sidney B. Brinckerhoff and Pierce Chamberlin, "The Army's Search for a Repeating Rifle," 28.
2. *New York Times*, March 20, 1892, p. 20:2.
3. Ibid., April 25, 1892, p. 8:3.
4. Ibid., June 19, 1892, p. 17:7.
5. Ibid., September 4, 1892, p. 15:4.
6. Ibid., April 21, 1893, p. 8:5.
7. Ibid., June 8, 1983, p. 8:2.
8. Ibid., August 20, 1895, p. 9:2.
9. Ibid., October 7, 1895, p. 5:6.
10. Ibid., December 27, 1895, p. 3:7.
11. Ibid., December 31, 1895, p. 6:3.
12. Ibid.
13. Russell F. Weigley, *History of the United States Army,* 309.
14. Frank Freidel, *The Splendid Little War*, 143.
15. John A. Garraty, *The American Nation,* 632.
16. Weigley, *History of the United States Army,* 305–306.
17. Margaret Leech, *In the Days of McKinley,* 380.
18. Barbara Tuchman, *The First Salute*, 4.
19. Much of the material on General Miles comes from Graham Cosmas's book, *An Army for Empire.*
20. Ibid., 61.
21. Ibid.
22. John Robert Elting, *American Army Life,* 163.
23. Philip C. Jessup, *Elihu Root,* 2 vols. (New York: Dodd, Mead, 1938),

vol. I, p. 240, as quoted in Weigley, *History of the United States Army*, 313.

24. Allan R. Millet and Peter Maslowski, *For the Common Defense*, 310.

25. Weigley, *History of the United States Army*, 320.

26. Corelli Barnett, *Britain and Her Army, 1509–1970*, 291.

27. Ibid., 334.

28. Ibid.

29. Ibid.

30. Ibid., 336.

31. Ibid., 340.

32. Ibid., 362.

CHAPTER 19

1. Quoted in David A. Armstrong, *Bullets and Bureaucrats: The Machine Gun and the United States Army, 1861–1916*, 117.

2. James Fallows, *National Defense*, 81.

3. Edward C. Crossman, *The Book of the Springfield*, 2.

4. *New York Times*, June 1, 1901, p. 3:3.

5. Ibid., October 4, 1901, p. 5:5.

6. Ibid., November 23, 1901, p. 5:4.

7. Ibid., p. 5:5.

8. Ibid., January 12, 1902, p. 1:4.

9. Ibid., Editorial, May 4, 1902, p. 6:4.

10. Ibid.

11. Armstrong, *Bullets and Bureaucrats*, 131.

12. Crossman, *The Book of the Springfield*, 9.

13. Clark S. Campbell, *The '03 Springfield*, 12. Roosevelt made the observation in a letter to Secretary of War Elihu Root.

14. The Springfield trap-door '88 rifle had featured a cleaning rod that would "pull out and snap into place to form a pencil-thin bayonet." Springfield Armory Fact Sheet No. 2, "The Trap Door."

15. Fallows, *National Defense*, 81.

16. Jack O'Connor, *The Rifle Book*, 52.

17. Campbell, *The '03 Springfield*, 49.

18. Ibid., 51.

19. *New York Times*, November 19, 1905, p. 9:1. The *Times* characterized the success of General Crozier's first term as COO as "conspicuous."

20. Ibid., November 12, 1905, p. 1:3.

21. Campbell, *The '03 Springfield,* 51.
22. Ibid., 52.

CHAPTER 20

1. George M. Chinn, *The Machine Gun,* 123.
2. John Ellis, *The Social History of the Machine Gun,* 33–34.
3. Ibid., 34.
4. Joseph E. Smith, *Small Arms of the World,* 107.
5. Ellis, *The Social History of the Machine Gun,* 36.
6. Smith, *Small Arms of the World,* 109.
7. Ellis, *The Social History of the Machine Gun*, 87, and Smith, *Small Arms of the World*, 110, puts the number at twenty thousand.
8. Ellis, *The Social History of the Machine Gun,* 86.
9. Smith, *Small Arms of the World,* 110.

CHAPTER 21

1. J. Browning and C. Gentry, *John Browning: American Gunmaker*, 73.
2. For more biographic data, see ibid.
3. Ibid., 152.
4. Joseph Smith, *Small Arms of the World,* 116.
5. David A. Armstrong, *Bullets and Bureaucrats,* 126.
6. Quoted in ibid., 117.
7. Aberdeen Proving Ground, *Welcome to the U.S. Army Ordnance Museum.*
8. Smith, *Small Arms of the World,* 117.

CHAPTER 22

1. George M. Chinn, *The Machine Gun,* 271.
2. *New York Times,* September 18, 1916, p. 4:2.
3. Colonel Lewis, testifying before the Senate Armed Services Committee, *New York Times,* December 22, 1917, p. 2:3.
4. Robert M. Calfee, attorney for Automatic Arms Company, *New York Times,* September 18, 1916, p. 4:1.
5. Colonel Lewis, Senate testimony, *New York Times,* December 22, 1917, p. 2:2.
6. *New York Times,* December 22, 1917, p. 2:2.
7. Robert M. Calfee, *New York Times,* September 18, 1916, p. 4:1.
8. Ibid.

9. Ibid.

10. Ibid.

CHAPTER 23

1. John Ellis, *The Social History of the Machine Gun*, 39.

2. Ibid., 119–20.

3. Ibid., 120.

4. Ibid., 121.

5. Ibid., 122.

6. Ibid., 127.

7. Ibid., 130.

8. Ibid., 49.

9. William Manchester, introduction to Dan Congdon, *Combat: World War I,* xvii.

10. Ellis, *The Social History of the Machine Gun,* 120.

11. Manchester, in Congdon, *Combat,* xvii.

12. John Keegan, The Face of Battle, 230.

13. Ellis, *The Social History of the Machine Gun,* 132.

14. Sir Llewellyn Woodward, *Great Britain and the War of 1914–1918,* 48.

15. *New York Times,* September 6, 1918, p. 1.

16. T. N. Dupuy, *The Evolution of Weapons and Warfare,* 199.

17. *Encyclopaedia Britannica*, vol. 23, p. 79a.

18. Dupuy, *The Evolution of Weapons and Warfare*, 218.

19. *Encyclopaedia Britannica*, vol. 23, p. 761a.

CHAPTER 24

1. *New York Times,* December 29, 1916, p. 12:4.

2. Ibid., January 26, 1916, p. 1.

3. Ibid., November 13, 1916, p. 3:3.

4. Fred H. Colvin, *Sixty Years with Men and Machines,* 184.

5. Ibid., 185.

6. Ibid., 187.

7. *New York Times,* March 24, 1916, p. 2:3.

8. Ibid.

9. John Ellis, *The Social History of the Machine Gun,* 75.

10. Ibid.

11. *New York Times,* September 18, 1916, p. 1:5.

12. Ibid., September 19, 1916, p. 7:1.

CHAPTER 25

1. *New York Times,* September 19, 1916, p. 1:4.
2. Ibid., November 11, 1916, p. 1:4.
3. Ibid., December 19, 1916, p. 10:8.
4. Ibid., July 22, 1917, pp. 5:7–8.

CHAPTER 26

1. *New York Times,* Editorial, September 26, 1917, p. 10:2.
2. Fred H. Colvin, *Sixty Years with Men and Machines*, 188–90.
3. Ibid., 191.
4. Ibid., 193–94.
5. *New York Times,* December 15, 1917, p. 2:6.
6. Ibid., December 18, 1917, p. 1:4.
7. Ibid., December 19, 1917, p. 1:8.
8. Ibid., December 20, 1917, pp. 2:2–3.
9. Ibid., December 21, 1917, pp. 6:4–5.
10. Ibid., December 23, 1917, p. 1:8.
11. Ibid.
12. Ibid., January 1, 1918, p. 13:1.
13. Ibid., January 2, 1918, p. 10:3.
14. Ibid., January 26, 1918. pp. 1:1, 4:1.
15. John Ellis, *The Social History of the Machine Gun,* 40, quoting F. W. A. Hobart.
16. *Encyclopaedia Britannica,* vol. 23, p. 775.
17. Maj. Gen. William Crozier, *Ordnance and the World War* (New York: Charles Scribner's Sons, 1920), 56, as quoted in Walter Millis, *Arms and Men,* 240.
18. As quoted in Ellis, *The Social History of the Machine Gun,* 56.

CHAPTER 27

1. Germany didn't have the $33 billion called for in the treaty.
2. See John A. Garraty, *The American Nation,* 692.
3. René Gimpel, *Diary of an Art Dealer,* 85.
4. Garraty, *The American Nation,* 693.
5. Russell F. Weigley, *History of the United States Army,* 411.
6. For more on Christie and his tanks, see Mildred Harmon Gillie, *Forging the Thunderbolt,* 274–76, particularly chapters 1 and 2.
7. Weigley, *History of the United States Army,* 410.

8. *Encyclopaedia Britannica,* vol. 15, p. 619d; see also Weigley, *History of the United States Army*, 412–14.
9. *Encyclopaedia Britannica,* vol. 15, p. 619d.
10. Ibid., vol. 15, p. 620a.

CHAPTER 28

1. Edward Clinton Ezell, *The Great Rifle Controversy,* 24–25; see also, Maj. Gen. Julian S. Hatcher, *Hatcher's Book of the Garand,* 34.
2. For "the many vicissitudes through which Mr. Garand and his gun passed during the hectic development years," see Julian Hatcher's *Hatcher's Book of the Garand*. General Hatcher was connected with the armory for many years and knew John Garand well.
3. Ezell, *The Great Rifle Controversy,* 21.
4. Hatcher, *Hatcher's Book of the Garand,* 54–57.
5. Ibid., 56.
6. Ibid.
7. Ibid., 66.
8. Ibid., 78.

CHAPTER 29

1. Maj. Gen. Julian S. Hatcher, *Hatcher's Book of the Garand,* 85.
2. Ibid., 100.
3. Ibid., 101.
4. Hatcher does not identify this officer.
5. Hatcher, *Hatcher's Book of the Garand,* 120.
6. Russell F. Weigley, *History of the United States Army,* 400–401.
7. Ibid., 403.
8. Ibid., 402.
9. Chapter 16 of *Hatcher's Book of the Garand* provides extensive notes and quotes on the M1's wartime performance.
10. Hatcher, *Hatcher's Book of the Garand,* 251.
11. Ibid., 242.
12. Ibid., 153.
13. Much of the following material is drawn from William J. O'Neill's A Democracy at War: America's Fight at Home and Abroad in World War II, 350–53. Professor O'Neill's book is a sobering study of America's combat record during the war.
14. In one of the great ironies of the war, the Ordance Department dis-

covered that it couldn't even copy a good idea, for when it tried to reproduce the German MG42, a mistake in converting metrics to inches produced an American duplicate that wouldn't fire properly. The error was discovered only after the war. For the curious, the American copy sits behind a glass case in the Springfield Armory Museum.

15. O'Neill, *A Democracy at War,* 411.

CHAPTER 30

1. Dr. Edward Clinton Ezell discusses this in both his *Small Arms of the World,* 16–17, and *The Great Rifle Controversy,* xvii, 58–59.
2. Edward Clinton Ezell, *Small Arms of the World,* 514–15.
3. Edward Clinton Ezell, *The AK47 Story,* 95.
4. Ibid., 104.

CHAPTER 31

1. Edward Clinton Ezell, *The Great Rifle Controversy,* 50.
2. Ibid., 42–43. "These specifications," Dr. Ezell notes, "were unrealistic . . . impractical without a change in ammunition."

CHAPTER 32

1. For a fuller biographic sketch see Edward Clinton Ezell, *The Great Rifle Controversy,* 65–68.
2. Ibid., 72.
3. Ibid., 75–77.
4. Gen. S. L. A. Marshall, *Men Against Fire.*
5. Ibid., 54.
6. Ibid., 57.
7. Ibid., 60–61.
8. Thomas L. McNaugher, *The M16 Controversies,* 34.
9. Ezell, *The Great Rifle Controversy,* 89.
10. Ibid., 92.
11. Ibid., 77.
12. Ibid., 80.
13. Ibid., 81.
14. Ibid., 165.
15. Ibid., 98.
16. Ibid., 108.
17. R. Blake Stevens and Edward C. Ezell, *The Black Rifle, M16 Retrospective,* 7.

18. Ibid., 8.
19. Ezell, *The Great Rifle Controversy,* 137.
20. Stevens and Ezell, *The Black Rifle,* 9–10; see also Ezell, *The Great Rifle Controversy,* 165–69.

CHAPTER 33

1. Edward Clinton Ezell, *The Great Rifle Controversy,* 119.
2. Ibid., 316, n. 33.
3. Ibid., 121.
4. Ibid., 124.
5. Ibid., 118, 124.
6. Ibid., 128.
7. Ibid., 317, n. 52.
8. Ibid., 135.
9. John Tompkins, "The U.S. Army's Blunderbuss Bungle That Fattened Your Taxes," True Magazine, 36–39.
10. John Tompkins, "Our New Blitzkrieg Rifle That's Clobbering Communists," *True Magazine,* 116.
11. Ibid., 90.
12. "Senate Unit Assails the Army's Policy on Rifle Purchases." *New York Times,* June 5, 1967, p. 1:4.

CHAPTER 34

1. Edward Clinton Ezell, *Small Arms of the World,* 30.
2. R. Blake Stevens and Edward C. Ezell, *The Black Rifle, M16 Retrospective,* 60; see also James Fallows, *National Defense,* 82.
3. John Tompkins, "Our New Blitzkrieg Rifle That's Clobbering Communists," *True Magazine,* 92.
4. Stevens and Ezell, *The Black Rifle,* 45.
5. Edward Clinton Ezell, *The Great Rifle Controversy,* 177.
6. Ibid.
7. Stevens and Ezell, *The Black Rifle,* 61.
8. Ibid., 66.
9. Ezell, *The Great Rifle Controversy,* 181.
10. Stevens and Ezell, The Black Rifle, 70.
11. Thomas L. McNaugher, *The M16 Controversies,* 67.

CHAPTER 35

1. R. Blake Stevens and Edward C. Ezell, *The Black Rifle, M16 Retrospective,* 71–72.

2. Ibid., 73.
3. Edward Clinton Ezell, *The Great Rifle Controversy,* 180.
4. Ibid., 182.
5. Stevens and Ezell, *The Black Rifle,* 75.
6. Ezell, *The Great Rifle Controversy,* 182.
7. Stevens and Ezell, *The Black Rifle,* 76.
8. John Tompkins, "Our New Blitzkrieg Rifle That's Clobbering Communists," *True Magazine.*
9. Stevens and Ezell, *The Black Rifle,* 74–75.
10. Ibid., 79.
11. This was a surprisingly long time after the Russians introduced this weapon in 1948—some eight years earlier. AK47s were used against U.S. troops in Korea in the early fifties. It seems unlikely that Springfield had not seen this weapon "unofficially" before then.

C H A P T E R   3 6

1. R. Blake Stevens and Edward C. Ezell, *The Black Rifle, M16 Retrospective,* 81.
2. Robert Macdonald's testimony before the Ichord subcommittee. *Hearings Before the Special Subcommittee on the M16 Rifle Program, 90th Congress, 1st Session,* Tuesday, August 8, 1967, pp. 4785–4812.
3. Macdonald's Ichord committee testimony.
4. Ibid.
5. For more on General LeMay's considerable small arms background, see Thomas L. McNaugher, *The M16 Controversies,* 78.
6. Macdonald's Ichord committee testimony.
7. Ibid.
8. Stevens and Ezell, *The Black Rifle,* 91.
9. Edward Clinton Ezell, *The Great Rifle Controversy,* 183.
10. Stevens and Ezell, *The Black Rifle,* 92.
11. Ibid.
12. H. G. Summers, Jr., *Vietnam War Almanac,* 30.
13. Stevens and Ezell, *The Black Rifle,* 100.
14. Macdonald's Ichord committee testimony.
15. Stevens and Ezell, *The Black Rifle,* 100.
16. Ibid., 107.
17. Ezell, *The Great Rifle Controversy,* 188.

CHAPTER 37

1. Edward Clinton Ezell, *The Great Rifle Controversy,* 140–41.
2. Ibid., 150.
3. Ibid., 152.
4. John Tompkins, "The Army's Blunderbuss Bungle That Fattened Your Taxes," *True Magazine,* 36–39, 114–16.
5. Ibid., 39.
6. Ezell, *The Great Rifle Controversy,* xii.
7. Ibid., 157–58.
8. R. Blake Stevens and Edward C. Ezell, *The Black Rifle, M16 Retrospective,* 111.
9. Ibid., 115.
10. Ibid., 116; see also Ezell, *The Great Rifle Controversy,* 189.
11. Ezell, *The Great Rifle Controversy,* 191.
12. Ibid., p. 191. Ezell notes that while this remark was later denied, McNamara was left with the problem of guessing how much bias had actually entered the tests.
13. Ibid.
14. J. A. Stockfish, *Plowshares into Swords,* 173. Three years later, at the deadline for the presentation of the new weapon, no new weapon had been created.
15. H. G. Summers, Jr., *Vietnam War Almanac,* 31.

CHAPTER 38

1. *Report, Special Subcommittee on the M16 Rifle Program, 90th Congress, 1st session,* Tuesday, August 8, 1967, p. 5332.
2. R. Blake Stevens and Edward C. Ezell, *The Black Rifle, M16 Retrospective,* 120.
3. Ibid.
4. Ibid., 125.
5. *Hearings Before the Special Subcommittee on the M16 Rifle Program,* pp. 4540, 4567 passim.
6. Edward Clinton Ezell, *The Great Rifle Controversy,* 199.
7. Stevens and Ezell, *The Black Rifle,* 134.
8. Ibid., 129.
9. H. G. Summers, Jr., *Vietnam War Almanac,* 32.
10. Stevens and Ezell, *The Black Rifle,* 142.
11. *Hearings Before the Special Subcommittee on the M16 Rifle Program,* pp. 4540, 4567 passim.

12. Stevens and Ezell, *The Black Rifle,* 142, 158.
13. Ibid., 162.
14. Summers, *Vietnam War Almanac,* 33.
15. James Fallows, *National Defense,* 91.
16. "Up to September 1966, about 99 million rounds of 5.56-mm ammunition were consumed in Vietnam, of which 89 million rounds were loaded with ball propellant." *Hearing Before the Special Subcommittee on the M16 Program,* p. 5369.
17. Stevens and Ezell, *The Black Rifle,* 190.
18. Ibid., 193.
19. Ibid.
20. Ibid., 213.
21. Summers, *Vietnam War Almanac,* 36.
22. Thomas L. McNaugher, *The M16 Controversies,* 138.
23. Ezell, *The Great Rifle Controversy,* 212.
24. Ibid., 213.
25. Ibid.
26. Ibid., 206.

CHAPTER 39
1. R. Blake Stevens and Edward C. Ezell, *The Black Rifle, M16 Retrospective,* 209.
2. James Fallows, *National Defense,* 91.
3. Edward Clinton Ezell, *The Great Rifle Controversy,* 218.
4. Fallows, *National Defense,* 92.
5. *Hearings Before the Special Subcommittee on the M16 Rifle Program, 90th Congress, 1st Session,* pp. 4509–10.
6. Ibid., pp. 4582–83.
7. Ibid., p. 4583.
8. *Report, Special Subcommittee on the M16 Rifle Program,* pp. 5349.
9. Kanemitsu ("Koni") Ito, Colt's Patent Firearms Manufacturing Company, *Hearings Before the Special Subcommittee on the M16 Rifle Program,* pp. 4585, 4643 passim.
10. Stevens and Ezell, *The Black Rifle,* 210.
11. James Fallows, *National Defense,* 91; see also Stevens and Ezell, *The Black Rifle,* 87, for phrasing from Colt manual.
12. *Report, Special Committee on the M16 Rifle Program,* p. 5369.
13. Gen. William C. Westmoreland, *A Soldier Reports,* 138.
14. Stevens and Ezell, *The Black Rifle,* 197.

15. Ezell, *The Great Rifle Controversy,* 206
16. H. G. Summers, Jr., *Vietnam War Almanac,* 40.
17. Westmoreland, *A Soldier Reports,* 138.
18. The full title was *The Special Subcommittee on the M16 Rifle Program, Committee on Armed Services, U.S. House of Representatives, 90th Congress, 1st Session.*
19. *Report, Special Committee on the M16 Rifle Program,* p. 5343, Index.
20. *Congressional Record,* vol. 13, pt. 10, p. 1338, Monday, May 22, 1967.
21. *Report, Special Committee on the M16 Rifle Program,* pp. vii–x, Index.
22. Colonel Harold Yount's testimony before *Special Subcommittee on the M16 Rifle Program,* pp. 4611, 4656, 4696.
23. Fallows, *National Defense,* 94.
24. Ibid., 77.
25. For a defense of Colonel Yount, see the Davis comments, Stevens and Ezell, *The Black Rifle,* 217.
26. Ibid., 188.

CHAPTER 40

1. R. Blake Stevens and Edward C. Ezell, *The Black Rifle, M16 Retrospective,* 274.
2. Edward Clinton Ezell, *The Great Rifle Controversy,* 226.
3. Ibid., 265–66.
4. Stevens and Ezell, *The Black Rifle,* 341.
5. Ibid.
6. Ezell, *The Great Rifle Controversy,* 271.
7. Stevens and Ezell, *The Black Rifle,* 356.
8. Ibid., 340–41.
9. Ibid., 348.
10. Ibid., 350.
11. Ibid., 356.
12. Ibid., 336–37.
13. Edward Clinton Ezell, *Small Arms of the World,* 65.
14. Stevens and Ezell, *The Black Rifle,* 368.
15. Ibid., 370.
16. Because the M16A2 fires bursts of three shots with each pull of the trigger, the weapon is categorized as a selective-fire automatic rifle.
17. Correlli Barnett, *Britain and Her Army,* 340.

BIBLIOGRAPHY

Aberdeen Proving Ground. *Welcome to the U.S. Army Ordnance Museum.* Aberdeen, MD, n.d.

Armstrong, David A. *Bullets and Bureaucrats: The Machine Gun and the United States Army, 1861–1916.* Westport, CT: Greenwood Press, 1982.

Austerman, Wayne R. *Guns at the Little Bighorn.* Lincoln, RI: Man at Arms Magazine Publication, 1988.

Barnett, Correlli. *Britain and Her Army, 1509–1970.* New York: William Morrow & Company, 1970.

Birnbaum, Louis. *Red Dawn at Lexington.* Boston: Houghton Mifflin Co., 1986.

Blair, Clay, Jr. "A New Rifle for NATO?" *American Rifleman* (September 1951).

Blay, John S. *The Civil War: A Pictorial History.* New York: Bonanza Books, 1958.

Brinckerhoff, Sidney B., and Pierce Chamberlin. "The Army's Search for a Repeating Rifle, 1873–1903." *Military Affairs* 32 (Spring 1968).

Browning, J., and C. Gentry. *John Browning: American Gunmaker.* New York: Doubleday, 1964.

Bruce, Robert V. *Lincoln and the Tools of War.* Indianapolis: Bobbs-Merrill Co., 1956

Buckeridge, Justin O. *Lincoln's Choice.* Harrisburg, PA: Stackpole Books, 1956.

Butler, David F. *United States Firearms: The First Century, 1778–1875.* New York: Winchester Press, 1971.

Campbell, Clark S. *The '03 Springfield*. Beverly Hills: Fadco Publishing Company, 1957.

Canfield, Cass. *The Iron Will of Jefferson Davis*. New York: Fairfax Press, 1978.

Casey, William J. *Where and How the War Was Fought: An Armchair Tour of the American Revolution*. New York: William Morrow, 1976.

Catton, Bruce. *Terrible Swift Sword*. Garden City: Doubleday and Company, 1963.

Chidsey, Donald Barr. *The War in the South: The Carolinas and Georgia in the American Revolution*. New York: Crown Publishers, 1969.

Chinn, George M. *The Machine Gun*. 4 vols. Washington, D.C.: Government Printing Office, 1951.

Clagett, Major Robert H., Jr. "How the Infantry Tests a Rifle." *American Rifleman* (October 1953).

Clark, Champ. *Gettysburg: The Confederate High Tide*. Alexandria, VA: Time-Life Books, 1985.

Colvin, Fred H. *Sixty Years with Men and Machines*. New York: McGraw-Hill (Whittlesey House), 1947.

Comparato, Frank E. *Age of Great Guns*. Harrisburg, PA: Stackpole Books, 1965.

Congdon, Dan. *Combat: World War I*. New York: Delacorte Press, 1964.

Cosmas, Graham A. *An Army for Empire: The United States Army in the Spanish-American War*. Columbia: University of Missouri Press, 1971.

Crossman, Edward C. *The Book of the Springfield*. Marines, NC: Small Arms Technical Publishing Co., 1932.

Cuneo, John R. *The Battles of Saratoga: Turning of the Tide*. New York: Macmillan, 1967.

Cunliffe, Marcus. *George Washington, Man and Monument*. Boston: Little, Brown, 1958.

Dixon, Brigadier C. Aubrey. "The NATO Rifle, A British Statement on the Development of a Shoulder Weapon for the North Atlantic Treaty Organization." *American Rifleman* (January 1952).

Drury, Ian, and Tony Gibbons. *The Civil War Military Machine: Weapons and Tactics of the Union and Confederate Armed Forces*. New York: Smithmark Publisher, 1993.

Dupuy, R. Ernest, and Trevor N. Dupuy. *The Compact History of the Revolutionary War*. New York: Hawthorn Books, 1963.

Dupuy, Col. Trevor N. *The Evolution of Weapons and Warfare.* Indianapolis: Bobbs-Merrill Co., 1980.

Ellis, John. *The Social History of the Machine Gun.* Baltimore: The Johns Hopkins University Press, 1975.

Elting, John Robert. *American Army Life.* New York: Charles Scribner's Sons, 1982.

Encyclopaedia Britannica. 1956 ed.

Ezell, Edward Clinton. *Small Arms of the World.* 12th rev. ed. Harrisburg, PA: Stackpole Books, 1983.

————.*The Great Rifle Controversy: Search for the Ultimate Infantry Weapon from World War II Through Vietnam and Beyond.* Harrisburg, PA: Stackpole Books, 1984.

————. *The AK47 Story.* Harrisburg, PA: Stackpole Books, 1986.

————. *Small Arms Today.* Harrisburg, PA: Stackpole Books, 1988.

Fallows, James. *National Defense.* New York: Random House, 1981.

Flexner, James Thomas. *George Washington and the New Nation (1783–1793).* Boston: Little, Brown, 1969.

Freidel, Frank. *The Splendid Little War.* New York: Bramhall House, 1958.

Ganoe, William Addleman. *The History of the United States Army.* Ashton, MD: Eric Lundberg, 1964.

Garraty, John A. *The American Nation: A History of the United States.* New York: Harper & Row, 1966.

Gilbert, Dave. *Where Industry Failed: Water Powered Mills of Harpers Ferry, West Virginia.* Charleston, WV: Pictorial Histories Publishing Company, 1984.

Gillie, Mildred Harmon. *Forging the Thunderbolt: A History of the Development of the Armored Force.* Harrisburg, PA: Military Service Publishing Company, 1947.

Gimpel, René. *Diary of an Art Dealer.* Translated by John Rosenberg. New York: Farrar, Straus and Giroux, Inc., 1966.

Green, Constance McLaughlin. "History of the Springfield Armory." Unpublished ms. Springfield: Springfield Armory Library, National Park Service, n.d.

Hastings, Max. *Overlord: D-Day and the Battle for Normandy.* New York: Simon & Schuster, 1984.

Hatcher, Maj. Gen. Julian S. *Hatcher's Book of the Garand.* Highland Park, NJ: The Gun Room Press, 1948.

Hendrick, Burton J. *Lincoln's War Cabinet.* Boston: Little, Brown, 1946.

Higginbotham, Don. *Daniel Morgan, Revolutionary Rifleman.* Chapel Hill: University of North Carolina Press, 1961.

Holley, Irving B. *Ideas and Weapons: Exploitation of the Aerial Weapon by the United States during World War I: A Study in the Relationship of Technological Advance, Military Doctrine and the Development of Weapons.* New Haven: Yale University Press, 1953.

Huntington, R. T. *Hall's Breechloaders.* York, PA: George Shumway, 1972.

Jensen, Merrill. *The New Nation, A History of the United States During the Confederation, 1781–1789.* New York: Alfred A. Knopf, 1967.

Keegan, John. *The Face of Battle.* New York: Dorset Press, 1976.

Kinsley, D. A. *Favor the Bold: Custer the Indian Fighter.* New York: Holt, Rinehart and Winston, 1968.

Leech, Margaret. *Reveille in Washington, 1860–1865.* New York: Harper & Brothers, 1941.

————. *In the Days of McKinley.* New York: Harper & Brothers, 1959.

McNaugher, Thomas L. *The M16 Controversies: Military Organizations and Weapons Acquisition.* New York: Praeger Publishers, 1984.

Marcot, Roy M. *Spencer Repeating Firearms.* Irvine, CA: Northwood Heritage Press, 1989.

Marshall, Gen. S. L. A. *Men Against Fire.* New York: William Morrow, 1947.

Millett, Allan R., and Peter Maslowski. *For the Common Defense: A Military History of the United States.* New York: Macmillan, 1984.

Millis, Walter. *Arms and Men: A Study of American Military History.* New York: G. P. Putnam's Sons, 1956.

Morison, Samuel Eliot, Henry Steele Commager, and William E. Leuchtenburg. *The Growth of the American Republic.* 2 vols. New York: Oxford University Press, 1969.

Neagles, James C., and Lila L. Neagles. *Locating Your Revolutionary War Ancestor: A Guide to the Military Records.* Logan, UT: Everton Publishers, 1983.

O'Connor, Jack. *The Rifle Book.* New York: Alfred A. Knopf, 1966.

O'Neill, William J. *A Democracy at War: America's Fight at Home & Abroad in World War II.* New York: The Free Press, 1993.

Ripley, Sarah D., ed. *James Wolfe Ripley.* Hartford, CT: 1881.

Smith, Joseph E. *Small Arms of the World.* 10th ed. Harrisburg, PA: Stackpole Books, 1973.

Smith, Merritt Roe. *Harpers Ferry Armory and the New Technology.* Ithaca and London: Cornell University Press, 1977.

Springfield Armory National Historic Site Fact Sheet. No. 2. "The Trap Door," n.d.

Smith, Page. *A New Age Begins: A People's History of the American Revolution.* New York: McGraw Hill, 1976.

————. No. 3. "Evolution of Springfield Weapons," n.d.

Stevens, R. Blake, and Edward C. Ezell. *The Black Rifle, M16 Retrospective.* Toronto: Collector Grade Publications, 1987.

Stockfish, J. A. *Plowshares into Swords: Managing the American Defense Establishment.* New York: Mason & Lipscomb, Publishers, 1973.

Summers, H. G., Jr. *Vietnam War Almanac.* New York: Facts on File, 1985.

Tompkins, John. "The U.S. Army's Blunderbuss Bungle That Fattened Your Taxes." *True Magazine* (April 1963).

————. "Our New Blitzkrieg Rifle That's Clobbering Communists." *True Magazine* (December 1963).

Tuchman, Barbara. *The First Salute.* New York: Alfred A. Knopf, 1988.

U.S. Congress. House. *Hearings Before the Special Subcommittee on the M16 Rifle Program, Committee on Armed Services, U.S. House of Representatives, 90th Congress, 1st Session.* August 8, 1967, pp. 4785–4812.

U.S. Department of the Interior. *Fort Sumter, Anvil of War,* Washington, D.C.: Government Printing Office, 1984.

Utley, Robert. *Frontier Regulars: The United States Army and the Indian.* Lincoln: University of Nebraska Press, 1973.

Valley Forge Briefs No. 35. Valley Forge, PA. Valley Forge National Historical Park, n.d.

Weigley, Russell F. *History of the United States Army.* New York: Macmillan, 1967.

Westmoreland, Gen. William C. *A Soldier Reports.* Garden City, NY: Doubleday, 1976.

Whittlesey, Derwent Stainthorpe. "The Springfield Armory: A Study in Institutional Development." Ph.D. dissertation, University of Chicago, 1920.

Woodward, Sir Llewellyn. *Great Britain and the War of 1914–1918.* London: Methuen & Co., 1967.

INDEX

Gatling and, 172
Hall rifle and, 55, 56–62
Hunt committee of, 145–46
Ichord committee and, 515–16
Krag-Jorgensen rifle and, 235–36,
    241, 266, 300
Lewis-Crozier clash and, 298–303,
    320–27, 329, 332–33
M14 production and, 477
and M14 vs. AR-15, 450–52, 454
MP44 automatic rifle and, 402–4
M16 "militarization" and, 488–89
McNamara's revamping of, 479, 481
NATO and, 422
ORO and, 431
patent infringements and, 272–78
postbellum era and, 212–13
Ripley's tenure with, 111–17,
    182–83
Sharps rifle and, 132
SPIW concept and, 485, 486
Studler and, 407, 408
TCC formed by, 489
World War II failures of, 392–93
Ordnance Regulations (1816), 60
Oriskany, Battle of, 10
*ORO-T-160: Operations Requirements
    for an Infantry Hand Weapon*
    (Hitchman), 430–31
Osman Pasha, 220–22
Otterson, J. E., 342–43

Palmer, William, 168
Patowmack Company, 27–29
Peabody, Henry, 196, 199–200
Peabody-Martini rifle, 221–24
Peabody rifle, 135
Pedersen, J. D., 369–70, 372–86, 420,
    520
Perkin, Joseph, 31–32, 34, 55
Pershing, John J., 311, 319, 321,
    333–35, 345, 347, 361, 533
Philippines, 250, 252, 287
Pickering, Thomas, 29, 30

Pig Board, 379–80, 382, 386, 406,
    429, 473, 474, 520
Plevna, Battle of, 196, 220–23, 227,
    228, 247, 291
Poinsett, Joel R., 68, 71–76, 78, 90,
    129, 130
Powell, Herbert B., 459–60
Prescott, Benjamin, 39–43, 47, 48, 50,
    64, 80
Princeton, Battle of, 13

Rafael machine gun, 165–67
Ramsay, General, 183, 192, 211
Rayle, Colonel, 436, 438
recoilless rifle, 407
Remington, Frederic, 248
Remington Arms Company, 219, 226,
    227, 409, 410, 411
Remington Model 51 pistol, 369
Remington Model 1910 shotgun, 369
Remington rifles, 135, 227, 369
*Report on Project NR2787, Evaluation of
    Small Caliber High Velocity (SCHV)
    Rifles,* 457
Ridgway, Matthew B., 436, 437, 439,
    448, 480
Rifle and Light Infantry Tactics (Hardee),
    105
rifles:
    Allin trap-door mechanism and,
        200–201
    American Revolution role of, 8–9
    "American System" and, 81–83
    automatic cam cocking mechanism
        for, 219
    Boxer cartridge and, 196
    breech-loading vs. muzzle-loading,
        126–38, 196–97
    European designs of, 129–30,
        196–97
    falling-block mechanism and,
        199–200
    Flobert cap and, 198
    gas-operated, 291–92